GODLY
LETTERS

GODLY LETTERS

THE LITERATURE OF THE
AMERICAN PURITANS

MICHAEL J. COLACURCIO

UNIVERSITY OF NOTRE DAME PRESS
NOTRE DAME, INDIANA

Copyright © 2006 by University of Notre Dame
Notre Dame, Indiana 46556
www.undpress.nd.edu
All Rights Reserved

Manufactured in the United States of America

Library of Congress Cataloging-in-Publication Data

Colacurcio, Michael J.
Godly letters : the literature of the American Puritans / Michael J. Colacurcio.
p.   cm.
Includes bibliographical references and index.
ISBN-13: 978-0-268-02290-7 (alk. paper)
ISBN-10: 0-268-02290-9 (alk. paper)
1. American literature—Puritan authors—History and criticism.
2. American literature—Colonial period, ca. 1600–1775—History and criticism.
3. American literature—New England—History and criticism.
4. Christian literature, American—History and criticism.
5. Puritans—New England—Intellectual life. I. Title.
PS153.P87C65   2006
810.9'001—dc22
2006012839

FOR LISA

who picked up the pieces

AND MAHNAZ

who found a way to make them fit

CONTENTS

PART THREE. REVISION

EPILOGUE

ACKNOWLEDGMENTS

Books written over a long period are indebted in more ways than even the most conscientious scholar is likely to remember; and the present book, though typed into the computer in a reasonable amount of time, has been growing in concept and style since the beginning of my academic career. At the University of Illinois, Edward Davidson taught me to write about the Puritans without generic embarrassment: philosophy and theology, sermons and histories, are literature; the only requirement is that they be thoughtful and spirited. Force at a distance, Perry Miller taught me—along with everybody else—that intellectual history does not have to look like A. O. Lovejoy. And Nathaniel Hawthorne proved that children of the Puritans need to know their fathers: Hawthorne is our first important reader of their Godly Letters, and my first book about them is about him. (It took a while to learn how to write that kind of book.)

Since that beginning, in the 1960s, I have had the curious pleasure of teaching the canon of Puritan literature with some regularity—surveys and seminars, as the trade would bear. A little less frequently as time went along: one sensed a declining interest in the once hot topics of the "Hot Protestants" and was well prepared to encounter resistance to the hegemony of the Anglo-Saxon; but it came as a surprise when an otherwise sensible graduate student offered a paper proving that *The Great Gatsby* is a better book than *Of Plymouth Plantation*. Of course it is not, but one had hardly expected the question to arise. Then it was, I suppose, that I knew I needed to publish the news that, read right and right along, Puritan writing is, like, good. And I need to thank the students who have, over the years, listened to me say so out loud—from Cornell, Robert Daly, John Gatta, Gary Williams, Carol Bensick, David Van Leer, Allan Emery, John Samson, James Duban, Lauren Berlant, and Christopher Newfield; from UCLA, Lisa Gordis, Geoffrey Sanborn, Laura Arnold, Martin Kevorkian, Maurice Lee, Luke Bresky, Joanna Brooks, Meredith Neuman, Andrew Rosenblum, Derek Pacheco, Sean Silver, Joe Rezek, Austin Graham, and (helping with the index) Brian Hayden. One learned from their faces, often enough, what could and could not be said.

Of the more professional influences, again, Perry Miller: he nowhere attempted the sort of literary criticism this book sets out to perform but, having invented the field of Puritan Studies, he both made me the place and left me the room. Of his followers and revisers, Edmund Morgan, Larzer Ziff, Norman Pettit, David Hall, William Stoever, Sargent Bush, Harry Stout, Philip Gura, Janice Knight, Michael Winship, and—from the list above, teaching the teacher—Robert Daly, John Gatta, Lisa Gordis, and Meredith Neuman. Andrew Delbanco, Emory Elliot, Albert Von Frank, and Tom Werge figure as both friends and coworkers in the field; so, preeminently, does Sacvan Bercovitch, whose energy and insight gave new life to that well-planted field, and who always said a kind word when one needed to hear it. So did Fred Newberry, who helped me cut some stutters and some echoes, and who is more of a Puritanist than he lets on. Karen Rowe is just the sort of Puritan scholar one is glad to have as a first-floor friend; Jeanette Gilkison, just the sort of departmental assistant. And, as if to prove the need for friends who are just that, there appeared Al Braunmuller, Barbara Packer, and Eric Sundquist: until the "dedicated" ones arrived in Westwood, they each took their turn at faith and trust. They could not imagine why I wanted to write this book but, because I wanted it so much, they thought it best perhaps I should.

Having eagerly solicited a not-quite-finished form of this book, Lara Heimert (formerly of the Yale University Press) shared the excitement of its completion and the chagrin of learning that an editorial board wished to reduce it rather severely. Barbara Hanrahan of the University of Notre Dame Press has been equally friendly—and has made good her belief that books need to be as long as they need to be. More formally, I need to thank the editors of *Religion and Literature* for permission to reprint, as chapter 3, an expanded version of an article that appeared there in spring 2000; and of *English Literary History,* where the material of chapter 7 appeared in fall of that same year. And finally, I want to remind my scrupulous reader that, except where I found some curious linguistic effect at issue, I have not hesitated to modernize the texts of the works I analyze—always when I am quoting from a seventeenth-century publication and often enough when a more modern edition is available. No doubt a point of scholarship may be lost here and there, but the gain in reader-friendliness seemed well worth the risk.

Godly Letters

If the case for the founding importance and prime historical interest of "the Puritans" has not by now been satisfactorily made, it is hard to see what further argument or evidence the practiced skeptic might yet require. One of the two or three most distinguished intellectual historians in the history of the world, himself a singular agnostic, devoted an entire career to the discovery of the inherent fascination and the predictive power of the several generations of New England writers who supposed that the completion of Holy History depended on the endurance of their inspired ecclesiological experiment and of the highly demanding theology it expressed. Others thought the frontier, or the revolution, or other aftereffects of the Enlightenment held the key to the American Difference; but against these more secular explanations, Perry Miller's commitment to his own flood subject remained fixed. And the power of his example—to inspire or to provoke whole programs of archival research and to authorize an entire field of academic self-definition—is all but unique in the history of the modern academy.[1] Not a monolith, as some have caviled to complain, but a foundation stone in all conscience.

Even today, while the scandal of race demands to be recognized as the lasting legacy of a continent's conception within that state of sin called empire, the puritanic books written in the wake of reformed theology and the revolutionary steps taken in the name of biblical destiny refuse to recant the name of "Origins." A truly multinational concern, imperialism everywhere cloaked itself in the dignity of some more or less reformed religion; if parliament outlasted pope, and covenant held on to vanquish king in the mobile and always revisable drama we call "the Holy Pretense," the reason can only be that the prophets of New England better understood, more fully enacted, and more frequently and memorably enunciated the mystic premise and the worldwide goal of their own especially civil religion. New Englanders rehearsed their Covenant long after they held any slaves. And even so late an arrival as Frederick Douglass would have to unlearn the structure of Bercovitch's Jeremiad before he could identify the unity of his own experience of a racism that recognized no region.[2]

All of this could be argued out, again and at great length: the distinguishing mark (if not the beauty) of intellectual work is that, while thought endures, the scholar's task is never done; just ask Melville, who kept beginning again, repeatedly, before he ever finished anything. And no doubt the attentive reader will find elements of this Puritans-first idea—in earnest as temporary conclusion or at play as enabling premise—scattered through the several chapters of this book, violating its other, more esthetic interests. Inevitably, perhaps: strong beliefs are like that. And yet my main interest is decidedly not to defend the proposition that the enduring politics or the essential morale of the united states of North America begins at Plymouth. Something important may well begin just there; and—if the historical analyses of William Bradford are to be credited—something precious may end there as well.[3] And though one may need to suspend some part of one's historical disbelief in order to appreciate first Bradford's visionary power and then, more lastingly, his elegiac pathos, his book is called upon to initiate something less grand than Authentic American Literature As Such.

Not that anyone should be too shocked to learn that, in these latter days of just about everything, one can begin an account of just about anything just about anywhere. As origins are indeed lost, so the very idea of a starting place is in theory suspect and in practice arbitrary. Not entirely a matter of convenience, perhaps, and needing to be rationalized, certainly; but only with arguments of interest—in our very own name or, if the narcissism seems by and large harmless, in the name of our cautiously socialized suspicion that a modest portion of the academic readership might be in some measure enriched by the figure of that private interest on suitable public display. Well deconstructed, the survey and even the narrative history reappear in the space between political resistance (to the attack on Affirmative Action, for example) and the now friendly terrain we call the Abyss.

Not, then, to put too fine a point upon it: the first generation of New England Puritans wrote a remarkable number of *excellent* books—even if, at the outset, they did not intend to be "writers." Among the historians, Bradford waited a long time before his contemporaneous observations acquired validation sufficient to run the risk of narrative form; and Winthrop's perspicacious record keeping grew only gradually from "journal" to "history." Only in the latter days did their heroic example arouse Johnson's antic muse to the task of original recapitulation. Among the preachers, the book-making project was even less direct: first in the Old and then in the New England, they preached a lively word to all who had ears to hear; only gradually did their accumulating sermons attain the form of an extended meditation, like Shepard's *Sound Believer* or Hooker's *Application of Redemption.* Even then the text might come from the faithful notes of an ardent listener, reviewed (where possible) by the author's own eye and published back home in England, which lacked now their living voice. And what seems less plausible, a priori, than that Cotton's provoked unfolding of sixteen compressed answers to sixteen tendentious questions should form itself into a definitive treatise on the distinguishing marks of Protestant experience? Yet there they all are— proving beyond all reasonable doubt that literature may work in strange ways.

Most of these works have been mined for social observations—and for religious arguments which have, over time, tended to take on a life of their own— but few of them are ever properly "read." Comprehensive, circumspect, determined, subtle, energetic, relentlessly intellectual, playful in spite of their cultural prohibitions, in spite of themselves even, they are in every way remarkable products of a culture which, if it did not anticipate the modern interest in "the literary" as such, assigned an extraordinarily high place to the life of words; and a number of dedicated persons, though they did not always publish in the ordinary way, evidently took time from the onerous task of church and state building to enunciate, defend, and make memorable the terms in which they conceived and executed their work and the events which bore the sense of its success or failure. Suitably impressed, perhaps even a little daunted by the outpourings of their founders, later generations cherished and preserved these remarkable products of original puritanic literacy.[4] And their survival into a less reverent age thus amounts to a kind of double dare to the modern reader: Fathers and Sons both require us to read before we decide what is so patently didactic as to be merely a document.

Bradford's *Plymouth,* to cite the founding example, is an astonishingly good book. Good enough, all by itself, to unsettle our more or less fixed sense of where to look for texts which reward serious study with rare intellectual pleasure, and to provoke a serious reconsideration of the entire question of just which "genres" we customarily account as "literary" on their first face. It is better than almost everything else that associates itself with the colonial beginnings of literate life in North America, and better than very much of what is (barely) taught from the corpus of seventeenth-century British prose. Better locally, in point of emergent sensibility and style; and better continuously, as a long text that means much more and much more richly as it goes on, in readerly time, to remember itself, to challenge its out-setting premises, bearing down on the beliefs that endure the in-look of conscience from one writerly moment (or "self") to the next, subtly amending the prejudices that further reflection has had the power to bend and stretch, and abandoning the tenets, indeed the dogmas, that simply could not stand the test of experience, including that special test of extended composition.

On the one side, Columbus, Cabeza de Vaca, Smith, Wood, Morton (and others) all retain their power to focus the attention of the colonialist on the problem of imperialism, but they move to the margins when Bradford writes himself boldly into the center; and it takes a pretty determined politics to bring them back again. On the other, Bacon, Brown, Burton, Bunyan, and Behn—even Walton, Milton, and Dryden—can fill up the stylish spaces literary history has allotted; some even get their full redemption from the greedy, competitive pen of Melville. But for the adequate prose treatment of a comparable subject, only Spratt's needful *History* of the amateur beginnings of professional science and Locke's foundational *Essay* on understanding and his timely *Treatises* on government deserve to be mentioned with Bradford's firsthand report on the fate of reformed religion in America. (Perhaps the canon of "English" requires more additions than just one.)

Bradford may be the signal instance of American literature's failure to insist upon itself, but his position is far from singular. Winthrop's *Journal,* which has finally undergone a satisfactory modern editing, makes an almost equal demand for some grown-up readership. Long the fundamental document in the historian's search for a neutral point around which to arrange the story of personal eccentricity and ideological strife in the founding and the formative years of the diverse and thriving colony at Massachusetts Bay, the *Journal—History* if one insists—may now present itself in terms of the control its own prose attempted to impose upon the "subjects" an opinionated but educable magistrate could not otherwise control.[5] That is to say: our established authority on the laws and the facts of the Puritans' unique, utopian attempt to discipline and punish is also worth knowing as an "author," who began by violating the requirements of legal discourse in the name of love and ended by leaving, as his monument to the unpredictable ways of faith, not a holy state but a stately book.

Thus launched, some prophet of "historical literature" might wish to go right on to a third "historical" effort, *The Wonder-Working Providence of Sion's Savior,* which redeems its repetitions with the energy of its prose. The seventeenth century's Great Justifier wrote out God's Ways in a syntax triumphantly adapted from the Latin and, less grandly, the Cobbler of Aggawam just loved them Inkhorn terms; but Edward Johnson writes a more rampant form of not-English than either. It is also true that Johnson—a better lover of the law than Winthrop even—has left us an intriguing example of what, in an increasingly worksy and anxious New England, a non-Antinomian enthusiast might have to crow about. But here too the test is unabashedly literary: we have to love the way he loves to make a sentence sound.

Trying to perform its esthetic task in as thickly described an historical context as possible, however, the present work leaves Johnson (and half of Winthrop) to somewhere near its end, when very much of what they have to write about has found expression in other, less cautiously retrospective forms. The ordering of texts may be as arbitrary as it is crucial, but surely Thomas Shepard's masterful *Autobiography* insists on placement just after Bradford: arriving in New England only after much of its novel Way was already laid out, requiring only his after-the-fact recognition and defense, Shepard nevertheless tells us, in as complete a form as we have and with all the detail we are likely to demand, what it was like to be a Non-Separating Puritan in England in the decades after Bradford and his Brownist brethren had been hassled in their innovative churches and harried in their conscientious departure. What was it like, that is, to have been a Gradualist rather than an Immediatist? How and how long might such persons "tarry"? And for whom? And what, in the tormented moment of that long postponed nonseparatist separation, would be the causes that drove those heroes of so signal a piety? To be sure, Winthrop has already written out his "Reasons," very reasonably, in the form of a list. But Shepard, ever wary of his own capacity for self-deception, situates his motives in the text of his own life story.[6]

Certainly this thematically arrogant yet personally modest little self-story is eminently worth studying in some old-fashioned literary way. Not ahistorically, of course, for the Puritan saint who rose from the blind towns of his youth to a fellowship at Cambridge—and then just barely managed to exchange the life of church-outed renegade in the hinterlands beyond the effective watch of Bishop Laud's "Anglican" police for an absolutely central place in the power structure and then the pantheon of New England—is as much the creature of time and circumstance as any near-great man we might care to name. Yet his interest is inherent enough to reveal itself with or without reference to the allied and no doubt derivative specimens of the personal narrative which Shepard saw fit to record as the record of the ongoing spiritual life of his exemplary Cambridge Church;[7] and this whether or not we decide to presume on our acceptance of autobiography as an unjustified "fourth" in the noble family of literary genres—the sort of poor relation that can always be called upon when poetry, fiction, and drama have nothing left to say on the issues that have organized our project of moment. For, whatever else may be true, Shepard has subtly shaped a story from some painful midway moment in the remarkable adventure of the redeemed-life-so-far. Which only the conspicuously dull will find prosaic and only the terminally distracted declare beside the point.

So far so good: after some preliminary disclaimers, Bradford, Shepard, and *some* of Winthrop at the beginning; and, since we are concentrating our literary attention on that momentous first generation of American Puritans, later Winthrop and Johnson reserved for the end. But that still leaves the hard part: How to find a plausible organization for that stately, churchly venture which Bradford only advertises, which Shepard enters in medias res, and for which Winthrop and Johnson are bound to provide the memorial analysis? And more basically still: How to discover the literariness of the rhetorical stuff which constitutes that complex social thing? In a society organized in opposition to the idea of systematic amusement, regular church attendance may well have counted as an entertainment; and in a land where the theatre had been illegitimated as such, many of the social functions of the early modern drama may have been absorbed into the dialectic of Puritan preaching. But neither the Sunday Meeting nor the Thursday Lecture was supposed to be an esthetic experience—so far as that rare and perhaps "learned" form of human pleasure was even conceivable in the early years of the seventeenth century.[8] And, though a preparationist practitioner like Thomas Hooker may not be representative in his desire to outrage the entire sensibility of the natural man, nor a witness like Edward Johnson typical in his desire to receive just such offense, it is hard to think of any Puritan sermon as written on purpose to please. Not even to teach by pleasing. Or please by teaching. Or pleach by teasing.

So I may meet some conservative resistance when, going right on with Shepard, I propose that, though the doctrinal explication of his *Sincere Convert* will instruct only readers just barely familiar with the special emphases of Protestant salvation theory, its proleptic—and passionate—asides into the more urgent matter of seeking and avoiding conversion may well astonish anyone reading merely for research; and that its complementary study, *The Sound Believer,* is a major work not only of the preparationist persuasion but also of the theological imagination as such. Equally compelling is his indefatigable sequence on the *Parable of the Ten Virgins,* which seeks to wrest the matter of the holy marriage away from the Antinomians, and which steadily reminds its primary audience that, as long as the saint endures life on earth as a form of holy waiting, for death or for some more general second coming of the Heavenly Bridegroom, sanctification itself is only preparation in another key, with ghostlier demarcations, keener doubts. To be sure, no man ever wished it longer; but just here the patient reader will learn to recognize Shepard as an accomplished master of steady attention to problems which had to be dealt with because they could never be quite solved.

None of these works is quite so pointedly succinct or dramatically memorable as Hooker's *Poor Doubting Christian,* which I take to be a more definitive and durable form of Protestant consolation than Bunyan's allegorical but less circumspect rendition of the role of human exertion in a world redeemed by faith alone;[9] nor so brilliantly formulated as Cotton's embattled but slashing *Rejoinder,* which I regard as the most subtle and resilient piece of Protestant argumentation ever written. But neither is far off the standard set by Hooker's great and crescive *Application of Redemption,* the vitality of whose ongoing drama has already received some suitable notice.[10] And both are, along with the other works just mentioned, quite good enough to be read through, in their entirety, by all who imagine themselves capable of taking pleasure in—and teaching—the way human tones reveal themselves in a language once vividly expressive but available to us now merely as writing; and in the way writers invent or arrange their own structures of thought in order to encompass other structures of thought, equally human in origin, whether Scriptural or merely systematic, and so to express and transmit the results of their private meditation and social conversation on the most serious of human subjects. To be read, that is to say, by any critic who has ever wondered, from time to time, whether there is more to a literary life than "Poems and Stories," and whether the readerly sensibility may not often possess itself in works less palpable and mute than, say, globed fruit.

Of course it cannot all be done by mere assertion: I see something you don't see and the color of it is, well, not all the monochromatic granite gray you have been led to expect. Nor do I mean that my case should rest entirely on the inscribed enthusiasms of a monastic education grown giddy with advancing age. Some hard questions will have to be asked; and answered—not definitively, of course, since by now we are supposed to know that Bacon and Kant (and Northrop Frye) are simply wrong in demanding that science arise on the ground of humanist discourse, but with such plausibility and suggestiveness as is usually permitted to pass in such matters.[11] But except for the few hints at definition already thrown out in this preliminary excursus, I mean to let general questions arise only when they do, to treat theory not as a body of necessary intellectual work done elsewhere and a priori, inventing and controlling the kinds of analysis that can be done in any and all supposable cases, but as an occasional challenge, a specter which only sometimes arises in the path of reading we may feel called upon to do, whether we can clear our motive and derive our practice from first principles or not; a sufficient answer to a pressing difficulty, not an abstract enabler of literary activity as such.

We shall no doubt have to think about what "we"—who never doubted that "organic unity" was a metaphor of critical expectation and never a sober account of textual fact, however uncannily an image here might consort with another image there, and who always felt a little ashamed to be caught in the posture of disinterested contemplation of the formal beauty of a work someone wrote to aid the Spirit, if not to save the Soul—what "we" can possibly mean by calling a work "good."[12] Can we mean anything more than that it probably served the social use for which it was originally intended? That it suitably threatened persons who knew themselves to be sinners? Or, more subtly, that it taught a tense but teachable populace to see its Self under the aspect of sin in the first place?—at last to be identified, where a guilty identity was better than none. Or that, on the other hand, it appropriately reassured those who dared think of themselves as saints? Or furnished the socially competent a language in which sainthood might be constituted? That it served these purposes well, counseling anxiety or constructing selfhood with more élan than we imagine was necessary for the local purpose? And that we can still notice the effects that caused some preachings to be reprinted?

Or can we significantly mean that, as apprehended then or represented now, a Puritan sermon can be, in its power to invent character and imagine situation, significantly "dramatic"? Or that a sequence of such sermons can emplot a fascinating narrative, which might almost redeem its longueurs by participating in the episteme of the epic? Or that certain puritanic probings and deep-self projections break free of the psychology of the faculties far enough to seem mythic in their encompassing power? Or that inspired Puritan utterance often outruns the comfortable rhetoric of the dichotomies and finds itself, breathless, in a landscape of ambiguity?[13] Or must we not also admit, as scholars, that the sermon has been, all along, a genre which an educated appreciation of the career of writing in America cannot do without? And to confess, as intellectuals, that it is thrilling to watch the instructed intelligence of an age press itself to the limits of its own discourse in a concerted and continuing effort to link the poetic word of God to the troubled life of man? And, in such an atmosphere, somewhat different from the one we now naturally breathe, can we find ourselves comfortable saying that something is better than something else? Can we, if only in the heat of some expressive moment, say "masterwork" without at the same time enslaving (or at least marginalizing) somebody or other? Can we learn to understand the best, or even the better, as anything but the enemy of the merely good? Is "Literature" always an Enemy of the People? Is literary history a zero-sum game?[14]

With a no longer governable desire to discuss Big Puritan Books in detail—and with art looking longer and life shorter every day—I have decided to limit my discussion to the Big Books of the first generation. I mean to make some ironical observations about the appearance and evolution of Puritans' poetry in my last chapter; but that I offer as an epilogue, as if to imply that *of course* the New Englanders would eventually find the need and the way to say their sense of the world is verse. But that moment comes a little late: Wigglesworth and Taylor are both "latter-day": both learn to thrive on the Declension, signaled if not invented by the infamous Half-Way Covenant of 1662. And though Bradstreet is indeed a Puritan original, her best efforts are not revealed until a posthumous volume of

1678. Taylor is certainly a literary giant, comparable to any figure of the first generation; but he implies the world of Mary Rowlandson, Solomon Stoddard, Cotton Mather, Samuel Sewall, and a whole new range of subjects and genres, intentions and accomplishments. Another time, perhaps; certainly another place.[15]

So the point is simple: Puritanism has, from one generation to the next, an absolutely fascinating history which, as others may continue to argue, either does or does not epitomize or inaugurate the project of American spiritual history as such; but it also has, at its very outset, a formidable literary product as well. Some Geist or other moved Bradford, Shepard, Hooker, Cotton, Winthrop, and Johnson to write books that both recorded and abetted the drive to make the individual and the group quite new on the ground a less literary adventurer had the luck to name New England. What they wrote both enabled and threatened many later attempts to reassert or to revise the project, even to rename the place. But all of these vigorous writers, whether strongly vindicated or silently transumed by later generations, intend and accomplish their own orders of meaning: unable to escape the concepts of Calvinist redemption theory or of Protestant *heilsgeschichte*—unable even to imagine what such an escape would look like—they wrote what they saw and what they heard and what they thought. With passion, as seems the fate of godly men. But with a complexity of imagination, a sudden suppleness of notice and of style, and an instinct for the pleasures and the pitfalls of extended composition that mark them as men of rare genius as surely as they were old-time dogmatists.

We may not wish to invoke the Spirit that enabled them to express themselves with such energy. Or—failing to "observe the mode of our illumination"—we may hesitate to equate it with our own concern for writing well. We may resist the idea that what they had to write was what we choose to call "belles lettres." But then we'll simply have to find another form of words.[16]

PROLOGUE

CHAPTER ONE

A COSTLY CANAAN

Morton and the Margins of American Literature

One founding fact of American literary history as we have known it is that the conscientious memorials of William Bradford have pretty well succeeded in marginalizing the more whimsical if also more "literary" observations of Thomas Morton. Morton has had his champions, from the timely editing of Charles Francis Adams to the eccentric advertisement of William Carlos Williams to the countercultural sponsorship of Richard Slotkin to the academic explication of Donald Connors; and Bradford has had his share of revisionists, reminding us that his wonderful manner of simple truth-telling covers some blatant misrepresentations, some of them probably deliberate.[1] But a quick roundup of the usual anthologies, including those whose canonic reformism is much in vogue, will quickly establish the point: beginning students of American literary culture are regularly asked to read much more of Bradford's *Plymouth* than of Morton's *Canaan*. And over in the research library, a quick "global search" of books and articles will establish a similar preference for Bradford among the scholars.[2]

It would not be difficult to protest, in the scale of this preference, a certain disproportion: surely Morton's Nature counts as much as Bradford's Grace in the unfolding of the national literary project. Or, with more political conviction, we could suggest that Morton does better by the Native Americans, in prose and (probably) in fact. Yet we ought also to ask ourselves whether the present critical situation might have been otherwise. Can we imagine that Morton might have won?—not the mock heroic encounter at the much renamed Mount of Merriment but, in the long aftermath, the more important contest for the loyalty of the New England generations and then of the larger American audience. Is this one of those cases—now famous in the literature of canon revision—in which reputation is shaped by the mere pleasure of persons with privilege of gender and power of the press? Or can we actually defend the clear cut of Bradford's victory?[3]

To ask the question at all is to risk the embarrassment of trying to rewrite Hawthorne's "May-pole of Merry Mount"; and to do that, as I have taken pains to show elsewhere, is to get caught up in the allegory in which, whenever faced with some dialectical opposite, Puritanism seems destined always to win. Suitably deconstructed, however, what Hawthorne's little story actually reveals is that Puritanism always wins because Puritans are always there to create the dialectic and to structure their story just so; and because, conversely, no line of prophets has arisen on purpose to dispute their claim, with comparable resources and equal vigor, wherever it should arise.[4] But even this tautological discovery is not without relevance—revealing, as it does, the fact that literary history is no less written than any other sort; and reminding us, perhaps, that Puritans tend to write more profusely, perhaps more uncontrollably, than other social types. But sooner or later we come back to the root question: Granted that history is written by the winners, can we yet discover any apolitical reason why Bradford's annals of certain weather-beaten Pilgrims have proved more largely repeatable than Morton's racier account of love and sport in the New World Canaan?

Surely Morton's text is not without its distinct pleasures; and some of these, it seems fair to observe, may lie closer to Renaissance traditions of witty writing that lent their pleasing example to the formulators of the notion of the beautiful-letters definition of "literature" in the next century. Yet British literature has been as happy to concede the playful Morton to their Americanist colleagues as they have the more sober work of Bradford himself. For the moment, at least, a small paradox: Morton's book is altogether more literary than Bradford's without being in any significant sense better. We need to locate the pleasure—or Bradford's victory will seem empty because uncontested. But unless we can also notice the problems, not much else in the literary history of New England will make sufficient sense.

————

Only by the famous "Third Book" do we realize that Morton's gift is not for anthropological insight or even for pastoral evocation but for satire, particularly in the emergent subgenre of Puritan-baiting. There, in an extended account of the author's Pyrrhic defeat at the hands of certain allegorically named Separatists, who seem to have marked him for some special enmity, Morton makes his bid to discredit the claims of an adversary whose culture he scorns and whose source of authority he hesitates even to name. But something of his whimsy appears from the outset, pleasant and playful, and suggestive enough to help us to misidentify the reasons why Morton has been able to make and maintain a modest canonical place.

After a verse prologue, assuring us that the rich resources of the New English Canaan are as eager to be ravished as any "fair virgin" (10),[5] Morton launches his hyperbolic praise of the geographic bliss of the Zona Temperata in which his wondrous discovery happens to lie. Zonas Frigida and Torrida are disqualified as easily as an unlucky demographic guess of Aristotle, and the knightly personage of "the noble minded . . . Ferdinando Georges" (15) is smoothly enlisted as patron of Morton's enthusiastic ideal of the "golden mean." New Canaan or not, New England is a middle-class opportunity, as Englishmen already knew from the less stylized evocations of John Smith. And, though students are often struck by the ethics of Morton's very next discovery—that New England's aboriginal population of "Infidels" are "most full of humanity" (17) than the Christians newly arrived—their sober sensibility is troubled by the quasi-puritanic complacency with which Morton confesses that a recent plague has indeed made this Canaan "more fit for the English nation to inhabit in" (24). And what (but unregulated satire) can anyone make of a zany classicism which discovers that, as the language of these New World followers of Pan is derived from Latin and Greek, so "the Natives of New England" may derive from the "scattered Trojans," after "Brutus departed from Latium"? (20). Maybe—someone having miscounted—they are the *thirteenth* tribe of Israel. Maybe they came from the moon.

Elsewhere, this not unloving anthropology notices that, though they have no religion properly so called, Algonquians at least have the wit to cover their nakedness. Less symbolically, they acknowledge a Creator and hope for a form of immortality. They are by no means a "dull or slender witted people" (43), and their senses are remarkably well developed. They may indeed incline to "drunkenness," but they have not, Morton insists, been abetted in this practice by himself or his associates. Then, in conclusion, and as if to specify the out-setting theme of the golden mean, the "Salvages" of this Canaan are seen to have been living, all along, an altogether contented life: poor only by some inflated standard of "civilized" luxury, they have learned, without the benefit of Thoreau's experiment, that it is "but food and raiment" that living men need and that "the rarity of the air" they breathe well displaces any imaginable "variety of sauces to procure appetite." Lacking nothing needful, why cannot these Natives "be said to live richly?" (56).

Nor is there any falling off from this will to appreciation as Morton moves into his Second Book, on "the beauty of the country with her natural endowments." Elsewhere, criticism might labor to found the episteme of modernism on Columbus' minimalist discovery that "the farther one goes, the more one learns";[6] but Morton's mantra is simpler still. His arrival in "June, Anno Salutis, 1622," may have been but one more "chance" in the life of a traveling man, but his response was, like any judgment of taste, altogether fatal: "The more I looked, the more I liked it" (60–61). Any justification of this judgment would have itself to be poetical, and thus Morton breaks into a short list of natural occasions for pleasure bordering on transport. Trees, hillocks, and plains, set down in haste, but also

> sweet crystal fountains and clear running streams that twine in fine me-
> anders through the meads, making so sweet a murmuring noise to hear as
> would even lull the senses with delight a sleep, so pleasantly do they glide
> upon the pebble stones—

all hurrying down, poetically, to "Neptune's Court." And then, as if to insist that diction alone cannot a poem make, this preliminary evocation of Pastoral Plea-sure and previous invitation to Romantic Joy, this fulsome praise of "Nature's master-piece" lapses to the meter of its own mimesis:

> Her chiefest magazine of all, where lives her store:
> If this land be not rich, then is the whole world poor. (60)

The "needless alexandrine," for those who stay awake to count in Lotus Land. But reason not the need: these lovely facts, themselves the greatest poem.

Or more nearly so, at any rate, than the familiar list of lists thus introduced: "Trees," so loved of old Columbus,[7] in daunting difference and numberless ex-cess; "herbs" (for "sallets"), if only in a line or two; "birds, and feathered fowls," including, for the gourmand, "turkeys," which can hardly keep from crowding themselves into our "cook room," and which are "by many degrees sweeter than the tame turkeys of England, feed them how you can" (69), and including also, for the American born too soon for a visit to the Jardin des Plantes in Paris, a cer-tain "humming bird, no bigger than a great beetle, that . . . lives upon the bee, which he eateth and catcheth amongst flowers" (73); and "beasts of the forest"; and "stones and minerals"; and "fishes," so abundant that the "inhabitants of New England do dung their grounds with cod," and which is yet, as Smith had clearly implied, "a commodity better than the golden mines of the Spanish In-dies" (86). And so forth. Until one comes to appreciate the wisdom of an honest book on the subject of this not-quite-settler literature: sooner or later readers will have to develop an esthetics of "the list."[8] Evidently it comes with the territory.

In spite of this generic demand, however, Book 2 manages a proper climax, on the "goodness of the country and [its] waters," especially those of the "Great Lake of Erocoise"; and it has proved strong enough to attract the bemused notice of that prophet of "Prophetic Waters," John Seelye. Everywhere the water "excelleth Canaan by much," and indeed "at Ma-re Mount, there was a water . . . most excellent for the cure of melancholy" (92–93). No "milk and honey," to be sure, but this definitional lack is more than supplied by the redundant overflow of every other good thing; so that no sensible man will "hold this land unworthy to be entitled by the name of the second Canaan." And then, while scholarship pauses to consider how studied may be this insult—to the self-denying Separatists, and to those later Puritan immigrants who stoutly insisted that the only proper fulfillment of Canaan's typological promise was that otherworldly paradise of heaven itself—Morton goes on to predict that the green and golden venue of some really Great Lake, as yet by him unseen, is surely "the principalist place for a plantation in all New Canaan, both for pleasure and profit" (97). Enticing prediction, indeed: less than is suggested by Seelye's evocation of "green fire," perhaps—and far off from Slotkin's intimation of violent redemption—but quite enough to indicate the possibility of a New World project most unlike *either* version of Miller's famous "Errand."[9]

But as it would be a mistake to stop reading Morton just here—before his climactic and carefully arranged confrontation with that very enterprise—so would it be misleading to think of the enticing and perhaps subversive Project of Nature as beginning with Morton's witty advertisement. Columbus himself was at times almost distracted from his overwhelming desire to discover treasure (or to meet the Great Khan) by the transporting sight of trees whose green is "so intense that it is no longer green." Indeed, as Todorov observes, "there is no end to the enumeration of all of Columbus's admirations," and the forms of beauty he encounters are everywhere a threat to worldly purpose of any sort: at one moment "the singing of the small birds is such that it would seem that a man would never willingly leave this place"; and again, in the report of Las Casas, Columbus "says that there was such a great pleasure in seeing all this verdure, these forests, and these birds that he could not bring himself to leave"; and again, most emphatically, "This was a thing so marvelous for him, to see the trees and the foliage, the crystal water, the birds and the sweetness of the places, that he said he . . . never again wished to leave the place."[10] The more he saw, the more *he* liked as well; so that Morton is not quite original in his discovery that pleasure may well compete with commerce and religion as enticements to emigrate.

Formidably a formalist, Todorov may be somewhat too interested in the "endlessness" of Columbus' New World admirations, defining his interest as a signal instance of the esthetic as such. "Trees," he suggests, "are Columbus's real Sirens: in their presence he forgets his interpretations and his search for gain, in order to reiterate tirelessly what serves no purpose, leads to nothing, and so can only be *repeated:* beauty." Static admiration is not the only feature of Columbus's admiration of New World Nature, to be sure, but it may be the one that has the longest and most productive literary life, especially in the works of explorers and would-or-would-not-be settlers who seek not to transfer some preexistent interest to the American scene but to discover some powerful reason of removal within the scene itself. It may seem a little tendentious to reidentify Columbus, not as the harbinger of empiricist method, but as an exemplar of that yet more recent "rejection of interpretation constituted by intransitive admiration, the absolute submission to beauty, in which one loves a tree because it is lovely, because it *is,* not because one might make use of it as a mast for one's ship or because its presence promises wealth." But it remains cogent to suggest that Columbus may well discover, in the simple fact of pleasure, "a motive that has inspired all the great travelers, whether it was unknown to them or not."[11] And, as the example of Columbus has a long history of echoes or uncanny repetitions, it will not do to overpraise Morton's rediscovery of the prime motive to move.

The New England scene is not much like that of Columbus' Asiatic Caribbean, but it would be hard to discover this fact from Morton; and this is only to specify what we learned from Howard Mumford Jones decades ago: we do *not* go to the literature of American advertisement for nicely differentiated descriptions of real and resistant landscapes.[12] Not quite a projection of pastoral, perhaps, the evocation of the terrain of natural pleasure has, everywhere, only the most general contours: plentitude, intensity, availability. Tempting, no doubt, to all tempers but the puritanic, which has, Endicott-like, made a business to identify and resist naturalistic fantasy as such. Succumbing instead, it may be, to fantasies of history and theosophy, but all the more resistant to the lure of Nature for that very reason.

Similarly, the tendency of discovery reports and settlement propaganda to dissolve both observation and argument into a list of lists, aiming at an effect somewhere between numerical exhaustion and the ecological sublime, is already well established. The soldierlike—but also merchantlike—John Smith is everywhere less self-consciously poetic than the leisurely Thomas Morton, but it is impossible to read his account of the rich supply of Nature's bounty, in Virginia and again many degrees of latitude north of the Tidewater, without sensing that even this unabashed booster is not immune to the poetry of the new place and its imaginable produce. Predicting Morton's via media, Smith places New England at "the very mean betwixt the North pole and the line"; and teaching his successor not to impose too strict a set of political conditions, he earnestly stipulates that, had he "but means to transport a colony," he would, "of all the four parts of the world[,] . . . rather live here than any where" (208–9). And though he introduces his many-stanza'd hymn to New World plentitude with social observations more worldly than Morton's prediction of Thoreau—consider what an edifice of more than Spanish wealth the most peaceful Hollanders rear on the humble foundation of fish—the Song of the Someplace Else cannot long be repressed.[13]

"First, the ground is so fertile, that questionless it is capable of producing any grain, fruits, or seeds, you will sow or plant"; even these "very hedges do naturally afford us such plenty." "All sorts of cattle may here be bred and fed in the isles or peninsulas securely for nothing." The famous New England cod abound in March, April, May, and half of June; and then "in the end of August, September, October, and November, you may have cod again to make cor-fish or poor-John." ("Hake you may have when the cod fails in summer.") And

> mullet and sturgeon, whose roes do make caviar and puttargo; herring, if any desire them: I have taken many out of the bellies of cods, some in nets; but the salvages compare their store in the sea with the hairs of their heads; and surely there are an incredible abundance on this coast. (211)

And "furs of price" and "mines of gold and silver," and woods in "plenty of all sorts," and so forth, past all the limits of reason and on towards the very hungers of the imagination.

Interrupting himself, for a moment, to estimate the "gain" sure to be realized, Smith starts it up again, several pages later: waters "most pure . . . from the entrails of rocky mountains," "herbs and fruits" to the length of another goodly list, and

> eagles, grips, divers sorts of hawks, herons, geese, brants, cormorants, ducks, cranes, swans, sheldrakes, teal, mews, gulls, turkeys, dive-doppers, and many other sorts whose names I know not.
>
> Whales, grampus, porkpisces, turbot, sturgeon, cod, hake, haddock, cole, cusk or small ling, shark, mackerel, herring, mullet, bass, pinnacks, cunners, perch, eels, crabs, lobsters, mussels, wilks, oysters, clams, periwinkles, and divers others, &c.

> Moose, a beast bigger than a stag, deer red and fallow, beavers, wolves, foxes both black and other, aroughcunds, wild cats, bears, otters, martins, fitches, musquassus, and divers other sorts of vermin whose names I know not. (216)

Do I repeat myself? Very well then, I repeat myself: I do indeed contain multitudes; so much, in fact, that there is nothing to do but let it all out. And almost nothing for the critic to do, it appears, but repeat the repetition. Even as the lists tend to repeat themselves, in spite of an increasing need for sober critique, from one amazed beholder to the next.[14]

Searching for an emphasis to end the endless listing of lists, Smith can only suggest that Nature itself seems to require hearty consumers in New England, in numbers, and as quickly as possible; for all this plentitude does

> here for want of use still increase and decrease with little diminution, whereby they grow to that abundance, you shall scarce find any bay, shallow shore or cove of sand, where you may not take many clams or lobsters, or both at your pleasure, and in many places load your boat if you please. (216)

And the same for isles and rivers, as it threatens all to begin again. To be sure, Smith is sober enough to confess that access to this luxuriant supply will require some work. Further, his emphasis on middle things is more steadily economic than geographic or meteorologic. So that his poems are human as well as natural, domestic as well as pastoral:

> Who can desire more content that hath small means ... than to tread and plant that ground he hath purchased by the hazard of his life; if he have but the taste of virtue and magnanimity, what to such a mind can be more pleasant than building a foundation for his posterity, got from the rude earth by God's blessing and his own industry without prejudice to any ... [?] (216–17)

A familiar religious motive begins to suggest itself at this point—the conversion of the "poor salvages" Morton declares to be rich enough. But if the goal is middle-class wealth, and the means are those well known to English virtue, the premise is nothing other than the poetic promise of Nature's New World bounty.

It even appears that the tendency of pro-settlement tracts to lapse from the prose of surplus productivity to a poetry that presses to an intimation of Nature beyond the pastoral may have become, by the time Morton had published his modest sally into the field of visionary economy, an occasion of parody. The possibility is certainly suggested by a moment of rare interest in the otherwise pedestrian *New England's Prospect* by William Wood. Consciously meaning to correct the many false, perhaps dangerous impressions left by earlier writers, including Smith, Wood promises to stick to facts, to tell the truth about the place to which not a few readers might wish to voyage in fact and not merely in vision. And for a number of brief chapters—"Bays, Havens, and Inlets," "Seasons," "Climate," and "Soil"—Wood is nearly as good as his word, to eschew the temptation to "voluptuous discourse" in favor of a "faithful relation of some few years travels and experience" (19).[15] But then, in chapter 5, a harmless looking, *omnium gatherum* account of the "Herbs, Fruits, Woods, Waters, and Minerals" of New England, something rather curious happens, something gratuitously "literary," which will happen several times more in the course of this expressly businesslike account, though never with quite the same sense of discursive paradox and rhetorical surprise.

Brief on the subject of herbs and waters, cautious on the matter of mines and minerals, Wood allows himself to grow expansive on the (Columbian) subject of trees. A long paragraph assures the prudential reader that nothing is lacking which worldly practice could possibly require. But then, as if only full specification could satisfy a certain class of readers, who need to know "what timber and wood of use is in the country," Wood agrees to "recite the most useful as follows": in twenty lines of iambic pentameter. Not a *great* poem, perhaps,[16] but quite a surprising stroke under the circumstances, and full of diction and device that seem contrived to emphasize the established and steady tendency of nature specification to lapse into poetry. That the oak is "long-lived" may be a practical (if well-known) consideration, but why do we need to learn again the established poetic fact that the cypress tree is indeed "mournful"? Just so, the ash remains as "brittle" as everyone knows, but what purpose is served by the observation that the aspens are "ever trembling"? And while thus we wonder, the modest but needless verse becomes expressive indeed:

> The knotty maple, pallid birch, hawthorns;
> The horn-bound tree that to be cloven scorns,
> Which from the tender vine oft take his spouse,
> Who twines embracing arms about his boughs. (39)

Taking next a plausible but unprepared-for turn to the fruits of these trees, the poem raises its own figurative stakes by calling all of wild New England's unregulated forest produce "this Indian orchard." And with this utterly Thoreau-vian reversal, we realize that poetry has indeed occurred.

Intent on its own oxymoron, the poem ends its account of what "it may be necessary for mechanical artificers to know" by assuring us that "The dyer's sumac, with more trees there be, / That are both good to use, and rare to see." "Rare" bears several senses, of course, but none of them implies a use more practical than some poem by Ben Jonson. But the boldest assertion—and nicest enactment—of the literary, in flat opposition to the announced dedication to the pragmatic, is nestled snugly, deconstructively, in the very center of the poem's self-constituting list: "Small eldern" are indeed "by the Indian fletchers sought"; but they have to accompany "the water-spungy alder" which is in fact "good for naught." Wood omits to observe that, in just-spring, the New England world is "puddle-wonderful" indeed, but we get the point no less: this Nature thing is just enough to turn a sober economic man poetical; and so the books come back to tell the news: the New won't always say its sense in prose.

Assuredly, now, the *Prospect* goes on to repeat its genre-defining effect of breaking into measured verse in the midst of chapters full of needful information. "Quill-darting porcupines" introduce a few lines of verse that help to specify the "beasts that live on the land" (41–42). But then as if, once admitted, the need for natural enjoyment had begun to insist upon itself, Wood employs quite a long poem—"The princely eagle, and the soaring hawk"—to introduce an account of the "profit and honest pleasure" to be had from the "birds and fowl of both land and water" (48). And then, self-consciously, the "fish" are accorded a verse account that leads from the natural heroism of "the sea-shouldering whale" down to the social comedy of an Indian squaw who digs for clams "whereby her lazy husband's guts she crams" (54). And then no more, for the three chapters that remain of part 1, on the country and its produce; and none at all for the twenty light-hearted but prosy chapters of part 2, on the physical appearance and the manners of the native population. Wood apologizes in his preface for treating the Indians in a "light and facetious style," contending that "their carriage and behavior hath afforded more matter of mirth and laughter than gravity and wisdom" (20); evidently it would require the example of Morton to suggest that Separatists might be the true object of laughter; and, from another quarter entirely, that of Roger Williams to demonstrate that Indians can be the subject of poems.[17] But a simpler point will suffice: Wood's wit goes only so far; and not in all ways so far as Morton's; but far enough, in all conscience, to notice that, again and again, at the site of discovery and praise of New World resources, poetry happens.

Less well prepared are the laws governing the literary treatment of immigrants who prove deaf to the poetry of American Nature and its natives and who, partly for that reason, mistreat settlers more sensitive. And this, finally, looks like the raison of the *New English Canaan,* as Morton worked out the logic of his own would-be Americanism. Brave critique might hold out for the staying power of Morton's very own vision—or, braver still, for the *expression* of that vision—as such; but in the longer view, of histories, and classrooms, and anthologies, Morton survives as the most curious of Bradford's many antagonists. Clearly Bradford dissents, if only implicitly, from the gathering consensus concerning the nearly self-sufficient appeal of landscape and ecology in the not uninhabited but not unavailable territory of New England; and so, with him and his not-quite-Separatist successors, one looks elsewhere for an original logic of immigration and settlement. The point, however, is not simple difference but confrontation; and that less over land than over ritual. The maypole is not *just* a tree. And it is on this ground, of more than available nature, that Bradford chooses to engage with Morton. Further, it is by winning there that Bradford wins the literary battle as, symbol for symbol, historical purpose has proven a more fertile premise than natural symbol.

One could say, of course, that Morton's maypole is every bit as cultural as Bradford's: that it, quite like the English prayer book, which Morton defends with equal vigor, signifies not Nature but the king's right to order all the ways of his subjects on which Scripture is silent; this is, after all, Merry Middle Earth and, as his own "Book of Sports" had seemed to say, my English people must have merry middle things; by the power of my patents and charters my people may indeed migrate, but they must not think to reinvent themselves thereby; May Games remain, a sign less of fertility than of fealty.[18] But such a critical claim, even when made by Morton himself, serves only to threaten the modest coherence of his book. Some of Morton's rhetoric may charge Bradford's Separatists with treason, but his best strokes identify them as spoilsports; and the logic of his chapters points to their inability to savor the appeal of the Indian Orchard they have invaded, to hear at all the siren song of Nature.

About as long as Books 1 and 2 together, Morton's historical-satirical Third Book bears the full sense of validation—so much so that we may wonder if this "Canaan" would ever have been memorialized as such if Morton had not had a run-in with "the people who are planted there," acquiring, thereby, some sense of "what tenets they hold, together with the practice of their church." Christopher Gardiner and other like-minded English knights in search of American adventure may well have wished for a logic with which to counter the mounting conviction and deployment of some Puritan Errand, but this work was already being done, quite well enough, by other hands; and Morton, if his own account is to be trusted, appeared to be enjoying his natural liberty too much to be encumbered by the arduous labor of making a book. Writing, he seems with Thoreauvian insouciance at first to imply, is "not what interests us."[19] But History, in the costume of Separatism, does indeed intrude on the little idyll of his own creation, as surely it does on the more fictional but more aggressively representative experience of the Lord and Lady of Hawthorne's socially constructed "May." Bradford and others go out of their way to make an example of Morton, and this fact, including, as it must, an offended but still humorous response, is our first intimation of the fact of Morton's radical dependency. Aroused at last to writing—and protest how he may—Morton's significance remains all but fixed, very near the point at which it found itself arrested. So criticism concludes that Morton was actually quite lucky to have made a literary enemy as powerful as William Bradford. Or else, less prejudicially, that Morton did well to write himself into relation to Bradford, without whose original and steady op-position he might have fallen even further from the center of our notice.

Relevant history—which for Bradford begins, long before the formation of a separatist church at Scrooby near Austerfield in Yorkshire, with the outbreak of Reformation, coupled, by some law, with a corresponding outbreak of persecution in sixteenth-century England, both in echo of what happened, long ago, at the beginning of the Christian era—begins for Morton with "a great league made with the Plymouth Planters . . . by the Sachem of [the] territories" (103). And then, before we find out who these Planters may be, or how their curious motives or various travels may have thrown them in the way of this great sachem, it moves abruptly to the arrival of "a company of servants" sent by a merchant named Thomas Weston "to settle a plantation there" (105). The uninstructed reader can tell that the "entertainment" of these sturdy good Englishmen, with "court holy bread," by the settled group referred to only as "the Brethren," was nothing but a "show," hypocritical at the outset and prejudicial in the aftermath; but the exact identity of all these participants is a little mysterious.[20] And we might ask ourselves what we would make of Morton's report of Bradford's "Brethren" if the *Canaan* provided our only account. Or if students of literary history were obliged to read it first—appearing in print, as it did, more than two hundred years before Bradford's much-traveled *Plymouth* finally became fully public.[21]

Significant uncertainties persist, even as portentous events now follow one another in profusion: a "battle"—puzzlingly said to be "between the English and the French"[22]—the preparations for which the author sets forth in an invented "oration" about what a sachem has seen in a "vision"; a "parliament," in which the

Weston group decides to put to death a man old and sick instead of the one who had actually committed an offense against Indian property; and a "massacre" of "salvages at Wessaguscus," made not by Weston's men, many of them admitted to be "lazy," but by those increasingly nefarious "Plymouth Planters." Some strategy there may be to this dizzying dose of action without prior characterization or emplotment, which we begin to sense only when, at the end of chapter 5, Morton proposes that

> the savages of Massachusetts that could not imagine from whence these people should come, or to what end, seeing them perform such unexpected actions; neither could they tell by what name properly to distinguish them, did from that time afterwards, call the English planters Wotawquenange, which in their language signifieth stabbers or cutthroats. (112)

We know them, that is to say, not by their a priori declarations, however pious, but after the fact of their own first fruits. A nice point in the logic of moral identity, yet the risk turns out to be very great. Modern students, who do not like to hear of massacres, on either side, are more likely to accept the historical fact of bloody crime than the ideal possibility of heroic virtue, and thus they often look for ways to translate Bradford's holy ends into worldly means; and those trained up as proper Marxists occasionally demand a more "material" account than Bradford provides; but no one with skill enough to read the idioms of seventeenth-century English ever responds to Bradford's careful identification and placement of his group of holy-historical protagonists by asking, simply, "Huh?"

Now savage, now sly, Morton means to write satire rather than proper history, we readily conclude; and no doubt some coterie audience back in London needed no scorecard to know the names and numbers of all the players. Yet satire itself is one of the most historical of the literary genres we know enough to name, and any writer banking on the long-term reception of the values that validate his mockery can scarcely afford to leave his eventual readers too much on their own; or, worse still, to trust that the *object* of the satire will somewhere identify himself without at the same time creating an identity rather more subtle than the reductive one required by satire as such.[23] What if some member of these "Brethren" should have the power to make good on exactly that claim to relational identity? To turn a term of polite scorn into the kind of strong value for which only the cynical manage utterly to lose respect? Unlikely, perhaps, as it might require nothing short of a sustained and convincing book to turn that trick; but you never know. As satire is always *of* something specific, and as posterity must indeed be the judge, it seems unwise to presume too much on the steady tendency of Royalist prejudice: one man's Cutthroat is another man's Pilgrim.

With the arrival of "the Merchant" himself, in chapter 6, the basis of Morton's opposition to the Brethren begins to be clear: receiving Weston with pretended "love and zeal," they inaugurate a policy to which they will adhere consistently, blaming the savages for the misfortunes that have befallen his people and insisting, furthermore, that as they are "a dangerous people, subtle, secret, and mischievous, and that it is dangerous to live separated, but rather together, and so be under their lee" (113–14). Pretending Christianity, they mind the main chance of the beaver trade, slandering the natives in the process, whom Morton himself has found "more full of humanity than the Christians." And to any who shall premise that "where two nations meet, one must rule and the other be ruled," Morton lets it be known that, in New Canaan at least, the pro-Christian bias might well be set aside; for in his experience, "the more savages the better the quarter, the more Christians the worser quarter"; and, he thinks, "all the indifferent minded planters can testify" the same. And then, while the Merchant wonders whose country he has come to now, the "sharp witted" Brethren confiscate his ship and goods, threaten to return him as a prisoner to England, and even declare him mad. And so was it believed by "those that did not know the Brethren could dissemble"; for are they not, "all of them honest men in their particular," and every one of them "bound to seek another's good"? (115).

Stung by the force of this perfect anticipatory mocking of Bradford's grandest claim, the instructed reader may find himself paging back through Bradford's *Plymouth*—and even *Mourt's Relation*—anxious to find a way to reconcile *this* version of the Weston story, some archival reason to split the difference. None readily appears[24] and, momentarily at least, a bit of literary luster is lost. But then that is exactly the way the reading of Morton has to work: on his own he has accused some corporate Somebody of blatant hypocrisy, small and large. But unless we know the Bradford story in advance, we have no real idea of who is being taken sternly if perhaps fairly to task—or, if the thought happens to occur, whose fair reputation is being slandered. The simple fact is that Morton nowhere works hard enough to establish and adumbrate the identity he would challenge, the reputation he would mar. We cannot praise duplicity, and we guess there must have been some of that in New England, spoiling at the outset the rich possibilities of Canaan's natural reinvention; but without Bradford's full-dress Christian pretense, we have no real idea what ox is being gored.

Nor is this protohistorical account of brotherly deception and inhumanity much more cogently circumstantial when it comes (in chapter 7) to Morton's own "entertainment at Plymouth." Lured there by "news of a Town that was much praised," Morton seems satisfied enough with his "sallet of eggs in dainty wise, a dish not common in the wilderness," but he is clearly upset when the (nameless) inhabitants of Plymouth seek to convince his servants that having their Master read from the Bible and "the book of common prayer" represents an altogether insufficient attention to the "means" of salvation; and he is especially irritated when this advertisement for the need of a plain and powerful preaching does "like the serpent . . . creep and wind into the good opinion of the illiterate multitude" (116–17), causing them to desire and then to plot ways of freeing themselves to join the holy community at Plymouth. Their plot—to desert this Master upon an island—is foiled by the Master's superior wit, but we cannot be entirely certain whether the Master in question is Morton himself or someone of greater authority (such as the Captain Wollaston of Bradford's account),[25] and we are left wondering just what sort of liberty these would-be deserters hoped to find at Plymouth, especially as Bradford will hold that the real temptation was for his own servants to run off to Merry Mount. All we can say is that Morton has, without benefit of Bradford, his own countertheory of how the subtle serpent "insinuates" himself and that, telling quite different stories, both men appear to agree, with D. H. Lawrence, on the prime temptation of New World settlement: "Henceforth be masterless."[26]

By now it appears that the person who reads Morton without benefit of Bradford has pretty much to trust to his instincts, including his sense of style: Morton steadfastly declines to make plausible (or even to identify) his adversaries, so that we have no standard by which to measure his political or moral intelligence; sharing or not his wish to embarrass the very godly, we either enjoy his manner of insider satire or we do not. The instructed reader, on the other hand, can readily learn that there can be another side to many of Bradford's stories, but he may have a hard time constructing a compromise version of what really went on in the years before the episode of the Maypole. And it will require of him an anti-Puritan bias at least as strenuous as Morton's own to conclude that Bradford loses in the battle of who, what, when, where, and why. Bradford the steady (if biased) historian identifies, situates, explains, emplots; Morton the sometime satirist merely presumes his own wit.

Morton's account of the careers of "Master John Layford [Bradford's Lyford] and John Oldham"—even when the reader can tell which exactly is which—is so brief as to offer even the Puritan-hostile reader far less evidence against Bradford than he himself provides: both writers agree that the religious loyalty of these mysterious, oddly Melvillean drifters is to the religion of England; and both agree that the Brethren suspect them of being spies; but Morton's account of Oldham's being forced to leave town between "a lane of Musketeers," receiving "a bob upon the bum" (120) by every one, is far less damaging to the Puritan cause than Bradford's confession of the Special Providence that led him to break into certain letters about to be carried back to England.[27] And the story of "Master Bubble," without any competing version in Bradford, continues to defy explanation. It gives Morton the chance to create a sort of independent "character": "approved of the Brethren" and sent over to be "Master of the Ceremonies," this mysterious personage commanded an oratory which could lull "his audience fast a sleep, as Mercury's pipes did Argus eyes," and once said grace "till all the meat was cold" (122–23). And—given the conscientious preservation of certain of Bubble's possessions by the Indians he affected to distrust—it serves to raise again the (rhetorical) question of whether the savages "are not full of humanity" and not at all the "dangerous people [that] Master Bubble and the rest of his tribe would persuade you" (128).

This, then, is the context which the prior portions of the *Canaan* will provide for the chapters which, thanks to the (de)mythological power of Bradford, continue to express our determination to tell "the other side of the story": temperate New England has all the appeal of another Canaan, whether the immigrant population shall approve this less-than-typological equivalence or not; the natives are altogether fit inhabitants of this rare and remarkable place, and their savage ways bid fair to embarrass the Civilized Men who might like to discredit or displace them; and evidently a certain falsely pious "Brethren" mean to do just that. Intemperate souls, dead to the appeal of place and people, their ways are almost entirely hurtful; yet their utter failure to fit the place where they have (somehow) arrived cannot altogether escape the mode of social comedy. And—Morton implies, trusting the established morale of an English party of church and court and king—we know who they are. Spoilsports, essentially.

And now, their predictable (though not quite intelligible) response to "the Revels of New Canaan." About which, for once, Morton appears to wax full and explicit:

> The inhabitants of Pasonagessit (having translated the name . . . from that ancient savage name to Ma-re Mount; and being resolved to have the new name confirmed for a memorial . . .) did devise amongst themselves to have it performed in a solemn manner with revels & merriment after the old English custom, prepared to set up a maypole upon the festival day of Phillip and Jacob: & therefore brewed a barrel of excellent beer . . . with other good cheer, for all comers of that day. (132)

Innocent enough, this *new* English celebration, unless we regard the violence of naming. Yet full of cultural matters enough to keep Anglican and Puritan busy attacking one another for a month of Sabbaths: solemnity through merriment, indeed. What Morton chooses to defend first off, however, is nothing about the propriety of maypoles themselves, or of decorating them with "a pair of buck-horns," or of covering their "country" significance with the fiction of a couple of minor saints, or of the survival of the Roman Catholic calendar in the properly Protestant Church of England, or of its projection into the wilds of New England; but something about the poem "fixed to the Maypole," which "puzzled the Separatists most pitifully to expound" (132–33).

Eager to get on to that literary performance, we may well forget to wonder why the Brethren are now referred to, for the first time, as "Separatists": have we come, at last, to a scene of religion and culture in which their separatism will express itself as such? And in which it begins finally to make anthropological sense? Nor will it help much to pause over the strategy by which the principal antagonist of these Separatists now begins to be referred to as "mine Host": is this indeed someone else or merely Morton's latest way of referring to himself as some subaltern third person? But somewhere between the actual response of Charles Francis Adams and the hypothetical one of Henry James, we give up and go on to the poem—not yet the insouciant "Io to Hymen" but the murkier "Rise, Oedipus" which, after ten couplets of mythological mishmosh, ends with the ordinary enough proclamation "that the first of May / At Ma-re Mount shall be kept holiday."[28] Perhaps the meaning is that May Day will be kept in New England *too*, whatever the objections of the "precise separatists . . . at new Plymouth" (133–34).

But if the Separatists do not quite know what to make of the poem—which Morton, fallaciously or not, will go on to "illustrate . . . according to the true intent of the author of these revels" (136)—they have no trouble recognizing the maypole itself as "an Idol," calling it "the Calf of Horeb," or in (re-)renaming the place "Mount Dagon, threatening to make it a woeful mount and not a merry mount" (134). For once our authors agree: symbolists chiefly in the mode of typology, Puritans see Paganism everywhere.

Next, in this same (long) chapter 14, comes the famous little song—"Drink and be merry, merry, merry boys; / Let all your delight be in the Hymens joys"—which, fashionably, "was sung with a chorus, every man bearing his part; which they performed in a dance, hand in hand about the maypole, while one of the company sung and filled out the good liquor, like Gammede and Jupiter" (134). "Like so many fairies, or furies, rather," Bradford will retort, "as if they had anew

revived and celebrated the feasts of the Roman goddess Flora, or the beastly practices of the mad Bacchanalians" (205–6). Bradford's terse reference to "worse
practices" may be homophobic, but to Morton this is nothing but the "harmless
mirth" of young men living "in hope to have their wives brought over to them"
(92). On the other hand, Morton's invitation to "lasses in beaver coats" may lie behind Bradford's charge that Morton's men somehow "abused Indian women"
but, though the language of the invitation may well be obscene, no "abuse" could
ever be proved against him. Possibly Bradford thought it consisted in inviting
them at all: Pagans they already were, he must have thought, by gift of American
Nature; but perhaps they could be spared from participating in that miscegenation of religion by which the cults of the classical world had extended their weird
half-life into the unreformed Church of England.

In the end, however, the surprising thing about the entire Maypole episode is
not that Bradford and Morton represent its motives and effects so differently, but
(as I have argued elsewhere) that Bradford's response to Morton in the *Plymouth*
is so unlike the one preserved in his earlier letters to England, explaining the reason of Morton's deportation. Furnishing the natives with guns and rum might
well constitute a clear and present danger, but the "foundation for a philosophical
romance" lies elsewhere—in Endicott's after-the-fact and indeed hysterical response to "the only maypole in New England";[29] and also, perhaps, in Morton's
(intervening) insistence, that the symbolic and ceremonious item in such a hot
and heavy question is not only innocent but also, like the forms of the *Canaan*
itself, quintessentially English. So that, even as Hawthorne implies, some choice
of national identity may lie barely disguised in the choice of cultural heroes at just
this point—the single point, it could be argued, where, adumbrating one another
in about the same degree, Bradford and Morton come close to being dialogic
equals.

Here, perhaps, but never again. For as Bradford marches on to the *other* occasions of triumph and then of sobering reversal that constitute his originary experience in, not Canaan, but an England made significantly new, Morton slides
back into his status as running critic of the alien persons and uncouth events that
seem, strangely, sadly, to possess a drive to success altogether foreign to his own
most uncompulsive lifestyle. Unable to arrange any other comparably symbolic
conflict, he manages only to carp and cavil for seventeen more chapters, ill satisfied with his marginal position but unable to command any other. And as he re-
treats, his manner becomes even more (annoyingly) literary than ever, as if in
recognition that his only victories will lie in satire's domain of reductive characterization and oblique allegorical naming. Bradford writes the will of God.
Morton seems intent to make himself into a book.

Identifying himself (rather than the maypole) as the supposed "great Monster" at Ma-re Mount, and still referring to himself as "mine Host," Morton accuses the Separatists of something like beaver envy—out of which, and to embarrass any further attempts to "advance the dignity of the Church of England" (138), they set upon him at Wessaguscus, make him a prisoner to show that they are now "become masters and masterless people," and reveal their inhumanity in making sport of a man who "meant them no hurt." He escapes, by superior wit, but is pursued by "their grand leader Captain Shrimp" (140), who is anxious to restore his military honor. Taking eight men with him, he (Standish) and they become "the nine Worthies of New Canaan" (141), to whom "mine Host" surrenders so as to avoid bloodshed. For their part, the Nine Worthies despoil Morton's plantation and, taking the (king's) "law into their own hands," order him "to be sent to England a prisoner"; when this cannot be immediately effected, they set him upon an island, where he is ministered to by the savages—"so full of humanity are these infidels before these Christians" (144–45). Eventually he takes ship for England, but "no man [there] being able to tax him of any thing," he returns almost at once, to the great dismay of the Separatists, who "hoped they had been rid of him" (145).

But then, before he can go on with his second round of misadventures at the hands of these grim Inhumanists, Morton must reprise the occasions of his complaint—as if repetition could compensate for lack of sufficient motivation or even lucid explanation. And so we have "The Poem" which recaps (and attempts to mythologize) his recent trial and also "The Illustrations" which explicate the poem. Mock-heroic in their imputed villainy, the Ma-re Mount offenders appear, as Hydra, before Judges Minos, Eacus, and Radamantus, for whom identification is possible but not especially useful.[30] Once again the Separatists play fast and loose with the laws of England and do not even live up to their own word; and once again the "beaver trade" is offered as the sufficient reason why the men of Plymouth regarded Morton as "a main enemy to their Church and State" (100). No one should conclude that Morton's stylish but inept account is all false and Bradford's plain-style presentations are all true. Indeed it is just possible—though past finding out—that the very reverse may be true. The point is simply that the losers, when they have the chance to write at all, have got to learn to write a better sort of history. Starting, in this case, with the prose.

———

Fourteen of Book 3's thirty-one chapters remain after Morton has his final say about the matter of the Maypole, but they are often murky, mostly tendentious when they are at all clear, and not always very funny. A newly arrived physician (Samuel Fuller) is said to relieve one unnamed patient "of all the wind he had" and Captain Littleworth (Endicott) "of a disease called a wife" (102). An unnamed minister, come over "to play the spy," is himself "spied out" (103) by the great Joshua (Winthrop). Then, as if to show that this congeries of ad hoc and, by now, largely ad hominem vignettes really can go wherever it wishes, chapter 20 takes us back to the scene of deportation and the subsequent failure of the Separatists to have Morton discredited in England. Next, the newly arrived and endlessly self-important Littleworth is accused of "making warrants in his own name" and of needing to be reminded that the "godly" laws of Massachusetts are not to contain anything "repugnant to the laws of . . . England" (159); even with this protection, however, mine Host prefers to keep his distance and so refuses to join a general-stock arrangement for the beaver trade. Retaliating, Littleworth creates a pretext under which he can relieve Morton of his copious supply of corn but, trusting to his gun, this resourceful Host is able to feast "his body nevertheless with fowl and venison."

Then, almost as an afterthought, this small personal triumph is moralized in a way that serves to remind us of the prior, less-than-legal-or-religious difference that separates him from the grim Separatists, namely, his sense of "the plenty of the country, and the commodiousness of the place affording means by the blessing of God," of a place "so much abounding with plenty of food for an industrious man" (162). Do they not understand—Morton stops just short of demanding—that there is or easily can be plenty of everything for everybody in this land of more than milk and honey? Why this insistence on conforming to a Way so much narrower than the Spirit of the Place? The corn and the wine having been dealt freely to all, be, henceforth, a little less compulsive.

Even as we tease it out, however, this naturalistic reminder is lost in the mock celebration of an event which Morton may have known would tell definitively against him: "A great bonfire made for joy of the arrival of great Joshua surnamed Temperwell into the Land of Canaan." Of course we cannot expect him to recognize the proper beginnings of a "Great Migration," and the rules of his defeatist literary game prevent him from saying, in just so many words, "Governor Winthrop, complete with charter and quorum of a General Court"; but we, who know this newer story from other memorials, can instantly see the writing on the wall. Moral sense may favor, but criticism can do little to abet or extend, the momentary effect of Morton's deconstructive protest:

What [!] are all the 12 tribes of new Israel come: No, none but the tribe of Issacar, and some few scattered Levites. . . . And here comes their Joshua

too among them, and they make it a more miraculous thing for these
seven ships to set forth together, and arrive at New Canaan together, than
it was for the Israelites to go over Jordan dry-shod. (162)

The last irony here is telling enough, but it cannot alter the facts—of a belief system powerful enough to motivate a mass migration and then to generate a history
whose masterful repetition will impose itself on successive generations, including
quite a few which will utterly reject its first religious premise. Indeed we may
even feel tempted to read amazement as well as scorn into Morton's satiric gesture. But if we should wish to alter his own "bottom line"—"Now you may think
mine Host will be hampered or never" (163)—it could only be to say, "And marginalized too, as part of the same bargain."

A proper court is promptly called and, caught this time in the "snare" of the
"despised" Book of Common Prayer, Morton is judged worthy of a second banishment.[31] Confiscating his goods and burning his plantation satisfies the powerfully augmented Separatists that "the habitation of the wicked [shall] no more be
seen in Israel," but it prompts the "harmless savages" to lament one more "inhumane deed" and Morton himself to remark that "The smoke . . . appeared to
be the very sacrifice of Cain." Then, as if to insist that typology is not *his* game,
he quotes Epictetus and Cicero on the jests of fortune. He might have made a
remark about "vanity," but that too he leaves to his Puritan supplanters—to Anne
Bradstreet, perhaps, mourning a fire of a rather different import. Yet if he with-
draws to the margins of the text of godly letters, he will not quit the field of religion entirely: staring (in memory) at the ashes of his fallen outpost of English
merriment, he calls upon "piety itself [to] add a voice to the bare remnant of
that monument, and make it cry for recompense (or else revenge) against the
sect of cruel schismatics" (164). Even if that pious voice will have to be entirely
his own.

The rest may not be silence—indeed it may even be history—but it certainly
is anticlimax. A more-than-Separatist hegemony being now established, nothing
remains to the twice-ostracized Morton but to wreak the revenge of satire. For
social comedy, see how the beaver trade has virtue to create a new gentry in New
Canaan; for invective, witness the brutal punishment of Mr. Innocence Fair-
cloath who, though an agent of Mr. Mathias Charterparty, had the blasphemous
nerve to suggest "the Devil was the setter up of [the Puritan] Church" (112). Less
well founded, a long chapter on "the practice of their church" begins with an
attack on unlearned men (and women) as voices in the church; back in England, Morton may have got word of Anne Hutchinson, but he has certainly not
noticed the influx, beginning in 1633, of a whole cadre of Cambridge-trained

intellectuals. A section on New England preaching tries to make fun of Puritan jargon and of the tendency to torture a text into a number of sections and subsections but falls flat for want of cogent examples. And a lengthy list of differences from established English creed and practice (178–79) might serve to confirm the suspicions of William Laud, but they will horrify only those who abhor religious divergence as such. Once again, outsider criticism has presumed entirely too much. And even the sympathetic reader may have to conclude that Morton has stayed too long at the fair.

Chapter 29 represents the political anxiety felt by the "Separatists"—who now include a large majority of conscientious persons prepared to deny they are any such thing—on the eve of Morton's actual deportation. Chapter 30 briefly recounts the unhappy experience of Sir Christopher Gardiner at the hands of Master Temperwell (Winthrop, without his Joshua hat) and includes "the sonnet" in which Gardiner admonishes the "Wolves in Sheep's clothing" to study their "own infirmities" and then "be mute,"

> Lest great Jehovah with his power,
> Do come upon you in an hour,
> When you least think and you devour." (185)

After which, in literary time at least, that Good English Gentleman "disposed of himself for England, and discovered their practices in those parts towards his Majesty's true hearted subjects" (185), warning them against any plan to make a home in land which Nature made so rich. And a final chapter presents the serio-comic spectacle of Morton posing as Jonah—lodged a long and dangerous while in the belly of some poor excuse for a seagoing vessel, and then emerging at last, to issue a prophetic warning to his personal tormentors, who are also, not incidentally, the fatal corruptors of Earth's Final Canaan.

The speech may be worth quoting at some length, for only so can we gauge what we may have lost—not, this time, by the inattention of literary historians, overcome by the cumulative power of Puritan self-definition, but by the failure of original criticism to make itself originary. Morton begins by instructing the captain of his ship of deportation to "tell the Separatists that they would be made in due time to repent [their] malicious practices"; as would this Captain Weathercock himself, come to think of it; but here Morton's figurative language (of baskets and basket makers) and his syntax effectively inhibit the will to quotation. In the next moment, however, Morton's prose turns clear enough to lodge its final protest and appeal:

And now mine Host, being merrily disposed, having past many perilous adventures in that desperate whale's belly, began in a posture like Jonas, and cried, Repent you cruel Separatists, repent; there are but 40 days; if Jove vouchsafe to thunder, charter and the kingdom of the Separatists will fall asunder; Repent you cruel Schismatics, repent. And in that posture he greeted them by letters returned into New Canaan; and ever . . . he was both heard and seen in the posture of Jonas against them, crying, repent. (188)

And more to the same effect: dramatic but mannered; admirable in sentiment but overconfident of audience and clumsy in persona; cogent but not inevitable because a little too simple.

We may sympathize with Morton's feeling that "it is fitter for him to play Jonas in this kind than for the Separatists to play Jonas in that kind as they do" (188) and yet wish mine Host had cultivated, here and elsewhere, a little leaner, steadier prose, further from the redundancies of England's putative "Renaissance" and closer to the order of "Early Modern." Less formally, we may wonder why, if Morton's piety has indeed turned serious, his appeal is to "Jove" in exactly the place where Gardiner had dared to name the great "Jehovah": does he mean to imply that the true part of earthly religion is to be humble about the historic intentions of the One True God? Or does he mean to flaunt, once again, the pagan sources of his own eclectic religion? Or does his "Jove" refer only to that very earthly monarch named King Charles, more distracted, just then, than God himself, but more likely to intervene, in any event, in affairs of the English realm? The answer to this question—as to so many of similar historical overdetermination—is simply *yes*: Morton hates (and has reason to fear) the arrogance of history's New Israelites and, though he may indeed hope for divine sanction, he looks for human solutions to historical questions. God may or may not be English, but Englishmen assuredly are; and Morton imagines only scornful reasons why those living in New England should constitute a separate case. And if you'll only look for him, not "under your boot-soles," but "at the next [English] market-town," he'll gladly pluck your ears and elaborate. Indeed he may even explain why, in the final line of this other-godly letter, he adopts a name antiquity gave Apollo rarely.[32]

Above all, therefore, we may wish for a better balance between mockery and knowledge. It might seem pedantic to insist, with Perry Miller, and as we regularly do to all our students, that the Puritans who begin to pour into Massachusetts Bay under the leadership of John Winthrop in 1630 are not so simply "separatists" as Bradford's group of doubly expatriated "Pilgrims"; but it is fair to notice that this is exactly the *kind* of subtlety the broad gauge of Morton's satire is likely to miss; and this failure may stand for Morton's more general inability to imagine that his enemies may have solid and sober reasons—for being in New England in the first place and for caring so passionately for who else might wish to establish a book-and-beaver enterprise in the same neighborhood. Morton's implied audience distrusts, expects the worse of all who actively protest the hegemony of Old England. But one need not be a Puritan to detect a certain complacency within a too well established status quo that is religious and everything else at the same time; and critics of culture may feel free to demur and even to disidentify. Reformers can all be "cruel," but sometimes the Separatists are right. And as to being "Schismatics," that is exactly what the pope had thought of King Henry; and worse than that of Luther, who could do no other than stand his ground. Morton wants his fling with American Nature, and a friendly partnership with certain American Natives, but he wants his Merry England too. Which, unless it could be explained, there need not always be.

But Morton loses—to Bradford and his successors, all waiting silently in the wings of that exile drama we know as New England historiography—not because his values are English, or because his cultural loyalties are oddly mixed with a widespread European fantasy about the ur-state of American Nature, but because he obdurately refuses to think about who his enemies really are. Ridiculous in language and private manners but cruelly determined in pursuit of public policy, they seem altogether improbable, incoherent even. The Native Americans may be entitled to wonder, in the beginning at least, "Who are these guys?" but an English Author had better get a theory. And quickly, as these more-than-Separatists are about to set up a New World writing shop that will threaten to turn a delayed English Reformation into a proleptic American Renaissance. Overwhelming by volume but also by energy the literary output of all comparable colonial undertakings, they make their own venture seem in fact incomparable. Surely they must have, somewhere, some point. Did they separate with a view to making themselves absurd? Or migrate to New England on purpose to be cruel? Or was there not a project which *some* reasonable men might find worth the effort, if not of rational discussion, at least of explicit critique? But if there was, one cannot learn it from the deft but often opaque satire of Thomas Morton.

There is, of course, always the danger of giving one's enemy too much credit, of entering too sympathetically into the spirit of his opposing thought: one's reader might make the wrong choice of sympathy; indeed one might even convert oneself. It happened to Perry Miller. But, in a literary sense at least, this danger is no greater than that involved in merely positing the object and presuming the standard of one's satire. Morton's *Canaan* has its moments, but even these depend to a large extent on knowledge we have from elsewhere. And if we have it from Bradford, who so patiently explains what the Separation was all about, we may well conclude that Morton's satire, occasionally energetic but often elaborately obscure, is really an unwarranted simplification, an untimely shortcut. Not to oblivion, by any means, whatever Bradford might have wished, but to the margins of Bradford's own page, and to the subplot of a story that can establish and discredit itself, well enough, all on its own.

———

Bradford's more self-sufficient accomplishment needs its own chapter, of course, but a word or two about his *relative* standing may serve to complete the present perspective. Nothing further on his opposite but equal rendition of the Maypole; only on the spirit and premise of his own project. Made plausible, perhaps, only by his own steadfast account, that premise is most unlike that of Morton and of many other writers of early American literature as well. And we need to mark if not to honor that difference.

It may seem almost enough, given the generally useful distinction among "Discoverers, Explorers, Settlers," to say that Bradford stands out as one of the very first English *settlers* of significant literary ambition.[33] Not given to fantasy-at-a-distance, or to wholesome propaganda from the source, he wrote of his American place almost entirely as it appeared to a man who knows that history will scarcely excuse him to move again. His most peculiar situation in the world has been a long time unfolding, and there is nothing now to do but embrace it. And strongly encourage his fellow migrants to do the same. We cannot forget, of course, that Morton may well have intended to take his own final rest at Pessonagessit/Wollaston/Ma-re Mount—if only he *could* get the name just right—and that it was only the inflexible counterpurpose of Bradford and others like him which prevented that fact: who knows what his little corner of Canaan might have become if the "cruel Schismatics" had indeed relented, or if Morton's earthly "Jove" had possessed the attention and the capacity to loose his threatened thunderbolt? Then too one can imagine (if not quite credit) political conditions under which John Smith might have been willing to remain in Virginia.[34] But facts are, and they make for significant differences in experience, purpose, and genre. Unlike Smith, Wood, Morton, and other writers vying for originary attention, Bradford settled in, fought off desperation, went to work in prosecution of the purposes that led him overseas, and (eventually) decided to tell the sense of just that story.

Concealed in this apparently simple fact of life and genre, however, is a sub-tler difference between Bradford and most who went before and not a few who came after: Bradford expresses almost no interest in the land as such and—though it is naive to discount economic motives—he lends none of his consider-able rhetorical power to advertising the richness of American Nature or the wealth it might be expected to produce. Trees almost seduce Columbus from the project of gold and emeralds; Smith and Wood recalibrate New World econom-ics in favor of commodities that favor the middle class without ceasing to revel in their overlapping versions of the ecological sublime; Morton weds English Cul-ture to the State of Nature. Lacking this well-publicized sense of "wonder" al-most entirely, Bradford lives and dies by the Reformation: he has no prejudice against wealth as such, and the crucial "New Deal" of 1627 makes him a rich man; but he did not know before the fact that this would be so;[35] and he learns to hate both the cattle market and the allure of land when they threaten to disrupt his particular Church, made up to look like a veritable Act of the Apostles and carried about like an Ark of the Covenant.

No one can now with a straight face say anything like "Ask not what your country can do for you" but, having had the rare good fortune not to know Camelot, Bradford dares organize his own purposes around the theme not of gain but of sacrifice. We cannot say for certain that he and his fellow Pilgrims were, in 1620, entirely proof against the pleasing if extravagant New World ad-vertisements of John Smith and others, but he certainly chose to repress this con-sideration when he came, in 1630, to look back over his twelve-year sojourn in Holland and his ten-year experiment at Plymouth. Indeed Bradford might be thought to be replying to Smith and his whole tradition at just that critical mo-ment of historical review. Not that he and his Pilgrims rushed to the New World headlong, expecting to suffer and probably die in the prosecution of utopian fan-tasy; but "Summertime, and the Livin' Is Easy" is just the song he never did learn to sing.

Any move out of Holland would involve, he knew, a "change of air, diet and drinking of water [which] would infect their bodies with sore sickness and griev-ous diseases" (26); and the American option conjures an expectation of "savage and brutish men which range up and down, little otherwise than the wild beasts" (25). Some of the Holland group represent Guiana, in terms we recognize, as "rich, fruitful, and blessed with a perpetual spring and a flourishing greenness, where vigorous nature brought forth all things in abundance and plenty without any great labor or of man" (28). But an Anglo suspicion of hot climates prevails, and so the decision is for the northern parts of Virginia—more temperate and not too close to the Church of England men already planted at Jamestown. And if the Brethren expected the regions around Hudson's river to be as lush and fruitful as those around the Orinoco, nothing is said of this fond belief.

Further, when the Brethren represent themselves to the London merchants, who have the capital (and may yet find the wisdom) to fund a plantation made by cautious and not unruly Separatists, heavy emphasis falls on their courage and proven endurance. Anticipating no easy time of their American venture, they nevertheless expect to measure up. Unlike the quarreling men who seem to be making a mess of Smith's Virginia,[36] they are, by reason of the covenant at the center of their religion, doubly and trebly unified in mind and practice. Furthermore, given the remarkable experience in Holland, they are "well weaned from the delicate milk of [their] mother country, and inured to the difficulties of a strange and hard land"; also to the purpose, they are as "industrious and frugal . . . as any company of people in the world"; and so, most generally, "it is not with us as with other men, whom small things can discourage, or small discontentments cause to wish themselves at home again" (33). A strong case, the merchants may well have thought, and from a fairly improbable source: one hardly imagined a separate sect could write so well.[37]

Most memorable, perhaps, is Bradford's justly famous but often misunderstood meditation on the aspect of land and reflection of mood at the moment of arrival. Written from the safety of 1630, when physical survival is assured, and ideological imitation seems to be publishing itself, Bradford can afford to make the prospect of 1620 as bleak as possible. The worse, indeed the better: for the degree to which a happy outcome seemed unlikely then is exactly the measure of the remarkable nature, perhaps even the miracle, of the success now enjoyed.[38] And so Bradford lets it all come out, plain as any Puritan stylist might require, but sure of its power, not of "blackness," exactly, but of a grim experimental realism thrown back in the face of Nature's bland deceit and theory's soft desire: a barely figurative "sea of troubles" behind them, they have, just now, no safe place to turn; not back to England or even to the ship, a May Flower most painfully misnamed in the gathering November and December of potential discontent;

> [N]o friends to welcome them nor inns to entertain or refresh their weather-beaten bodies; no houses or much less towns to repair to, to seek for succor. . . . And for the season it was winter, and they that know the winters of that country know them to be sharp and violent, and subject to cruel and fierce storms, dangerous to travel to known places, much more to search an unknown coast. Besides, what could they see but a hideous

and desolate wilderness, full of wild beasts and wild men—and what multitudes there might be of them they knew not. (61–62)

Leaving Thoreau to turn New England's winter back into Morton's summer, Bradford goes on with more to the same, deliberately dismal effect: the more desperate the "natural" condition—including, emphatically, the condition of physical nature itself—the greater the need, then, for only faith to save; and, not incidentally, the greater the evidence, now, that this faith indeed had saved.

One might go on, of course, to the starving time when, by Bradford's self-conscious account, it was not the land but only God and a spirit of self-sacrifice that preserved any of them from the ravages of starvation and disease in the first New England winter. But by now the point should be clear: never a poet of plenitude, Bradford writes American literature under the sign of natural lack and spiritual longing—and of a religious project that may compensate the one by richly fulfilling the other. The choice of some region in "America" seems to have been conscious and deliberate, but Bradford is simply not interested in the attractions of the Nature that the literature of early American representation had draped with such allure. For this moment at least, the project of Reformation is vastly more important than any quality in the land. Repeatedly imagined as a yet unspoiled locus of Nature, and often inhabited as a place of actual refuge, Bradford's New England is simply the scene where ancient Scripture may presently be enacted.[39]

Adventure, wonder, even pleasure to the contrary, surely Smith speaks the implicit sense of whole choirs of "Discoverers" and "Explorers" when, expressing the gathered wisdom of the worldly wise, he stipulates that no "other motive than wealth will ever erect . . . a common wealth, or draw company from their ease and humors at home to stay in New England" (219). So comprehensive is this one brief sentence that the only question is deciding where exactly to lodge the emphasis. Not much given to indulge their "humors," in plays or in dead earnest, the Pilgrim Brethren have been off from "home," as they have told the merchant adventurers, for some time now; and "ease" never having been either their ideal aim or their actual condition, perhaps the economic challenge does not apply. But supposing it does indeed survive the Separatists' collection of very special conditions, Bradford's answer is ready to hand and very nearly explicit. It prefaces all the distress and potential discouragement that constitute the substance of Bradford's account up to and including the landing and the starving time. Not in it for wealth—not even for that "esthetic" richness which elsewhere either grounds or disguises or distracts from the lust for king's gold or entrepreneur's cod and beaver—Bradford expects to pay a very high life cost for his curious venture. Not ease but hardship, and no wealth except the rare satisfaction of doing right.

Bradford's strong thematic claim comes early, just after his summary outline of what reformed churches do and do not look like, and just before he announces the formation of "two distinct bodies or churches." Dropped as a dare to the cynical reader, it may also be read as an answer to Smith and all others who dream an America of natural richness. At first the conscious claim may seem all jargon, the kind from which a man like Morton must decently avert his gaze: awakened sinners shake off their

> yoke of antichristian bondage, and as the Lord's free people [join] themselves (by a covenant of the Lord) into a church estate, in the fellowship of the gospel, to walk in all His ways made known, or to be made known unto them, according to their best endeavors, whatever it should cost them, the Lord assisting them.

But then comes the differential boast, in the plainest possible English: "And that it cost them something this ensuing history will declare" (9). Whatever else you may have read, dear reader, expect the story of these pages to emphasize not disinterested pleasure or covetous gain but actual human cost; or, if gain should yet become the leading fact this history has to name, then turn away and read some other book.

To emphasize this daring claim is not at all to suspend economic suspicion or to forswear material analysis. Indeed Bradford's text is everywhere full of financial detail; and—as Robert Daly has ably argued—Bradford is himself the first to notice that his express ideal of self-sacrifice in the name of holy community goes sadly unfulfilled.[40] It is simply to notice that there is a thematic as well as a generic difference between Bradford and a whole host of wood 'n' water prophets. Accordingly, the interest in his narrative cannot concern the question of whether the Canaan place did or did not live up to a certain set of all but a priori expectations; it must concern, instead, the way a project hatched out amidst the complex politics of Old England—a plan "to live ancient lives,"[41] perhaps—could be made to work within, perhaps even to create, a simpler politics in the New. And if it could not, whether any of the reasons for the failure might be called *geo*political. And it is to argue that, fair or not, the vague self-defeat of William Bradford's hopes makes a more self-sufficient narrative—and marks the beginning of a story more fraught with consequences—than the final, perhaps brutal check handed to those of Thomas Morton.

But to say that Bradford thus marginalizes Morton is not to suggest that he in any sense destroys or obliterates him. Rather, Bradford puts Morton squarely in a place of an ancillary yet in some ways necessary paratext (pre-text, if one recalls that Bradford can have read Morton and not the reverse). More than that, perhaps, Morton may be lucky to have been put in just that place; for, given the difficulties we face in trying to read the *Canaan* all on its own—including the not insignificant problem of a decidedly premodern "style"[42]—far more people seem to read Morton for Bradford's sake than for his own gnarly and not quite hilarious reason. In any case, the American canon—and even the Puritanist project— is only the richer for the fact that Bradford's long-arriving book inevitably points to its own critique, less well accomplished, but perched always at the margins of his own.

Nor should it be imagined that Bradford has the power to displace *all* books seeking pride and primacy of place. Some day, when we know what the project of an Inter-American literature would have to look like, or when we find a credible way to begin the national story itself with the Spanish in Florida or New Mexico, Bradford may slide toward the middle of a story beginning with Columbus and other discoverers but featuring the truly remarkable exploratory *Adventures* of Cabeza de Vaca, who also writes under the sign of "cost." Sent to keep a record of an expedition bent on discovering whole cities of gold, Cabeza is forced, by a fortune barely recognizable as Providence, to rehearse instead the story of his bare survival and the nearly unbelievable tale of a cultural adaptation that gave him an odd but not dishonorable place in a set of native societies which kings and conquerors could scarcely credit. The cost is to his body, that is to say, but also to his ready assumption of national (and racial) superiority. Even more telling, however, is Cabeza's account of the cost, to the natives, of colonial intrusion itself.[43] This fundamental consideration is all but absent in Bradford, who imagines his project is altogether metahistorical; and it appears only intermittently in Morton, who harshly judges the Separatist supplantation but seems largely to overlook his own curious but not altogether innocent efforts at cultural miscegenation—as if an Algonquin people, full-time hunters and sometime farmers, were naturalists enough to grasp at once the symbolic sense of their worldly being in the erection of a maypole.

Bradford's firm rejection of what Morton called Canaan bespeaks a foundational abstinence from the rare and remarkable pleasures of a wonderful place, abundant in supply if imaginative in form. Yet the finality of this refusal produces not the absence or the dullness of sensibility that Morton seems to have supposed but an astonishing fullness of another sort, also recognizable, perhaps, as imaginative in kind. Less heroic than Cabeza's rare willingness to join and then to speak for the autonomy of a native people scratching out what some might call a marginal existence at the edges of a most unforgiving landscape, Bradford initiates not the master narrative of European Man in America but only the lesser yet much denser story of British Zealots in New England. A literary story. A story of many books, all turning their attention not to a wonderful land or the strange persons living there but to worldly purposes of a God they seem always and never to have known; and to themselves who, apart from those godly purposes, they could not hope to know at all. Nobler projects are possible, no doubt, but none we see so fully written out. Godlier ways we are free to imagine, but godlier prose we are not to expect.

PART ONE

VISION

CHAPTER TWO

ADVANCING THE GOSPEL, DIVIDING THE CHURCH

Design and Vision in Bradford's *Plymouth*

I. THE TRIUMPH OF DESIGN

Nothing could seem more telling, at first glance, than the structural division by which William Bradford organizes the materials in the remarkable account of his community of doubly exiled Separatists. "The First Book" sets out, in ten brisk, topical chapters, the events leading up to this momentous New World plantation: a religious awakening that spurs the formation of extralegal churches, the persecution provoked thereby, the impeded flight to toleration in Holland, the critical decision to leave that pluralist domain, the various steps leading up to the perilous ocean voyage, the climactic arrival scene, and (less rhetorically) the first efforts at securing the basis of the group's transplanted life. Then, in "The Second Book," beginning in 1620 with the famous "Mayflower Compact," Bradford offers a set of yearly entries, or "annals," which record "the heads of principal things . . . as they fell out in order of time, and may seem to be profitable to know" (73).[1] Eventually, of course, every reader must puzzle to infer the law by which Bradford discovers things to be "principal" and "important to know," and this in *both* parts of his self-divided history. But his own design suggests that everything leading up to the actual planting of the Plymouth colony, including that "weighty voyage" itself, is merely preparatory. Had the little band of Saints failed to establish a viable outpost of Reformed Christianity, Bradford could scarcely have imagined the vicissitudes of his group were worth the telling; for he hardly strikes us as a man who, like Columbus or John Smith, was tempted to regard adventure itself as the end of travel and indeed of life.[2]

37

But Bradford's masterful history, *Of Plymouth Plantation,* admits of another sort of structural self-division, not so immediately visible as a feature of explicit authorial design, but even more important to the experience of reading and absolutely crucial to the writer's silent sense of his own task. I refer, of course, to the fact that Bradford began formally to write his history not in 1608, when his odyssey first began, and not in 1620, at the moment of arrival in New England, but only in 1630, when quite a lot of New World experience had already been logged. What this delay suggests, I think, is that Bradford was even more self-restrained than even his modest habits of style have always suggested; that he waited and waited and watched and watched until events should have proven the larger significance of his unusually ragged life experience so far; until only a settled skeptic like Thomas Morton could doubt that a sequence of Puritan successes in New England had to "mean" something.[3] Something important, in which God almost certainly had a hand.

Able criticism has already suggested that the events in the Plymouth history get harder and harder for Bradford to "read" as the New England decades wear on, and this may indeed have as much to do with the lack of adequate retrospect as with the increasing complexity of the events themselves.[4] But it is just as important to be explicit about the precise emphasis the retrospect of 1630 positively enables, in the annals of the 1620s as well as the more narrative chapters before that. For to understand exactly what sort of a book Bradford actually writes, it is necessary to consider well the moment when he decided he had one to write. What his well-tempered idealism required, it appears, was not just safe arrival, however fortunate, or survival of the starving time, however revealing of the pilgrim character; not just a couple of crucial adjustments in the arrangement of the Plymouth economy, or the timely exposure of spies and their plots; but nothing less than full and explicit assurance that his Separatist sympathies had been premature only in the positive sense of being well ahead of their time and that his singular community was in fact coming to serve as a signal example. Otherwise, one risked corporate egotism on the one side and curious irrelevance on the other: divine redirections of history were precious rare, after all, and of the making of books of natural men's natural experiences there appeared to be no end.

———

A prime question involving the "chronology" of Bradford's account has been mentioned in chapter 1—the problem of what we might call the "pessimism" of the famous arrival scene. Surely the gloom is strategic: the arriving Pilgrims may or may not have fallen "upon their knees" to bless "the God of heaven who had brought them over the vast and furious ocean," but probably their mood was, at some such moment, indeed "joyful" (61).[5] It is only some authorial "I" who, looking over their heads, as it were, can see past this moment of joy and face the daunting circumstances that loom like shadows cast by the pale sun of present deliverance. And even this sadder and wiser observer would hardly dare interrupt the joy of his fellows with a solemn preachment on the terrible text of his own discouragement; indeed it seems unlikely that he himself would have had either the perspicacity or the nerve, just then, to face them himself. Speaking in the historical rather than the literal present, he looks back from the safety of 1630 to the danger of 1620: the knowledge of eventual success liberates a realism which the weakness of the flesh was *then* strong enough only to repress; and the frank evocation of the odds against that little band of true believers serves to lift the fact of their success out of the realm of chance and into the world of faith.

It is a rare moment in the history of religious literature. And Bradford, who everywhere tells us what he must, for the sake of brevity, and must not, for the sake of truth, omit, is never on a surer ground of professed necessity: his brief and stylized account of the "weighty voyage" decides "to omit other things (that I may be brief)" (59); but here he cannot omit. Knowing what he knows about what might be required to achieve the success that *has been* achieved, he pauses to suffer and to savor the moment this double vision can alone create; and to invite his reader to do the same:

> Here I cannot but stay and make a pause, and stand half amazed at this poor people's present condition; and so I think will the reader, too, when he well considers the same. (61)

The invitation is really a dare, of course—to the reader of Smith's natural economy, it may be, or of Morton's natural pleasure—to enter the spirit of this complex, constructed moment; and to read anything *but* divine purpose into the one-try success of anything so chancy; to name the writer's representation of the people's mixture of repressed foresight and sad memory as anything but faith. No wonder if the children were indeed impressed by the "wonderful works" of their fathers' God; or if some of his valeur rubbed off on them.[6]

But we, who are agreed to read literature and not confess faith, may find the loaded and explosive word in Bradford's most immemorial passage not any magical invocation of favoring providence or fond posterity but only the simple-appearing temporal marker "now": "What could *now* sustain them but the Spirit of God and His Grace?" (62–63; my emphasis). Not the *now* of his writing, in 1630, obviously, though we may be certain that Bradford hoped he was bearing witness to the enduring reality of that self-same favor; but not an innocent chronotrope for the *then* of 1620 either, though surely Bradford could recall *some* sense of trouble in the midst of their arriving joy; and not merely the polite, literary fiction of historical recovery, as writers boldly leave the now of now and live again the now of then. But also the rare figure of the mind truly grasping now what was fairly hidden then: the faltering but not failing faith that could not see its present victory; the triumphant now, refusing to believe that only time had gone between. A remarkable moment. So read, the long list of insuperable difficulties— of being all but abandoned and alone in a strange, unsettled, and even savage land, full of hostile inhabitants, at a season never represented in the propaganda of American Nature—actually gives the moment of arrival an air not of pessimism but of exhilaration. Each impediment becomes in fact a further glory. What but faith *could* sustain them? And, as they were indeed sustained, their faith had to be real: itself a gift of God, that faith was hardly different from the gracious protection that enabled them to come as far by 1630 as Bradford knows he will shortly be writing to show. Daring to contrast his plight with that of "the Apostle" Paul in his evangelical mission and then with that of Moses in his exodus (61–63), Bradford subtly manages to imply a place for his own enterprise within the sublime context of holy history: if it succeeds, it means a share in God's eternal plan; if not, it means nothing at all; and, at the moment of writing, it seems to be succeeding beyond belief.

Explicitly denying that anyone "then," wandering alone in the latter days, when miracles may indeed have ceased, could "go up to the top of Pisgah to view from this wilderness a more goodly country to feed their hopes" (62), Bradford actually succeeds in providing an inverse of such a vision "now." Possession of that "goodly country" has had the effect of liberating the story it were folly for any good man to tell too soon. And though the first-time reader does not yet know the Pilgrim's timely success against the frivolous Lyford and Oldham—or the mythic one against the provocative Morton—and though he has only a momentary hint that, by 1630, the Bradford group will indeed have served as "stepping-stones unto others" (25) in the performance, in America, of the last-days business of completing the Reformation, he knows that Bradford at least has escaped the looming death to tell the tale; which fact, given the chances Bradford spares no prose to name, may seem like miracle enough. But something else is true as well: something in the assurance with which Bradford heaps it up assures us that he is "now" quite safe and, in a guarded sense, proud. Had the Pilgrims all disappeared, like the vanished inhabitants of Roanoke, no word at all; and had their mission simply failed, prose like this would never dare.

Glad enough to have set foot on dry land, no arriving Pilgrim could be at all assured that triumph lay ahead, as if the type should know itself as such. And no succeeding saint could dare exult in present good achieved, as if to value pleasure over pain; or else, at the very least, to tempt the God that turned the fates away. But how avoid the godly task to turn and look behind? The vision is not of a promised and predicted land from Pisgah's desert mount but, Puritan-wise, a backward glance from safety to the wilderness behind. A somber look, no doubt; unsurvivable, perhaps, if truly taken then and there. But full of faith fulfilled and hope restored if taken "now"—when Bradford lets his present work its magic on the past. A post- and anti-Pisgah vision that makes the present glow by shadowing the past; and hides within the past a seed of hope that dare not name itself as such. Achieving something more "amazing" than a Pisgah vision, Bradford turns a lavish list of insuperable difficulties—which have in fact been overcome—into the one sort of luxuriance the Puritan imagination dare indulge: to learn the transport by the pain.

But if the arrival scene does indeed epitomize the strategy of Bradford's work of retrospect—a first part ending more truly in 1630 than in 1620—it is hardly the only moment when the confidence of achieved success redeems the ragged sense of work in progress. Consider, for example, the instinct prompting Bradford to insert, as part of chapter 8's account, "Of the Troubles that befell them on the Coast, and at Sea" (52), a despairing letter by Robert Cushman. As we have seen in the case of the letter that Robinson and Brewster sent to Sir Edwin Sandys on behalf of the London adventurers, Bradford is never too proud of his project to allow other persons to speak in their own voices, especially when they truly express the *sensus communis*. Indeed, when these letters are particularly well written, he may be thought of as half-consciously enhancing the effect of his own verbal production. But such is not the case with Cushman's (Aug. 17) letter to Edward Southworth ("a member of the Leyden congregation who did not emigrate"):[7] grumbling rather than professing, this letter lacks both the faith and the passion of the Robinson-Brewster credo; and Bradford is far from suggesting that Cushman's John Smith–like complaints represent the mood of the group at the moment of migration.

His point is simply that someone—not this time Bradford's own divided self—has the wit to notice and the courage to say out loud that there is no *natural* reason to suppose the Pilgrim adventure can possibly succeed. And so, for the moment, Bradford lets Cushman speak for that ordinary human point of view:

Friend, if ever we make a plantation, God works a miracle, especially considering how scant we shall be of victuals, and most of all ununited amongst ourselves and devoid of good tutors and regiment. Violence will break all. Where is the meek and humble spirit of Moses? . . . Is not the sound of Rehoboams's brags daily here amongst us? Have not the philosophers and all wise men observed that, even in settled commonwealths, violent governors bring either themselves or people or both to ruin? How much more in the raising of commonwealths . . . ? (56–57)

Passing over the question of the identity of the braggarts and conceding that Cushman appears to be denying exactly what the Robinson-Brewster letter so passionately affirmed, and what the farewell letter of Pastor Robinson had so explicitly instructed—"that with your common employments you join common affections truly bent upon the general good" (369)[8]—we "cannot but" pause over Cushman's jaundiced view of the prospect; and over his unguarded use of the word *miracle.*

There is some reason to think that, modern enough to include a whole range of relevant documents in his avant-garde history, Bradford may also be honest enough to present evidences that are embarrassing along with those that fairly shine: notice, dear reader, we were not, all of us, always so full of faith and hope. Then, too, there is reason to notice that Cushman's despair is not ultimate, that his letter comes around to the side of piety after all: "[P]ray you prepare for evil tidings of us every day. But pray for us instantly, it may be the Lord will be entreated one way or another to make for us" (57). Another up and down, perhaps, in a faith not fully proof against the world. But another commentary seems called for as well.

The moment of Cushman's writing is of course 1620 and, supposing Bradford first saw the letter then, there is no way of knowing how Cushman's gloomy mood or his practical theology affected him at just that time. No one could foresee that Thomas Morton would soon be preparing to pounce on any possible Puritan pretense of miracle, but surely all the principals had thought long and hard on the reason and the method of God's ordinary and also his special Providence; and no doubt they would all be in sympathy with John Winthrop's later, uneasy attempt to deflect the charge that the odds against success are so great that "we must look to be preserved by miracle if we subsist, and so we shall tempt God."[9] Evidently Cushman has raised the stakes to the highest level; nor can Bradford include his letter without being drawn into a dangerous logic. Not predictively, of course, as at the moment of Cushman's original doubt and prayer, but retroactively, reflexively, as the triumphant knowledge of 1630 disciplined the legitimate fear of 1620.

For what might have seemed outrageous in 1620—a daring of God to look with favor on one small and damaged ship in the throes of the angry North Atlantic, and a presumptuous hope that he might not incline his ear to what things were being praised or blamed on that ship of more than fools—appeared in quite another light by 1630. No one dare put himself in the position of requiring or even begging a miracle of God; and if Cushman has placed himself in that most unenviable position, then charity's self can do no more than forgive, within the swing of human hope and desperation, a moment's mood of last resort.[10] But judging of potent cause after the fact of remarkable effect presents an altogether different problem; and who can deny the right of piety to confess God when a favorable outcome could in no way have been expected? Indeed, one might consider defining "miracle" in just that way: an event confirming faith that hope itself could not predict. Again, the more credibly pessimistic seem the informed predictions of a seasoned skepticism, the more glorious the happy effect. So that Bradford's own commentary seems modest indeed. The real-life gloom of the fathers is included so "that their children may see with what difficulties their fathers wrestled . . . and how God brought them along, notwithstanding all their weaknesses and infirmities" (46). Here again, in its simplest form, is the formula that explains the force of Bradford's retrospect: the weaker then, the stronger set in faithful knowledge now.

So important are the events and attitudes embraced by this formula that they may come to count for more than the glaring but more local instances of unusual divine intervention: the salvation of John Howland, whose apotheosis leaps straight up from the ocean perishing of another, nameless, but equally "lusty" (58, 59) young man; the unlooked-for discovery of a buried cache of corn and seed (65–66);[11] the deliverance from a "first encounter" with a band of armed natives (69–70), itself closely followed by the friendly appearance of first Samoset and then Squanto (79–81). Credulous rather than critical, in the manner of a saint, Bradford regards these accidents as more significant than they would be in the life (or in the book) of a less godly settler in the unfamiliar world of New England—of John Smith, for example, who may have made up the story of his own salvation at the hand of King Powhatan's "dearest daughter" but who did not in any event presume to offer it as a special manifestation of divine favor.[12] And the discovery of this difference, of faith as of mission, marks a recognizable feature of godly letters in the (American) seventeenth century. Yet not, perhaps, the most essential one.

For the confidence that led Bradford to write his book at all, in 1630, and at various times thereafter, was arrived at not by the calculus that needs to find an infinite sum for all its finite instances. That confidence rests, rather, on the more probablist (more psychological) logic we have been noticing: no one had the nerve, in 1620, to make much of what a small, self-divided sect of religious dissidents might hope to accomplish by moving half their number from one place of exile to another; and *almost* no one, then, had the courage to say out loud how slim were the odds of accomplishing anything at all. No one paying attention to the infant state of the English colonial enterprise would have been surprised if the Pilgrim ship had sailed off into oblivion; or if the Separatists had been massacred the day they violated a native grave site; or if none of them had survived a first winter of starvation. But they made it—through all that and a number of other difficulties that no one's colonialist imagination could predict a priori. And someone, Bradford thought, had better make the most of that.[13] Especially as, by 1630, the moment of conviction and hence of initial writing, his little band of "stepping-stones" (25) could see themselves as turning into the cornerstone of Reformation's New World meetinghouse. And if, for this truly transcendent success, Jehovah is to "have all the praise," the reason can only be that the wondrous work has been beyond the strength of any arm of flesh. Talk of special providences, as Emerson might say, it is *all* providence: "all design[,] . . . all beauty[,] . . . all astonishment."[14] And all of it worth, if truth be told, "whatsoever it [had] cost" (9).

———

Also implied by the fact that the visionary, the literary *Plymouth* began at the moment of triumph in 1630 is the correction of an error profound enough to have been made by Perry Miller. Recent criticism has been attentive to the question of *when* the American Puritans first glimpsed the shape of their famous "errand": was the hope to complete history by perfecting the Reformation a significant part of their out-setting motivation? Did it develop gradually as time went by and events went well? Or was it a late but all-at-once creation of the second generation, a way of explaining what they were doing in a world they held but never had quite sought? Miller, however, was satisfied to inquire *what* they imagined their highest purpose precisely to be—and about their use of the very word *errand* to call it by name: Did "errand" signify some duty a subaltern might perform on behalf of an agency more fully valorized? Or were they acting entirely for themselves? Were they nothing but "errand boys" acting in the name of the Church of the Future in England? Or had they claimed to be their own knights errant?[15] At issue, in the long run, was the possibility that America might be an afterthought. Perhaps even a mistake.

One thing, in any event, seemed perfectly clear to Miller: *no* version of the errand problem applied to the Bradford group. This was indeed "the charm about Plymouth: its clarity." "Reluctant voyagers," the "Pilgrims" had departed only when the "authorities made life impossible for Separatists." Their escape to Holland was nothing but an unhappy necessity, and "neither can we extract the notion of a mission out of the reasons which . . . persuaded them to leave Leyden for 'Virginia.'" To be sure, Miller pays his respect to these heroes of conscience when he reminds us that they left England because the idea of ceasing to be Separatists "simply did not occur to them." But the real force of his argument comes in his gritty, almost cynical account of their second departure, the one which watchful Bradford finally knew required a book: as the "war with Spain was about to be resumed, . . . their migration was not so much an errand as a shrewd forecast, a plan to get out while the getting was good."[16] And with this wave of the hand—part admiration and part dismissal—Miller moves on to the vexed question of the motives to migrate to Massachusetts Bay.

Excluded by this haste, unfortunately, is not only a fully nuanced reading of exactly what Bradford does in fact offer as "the Reasons and Causes of their Removal" (23) but also, more crucially, a sense of what light the achievements of 1630 cast backward on the motives of 1620. A less assured reader than Miller can find much to puzzle over in the ample list of considerations Bradford projectively remembers as bearing on a migration more momentous and memorable than the flight from England's religious police in 1608. A mixture of motives is well revealed and, possibly, an intention to make some unsettling distinction between "Causes" and "Reasons." Most important, however, is the strategy by which a retrospectively assured Bradford decides merely to hint, as of 1620, at the power of an explanation which, by 1630, he knew to be the necessary and sufficient condition of the Pilgrims' truly epochal decision. In the discussions of 1620, that decision might have meant many things or just nothing at all. In retrospect, however, it meant the errand.

If there is, in 1620, a single operative "cause" of the removal from Holland, that certainly is the one which Miller makes so plain: the end of "that famous truce between that state and the Spaniards" (23). But, if our criticism is to be in any sense literary, we can hardly let it go at that. No more than Bradford himself. No more than Winthrop or Shepard when they, in their turn, find the need to set out a list of "Reasons" to embrace a course they seem increasingly powerless to resist. Beyond the moving *cause,* a forecast of war and peace, there must be, in all reason, *reasons,* assuring men that what they must they plainly also may. "Rationalization," it may seem, to a century more inclined to take full praise for its happy decisions and, more important, to give full credit to the process by which we seem to be making up our minds. To these earlier analysts of human motivation, however, the process may have seemed a little more "Melvillean."[17]

Of "reasons," then, Bradford lists four, the first three of which collapse into a single encompassing consideration and a fourth which, taken all by itself, is easy to misunderstand. First, from "the hardness of the country" they already notice that only a few new members will "come to them" and, of those, not many will "bide it out and continue" (23). Second, though the original group remains stout of purpose, Bradford can already see "old age [beginning] to steal on many of them," and can predict that "within a few years more they would be in danger to scatter, by necessities pressing them, or sink under their burdens, or both" (24). Third, there is the question of "their children," beginning here and never far off hereafter: the same hardness of life shows many becoming "decrepit in their early youth"; and worse, from Bradford's point of view, many others, imitating the "great licentiousness of youth in that country," are falling prey to "the manifold temptations of the place"—becoming soldiers, departing on sea voyages, or in other ways "tending to dissoluteness and the danger of their souls" (24–25). Taken together, these three reasons indicate that Bradford is already concerned about the survivability of his group as such, his prime consideration.

On this reading, the approach of war only forces into the open what the suitably concerned observer must already be thinking: unless something is done, the exemplary distinctness of our covenanted church—for the sake of which we find ourselves self-exiled in the first place—will soon be overtaken by that set of inevitable forces which saints everywhere call "the world." At worst, the children will rebel and live their lives according to other values entirely; and at best, the entire group will simply blend into the current of the tolerant and otherwise unterrible life in busy and bustling Holland. And whether any big bang had been expected or not, that surely were to end with a whimper. There is no doubt that those awakened souls who, in the fateful years of 1607 and 1608, formed themselves into "two distinct bodies or churches" (9), did so partly for what Bradford elsewhere calls "Christian and comfortable fellowship" (253): in a world that seemed less and less familiar and secure, they hoped that this covenanted group of "professors" might be, each to each and all to all, more truly a family than those the world tears asunder—or which one voluntarily leaves when called to follow Christ. Probably Bradford and a few other like-minded saints could have straggled on, keeping the souls of one another warm, in Leyden as well as elsewhere. But would that cozy little outcome be enough?

To say *no* to this unavoidable question is to concede that there is already, in Bradford's reformist purpose, some inceptive version, if not of "*the* errand," then at least of a sense of "*a* mission": Reformation might begin with a church that was "particular" in its formation and function, but it did not end until this local ideal showed forth, in the very fact of its local repetition, some power to heal the world. That is to say: the Separatist church may have been entirely particular in its "polity," but its worldly reach was wide indeed. Separatist Reformation was to begin *now*—at this very moment, "without tarrying for any"—but no one can suppose Robert Browne would be satisfied with a local church or two.[18] And we probably misread Bradford at this point unless we realize that he wished his congregation to be not only perfect, according to the Bible plan, but *exemplary* as well. And what could one make of an example grown too dim for any but the aging eyes of its own members to see?

With this question in mind, perhaps we can read Bradford's last reason, which he assures us "was not least," to mean something other than a weak and easily abandoned wish to convert the natives of the northern parts of Virginia or, as it turned out, of New England, to some brand of Western Christianity. It is easy to be misled, just here, by the pro forma appearance of that motive in virtually every writer, from Columbus to John Smith, who felt the need to justify intrusion into a world where things were working well enough, if a little differently, all on their own. For if Bradford intends nothing more than to repeat this pious minimalism, his formulation seems a little overwrought:

> A great hope and inward zeal they had of laying some good foundation . . .
> for the propagating and advancing the gospel of the kingdom of Christ in
> those remote parts of the world; yea, though they should be but even as
> stepping-stones unto others for the performing of so great a work. (25)

Noticeably, no form of the omnipresent word *conversion* is used here; nor, for the moment, is any mention made of the Native Americans. In the next paragraph, they show up as "savage and brutish men" for whom conversion might not even be a live option. To be sure, any advancing of "the gospel of the kingdom of Christ" must presume the winning of a fair number of souls to the knowledge of the Divine Redeemer and of the place of his atonement within the logic of predestination, but Bradford's emphasis may *still* be on the church; he may well be implying that, unless one wished to concede a vast new territory to the policy and the priests of Roman Catholicism, the cause of reformation requires not a few Protestant "missionaries" but some visible outpost of reformed polity in the American world.

What assures this reading, however, is the language that reflects Bradford's later but originary understanding of the larger-scale Puritan events of 1629–30: rightly or wrongly he comes to understand his own endeavor as the stone on which later, more numerous and powerful migrations have needed to place their unsteady feet in order to make *some* sort of separation from the insufficiently reformed churches of England; and the modest but awkward qualification which reduces "laying some good foundation" to "at least to make some way thereunto" points more precisely to the comparative, perhaps competitive moment of the migration of John Winthrop and his associates than to the homelier one of 1620. This later purpose, he more than implies, has been his own as well. And converting the natives is largely incidental to the rationale of men like Endicott, Winthrop, and Dudley.[19]

One might argue that Bradford's fourth reason tells us almost nothing about the earlier moment. Clearly the "Pilgrim" migration is more than satisfactorily accounted for by supposing that the end of Holland's truce with Spain may have clarified the growing suspicion that the safety of Holland had not solved all of the problems of maintaining an exemplary Christian identity, that it may in fact have precipitated the decision to make some sort of move. The wish to volunteer for the task of manning an outpost of what would be called "congregationalism" in the New World, to offset and if possible to retard the spread of Catholicism there, may have been little more than inchoate in the discussions Bradford recounts in his crucial fourth chapter. Probably the situation was a trifle more complex than Miller makes it appear; but even that reading, of the utter simplicity of Pilgrim motive in 1620, can be maintained so long as we recognize that, by 1630, Bradford is clearly committing himself to the idea that—cause or motive—some fit preparation for the large-scale movement of persons and property, real and ideological, we have come to know as the "Great Migration" had become and deserved to survive as the "meaning" of that earlier, less populous, less theorized translation of saints. Even if we should suppose, therefore, that Bradford intended *nothing* but a timely escape in 1620, still he had, a decade later, entirely incorporated "the errand" into his own project.[20] And that as the necessary condition of his decision to write.

We will need to look carefully, then, at the series of events leading up to the climax of Bradford's conviction and the origin of his writing. For whether we take them to confirm or originally to suggest some world-class motive, they turned Bradford from an elder in a Separatist sect (which Thomas Morton felt sure he could mock almost without naming) into the prime author of "Early American Literature"; from a stray dissenter who seems somewhere to have acquired a little learning and may have had a penchant for saving letters and making notations into the founding father of literary New England. Yet one more word—on Bradford's actual, verbal beginnings—may not be out of place.

In this regard, Miller's wish for Plymouth to be simple may conceal a less innocent desire—to keep Bradford's story as secular as possible. The evidence appears in his way of representing Bradford in his widely used (and imitated) anthologies. No one who has tried to teach *Plymouth* to the multiply distracted survey students of latter-day America can possibly object to the idea that some judicious selection needs to be made. But they will be as revealing of the editor as of the author. Just so, a selection which begins, not at Bradford's literal beginning—"It is well known unto the godly and judicious" how tortuous has been the history of Reformation in England—but at the later, more local and personal place—"When as by the travail and diligence of some godly and zealous preachers" some word of Reformation reached even the "North parts"—is doing more than saving five pages of (very thin) paper.[21]

Clearly Bradford's story, of personal conversion and then a life devoted to the cause of church reformation, has a prehistory, and even a meta-history, which the author works very hard to compress into his first few pages; and if they seem a little credulous, they are nevertheless all we are given as background to the curious fact that certain English rulers, Protestant as well as Catholic, have seemed so resolutely opposed to the cause of organized saintliness. Indeed, one might almost expect some sort of conspiracy. But while we may wish to spare our students the embarrassment of Bradford's overcommitted religious-historical conviction, we also run the risk of placing ourselves outside the circle of intended readers: do we wish to be *un*godly and *in*judicious? To be sure, by declining to name Satan as the leader of Bradford's worldwide conspiracy, we may forestall our students' observation that Bradford's politics seem a little paranoid; but we will also blunt the force of a conclusive moment of self-recognition, when Bradford finally confesses that the marplot of Eden has deceived even him.[22]

Simply put, Bradford names Satan as the counterforce which appears whenever Reformation seems about to have its way: "the world" and "the flesh" go a long way toward explaining humanity's resistance to its own salvation, but Bradford must be numbered among those who count in "the devil" as well. Active at the first institution of the Christian religion, active again since the first outbreak of Reformation in England—which Bradford names, not quite inevitably, as the "first of nations" to begin to escape "the gross darkness of popery"[23]—Satan appears to employ two classic strategies: persecution, until it appears that the "truths of the gospel" are actually "watered with the blood of the martyrs" (3), and then what we might call "theory." Thus it was in the beginning, as witness the *Ecclesiastical History* of Socrates the Scholastic; and thus it has been in England, as is clear from the richly suggestive pages of Foxe's *Book of Martyrs:* when, in the reign of Queen Mary, the "old serpent could not prevail by those fiery flames," he "then began another kind of war," hoping to discredit Reformed Christianity "by kindling the flames of contention and sowing the seed of discord and bitter enmity among the professors and, seeming reformed, themselves." These disputes consumed the attention of very many of those Protestants who went into exile, at "Wesel, Frankfort, Basel, Emden, Markpurge, Strasburg and Geneva, etc." (5), with one side laboring to recover "the simplicity of the gospel, without the mixture of men's interventions," and the other trying "to have the episcopal dignity . . . still retained" (5–6).

Nor was this dispute—about more or less Reformation—left behind when, at the accession of Queen Elizabeth, the Marian exiles returned home to England. "Preferred to bishoprics and other promotions according to their aims and desires" (6), the moderates quickly branded as "Puritan" all those smitten with the image of Gospel simplicity, even as they counseled the Protestant monarch that only the most "fundamental points of religion" needed to be preached "in those ignorant and superstitious times" (6). And further, they smoothly reasoned, that "to win the weak and ignorant they might retain diverse harmless ceremonies; and though it were to be wished that diverse things were reformed, yet this was not a season for it. And many the like, to stop the mouths of the more godly, to bring them on to yield to one ceremony after another, and one corruption after another." So successful were the sponsors of this policy of moderation that in time it became possible for them "to persecute all the zealous professors in the land" (6–7). And so indeed it all happened, belatedly, to Bradford and his fellows:

> When as by the travail and diligence of some godly and zealous preachers, and God's blessing upon their labors . . . many became enlightened by the Word of God and had their ignorance and sins discovered unto them, and began by His grace to reform their lives and make conscience of their ways; the work of God was no sooner manifest in them but presently they were both scoffed and scorned by the profane multitude; and the ministers urged with the yoke of subscription, or else must be silenced. (8)

And so forth, now, in almost any anthology: to Holland, to live the *communal* life of true Christianity; and thence, in the fullness of time, to New England, to *exemplify* that same hopeful possibility.

Bradford goes on, of course, to outline his sense of the content of radical Reformation: after that most necessary discovery of sin, the awakened Christian moves on to realize the outrage of the "base and beggarly ceremonies" left over from Roman days, the continuing "power of the prelates," who enforce a "profane mixture of persons" (8) as well as of things in the worship of God; and then, leaving all such human inventions behind, he joins himself to others of like mind "by a covenant of the Lord into a church estate" (9). But what has gone before in the history of the church, especially in the name of Reformation in England, is surely the necessary context for this local event. With or without Satan, one has to provide students with some of this "historical" information anyway and, as Bradford's own beginning provides the occasion and even the outline of the required lecture on "backgrounds," we might consider letting him say the words himself. Especially as they indicate, if only by way of some well-chosen footnotes, precisely the tradition of Christian history and purpose in which he means to place his own ecclesiastical efforts.

Eusebius (7), Socrates Scholasticus (4), and John Foxe (5) may not make up a complete set of anything in the history of ideas but, as Robert Daly has observed, they stand together pretty well as ancestors of Bradford's particular "vision of history."[24] Foxe, of course, is the prime figure in establishing the idea that Britain— "the first of nations" in the matter of Reformation—might itself have some holy destiny as an "Elect Nation." And the credibility of any such form of political religion depends on the survivability of the belief, of Eusebius and the Scholastic Socrates, that the rise and fall of nations is not utterly divorced from the Progress of Salvation and the Fate of the Visible Church. Augustine—to whom the English Puritans were indebted in many *other* ways—would teach explicitly otherwise: souls are saved, in some awkward, catholic way, without regard to the rise and fall of nations; and further, the City of God being within, nothing "spiritual" can be inferred from the success or failure of one's secular affairs. Unwilling to accept this entire separation of the secular from the spiritual, the Puritans who settled New England maintained a holy-historical place for their "errand," otherwise intelligible as but a love of travel, and steadfastly insisted that all their lucky escapes were special providences.[25]

And just so, the same Bradford who greets the Great Migration by beginning to write a book on the worldly fate of his own religious enterprise begins that book with a nod in the direction of the very theorists who make that worldly fate a godly fact. Call it dumb, call it funny, but Bradford comes to hold the belief—for the time it takes to write from 1608 to 1630—that God is smiling down on those who love his church.

———

Not surprisingly, the year 1620 is crowded with events that "seem to be profitable to know" (73) and—what amounts to the same thing—are early parts of the attempt to convince the reader, as they had come to convince Bradford himself, that he and his fellow Pilgrims were no ordinary travelers. Yet Bradford's disposition of emphasis throughout the pivotal chapters 9, 10, and 11 is not always easy to predict. Haste might account for some of the surprises, as Bradford had more to do with public affairs than many an aspiring writer. But here and there we may suspect the subtle force of art.

Most remarkable, perhaps, is chapter 9's brief and indirect treatment of the "weighty voyage"—explicitly prepared for throughout a number of prior chapters and, by all odds, the most powerfully life-changing experience in the altogether unusual lives of these wayfaring reformers. Three paragraphs only, and two of them devoted to a couple of very specific instances which must epitomize, if they are not to displace, a "useful" account of "how they Passed the Sea." In the first paragraph, the death "in a desperate manner" of a "lusty" but also "proud and very profane young man" appears to be a fit punishment for his unabated scorning and threatening of Bradford's "poor people." Bradford himself names the event "a special work of God's providence" but gives the bottom line to the sailors, who "noted it to be the just hand of God upon him" (58). More conventionally, but with a kind of formulaic minimalism, the second paragraph mentions "many fierce storms," which seriously damage the ship and lead to "mutterings" among the crew. But makeshift repairs are ingeniously made and, when human effort had done its best, the frightened but trusting Pilgrims "committed themselves to the will of God and resolved to proceed" (59). Then, in one of those fierce storms, the story of a second "lusty" young man, who fell overboard and was towed along for a time "many fathoms under water" but was eventually rescued; and "although he was something ill" with his experience, he yet recovered and went on to become "a profitable member both in church and commonwealth" (59).

Evidently Bradford thinks the voyage *itself* can pass almost without notice: there were difficulties, fears, and alarms, but there was also faith and, whatever the lover of adventure might require, the "godly and judicious reader" can name this tune in almost no notes. The emphasis—and the art—is in the two particular, *not quite parallel* instances. The lusty young man who is nameless is punished in a way, and for a sin, that even his fellow Strangers can recognize. But the other, equally lusty, is not distinguished by any particular virtue, equal and opposite to that of his profane counterpart. In a stroke of practical Calvinism, he is saved not by his own merit, for something he is or has done, but for something he will go on to be, a useful member of the planting enterprise. For this alone he needs to have his name inscribed. And this little lesson in theology has to serve as a conclusion to Bradford's curious account of the voyage "itself"; for then, "to omit other things . . . after long beating at sea they fell with the land which is called Cape Cod" (59). And *now* Bradford "cannot but stay and make a pause" over the scene of arrival, which we may fairly take as both the climax of a long preparation and the first of several beginnings of the planting of Plymouth. A beginning in the Spirit.

The surprising thing about the transition from the First to the Second Book of *Plymouth Plantation* is not that the second part begins with the makeshift political triumph known as the "Mayflower Compact," the third of three possible beginnings, but that the first part is not concluded with the highly charged ending of the arrival scene: "May not and ought not the children of these fathers rightly say" all sorts of wonderful things about those fathers and their God? Should they not "praise the Lord" and confess "His loving kindness and His wonderful works before the sons of men" (63)? Rhetorical to a fault, the passage blames its excitement on the rhetoric of Scripture: Deuteronomy, at the outset, to let the reader know that Hebrew poets were not at all "Augustinian" in the expectations they held of their God; and Psalms, in the end, to spread the word that saints know when to sing. The big finish, surely. How could any "Book" say so much, with such an access of literary energy, and still go *on*?

Yet "The First Book" does indeed go right on—from the arrival scene, which concludes chapter 9, to a much more prosaic tenth and final chapter. Providences abound as the saints—who have arrived more or less safely in the American world but not at all where they had expected to plant—have to decide, under mounting pressure, where exactly to set themselves ashore, how to begin to feed and shelter themselves in their unreceptive new place, and how to relate themselves to the native population. Evidently getting to "America" is only part of the problem: one still has to make a "plantation"; and winter is icumin in. At first glance, therefore, it appears that this sense of anticlimax is all Bradford has in mind as he moves, without modulation, from the drama of the arrival to the workaday business of getting settled. And the effect seems typical of Bradford, who has learned that even Salvation History is not all Prayer and Song.

Yet even this low-concept chapter ends with its own little *coup d'art*. On the fifteenth day of the Massachusetts December, they attempt to bring their ship to the place where they mean to begin their life anew; but adverse winds keep them an extra day out of harbor, and only on the sixteenth day do they resolve "where to pitch their dwelling." And then, with deadpan only Thomas Morton could confuse with sourpuss, on "the 25th day [they] began to erect the first house for common use to receive them and their goods" (72). It takes another year to learn that Bradford knows we know he knows; for on "the day called Christmas Day" of 1621, a party of men playing at "stool-ball" (97) are soberly reminded that the calendar of mirth has all been left behind.[26] *Ici on parle le moralité protestante:* no knocking off to play while better men go out to work.

It begins, then, this new order of the world, on a Christmas Day that will not name itself as such. Sabbaths are real, but "holy days" are popish trash: no one really knows the day the Son was born; only some recall the time when pagans thought the sun might turn and come again; and besides, the birth to celebrate is not the month when Jesus came to Bethlehem but the day when Christ comes to the soul. And yet if anyone should notice, let them notice that this new order begins in work and not in play; not even in that rarest form of play called worship: houses needing to be built will not erect themselves. And if the people work on the day which some call Christmas, the end is no one's private good. Despite the doubts of Cushman's letter, they remain the corporate thing they advertised themselves to be: "knit together"—not as a garment is sewn, but as a body heals the rents of flesh—

> in a most strict and sacred bond and covenant of the Lord of the violation wherof we make great conscience, and by virtue whereof we do hold ourselves straitly tied to all care of each other's goods and of the whole, by every one and so mutually." (33)

"Communists," if earnest bearded men had not absconded with the word; "Brethren," if Morton would but hold his tongue; Members of the Body of Christ, as Winthrop may give the necessary gloss; they work that day to build a "house for common use." If the afterworld should need to build a symbol, build that. And now, after this second beginning—practical yet full of moral implication—"The Second Book" can well begin.

Whenever it was written.[27] And even if it needs to "return back" a little, to "a combination made by them before they came ashore" (75). Politically, Plymouth begins with yet another covenant—outward this time, uniting a ring of men who love the law whatever they may know of saving grace. Overly famous, once, in the mythology of "Puritanism and Democracy,"[28] the Mayflower Compact is founded on the consent of much less than all of the governed; and indeed it speaks not an original clarity of contractual politics so much as a confused, or at least a double, sense of the nature and source of political sovereignty. Had these religious Pilgrims landed in their allotted place, near Hudson's River, they might well have agreed that the king's patent supplied them with all the authority they needed, to choose some form of leadership and make the laws their enterprise required; for they were, at all events, happy enough to receive a second, improved patent, when it came to them. In this context, therefore, sovereignty was something the king possessed and might reasonably hold or grant in part away. But their decision to settle in some *other* place caused "some of the strangers amongst them" to assert that, once ashore, they might fairly "use their own liberty," the patent "being for Virginia and not for New England" (75). Now obviously these renegade Strangers are no party to an instrument designed to bind them fast to whatever government the Saints shall invent; the purpose of that instrument is merely to suggest that sovereignty can be contractually invented as well as accepted of long-established authority.

The point here, however, is not sovereign theory but successful practice: the plantation of Plymouth is not entirely begun until a workable "Civil Body Politic" (76) can be successfully imagined—credible enough to convince the leaders of the movement that they had the right, as they had indeed the power, to insist on a way of law and order. And Bradford sets out the solution to this first crisis of authority as an important instance of social success: "In these hard and difficult beginnings they found some discontents and murmurings arise amongst some[,] . . . but they were soon . . . overcome by the wisdom, patience, and just and equal carriage of things, by the Governor and better part, which clave faithfully together" (76–77). How close they came to political disaster Bradford does not elect to say. Choosing to emphasize instead the happy outcome, he more than implies that adherence to the Robinson-Brewster principle of loving unity may knit the whole where political argumentation may only deconstruct. Surely they are well begun.

But then what? Here they are, safe from death on the ocean and from the threat of internal dissention, but not at all inured to their new place and not very reliably supplied by their partners in London. What can happen, and who will care? Who indeed will know? It needs somewhat more than common belief in the future to write this sort of present. But evidently Bradford has what he needs. So he bravely records that "in two or three months' time half of their company died." And, though forced to confess that Saints and Strangers died together, they did not die alike. "Brewster, their reverend elder," and "Standish, their Captain," were especially forward in their care of others and, though they nursed the sick and the dying, "the Lord so upheld these persons as . . . they were not at all infected." And other Pilgrims too: "whilst they had health . . . they were not wanting to any that had need of them" (77–78). Critics merely, we well may doubt "their recompense is with the Lord"; but we are required to lay this firsthand account beside the sharp critique of Thomas Morton and make some sort of guess. What manner of fiction would lead Bradford, long after the fact, to remember that when he himself desired of a Stranger "but a small can of beer" the answer was *no*, not "if he were their own father"? Or dare invent a Stranger's stark

comparison: "Oh!" (saith he) "you, I now see, show your love like Christians indeed to one another, but we let one another lie and die like dogs." And was it
Morton's comic muse that aided Bradford to recall how "Another lay cursing his
wife, saying if it had not been for her he had never come on this unlucky voyage"?
(78). Even zealots sometimes tell the truth.

Perhaps it was not God but Samoset who pulled the Pilgrims through—and
Squanto too, and then the very Hobomok, rejoicing in an evil name until the call
of sex and sentiment revised the Anglo's moral scheme.[29] However: a pact of
peace occurred; the native guides held true; and no one has ever accused Bradford of trying to round up the natives who survived an English plague and "sell
them for slaves in Spain" (81). Maybe it was not entirely the "Brethren" who
dazed the native moral sense. Whatever: the dying ran its course, and either God
or the Spring "put as it were new life" into those who remained of the little band
whom the idea of a primitive church had joined together and then driven off to
view some primal scene. And if it was indeed "the Lord which upheld them," the
miracle or the providence began with a prior fact: he "had beforehand prepared
them; many having borne the yoke, yea from their youth" (84). Indeed, considering what their improbable venture had "cost" so far, the known result must seem
wonderful indeed.

———

The years 1621 and 1622 contain very few passages in which Bradford permits his
after-the-fact confidence to excite his rhetoric. Squanto's timely instruction in the
mysteries of New World agriculture is presented as a matter of fact; Governor
Carver's death gets only one short paragraph, and his replacement by Bradford
gets even shorter shrift; and though Bradford's defense of civil marriage may be
written back against Morton, its tone is pedagogical rather than passionate. An
approach to "their new friend Massasoit" (87) leads to a greater familiarity with
the beaver-rich territory around Massachusetts Bay, and some of the group wish
"they had been there seated"; but Bradford's advance knowledge assures him that
"the Lord, who assigns to all men the bounds of their habitations, had appointed
it for another use" (89). A successful first harvest produces not a "First Thanksgiving"[30] but only a modest endorsement of certain reports of plentitude. An arriving ship brings, along with a supply of somewhat "wild" new residents and a
second patent, an accusatory letter from Weston to Carver, which Bradford must
answer in his stead. A symbolic challenge from the Narragansetts must be met in
its own symbolic kind. And the hopeful year of 1621 ends with a little "mirth" at
the expense of those who wish to recreate "on the day called Christmas" (97).

Particularism governs the annals for 1622 as well: in the midst of a second attempt to trade with the Massachusetts, an intrigue springs up between Squanto and Hobomok; then follow a number of letters concerning the willingness of the adventurers to send only more mouths to feed. The death of Squanto is dramatic enough—he "desiring the Governor to pray for him that he might go to the Englishmen's God in Heaven," and the Governor (as Bradford now inscribes himself) conceding that "of [him] they had a great loss" (114). Leaving this understatement, however, Bradford ends his year by turning to the politics of food: his own people have traded fairly with the natives, but Weston's thieving men are the reason of a "conspiracy against the English, of which more in the next" (115).

But the annal for 1623 is dominated not by the spectacle of Weston's wastrels, or indeed by the arrival of the troublemaker himself in "the disguise of a blacksmith" (119), but by Bradford's spirited account of a change in the regulation of the group's agricultural economy. God and the natives have done their part; and Samuel Eliot Morison hastens to designate the "fur trade" as the "economic salvation of the Colony" (89); but Bradford rallies his own emphasis in favor of the decision to end the "common course and condition" as it applied to the growing of foodstuffs. "All this while," Bradford reminds us, "no supply was heard of"; and, the early moment of plenty having slipped away, "they began to think how they might raise as much corn as they could." And so,

> after much debate of things, the Governor (with the advice of the chiefest amongst them) gave way that they should set corn every man for his own particular, and in that regard trust to themselves; in all other things to go on in the general way as before." (120)

Communalists they will remain, that is to say, in every way except that which governs the means of primary production. No wonder if Bradford sounds at first a little defensive: other wise heads were indeed consulted and, rather than sponsor the decision, the governor merely "gave way."

But for the moment, at least, the new plan works very well; so well, in fact, that a not *so* reluctant Bradford calls in God to witness the spirit of private enterprise. To every (extended) family their own "parcel of land, according to the proportion of their number," and behold, "all hands [become] very industrious," planting more corn, and that more willingly than by any other means "the Governor or any other could use." Indeed, "the women now went willingly into the field, and took their little ones with them . . . which before would allege weakness and inability; whom to have compelled would have been thought great tyranny and oppression" (120). Torn between nostalgia for the Acts of the Apostles and curiosity at the collapse of Soviet socialism, the critic can only stand aside and let Bradford rush ahead: he knows, as he writes, of the triumph of 1630 but not yet, it plainly appears, of the distress of 1632 or the discouragement of 1644—the seeds of which, one sadly suspects, are being sown just here.

Complacently, then, Pilgrim experience "may well evince that conceit of Plato's . . . that the taking away of property and bringing [all] in community . . . would make [men] happy and flourishing"; for "this community (so far as it was) was found to breed much confusion and discontent." The student of communitarian movements in the nineteenth century will smile to learn that many thought it "slavery" to have men's wives "commanded to do service for other men, as dressing their meat, washing their clothes, etc. . . . [and] neither could many husbands well brook it." One cannot easily forget the author's determined burial of economic communalism: "God in His wisdom saw another course fitter" (120–21) for fallen mankind. But he may also recall, with discomfort, the conclusion of one less assured observer: "More and more I feel we had struck upon what ought to be a truth. Posterity may dig it up, and profit by it."[31]

In any event, Bradford has put his thumb rather heavily on the scales just here; and we may remember both his solution and his tone when we have forgotten many of the details of Pilgrim life and business in the mid-1620s. Out of which, small successes and mild discouragements now come in a flood: supplies from home remain short and starvation continues to threaten, at least until the full effect of the new order of "particular" planting begins to be felt; newcomers arrive, to live within or without the Plymouth plantation, and all these new complexities must be handled in a way that is more or less politic; objections "made by some of those who came over on their particular and were returned home" (142) must be answered. The years 1624 and 1625 are largely devoted to the duplicity and the eventual downfall of John Lyford and John Oldham—faithful members of the Church of England, by Morton's patriotic account, but malcontents, perhaps even spies, in the view of the Plymouth faithful. Both Lyford, the would-be minister, and Oldham, a discontented Particular named a "Mad Jack" by Thomas Morton, play to the sympathies of the Plymouth group, making smarmy confessions of Separatist faith and personal loyalty, only to be exposed, by their own letters home, as part of a plot to overthrow the dominion of the Separatists and to replace it with a more properly inclusive, more sacramental, more "English" regime. Oldham comes out right in the end, appearing genuinely to repent his efforts to unseat a godly community and to maintain, thereafter, "an honorable respect of them" (166). Lyford, however, despite his repeated and tearful confessions, remains reprobated to the end; and the discovery of his many sexual transgressions appears to embarrass even Bradford's "chaste ears" (168).

Delivered apologetically, his account of the defeat of these all-but-internal threats is full and detailed. The reason may be that, despite his claim to have acted "as a magistrate" (152) and so necessarily, Bradford may feel uneasy about the fact that, to expose the intent of these malign detractors, he has had to break into their letters. Or perhaps he may have sensed that some of the slanders of these conscious opposers might defend themselves on the ground of "truth."[32]

In any event, however, the elongated account of this timely double exposure has nothing about it of stirring or representative triumph. Bradford is glad to have won out, in a contest fraught with dangerous consequences; and he senses that, with enemies waiting word and agents eager to comply, the completeness of his victory has been fortunate indeed. So far, so good, as history with an "end" must always read its own unfolding plot. But Bradford has yet to relate the episodes on which his case can rest—a case not of luck but of providence; not of the local virtue a separate group may migrate to preserve but of the transcendent meaning only godly letters dare inscribe.

Nor is there as yet any way to predict, from the passage of time and the accumulation of detail, when that luminous moment might arrive; not even to suspect when Bradford may again step aside from his task of dutifully recording the curious, unfamiliar, yet not entirely unpredictable events in the common life of a body of corn-planting believers to note again some spare irruption of the real. The final word on the Lyford matter is followed by the unhappy news of the breakup of the Company of Adventurers—the cause being "want of money" and the reason "that you are Brownists" (173). Supplies will still be sent, from time to time, by individuals who remain convinced that Bradford and his associates are still "the people that must make a plantation in those remote places when all others fail and return" (174); but they must be paid for, in cash or in kind, it being now clear that it may take seventy times seven years for Plymouth to make a proper return on the corporate investment. Just so, a ship full of commodities meant to make some payment on the heavy debt "was unhaply taken by a Turks' man of war" (176). And all we have by way of hopeful balance is the assurance that it now "pleased the Lord to give the plantation peace and health and contented minds"—bolstered, perhaps, by an editor's note that "Bradford wrote to Cushman 9 June 1625 that the Pilgrims 'never felt the sweetness of the country till this year'" (178).

The brief annal for 1626 has to notice, by way of a letter out of Leyden, the recent death of King James, with whom the Separatists have had to deal, honestly or not,[33] and the less historic deaths of John Robinson and Robert Cushman. Robinson died in the midst of his faithful duties to the congregation back in Leyden, who promise by letter to "hold close together in peace and quietness" (179); and

Cushman died worrying how the plantation could survive without his agency. Of the mortal passing of King and Pastor, Bradford observes, tersely, "Death makes no difference"—by which he appears to mean more than that it comes to all alike; for his remarks on Cushman recognize that his death will make, to Plymouth, a great difference indeed; and in the face of this recognition he can only observe that "man's ways are not in his own power." Just so, many other letters out of Leyden profess a great willingness to join the Plymouth group but see no "means how it might be effected" and dismally conclude "that all their hopes were cut off." Particularly as "many, being aged, began to drop away by death" (180). Even as predicted.

And then, all suddenly, when the depth of mortal weakness has fairly and in the way of history been sounded, Bradford, who trusts God—and who knows better, in 1630, of the chances they will all have to reunite—plays again, and more explicitly, his old game of daring hope in the face of despair: "All which things before related, being well weighed and laid together, it could not but strike them with great perplexity." Indeed, Bradford insists, working his "pessimism" for all it is worth, "to look humanly on the state of things as they presented themselves at this time,"

> It is a marvel it did not wholly discourage them and sink them. But they gathered up their spirits, and the Lord so helped them, whose work they had in hand, as now when they were at their lowest they began to rise again, and being stripped . . . of all human helps and hopes, He brought things about otherwise, in His divine providence, as they were not only upheld and sustained, but their proceedings both honored and imitated by others. As by the sequel will more appear, if the Lord spare me life and time to declare the same (181).

Echoed here, obviously, are both the letter of Cushman and the arrival scene. Parodied, it appears, is the call to self-reliance offered by a remnant of the adventurers: "Go on, good friends, comfortably; pluck up your spirits, and quit yourselves like men" (174). And oddly introjected, it may be, are the sickbed anxieties of Cushman, whose fear of dying before the safety of Plymouth is assured reappears as Bradford's prayer that he live to write the moment of his own beginning to write; for otherwise his tale will seem curious but vain.

More explicit, now, about the difference between looking at things "humanly" and with the eye of faith (or retrospect), Bradford also names the end toward which his writing has all along been driving, the moment not only of honor but of imitation. And with this new directness, we sense a new proximity as well:

any further intimations of the way his godly ends redeem his worldly means might seem not artful—in humble imitation of the way God's purposes hide out in the accidents of men—but merely coy. And so we read of matters fairly called "Down-East Trucking" (181)[34] with a renewed sense that, though Bradford's loyalty to the vicissitudes of seasonal life and economic venture will permit no rush to redemption, it is only God who may cut him off too soon. And against that unlucky event Bradford has nothing but faith.

Not panic, then, but steady and faithful dedication carries Bradford through the annal of 1627—dominated, clearly, by a brave new financial arrangement. The London "Adventurers" agree to sell, to the planters of Plymouth, their entire holdings in the joint-stock partnership begun in 1620, for the lordly sum of 1,800 pounds; the planters readily agree, and an attempt is made to divide among the planters the goods they hitherto held in common. The planters themselves agree to allow a consortium of their principal men to undertake to pay off this debt, within six years, in exchange for exclusive trading rights abroad during that same period. Avidly concerned for the rough justice of this "New Deal,"[35] Bradford nevertheless declines either to celebrate or to lament a further erosion of the communistic basis of his community. He can read legalese with the best, it appears, and he remains committed to his duties as the Protector of Plymouth. Yet the restraint of his economic account seems to imply that the business of Plymouth is somewhat more than business. And the moment of exemplary reformation is yet to arrive.

———

Extending from the confrontation with Morton in 1628 to a time just after the arrival of the Winthrop fleet in 1630, the "moment" is anything but instantaneous. And though in the complex affair of Merry Mount Bradford momentarily loses his established ability to name the things themselves, he does not at all rush his account of the several, interrelated events which he has been trusting, all along, to redeem the history of Plymouth as a plot of God. The annal for 1628 begins and ends, as we sense it must, with the worldly and (so far) faithful agency of Isaac Allerton. But in between falls the "allegory" it needed less than Hawthorne to define; and with that, linking smaller things with great, the ghostlier agency of Endicott.

Freedom of response to the contrary, readers of Bradford's account of the misdeeds of Thomas Morton need to keep reminding themselves that there are *two* Merry Mount occasions.[36] At the first, early in 1628, Miles Standish, acting on behalf of a number of separate plantations, all more or less upset by the suspicion that Morton was offering the natives guns and rum in exchange for beaver skins, took Morton into custody against the time when the officials of Plymouth could find a way to deport him. At the second, much later in the year, when the troublesome Morton was no longer at large, Endicott, the leader of a newly arrived advance guard for a further migration of Puritans, aimed at Massachusetts Bay and regions to the north, performed the largely symbolic deed of "caus[ing] to be cut down" (206) the maypole Morton and others had earlier erected at Ma-re Mount. Not unintelligibly, therefore, Bradford wrote two quite different accounts of the Morton problem. The first, a letter directed to the Council for New England, is a terse attempt to explain the ground of the paralegal action against a clear and present danger; the second, the lavishly rhetorical invention we encounter in the *Plymouth*.

What needs no explanation, of course, is the fact that Bradford's letter makes no mention of the maypole or the attendant behaviors that seemed to spray forth, like streamers, from that truly centric moral outrage. For May Games were not only an honored part of the rural life and courtly poetry of Merry England but also had been personally endorsed by King James himself;[37] and the loyalty of New England Separatists was already being called into question. What may call for some comment, however, is the fact that, for all the scorn his aroused rhetoric is eager to pour on Morton and his amoral associates, Bradford did not pull down that symbolic pine tree himself; or instruct Standish to do so in his encounter with Morton. Perhaps he was not aware, in the first, literal instance of anti-Mortonism, that the thing had come to carry symbolic weight. Or perhaps his own opposition to traditional English ways—making not savage indignation but only "mirth" of a transplanted fondness for Christmas—required something like "the example of Endicott," some aroused awareness of the power of symbol and the meaning of the moment.

Certain it is, however, that Bradford comes to understand the destruction of what *Hawthorne's* Endicott calls "the only may-pole in New England" in perfect accord with other, less symbolic events transpiring at about the same time. What happens, in fact, is that Bradford reaches ahead of himself, borrows Endicott from a moment in the future, and makes him a central figure in an account that, wishing to emphasize the moral of the maypole over the politics of guns and rum, actually seems to reverse the order of the two historical episodes. Which order and emphasis, as I have elsewhere observed, took a very long time to straighten out and are not to be left out of any grown-up reading of Hawthorne's own little "May-pole."[38]

Wollaston arrives, "provisions" in hand and "many servants" in tow, changes the Indian name Pessonagessit to the self-referring "Mount Wollaston" (204), and then moves off toward Virginia, taking with him "a great part of the servants" and eventually "selling their time to other men." When the rest of the servants are sent for, Morton plies them with "strong drink" and then foments a small-scale servants' revolt, inviting them and all comers to "feast," "be merry," and, if D. H. Lawrence is correct, "Henceforth be masterless."[39] After this—though the passage is almost too famous to quote—all hell breaks loose: "licentiousness," a "dissolute life" expressing itself in "all profaneness"; Morton himself "became Lord of Misrule, and maintained (as it were) a School of Atheism" (205). Worst of all, in a view of things Bradford may have learned from Endicott,

> They also set up a maypole, drinking and dancing about it many days together, inviting the Indian women for their consorts, dancing and frisking together like so many fairies, or furies, rather; and worse practices. As if they had anew revived and celebrated the feasts of the Roman goddess Flora, or the beastly practices of the mad Bacchanalians. (205–6)

Then comes the further insult of Morton's poetry, obscene or merely absurd, but affixed, at all events, to "this idle or idol maypole," and properly execrated, as the pun implies, in either case. Finally, to complete this "allegoric" version of the story, another metonym: "They changed also the name of their place, and instead of calling it Mount Wollaston they call it Merry-mount, as if this jollity would have lasted ever" (206).

Never absent from any anthology that includes Bradford at all, this passage, every bit as famous as the arrival scene, has always stood for the *essential* Puritan response—to Morton, who never could be made to stay away, and to the "Cavalier" life in general. So far, at least, no problem: Morton allies his Maypole not only with an English love of mirth but with the theopolitical cause of the Prayer Book; Bradford reduces it to the phallic center of pagan worship. With no real evidence beyond the literary on either side, readers seem free to take their choice: Reveler or Puritan. And to take it again, when they come to Hawthorne.

The next moment, however, things grow complicated. Thus far, with Morton at the center of the outrage, readers naturally assume that Bradford is speaking of the earlier encounter between Plymouth and its Symbolic Antagonist; but what then are we to make of the sudden intrusion of Endicott, who came along only later, who was not yet *in* New England when Morton was first placed under arrest? To be sure, Bradford tries to make clear that he is collapsing two episodes into one, his emphasis falling upon the fact that Merry Mount was *indeed* shut down:

But his continued not long, for after Morton was sent for England (as follows to be declared) shortly after came over that worthy gentleman Mr. John Endecott, who brought over a patent under the broad seal for the government of the Massachusetts. Who, visiting those parts, caused the maypole to be cut down.

Bradford probably means his parenthetical "as follows to be declared" to refer to the deportation of Morton, which did indeed take a little time to accomplish; but it clearly applies as well to Endicott, whose arrival makes up an important part of the next annal, for 1629. But rather than spell this out in historical detail, Bradford turns instead to the allegorical fact that somebody or other has now "changed the name of their place again and called it Mount Dagon" (206).

Nor is this the only confusion the double stimulus of Morton and Endicott has inflicted on Bradford's text. Aroused, if not rattled, Bradford begins his very next paragraph with a second rare usage of what deserves to be his most famous word: *now*. "Now to maintain this riotous prodigality," he tries to explain, Morton engages in the practice of trading "pieces, powder, and shot to the Indians"; and he follows this charge—never proved back in England[40]—with a long and highly rhetorical effort "to bewail the mischief that this wicked man began." "O, the horribleness of this villainy," he exclaims, that our "neighbors and friends are daily killed by the Indians, or are in danger thereof and live but at the Indians' mercy" (206–7). In consequence of which, as Bradford proceeds with his "now" disrupted tale, a number of "straggling plantations" (208) agreed to support Plymouth in its decision "to send Captain Standish and some other aid with him, to take Morton by force" (209). Which is to say that Bradford now gives, in his *second* place, a clear (if biased) account of what happened *first*, before Endicott ever appeared.

Clearly, Bradford's "now" is a causal and not a temporal. It marks the place where he decides to explain how the strayed revelers at Merry Mount were able to finance their New World party. Indeed, he had begun that explanation several pages earlier, just after his evocation of Misrule and Atheism: "after they had . . . got much by trading with the Indians, they spent it as vainly in quaffing and drinking, both wine and strong waters in great excess (and, as some reported) £-10 in a morning" (205). But then, as he began to unleash the fury of his moralism, he evidently felt that the luminous symbolic deed of Endicott was more edifying than the awkward police action of Standish. Rushing ahead to the "fit" conclusion of the moral outrage, he can only go on, in the next place, to tell the tale of local politics.

Writing in the interest of fairness to all, a sober historian has disputed the credibility of the reported figure of "£-10 in a morning";[41] but the literary critic may spare himself to notice other things. First, that Endicott's deed of symbolic destruction so impressed itself on Bradford's imagination that he decided to give it pride of place in his handling of the Morton affair, even though this emphasis involved a compromising of the sort of chronology on which a series of "annals" might be thought to depend: no wonder Hawthorne saw allegory. And second, that Bradford's literary reversal misled virtually all the redactors who sought to retell the Merry Mount story, often with the aid of his own manuscript: they all place the matter of "guns, powder, and shot" second, in chronology as well as interest, to that of allegorical paganism, deemphasizing, often apologizing for the inclusion of, and finally leaving out of account altogether, the worldlier question of who was profiting most by contact with the native population. And how. But if Bradford allows his runaway emphasis to confuse certain local events of 1628 and 1629, his macropolitics are absolutely clear and assured. Considered in itself—or as the act of Standish—the victory over Merry Mount is by no means unimportant: whatever the facts of the local commerce, Bradford and others probably believed that Morton was trading with the natives in the way he indicates; and surely the arrest of Morton was no less significant than the exposure of Lyford and Oldham, or the thwarting of the protesting Particulars. Considered as the act of Endicott, however—symbolically, that is to say, and as a harbinger of things to come—the Merry Mount episode stands out as the most important event recorded so far. Survival, certainly, or no other tale to tell. A timely dose of economic individualism, or survival itself remains the only issue. Lies, sex, and videotape: the world is that much with us. A few really distinguished planters become themselves adventurers—no department stores to inherit, so why not? But where's the playground, Susie? Then in strides Endicott, and all bets are on.

Clearly it is Endicott who, appearing out of time and place, links the rhetorical and clearly symbolic triumph of 1628 with the surprising, confirmatory events of 1629 and 1630. For, before Endicott could appear at Merry Mount (though not before the face of Morton), this "Puritan of Puritans" had first to arrive in New England at all. And not by himself, as it turns out, but as the first note of a song Bradford almost knows to name "The Saints Go Marchin' In." First off, in the annal for 1629, there arrive—all unpredictably, except for the tone of 1626—a company of "the Leyden people." Brought over on the ships that came to Salem, bearing "many godly persons to begin the . . . Churches of Christ there and in the Bay," their arrival, though long delayed, amounts to a kind of "double blessing": reunion with their friends and fellow saints, "when all their hopes seemed to be cut off," but also, with them, "many more godly friends and Christian brethren as the beginning of a larger harvest" (213)—by which he means not conversion of the natives but "now," as he approaches his moment of full consciousness and present confidence, the "errand."

What we are asked to contemplate is not only the comfort of Christian re-union but also the first formulation of a (meta)historical meaning that had to await the time of its own confirmation:

> In the increase of His churches and people in these parts, to the admiration of many, and almost wonder of the world, that of so small beginnings so great things should ensue, as time after manifested. And that here should be a resting place for so many of the Lord's people. . . . But it was the Lord's doing, and ought to be marvelous in our eyes. (213)

The initiate may wish to observe that Bradford's "resting place" has some of the same ambiguities as "the errand" itself: is it (short of heaven) a *final* resting place or only a temporary one, until the "scourge" of England shall be lifted? But only the novice will need an editor's footnote to realize that "This [is] the beginning of the great Puritan migration to Massachusetts Bay."[42] And only the tone deaf will miss the fact that, by the "now" of this event, the "lesser" migration of 1620 meant much more than a prudential escape.

But though Bradford can lurch ahead, to identify the advance man of this new episode in Puritan history as the proper agent in the "truest" story of Merry Mount, and though he can, as he now explains, handle two separate arrivals from Leyden in one place,[43] still his customary pace is quick to return. The annals for 1629 and 1630 contain a whole series of confirmatory moments, following from or closely associated with the "double blessing" of this compound-complex arrival, but Bradford is careful to retain his loyalty to another class of events as well. His sense of pace, that is to say, is really an epistemology: he knows, in retrospect, exactly which events go with which others; and he seems convinced that the "marvelous" will more truly appear so if kept in a kind of alternating tension with events altogether ordinary. However occluded may become our sense of drama, and however his own faith would like to break free and sing, Bradford remains as loyal to men's purposes as to God's dispositions.

Accordingly, before we can learn of any more important arrivals and the confirmatory events that followed from these, we need to hear that the heavy expense of transporting two sets of migrants from Holland—by way of England and then of Salem—was borne by the established planters without a murmur;

that the newcomers were reluctant to pay, and were in fact never charged, the recently imposed tax of three bushels of corn a year. Then there is the complex and ever-growing problem of Allerton who, though rendering the plantation "faithful service" (202) for a time, now begins to reveal himself as the man who "used his fellows even worse than did the merchant adventurers."[44] Having furnished the Plymouth congregation with a minister discovered to be "crazed in his brain," Allerton was also noticed, in the annal for 1628, to have "brought over some small quantity of goods upon his own particular, and [selling] them for his own private benefit" (211). Now, besides failing to resolve the matter of a patent for Kennebec and continuing, against all instructions, to import and sell "retail goods . . . on his own account" (217), he commits the unpardonable sin of ferrying Morton back to New England, causing Bradford to waste a long paragraph on the after-career of a problem he thought he had solved. And though it taxes his patience, Bradford does indeed detail a fur-trading venture at Penobscot in which Allerton has rashly involved the planters who have undertaken the Plymouth debt.

In all of this Bradford may perhaps be thought of as delaying his climax; or of forcing himself to give the flesh equal time with the Spirit. But if so, the spiritual climax of the annal for 1629 is a little more complicated than we might expect. It involves but in no way "features" the arrival of a long-sought minister to serve the Plymouth Church. Part of the reason for this deemphasis may be that the Rev. Mr. Ralph Smith proved to be, in the words of the Plymouth Church Records, a man of "very weak parts."[45] Still, Bradford gives him his paragraph of respect, concluding that he "exercised his gifts among them and afterwards was chosen into the ministry and so remained for sundry years" (222–23). And there are other, more cogent reasons why other events conclude the momentous year of 1629. First, as the experience of the Quakers will prove, a New Testament church can get along quite well without a designated minister; indeed, one might even infer, from Bradford's own account, that where the members live their daily lives by the law of love, what happens on Sunday may not matter much at all. And second, what has come to matter most to Bradford is not the in-house perfection of his church but the imitability of its inception in covenant and its prosperity in fellowship. As the true climax of 1629 clearly demonstrates.

As the example of Cushman should certainly have taught us, we have to resist the temptation to skip over the letters embedded in this extremely well-formed text: though indeed an "author," in a sense much scorned by academics who nevertheless insist on collecting their own royalties, Bradford is extraordinarily sensitive not to the rule of discourse but to the cogency of quotation. And because he clearly sees his own role as exemplary rather than conclusive, he is most happy to hear the voice of those who get the message. Nor is any letter in the *Plymouth* more carefully introduced than that written to Bradford by "Your assured loving friend, John Endecott, Naumkeag, May 11, Anno 1629."

As "was before noted," some of those who arrived of late from Leyden "came over in the ships that came to Salem, where Mr. Endecott had chief command." Now, "though our people through the goodness of God escaped it," many of these others grew ill with scurvy or some infectious fever. Hearing that there was a man of some medical ability among the Separatists (Thomas Fuller), Endicott wrote to Bradford requesting his services at Salem. And now Bradford—and Endicott—must speak for themselves.

> The Governor here sent him [Fuller] unto them and also writ to him from whom he received an answer, the which, because it is brief and shows the beginning of their acquaintance and closing in the truth and ways of God, I thought it not unmeet nor without use here to insert it:
>
> RIGHT WORTHY SIR: It is a thing not usual that servants to one master and of the same household should be strangers; I assure you I desire it not. . . . God's people are all marked with one and the same mark and sealed with one and the same seal, and have for the main, one and the same heart guided by one and the same spirit of truth. And where this is there can be no discord, nay here must needs be sweet harmony. (223)

And more to the same unific effect. Bradford must surely have rubbed his eyes: the speech, which might have been written by Pastor Robinson, or indeed by Bradford himself, not only celebrates Christian unity in the same way the Separatists had learned to value it among themselves but also declares that old migrants and new belong to the selfsame circle of saints.

Notwithstanding the fact that the Bradford group has been scorned all over England as the sort of "immediatists" who eschew the arduous task of reforming an entire nation, and that "politically," or that the later, greater migrants never *would* admit that going three thousand miles to do things differently, illegally, makes you a Separatist de facto,[46] here is the newly imperious Endicott warmly greeting, indeed amply courting the ever modest Bradford: don't be a "stranger," as if he knew the other's term of art. In debt to Bradford, momentarily at least, Endicott briefly thanks him for the loan of Fuller's pharmacy. But more is on his mind than that. Not quite sure, perhaps, exactly what a sort of thing a "Brownist" may be, especially when let loose on a new continent, and unable to predict his own career as ravager of churchly cross from flag of state, Endicott admits to being reassured by Fuller "touching your judgments of the outward form of

God's worship" (223–24). Sounding more than a little like an equally complacent King James in quite another context,[47] he happily concedes that the Way of Plymouth is "no other than is warranted by the evidence of truth" and is, in very fact, "the same which [he has] professed and maintained ever since the Lord in mercy revealed himself unto [him]" (224). For which relief, Bradford might have mused, much thanks. Unless a more important thought were in his mind.

For, whether he realized it or not, here was the key to the odd reciprocity— or temporal "borrowing"—between Bradford's notes on 1628 and 1629. Here, in just so many words, Endicott pays congregational homage to the works and days of Bradford's Plymouth. But—fair is fair—Bradford has already paid his own homage in the opposite direction. Endecott offers Bradford the important political compliment of formally recognizing, on May 11, 1629, the full legitimacy of the separated and long minister-less church at Plymouth, but Bradford has already offered, in our reading of his annal for 1628, or will soon offer, sometime in the now of his beginning to write, the enormous literary compliment of allowing Endicott to occupy the symbolic center of, indeed in some measure to "write," the indelible story of "The May-pole of Merry Mount." Of course, it may have happened, to Bradford, all at once, at a time we can only imagine: by God we *are* all up to the same thing: churches made by covenant are, always and of their nature, separate from the maypoles of the culture that surround. Culture is Nature, ill disguised, and never worse than by Morton. Churches withdraw, therefore, not to seek after or to invent another culture but merely to point, always, to some place of Grace. Internal largely, but not entirely: just in case souls really are to be saved in bundles.

And then, in fact to end the quite explosive annal for 1629, a "second letter [which] showeth their proceedings in their church affairs at Salem, which was the second church erected in these parts; and afterwards the Lord established many more in sundry places" (224)—even if it shall require the *Wonderbook* of Edward Johnson to tally the total.[48] Bradford's editor thinks it might be more proper to call Salem the New World's *first* properly constituted congregational church, since Bradford's was covenanted, years ago, in England, and since it might still be thought of as but a branch of the Leyden congregation.[49] But Bradford insists: *second*. More than that, he lets a second letter, carefully detailing the entire procedure of forming a church and electing its first pastor and teacher, clearly imply that the men of Salem are looking to Plymouth not just for fellowship but for sanction:

> And now, good Sir, I hope that you and the rest of God's people (who are acquainted with the ways of God) with you, will say that here was a right

foundation laid and that these two blessed servants of the Lord came in at the door and not at the window. (225)

What further need of witness? The example of Scrooby, of Leyden, of Plymouth, or only of Bradford's fond imagination—an example of separation but also of love—was coming true at large. How *not* write a book? Big problems lie sleeping here, big enough to have spurred Perry Miller to devote much of his *Orthodoxy in Massachusetts* to refuting the notion that Salem learned the ways of church formation from either Thomas Fuller or the Separatist example at large. But the vexed (and often tedious) question of "Non-Separating Congregationalism" need not detain us here.[50] Bradford is gaining the evidence he needs; and also, in some order of time, explaining the logic of the work he is emboldened thereby to write. One more (brief) annal should do the trick.

Somewhat more on the bizarre economic adventures of Allerton, who threatens to become Bradford's latter-day obsession. Then the execution for murder of one John Billington who "came over with the first" and in whose trial the socially deferential leaders of Plymouth have taken the "advice of Mr. Winthrop and other the ablest gentlemen in the Bay . . . that were then newly come over" (234). But if this rather casual mention is the first we hear of the name of that truly great migrant, the reason is not that Bradford has turned his attention away from events occurring some few miles to the north, where the prediction of Endicott's Salem has been fulfilled, at Winthrop's Boston, by the arrival of Puritans in their numbers. And so the confirmation appears to continue, in polite letters as in demographic fact.

Better if the letters had come from Winthrop, or Dudley, or some other principal man from the Bay, but history has to make do with whatever it can find. And so Bradford ends the annal for 1630, the year given ever after as the beginning of the *Great* Migration, with letters from the Plymouth men who happen to be present at this next, a third, creation. The first letter reports the predictable bout of sickness among the newest arrivals and cordially invites the members at Plymouth to join their neighbors to the north in a Day of Humiliation; and especially so since, later on that same day, a due number of the recent arrivals mean "solemnly to enter into covenant with the Lord to walk in his ways." Accordingly, these new men "do earnestly entreat that the Church of Plymouth would set apart the same day . . . , beseeching the Lord as to withdraw His hand of correction from them, so as also to establish and direct them in His ways" (235). Again, the appeal is made in brotherhood; which is to say, in equal spiritual dignity.

And then a second letter, from one day later, implying ever so much more. So that it may well be quoted at length:

The sad news here is that many are sick and many are dead, the Lord in his mercy look upon them. Some are here entered into church covenant. The first four, namely the Governor, Mr. John Winthrop, Mr. Dudley, Mr. Johnson, and Mr. Wilson. Since that[,] five more are joined unto them, and others it is like will add themselves to them daily. . . . Here is . . . one Mr. Coddington . . . who told me that Mr. Cotton's charge at Hampton was that they should take the advice of them at Plymouth, and should do nothing to offend them. Here are divers honest Christians that are desirous to see us, some out of the love which they bear to us, and the good persuasion they have of us; others to see whether we be so ill as they have heard of us. We have a name of holiness and love to God and his saints; the Lord make us more and more answerable and that it be more than a name, or else it will do us no good. (235–36)

Certainly John Cotton knew, as well at least as Perry Miller, that the Puritan intellectuals who would eventually decide for New England had no need to learn the reason or the outline of the particular, the covenanted church from the likes of Elder Brewster or Pastor Smith, let alone the bloodletting (and gas-relieving) Thomas Fuller.[51] And yet Bradford himself could not have drafted for him a more satisfactory or, for the sake of Bradford's "design," a more climactic utterance: honor the men of Plymouth, as those who ran before to show the way; indeed, "take advice of them." No wonder if Bradford should decide to end his annal here. Or begin his book just "now."

Yet not without a word of his own, to gather up and set the seal on all that has happened in the last three annals, and to remind us of the reminders encountered so far: "stepping-stones," at the moment they decided to leave Leyden; "miracle," by the uncautious remark of Cushman; "wonderful works," at a very sober moment of arrival; rising spirits in 1626, just when they were stripped of all "human helps"; and the "great things" from "small beginnings" of 1629, amounting *almost* to the "wonder of the world." And now, the bottom line, serving to advertise not the mood of migration but the design of the *Plymouth* so far:

That out of small beginnings greater things have been produced by His hand that made all things of nothing, and gives being to all things that are; and, as one small candle may light a thousand, so the light here kindled hath shone unto many, yea in a manner to our whole nation; let the glorious name of Jehovah have all the praise. (236)

Reading this, one wonders if Miller ever really *read* the *Plymouth*. For in the face of the vision here achieved, it scarcely matters what a ragtag remnant once had hoped or feared. And, given the book we have thus far, we, who know much better, may almost forgive Bradford for putting God and the Christian example of his own community in the place of a half century of "Reformed Dogmatics." For, in the view of the literary critic, at least, the problems all begin just now.

II. The Failure of Vision

By the logic of this essay, a "first part" of Bradford's *Plymouth* may easily be thought to end in 1630. Not that Bradford should have placed his formal marker ten years later than he did: the soul's emphasis may *not* always be right, but art has its reasons; and, in the long look of early American literature, Bradford's art is well assured. It is just that all of the narrative up to 1630 seems to have been imagined from that moment's clarity and confidence. And also, in some relation to that fact, things after 1630 began to look worse than things before. Not that they were all *really* worse, necessarily, any more than Puritan piety really left the Massachusetts world in 1662. It is just that, after the confirming moment of 1630, Bradford may have no further point of triumph to write himself *toward*. To be sure, he might have waited, to see if any other powerfully authorizing event might come along. Indeed, he may well have done just that; for, though he almost certainly continued to make notes toward further annals as he went along, he seems to have enjoyed—or more likely suffered—another extended moment of composition in the 1640s.[52] And yet, as he could not find much of a hopeful nature to distinguish the latter days of the Plymouth experiment, he may well have decided simply to go *on,* to finish, if possible, the thing so well begun.

   In fact, of course, he never did finish his account—bipartite, however we decide to mark the break—of the life and Christian example Of Plymouth Plantation; and the spectacle of his final few blank pages has come to stand for the gathering discouragement he seems to have felt, as his years at Plymouth wore on, in the face of specific evils and, worse, perhaps, a certain mounting ordinariness. Puritan affairs, at the Bay of Massachusetts, continued to bustle along and, if John Cotton stood somewhat alone in predicting that the end of the world was set for 1656, still no one there seemed inclined to renounce "the errand."[53] Yet that may have been exactly what Bradford felt himself called upon to face—not, perhaps, the end of some large-scale mission in America, but the end of whatever part Plymouth had been called upon to play. As Bradford's prime disciple in the writing of Holy History in the New World would later propose of the whole of New England, perhaps its only purpose had been to give the world "a specimen of many good things"; that done, who knows "whether the plantation may not, soon after this, come to nothing."[54] Worldly wealth grew, to be sure, at Plymouth as at Massachusetts Bay; congregational churches seemed to multiply and flourish; and, in the decade after 1642, at least, all England seemed positioned to benefit from the New English example. And in all this the old planters and their children seemed entitled to take a certain comfort if they could. Bradford, somehow, could not.

Perhaps he preferred the hour of trial to the days of success and orderly progress it needed no man's faith to recognize. Perhaps he was, this essential Pilgrim, something of an adventurer after all, if only in the "spiritual" sense that prefers wayfaring and warfaring to all comfort and security. Perhaps getting a corner on the beaver trade was less than Morton cracked it up to be. If so, perhaps Bradford should simply have ended his *Plymouth* in 1630—ended the narrative, that is, exactly where the brilliant hindsight had made him take it up: one small candle lights a thousand; Jehovah must have all the praise.

But he did not. Unable to finish his "Second Book," Bradford was neither farsighted nor self-protective enough to avoid starting and indeed continuing it throughout the messy decade of the 1630s and on, well into the 1640s, when events—some sad and some shocking without being at the same time entirely a surprise—seem to be stretching out beyond the power of vision to redeem. Yet it may be a mistake to refer the defeat of this first great New England writer to any gross evil or painful loss. More subtly, perhaps, his discouragement may come from nothing more than a dying back of some spirit that had made the sojourn in Holland and the venture at Plymouth, not fun, to be sure, for that was the special preserve of Thomas Morton, but keen and sweet to the sober (*Puritan*) sense of life. Bradford stops telling his story when it had become, quite simply, "uncomfortable." And if we ask, was it the writing or the life from which the life seemed drained? the answer once again is *yes*: he would not write what he could not love.

American writers are supposed to have within them only one real book. Never *entirely* an American, perhaps, Bradford was quite good enough for a book and a half: first, a full-dress account of the curious experience leading up to the unlikely triumph of the Separatist example in 1630; and then, more briefly, the unfinished record of the less than exemplary events which ensued. Literary fragments have their own interest, of course, and Bradford's has much to tell us about the tenor of Pilgrim life in New England "After the Surprising Migrations." But even more about what it was, now gone, we should have seen before.

———

It seems impossible to say how intensely surprised Bradford may have been by the wonderful way the Puritan World came beating a path to the doorstep of Plymouth in 1629 and 1630.[55] Certainly the spirited recognition by Endicott and others was the most he could have hoped for, and no doubt hope itself was well prepared to accept much less. What could scarcely have escaped his attention, however, is just exactly how fast this success turned into failure—and in just about the same terms. Success meant being followed, imitated, and not by other straggling bands of self-marginalized malcontents but by rank on rank of zealots from the body of the "sociologically competent."[56] To be sure, Christ himself was there wherever two or three saints would join together; but notwithstanding this Brownist minimalism, success meant numbers. Not more than might enter in at the straight gate of godly motivation, of course—not vast numbers, that is to say, but more than might crowd into one or two early modern sailing ships.[57] But when they came, in their numbers, they swiftly became, for life at Plymouth at least, as clearly a part of the problem as they were of the solution. And Bradford notices the fact as early as 1632.

The annal for that year begins, unhappily enough, with a matter that had begun to concern Bradford several years earlier and which indeed occupies most of the pages for 1631: the economic behavior of Isaac Allerton. Agreeing with most readers that Allerton has involved himself and his Plymouth partners in a very "tedious and intricate . . . business" (238), Bradford nevertheless struggles to make sense of it all. The affairs of Allerton "amaze and trouble" (229) him but, because they bear on the matter of the debt he and a few others have "undertaken" to discharge, Bradford cannot simply let them pass. It may be, as well, that the increasingly irresponsible behavior of this former member of the Brethren fascinates Bradford in its own terms, leading his conscience outward, as it were, in an economic (even capitalist) direction at just the time when matters more "internal" to his loving community begin to disappoint his most cherished expectations.

First, there was Allerton's (1629) plan of a trading outpost at Penobscot— under the command of the "profane" Edward Ashley, known to have lived and gone naked "among the Indians as a savage" (219)—and certain to compete with one already established at Kennebec. But because Allerton has begun this enterprise with the support of Plymouth's creditors, they have reluctantly decided "to join in the business"; the best they can do is send one of their own men to "keep Ashley in some good measure within bounds" (220). Worse yet, with two newly purchased ships, one or both of which would have to be charged against the Plymouth account, Allerton has attempted (in 1630) to involve the Undertakers in the business of bass fishing, which Bradford is sure will "turn to loss" (229).

A shrewd enough economic intelligence, Bradford is anxious to pay off the debt of the Undertakers as soon as possible, but he is unwilling "to have any accounts lie upon them but about their [own] trade" (231). No proper capitalist, his fascination can see nothing but self-interest in Allerton's adventures, especially as this once-trusted agent has "abused them in England," regularly intimating that these simple souls would "never be able to repay their moneys" (232). And so Bradford is pleased to begin the annal for 1631 by reporting that "Ashley being . . . by the hand of God taken away, and Mr. Allerton discharged of his employment for them, their business began again to run in one channel" (237).

Yet he cannot let it go at that, as nearly all of 1631 is given over to a casting up of accounts between Allerton, the English creditors, the Undertakers, and the plantation at large. First, the two new ships and their proposed use were Allerton's idea; without them, he seems to have claimed, the plantation could never "repay their moneys" (238). Second, in this matter, as in others, he "might think not to wrong the Plantation in the main, yet his . . . private ends led him aside in these things"; for he had, in the first several months of his employment by Plymouth, "cleaned up £-400 and put it into a brewhouse of Mr. Collier's in London." Therefore, third—in a conclusion likely to sow "discord" where there needs to be "sweet harmony"—as it was Allerton who brought the plantation into ambitious "new designs" which seemed promising but only led to "loss and decline," so it would be "more meet for the Plantation to bear" those losses than the Undertakers alone. Finally, however, not an economic inference but a moral lesson:

> With pity and compassion touching Mr. Allerton, I may say with the Apostle[:] "They that will be rich fall into many temptations and snares . . . for the love of money is the root of all evil." God give him to see the evil in his failings, that he may find mercy by repentance, for the wrongs he has done to any and this poor Plantation. (239)

The moral has become trite over the years, but it may apply closer home than Bradford has occasion, just here, to notice. For though he regularly characterizes both his people and their plantation as "poor"—lacking, that is, in the resources usually thought necessary to accomplish the task they have set themselves—he is about to face up to the fact that, in strictly economic terms, some of his friends are less poorly provided than once upon a time. And surely he knows.

Other matters manage to separate this sharp pointing of an economic lesson from the moment of its wider application, much of it applying to Allerton's accounts, "so large and intricate they could not well understand . . . much less examine and correct" them (241), and all tending to the conclusion that "if their business had been better managed they might have been the richest plantation of any English at that time" (242). And indeed the now-compulsive listing of Allerton's sins—including the observation that, "having brought them into the briars, he leaves them to get out as they can" (244)—is itself interrupted, by a lively and momentarily distracting account of the carryings on of Sir Christopher Gardiner: posing as one who came to New England by way of "forsaking the world" (247), but in flight from some answerable charges at Massachusetts, Gardiner is exposed, when some notes fall out of his pocket, as a Roman Catholic and probably a spy for Sir Fernando Georges; Bradford commands the local Indians to spare his life and, upon returning him to the authority of Governor Winthrop, is happy to agree with that exemplary Christian that "It was a special providence of God to bring those notes of his into our hands" and that indeed "The good Lord . . . hath always ordered things for the good of His poor churches here" (248). Evidently Bradford has taught the much richer Winthrop himself to say "poor." But even if we fail to regard this quasi-economic usage as a structural providence, we cannot forget that a long and multiform meditation on rich man/poor man serves as the backdrop to the crucial entry for 1632 which Bradford's apologetic editor has titled "Prosperity Brings Dispersal of Population" (252) but which might read better under the head of "Increased Population Breeds a Love of Money That Causes a Dividing of the Church."

Sure of his emphasis, however, Bradford builds to his point slowly. In spite of the worst that Allerton could do, Bradford premises, the Lord so "prospered their trading, that they made yearly large returns" and, had they otherwise been dealt with fairly, they would soon have "wound themselves out" (252) of all their debt. Then, as if there were no distinctions to be made: "Also the people of the Plantation began to grow in their outward estates, by reason of the flowing of many people into the country, especially into the Bay of the Massachusetts" (252–53). Any student of "modernization"[58] can easily infer that something fundamental may have happened to the morale of Plymouth when its inhabitants were permitted to raise food each on his own particular; or when, several years later, the leaders constituted themselves as an economic oligarchy and began to play the part, however reluctantly, of adventurers themselves. And though the small-group dynamics of original Plymouth might possibly have survived the modest enlargement brought about by the arrival of the latecomers from Leyden, there is no reason to suppose their fundamental values will not be challenged by the entry into their "market" of a large number of migrants who bring specie but are short on just the supplies the old planters are now very good at producing. The only question concerns their access to the necessary means of production—

in this case, land, on which to grow more feed for stock and food for saints. And so it seems to happen all at once: all of a sudden none of the old planters has enough land.

And Bradford seems surprised, not by the occurrence of the question, but by the need to take the tone he does. Keen analyst of mercantile motive come loose from social obligation, he seems unprepared to find the "love of money" so much closer home. Yet his logic, however old-fashioned, is impeccable. By virtue of so many new buyers, "corn and cattle rose to a great price, by which many were enriched and commodities grew plentiful. And yet in other regards this benefit turned to their hurt, and this accession of strength to their weakness."

> For now as their stocks increased and the increase vendible, there was no longer any holding them together, but now they must of necessity go to their great lots. They could not otherwise keep their cattle, and having oxen grown they must have land for plowing and tillage. And no man now thought he could live except he had cattle and a great deal of ground to keep them, all striving to increase their stocks. By which means they were scattered all over the Bay quickly and the town in which they lived compactly till now was left very thin and in a short time almost desolate. (253)

So much for "wealth" and "dispersal." But it is a distinguishing mark of the *godly* element in Bradford's historical vision that he will not let it rest at that.

For to Bradford this "Dispersal of Population" signifies not successful resettlement but a very unhappy division of the church, that Ark of the Covenant he and his Pilgrim brethren have carried about in their hearts so long.

> And if this it had been all, it had been less, though too much; but the church must also be divided, and those that had lived so long together in Christian and comfortable fellowship must now part and suffer many divisions. First, those who lived on their lots on the other side of the Bay, called Duxbury, they could not long bring their wives and children to the public worship and church meetings here, but with such burthen as, growing to some competent number, they sued to be dismissed and become a body of themselves. And so they were dismissed about this time, though very unwillingly. (253)

Bradford's editor intervenes just here to apologize: "Bradford's efforts to stop what would now [1952] be called 'progress' are amusing and pathetic"; but this may prove only that Perry Miller was not the only Harvard professor who could not quite read godly letters.[59] However that may be, the force of Bradford's rhetoric—not to mention "the truth of history"—requires us to make what we can of his reactionary pathos.

What we notice, first of all, is that Bradford's church is not the sort of thing one could leave in a casual or whimsical manner; and we can imagine that the discussion of the "causes and reasons" why certain individuals felt they had to break away from the main body at Plymouth must have gone on for a long and painful time and that Bradford *under*states his own feelings when he characterizes the eventual permission as "very unwillingly" given. It is not, to be sure, a question of their wishing to abandon the ideal of Christian community altogether; no one is going off to Merry Mount or to live naked among the natives. Duxbury and then Green's Harbor will have, soon enough, their very own congregations: "wherever two or three are gathered together." And if it should take them a good long while to have their very own minister, they could point of course to the founding example of Plymouth itself. Nor, on the other hand, is this resistance to division *entirely* a matter Bradford's own (orphan's) wish to have and keep about him, in "Christian and comfortable fellowship," all those with whom he had shared so much, from the heady days of effecting a local reformation "without tarrying," through the hardships of Holland, the "weighty voyage," the starving time, right down to the blessed reunion with those kept back in Leyden so long. Partly this, no doubt, for though the *idea* of community is emphatically no respecter of persons, its effective practice may depend much more on real familiarity than on ideal dedication. Yet what troubles Bradford most is the motive propelling the division: called "necessity" in the politeness of indirect discourse, its real name would seem to be "love of money," which many seem to be setting ahead of love and friendship.

Duxbury, today, is as lovely a New England village as the casual tourist can discover. Tall old trees shade streets lined with houses bearing the names of the founders, if only by way of their children's historical sense: Alden, Standish, Brewster, Prence, and others, just less famous because less original. Yet the reader of Bradford can scarcely drive down those streets without sensing an ending as well as a foundation. The center could *not* hold. The living voice of Bradford's pathos notwithstanding, "they must of necessity go to their great lots."

Nor, as Bradford goes on to make clear, were those who held on firm to the original place of Pilgrim comfort able to prevent further disaffection. A new policy of distributing "some good farms to special persons that would promise to live at Plymouth," there to be "helpful to the church or commonwealth" (253), quickly proves a remedy . . . worse than the disease; for within a few years those that had thus got a footing there rent themselves away, partly by force and partly [by] wearing the rest with importunity and pleas of necessity, so as they must either suffer them to go or live in continual opposition and contention.

A fine community *that* will make—when the main topic of discussion is how soon, in despite of promises strictly undertaken, some of us can break away under cover of necessity but in the name of wealth. All right, then: go. Down the slippery slope. For others still "broke away under one pretence or another, thinking their own conceived necessity and the example of others a warrant sufficient for them" (254). A painful "family" moment indeed: but you let *them* go.

Yet it takes a conscience somewhat less than Puritan to hear Bradford retort: that's not funny. It wasn't funny in the case of Allerton, who lived so long among the adventurers he forgot that life is a Pilgrimage; and if he began to seek wealth of necessity, he soon came to enjoy the game for its own sake. And it isn't funny here, as people sworn to love God above all things and their covenanted brothers and sisters—as well as both themselves and the pretended necessities of their natural families. Editors smile, and classes in American literature move uncomfortably in their seats, but the idea of Christian community is what the venture for an abstraction called "the church of Christ" is all about. Or *was*. For it may be this manuscript is all that will survive to tell that tale intact. In which case, let this ragged second book here prophesy and then record its deepest fear: namely, that this breaking of covenants, necessitated by nothing more than a people's wish "to grow in their outward estates" (252), "will be the ruin of New England, at least of the churches of God there, and will provoke the Lord's displeasure against them" (254).

One can only guess whether this passage was written with the more famous "breakup" scene of 1644 in mind. If so, then it may be possible to think of Bradford's "Second Part" as having a teleology of its own. Yet not a happy one, as Bradford could do no more than write toward the fulfillment of his own dire prophecy, inverting the method and the mood that made him write at all. In any event, it probably requires two or more exposures for the reader to sense the dismal potency of the passage just rehearsed. Bradford quite means the economics of his reaction, in spite of the logic that led him out of Holland: better one church really dedicated to the spirit as well as to the form of renewed Christianity than a meetinghouse popping up on every corner of every town in a land where land rules. Perhaps the decision for America had been indeed a mistake. If not, then how explain the overriding paradox that their success had been indeed their failure? For at no time during the 1620s did anyone even dream of the need for "great lots"; but only when the arrival of many more saints—following the Plymouth example, as it seemed—made it possible to dispose of farm surplus at a neat little profit.

And there we are: meaningful Reformation requires more saints; newly arrived saints have material needs; established saints have it in their power to meet these needs; meeting these needs means going out to farm where the land is abundant; going *out* to farm makes coming *back* to church somewhat inconvenient; so why *not* separate and then regather? It might not win the West, but surely it would settle New England. How *could* Bradford resist a logic so inexorable? Only if he saw, somewhere in this chain of propositions, a change in the ruling motive of his fellow reformers. Having agreed to trust them, some time back, to farm for themselves in the name of community survival, he now agrees, "very unwillingly," to let that community be divided for the sake of particular wealth. And he predicts the worst. He does not explicitly say, in the last paragraph of his annal for 1632, that their loss of a ship full of beaver has any connection to the colony's failure to regulate its "love of money"; but he does note that this was "the first loss they sustained in that way" (255), and the juxtaposition looks suspicious.

As do losses and crosses to follow. Because Bradford has decided to "handle things together that fell out afterwards" (253), we need to remind ourselves that the emptying out of the town and the church of Plymouth was not the isolated instance it may first appear. Taking place not all at once but over a number of years, it was not a single flat announcement and enactment of large-scale defection but a gradual and repeated "wearing the rest with importunity." As such, its toxic discouragement may infect the mood—and even the logic—of much that falls between the prolepsis of 1632 and the most unhappy retrospect of 1644. Certainly that latter entry formally remembers its earlier prediction. And whether or not the earlier one consciously predicts its literary fulfillment, its chastened expectation of divine "displeasure" is never very far from the history that lies between.

———

Much of what follows the predictive entry for 1632 concerns questions of land on a scale much larger than the pouring out of Plymouth into Duxbury and Green's Harbor. And if it requires Bradford's special insistence to perceive the microeconomics of that movement as not entirely innocent, certainly no very great preci-

sion of conscience is necessary to see the sin at large. Casting the pall of a generalization over the "strange opinions" (257) of Roger Williams, Bradford spares
himself consideration of one of Williams' prime ideas, that the patents of the European potentates were pieces of paper merely, and that settlements were legitimate only if their land had been fairly purchased from its native inhabitants.[60]
But if Bradford can handle Williams as a moral case—to be "pitied and prayed
for" in the hope "he belongs to the Lord"—no such piety can cover the eminence
of the domain question touching "a river called by [the Dutch] the Fresh River,
but now . . . known by the name of Connecticut River" (257).

Formerly, these same Dutch had recommended this fertile territory to the
men of Plymouth, as a handy solution to their own land problems. Now comes "a
company of . . . Indians" banished from that attractive internal region—by the
Pequots, we unhappily hear—to encourage the Brethren once more. Again, not
much interest. So these Indians, hoping to have the English shield them from the
Pequots, turn to "them of the Massachusetts" (258). Unaware, it appears, that the
Connecticut Valley is destined to become a prime bastion of Puritan empire, they
too demur, agreeing at a conference to allow a few Plymouth individuals "to
make a beginning there"; and these were "the first English that both discovered
that place and built in the same" (259). Meanwhile, however, the Dutch have
changed their minds and are trying, by the construction of "a slight fort," to keep
the English out. Episodes of saber-rattling ensue, but when the Dutch confront a
reinforced garrison, they come in "to parley" and then return to New Amsterdam in peace. "And this," Bradford summarizes, was "their entrance there." The
people of Plymouth "did the Dutch no wrong, for they took not a foot of any land
they [had] bought, but went to the place above them and bought that tract of land
which belonged to these Indians." And they certainly deserved to have held this
land, "and not by friends to have been thrust out as in a sort they were as will
after appear" (260). Evidently the "stepping-stones" are about to be stepped upon.
And even now, as the macroplot of Land begins to unfold, political affairs are
getting more complicated than Bradford might well have hoped.

Not yet oppressed by intimations of this political future, however, Bradford
ends his short entry for 1633 with an unmoralized account of "an infectious fever
of which . . . upwards of twenty persons died," including sundry of "their ancient
friends" from Holland. Significant, perhaps, but only as natural science, is the
fact the fever had been preceded by a swarming of the seventeen-year locusts,
from which the Indians had predicted a period of sickness. Bradford will risk
only the safe formula "It pleased the Lord" (260). Is it strategy, then, or lack of
invention, when Bradford repeats the same formula to introduce a fact which

might have a quite different bearing on the healthy endurance of the Plymouth group? "It pleased the Lord to enable them this year to send home a great quantity of beaver . . . which good return did much to encourage their friends in England" (260–61). Oddly, the encouragement mentioned is foreign rather than local and, for the moment at least, some of the zest seems to have gone out of Bradford's economics. One wonders if he is feeling tempted to regard all his summary events—a killing pestilence, a swarm of constantly "yelling" locusts, and one quick upturn in the beaver market—as "remarkable," in some literary sense, but as all belonging equally to the order of *ordinary* providence. If not here, soon.

Though the political year of 1634 is entrusted to the governorship of Thomas Prence—not *yet* gone off to Duxbury—it falls to Bradford to explain a double murder on the perimeter of Plymouth's expanding sphere of influence. Not at the Connecticut, this time, but at the Kennebec, their authority is deliberately and provokingly challenged by "one Hocking, belonging to the Plantation of Piscataqua" (263). Shots are fired, and one is killed on each side: All's fair in love and beaver trade: no harm no foul. Except that, as the Piscataqua Plantation is the overseas interest of some very important persons, "all New England was concerned to see that justice was done."[61] So concerned are the officials of Massachusetts that they hold John Alden in prison for a time as something like a material witness. Governors Dudley and Prence eventually resolve matters in favor of the men of Plymouth, thanks largely to the failure of any representative of Piscataqua to appear at an oyer and terminer; but in the meantime Bradford has to record a serious strain on the "harmony" that ought to exist between the several avatars of God's own people. Also, at the outset of his account, he must turn back to show that his people have clear patent rights to trade on the Kennebec. Earlier, he had made it clear they were drawn into business there with great reluctance; now, it appears, they are quite committed to their claim to do business in that area. The affair ends with "love and concord renewed," and with Winslow carrying off to England not only a full explanation to "the Lord Saye and others" but also 3,738 pounds of beaver and 234 otter skins "which together rose to a great sum of money" (268). But none of this eventual success can quite annul the sentence with which Bradford had begun: "I am now to enter upon one of the saddest things that befell them since they came" (262).

Nor do the other matters of 1634 add much by way of uplift. First, the entire party of a certain Captain Stone is killed by Pequots in the Connecticut River region. Next, in an incident unrelated except perhaps ethnographically, "it pleased God to visit" a whole tribe of perfidious natives "with a great sickness and such a mortality that of a thousand, above nine and half a hundred of them died, and many of them did rot above ground for want of burial" (270). Then too, in the spring, another group of Indians "fell sick of the small pox and died most miserably": their many oozing sores stick to the mats on which they lie, so that when they try to turn themselves, "a whole side will flay off at once as it were, and they will be all of a gore blood, most fearful to behold" (270–71). The English in the region give these natives all the help they can, and Bradford regards it as a "marvelous . . . providence" that none of them is "in the least measure tainted with the disease" (271). But if Bradford had wished this emphasis alone to survive, he probably should not have made his descriptions of sickness and death quite so graphic. And as Native Americans begin to kill Englishmen emboldened to penetrate and compete for the interior of New England, neither author nor reader can expect the uneasy peace to continue.

Ordinary or special, the providences of 1635 seem distinctly unfriendly. Back in England to explain the death of Hocking, Winslow is pleased to observe both a setback to the plan of sending over a general governor, "to disturb the peace of the churches here" (273) and an official rebuke of Thomas Morton; but his answers to questions about religious practices in New England so infuriate Archbishop Laud that he is imprisoned "seventeen weeks or thereabout," during all of which time important plantation business lies suspended. Back in New England, the Plymouth men lose a trading post to the French and lose both their trouble and their investment in a hapless attempt to retake it by force; nor can they persuade their neighbors at the Bay to aid them in any material way. Happily—as it almost seems—a great hurricane comes along to separate one account of frustration with Massachusetts from another. For when the winds die down, there is nothing for Bradford to do except chronicle the loss, to avid migrants from the Bay, of all but a token presence on the Connecticut. Predicted at the end of an entry for 1633, and resisted by strong arguments both there and here, this loss is one more indication that the "great" migration was no unalloyed blessing.

Both sides appeal to providence; each warns the other—in what ought to have been a learning experience—not to abuse that claim. And when the authorities of the Bay refer to the disputed territory as "the Lord's waste,"[62] they are reminded that if it once indeed seemed so, "it was themselves that found it so and not they"; and furthermore, since the time of their first discovery, they "have since bought it of the right owners, and maintained a chargeable possession upon it all this while" (282). But several Massachusetts congregations, originally denied permission, are now in the very act of relocating. Evidently they have worn down Winthrop and his General Court in much the way the settlers of Duxbury eventually wore down Bradford himself—"with importunity and pleas of necessity."[63] And so, as the type must always accede to its completion, Plymouth caves in once again:

To make any forcible resistance was far from their thoughts—they had enough of that about Kennebec—and to live in continual contention with their friends and brethren would be uncomfortable and too heavy a burthen to bear. Therefore, for peace sake, though they conceived they suffered much in this thing, they thought it better to let them have it upon as good terms as they could get. And so they fell to treaty. (283)

Thus end any hopes the planters of Plymouth had of removing, as a body, from their own lands, now regularly referred to as "barren," to the richer soils of the Connecticut Valley. And though it requires the force of commentary to get Bradford to say that there are now too many saints running around here, it is his very own language that speaks of a "fall": saints encovenant; soldiers make war; but only the miserable are reduced to treaty. (And by the way, we failed again to obtain a proper minister: we rather liked Mr. Norton, but he went off "to Ipswich, where were many rich and able men" [285].)

Reversing this ill fortune, 1636 presents the Plymouth Separatists with a satisfactory minister at last, the "able and Godly" Mr. John Rayner (293). Unfortunately, however, this fact ends the report on a year less satisfactory in other ways. An outbreak of the plague in London interrupts the ordinary flow of business and the ongoing attempt to clear up the Plymouth accounts. Two ships bound from the Massachusetts to the settlements newly spun off in Connecticut are driven aground in Plymouth harbor, which "some imputed as a correction from God for their intrusion, to the wrong of others, into that place"; but Bradford, not sure what God might decree in a contest *among* saints, confesses he "dare not be bold with God's judgments in this kind" (290). And word from the Bay indicates that a "Pequot War" may not be easy to avert. It strikes in 1637, of course, as every student of the history of American "genocide"[64] must surely know. Bradford begs to be excused from a complete account of the prosecution of this brutal conflict because he expects "it will be fully done by themselves who best know the carriage and circumstances of things"; but as his own colony has played a large (if losing) part in the disputes that led up to the outbreak of hostilities, and as the court at Plymouth agreed "to send fifty men at their own charge" (295), he can scarcely avoid it altogether.

Bradford begins his annal for 1637 by noting that "the Pequots fell openly upon the English at Connecticut, in the lower parts of the river," but he can hardly be unaware that his own earlier accounts of the competitive spreading out of various groups of traders and settlers amount to a kind of one-sided prehistory of the conflict. The arguments by which the Pequots try (and fail) to win the support of their longtime enemy, the Narragansetts, strike Bradford as "pernicious," but the faithful historian in him cannot set them aside. "The English," argued the Pequots,

> were strangers and began to overspread their country, and would deprive them thereof in time, if they were suffered to grow and increase. And if the Narragansetts did assist the English to subdue them, they did but make way for their own overthrow, for if [the Pequots] were rooted out, the English would soon to take occasion to subjugate [the Narragansetts]. (294)

Tempted by these arguments, Bradford suggests, the Narragansetts were "half-minded to have made peace with them," but when push came to shove, they remembered "how much wrong they had received from the Pequots," and "revenge was so sweet unto them as it prevailed above all the rest, so as they resolved to join with the English against them, and did" (295).

So much for the logic of the hostilities. What follows next is a scene of suffering so intense that, like the earlier one involving the "flaying" of Indians stricken with smallpox, only a sensibility steeped in the pious carnage of the Old Testament dare mention it and God in the same breath. Surprised by the English (and their Narragansett allies), the Pequots offer "sharp resistance," with arms and also in hand-to-hand conflict. But then, once their huddled dwellings were put to the torch,

> all was quickly on a flame, and thereby more were burned to death than was otherwise slain; . . . those that escaped the fire were slain with the sword, some hewed to pieces, others run through with their rapiers, so as they were quickly dispatched and very few escaped. . . . It was a fearful sight to see them frying in the fire and the streams of blood quenching the same. (296)

As Bradford cannot have witnessed this scene, one wonders whose firsthand observation lies behind his fearful account; or perhaps Bradford merely loosed his imagination on the scene of hell, outdoing Wigglesworth, in advance.[65] In any case, Bradford spares us nothing of his "theology":

> horrible was the stink . . . thereof; but the victory seemed . . . sweet sacrifice, and they gave the praise thereof to God, who had wrought so wonderfully for them, thus to enclose their enemies in their hands and give them so speedy a victory over so proud and insulting an enemy. (296)

Anxious to clear his people of the charge of murder in the case of Hocking and eager to present himself as a man of peace in disputes with Massachusetts, Bradford here discovers an enemy he feels free to treat as "other."⁶⁶ And with that he seems to recover his old interpretive confidence.

Yet he continues to give us much more than we need to see God's terrific hand aright. The Narragansett response, for example. Hanging back from active participation in the ferocious danger of the battle, they come alive when the truly apocalyptic outcome begins to be clear.

> Insulting over their enemies in this their ruin and misery, when they saw them dancing in the flames, calling them by a word in their own language, signifying "O brave Pequots!" which they used familiarly among themselves in their own praise in songs of triumph. (296)

How does Bradford imagine the "children" are supposed to respond to *this* revelation? Vanity of vanities? Those who live by the arrow will die by the fire-next-time? "Wonder ye then at the fiery hunt?" Hawthorne will gain a modest fame, years later, for teaching his Puritans to say "Woe to the youth . . . who did but dream of a dance." But who inspired Bradford with the Melvillean vision of savages "dancing" in the flames?⁶⁷

And if *Moby-Dick,* then "Benito Cereno" as well. For if not, then why must we learn that "the Pequots' chief sachem being fled to the Mohawks, they cut off his head";⁶⁸ and whether this was "to satisfy the English or rather the Narragansetts (who as I have since heard, hired them to do it) or for their own advantage I well know not; but thus this war took end." The war, no doubt, but not the ongoing contest of culture; for, unhappy that some surviving Pequots avoid slavery by joining themselves to the Mohicans "with the approbation of the English of Connecticut," the Narragansetts now seek to "raise a general conspiracy against the English" (297). It is lamentable, of course, that Bradford cannot be got to call that "conspiracy" the just resistance of a native people unwilling to abet their own supplantation. For that insight we have to rely on the Pequots and on Roger Williams.⁶⁹ What we get from Bradford is only the bare evidence that savage "revenge" and saintly "sacrifice" do not look much different. And the silent suggestion that "de god what made shark" may also have made, "in a moment contraband" the nature of Red and White alike.

But if the annal for 1637 records, in a language that may know more than Bradford "himself," one fiery climax of a cultural conflict expressing itself in a variety of claims upon a contested continent, the next year's entries suggest a kind of ongoing parallel between the larger and smaller versions of the "land" problem. Bradford's account of the execution of an Englishman for the murder of a Narragansett reveals that the culprit, "out of means and loath to work," had been "one of the soldiers in the Pequot War" (299), and that his deadly deed recalled to some the truth of the Pequot warning that "the English would fall [next] upon them" (300). Accordingly, Bradford takes some satisfaction in recording that the murderer's execution gave the Narragansetts "and all the country good satisfaction." More locally, however, he has also to confess that the affair was "a matter of much sadness," being "the second execution which they had since they came" (301). Then, in that same range, he returns to the problem of 1632: wealth, scattering, and the possibility of divine displeasure. Uneasily, it appears, but with a sense that this may be his proper prospect.

"It pleased God," he begins, in a phrase that is coming to express some *skepticism,* as if, Hawthorne-fashion, it might preclude rather than invite further interpretation:

> It pleased God in these times so to bless the country with such access and confluence of people into it, as it was thereby much enriched, and cattle of all kinds stood at a high rate for divers years together.... By which means the ancient planters which had any stock, began to grow in their estates. (301–2)

The language is much the same as that for 1632: one braces oneself for the old analysis and prediction; for, since that time, the "access and confluence" of various peoples has proven anything but a blessing to New England at large. But Bradford maintains a deliberate calm: many of the old planters are losing interest in anything but corn and cattle; so that a new combination must be formed to maintain the fur trade at Kennebec. And that with good results: they tax themselves at a rate of one-sixth," with the first fruits of which they built a house for a prison"; and, more generally, they hedge the colony against the likelihood that "these high prices in corn and cattle would not long continue" (302).

For the reader who remembers Bradford's "sadness" over the two murders, the detail about the prison as a first fruit of capital wealth adds a troubling social note to this account of complex economic success—as if Bradford would rewrite the first chapter of *The Scarlet Letter* in the manner of a Marxist.[70] But the explicit turn is yet to come. This same year, "about the first or second of June, was a great and fearful earthquake": rattling dishes rather than overturning houses, whether prisons or trading posts, the noteworthy thing about this rare phenomenon was not its destructive power but its peculiar timing:

It so fell out that at the same time divers of the chief men of this town were met together at one house, conferring with some of their friends that were upon their removal from this place, as if the Lord would hereby show the signs of his displeasure, in their shaking a-pieces and removals one from another. (302)

"As if," indeed. As if the same "Deuteronomic" God who smiles approval on godly endeavor may not, with equal power, take note of studied deviations.[71] For even "friends" must know "the mighty hand of the Lord" can make "the mountains to tremble before Him, when He pleases" (303).

But then, as if to stop himself from turning in anger on the faithless ones he loves, he manages a strategic retreat into skepticism:

The summers for divers years together after this earthquake were not so hot and seasonable . . . as formerly, but more cold and moist, and subject to early and untimely frosts by which, many times, much Indian corn came not to maturity. But whether this was any cause I leave it to naturalists to judge. (303)

A skepticism but also an irony, and quite advanced for a book begun in search of "simple truth in all things" (3); for the real question is *not* whether the earthquake ran before the cooler summers in the manner of a cause but whether both these "threatening" natural phenomena are to be interpreted, together, as warnings to those men who would shake the foundations. And if Bradford declines to say so emphatically, the reason can only be that he is not quite ready to give up on his friends. Or on the idea that he is still writing a proper continuation of the book he began, in 1630, not in faith unaided but in hope fulfilled. Against the evidence, now, he holds out as long as he can.

———

Powerful as they have been, none of the discouragements so far has had the power to turn Bradford from the course he has set himself. Indeed, none of them might matter much at all—to his vision, at least—if they were being written from some end point of future triumph. If England had adopted, sometime in the middle or late 1640s, some version of "The New England Way," or if New England itself had undergone, at some time before Bradford's death in 1657, the sort of revival that made all the professedly godly think more, once again, of their common covenant obligations than of their separate economic interests, the story of Plymouth in the years after 1630 might sound different. But then, of course, supposing natural life on earth went right on, beyond the new moment of triumph, the possibility of a "third" part or section would come dauntingly into view.

The point—and we will see it again in Shepard's "Autobiography"—is simply that accounts of some segment of human experience as an intelligible "plot" can be *sanely* written only from a point of confident retrospect. Quite like accounts of personal conversion. Anything else must prove either too variously empirical to be truly godly or else too mindlessly godly to be credible or interesting.[72] The problem, then, is never that of starting up or of "catching up," supposing that something truly remarkable has happened but, always and of necessity, of going on beyond the point of historical—which is to say, "literary"—confidence. And so as we commit ourselves to go *on* with Bradford's account of going on, the suspense will not be in the expectation that something else truly spectacular will yet occur; for if that were going to happen, we would know it already, from the tone which an ex post facto design must always confer on intimations of discouragements to faith. The interest will be, rather, in "what to make of a diminished thing." And not just arithmetically, as every day in every way we do seem to be getting ever so slightly worse; but metaphysically too, as what began in godly design seems destined to end with some quite familiar patterns of human repetition. How then will Bradford end? we need to ask. Which is really to inquire: when?

Not yet in 1639 or 1640, though Bradford's interest seems flagging: "These two years I join together, because in them fell not out many things more than the ordinary passages of their common affairs" (304). A dispute with the Bay Colony about its border with Plymouth drags on for two unedifying years and ends with Plymouth capitulating as usual. And an extended discussion about how to wind up affairs with the creditors in England reaches no conclusion, in spite of the fact that the partners at Plymouth, now well along in years, are "loath to leave these entanglements upon their children and posterity, who might be driven to remove places as they had done" (310–11). Perhaps the annal for 1641 might have been merged as well, for it takes Bradford only a few paragraphs to detail the inventory taken in preparation for their settlement with the overseas partners, and to abbreviate a three-year controversy with the Reverend Charles Chauncy, whose strict scriptural conscience insisted on baptism by total immersion, even in the chilly latitudes of New England.[73] And then, returning to the subject of "dispersal," a single paragraph, naming for the first time the defections of Winslow, Standish, and Alden, and worrying about still others "dropping away daily," greatly weakening the original settlement and setting "the thoughts of many [more] upon removal" (315). And just so the stage seems set for a slow decline leading toward the sort of onetime removal that may make a *literal* end of Plymouth Plantation.

But not quite yet, for the surprising events of 1642 seem to arouse Bradford's literary energies once again, as if even a tale of gross wickedness were somehow preferable to the ongoing report on wearing disaffection. "Marvelous"—begins the preface to an animated account of the flourishing of irregular sexual practice in both Plymouth and Massachusetts—"to see how some kind of wickedness did grow and break forth here," in spite of the strictest early modern standards of discovery and punishment, to the point where even "moderate and good men" have censured them for their severity. Yet all this surveillance

> could not suppress the breaking out of sundry notorious sins. . . . Not only incontinency between persons unmarried, for which many both men and women have been punished sharply enough, but some married persons also. But that, which is worse, even sodomy and buggery (things fearful to name) have broke forth in this land oftener than once. (316)

Surprised at first, perhaps, that Bradford has made no mention of such things before, we quickly remind ourselves that possibly he thought of these matters as falling outside the category of "news that's fit to print"; or else, more likely, that he was hesitant to regard the unfailing evidence of human depravity as part of his largely public account of a people bent on "advancing the gospel." Still, as meaningful Reformation presupposed a certain *number* of Saints, it probably required as well a certain *level* of moral behavior—among the Saints themselves, first of all, unless they should choose the way of the Antinomians, but also among the Strangers, who might be thought to have opted for a sort of virtue by association.

In any event, the suppression of vice having failed, the literary repression is lifted as well. For Bradford—bored at last by the details of an economic partnership that cannot order its records, and heartily discouraged by the mounting evidence that he is the only communitarian left in Plymouth—cannot come to the end of his fascinated attempt to comprehend an impulse his rules have failed to rule. Still working a priori, before any historical facts have been set forth, Bradford tries hard to name the reason of the scandal. First of all, obviously, we should all "fear and tremble at the consideration of our corrupt natures" which cannot be "bridled, subdued and mortified . . . by any other means but the powerful work and grace of God's Spirit." Besides that, however, we may need to thank the

Devil—full of "spite against the churches" here in exact proportion to their "endeavor to preserve holiness and purity amongst them," and hoping thereby to "cast a blemish and stain upon them in the eyes of [the] world." Absent from the *Plymouth* for many pages, the Devil has been permitted to fade into the background of the book's epistemology, a figure of premise and prehistory, as we almost come to think; so that his reappearance may signify the return of a force Bradford himself had heartily wished to repress.

For he has other, more modern explanations as well—still in advance of any specific case. Perhaps it is "as it is with waters when their streams are stopped or dammed up": "When they get their passage they flow with more violence and make more noise and disturbance than when they are suffered to run quietly in their own channels" (316). Or perhaps there are *not* indeed more evils of this kind here, "nor anything near so many by proportion as in other places; but they are here more discovered and seen and made public by due search, inquisition and due punishment; for the churches look narrowly to their members, and the magistrates over all, more strictly than in other places" (317). How *very* strictly we are tempted to infer from the redundancy of the prose. In any event, it is only after he has turned to social science for excuse as well as explanation that Bradford is ready "to proceed"—with the details of "a letter from the Governor in the Bay to them here," with the answers he and the other "Elders" of Plymouth have seen fit to return, and to a case of "bestiality" in the venue of Plymouth itself.

The letter itself is actually quite various, mentioning the question of political relations with the growing society of outcasts at Rhode Island and the "maintenance of the trade of beaver" (318), as well as the subject of Bradford's own acute interest, the punishment of certain "heinous offenses in point of uncleanness" (317). The occasion, it appears, is the sad case of the statutory rape of two prepubescent girls. The question burning itself into the record of two Puritan colonies is not the psychological damage done to the young girls but a much more technical consideration: does not the fact that both girls are below the age of possible conception turn any copulation with them into an "unnatural act," quite like the congress of male with male or of male with a female animal? The author of the letter is Richard Bellingham: himself about to become the subject of a sexual scandal that helps to invent *The Scarlet Letter*.[74] Bellingham writes to all New England congregations to learn the local consensus about the death penalty in cases of irregular sexuality. Bradford's own answer is most modest: he defers, first of all, to the greater learning of the elders in the Bay colony; he then indicates his own belief, that as in the case of adultery, sodomy and buggery are capital offenses only if there is "penetration." Other elders from the plantation disagree—arguing in Latin that "*frictatio usque ad effusionem seminis*" is, by Scripture warrant, quite enough to warrant capital punishment. And Bradford includes these letters as well as his own.[75]

And then goes on to his local case. "After the time of the writing of these things befell a very sad accident of the like foul nature in this government": Thomas Granger, "servant to an honest man of Duxbury[,] . . . was this year detected of buggery, and indicted for the same, with a mare, a cow, two goats, five sheep, two calves and a turkey"—the partridge, it appears, had escaped into a pear tree. But if one's students rather expect some such joke, they have only themselves (or their Chaucer class) to blame; for Bradford is quick to assure us of the chastity of his own interest: such things are "horrible . . . to mention, but the truth of history requires it" (320). Were he to avoid the question, he might well suspect himself of *historical* suppression, exactly where the other sort had failed. And beyond that, in this chapter particularly, Bradford seems to have set his heart upon honesty. And so, after a number of free confessions, before a variety of inquiring panels, the unhappy Granger identifies all of the violated animals, whereupon each is "killed before his face, according to the law, Leviticus xx.15; and then he himself was executed" (320). A modest inquiry into the source of the knowledge of such "bestial" practices throws the blame toward "old England," and evinces the warning about "what care all ought to have what servants they bring into their families" (321).[76]

Yet Bradford can hardly let it go at that. Something here requires further explanation. Suppose an unfriendly reader—something he imagines very rarely—should demand how "so many wicked persons . . . should so quickly come over into this land and mix themselves amongst them?" Especially as "it was religious men that began the work and they came for religion's sake." A thing to marvel at, Bradford concedes, especially "in time to come," when many of the relevant facts shall have become obscure. And so he provides another list of possible explanations. First, all Christians need to remember that "where the Lord begins to sow good seed, there the envious man will endeavor to sow tares"; this "envious man" sounds a lot like the very Devil mentioned in the former list, but perhaps Bradford refers to human enemies anxious to ship their indentured troubles abroad. Then too, Bradford hastens to add, men "come over into a wilderness . . . were glad to take such [help] as they could." Further, men involved in the trade of transporting Saints but who could not always fill their ships with just such persons might "make up their freight and advance their profit" with "unworthy persons" (321) of all sorts. Finally, as many people had followed Christ for the loaves of bread he was known to multiply, so here: many Strangers followed the Saints with a hope to share in the blessings that usually follow God's people "in outward as spiritual things" (322).

Anxious to get this last explanation exactly right, Bradford hastens to remind himself that the prosperity of Saints will have "afflictions . . . mixed withal."
And the effect of this is certainly to remind the reader that neither prosperity nor
the increased population (even of Saints) from which it grew has proved altogether a blessing. Nor does Bradford himself seem entirely satisfied with his
largely naturalistic attempt to explain a set of behaviors he well might wish away.
For he ends his long discussion of the "wickedness" not with any sense of sufficient justification but with a single self-conscious and damaging admission: "thus,
by one means or another, in 20 years' time it is a question whether the greater part
be not grown the worse." He means the entire, mixed population, of course, not
just the core of Saints; but one could hardly be encouraged if that rare ingredient
had proved insufficient to leaven the whole lump. Perhaps that is what one would
mean by "declension." So it comes as no surprise that the matter which ends the
annal for 1642—"the conclusion of that long and tedious business between the
partners here and them in England" (322)—should seem brief but still tedious.
One might almost think Bradford welcomed the "wickedness" as a relief from a
story that was becoming merely ordinary.

Nor will any of the matters for 1643 quite reverse the sense of falling back
into the predictable. First, the peaceful "falling asleep" of "their Reverend Elder
and . . . loving friend Mr. William Brewster"—in proof, it would seem, that
though God is wont to reward his faithful servants with a life that endures in
spite of hardships and perils, not all such Saints can be expected to live right on
into the moment of God's final intrusion into earthly life. Bradford makes Brewster a type of the very thing a latter-day New Englander, also interested in the
problem of "biography," could never quite conceive, a *holy hero;* and, in spite of
Emerson's disbelief, Bradford's "Life of Brewster" easily established itself as the
model of such writing for at least two centuries.[77] An upright and faithful servant
to men of station before he ever became a Saint, Brewster never did seek a fugi-
tive and cloistered virtue but remained committed to a life of appropriate work in
the world. Driven into Separatism by his insight into "the tyranny of the bishops"
(326), he was forced to change careers both in Holland and again in New England, but this Pilgrim for all seasons exhibited, in both places, all the competence required; and, because the Church is not opposed to the World in all senses,
the abilities he exercised as teaching elder at Plymouth kept the congregation as
well furnished, for many years, as if they had a minister properly so designated.
A loving and beloved man, he lived long and, in all proper senses, did indeed
prosper.

Yet he did in fact die. Bradford is moved to exclaim, in a formula much used
in earlier years, that he "cannot but here take occasion to admire the marvelous

providence of God" in ensuring that Brewster and so many other of the Plymouth faithful were granted so long a life. Surely, given all the changes of air, of water, of diet (down to the point of famine), and given their experience of "perils" of truly biblical form and proportion, this longevity "must needs be more than ordinary and above natural reason" (328). But he can in no way evade the mortal fact itself. Dangerously, he asks a version of his old question: "What was it then that upheld them?" Probably Bradford's *then* is still not a temporal marker, but the change leaps out just the same. As does the fact that he must now *answer*, for himself, his own most rhetorical question: surely "it was God's visitation that preserved their spirits" (329). The Teller answers for himself because he knows he can no longer trust the Tale to do the work instead.

Bradford is *our* Pilgrim Saint but, as we learn from this astonishing eulogy, Brewster was *his;*[78] and no scorning of "good and dainty fare" and no appeal to the career of Daniel or of Jacob can belie the fact that this prime Saint has died. "In his bed, in peace, amongst the midst of his friends," without Melvillean ravings, without indeed "any pangs or gaspings," but without any Pisgah vision to guarantee that the future of Plymouth Plantation will in any manner fulfill the promise of a past over which the spirit of Brewster so long presided. Or none at least that Bradford finds himself in any position to provide. His unstinting praise of Brewster is "now" in fact an evocation of the richly rewarded past. Brewster may have "sweetly departed this life" but he has also departed this plantation. Gone "unto a better" life (324), no doubt, but he is no less gone from ours. Gone at a time when special providence may effectively have ceased. For if he *was* preserved over so long and fateful a past, his death might well mark a term. Past which, for better or for worse, Bradford has decided to go on writing. Until he could find, perhaps, a reason to stop as cogent as the one that led him to begin. Or, failing that, a note on which to end.

Not the grisly euthanasia which the New England Federation permits the still-vengeful Narragansetts to administer to Miantonomo, though that blow of less than grace might stand for Bradford's idea of the state of an American Nature neither Pilgrim nor Puritan could quite redeem.[79] And not even, in 1644, the final, long-dreaded breakup of the Plymouth church. Bradford can see the end of his own most vital religious connection in that event, and his prose spares us nothing of his personal pain. But he hesitates to blame those who had made that connection possible in the first place; and he can see no way (yet) to accuse himself.

Though the dispersal of the Plymouth population has been noted at various points in Bradford's text, counterpointing the grosser instances of disaster predicted by the spreading of the white population, it is the compressed epitome of 1632 to which the sad entry of 1644 looks back. Many having left Plymouth already, finding "accommodations elsewhere more suitable to their ends and minds, and others still upon every occasion desiring their dismissions,"

> the church began seriously to think whether it were not better jointly to remove to some other place than to be thus weakened and as it were insensibly dissolved. Many meetings and much consultation was held hereabout, and divers were men's minds and opinions. Some were still for staying together in this place, alleging men might here live if they would be content with their condition, and that it was not for want or necessity so much that they removed as for the enriching of themselves. Others were resolute upon removal and so signified that here they could not stay; but if the church did not remove, they must. (333)

Again Bradford sounds the note of disharmony—many wearing meetings in which, in place of sweet accord or even hard-won consensus, many men had many minds. Finally, however, something like a plan: the whole church will remove if (and only if) a "fit place could be found that more conveniently and comfortably receive the whole, with such accession of others as might come to them." And so—the Connecticut opportunity long lost—"the greater part consented to a removal to a place called Nauset" (333).

In the midst of regret "that they had given away already the best and most commodious places to others," they quickly discover that Nauset, "about fifty miles from hence, and . . . remoter from all society," cannot accommodate "the whole body, much less . . . any addition or increase." Unable to meet the necessary condition of group removal, they seem required to "change their resolutions." But no: "such as were before resolved upon removal took advantage of this agreement and went on, notwithstanding; neither could the rest hinder them, they having made some beginning" (333–34). What sense could one make, after all, of a covenant of complainers? Or a community of Christian coercion? Yet what Bradford offers, in place of logical critique or personal attack, is something very like what another century would call "sentiment"; not tears, perhaps, but a noticeably "feminine" appeal to domestic emotion:

> And thus was this poor church left, like an ancient mother grown old and forsaken of her children, though not in their affections yet in regard of their bodily presence and personal helpfulness; her ancient members being

most of them worn away by death, and these of later time being like children translated into other families, and she like a widow left only to trust in God. Thus, she that had made many rich became herself poor. (334)

Bradford's "rich" and "poor" are just literal enough to prompt some suspicion of Puritanism and the rise of entrepreneurial wealth in the New World. Though it may be more to the sentimental point to wonder if it is not Bradford *himself* who feels like the abandoned mother—as if the Saints of his very own church, with whom he grew up and grew old, were the truest family this orphan were ever to enjoy.

Certainly Bradford makes it sound as if he is almost the only one left. Little by wearing little, the "children" of this most fostering of men have left him behind. For other churches, to be sure, and this could be seen as the way it pleased God to advance the cause of Reformation in these remote parts of the world. But where others might see departures from Plymouth as advancing the Gospel beyond its first New England basis, Bradford can feel only the pain inflicted by those who, for reasons he briefly indicates but will not press to analyze, are in fact dividing the church their covenanting oath once placed beyond the reach of any other motive. For if the defections from Plymouth regularly covered themselves with the name of "necessity," still none of them dared to cloak themselves in the mantle of Reformation. Nor would it require a Perry Miller to expose them if they had.

Bradford tries to be charitable: Plymouth remains alive in the "affections" of its departing members. But the force of his logic survives the recollection of friendship: certain New World migrants, once recognizable as "pilgrims" indeed, have grown rich on a large-scale Puritan rush to follow the example of their wilderness church; and then they have all gone off, one by one, to discover some place more like a garden. Leaving the reader to ponder what will sustain them *now*: wealth, according to the middle-class appeal of John Smith? Wonder, at the plentitude of the natural world, even in New England? Or merely the memory of a corporate mission that once seemed vital enough for them (or their Fathers) to have risked coming over on the *Mayflower*? All of these in some measure, no doubt, but on no account would the mixture be godly enough to inspire a book like Bradford's *Plymouth*.

———

Quite long enough to dramatize the sources of its own discouragement, the "second part" of *Plymouth Plantation* labors on for a few pages beyond the recognizable lapse of its reason for being. As if writing for the record were all Bradford had left. Dutifully, therefore, he recounts the combination of diplomacy and military preparedness by which the "Commissioners" of the now "United Colonies of New England" manage to avert war with the Narragansetts and their potential allies; but he seems convinced that things will not long go well between the English and these "children of strife" (341). Halfheartedly he retails the fatal outcome of an ugly quarrel between the captain and an unruly crewman of a ship commissioned for piracy. Then, at the end of the entry for 1646, and with as little tone as possible, he outlines the nature of Edward Winslow's mission to England, noting that by 1650 he has still not returned. What follows this inconclusive account of an open-ended and faltering errand—as criticism has suitably advertised—are blank pages labeled "Anno 1647" and "Anno 1648."

Something happened in those years, no doubt, and in the years after that, up to and including the year of Bradford's death in 1657. But nothing, it would appear, of sufficient moment to compel the historian who had begun his work in the plain sight of God. And if it seems a little pious to say that he gained his book in losing it,[80] we may have to wait a while before feeling tempted to sound that note again. For the implication, and even the "meaning" of Bradford's inconclusion, is arresting indeed. He might of course simply have gone *on,* with all such matters as survive the breakup of his beloved church community; but that would have been to concede that what he was writing was, after all, not holy history but only what one critic calls a "mercantile epic."[81] Or he could have contrived to lie, searching everywhere for providences to prove that 1630 had been but the *beginning* of the Age of the Spirit; even claiming, perhaps, that the defections were really important repetitions of the Covenant gesture itself. Or, supposing this third alternative is adequately distinct from the second, he could himself have invented the New England Jeremiad; for clearly he has conveniently at hand, right there in the middle of the 1640s, all the evidences—of declension mixed with denial—anyone would ever need.

Though Bradford says so only in metaphor, the problem clearly is the "children" who are being "translated" as it were to other "families." Granting the figure, however, all the members of a given congregation are equally "children" of the one "mother" church, even if their ages were equal to that of Elder Brewster. But with Alden, Standish, Brewster, and Prence long gone for Duxbury, and with Winslow away in England, just who do we imagine Bradford is talking about when he writes, in 1646, his entry for 1644? To be sure, these children of Plymouth have had no strict test of "saving faith" to determine whether they are living up to the parental norm; the best they can do by way of generational rebellion, it appears, is "sue for dismission" from the church of their baptism. And even if we reject the idea that Bradford's "children" is a Freudian metonymy for *children,* the case will look much the same. For surely it has been in the *name* of the children—more mouths to feed, more land to bequeath—that most of the removals were carried out.[82] If it were any otherwise, the euphemism of "necessity" would fool nobody: one great advantage of having children, surely, is that they provide parents with a blameless excuse for their own expanding ambition.

Yet Bradford need not have turned on any of the children directly. He need only have cried out, in a painful warning that ill conceals his fervent hope—or indeed his fixed ideological conviction—that the waning of original piety had to be only a temporary thing; that God could not have led his open-boated people through such a sea of trouble only to withdraw his grace in the end. This, after all, is the way the Jeremiad worked, so long and so well, for generations of children at Massachusetts Bay: the providential protection that enabled the religious accomplishments of the first generation could hardly have been for nothing, or for its own sake alone; and any aroused moment now the tide might turn, from Declension grown familiar to Reformation once more. Or else, at the very least, Bradford could have continued to celebrate the miracle of preparation by which Plymouth made way for Massachusetts and, in doing so, anticipated the gesture by which Cotton Mather seemed willing to exchange New England for America.[83] And given the willingness of American Studies to make the best of whatever it finds, it could have worked.

But surely that gain would have been our loss. For one thing readers have always prized about Bradford is a sense of the difference between his ragged "pilgrim" identity and the elaborately endowed ideology of Puritan Massachusetts. To be sure: Bradford decides to write only when it appears he can fairly plug his project into theirs; but he stops when he honestly understands that, though Massachusetts might absorb or subsume Plymouth, it can in no way redeem it. That Model City by the Bay is having its own problems, as Bradford began to sense when these land-hungry upstarts beat his old-comers out of the chance to resettle in Connecticut. And whatever might be true of the macropolitics of church and state in the "United Colonies of New England," nothing could ever compensate Bradford for what he saw as the failure of loyalty within his very own congregation. They broke their promise, he keenly feels—to him, it seems only fair to admit, but to one another as well. As he saw it, they had all sworn, before God, and each to every other, that nothing could matter more than the faithful following out of God's will for the world; and that, to ease the difficulty involved in following that godly path, they would place care of one another above self-interest in any form.

Perhaps each one had promised too much; but all were supposed to have seen enough of the world to know how badly it runs when left to the worldly. And indeed they did promise: all for one and one for all, with or without the muskets. Then, one sudden rise in corn futures and it was every man for himself. "Necessity," indeed "Progress," in an editor's eye. Not even Declension could cover the case of an eminent worldliness where familiar love had been. Others might find what names they could to hide the failure, but Bradford would stick to his own unhappy truth: they broke their promise.

But not to that alone, for it is characteristic of Bradford's honesty that, however he might stack the cards against Lyford or Morton, or undervalue the culture of the Native Americans, he will not easily overlook the part he himself may have played in the failure. Perhaps he had not been "unwilling" enough, in 1632, to permit those who "sued to be dismissed and become a body of themselves" (253); perhaps even he, economic patron that he was, was too easily swayed by the "pretence" of "necessity" (254). Or perhaps the problem went back even further than that, into the 1620s, the decade of multiform success. Had it been altogether wise for him and a few others to assume the accumulated debt of the entire enterprise, in exchange for exclusive trading rights? Possibly this new freedom from common obligation (and opportunity) had helped to loose the selfish impulse. And, further back than that, was it not himself who preached that little sermon on the "confusion and discontent" (121) of communism as a basis for Christian community; himself who had seen divine "wisdom" in economic particularism? Perhaps that had been a mistake—in tone, at very least; an act not of original insight but of hubris. Perhaps "the Governor," with or without the advice of the other leaders, "gave way" too easily. Perhaps it was a snare and a delusion to imagine that "in all other things" they might "go on in the general way as before" (120).

But if these self-accusations must be teased out from an uncertain word or two in the text, there is one encompassing passage that puts the case of *personal* failure more starkly—and more movingly—than any rhetoric the critic can arrange. Well worth quoting at length, it is the marginal note that Bradford, in one of his last acts of composition, added to the (1617) letter from Robinson and Brewster to the London Adventurers, making the best possible case for Separatist trust and dependability. Indeed the text itself is worth repeating along with its gloss:

> We are knit together as a body in a most strict and sacred bond and covenant of the Lord, of the violation whereof we make great conscience, and by virtue whereof we do hold ourselves straitly tied to all care of each other's good and of the whole, by every one and so mutually. (33)

If this account were to appear in a freshman paper, most teachers would probably mark it as "redundant," but saints have their reason: repetition is the mother of conviction as much as of emphasis. They really *mean* it. God knows whether we are truly saints, but we can attest that we are a community bonded for mutual aid and comfort, sworn before God and not apt by any human means to be put asunder.

So there it was: the promise broken. And though it is poignant, it is not at all surprising to find that "Bradford wrote the following in his aged hand on the blank page opposite:"[84]

> O sacred bond, whilst inviolably preserved! How sweet and precious were the fruits that flowed from the same! But when this fidelity decayed, then their ruin approached. O that these ancient members had not died or been dissipated (if it had been the will of God) or else that his holy care and constant faithfulness had still lived, and remained with those that survived, and were in times afterwards added unto them. But (alas) that subtle serpent hath slyly wound in himself under fair pretenses of necessity and the like, to untwist these sacred bonds and tie[s], and as it were insensibly by degrees to dissolve, or in a great measure to weaken, the same. I have been happy, in my first times, to see, and with much comfort to enjoy, the blessed fruits of this sweet communion, but it is now part of my misery in old age, to find and feel the decay and want thereof (in a great measure) and with grief and sorrow of heart to lament and bewail the same. And for others' warning, and admonition, and my own humiliation, do I here note the same. (33)

And here it is: a testament of failure more searching than any Jeremiad; a song of loss more grievous than any elegy; an accusation of complicity—no, the word is *participation*—as painfully honest as the confessions of the world have to offer. And no *bad* place to begin American literature, if that were any issue.

The first thing to note, perhaps, is the finality of the failure: what was uneasily predicted in 1632, as a sort of self-punishing worst-possible-case scenario, and what was merely implied by the tone of 1644, is here a fixed fact: "their ruin," well seen in its approach, is now upon them. Yet even before we get to the last sentence, the tone reveals that *them* means *us*; unlike the "blaming" passages of 1632 and 1644, the "they" here is the exact same third person Bradford always uses to discuss the affairs of his group as such. In spite of the commonality of this responsibility, however, one can still make out that the "children" were indeed a special problem: if only the "ancient members had not died." It seems quite possible that Bradford may once have thought, like the earliest Christians, that some of them at least might live on into the "new heaven and new earth" which Christ's return would usher in. But in any case, as the old world wore right on, even in *New* England, the children and other new recruits failed to know that their only true life was the one they led in common. In some sense, God himself might be to blame, for "his holy care and constant faithfulness" seemed indeed to have been withdrawn. But wherever that question—"whether deity's guiltless"—might tend elsewhere, it signals here only the fact that the season of special providence is over. If there had indeed been such a thing to begin with. For that too might have been a glorious delusion: some ships do make it across some oceans, however their voyage might be manned or motivated.

Only after some grievous time does Bradford think to mention Satan, not by name, but under the figure of the "subtle serpent" who is always winding himself in where least expected. But when he does appear, it is not as some *other* agency to blame—certainly not as the marplot whose subtle devices must share equal responsibility with the failure of God's holy care. The aged Bradford may be skirting the edges of blasphemy here, but not of the systematic, "dualist" sort. The serpent always opposes God, of course, but what he does here, more specifically, is to provide a name for the fact that mistakes can be fatal. All sorts of things that must have seemed like a good idea at the time—like setting persons to sow and to reap on their own particular—may turn out to have been a work of Satan after all. And so Bradford does indeed accuse himself—who listened so patiently to those "fair pretences of necessity and the like," only to discover, now too late, that the moving pleas of his own dear comrades were part of a subtle trap. Yet how was he supposed to resist? by playing the "tyrant" after all? What sort of community would that have fostered?

The point, of course, though Bradford may not quite realize this himself, was that there probably was nothing else he could have done: knowing what he *now* knows he might discover some way to act differently, but given about ten chances *without* the rare benefit of holy hindsight, he would probably do about the same thing. Perhaps that was the devil of the matter. With exquisitely painful effect, therefore, Bradford's language hauntingly echoes that of the entry for 1644. There, the most cautious interpersonal diplomacy had tried to find a way to keep the church from being "as it were *insensibly* dissolved." But it had failed. So it must be concluded here—in the *now* of last possible interpretation—that the serpent had found a most subtle way "as it were *insensibly* by degrees to dissolve" the unity which alone had made writing about Plymouth seem a suitable distraction from the beaver trade. And now no more.

For which lapse Bradford here assumes his fair share of guilt. Somewhere beneath his theological paradox of not knowing then what is inescapably clear now—and of having had to act on that not-knowing—this remarkable passage of critical afterthought may express a pain even greater than its very considerable guilt; but it will not do to conventionalize the more-than-Johnsonian act of "humiliation" here. Whether Bradford used the word to name a needful step in the process of "preparation,"[85] or whether he wished to suggest, according to some older usage, that he might fairly go about in sackcloth and ashes, the gesture is both conscious and strong: he accepts the blame for not being able to identify the Devil in his subtler forms. In the persecution of God's saints, then or now, the serpent showed his naked form; and only those in love with human learning could miss his spirit in quarrels that went beyond the plainest sense of Scripture's saving lore. Recognizable too were his attempts to foster strange lusts within a society of pure love. But what was one to say when dearest friends offered familiar need as a reason to desert the church?—placing the naturally occurring unit, that is to say, in place of one that had to be chosen from deepest spiritual need. Not a nice place to be in, to be sure, but "let's not go there" was not an option. There he was in fact, and he got it wrong. What if good is not always nicer than bad? How in the end could one know?

Yet even those who will not share the guilt may find a way to feel the pain. Which we had better call *spiritual* or nothing else will make sufficient sense. Including Bradford's reasons for writing at all. Bradford is not, as all agree, a very "subjective" writer.[86] Perhaps no Puritan is truly so in a modern sense, but even among his fellows he may be a special case. Trying to tell the public story of a group enterprise, Bradford has not written much about how it felt for him to have been a member of that group; personally, he is "the Governor," where that political designation is appropriate, and at other times his thoughts and deeds are simply a part of what "they" thought or did. A consummate master of tone—as this long chapter has tried to suggest—he feels no need to say when the corporate "they" are happily of one mind and when their treasured unanimity begins to wear a little thin. When the corporate author is successful, the reader can tell. When Bradford's prose is hard to follow, as it occasionally is, the reason is that there are too many different "they's" in the same sentence or paragraph. And yet the motive is clear: so impersonal is his concern that he refuses to say "us." Let alone "I." So we really are quite unprepared for the cri de coeur which sounds along with the profession of corporate faith and the confession of personal guilt in Bradford's side note to the credo of Robinson and Brewster.

There is, to be sure, the daring figure of abandoned mother of the annal for 1644. And for the year before that, Bradford's formal and most proper eulogy for Elder Brewster has a strong personal undertone: Bradford *loved* Brewster and, beyond that, he treasured the life of the Plymouth church—in the regular repetition of its stripped-down Sabbath exercises, and as the spirit of those exercises had flowed out into the work of the week. And readers who miss these intimations of personal sentiment, or weight them less than ledger books full of financial detail, are reading the letter without the spirit. But if only the "sensitive" are prepared to witness Bradford salute the "sacred bond" in full apostrophe, or even to recall its wholesome social effects as "sweet and precious . . . fruits," still *no* reader can possibly anticipate the confession, in advance of the guilt, "*I* have been happy, in my first times, to see, and with much comfort to enjoy, the blessed fruits of this sweet communion"—as if the chief executive officer of the Planters (and then the Undertakers) of the Plymouth Plantation had suddenly thought to write the pain of Edgar Poe. And if happiness once, then "misery" now, in "*my* old age," to know the passing of the splendor. Not from the grass of Wordsworth or the trees of Columbus, but from the social world, where loving sweet "communion" was a fact, whether minister was there to break the bread or not.[87]

And then, as if to show that even *religious* genius will out, the final lapse from lament to confession; from personal pain, endured so well, repressed so long, to personal guilt, discovered only now, as then it failed to know itself as such. So sure is this transition that in any lesser man we might suspect the fine hand of artifice: corporate purpose, common failure; private pain, personal guilt. There's a legacy, if anyone could notice: our errand failed; I see precisely how, but cannot say exactly why. And if I suffer loss, I publish guilt as well. Mea culpa.

Closer by far to Elegy than to Jeremiad,[88] Bradford's "history" of Plymouth Plantation invents and exhausts the possibilities of a form we find it hard to specify; for even if we could name the note on which it ends, we would face the problem, still, of deciding whether it is proper to allow the personal gloom of 1646 to infect the providential glory of 1630, as that glory redeems the daunting discouragements of 1621. Unwilling to regard the undoing of the Plymouth covenant as a temporary failing—and utterly incapable of imagining that the lapse of Christian love might be offset by the triumph of congregational polity— Bradford stops, well short of lying. Not short of lament, perhaps, but not the strategic lament of those who invoke a glorious past as an earnest of a more perfect future; and not the shameless lament which asks to be "literature" in the name of the poignancy of its own suffering and regret. In Bradford's *Plymouth,* providence underwrites suffering and redeems despair for as long as promises are kept; providence fails exactly as other motives come more prominently into view.

And Bradford stops writing the moment he knows that the promises are indeed a memory and that nostalgia can neither assuage his pain nor disguise his responsibility. The failed vision we may suitably identify as but a local variant of the "Protestant Theory of History." The one which takes its place we need to recognize as Bradford's own.

CHAPTER THREE

"A STRANGE POISE
OF SPIRIT"

The Life and Deaths of Thomas Shepard

Not quite the transcendental imagined by the New Critics, literary completeness is nevertheless a condition real enough to defy subtle intimations of changing design and even the glaring evidence of fragmentation: a literary thing is over when it has done all it can; we call it complete if it has done all its law allows. So it is with Bradford's *Plymouth:* it stops when it realizes it cannot conscientiously go on with the thing it thought it was doing. And though our literary conscience may have to learn to praise examples of a more abiding faith in the possibility of holy history, the morale of our private expectation is hardly undone when we find some perfect knower in the act of suspecting that things may work some other way. Bradford begins—when he does indeed begin—with a perfect (if circular) assurance that the ways of God alone could explain how Plymouth came so oddly to be and then so grandly to be seen. And he stops when—History having indeed moved on—the residue of Providence seems a little too ordinary. Thus it always ends, we seem to see: awakening, aspiration to the truer life, endurance beyond the reach of all design, a lapsing to the world we always knew. The Fate of Puritanism? The fact of life. Which Bradford knew only too well.

The problem with a *perfect* completeness of this kind is that it leaves us scarcely knowing where to turn. "That's the name of that tune," we hear ourselves saying, with a finality (also circular) that prevents history and appears to separate the experience of the literary from an involvement with discourse of every other kind. Dreary repetition seems not only possible but inevitable: literary history as a series of small embellishments or nominal revisions of the one heroic text. Why not look for a replenished sense of being in some truly *other* place? Surely there was *maize* before our tears did drown it. Or maybe Philadelphia will have a project.

Yet it has been the surprise of Americanist literary study to discover writings of lucid human intelligence in precisely the place where religious masterwork had seemed to say the final word. And in the seventeenth century no less than elsewhere. Anything but a monolith, the "Puritanism" of original New England generated sharp and interesting differences in religious doctrine, philosophical premise and implication, genre of visionary expression, and even in what we might call the "sense of life," where opposition to the pleasures of play for its own sake and a keen eye for the failure of zeal are only part of the story. Failure may wear more than a single face, and silence may not be its only tone. But even if we should hold fast to our suspicion that, in spite of all that has been said about the *optimistic* meaning of "the American Jeremiad,"[1] the various versions of the Puritan story always end the same way—in a spiritual disillusion that will not quite admit itself as such—there remains the question of beginnings.

Bradford's literary career began with an overwhelming sense that, in the imitative fact of a Great Migration, the vagrancy of his Separatists had been redeemed as pilgrimage. And, given the power of his masterful manuscript, later historians were only too happy to see their own beginnings in his rare after-the-fact prolepsis. Nathaniel Morton indicated the pattern and Cotton Mather set the seal: New England begins at Plymouth.[2] But surely one might look for other inaugurations as well: wherever two or three had joined together; or, if that dangerous act were slow to repeat itself in the lives of those who were trying to reform the English church gradually and from the inside, in the moment when some all too-loyal individual or group was forced to the painful—life-changing, logic-disrupting, and identity-threatening—conclusion that, for the time being at least, a separated approach to the problem of Reform was in fact indicated.

Indeed, it is precisely here that the once vexed, now tedious question of "Non-Separating Congregationalism" takes on a vital significance. For whatever may be true of the relation of nonseparating theory to separatist practice of church formation and discipline,[3] and however much the Great Migrants of 1630 may have deceived themselves about the nature of their loyalty to the Mother Church of England,[4] this one prime difference insists upon itself: nonseparating migrants to New England stayed in England longer. Far too long, if any of them had thought to consult the conscience of John Robinson or William Brewster. And not nearly long enough, in the view of those stay-at-home Puritans who studied to erect their own platform at the Westminster Assembly of 1642. But then that was exactly the problem: when *was* a moderate man justified in concluding that the brotherhood of internal reformers was in fact losing out to a powerful combination of more overtly political men who wished to lead the Church of England in another direction entirely? Surely, in the face of Bishop Laud, these moderates must have their own story.

Bradford's Immediatism we know. But how did it feel to be a Gradualist—one who "tarried" in the hope that Parliament, eager to turn the king of England from a sovereign ruler to a constitutional monarch, might also enact a reformation which would take the organizing and disciplinary power of the church and hand it over to its own members and officers, and would then enlist the full and vigorous power of the state to protect this precise form of disestablished establishment? Such pious hopes can seem a little naive—unless one counts in the problem involved in Separatism as such. In the minds of the Gradualists, it was the Immediatists who were being naive; for how could the dispersed noncooperation of local dissent ever hope to reform a nation and beyond that a world? Secular governments might indeed wither away in the bright blaze of an imminent millennium, but that time was not yet; and meanwhile one required "a due form of government, both civil and ecclesiastical." And even John Winthrop had only faith and hope to assure him, in the face of his own lively sense and exercise of power, that *exemplary* did not mean simply *deluded and irrelevant*.[5] Reformation, on this account, was as much a matter of efficacious power as of faithful insight. What wonder, therefore, if Puritan reformers were not all visionary idealists from the outset?

Yet the tarriers did not hold back forever. Slow learners they may have been, but even these "duller scholars of the Mysterious Bard" somehow divined that salvation can begin to organize itself without the timely aid of existing statecraft. While they were learning, they no doubt followed their consciences as well as they could. Trying not to be "absurd and pedantic in reform," they wore the surplice and used the prayer book until these familiar symbols became the establishment's very substance. Hoping for an established living among persons known to be like-minded, or seeking to discover the shape of an elite congregation within the mixed multitude of a parish, or angling for an independently endowed lectureship when the position of pastor was no longer available, they fought the fight for reform in and for England until it seemed clear that the cause of England was either lost or not in any event to be won in that way. And so the famous "errand"—to perform the work of Reformation in the Wilderness, which God seemed to be demanding and which England might decide to imitate or not. That is to say: they took the step they meant to take, whether they too were to be "stepping-stones" or not.[6]

More eager to "relive ancient lives" than to imitate Bradford, the reviving spirit of these discouraged Gradualists also required some evidence to turn their sense of an immense destiny from a quiet hope to a shameless assertion. And though their historians might draw sanction by aligning their own story with Bradford's masterplot, the first few waves of Great Migrants could do no such thing. For them success meant not fulfilling the (largely literary) promise of Plymouth, a work still in progress (and indeed in manuscript); and not winning the admiration of the remnant which remained in England, where the opportunity for inspired imitation would not arise for a dozen or more years. It meant, instead, witnessing the realization in a New England of exactly those hopes that had been baffled in the Old. And this success involved much more than demonstrating, once again, that with a little luck you could, like Hawthorne's arch-Separatist "Man of Adamant," go off by yourself and do pretty much as you pleased. First off and absolutely, it required local proof that "congregational" principles could vitalize enough seriously godly persons in any given area to make a select "congregation" of saints seem as legitimate as a comprehensive parish of sinners; and, given the "greatness" of the gradualist migration, it required at least the beginnings of a sense that several self-consciously self-sovereign congregations could find a way to live in the near neighborhood of one another without the wearing fear of hierarchy or the sickening dismay of scandal.

The place to watch the unfolding drama of this complex experiment in self-conviction is the terse but revealing first-decade record of John Winthrop's *Journal*. And indeed it would be natural enough to move "on," from Bradford to Winthrop, in just this way. But the urgent beginnings of this story—of prolonged failure followed by quick success—are back in England. While Bradford's Immediatists were sojourning in the safe haven of Holland and then spreading out in the marshy fields just north of Cape Cod, the Gradualists were discovering and then pressing the limits of Reformation in England. And their story— fascinating for its own pace of insight, experiment, suppression, and discouragement—is also the proper foreground of their own unexpected encounter with the wonderful works of the Lord in New England. Certain elements of this story might be worked up out of Winthrop's "Reasons for Forsaking England,"[7] but his brief account presents only a layman's list of justifying arguments. For the narrative of unexpected insight and cumulative conviction, experienced most keenly by a person who began adult life as a professional minister and not just a faithful member of the Protestant Church of England, we must turn to the remarkable "Autobiography" of Thomas Shepard.

Fiercely compressed—indeed, cryptic by the standard of Augustine or Rousseau—this brief life does all it dares by way of explaining, to a son who may have troubles of his own, how its author came to be personally identified with the perilous yet self-fulfilling project of reform in New England. Lest that son forget. Or lest he or his figurative equivalent, living on into an age of comfort and cynicism, begin to suspect that, though here and there they may have the bad luck to suffer persecution for the sake of conscience, ministers of the Gospel mind the main chance in about the same degree as everyone else. Careerists, all. For unless that son (or, again, his figurative equivalent) can believe in the father's belief in the God who made New England, the mind of that father, effective enough to forge a local reputation for biblical learning and spiritual acumen, will seem not only somewhat delusional, in the familiar providentialist manner, but also a bit self-important. As if the individual could ever know his part in God's mysterious plot.[8]

Many students do not like to read autobiographies: they find them egotistical. A few of these purists can be got to admit they would like Bradford a little better if his book were more "personal," if he somehow found a way to include more of his own thoughts and feelings; but this particular admission in no way qualifies the generic suspicion. Some few can be jollied out of their superior conviction by the Thoreauvian suggestion that the habit of self-expression, explicit or not, is endemic and not optional. And a few more can be enlisted in favor of works in which a single human subject essays to represent the neglected interest of an oppressed class. But the prevailing prejudice remains. And when these "exacting children" read a life like that of Thomas Shepard, in which an unsuspecting son is being bound to love the thing an awesome God has condescended to teach his father, it bristles up with a moral vigor suddenly sure of its tone: Is there no end to this arrogance? Where does this guy get off?

Sometimes, well after the fact, these students will read of the difference between the "majestic idea, that the destiny of nations should be revealed . . . on the cope of heaven" and the "disordered mental state" in which an individual man has "extended his egotism over the whole expanse of nature"[9] and say *yes:* that is what I mean exactly: Bradford's providence guides a whole group, a biblical "people" aspiring to become an end-time "nation"; in Shepard God stoops to the reform of a man and his family. And even the professional apologist, well protected by his doctrine of historical criticism as a needful lesson in "otherness," can hardly pretend not to see what they mean: by God's design, beloved persons lose their lives to teach their ardent lover not to love too much; and even more than in the famous case of Emerson, perhaps, "the costly price of sons and lovers" is never quite enough to introduce the author to the affect of divinity.[10] Thus critique may see its work cut out: What singular events can have persuaded Shepard that, amidst the wreck of so many others, his own peculiar life was worth the saving? What love was this that seemed to tempt the Christian God more pointedly than hubris threatened Zeus? And what part can the poor surviving son be made to play in a drama in which Protestant Providence finds time to sharpen up the rules of Puritan Romance?

Most obviously, Thomas Shepard Jr. (or Thomas Shepard III, depending on how we count) serves as the first figure of relevant audience for a manuscript written very close to the author's private heart and probably not intended to serve as anything like an *apologia*. Yet in spite of the explicit dedication—"To my Dear Son Thomas Shepard with whom I leave these records of God's great kindness to him" (33)[11]—one hesitates to say, without the clutter of a dated literary terminology, that the literal son *is* the literal audience for a father's literal confession, of purpose faithfully undertaken and of lapses honestly recognized; for, even if audience is *not* "always a fiction," a number of relevant considerations complicate the exigent Shepard case.[12] First, though Shepard clearly suffers all the anxiety a Calvinist father may be forgiven to feel for a son whose title to salvation runs through loins other than his own, it is hard to believe that Shepard is innocent of the concern for the offspring of New England more generally. A Father can hardly bear to lose a Son, but Reformation is a cause more general than that; and it would be a little cruel to imagine Shepard committing, in the first few words of his life story, the very "familiar" sin his story sets out to repent. And besides, Shepard Jr. is, at the moment of his father's writing, not quite old enough to get the full effect of the story; he needs to grow up to be its proper reader; indeed, a proper reading will be the proof that he has in fact grown up. Perhaps he is to read it "now," in the moment of inscriptive dedication, and then again (and again) in the years to come; in which case it will be the work of the text to make him into its own proper audience. Thus even the godliest epistle may require a scrap of what remains from the science of letters as such.

And also, perhaps, a little patience; for it takes a while to discover why Shepard has needed to lay the trip of his own guilt so heavily on the head of the second son of his own first name. We may pass over, on first reading, the curious fact that Shepard explicitly locates his subject in God's kindness "to him," the son, and not to himself, the father and author. What we notice instead, perhaps, is that this momentary cancellation of the autobiographical self seems well atoned in the next clause, which more than authoritatively invites the son to "learn to know and love the great and most high God, the God of his father" (33); for we do not need our students to tell us that this formulation does more for the humble father than for the most high God. But sooner or later we do need to recognize that Shepard's little preface is nothing but a dramatic culling out, a repetition in advance, of some of the central facts of the narrative itself; and that these same astonishing facts—of the painful death of first son and the almost equally painful birth of a second, of the sickness and recovery of that blessed survivor, of harrowing dangers and narrow escapes, of balked plans and eventual success against all odds—will all be narrated, in a far less threatening manner, at their proper place in Shepard's (otherwise) strictly chronological account. Nothing new is being added here, that is to say, except the tone of grave paternal instruction. And before we decide just how much (Oedipal) scandal is to be taken, perhaps we ought to wait to see what context may have prompted a prefatory tone so aggressively unsentimental.

Yet no reading can fail to notice that Shepard's rhetoric seems determined to set the stakes as high as possible:

> And therefore know it: if thou shalt turn rebel against God and forsake God and care not for the knowledge of him nor to believe in his Son, the Lord will make all these mercies *woes* and all thy mother's tears, prayers, and death to be a swift witness against thee at the great day. (36)

Close examination of Shepard's theology will assure us that this passage deploys the rhetoric of Calvinist self-fulfillment more securely than it implies a logic of Arminian conditionalism: as ever, your attitudes and actions will reveal your nature, regenerate or not.[13] But will there not be in this case a certain *sting?* For the "mercies" of the paragraphs preceding have been not only to save and instruct the father but also to preserve the fragile life of the mother, already bereft of one same named Thomas, until a second son of that name shall have been born and delivered up for baptism in a properly reformed church in New England. Predestination, it turns out, can breed some ironies of its own. Indeed, one almost suspects that the real target of Shepard's hostility is God: "Were we led all this way for / Birth or Death?"

But if the theological plot is somewhat too thick wherever we elect to take it up, perhaps it may help to remind ourselves that Shepard's son grew into a New England life about as effective as any other in the second generation; that in fact his 1672 sermon called "Eye-Salve" completes the Jeremiad analysis of Samuel Danforth's "Errand" so effectively, indeed so brilliantly, as to assure us that the literal as well as the figurative son had introjected without trauma the fierce reminders and prohibitions of the father.[14] Closer to the rhetorical point, however, is our faint intuition that, where we sense only aggression, the son was supposed

to hear wonder. Almost certainly written last, Shepard's preface is constituted of
nothing but a personally pointed rehearsal of the very turning point of his story—
the densely packed and well nigh incredible ending of his long maintained and
finally failed attempt to live the life of a conscientiously dissenting minister of the
Gospel of Christ within the Church of England; and of his involvement, thereupon, in a complex, intrigue-filled, at first ill-starred and then very lucky attempt
to get away to Massachusetts. What draws the son into the plot is less the father's
angry expectation that *of course* the son will not understand "what the father
went through" in the interest of godliness than the uncanny way first one son,
who died just when the father fondly thought that prayer might intervene to
spare his life, and then another, who lived in spite of the illness his chastened father "did expect would have been his death" (35), were themselves woven into a
plot that pointed—beyond the private loves of any man—to the churches of New
England as its only proper denouement.

And thus, whatever the comparative burden of guilt, Shepard charges his
son—and all who may feel his fate as a figure of their own—with exactly the
same task of interpretation he himself has had to face: What is the faithful man
supposed to say when the ways of the very God dip down to touch his humble
self? Are we to suppose that, in these latter days, God's converting power may
touch the private heart alone, and never point the way to some proper task in life?
Is this not a question that may occur to a moderate man as well as to a zealot?
Perhaps the students have been too secure in the assurance of their tone.

To think so is to propose that Freudian outrage is only one avenue by which
to approach the "Autobiography" of Thomas Shepard. Competent fathers challenge uncertain sons along a spectrum that runs all the way from "Not at all,
so far as I could help it," to "No way less than God himself might ask"; and
probably—if we could ever really know this sort of thing—Shepard's son would
have been perplexed if, morally speaking, his father had left him anything less
than a personally emphatic version of the task to be faced by the soul of the Calvinist as such. Of *course* he would grow up to make his father proud—and to redeem the deaths of his mother and older sibling as well; churlish it were to think
any otherwise. But what sense would this New World son make of his father's
gradual, beclouded decision for New England? One option among many, for
"life is very long"? A "happen," like Emily Dickinson's finding her way into the
seclusion of a lonely upper room? Another, later instance of getting out "while
the getting was good"? A "prudent forecast on the probable issue of the great
questions of Pauperism and Poverty"? A "yearning for peace and security beyond
the reach of Laud's long ecclesiastical arm?"[15] Or something more: could the
son in fact believe, with his father's conviction hard-won, that the same (great)

migration which persuaded Bradford to loose his pen in the service of holy history had been sufficient to persuade those he supposed to be following his example? That the structure of these events reached further down into the lives of individuals than even the sympathetic outsider could well imagine? And that arrangements of these events had touched his own infant self—by design as well as implication—in just the way his father's finally aroused faith had dared suppose?

Biographically, historically, the answer would seem to be *yes*: the public life of the son did full justice to the private faith of the father; and also *no:* the reality—or even the rumor—of "declension" proves that design in the womb or at the breast is not the same as adventures among pursuivants or upon the high seas.[16] So that the *literary* argument turns back on the text of the father himself: how heartily has he received, how cogently arranged the evidences of design? And, more searchingly, what in the face of that design can he make of his own ("non-Separatist") delay? Perhaps one tarried on purpose to resist the call to be a saint. The life of which provokes resistance of its own.

———

Far more than Bradford, Shepard turns out to be a writer whose signifying system it is dangerous to enter without the protection of unfailing prejudice. Salvations are everywhere; without them his life simply disappears. Before the elongated and painful conversion at Cambridge, they figure as needful preparations; afterward, as so many reminders that he, like Bradford's John Howland, was saved not for anything he was or had done but only for what God would set him yet to accomplish. So prevailing is the design of Shepard's life that we may have to keep reminding ourselves that the effect is one of retrospect and possibly of writing itself; otherwise, Shepard should have seen the meaning of his life long before that moment (in the mid-1630s) when, noticing he "had been tossed from the south to the north of England and now could go no farther, [he] then began to listen to a call to New England" (55).

Cynicism can turn this "call" into opportunism, of course, and the "Reasons" which follow (55–56) into that flimsy self-deception by which one can always blame God (or Reason) "for every thing one has a mind to do." But then if cynicism is what suits us best, we will have to begin much earlier: what *really* saved Tom Shepard was the series of lucky breaks that got him into Cambridge. For evidence, just count the "blind" towns he left behind before he found his way to the New England village rejoicing in the same numinous name; not London or Westminster, to be sure, but not bad for a little orphan boy from Towcester. But then we might have to explain how his life would have been different if the scholarship had been to Oxford. The rejection of his "Sophister" achievements as the pratings of a man "foolish and proud" (40) might be written off as a "sophomoric" echo of Augustine,[17] whom lettered men might read in any corner of the kingdom; but for the equivalent of that series of faithful, heartbreaking preachers whose task it was indeed to break the natural heart of Thomas Shepard—Chadderton, Dickinson, Preston—one might search the Oxford lists in vain. A Shepard who went to the royalist university might well have enjoyed a useful career as one more midwife assisting at the birth of "Anglicanism"; but for the sense of his "life" we would probably have had to wait for the *Athenae Oxoniensis* of Anthony à Wood.[18] But then everything would indeed have been different if Shepard had not been a Puritan; from which we may learn the wisdom of letting Shepard name his own trump.

John Albro, Shepard's reverent nineteenth-century biographer, is convinced that we should list "a pious mother" among the earliest examples of a providential ordering of the life of his subject; but clearly it is sentiment that has generalized "a woman much afflicted in conscience, sometimes even unto distraction" into an enveloping atmosphere of soft maternal discipline.[19] Shepard is quick to assure us that his mother was "sweetly recovered" from her religious distraction before she died (in his fourth year) and that, probably at her death, she made many prayers for this her youngest son; but he makes almost as much of the example of his father, a "peacemaker" who, when he became competent to do so, "resolved to go and live . . . under a stirring ministry" (37–38). And what he appears to remember best is that while his own mother was yet alive, he was sent away, during an outbreak of the plague, to live (and keep geese) with grandparents in "Fossecut, a most blind town and corner"; and from there to "Adthorp, a little blind town adjoining," where he learned—dangerously, in Albro's view—"to sing and sport as children do in those parts and dance at their Whitsun Ales." And afterward, that his father's remarriage introduced him to a "woman who did let [him] see the difference between [his] own mother and a stepmother" (38).

Even more poignant, perhaps—and most pointedly similar to the travails of his adult life—is the memory of the moment, some years later:

> I do remember I did pray very strongly and heartily for the life of my father and made some covenant, if God would do it, to serve him better as knowing I should be left alone if he was gone. Yet the Lord took him away by death, and so I was left fatherless and motherless when I was about ten years old. (39)

Here, plainly, is the kind of sentiment Shepard is unwilling to lavish on the image of his "Dear Son," better protected from the uncertainties of childish life, as he may have thought, by the stability of his fatherhood. But if the death of either parent is part of an "affliction," designed to wean even the affections of the child away from the loves of this world, Shepard does not say so. Nor will he have learned the appropriate lesson by the time he is afflicted with the death of his first son. Years away, at this point, from his effective conversion, Shepard is evidently willing to let the feelings of the natural man speak for themselves—an indication of the emotional inertia that the call to sainthood must overcome; and a silent confession, perhaps, that preparations for salvation are not always recognized as such.

The same history of "unsettlement"—a motive to Puritanism, in the mind of Shepard's modern editor[20]—continues yet a while. The stepmother seems to have been willing enough to manage the young boy's inheritance but not to supervise his education; seeing this, his brother John intervenes with an informal adoption and, after an unhappy episode with a "cruel schoolmaster," Shepard is finally set upon a path that may lead to places other than hell or oblivion. The second schoolmaster, "an eminent preacher in those days," eventually turns into "a great apostate and enemy to all righteousness"; but though Shepard fears in retrospect that this man did indeed go on to "commit the unpardonable sin," he cannot deny the wholesomeness of his influence at the time of his teaching. Reprobate or not,

> it so fell out by God's good providence that this man stirred up in my heart a love and desire of the honor of learning, and therefore I told my friends I would be a scholar. And so the Lord blessed me in my studies and gave me some knowledge of the Latin and Greek tongues.

Thus, strangely enough, does Shepard begin to employ the discourse of providence. And though he is quick to remind us that his motive so far is only "ambition," it appears that even this unregenerate passion may lead on to something more. Pained at his inept inability to take notes on sermons, he "prayed the Lord earnestly" for just that ability; and then—for which he sees "cause of wondering at the Lord's providence"—the very next Sabbath, he "was able to take notes who the precedent Sabbath could do nothing at all that way" (39).

Wonderful too is the memory of how "it pleased the Lord to put it into my brother's heart to provide and to seek to prepare a place" at the university. And it is this large fact—of Shepard's being admitted a pensioner to Emmanuel College (on February 10, 1619/20)—that gathers together many of the other, smaller ones and lifts them out of the realm of the ordinary. And, as Shepard himself makes the point for us, there can be no ungodliness in recognizing Cambridge as the pinnacle of his "preparation":

> For I have oft thought what a woeful estate I had been left in if the Lord had left me in the profane, ignorant town of Towcester where I was born, that the Lord should pluck me out of that sink and Sodom, who was yet the least in my father's house, forsaken of father and mother, yet that the Lord should fetch me out from thence by such a sweet hand. (40)

A university education is by no means required for the salvation of a Puritan soul, but an educated ministry was becoming something like the chief glory of every reformed people; and for the founding prophets of Massachusetts, Cambridge was the necessary school.

"Conversion" there was not automatic, of course, and Shepard managed both to show off and to play around some before he began to get the ambient message. But when he did indeed begin to hear it—the bad news of sin that ran before the good news of grace—he felt the blast full bore: "the misery of every man out of Christ, viz., that whatever they did was sin"; which might apply to his sophomoric disputations as well as to his "lust and pride and gaming and bowl-ing and drinking." And even on that fateful morning after he was carried to the room of a friend "dead drunk," when shame itself proposed "a course of medita-tion about the evil of sin and [his] own ways," the work which Thomas Hooker would call "a holy kind of violence" was just beginning. The drama of this epi-sode has seemed literary enough to find its way into the large and then the small collections of Perry Miller, as if this were the memorable moment of all the rest.[21] But the unforgiving retrospect of the author himself suggests otherwise: for "al-though I was troubled for this sin, I did not know my sinful nature all this while" (41). And we ourselves, a section or two hence, will have to sound the depths of Shepard's self-rejection. Without which, all talk of Providence were shameless self-regard.

For the moment, however, it is enough to notice that one consequence of Shepard's "Augustinian" conversion is to associate him with several generations of ministers who underwent similar experiences at Cambridge; and though not all the members of this "brotherhood" made their way to New England, virtually all went on from their "true sight of sin" to a truer sight of the function of the church. For no surplice could suffice to whiten the heart of an unregenerate min-ister, and no amount of sacred ritual—even the kind called "sacrament"—could substitute for Augustine's radical "turning" from love of self to God.[22] And, though Shepard does not throw himself at once into the movement of radical church reform, it does not take him long to realize that his "Puritanism" will have serious consequences for his ministerial career.

Indeed his mentors seem to have joined him in his worry about "what would become of [him] when [he] was Master of Arts." Serious deliberations attend the idea that a privately financed lectureship[23] might be assigned to "a great town in Essex called Coggeshall," with Shepard as its first endowed occupant. Only Hooker advises in the negative—knowing that the regularly established minister in the town is "old yet sly and malicious" and arguing that "it was dangerous and uncomfortable for little birds to build under the nests of old ravens and kites" (46). But then, at the very time and place of this debate about policy, representatives of Earle's Colne request the lectureship for their own town; by which providence this new-fledged preacher, "who was so young and weak and unexperienced and unfit for so great a work," was called to it by the unanimous decision of "twelve or sixteen" very accomplished ministers of Christ. Blessing upon blessing, for he might have been "cast away upon a blind place," or sent to be corrupted by the sins of "some gentleman's house"; instead, however, it otherwise pleased the Lord, who had already led him "from the worst town . . . in the world to the best place for knowledge and learning, *viz.,* Cambridge," staffed, just then, with "the most able men for preaching Christ in this latter age."

> And when I came from thence the Lord sent me to the best country in England, viz., to Essex, and set me in the midst of the best ministry in the country by whose monthly fasts and conferences I found much of God. And thus the Lord Jesus provided for me of all things of the best. (47)

This might be pride but, as some Hawthorne narrator might observe, it is performing the work of humility: The wonder is that God should touch the lowly.

Nor is there any reason to suppose Shepard was enacting pride when, in 1627, he left his residence with Thomas Weld and went to the newly created post at Earle's Colne. He may not have considered his "taking of orders" a "sinful" (47) compliance at that very time. Certainly he knew that a lectureship was a way to work around England's tightening control of its parish system and that, given the workings of that ingenious subterfuge, he was faring very well indeed. But someone has to get the lucky breaks, and Shepard's "life" has not yet caught up with the moment of its own inspiration. Which can hardly have come before the decision to leave for Massachusetts and may not have been confirmed until he realized his new identity as an exemplar of the New England Way. Others might be content to look back and see their lives as a thing built up work by work, but Augustinian autobiography involves the interpretation of the works and days of an old self from the standpoint of one made new by grace.[24]

Yet now, as Shepard moves into the career of a minister working within the system but closely associated with older men working toward its subversion, his need for timely rescue can be predicted to increase. The work of "lecturing" at Earle's Colne—on the "misery" of a people in sin, on "the remedy, Jesus Christ," and on the behavior "answerable to [the] mercy [of] being redeemed by Christ"— goes very well; and this fact throws Satan predictably into a rage:

> [T]he commissaries, registers, and others began to pursue me and to threaten me, as thinking I was a Nonconformable man (when for the most of that time I was not resolved either way, but was dark in those things). Yet the Lord, having work to do in this place, kept me, a poor, ignorant thing, against them all until such a time as my work was done.

For the moment Shepard is willing to cast the veil of a generalization over these salvations—from machinations his naïveté may little have understood: "By strange and wonderful means . . . the Lord had one way or another to deliver me" (48). But we get the idea that, in retrospect at least, the entirely prepolitical work of preaching salvation in Christ crucified, even by a "poor, ignorant thing," is coming to seem a task altogether worthy of the divine protection. And in the next moment the dangers become specific indeed.

As the lectureship at Earle's Colne expires after its term of three years, the grateful people of that town gather their own funds to keep their "extraordinary" preacher among them, even as its sponsors had hoped they might. For his part, Shepard sees that the endowment is now placed in the service of his native Towcester. And now, suddenly, he comes into sharp personal conflict with the authorities whose system he has been more or less consciously undermining. He blames some failing in himself for incurring, by God's will, the shame of an official rebuke; but he leaves no doubt about the agency of his discipline: Bishop Laud is a "fierce enemy to all righteousness and a man fitted of God to be a scourge to his people" (49). Abruptly and angrily forbidden to exercise any sort of ministerial function within the diocese of London, Shepard lives for a time with friends, who are to him as "so many fathers and mothers"; and while meditating the full meaning of his humiliation, "the Lord let [him] see into the evil of the English ceremonies, cross, surplice, and kneeling" (50). Thus—if Shepard's memory is faithful and honest—Laud has turned a moderate, possibly even a "conformable" man into a Puritan properly understood: for "Anglican" things cannot be "indifferent" so long as the word of man has made them a test of faith.[25] So it is with a kind of odd appropriateness that Laud, on a tour of Essex, cites Shepard to appear a second time; and this time the angry prelate orders him out of his jurisdiction altogether.

Unable to return to the university in accord with Laud's dismissive suggestion, the pious young minister, so well launched and so favorably received, has now, literally, no place to turn. To complicate matters already difficult, Shepard now informs us—routinely and in the midst of sentences devoted to other weighty matters—that he "had about this time a great desire to change [his] estate by marriage." Confessing, in a way that speaks volumes for the ways of a social world well lost, that he has been praying for three years that "the Lord would carry [him] to such a place where [he] might a meet yoke fellow," Shepard seems to be implying that just about any means of support would be welcome at this time. A call to Yorkshire "to preach there in a gentleman's house" suggests itself; so too does the possibility of New England; or of Ireland by way of Scotland. The outskirts, surely: well enough for the kid from Towcester, one supposes, unless that kid has been to school in Cambridge and to work in Essex County. But while these heavy matters hang in the balance, Shepard and his friend Weld are delegated by the local brotherhood to confront Laud publicly, before he has left their turf: was it, after all, acceptable "to let such a swine to root up God's plants in Essex and not give him some check" (50)?

But Laud can play the game as well. And as the young protesters approach his person, Weld, already under sentence of excommunication and hence risking checkmate, is "committed to the pursuivant and bound over to answer . . . the High Commission" for daring to appear on holy ground. As he tries to explain himself, Laud asks him if he intends to go to New England and, if so, will he please take Shepard with him. And now it is Shepard's turn:

> While he was thus speaking I came into the crowd and heard the words. Others bid me go away, but neglecting to do it, a godly man pulled me with violence out of the crowd. And as soon as ever I was gone the apparitor calls for Mr. Shepard, and the pursuivant was sent presently after to find me out. But he that pulled me out . . . hastened our horses and away we rid as fast as we could. And so the Lord delivered me out of the hand of that lion a third time. (51)

Lions do not always have hands, but Shepard's metaphor is dead in only the technical sense. Fresh and lively here is the biblical echo: "your enemy is as a lion, going up and down, seeking whom he may devour." Implied as well is a keen sense that Shepard's first two encounters with Laud had involved deliverances as well; that given the power of the office and the mood of the man, this is now the *third* time the upstart has escaped arrest by officers of the state, in the service of a church, whose odd Latinate names appear nowhere in the Acts of the Apostles, and whose ironic function it may have been to create or to confirm Puritans as well as to arrest them.[26]

However that may be, Shepard finally understands that he can delay—one had almost said dally—no longer. Interpreting a series of invitations from private persons in Yorkshire as "the voice of the man of Macedonia, Come and help us," he resolves "to follow the Lord to so remote and strange a place, the rather because [he] might be far from the hearing of the malicious Bishop Laud." Magical rescue and urgent call aside, however, the tone of discouragement remembers itself: "with much grief of heart I forsook Essex and Earle's Colne and they me, going, as it were, now I knew not whither" (51). Cambridge behind, remoteness and uncertainty ahead, what could now sustain this brilliant young failure but God and his grace?

Of which there appears to be no lack. Saved by a "wonderful preservation" from a violent flood on the way to Yorkshire, Shepard is now made to profess that he "looked now upon [his] life as a new life given unto [him], which [he] saw good reason to give up unto [the Lord] and his service," and this even though— or because?—"the Lord that had dealt only gently with me before began to afflict me and to let me taste how good it was to be under his tutoring" (52). This odd preference for affliction may suggest a certain religious masochism. It certainly appears to forget the moments of near-despair in the dark night of the conversion at Cambridge; and if the forgetting is at all strategic, the suggestion may be that the entire experience there was initiatory rather than final; that Shepard has not *entirely* entered into the life of redemption. Perhaps that finality will come, whatever we decide to call it, when he shall have arrived at some confirming sense of why his fragile life and wayward soul were deemed worthy of saving in the first place.

Meanwhile, however, natural life goes on: moral affairs at the house of a gentleman of Buttercrambe are quite as bad as he once imagined such things might be; and, amidst a cast of characters with names that predict some Restoration comedy, only the faithful attention of a few sincere souls can alleviate the depression into which the exiled Shepard has understandably fallen. A sermon preached at the "marriage of one Mr. Allured, a most profane young gentleman," to the daughter of his patron, Sir Richard Darley, has the reassuring effect of touching both her heart and that of Mistress Margaret Touteville, soon to become Shepard's wife. Following these early examples, the whole Darley family is brought, if not to Christ, at least to such a favorable estimate of Thomas Shepard that they present their kinswoman to him not only freely but with an enlarged portion. And thus, says Shepard, the Lord answered his desires by giving him "a wife who was most incomparably loving to [him] and every way amiable and holy and en- dued with a very sweet spirit of prayer" (53). But though Shepard credits the Lord for being best unto him just when his "adversaries intended most hurt," those adversaries press on him nevertheless; and, with the Laudian "Bishop Neile com- ing up to York, no friends could procure [his] liberty . . . without subscription" (53–54)—without, that is to say, his unambiguous profession of loyalty to the church of Laud and of Charles I. And for this reversal of tendency there is now no chance.

Happily, therefore, the Lord gives Shepard a call to a town in Northumber- land—not "a place of subsistence with any comfort" but "far from any bishops." Fit audience is found, however, and it is here that this determined preacher of sin and grace comes to understand the politics of Puritanism properly so called— "the ceremonies, church government and estate, and the unlawful standing of bishops" (54). Clearly we are coming to the end of something; and so, when he is once again forbidden to preach in public, his attention is turned at last toward New England—where Cotton, Hooker, Stone, and Weld have gone, where in consequence "most of the godly in England" (55) were now intending to go, and where—God knows, and Shepard too, though only in retrospect—his life has been tending all along. Following a call, then, "by diverse friends [already] in New England to come over and many in old England desiring me to go over and promising to go with me, I did thereupon resolve to go thither" (55). Yet there seems little enthusiasm for the errand of Reformation; for what were now his op- tions? Sooner or later, one fears, he will have to do better.

The birth of a "son called Thomas, anno 1633," would seem to complicate the real-life arrangements, and surely Shepard might cite him as a reason for his lack of enthusiasm for a three-thousand-mile voyage to God knows what. But as Shepard is nearing the crisis of a "life" written to highlight manifold human fail- ings in spite of redundant divine mercies, he is more caught up in the memory of his fear of his wife's death at the hands of an unskillful midwife:

> But as the affliction was very bitter, so the Lord did teach me much by it, for I began to grow secretly proud and full of sensuality, delighting my soul in my dear wife more than in my God, whom I had promised better unto, and my spirit grew fierce in some things and secretly mindless of the souls of the people.

"And so," he concludes, as if unaware of the non sequitur, "I then began to listen to a call to New England" (55), as if that momentous public decision figured chiefly as a way to atone for personal pride and sensuality.

Perhaps we should not be surprised when the first attempt at secret emigration does not prosper. God may or may not be resisting Shepard's moral logic, but Shepard himself, catching up, now, with his own preface, and looking back on an attempt that failed and then one that succeeded—disturbingly like a child who died and then one who lived—may be searching for an explanation of why his life has required him not only to put the Creator ahead of all his lovely creatures but also, as a consequence of that, to put the interest of the churches of New England ahead of the safety of his own soul. The hard part of Shepard's "Autobiography," that is to say, is not what Providence provided but what Reformation required. And it may clear the mind of cant to examine the conditions of a test we never ask ourselves to pass.

————

The "reasons" which sway Shepard to New England are no more and no less interesting than most such exercises in the norming of affect: feelings are feelings, and the bias of the nervous system informs but does not consult the numbered list. But Shepard's mental scheme names other "faculties" and, as we may surely sense, Puritans routinely measure the *must* by the terms of the *may*. And so the prime consideration—"I saw no call to any other place in old England"—is supplemented by the desire of friends, the sight of the Lord's departure from England, an increasing sense of "the evil of ceremonies" and of "mixed communion," the "duty to desire the fruition of all God's ordinances," the wishes of his wife, and no clear conviction of the need to "stay and suffer" when "the Lord had opened a door of escape" (55–56). A mixed bag, as Shepard honestly recognizes. Trying to fan the spark of a *duty* into the flame of a *desire,* he sets the concern for his "own quiet" against a vision of "the glory of those liberties in New England" and solemnly promises, in language that recalls the "new life" of his escape from drowning on his way to York, "[I]f ever I should come over, to live among God's people as one come out from the dead" (56). Evidently the body of a list served the spirit of "meditation"—itself designed to make the good reason into the real.[27]

And the process continues. Friends "desire [him] to stay in the north and preach privately," but a list of considerations countervails: fear of impending "trouble from King Charles"; no reason to work privately when he might "exercise [his] talent publicly in New England"; the hope that these very friends might follow him there; a distaste of inflicting "that rude place of the north" on his wife and child; and, finally—back to the head of both lists—his "private liberty was daily threatened" (56). Having thus "decided," he both preaches and privately bids farewell to his friends in the north and proceeds, "in a disguised manner," to Ipswich and then to the familiar territory of Essex, there to wait the moment of Escape struggling to inscribe itself as Errand. That this is the "most uncomfortable and fruitless time" of his entire life, Shepard credibly confesses, and not the least because his wife is again pregnant—with a child who would have to be baptized, to the delight of the discovering pursuivants; or *not,* to the scandal of many sound, sacramental Christians. "And therefore," he concludes, in prosecution of a purpose still somewhat hypothetical, and spurred on by the fact that "diverse godly Christians [were] resolved to go toward the latter end of the year if I would go, I did therefore resolve to go that year, the end of the summer I came from the north" (56–57).

Very well, then: nothing truly difficult is ever easy. But surely exhaustion of the audience has not been Shepard's primary purpose here. What he seems to intend, rather, is partly to imitate the stuttering effect of conflicted behavior; but also, and more important, to suggest that the decision was not at all easy to make and was anything but hasty or ill considered. Just in case anyone should happen to ask. His surviving son, for example, who might want to know why he was not destined to go to the *real* Cambridge; or else, should his private story ever become public, some godly minister who had decided to stick it out in England, come hell or high water. To keep hiding out, if that is what it required, or to rot in prison, confirmed in the knowledge that suffering for the right is never in vain. But if the well-remembered reign of Mary had produced its list of Martyrs, had it not produced as well a share of Exiles? And had not the ones been about as well motivated as the others? And so Shepard is being careful to the point of redundancy.

Having just here caught up with his preface—abstracted in advance, and specially tailored for the fierce edification of the son just now to be inconveniently born—Shepard has in mind the keenest issue raised by the Great Migration considered as a desertion of Mother Church in her hour of greatest need, as a separation in undeniable fact if not in debatable theory. Recognizing the pressure of this issue, Albro interrupts his running elaboration of Shepard's own account to quote at length from the 1649 preface to the *Defense of the Answer* which Shepard appears to have cowritten with John Allin; and Perry Miller's anthologies, which gracefully slight the "Autobiography," resolutely insist on this text, quite probably with the example of Albro in mind.[28] While the body of this work tries to defend, from the explicit attack of "Presbyterian" reformers in England, the explicit workings of New England's Congregational Way, Shepard's preface seeks to answer the more fundamental question of the very presence in New England of not-*quite*-exiled English Puritans: not "what sorts of things are you alienated radicals doing over there?" but "what in God's name are you doing over *there* in the first place?" And though some ten years separate the "Autobiography" from the *Defense,* Shepard is already sounding his special note—not instantaneous revelation of a blindingly clear errand in the wilderness just begging for typological translation but, given the "terrible paucity of alternatives," emigration as an option a sane man might have to learn to love.

Which he did. Not of himself, perhaps, and not all at once, but in due time and to good effect. Evidently New England had not been at all his own first choice but only God's; and a fact like that the sane might not discover all at once. But what indeed *were* the alternatives? Inventing distinctions of reason to salve the conscience of compliance? As if the body of an English parish might house the soul of a covenant. Learning to "live without God's ordinances" and (as Shepard recalls his debt to the moral support of other conscientious persons) without the "Communion of Saints which he called us unto, and our souls breathed after"? Joining together in "private separated Churches"? At some point, as we hear it in the prose, a strong conviction has replaced the tautological listing and the stammering hesitation. Perhaps this is just where, like the second son, it had begun to be born. On one very sensitive point the skilled apologist even seems to echo and at the same time to strengthen the troubled confessor: as 1639 looked back to 1633–34, suffering for Christ was a possible but not an inevitable option, for "the Lord had opened a door of escape" (56); a decade later the alternative to finding a way "to have filled the prisons" has become "a wide door . . . set open of liberty otherwise."[29]

Yet Shepard's main point in the *Defense* is not quite the inevitability or even, in the wake of a success they only dreamed of at Plymouth, the resplendent glory of the New English alternative. Rather—as if the subjective bias of the autobiographer had gone along to keep the mind of the disputants fastened on the thing that makes religion meaningful in the first place—it is the almost paralyzing seriousness of those who took that option: the Lord alone knows "what prayers and tears," what whole days of "fasting and prayer," what "longings and pantings of heart," what "serious consultations with one another" lay behind the conviction of so many godly persons that the risk of making it new in New England was an idea acceptable in heaven. It will embarrass our own sense of appropriate professional diction to read very much self-defense of this sort—this daring of God to judge the place where one of necessity stands, or in a pinch decides to go—but then that might be part of the point of reading godly letters in the first place. Nor will Shepard let it rest with an account of Puritan deliberation. For in the end the talking mattered about as little as the lists. What mattered was the *mood*—what Shepard's psychotheology calls the "strange poise of spirit the Lord hath laid upon many of our hearts."

"Poise," on first reading, might be archaic for *stasis,* some sense of being caught up in a moment of motivation degree zero; and that, except for Shepard's wish to generalize the case, will stand very nicely for the mood and the manner that ran before the moment when he came to cast the die of his own volition. But in fact he seems to intend the more ordinary meaning of confidence based on competence. And strange it must have been, for what confidence could any of them have? And based on what competence? Those that can, do; the rest may only preach and duck. Wondering not at the sudden apparition of an apparitor, nor at the fiery hunt of a pursuivant, they could not "but wonder at [them]-selves,"

> that so many, and some so weak and tender, with such cheerfulness and constant resolutions against so many persuasions of friends, discouragements from ill report of this country, the straits, wants, and trials of God's people in it, . . . should leave our accommodations and comforts, should forsake our dearest relations, parents, brethren, sisters, Christian friends and acquaintances, overlook all the dangers and difficulties of the vast seas, the thought thereof was a terror to many, and all this to go to a wilderness, where we could forecast nothing but care and temptations, only in hopes of enjoying Christ in his ordinances in the fellowship of his people.[30]

The passage runs on, but that is the nature of its (antisublime) structure: no amount of difficulty then could disturb the resolve of these emigrants; and no analysis can now quite account for the way the calm had come about. Perhaps—after all discussion subsided—they gave it to one another. Perhaps that is what used to be meant by being "in the Spirit."

It may seem unfair to have leapt ahead to read the gloss of 1648 as a gloss on the gloss of 1639, but Albro did it first; and even Perry Miller may have known what he was doing. The point, perhaps, is that this is what a man cumulatively convinced (and repeatedly saved) could not *quite* say in the earlier moment. Not that it was not true—and made up much later as a sort of lying for the right. But that it may have taken Shepard that long to realize what (he thought) was really going on. Remarkable providences there unmistakably were: any fool could see when luck ran long or too often in his own favor. But maybe it took somewhat longer to notice how God might move in the mind of a group. What we need to remember, in any event, is that what Shepard tells his son—not yet part of the noosphere—is only a part of the truth.

What, then? Circumstances delay departure until quite dangerously late in the season, and the Lord—"to chastise us for . . . hazarding ourselves in that manner," and also (for he loveth cliches) to teach us "never to go about a sad business in the dark" (57)—sends a powerfully adverse wind; navigational catastrophe ensues, but not without providing the certain loss and then surprising salvation of a sailor "never able to swim but supported by a divine hand" (58). And "this man's danger and deliverance is a type of ours" (58), insists Shepard who, from the attention he gives to this first ill-fated voyage to New England, may himself have been one of those in "terror" of the sea. Catastrophic dangers persist, in any case, threatening all with death, driving the godly to prayer, and inspiring a "drunken fellow" named Mr. Cock to persuade the seamen to cut down the mainmast. This helps but, like many a second cause all by itself, not enough; so Shepard and his colleague John Norton lead the crew and passengers in committing their "souls and bodies unto the Lord that gave them"; and only *then* did "the wind beg[i]n to abate" (60).

So far, perhaps, we can hardly imagine any scenario significantly different: lots of people will pray when nothing else seems to be working. But Shepard goes on to register his difference from most people, then and now, insisting that he will *remember* this ultimate terror and rescue beyond the moment when such a thing seemed possible. Indeed, he will even renew his now-familiar promise of newborn dedication:

> This deliverance was so great that I then did think if ever the Lord did bring me to shore again I should live like one . . . risen from the dead. This is one of those living mercies the Lord hath shown me, a mercy to myself, to my wife and child then living, and to my second son Thomas who was in the . . . womb of his dear mother. (60)

We may here begin to resist Shepard's incipient attempt to capture the conscience of the unborn with a dramatic confirmation of his own faith, but this application is hardly separable from Shepard's general orientation to the future. He knows that a man like himself—so "full of many temptations and weaknesses"—is hardly worth saving as such; and so he feels it as the part of gratitude properly considered to dedicate all future versions of himself to the work to which he is seeking to join himself. From the point of view of the work yet to be accomplished, his unborn son is hardly more a prolepsis than his own future self. And so, if it seems inescapably prejudicial, in the manner of any strong parental belief, it is at least intelligible that Shepard should "desire this mercy should be remembered of [his] children and their children's children when [he] . . . cannot praise the Lord in the land of the living anymore" (61). The more so, perhaps, because the effect is cumulative; for at this period the Lord simply kept *on* touching the entire family.

And so, as if the "waters" of affliction were sufficient to purify the mixed intentions of the once competent but now hapless Thomas Shepard, the Lord sends the "fire" of a vomiting sickness to the son already in life. Aware of his own "fear, pride, carnal content, immoderate love of creatures and of [his] child especially," Shepard tries to barter repentance in exchange for the child, "but the Lord would not be entreated" for its life; nor can a grieving—and possibly puzzled—Shepard be present at the funeral, "lest the pursuivants should apprehend [him] . . . which was a great affliction and very bitter to [him] and [his] dear wife." Who could also be taken away, as the future would prove. Understandably enough, therefore, Shepard begins to wonder if the decision for New England were not perhaps a mistake. Yet still there is the sight of that "door opened of escape"; and still, it appears, a certain "poise of spirit" in spite of everything. From which he concludes that the decision was indeed correct, but only the man himself was "unfit": "with such an un-mortified, hard, dark, formal, hypocritical heart . . . no wonder if the Lord did thus cross me" (61). Shepard is, of course, being as hard on himself as possible; every bit as hard, it would appear, as on his son. And before we complain that such formulaic self-accusation is a small price to pay for the assurance that God has involved himself in one's very own life, we ought recall that Shepard is appealing to God's providence not as a reason for self-congratulation but as an occasion of enhanced self-demand.

In this crisis at least, God intervenes not to reward and not even to reassure but only to discipline and to challenge—to dare a man ready enough to settle for such virtue as may fall in the way of his professional exercises to look further into the various guises of own self-satisfaction and to require of himself the highest standard of public dedication. New England is God's idea, not Shepard's own. Nor has God decided to make the pursuit of reform abroad an obvious choice or an easy action. Others would decide as they must, but Shepard needs to be sure he is neither "running too far in a way of separation from the mixed assemblies in England" (62) nor seeking New England as a scene of peace, for himself and his precious family. Small wonder, then, if God should think to afflict him in just that area. For if souls are indeed saved in groups, the scene of that salvation is the congregation; beside which, the nuclear family is an idol which—as Edwards' rare lucidity will show—only sentiment will refuse to recognize as such.[31]

And so it takes a while. Friends are happy to provide for this family that would be holy all winter long and, in London in the spring, the Lord provided "a very private place for us where my wife was brought to bed and delivered of my second son Thomas" who—like Cotton's famous son Seaborn—"was not baptized until we came to New England" (62).[32] Other providences also seem worth recording: the expectant mother falls down a flight of stairs without harm to herself or the child; and a timely change of houses keeps Shepard one step ahead of the pursuivants. Soon enough, however, it comes time "to prepare for a removal once again to New England," and once again there must be reasons, the chief of which is that the lesson of "unfitness" has been learned. The voyage finds Shepard mercifully protected from "the violence of sea sickness," but in one of the many storms his wife "took such a cold and got such weakness as that she fell into a consumption of which she afterwards died" (63). But not yet; and in the meantime this nursing mother that would be in Israel was spared again when, in a violent shaking of the ship, "her head was pitched against an iron bolt" (63–64).

For the rest of these personal matters we must return to the preface: the second son's failure to thrive; Shepard's arguing, indeed bargaining with Him who giveth and taketh away; the sudden and strange healing, after that, of the "sore mouth which [he] did expect would have his death" (35); the wife's instantaneous rescue by an invisible hand but also her more general preservation, from the consumption which threatened, until the safe arrival in New England could provide for the living son of Thomas Shepard both a tender nurse and a proper baptism; the challenge to that son to know and serve the God of that baptism, lest the much-disrupted life of his father—and the untimely deaths of both his mother and an older brother of his very name—should seem undergone in vain. A heavy trip, even by the standards of an age less sensitive to the autonomous being of the child.[33] In the context of the narrative itself, however, the omission of this climactic stroke of guilty legacy has the effect of throwing the emphasis on matters more public, indeed more properly Puritan. And we need to remind ourselves that, however it turned out in literary fact,[34] the prime motive of those who sought reform in New England was not to entrap and then hamstring their offspring.

Contrasting with the condition of leaving England, the kind reception by friends indicates that the future will be different from the past. And, as if to keep this fact from seeming selfish, Shepard records the fulfillment of a "great desire" of his (dying) wife: "to leave me in safety from the hand of my enemies and among God's people, and also the child under God's precious ordinances" (64);

we guess she was indeed a "most incomparably loving" wife. More genuinely public is the fact—innocent to Shepard if not to those more deeply involved in a plot already in medias res[35]—that the congregation at Newtown is just then beginning its "removal to Hartford at Connecticut." Thus Shepard and his party find "many houses empty and many persons willing to sell"; and finding the situating mostly satisfactory, many of them "did desire to sit still and not to remove further." Within a few months of their arrival, therefore, "there was a purpose to enter into church fellowship, which [they] did . . . about the end of the winter" (64). Which ought to bring an important phase of Shepard's life to what Henry James might call a "formal conclusion"; for surely the proper accomplishment of this new beginning is both the goal which migrant Puritanism everywhere discovers itself to have been seeking and the end which authorizes the autobiographical gesture in the first place—raising it, if only just barely, out of the level of the personal and onto that plane where the life of the saint may fairly merge with the fate of an enterprise in which Providence itself must take an active role.[36]

Complicating this happy merger of the personal with the public, however, is the unhappy but unblinkable fact that

> a fortnight after [this founding] my dear wife Margaret died, being first received into church fellowship which, as she much longed for, so the Lord did sweeten it unto her that she was hereby exceedingly cheered and comforted with the sense of God's love, which continued until her last gasp. (64–65)

Not the last nor yet the most sharply sorrowful of the deaths Shepard will have to record, it is in fact noteworthy for its extreme "composure": never one to "rail," Shepard seems more willing to accept this death than that of his first son, already, or that of his second wife, in the future. Surely not an event Shepard could in any sense have desired, it seems nevertheless one for which he has prepared himself and for which, at the time of writing, he has already been compensated, by a second very loving wife. Then too, it is "balanced" by other, happier facts of saintly life: the safe arrival in the land of mission, the survival and baptism of the son who has somehow become identical with the second, successful attempt to reach that land, and the foundation of yet another reformed church. For which the loving Margaret seems as grateful as the worried Shepard himself. But what makes her death bearable, finally, is the way she herself is able to bear it—full of joy that her husband and son and herself are all safe in the church, the point of it all in the first place.

Probably Margaret Touteville Shepard could not have predicted that acceptance into a church which, most unlike the "mixed assemblies" of England, was instituted on purpose to receive only tried and tested saints into its communion would be an occasion of overflowing joy; but, unless her husband is faking his facts, she seems to have found that acceptance comforting indeed. Worth dying for, almost. Or, if that thought were a little morose, worth living an entire life in the struggle to discover and to realize. No record of his wife's confession of faith appears among those that now enlarge and adorn the modern edition of Shepard's "Autobiography"; perhaps her redundantly verbal husband gave one on her most modest behalf.[37] But it is almost as if the still ardent but now strangely fulfilled Margaret knows the meaning of her husband's life better than he does himself. Unless we recall that, as Shepard is reflectively writing rather than originally living that life, he may have found in her, for the moment at least, his own necessary symbol. Lovely women dying seem perpetually to be running that risk. And unless our theory of the family romance has failed us completely, the fate of the wife may be preferable to that of the son.

But while we puzzle over the choice between dying into and living out the life of the most patriarchal (if not very patristic) Puritan church, the events of Shepard's compressed yet variable narrative move right along. And not to any swift resolution either, as a new and disturbing set of historical questions—proper to the life of the churches but unexpected in a place that had been sought as a realm of answers—effectively disrupts his moment of spiritual poise and literary composure:

> No sooner were we thus set down and entered into church fellowship but the Lord exercised us and the whole country with the opinions of the Familists, begun by Mistress Hutchinson, raised up to a great height by Mr. Vane too suddenly chosen governor, and maintained too obscurely by Mr. Cotton, and propagated too boldly by the members of Boston and some in other churches . . . (65)

The unusually long sentence goes right on, inventing further parallel constructions to specify the deleterious *effects* of this multiplicity of personal causes, but the reader needs only the reference to the troublemakers as "Familists" to understand that Shepard's outrage can hardly pause to be fair.[38] But what energizes this passage is more its irony than its anger. Indeed, Shepard's effect is almost uncanny: "no sooner" had we reached the place the Lord himself provided for perfect Reformation Practice than that same Lord "exercised us" with problems in the area of Salvation Theory we thought well settled and left behind. And as the pilgrim for "peace" is forced to discover that its time is not yet, we hear a tone that asks if not a resentful "Why me?" at least an exasperated "What next?"

Shepard's account of the "principal seed" of the Antinomian (or "Free Grace")[39] Controversy is complex and multiform; and one incidental effect of the study of godly letters might be to make its contours of such old-time controversy a little less mysterious. For the moment, however, it is enough to notice that some considerable persons seem to be putting forth a theory that would place sinful man's timely discovery of his eternal "election" by God not at the end of a long and painful process of sorrowful introspection and (as it were) despair of one's ability ever to deserve the favor of the Most Holy God; and not even, after that, in the midst of a process by which persons discover a newfound ability to perform some "spiritual" work which Scripture marks as a sort of condition (if not quite a cause) of salvation; but only as a wonderful fact all by itself; or, as Shepard puts the detested position, "by an immediate revelation in an absolute promise" (65). Saints do not infer their salvation—Shepard is horrified to hear—from any other process, fact, or condition; they know it directly, rather, as God makes it known to them as such. And of course there was, as the reader may properly fear, much to be said on both sides.

Much of what Shepard has to say—on the side of a painful "preparation" for salvation and on human activity as an indispensable condition—is argued in the lengthy sermon sequences he delivered while trying to stay a step ahead of the pursuivants in England and was able much later to put into print.[40] The point here is simply that, as Shepard's experience of religion was marked by "anxiety" at every turn, he could scarcely be expected to favor the "way" of spontaneous insight and perfect assurance. It is even possible to imagine that Shepard's retrospective account of his grinding, seven-stage conversion experience at Cambridge was written with the prophets of the "Faire and Easie Way"[41] in mind.

———

Like Jonathan Edwards, perhaps, Shepard had "a variety of concerns and exercises about [his] soul" before he could mark the efficacious beginning of his conversion as such.[42] The earnest prayers for the life of his father seem to have begun a process in which he thought he could see "the spirit of God wrestling with [him]" (40). And at Cambridge, afterward, he was somewhat moved by the preaching of first "old Doctor Chaderton" and then, "half a year after," that of Mr. Dickinson. Then too, in the midst of a falling away from these salubrious influences, there was the peripatetic dialogue with the "godly scholar" we have noticed before—a timely reminder, from the voice of a social peer, of the hopeless predicament of "every man out of Christ" (40–41). But this sort of on-again-off-again religion might have continued indefinitely if it had not been for the stiff dose of self-revulsion that resulted from waking up, one Sabbath morning, "sick with [the] beastly carriage" (41) that caused him in fact to be "carried," unconscious, to the room of a sympathetic fellow scholar. One almost imagines that this suspension of consciousness was somehow necessary—a parodic reminder, perhaps, that there can be interruptions in the activity we reify and then thematize as the "self."

Even for a modern student, such a dramatic lapse might be enough to turn the life around. For Shepard, however, it leads not to the confession one is asked to make before other reforming alcoholics but to an extended moment of self-revelation "in the cornfields" where he had gone—like Adam, perhaps—to hide from God. And though he can plainly see, in painful retrospect, that he "did not know [his] sinful nature all this while" (41), this moment of predictable shame verging toward an efficacious sight of an ingrained sinfulness seems effectively to have begun the process by which his soul was turned from the life of sin to the love of God.

It is, however, *only* the beginning; and though the seven stages which follow involve some heavy going, it is a serious mistake to stop reading just here. For without some sense that Shepard's rendition of a powerfully private experience is written honestly *and* in animation of a technical understanding, of something scholarship has learned to call a "morphology of conversion,"[43] nothing else about the remarkable thought-experiment of New England will make much sense. Dauntingly sincere, Shepard must nevertheless write his drama of religious crisis and resolution into a pattern which could stand the test of public scrutiny: not "I'm saved, I have God's own word for it"; but here, in a series of stages, which make sense in relation to one another and to Scripture's definition of the end to be achieved, is the process by which I, like others before me, and as a model (perhaps) for those to come after, came to understand what Scripture means by "sin" as an inherent condition from which we need to be saved and by "faith" as the only means by which.

Of course, it *could* happen all at once: "What I choose is youse."[44] But such has been not at all Shepard's own experience. Nor does it correspond very well with the (complementary) way his salvation taught him to read Scripture's assembled account of how a Sovereign God has in fact decided to make known the otherwise mysterious decree of predestination—with and not without, in the overwhelming majority of cases, some painful period of prior preparation; for how could the subject of salvation appreciate (or for that matter even understand) the meaning of being saved without first realizing that he was indeed lost? And, more emphatically still, in the act of accepting a gift freely offered. True, that acceptance had to be an especially enabled and not a naturally available ("free") choice or the scheme ceased to be "Calvinist."[45] But an important point was being made nevertheless: one realized salvation not "anyhow" but only in the newfound ability to answer a call one never could before; to accept, as it were, a new identity in exchange for the one self-love had loved so long. And if something such were indeed the nexus of God's plot, then the Sectaries who announced themselves "no sooner" than the moment of his arrival would soon find Shepard a formidable opponent indeed. Certainly no one holding their "immediatist" theory should attempt to join the particular church to which this tough-loving pastor (and his like-minded followers) held the keys. For when assurance has been barely and dearly wrested from prolonged anxiety, the tale of spiritual self-evidence is likely to sound not poised but merely complacent.

In a second distinct step, then, it begins to be borne in upon the loose-living yet vividly impressionable Thomas Shepard that, in calling for the hearer of its word to "be renewed in the spirit of your mind" (41), the New Testament is requiring of the convert nothing less remarkable than a change of the image of self-identity and of the basis of motivation—a "personality change" if ever there was one. Accordingly, as Shepard listens to this call for renewal preached out of "Romans 12," he seems to hear—in a frontal attack on the self-deceptive self-regard of the natural man as such—"the secrets of my soul . . . laid open before me," as if someone had told the preacher "of all that ever I did, of all the turnings and deceits of my heart" (41–42). By all accounts Shepard's evangelical genius will master the lesson of this preaching, the trick and the truth of learning "to believe that what is true for you in your private heart is true for all men"; for the moment, however, he is ready to account Doctor Preston as "the most searching preacher in the world." And, for that same moment, he must recognize that Preston has succeeded only partially in the game of "killing me softly." For though Shepard may fitly "bless God [he] did see [his] frame and hypocrisy and self and secret sins," the logic he is learning forces him equally to confess that he finds as yet a "hard heart" that could not be appropriately "affected" (42) by that sight.

And this is to say, in the terminology of his own sequence of sermons on "The Sound Believer," that he has undergone the preparatory phase of "conviction" but not yet that of "compunction."[46] Students often affect not to understand this difference—between the clear intellectual recognition that one is indeed a sinner, "by nature," and so continuously and without remission, and the passionate hatred of that very condition. Nor are they always assisted by reference to this pair of preparations as the inevitable outcome of the scholastic division of "faculties" into intellect and will, or yet as the creation of the Ramist bias of the binary.

What they wish to know, it seems, is how *could* one see oneself as inevitably, and as it were hopelessly, involved in a world where every available option meant nothing but Self in one clever disguise or another and not be, well, moved by the discovery. Perhaps they ought to read their Hobbes as well as their Calvin; or their Hume; for humanistic self-acceptance may suffice if there truly is *no* alternative. What Shepard seems bound to believe, however, is that a full-blown religious renewal—the gradual conversion of Saint Augustine if not the instantaneous calling of the Apostle Paul—provides the possibility of self-overcoming; and that though one could, at the beginning, only undergo the regenerating process, it made good sense to do everything one could, if not to abet, then at least to contextualize the divine activity required.

Accordingly, therefore, Shepard hastens to make the shameful gap between the adequate perception and the appropriate hatred of himself as "sinner"—*toute craché* if not *par excellence*—"the work of daily meditation" (42). And now the process appears to begin in earnest; for, whatever may be the modern tuition on the subject of the innocence of "feeling" as such, the psychological world of the sixteenth and seventeenth centuries makes no sense apart from the deeply held belief, of Reformation and Counter-Reformation alike, that one was well advised, not to feel the full force of one's feelings, for that were tautology indeed, but to try to bring one's forceful feelings into something like an appropriate relation to one's crucial concepts. Sin is bad, granted. The worst, I hear you say? I guess you may be right. Well then, Sucker, is not your stupid, grinning affect just a little out of place? The dialogue is internal, of course; for, unlike an aroused conscience, Thomas Preston could hardly follow you around the entire day. Except as his preaching could be fairly internalized, precisely as "meditation." So Shepard's mind bears down on itself, in themes no less unsettling than they have come to be predictable:

> The evil of sin, the terror of God's wrath, day of death, beauty of Christ, the deceitfulness of the human heart, etc.; but principally I found this my misery: sin . . . did lie light upon me as yet, yet I was much afraid of death and the flames of God's wrath. (42)

He knows the evil of sin, that is to say, but he does not yet *feel* it. But, as meditation and writing are forever wedded, he takes a little book with him into the fields, to write down "what God taught [him] lest [he] should forget." This process involves growth, he admits, but only in the awareness of his own confused questionings—"whether there were a God," "whether Christ was the Messiah," "whether the Scriptures were God's word"; and whether, had he been educated differently, he might just as well have come to believe that "Popery" or "Turkism" (42) were the very truth; or even Grindletonian perfectionism, according to which the conscientious teaching of his mentors was all so much legalism. Shake on that, Sister Hutchinson.

Delivered from that fatal error, after many prayers, the Lord let him see "the three main wounds in [his] soul":

> (1) I could not feel sin as my greatest evil; (2) I could do nothing but I did seek myself in it and was imprisoned there, and though I desired to be a preacher, yet it was honor I did look to . . . ; (3) I felt a depth of atheism and unbelief in the main matters of salvation and whether the Scriptures were God's word. (43)

If the last of these self-accusations seems a little nonspecific, we should notice that in Shepard's case it went to the extent of "secret and hellish blasphemy" whenever he read Scripture accounts of "Christ's miracles," with the result that he began to wonder if he had not "committed the unpardonable sin." And so

> for three quarters of a year . . . I had some strong temptations to run my head against walls and brain and kill myself. And so I did see, as I thought, God's eternal reprobation of me, a fruit of which was this dereliction to these doubts and darkness, and I did see God like a consuming fire and an everlasting burning, and myself like a poor prisoner leading to that fire.

Clearly in extremis—and not knowing what *else* to do—Shepard tries the bold experiment of imitating Christ: "when he was in an agony he prayed earnestly" (43).

A good sign, this earnest praying, but not as yet "compunction." For the fear of damnation seems to be counting for more than the pure detestation of the infinite evil of sin—a God-insult—precisely as such. Only within the prayer itself does Shepard begin to sense the problem: "myself so unholy and God so holy" as to make mediation seem quite out of the question. But this thought, instead of deepening or fixing the despair, calls forth instead a "spirit of prayer . . . for free mercy and pity"; so that the entire process so far can be seen as the Lord's way, he says, of "helping me to see my unworthiness of any mercy and that I was worthy to be cast out of his sight and to leave myself with him to do with me what he would, and there and never until then I found rest" (43–44). A later generation of the New England Theology has taken credit (then blame) for defining the sentiment of salvation as a "willingness to be damned for the Glory of God"; but if the awesome thought required august parentage, surely one might father it here.[47]

And if one were to accuse Shepard, just now, of having gone *beyond* compunction's killing sense to some relief from the tricky problem of achieving some infinite negative affect, surely he might argue in his own defense that things come out even only when, one's sinfulness being realized as indeed infinite, the entire question is left up to God alone.

Then too, the process is by no means over; for though Shepard "went with a stayed heart unto supper late that night," it was not long before he again felt his "senselessness of sin and bondage to self" and his "heartlessness to any good and [his] loathing of God's ways" (44). But even as we begin to grow restless with this process of advancing and falling back, the Lord intervenes with a paradoxical suggestion that may be just exactly the "grace" one needs in a system the unregenerate find utterly counterintuitive: "Be not discouraged . . . because thou art so vile, but make this double use of it: (1) loathe thyself the more; (2) feel a greater need and put a greater price on Jesus Christ, who only can redeem thee from all sin" (44–45). This peculiar strategy—ac-cen-tuate the negative—proves successful enough to suggest that Shepard may be learning to "beat Satan as it were with his own weapons," to imagine that the "despair" of one's own virtue may be but a necessary stage in a complex and relentless process. And he is pleased to observe that he was taught this "negative" way of working, from God himself, "before any man preached any such thing unto [him]" (45). And so, as the work of compunction begins to discover that hatred of sin is identically hatred of self, Shepard goes on to cultivate rather than repress that precise affect: "Why shall I seek the glory and good of myself who am the greatest enemy, worse than the Devil can be, against myself, which self ruins me and blinds me, etc.?" (45).

One might object that there is at least one too many "selves" here, that Satan's guile and God's grace cannot both be targeting the selfsame entity; but this discovery would only serve to confirm, slightly in advance of Shepard's own meticulous observation, that in spite of the hellish natural self, a regenerate Christ-self is in fact in the process of being born. And to remind us, perhaps, that some such multiplication of entities is a perfectly generic feature of all self-writing in the "Augustinian" tradition.[48] Still, as we are dealing with a process rather than an instantaneous fact, Shepard goes on to confess that, though grace seems now to be guiding his inward motions and outward behaviors, "I had [yet] no assurance Christ was mine." And "therefore"—as the fourth stage dares to introduce itself—"the Lord . . . brought Dr. Preston to preach" the word in season, namely, that "all the good" of the redeemed is from Christ alone. The sinful human case is of course hopeless of itself: that is precisely why there is a Redeemer at all.

Simple enough, it would seem; nor was there anything here a Cambridge lad had never heard before, more times than once. But never before, it would appear, had he ever been so perfectly prepared: for how could anyone be saved before he had really come to feel his own utter loss? And never before, in any event, had Shepard been able to accept terms or keep the condition of the wondrous offer from beyond and in spite of the fallen self.

> I had heard many a time Christ freely offered by his ministry if I would come in and receive him as Lord and Savior and Husband. But I found my heart ever unwilling to accept of Christ upon there terms; I found them impossible for me to keep that condition, and Christ was not so sweet as my lust. (45)

As "lust" here comprehends more than unruly sexual desire, so the construction of gender is not the only issue raised by the need for Shepard to accept Christ as "Husband." The "feminization" of the soul by reason of its utterly dependent relation to a masculine Christ will no doubt have the widest possible implications for Puritan social policy;[49] but here it is enough to observe that what Shepard's unregenerate will has been resisting is dependency as such. Evidently his wish not to be a woman is not much different from his need to feel he can somehow save himself.

To be sure, he must accept terms and keep conditions, but they are identically the ones he has been so glaringly *unable* to accept and keep before. If he must freely accept an offer freely made, it must be thought that it is precisely the regenerate will (or self) which accepts, now, an offer no former or lesser self could bear to entertain. Indeed, it is in the act of accepting the offer one never could accept before that the saint begins to know himself as such. One might argue with some cogency that Shepard's self-authorized account of the process of salvation presents a pattern more complicated than anything one can find in the lucid pages of Calvin's *Institutes;* and even, from an older perspective still, that his "enabled activism" requires him to reduplicate the order of God's redemptive activity—so that, in one (biblical) act, God must "graciously" offer a salvation well beyond anything required by justice and then, in another (psychological) moment, provide the assistance required to enable acceptance of an offer not "naturally" adapted to the fallen human faculties.[50] But then the stress of one's system always appears *some*where. And what Shepard's activism wishes above all to emphasize is that salvation does *not* come in an "immediate revelation"— conveyed to or as it were imprinted upon a passive receptor.

Elsewhere, of course, he is perfectly clear that it does not come by the natural man's choice as such: "after my conversion [I] was never tempted to Arminianism, my own experience so sensibly confuting the freedom of will" (73). Shepard might well agree with his sometime mentor Thomas Hooker, that the natural man was "as free to go to the meeting house as to the alehouse," but neither man supposed this common sense of things told anything about what enabled one person to choose and another to refuse "Christ freely offered by his ministry" (45).[51] And even here Shepard is being about as careful as the recollection of one self by another may well permit: "I found therefore the Lord revealing free mercy" and knew that my only help was for him "to give me Christ and enable me to believe in Christ and accept of him, and here I did rest" (45). Not, yet, as in an end attained, but in the efficacy of a process—involving the human will—that would work if only God so willed. Accordingly, therefore, Shepard comes to understand that Christ's perfect righteousness is the systematic counterpart to and substitute for the "poor sinner's ungodliness," while yet questioning "whether ever the Lord would apply this and give this unto [him]" (45).

Until the very end, then, the issue remains unresolved. Hypothetically, still, the Lord lets Shepard see that to "so many as receive him, he gives power to be the sons of God." "And"—he says, uniting clauses in which the eye of philosophy may detect a little slippage—"I saw the Lord gave me a heart to receive Christ with a naked hand, even naked Christ, and so the Lord gave me peace" (45–46). Again, the sexual relevance of all this nakedness must sooner or later have its due, but in the first (consciously contextual) place one hears Shepard trying to place himself beyond the criticism of even the most radical Protestant salvationist. A baffled and balked Edward Johnson will ardently complain that "here"—in the midst of the so-called Antinomian Crisis—I am told that "I must take a naked Christ. [But] woe is me[:] if Christ be naked to me, wherewith shall I be clothed?" Making a nice rhetorical point, in language more redolent of Luther than of Calvin, he means that unless privileged to wrap himself in the righteousness of Christ, he will be altogether unable to claim salvation. What Shepard wishes to stress, however, is that his interest in Christ, though clearly "enabled," is in no way "extrinsic," and that it is without ulterior considerations of any kind.

To say that his own hand is naked is to remind himself that he has of himself absolutely nothing to offer God or Christ in "condign" exchange nor as "congruous" inducement to the "bargain" of salvation.[52] All he ever had he has needed to let slip away, and now—peace, Frank—"without himself, then he has naught": for only so can this greatest gift be thought to be entirely free. And Christ himself is naked to signify that Shepard loves and accepts and embraces him not, crassly, to validate his career as able minister of the Gospel, nor yet, with a little more finesse, to share in the plentitude of spiritual gifts which the Father has heaped on the head of his only-begotten Son, the first epitome of all creation.[53] Perhaps we are to hear Shepard saying, in the analogy one of his colleagues loved to press, that he has accepted Christ as the woman elects her husband, for the beauty of "the bare man himself" and not for any of the gifts he may well bestow; and, if we are willing ourselves to press the paradox of a "willingness to be damned," perhaps he is implying that he loves the loveliness of the Christ-idea whether he finds himself saved therein or not. Certainly, as he will demonstrate in his extended exposition of the Parable of the Ten Virgins, he is not willing to be thought of as the sort of legal professor who lies "poring on the law which Christ has abolished."[54] And, as *no one's* assurance is ever perfect, perhaps Shepard's "rest" and then his "peace" are those which lie—as Edwards would suspect and Emerson straightly teach—beyond *every* sort of concern with human personality, redeemed or not.

But however we decide issues of such extremity, the length, the conceptual specificity, the controlled activism, and the all *but* ultimate discomfort of Shepard's experience is more than enough to prepare us for his utter impatience with the way of immediacy. We may wonder that the "Autobiography" makes no reference to the active part Shepard took in the exploratory questioning of John Cotton, or in the notoriously mixed medium of the civil trial of Anne Hutchinson; and we may wince at his analogous discovery that Pequots and Opinionists "did arise" and "began to be crushed" (66) at about the same time. But his *ironic* handling of the arrival scene makes perfect sense in light of what has gone before— as if one had lived out the career of painful education involved in properly deciding on and then faced the staggering difficulty of getting to this place of peace, only to discover its equal mind upset by vulgar strife; and as if the soul-making discovery of salvation at the cost of self led only to a place where zeal beyond all public poise called even this killing condition "a way of works" (65). As if this newly arrived Shepard were not at all a faithful guide. As if his self-denying meditation—long inscribing itself, whenever it began to be written—needed to start anew, from different premises altogether. As if this "Autobiography" were but a travelogue: whose country had he come to now?

———

Published for the first time in 1832, Shepard's "Autobiography" is not quite the "fair copy," "author's last revision" we might wish. Some finite literary entity appears to end a few pages after the climactic yet puzzling arrival in New England; and though this brief section stretches out to include the death of Shepard's second wife in April 1645, it must both rush through and pass over many intervening matters to do so. And then, as if he were beginning to provide the sort of anticlimax Bradford achieves in writing on beyond his clear point of originary coherence, Shepard sets down several pages of numbered notations for "Anno 1639"—from which we learn, among other things, that "Mr. Cotton repents not, but is hid only" (74). After this annal there follows, in the "full correct text" of Michael McGiffert (1972), a "Journal," edited from a different manuscript and covering, in a series of discreet entries and at a length about twice that of the "Autobiography," the period from November 25, 1640, to March 29, 1644; it presents the kind of thing we would expect to find in a diary never subsumed by the powerful form of thematic narrative.[55]

This "Journal"—a sort of ongoing afterword—might possess great interest for anyone who wishes to learn the variety of moods in which Shepard lived out the years following his climactic arrival in the haven God provided, even for those who did, for a good long time, seem only to stand and wait. And, because even the best-made "text" bleeds over into something else, it is perfectly proper to imagine a larger project called "The Self-Writings of Thomas Shepard."[56] Yet the "Autobiography" has a formal impact all its own: Where Bradford's "history" succeeds in its very failure to press its teleological premise to a formal conclusion, Shepard produces, among other things, a connected and surprisingly coherent account of a life dominated by the progressive discovery, of a proud enough natural man, that God does indeed have Saints, called first to accept Christ in place of their own good gift and then again to carry out his work in the world.

It may look from the outside like "Heroism," in which the self makes good to strive beyond itself; but inside it has to feel like "Holiness," wherein the will gets on by giving up. And woe to them that lose the sense. Suspicious it must always be, particularly in a professed Christian, to seem to learn the lesson once and for all; but friendly to our mortalities, on the other hand, when Saints are such despite themselves. One especially grim year at Cambridge may get you started on a path that leads to the lair of the Lion; and one season's poise of spirit—when breeding bodies might seem concern enough—and you find yourself in the Wilderness, adding your individual mite to History's gathering sum, bolstering thereby the uncertain confidence of those who went before, but discovering yourself (if only as a grammatical marker) in the middle of a sentence with many clauses already written out, demanding your tardy pronoun to agree; or dangle. *Why* were Hooker and Stone moving off to Connecticut? And why were the "members of Boston" *so* eager to propagate the opinion that "conditional evangelical promises to faith or sanctification" could never count as "first evidence" (65)? First evidence of *what*? And why this need to *know*? Was *everyone* in New England writing a spiritual autobiography?

The answers lie dispersed, in works Shepard was not privileged to write. But if his own story—beginning in some "blind town" overseas—delivers him to a

New England he himself did not invent, that story does not quite end with the bewildering arrival toward which his whole "life" had been made to point. The Sectaries elicit a distress that almost hides itself as scorn; the destruction of the Pequots figures as a "most dreadful" deliverance but, as Indians burn and bleed, the "hot fight" (67) tempts Shepard to dip his own pen in patriotic gore; and the wondrous gift of Harvard College lands in Shepard's own town, which Providence kept "spotless from the contagion" (68) of the Opinionists. A divinely displaced person, Shepard sinks very low after the death of the ever ready Mr. Harlekenden, his "dear friend and most precious servant of Jesus Christ" (69); but the Lord is swift to revive him and even to bless his labors—as a preacher to his transplanted congregation and as an author published in England as well. And so, unlike the sobering example of Bradford's *Plymouth,* it begins to look like a success story after all: "We march with Providence cheery still."

Yet not to the very end. And not in the most personal terms. For though Shepard is only too willing to allow his public life to be gathered up into the project of New England, there to be authorized by a Province that really does know the difference between the life of a man and the fate of nations, he is also careful not to allow the evident success of a holy state to cover over the sins of a man who, for all the importance of his enlisted public identity, cannot quite keep his soul in order. And so the "Autobiography" proper ends not with New England's triumph over enemies—and certainly not with its author's satisfaction at the appearance of his *Sincere Convert* and *Sound Believer*—but with Shepard's continuing inability to learn the difference between the initial and the celestial love. For the Lord who, after the untimely death of one son and the unlikely survival of a second, took away, in his own time, the "incomparably loving" mother of both seemed to repay it all by providing a second wife in the person of "the eldest daughter of Mr. Hooker" (69). Yet only to carry her away as well—again, in His own time—though not before she bore her part in three further births and two further deaths. As if some pregnant verses "Upon Wedlock and the Death of Children" were less the private consolation of some grievous metaphysical than the always already twice-told tale of Puritan love and death.[57] Surely this too was not without meaning.

The death of New England it could not signify: too many public signs said otherwise. Nor was there now any further reason to insist on its true meaning. The first son named Thomas may have died to express the sense that, as churches and not families were to be the building blocks of the Puritan Utopia, one had better regard children in the promise and not in the flesh. But this lesson had surely been learned—well enough, if the spirit of the dedication to the second son Thomas is any indication; all too well, in the view of those students who regularly observe that the most dangerous thing that can happen to an American Puritan is to be loved too much by Thomas Shepard. And perhaps silence is indeed the best commentary on Shepard's confession that it "was no small affliction and heartbreaking to me that I should provoke the Lord to strike at my innocent children for my sake" (69–70). But the literary effect of Shepard's account of the death of his second wife can survive the discovery, in any tone, that the God who giveth and taketh away may be regarding ends other than the observer's needful education. The facts are simply that Joanna Hooker Shepard does die, that Thomas Shepard hates this fact about as much as any of us can possibly imagine, that this natural hatred cannot fail to constitute an occasion of blasphemy, and that—why-ever the hell she is dying—Shepard has to say something other than God damn God. For Ahab is not yet.

The moral context of the well-composed death scene is Shepard's sense of his life as a curious, almost a poised mixture of blessing and affliction: death of children but, after the death of the Pequots, "continued peace to the country," most noticeable "when all England and Europe are in a flame."[58] Blessed he is, therefore, to find himself and his now expanding, now contracting family in "a land of peace," even though it is also "a place of trial." Stumbling over his own transitions, Shepard tries to write out a formula: "But the Lord hath not been wont to let me live long without some affliction or other, and yet ever mixed with some mercy." And then, though the logic of his proposition is like a second nature, his recollection of persons utterly defeats the will to generalize:

> and therefore, April the second, 1646, as he gave me another son, John, so he took away my most dear, precious, meek and loving wife in childbed after three weeks lying in, having left behind her two hopeful branches, my dear children Samuel and John. (70)

The account is going to get more painfully moving, but already we begin to believe the truth of what we have always said: zealots though they were, Puritans did indeed love their spouses and their children and—dare we notice it?—not always in moderation. Certainly Joanna Hooker, first introduced in terms of her heritage, has come on to evince a passion more fierce and tender than the worshipful bride of Shepard's youth; and, as we begin to assemble an anthology of subjects on which the New England saints will risk all the poetry their prose can command, we should remind ourselves that woman is often more than a match for saint.

The mark of such poetry is that it starts and stops a number of times—reaching out for premature conclusions that will not stay put and having then to try again, learning along the way that "meditation" is itself part of the problem; for nothing one can say will cover the case entirely and, meanwhile, the activity of consciousness merely keeps alive the pain that will not be assuaged. If the issue were what Freud has taught the fashionable to call "mourning," the process might well have an end; and surely *some* poem could be written from the moment when one has finally felt his feeling long enough.[59] But in the midst of Puritanism's "great pain," no such "formal feeling" will seem to come; so that, as often as not, the poem of (un)weaned affections has to end not with some hard-won resolution, proving to reader and writer alike that writing really can regulate desire, but with the baffled recognition that, say what one will, the pain remains about the same. Apostasy is possible—No, God, her death is *not* all right—but not even Emily Dickinson can get that note quite right. And in the seventeenth century this love that hates is one that dare not say its name. So the poem ends when it has done all it sanely can, when earthly love has been remembered well and then rebuked about enough.

Within the circumscribed but correspondingly intense possibilities of this discursive world, Shepard dares all he dares:

> This affliction was very heavy to me, for in it the Lord seemed to withdraw his tender care for me and mine which he graciously manifested by my dear wife; also refused to hear prayer when I did think he would have harkened and let me see his beauty in the land of the living in restoring her to health again; also in taking her away in the prime of her life when she might have lived to have glorified the Lord long; also in threatening me to proceed in rooting out my family. (70)

Shepard tries to balance this rather long list of negative evidences by reminding himself that if he had "profited by former afflictions of this nature [he] should not have had this scourge"; and also, at a somewhat higher level of argument, "I am the Lord's, and he may do with me what he will." But then, as he remembers Joanna herself, in a relationship requiring very little of meditation to enliven, it becomes clear that the necessary work of weaning is yet to be done:

> But this loss was very great. She was a woman of incomparable meekness of spirit, toward myself especially, and very loving, of great prudence to take care for and order my family affairs, being neither too lavish nor sordid in anything, so that I knew not what was under her hands. (70–71)

Criticism might judge that the glaring need of Thomas Shepard is a little too heavily intertwined with the surpassing virtue of Joanna Hooker, but then that is precisely the point: he cannot let go a person who had become essential to his sense of well-being. Would the Lord require him to face his life alone?

For it was not as if her virtues were exclusively domestic. Surely a sufficiently attentive God would know that "she loved God's people dearly and [was] studious to profit by their fellowship, and therefore loved their company. She loved God's word exceedingly and hence was glad she could read my notes which she had to muse on every week" (71). This time the voice of criticism wants to address Thomas Shepard directly: How nice for you. How very lucky you were to find— the second time around—a partner who found yourself so much like both her God and her saintly father. By now, however, Shepard is beginning to work toward a way of loving his Joanna in just the way she is loved of God. And toward the discovery that, standing together, he and God can withstand our cynicism and even our jokes.

> She had a spirit of prayer beyond ordinary of her time and experience. She was fit to die long before she did die, even after the death of her first-born, which was a great affliction to her, but her work not being done then, she lived almost nine years with me and was the comfort of my life to me, and the last sacrament before her lying in seemed to be full of Christ and thereby fitted for heaven. (71)

The personal note remains ("the comfort of my life to me"), but now, instead of holding out for "his" beloved Joanna—together with him against God, as it were—Shepard is trying to learn, from her luminous example of patience in the face of loss, that human love need not be idolatrous to be "true."

Doubtless he knows he *must* learn precisely this lesson before he sets out to record this last, most difficult chapter in his life as thematized to date, but it is surprising how far his pen will follow his memory in the direction of feelings that are simply ungovernable. Visited by premonitions that she would not survive this next experience of childbirth, she tells her husband, "[W]e should love exceedingly together because we should not live long together" (71). And though Shepard can hardly bear to think she may be right, surely he treasures this poignant, desperate sentiment beyond anything else she could have said under the circumstances—love to be made not in vain but the more intense from the thought that it soon will end. Shepard omits to say the words but, given the situation, nothing of his could prevent our own conclusion: If only she could hold that thought up to the end, the memory of love's endurance might almost compensate the loss. It may not be surprising to learn that her dying mind moves on to other themes, but it requires more than the ordinary distaste for "superstition" to dispel the power of the deathbed drama that results.

Predictably, "her fever took away her sleep"; and though this fevered state seemed to fill her head "with fantasies and distractions," it was all, Shepard insists, "without raging." And then, beyond this denial of an unhappily predictive moral insanity, Shepard turns his wife's last dissociated moments into a paradigm of spiritual sight so lucid as to convict himself of sentimental misdirection one last time.

> The night before she died she had about six hours unquiet sleep, but that so cooled and settled her head that when she knew none else so as to speak to them, yet she knew Jesus Christ and could speak to him, and therefore as soon as she awakened out of sleep she brake out into a most heavenly, heartbreaking prayer after Christ, her dear redeemer, for the spirit of life, and so continued praying until the last hour of her death— Lord, though I unworthy; Lord, one word, one word, etc.—and so gave up the ghost. (71)

The final clause here suggests that Shepard is not everywhere victim of the overlay of Greek metaphysics on Christian hope: she died and no doubt. For the rest, she died affirming the reality of a world Shepard wishes he himself knew better or at all events more directly; and reminding him, with the painful directness of a deathbed reversal, that human loves cannot come first or be remembered last.

The question, emphatically, is not whether Joanna Hooker has "really" seen Christ or, as psychic science must suspect, was merely wandering further into the hallucinatory wonders of her own "near-death experience." It is, rather, that Shepard is utterly convinced that she has; and that he regards this fact as the fittest possible ending for her exemplary life, even though it balks his interest as a loving natural man. What that man wants, surely, is for this memorably loving person to assure him that he himself is the last thing she will remember in life; and to know that her deepest hope is that he will remember her, with love, through all the days of duty that remain. And yet he knows that Joanna has another, a heavenly spouse whose claim is absolute. To love anything—or indeed anyone—better than this perfect soulmate is the simple standard by which all other sin is measured. And so Shepard must come to love the fact that, in the end, his dying wife loves bridegroom Jesus more. Differently, if one insists, yet throughout a life of loving service it might have been difficult to show that Joanna Hooker was beyond worshiping God in the image of Thomas Shepard. But now, as death breaks in with a lucidity all its own, Joanna forgets Thomas and remembers Christ.

Neither the outcome nor its interpretation is quite inevitable. Surely orthodoxy itself could imagine a space in which Joanna's last words were not "Lord,
one word," but "Thomas, pray with me, for favor with the Lord"; or even "Pray
with me, Thomas, for our reunion in the Lord."[60] And clearly Shepard knows
enough about the distempered mind to know that the name of the Lord is no
guarantee against fantasy and distraction; God's ways being strange, deathbed
scenes may mean just nothing at all. Typically, however, Shepard is trying to do
the very best with what he has been given. And that is to prove to himself that he
cannot merely accept but positively love the fact that his wife loves husband Jesus
more. This indeed will be the climactic trial of his affections: his are weaned exactly to the extent that he can heartily endorse her final weaning of her own.
Surely "we should love exceedingly together." "My most dear, precious, meek and
loving wife." "Lord, one word." Not my name but Thine be spoken.

———

Do we need to say that Shepard seems only moderately successful at the task
he has set himself, here, at the end of his "Autobiography" proper? That the
dramatic posing of his problem is more moving than anything his prose can
conclude? Or that the point to emphasize—here and elsewhere in Puritan
literature—is not whether writers can persuade us that, with effort and in grace,
they are capable of perfect self-transcendence but only that they regularly set
themselves that precise standard and do not readily forgive themselves the failure? We, no doubt, can think of ways to avoid Shepard's painful but typically Puritan conflict: atheism, for one; affective incoherence, for another. Yet it may be
useful to remind ourselves, from time to time, that it once made sense for men
(and women) to take responsibility for their feelings as well as their actions. And
that our own ethic—of "Love Among the Ruins"—may be no match for the
analytic prediction that passionate commitment to anything less than "Being-in-
General" is going to create as many problems as ever it can solve.[61]

In fact, given the drama of his final scene, Shepard's concluding summary
seems a little less than brilliantly climactic. The will to (prayerful) resistance having subsided, and no flood of personal assurance there to offset the loss, Shepard
seems left with nothing better than a moral:

> Thus God hath visited and scourged me for my sins and sought to wean
> me from this world, but I have ever found it a difficult thing to profit even
> but a little by the sorest and sharpest afflictions. (71)

We of course are far less sure than Shepard that this or any of the others he had to endure can truly qualify as "afflictions"—losses sent on purpose to try the faith of the saint whose motives seem a little various. But no theology of ours can deny him the right to learn what he can from such losses as do occur. Love them he cannot, despite love's best example. To regulate his resistance he must heartily try. And try again. For to man's desire to have life his own way there seems no end.

To try, therefore, and still to confess the failure: this seems the agitated center of Shepard's midlife stasis. To be sure, he is poised, now, among God's people in New England, and the lifelong call to draw him there is one he never can resent; for surely a saint's work is worth more than a man's peace. But as a saint would seem to be a man for all that, should it not please God to comfort him with modest family joys? To which it seems as yet there is no answer. So that lovers of resistance and of open form may take comfort from the first "coda" to Shepard's "Autobiography"—a list of "good things I have received from the Lord" which, though daunting in its length, omits family blessings almost altogether. No mention here of sons and lovers; only of

> the God who took me up when my own mother died, who loved me, and when my stepmother cared not for me, and when lastly my father also died and forsook me, when I was young and little and could take no care of myself. (71–72)

That, it would seem, is the personal life for which Shepard is forced, a little grimly, to settle: a God—and His People in New England—in place of nearer loves that would not last.

"Poise of the Spirit," that is to say, in place of comfort of the flesh. Perhaps we should not wonder, therefore, that Shepard tried so hard to give that first surviving son to God. Or that "weaned affections" came to seem less a first principle within the "Augustinian Strain of Piety" and more a tactic of survival in the real world. For even if Deity were indeed "guiltless" in the deaths of Thomas Shepard's mortal family, the lesson seemed hardly less severe: one never lost so much as not to lose so much again. At least one still kept, in this case, the church.

CHAPTER FOUR

THE CHARTER AND THE "MODEL"

Writing Winthrop's Holy State

If New England has a story that can be told from major texts, it begins with Bradford's *Plymouth*: no other work from the colonial period offers so determined an account of what a self-conscious origination would look like; nor, in the end, so un-self-sparing a report on how it felt to learn that, as historical action obeys more laws than founders can write down in a covenant, first-comers will cause more effects than their faithful annalist may be willing to underwrite. Separatist by design and supplantational only when its own separations proliferated in the name of economic necessity, *Plymouth* rehearses a tale of success and failure—of success-as-failure—that could stand for some department of "America" even if nothing else were written before the age of Edwards and Franklin. Bradford wants to be first. And, sadly, he is.

But Shepard is second only if we say he is. Only, that is, if we choose to honor the story of those conscientious persons, including many famous ministers, who remained in England as long as they could; and only if we are willing to let Shepard deliver us to a new town in New England in medias res. Something always goes before, of course, but Bradford needs to invoke the example of Eusebius and Foxe more essentially than to consult the map of Captain John Smith; and the church at Salem had more need to reckon with the later one at Boston than to seek the sanction of the earlier one at Plymouth. Shepard, however, finds himself moving into a space already being evacuated, quite literally, by another minister of the same or similar persuasion: what is that about? Nor had Thomas

Hooker, the precursor at Newtown, been himself one of the founding presences in an enterprise already "great" enough to fulfill the promise of Plymouth. Indeed, Winthrop's 1630 migration is often characterized as a "lay movement"; and Shepard is only the most recent minister to arrive at a place where a great deal of human invention has gone on in the name of biblical recovery and where the political reactions to originary decisions have almost seemed like logical implications.[1]

The place to study the foundation and evolution of the world which Thomas Shepard (and other migrating ministers) might endorse and defend but did not help to inaugurate is, of course, the first pragmatic and then increasingly ideological record of John Winthrop. Begun, noticeably, as a "sea journal," it finds reason to go on, beyond the moment of safe arrival, to record—tonelessly, as it seems at first—the events that occurred and the decisions that had to be taken in the course of a suitably implemented and well-coached but still fairly ragged attempt to make and to mark a new, indeed an exemplary beginning of godliness—away from England, to be sure, but well within the world. Then, slowly, and by the pressure of its own implication, it begins to realize that its private inscriptions are expressive as well as notational; and that, in the authoritative formulation of Winthrop's most recent editor, the "journal was turning into a history."[2] One could of course read this remarkable document-turned-text in the second place—crescively, from beginning to end—and then go back to let Shepard elaborate his own moment of entrance into the Winthrop construct. But that would be to move the story of an increasingly anti-Puritan England in the 1620s and early 1630s even further into the "background"; and it would mean risking an encounter with a very difficult literary form before we were quite sure of our commitment. Autobiographies we come to grant: personality if not quite author; and Shepard does not disappoint. But dated entries we doubt and distrust: *write* if you're going to write, Mr. Winthrop. And it has taken us an unusually long time to discover that he really has done so.

And yet—though Winthrop's matchless account of the unfolding of events in and around the Bay of the Massachusetts is often referred to as "The History of New England"—it is important for criticism to remember that it begins as a journal. We cannot know whether Winthrop thought of revising his manuscript for publication, but it seems clear that the work we have is *not* a more polished version of something rougher than went before. What we have is what there is: moving from a staccato series of brief notations written very near the moment to be recorded and toward a smaller number of longer, more essaylike entries written less frequently and often with some sense of completion or retrospect; and edited, now, in that "scientific" way which makes it possible to reconstruct the look of the manuscript itself.[3] But even the older representations of this precious record have provided colonial historians with information and insights available nowhere else. And they might have provided much more, if garden variety Americanist critics had felt more comfortable with a public man's private "document." It is to our credit, perhaps, that we have been willing to confer on even miscellaneous notations of the early "Journal" the status of a full-dress "History." But we have been a little slow to read it as a book.[4]

Perhaps it will not be altogether unfair to read it, in two places, as two books. Though we are no doubt justified in supposing that, even in the beginning, Winthrop's notations are not really miscellaneous, it may be that the earlier portions of the "Journal" are best read not aggressively, as narrative or even as a set of traces out of which a powerful literary agency may be inferred or constructed, but cautiously, as a series of contextual markers, identifications of points or places of particular interest. As the selection of these loci (and would-be *topoi*) is in a certain sense arbitrary, so they are most certainly indicators of private personality as well as of political interest. But though not given as inevitable, they must certainly be accepted as privileged: we always begin a new study in the grip of someone's authority, and of the world Shepard entered in the winter of 1635–36—and where Hooker and Cotton had appeared the year before—Winthrop has been the designer, the theorist, the ruler and, so far at least, the principal record keeper. He may not at first give himself the opportunity to worry much about the "meaning" of his experience in New England, or exactly what his early entries might most importantly teach some potential or eventual reader, but surely no equally literate person has ever been more vitally present at so significant a human creation. The Puritan church, we may yet concede, is Christ; *mais l'etat, c'est John Winthrop.*

Leaving to a later chapter, then, the question of Form and Theme in Winthrop's "Journal"—and even of Winthrop's changing vision of New England—let us begin with a modest attempt to understand the reason of Winthrop's early habits of observation. After the blustery yet in the end successful voyage, what? What religious observations from the man who once "did seriously consecrate [his] life to the service of the church"? What discoveries from the leader who was given to understand, back in "evil and declining England," that "in all probability the welfare of the plantation depends on [his] assistance"? What reflections from the visionary who proposed that the end of his group was "to do justly, to love mercy, to walk humbly with our God"; and who inferred that, in the prosecution of that end, they "must be knit together . . . as one man"?[5] A self-transcending vision, truly. But perhaps it will be enough to begin by looking, more modestly, among the apperceptive observations of Winthrop's "Journal," for that transcendental unity which seems always to deliver us an author.[6]

———

As the quotations above were meant to suggest, one need not begin—"Anno Domini 1630, March 29[,] . . . Easter Monday"—with Winthrop "Riding at the Cowes near the Isle of Wight in the *Arabella,* a ship of 350 tons whereof Captain Peter Milbourne was master" (Y, 13).[7] For the opening twenty-four pages in Winthrop's first "notebook" do indeed constitute a "sea journal," familiar in kind and useful no doubt to persons thinking of undertaking a similar ocean voyage, but tedious enough to those with no such literal intention. The voyage was "windy," it appears, but not from this account very "spiritual"; for no mention is made of the famous "lay sermon" Winthrop (almost certainly) delivered to fellow seafarers, instructing them, with the advantage of the available metaphor, on "the only way to avoid [the] shipwreck" of playing false with God and failing their posterity.[8] By the time we are ready for a cumulative and thematic reading of Winthrop's journal-as-history we will have to ask if what criticism calls "Winthrop's Boston" ever did shine forth, in the view of its founder, "as a city upon a hill"; or if, more literally, it even satisfied the strict demands of his "Reasons for Forsaking England." Here, however, it may be enough to notice that Winthrop's safe arrival in New England marks the end of one sort of record—a detailed yet predictable account of the weathers that hindered or prospered a sea voyage and of the seamanlike responses to these vicissitudes—and the beginning of another, whose purpose might not be immediately obvious, even to the writer, and whose system of notice might therefore have to discover itself in the very act of writing.

To say this much is to imply that "journal" may identify not one elementary genre, with rules too primitive to require enunciation, but quite a variety of writerly possibilities, the very plurality of which gives the lie to the notion of quotidian observation as an altogether literal activity or as an exercise of imagination in the degree zero. Obviously, journals will vary with the activities of day-to-day existence; thus journals of travel come into existence a little more naturally than daily records of a single scene. Beyond this, however, journals can be more or less "private"—offering an imitation of events as their quality and meaning might have been received by virtually any member of the group needed to constitute an "event" in the ordinary sense; or, reconciled to its own subjectivity, determined to filter the events of the public sphere though the strongly coloring lenses of personal conviction; or, at some far extreme of publishable privacy, content to treat the common world as little more than an occasion of self-expressive reflection.

Further, in less "Romantic" terms, journals can exist to test some ideal hypothesis by the standard of daily experience; and they can do so along a scale that runs from a dogmatism so strong that self-confirmation seems inevitable, indeed generic, to a curiosity so fluid that conviction, indeed personality itself, seems at the mercy of historical accidence. Journals will also vary according to the level of significance a writer is prepared to demand of, or to discover within, his own works and days: big things may often happen or always impend; or else, God (or the Devil) will be in the details. And with the near knowledge that Shepard's "Autobiography" went right on into a further phase of spiritual record keeping, it seems well to remember that a journal certainly can be a faithful form of godly letters.

A priori, then, we might expect the "Journal" of so prime a Puritan as John Winthrop to be devoted to the project of Salvation—or at least of Reformation—from the outset. Perhaps it is, but only in some sense too deeply reserved to find expression at once. Equal-minded consideration marks the spirit of Winthrop's "Reasons for Forsaking England"; but the balance tips, finally, toward arguments in favor of a religious mission. Similarly, the "Model" begins as a rehearsal of a social and economic conservatism so familiar that its remarks about those "high and eminent" versus those "mean and in subjection" might indeed have been indited by discursive possibility itself; but it moves to its end with an overflow of spiritual ardor sufficient to inspire the most "fervent love" in the most zealous "pure heart."[9] Yet if Winthrop is moved to continue, beyond the legitimate scope of his sea journal, precisely because of the overbeliefs already expressed, the distinguishing marks of his account of arrival and establishment are perspicacity and restraint. His "Journal" may yet evolve a "History" as committed as *Plymouth* itself, in the moment of its literary invention, but at the outset it is less expressive than any the first reportings of *Mourt's Relation*.[10] As if the political conclusions reached in England, or the religious logic made vivid by the perils of an ocean crossing, could emerge in a journal of experiment only if they should fairly appear in the writer's experience.

Thus—if our own suspicion may be so bold—nothing exemplary is made of the fact that "[a] woman was delivered of a child in our ship, stillborn"; Winthrop merely records the further discovery that "the woman had divers children before but none lived, and she had some mischance now which caused her to come near a month before her time; but she did very well" (Y, 26). There is, of course, no reason for John Winthrop to be a proleptic version of Thomas Shepard; or for us to praise him if he were. And it will take many pages before we can discover if Winthrop shall evince a more than usual interest in the mishaps of childbirth. All that appears is Winthrop's ability to notice natural suffering; and its endurance. Nor is anything but maritime geometry at issue in Winthrop's report that, at its first sighting, "the land appeared thus to us in the center of this circle" (29). The first union with Puritans already on the scene—including Peirce from Plymouth and Endicott and Skelton from Salem—is remembered chiefly as the occasion for a select party of "the assistants and some other gentlemen, and some of the women and our captain" to enjoy "a good venison pasty and good beer"; and for the rest of the company, meantime, to gather a "store of strawberries." By way of his own "first encounter," Winthrop says only that "An Indian came aboard us and lay there all night"; and then, in the morning "the Sagamore of Agawam and one of his men came aboard our ship and stayed with us all the day" (Y, 28). There are, as yet, no other "Records of the Massachusetts Bay Company," and this is indeed the elected governor speaking. He clearly assumes, a priori, the pre-eminence of the men his Old World Charter refers to as "Assistants," but he is also teaching himself to use New World words, like *strawberry* and *Sagamore;* and he seems content at first to pronounce the natural sense of his new world in a few simple sentences. More like a tentative Smith than a validated Bradford.

Within several days of their arrival, Winthrop and his *Arabella* group begin to look for their own planting place. His modern editor properly suggests that the brief entry here is "among the most tantalizing in the whole journal," sliding over important—disputed—questions about one settlement or many and about exactly where in any case; for the governor says only that his party proceeded "to Mattachusetts to find out a place for our sitting down" and "went up Misticke River about 6 miles" (Y, 29).[11] Granted the existence of a journal, this foundational event demands its own marker; but just as clearly Winthrop is determined to give it only so much. The details of saintly infighting may or may not be fit to print, but the man who stands at the elected center of these inaugural debates has not yet committed himself to be their historian. For the present, at least, it is enough to mediate and then simply to record. For the rest, perhaps, the governor is content to keep his own counsel.

Presently, in the midst of marking the safe arrival of a number of ships important to the full establishment and early survival of this Massachusetts plantation, the "Journal" faces and resists its first temptation to swerve in the direction of the personal under the cover of the disciplinary. The notice of the accidental death of his scapegrace son Henry is pointed and painful in Winthrop's letter to his wife;[12] but its more official recording is carefully shorn of anything like tone, and it is immersed in a context which dares anything like private affect to appear:

> July 2, Friday. The *Talbot* arrived there. She had lost 14 passengers. My son
> H. W. was drowned at Salem.

Saturday, [July] 3. The *Hopewell* and the *William and Francis* arrived.

Monday, [July] 5. The *Trial* arrived at Charleston, and the *Charles* at Salem.

Tuesday, [July] 6. The *Success* arrived. Many of her passengers were near starved . . .

Thursday, [July] 8. We kept a day of thanksgiving in all the plantations. (30)

An editor's note reminds us that the Thanksgiving was "for the safe arrival of the ships from England"—which Morton thought the likes of Winthrop regarded as a "miracle"—but that, because "so many of the colony were sick and dying," a day of Fast had to be held as well.[13] We have heard, of course, that the Lord taketh away no less than he giveth. Beyond that simple tuition, however, and beneath the white noise of our own cynicism, the all but poetic shape of Winthrop's entry appears silently to teach the equality of death in any decently Christian community. Not quite that "it tolls for thee"; and not nearly that everybody is somebody's child or parent; but quite pointedly that some modes of thought need to make as little as possible of the difference between the private and the social. And some forms of writing as well.

Laconic merely is Winthrop's notation that, sometime between August 20 and 27, "We kept a Court" (Y, 30). Only with the aid of annotations directing us to the *Records of the Court of Assistants of the Colony of the Massachusetts Bay, 1630–1692,* can we estimate the significance of this first enactment of the terms of a royal charter which, by reason of its transportation to New England, is being transformed from a set of rules for conducting the affairs of an overseas plantation to a ground plan or indeed the "constitution" of a semiautonomous English province with what Winthrop will dare call a "Parliament" of its own. Something further *must* follow from this elliptical beginning, we correctly sense, but it will be hard to decide whether Winthrop's strongest motive is to celebrate the creative unfolding of a carefully restrictive set of orders into a flexibly workable government of which he is the prime guardian as well as the principal officer or to conceal the extent to which this very unfolding could be seen as a deliberate flaunting of first the letter and then the spirit of that curiously enabling document.[14] At issue, finally, is his understanding of "sovereignty." Was it rightfully and properly the king's, to be parceled out as His Majesty alone saw fit? Or was it something God's people might discover and claim in the moment of their mutual self-discovery? What exactly are the politics of these Puritans who have removed themselves without officially separating? Will it prove, in fact, just as awesomely easy to invent a holy state as to evoke a particular church?

But if these issues are insufficiently advertised in this first record of overseas political foundation, the very next entry—on the formation of the Boston church—gives a clear sign that Winthrop will not long satisfy himself with notation alone. His record is private, of course, yet it seems written with an eye toward English suspicion, from which he seems more than a little anxious to clear himself:

> We of the congregation kept a fast and chose Mr. Wilson our teacher, and Mr. Nowell an elder, and Mr. Gagar and Mr. Aspenall deacons. We used imposition of hands, but with this protestation by all, that it was only as a sign of election and confirmation, not of any intent that Mr. Wilson should renounce his ministry he received in England. (Y, 30–31)

Presumed here, obviously, is the difference between "the congregation" and the rest of the migrants, of whom the "Model" seemed to demand no lesser standard of behavior, and who may already have been regarded as belonging to some encompassing unit called "the church."[15] More noteworthy, perhaps, is the implication that, though the religious officers of this experimental group do indeed require a special, "congregational" calling, the Reverend John Wilson at least is not willing to renounce his full-dress ordination in the Church of England. And we might name "the anxiety of separation" as the first of a limited number of concerns which begin to tease a most cautious and circumspect observer out of notation and into prose. As if an experimental (and cautious) Winthrop were discovering the "self" of his "Journal" in the curious mode of proleptic self-defense.

The death of the important assistant, "Mr. Isack Johnson," calls forth a eulogy that is brief in sentiment and mixed in import: "He was a holy man and wise and died in sweet peace, leaving a good part of his substance to the colony" (Y, 31). And the first mention of Thomas Morton is as cryptic as some of his own "identifications": he is judged worthy of banishment, yet a certain "Capt. Brooke . . . refused to carry him" (39). Winthrop takes credit for restraining the drinking of toasts and, briefly too, God gets the praise for the bad-weather rescue of three of the governor's servants. The first lengthy comment on matters internal to the colony concerns the decision to "build a town fortified upon the neck between [Roxbury] and Boston" and then, upon further consideration, to consider "other places" instead. The matter ends with a meeting at Watertown where, "upon view of a place a mile beneath the town, all agreed it was a fit place for a fortified town" (Y, 32). It may require a footnote to explain that this discussion covers over an ongoing "tug-of-war" between Winthrop and his deputy governor, Thomas Dudley;[16] and it might be too simple to identify Dudley as more than just another of Winthrop's motives for writing. But already it comes as no surprise to learn that Winthrop tends to expand whenever he senses disagreement. And, given the macropolitics already implied, one could always wonder who or what this disputed town was being fortified against. For, as it begins to appear, Winthrop often omits sensitive matters, even where he elaborates.

Then, as if to insist that he is no less open to natural wonder—and divine rescue—than to political anxiety, Winthrop makes a lengthy record of the experiences of several persons overtaken in the midst of their travels by a winter turned suddenly fierce. Three of the governor's servants are forced to stay abroad at night "without fire or food," yet "through God's mercy" they all return safe, with only fingers "blistered with cold" to show for their ordeal. Not so fortunate are the six persons who "went towards Plymouth in a shallop against the advice of [their] friends." Just when they have given themselves up for lost to the icy winds and the freezing water, "God's special providence" carries them "through the rocks to the shore"; yet some have to be cut out of the ice into which their legs have frozen and, "having no hatchet," they can gather wood for only a very small fire. Setting out for Plymouth by land—"near 50 miles from them" and not the "7 or 8 miles" they suppose—two of their number encounter "2 Indian squaws" (Y, 33) who enlist their husbands in the project of rescue. Despite this timely assistance, however, two of the four persons who remained with the shallop die of the intense cold, as do the two who were assisted in reaching Plymouth; and one of the two survivors, "a godly man of the congregation of Boston, lay long under the surgeon's hands." The theme of Providence tries hard to redeem this "harrowing tale of winter life in New England,"[17] but the details of persons "being so frozen as they could not stir" and of "the ground being so frozen as they could not dig [a] grave" are managing to hold their own; and when we learn that the Indian savior has to cover the corpse in question with "a great heap of wood to keep it from the wolves" (Y, 34), we see the literary issue being resolved in favor of the natural gothic.

Less pious still is the very end of the passage, which names "the cause of [this] loss" as the fact that the shallop had not been "well manned" (44). So that, while it may be fair for criticism to notice the passage in which the providential mouse slays the allegorical snake—or eats up the Prayer Book but leaves the Testament untouched[18]—it seems necessary also to emphasize Winthrop's attention to the frailty of the human condition. Houses burn, at Dorchester and Watertown, without mitigation. "The poorer sort of people" are "much afflicted with scurvy" and, though many associate death from this disease with discontent and a lingering desire for England, Winthrop makes clear that its cure depends on the timely arrival of a ship that "brought store of juice of lemons." Provisions brought by the same ship are sold "at excessive rates," but the reason for this hardship is entirely economic, "the dearness of corn in England"; and "the day of thanksgiving for this ship's arrival" (Y, 35) appears to follow a law almost as natural as the one by which a wind blowing twelve hours from the east "brings rain or snow in great abundance" (49). When a neighboring Sagamore arrives "with a hogshead of Indian corn," it seems only customary for "the governor [to] set him at his own table" and to observe that "he behaved himself as soberly . . . as an Englishman" (Y, 36); and when these friendly visits continue, Winthrop even arranges to have his own tailor provide this friendly native leader with "a very good new suit from head to foot" (Y, 37).

But if Winthrop's "Journal" early discovers a tendency to take most events in stride, it never goes very long without reminding us that its author is the chief executive officer of an important and still perilous political enterprise. It duly notes the departure from the colony of some of its most important personages—including "Sir Rich: Saltonstall & his 2: daughters & one of his younger sons" who "came down to Boston & stayed [the] night with the Governor" on their way to the ship riding at Salem. Even more significant are the departures which, though expressly temporary, bear hard on the life of the fledgling Boston church:

> About 10 o'clock, Mr. Coddington & Mr. Willson & diverse of the Congregation met at the Governor's, and there Mr. Wilson praying & exhorting the Congregation to Love, &c, commended to them the exercise of prophesy in his absence, & designed those whom he thought most fit for it, viz. the Governor, Mr. Dudly & Mr. Noell the elder[.] Then he desired the Governor to commend himself & the rest to God by prayer, which being done, they accompanied him to the boat. (48–49)

In the words of Winthrop's editor, "The *Lyon* was carrying away four of the colony leaders."[19] Most crucial, perhaps, is the departure of Pastor Wilson, who will be gone for thirteen formative months in the life of the colony. Yet granting this further strengthening of lay leadership, affairs could hardly be left in more trustworthy hands; for Winthrop well understands that, though church and state have separate offices and functions, the overruling end of Reformation requires not competition but loving cooperation.

Indeed, it may come to appear that "Governor" Winthrop is the most important "religious" influence on the Massachusetts colony before the arrival (in September 1633) of John Cotton and a number of other famous Puritan clergymen. For, as we shall see, it was his court which was to make the landmark decision to extend the Charter-based status of "Freeman" to all male church members; and, at the outset at least, it was the power of his own personality which held out against the determined critique of Roger Williams. Arriving on the same ship that brought the overpriced commodities, Williams was at first greeted by Winthrop as "a godly minister" (Y, 34). A short two months later, however, Winthrop could recognize Williams' Separatism as a sectarian threat to the chartered evolution of a unified Puritan state. And once this crucial problem begins to take form, it becomes a necessary interest—in a "Journal" first marked by accidental variety.

———

Formal Separation has, of course, already been formally denied: the "call" Wilson received to the congregation at Boston was not meant to imply a repudiation of the "orders" he had taken in the Church of England. Now, with Wilson unavailable for advice and consent, it falls to a more or less uninstructed "court holden at Boston" to write, to Mr. Endicott of the Salem church, what amounts to a letter of reprimand for their implicit endorsement of Separatism:

> whereas Mr. Williams had refused to join with the congregation at Boston because they would not make a public declaration of their repentance for having communion with the churches of England while they lived there, and besides had declared his opinion that the magistrate might not punish the breach of the Sabbath nor any other . . . breach of the First Table, therefore they marveled they would choose him [as teacher] without advising with the Council, and withal desiring him that they would forbear to proceed till they had conferred about it. (Y, 37)

It is hard not to recognize "they marveled" as a powerful understatement; and even the uninitiated can identify *some* sense of urgency in this curious rhetorical exercise—of copying or paraphrasing a letter not recorded in the court's official minutes.[20] Indeed, the meanings are almost too many.

The passage announces the beginning of "the public breach" between Williams and the Boston congregation, which maintains a policy of "nominal allegiance to the mother church." Or it portrays the menacing first moment in the campaign to suppress the forces of radical dissent, of which Williams is always made to seem the captain. Or it marks the first time the Massachusetts magistrates think to intervene in the affairs of a particular (supposedly autonomous) church; and indeed Winthrop seems to imply that his most secular "Council" ought to have some sort of veto power in church appointments.[21] Most pointedly, however, it announces Winthrop's determined opposition to any word or act which would give the lie to the protestations of loyalty made by the migrants he led out of England in 1630: reformers they were known to be; but having drunk in their first "hope and part . . . in the common salvation" from the breasts of a "dear Mother" church,[22] none need repent not having been a Separatist in theory before the group decision to become part of an overseas reformed congregation. The reason might be ideological—the Church of England was a corrupted but still a true church; or merely pragmatic. There was absolutely no point arousing, back in England, determined opposition where there had been only insufficient attention. Or it might be, in the last supposable sense of the term, political: Separatism stood for the need to sign off from discussion with those who thought otherwise; to run toward that extreme at which all parties could have all matters their very own way, provided only their willingness to let their interest group become as small as it needed therefore to be. Not so much "a pope in every parish," as they would learn to worry back in England; but every conscientious man his own pope, bishop, minister, and congregation. A place Winthrop was determined not to go.[23]

But if Winthrop holds back from a full explanation of his opposition to Williams' perilous "foreign policy," he is positively tight-lipped on an internal matter of equal significance. The official *Records* of the Massachusetts Bay Company report that on May 18, 1631, it was agreed that "for time to come no man shall be admitted to the freedom of this body politick, but such as are members of some of the churches within the limits of the same."[24] And of that same meeting Winthrop's "Journal" records only the (prior?) fact that "all the freemen of the commons were sworn to the government" (Y, 38). If any of these newly sworn freemen were not, at that moment, members of any church, then Winthrop could well have been guilty, in Williams' eyes, of entering into a prayerful relation with the unregenerate. The more astounding fact, however, is that the term "freeman" is being completely redefined and, with that verbal change, the charter of a trading company is being transformed into something like a constitution. By "freeman," the king's charter seemed to mean something like "stockholder"—anyone who held shares in the "Company of the Massachusetts Bay," incorporated to encourage and to regulate, from England, a profitable overseas plantation.[25] Now it has to mean something like "duly enfranchised citizen."

As Edmund Morgan has lucidly explained, Winthrop and a few of his fellow investors could, by right of charter, have decided to rule the colonial territory of Massachusetts as their very own little oligarchy. The small band of investor-freemen who had actually emigrated would be required to meet four times a year to make all needful laws ("not contrary" to those of "our realm of England")[26] and to elect, once a year, a governor, a deputy governor, and a maximum of eighteen assistants; and the same few men could have gone right on choosing themselves from among themselves. But they did not. Guided by Winthrop, no doubt, they opened the status of freeman to some 116 male citizens at that meeting in May 1631 and, henceforth, to all male citizens who should be able to meet the entrance requirements of some Massachusetts church. To be sure, these requirements were about to become quite stringent, and it has been possible to criticize Winthrop and his associates for setting up a religious test for citizenship; or, for those who wish to follow the political plot in all its thickness, for stipulating that the newly enfranchised freemen should elect only the assistants and that this standing council should elect a governor and a deputy from its own ranks. To these charges of liberal default it has seemed relevant to reply that, even so circumscribed, the franchise was more widely available in New England than in Old. But Morgan's own emphasis remains cogent: the sense of community outlined in the "Model"—of a civil society designed to protect that "most perfect of all bodies," made up of "Christ and his church," seemed to require a saintly quorum.[27] And so the principle of "Member Franchise," the first plank of an effective "sanctocracy," was firmly if quietly put in place.

Quietly even in the privacy of a journal, as if even there Winthrop hesitated to say out loud that the king's charter, in which persons on various sides of all sorts of emergent issues would place their trust or rest their case, was not in fact being followed out to the letter; or perhaps that he himself—the quintessential "magistrate," as he appears in many thumbnail accounts[28]—had almost as keen a sense as Roger Williams himself that there had to be a Spirit beyond all the Laws. It might be a little precious to say that the alarmingly brief entry for May 17, 1631, speaks volumes for Winthrop's political caution. But it is certainly true that not much of the rich "constitutional" material that follows can be understood without some grasp of what that brief entry reveals and conceals. Indeed, the memory of the spiritual generosity just barely marked in this place will control the tone of much of the political recording that is to follow. As if Winthrop would remember much more than he would dare record.

Meanwhile, distractions abound: "one Philip Ratcliffe" must "lose his ears, and be banished" for his "scandalous invectives against our churches and government" (Y, 38); letters from Ferdinando Gorges to Christopher Gardiner and Thomas Morton discover the ever-present threat of conspiracy; a neighbor congregation falls into the belief that "the churches of Rome were true churches" (Y, 39), and one "man of a very violent spirit" (Y, 42) maintains his position loudly enough to draw in the magistrates; a "young fellow" is whipped "for soliciting an Indian squaw to incontinency" (Y, 40); the governor himself gets lost for a night and takes refuge in the "little house of Sagamore John" which he has to hold against an Indian squaw (Y, 40–41). More personally still: "The governor and some company with him" set about exploring the adjacent neighborhoods, comfortably naming the features they pleasantly observe—"Beaver Brook," "Adam's Chair" (in honor of Winthrop's eleven-year-old son), "Masters Brook," "Mount Feake," "Spott Pond," "Cheese Rock" (Y, 43–44). John Seelye reads the pleasure of these latter passages as evidence of a certain esthetic of landscape holding out just below the Puritans' more famous and more determined sense of typological self-placement.[29] But this easy appropriation of the happily natural is only one note among very many. And none of these miscellaneous interests is allowed to last for very long.

Presently, Winthrop needs to deal with persons protesting something like taxation without representation. Ordered by the General Court to pay their share of the cost of "the fortifying of the new town," the principal men of Watertown "delivered their opinions that it was not safe to pay moneys after that sort, for fear of bringing themselves and posterity into bondage." Summons follow, vigorous debate occurs, and the protesters finally declare themselves convinced. But Winthrop, wary enough of recording too much, sees also the danger of explaining less than he knows for sure. So he takes the occasion to provide a little unit of political instruction:

> The ground of their error was for that they took the government to be no other but as of a mayor and aldermen, who have not power to make laws or raise taxations without the people. But understanding this government was rather in the nature of a Parliament, and that no assistant could be chosen but by the freemen who had likewise the power to remove the assistants and put in others, and therefore at every General Court . . . they had free liberty to confer and propound anything concerning the same, . . . they were fully satisfied, and so their submission was accepted and their offence pardoned. (Y, 44–45)

Nothing ever pleases Winthrop better than the reestablishment of just this sort of sweet consensus, and so the moment passes.[30] But it is one the later governor-historian Thomas Hutchinson might well have included in his chronicle of American constitutional mistakes. Indeed, had there been present some hostile witness—Thomas Morton, for example—he might have asked Winthrop what exactly he meant by the phrase "in the nature of a Parliament"; and, depending on the answer, he might well have anticipated the antic Loyalist Peter Oliver in suggesting that the American Revolution had begun *ab origine*.[31]

Leaving the future to answer these questions, however, Winthrop moves on to another constitutional matter, this one with an intensely personal edge. Recording what transpired at a court in April 1632, Winthrop notices the beginning of the most *un*consensual behavior of Thomas Dudley, who "went away before the Court was ended," and then sent a letter declaring "a resignation of his deputyship and place of assistant." The entry ends with the curt remark that the resignation "was not allowed." Aware of the rivalry between Winthrop and Dudley, the abridged edition of the "Journal" leaps to the next episode of this important story: on May 1, 1632, "[t]he governor and assistants met at Boston to consider of the deputy his deserting his place" (Y, 45). But the full entry for April 3, 1632, reports that "At this court an act was made expressing the Governor's power" (64), and surely this question bears directly on the other; for Dudley's most purely political grievance has precisely to do with Winthrop's interpretation of his own powers. The act itself is unrecorded in the court minutes, probably because it expressed some further interpretation of the charter's "General Court" as something "in the nature of a Parliament"; and one is left to wonder whether it was approved before or after Dudley's surprising departure.

What the follow-up meeting determines is that, though the principal motive of Dudley's resignation had been an honorable concern for "public peace"—"he must needs discharge his conscience in speaking freely and he saw that bred disturbance"—still "he could not leave his place except by the same power that put him in." Yet the court of assistants cannot persuade this stubborn man "to continue till the General Court" (Y, 45), a bare eight days away. And then, in the most revealing single entry of the "Journal" so far, there breaks loose the all-hell of personal difference. Reminded of some sharp bargains he had made "with some poor men" who were "members of the same congregation," Dudley replies in "hot words" that he had not come to the court to be insulted and that the governor's mind was showing a "weakness" in the area of market economy. Loath to quote himself, perhaps, and bearing these speeches "with more patience than he had done . . . at another [unspecified] time," the governor refrains from pointing out that, though his "Model" had meant to invoke a rule of "Charity," it nevertheless assumed, a fortiori, "the doing of mere Justice to a poor man in regard of some particular contract"; for otherwise "the poor, and despised" might indeed "rise up against their superiors, and shake off their yoke."[32] But Winthrop does not hesitate to raise (again) the question of Dudley's bestowing too much "cost about wainscoting and adorning his house in the beginning of a plantation." Dudley defends his house on the grounds of "warmth" and reminds the governor that nothing is at issue beyond a few "clapboards nailed to the walls." And all this unwonted expression of the personal transpires "before dinner" (Y, 46).

"After dinner," the governor advises the assistants of an important political rumor—that "the people" mean to suggest "that the assistants might be chosen anew every year, and that the governor might be chosen by the whole Court and not by the assistants only." The very idea throws a certain Mr. Ludlow into a "passion" of political denunciation and, despite the sober reassurance of the rest of the assistants, into a determination to "return back into England" (Y, 46). Nevertheless, the proposal is duly enacted one week later; and this important reversal of a decision made "at [their] first coming" brings the actual government of Massachusetts into closer alignment with its founding charter. Probably Winthrop had thought, at the outset, that a "republican" restriction on the vote for the governorship was a more than fair exchange for the "democratic" expansion of the franchise; but he evidently did nothing to oppose the present revision because "the old governor Jo. W. was chosen over all the rest as before" (Y, 47). This elective outcome will not hold forever, of course, and the generously enfranchised freemen will soon be demanding to see what other powers the charter may actually have assigned them, if only by way of their stockholding precursors; but for the moment Winthrop has no quarrel to pick with his increasingly curious constituency.[33]

Winthrop even manages to make up with his personal rival; and, in general, he composes a scene of perfect harmony and goodwill:

> The deputy governor, Thomas Dudley, Esq., having submitted the validity of his resignation to the vote of the Court, it was adjudged a nullity, and he accepted of his place again, and the governor and he being reconciled the day before, all things were carried very lovingly amongst all, and the people carried themselves with much silence and modesty. (Y, 47)

What indeed could be more lovely, more in accord with the spirit of the "Model," than this scene of reconciliation—of "familiar commerce together in all meekness, gentleness, patience and liberality"?[34] Utopian government, it begins to appear, depends on the love of the governed. And on the governor's loving in return. Lovingly, therefore, Winthrop turns aside a proposal that "every company of trained men might choose their own captain and officers"; and, as part of the same postelection speech, this much-gifted governor lets his lovers know that in the future he will have to "refuse presents from particular persons except they were from the assistants or from some special friends" (Y, 47). He later learns "that many good people were much grieved" at this decision of his "trembling heart," but this fact only adds to the people's sense of love—toward a man who "never had any allowance toward the charge of his place" (Y, 47–48).

Reality returns, perhaps, with the need to advise the congregation at Plymouth on whether "one person might be a civil magistrate, & a ruling elder at the same time" (71) and to notice the continuing strife at Watertown, where a certain John Masters remained "obstinate" in his Separatism, refusing the Sacrament because the congregation had "admitted a member, whom he judged unfit" (72), and where (in fact) a mouse killed a snake.[35] Nor will the grievances of the conscientious Mr. Dudley remain long allayed. This time they will require of Winthrop his longest single entry so far, and of us the suspicion that the problem is more than just personal, that Dudley's ongoing critique of Winthrop's constitutional good faith and evolving political style may represent the threat of a breach of consensus—a separation, so to speak—more fundamental than any that has suggested itself thus far.

Much heat is being generated over Winthrop's refusal to remove his principal residence from Boston to "Newe towne," so much indeed that a panel of ministers returns the opinion that, even if the deputy has himself been responsible for discouraging many other "Boston men from removing," the governor erred in not "conferring with . . . the rest of the assistants" (Y, 49).[36] Winthrop humbly accepts the reprimand from "so many wise and godly friends," but the matter is not allowed to rest there; for Dudley has also charged that the governor has repeatedly assumed "too much authority" and, "after dinner," the Deputy demands—"in love & out of his care of the public . . . and not by way of accusation" (74)—to know "the grounds and limits of his authority, whether by the patent or otherwise."[37] Ever mindful of King Charles, Winthrop takes his stand on the patent alone. In that case, Dudley responds, he should have "no more authority than every assistant (except to call courts and precedency for honor and order)" (Y, 49–50). Sounding just a little less Protestant, Winthrop lays claim to "whatsoever power belonged to a governor by common law or the statutes"; and Dudley, balked perhaps by a fear of superior legal knowledge, flies into a "great fury and passion," which the author of the majestically calm "Model" confesses himself only too willing to match. "Mediation of the mediators" (Y, 50) is required before the deputy can proceed to his "particulars" (74): seven in number, they will try the patience of all but the closest student of local history; the more general reader will be satisfied to observe that Dudley's challenges are launched, predictably, from the platform of strict construction and that Winthrop's answers assume the implied powers of gubernatorial necessity.

Equally predictable, perhaps, is the governor's confident conclusion that his commonsense answers have refuted all charges, inappropriately made against a man who could not be accused of an intent to "wrong any man, or to benefit himself" but who, contrariwise, had been known to disburse "all common charges from out of his own estate"; and who, given his own knowledge of the charter's theory of governmental review, might have refused to answer these annoying charges at all. Indeed, his willingness to respond has spoken of his clear "desire of the public peace" and his wish to disabuse the deputy of his entirely counterfactual suspicion that the governor wished to "gain absolute power, & bring all the assistants under his subjection." Most happily, therefore, this unusual meeting ends amicably and with a prayer. After which, Winthrop remarks, "every man went to his own home" (77). Wainscoted or not.

Yet Winthrop went to a home in Boston and Dudley to one in Newtown, where Winthrop had promised and then decided not to move. The geographic separation itself might comment unfavorably on Winthrop's original wish for a single tight-knit community; or it might invoke the need to "account our selves knit together by a bond of love, even though we were absent from each other many miles."[38] But in any event it will require still another ministerial intervention to make "an end of the difference between the governor & deputy" (79);[39] and just now, with a little less grace in one quarter or another, Dudley might as easily have declared himself altogether unappeased by the governor's self-exculpations. It may be too much to imagine that a fixed sense of Winthrop's extraconstitutional behavior might have caused him to consider the possibility of a separate government within the chartered territory of the Massachusetts. But he might well have gone even more public with his views of Winthrop's unpatented exploits; and the resulting discovery of a procedural and indeed a theoretical disagreement at the very top of a government founded, ambiguously, on the letter of the king's charter and supported, perilously, by the spirit of the saints' own love, might have delivered a heavy blow to an evolving constitution of consensus. Than which, just then, revolution itself could hardly be much worse.

Thus it appears that Discord has more names than that of Roger Williams. And that some threat of Separation may shadow the procedure of the Chartered State as well as the logic of the Particular Church. It might be too much to say that Unity becomes the desired "literary" condition of Winthrop's eclectic and highly various journal. But—with or without reference to the pretext of the "Model"—it begins to look very much like a theme.[40]

———

With Dudley professing himself "well persuaded of the Governor's love to him"— and with both parties agreed to meet about public affairs "without any appearance of breach or discontent" (80)—the "Journal" appears ready to resume its miscellaneous ways. Rumors of a Narragansett "conspiracy" (Y, 50) threaten to spoil its pursuit of American happiness, but apparently the threat is not pressing enough to provoke a fast; indeed, "the prosperous success of the king of Sweden" and "the safe arrival of [the last] ship and all the passengers" are sufficient to tip the balance in favor of a "day of thanksgiving" (81). Williams appears in the next entry but only as part of an extended love feast at Plymouth. "Very kindly entertained, and feasted every day at several houses" (Y, 51), the men of the Bay, as if to prove the spirit of their own non-Separatism, participate in the Sunday service as well, partaking in the "sacrament" and also bearing their part in a sort of oratorio of prophesying orchestrated and conducted by the arch-Separatist himself who, excluded from the Salem church, was serving as teacher at Plymouth.[41] Yet—as Williams seems happy enough to commune with *them*—it all goes off without a hitch.

Untroubled too is the spirit in which Winthrop names a river crossing for the man who had seen them over and back. He also sees to it that a place called "Hue's Crosse"—almost certainly in the sense of "crossing" and probably not in his own jurisdiction in any case—is renamed lest "the papists [find] occasion to say that their religion was first planted in these parts"; but the new name, "Hue's Folly," may indicate the prevailing tone. And certainly it is not with theopolitical anxiety that the governor welcomes his own party to "Wessaguscus where they were bountifully entertained as before with store of turkeys, geese, ducks, etc." (Y, 52); and then, the next day, safely back to Boston.

More serious matters also pass without disturbing the composure: the Dudley family are preserved from the burning of their "house at new town" by a "marvelous delivery"; John Eliot accepts the call to become "teacher to the Church at Rocksbury," despite the efforts of the Boston church to retain him; the people of "Charles town," having secured a minister of their own, are duly "dismissed from the Congregation of Boston"; "the Congregation of Waterton" finally get around to discharging their unruly "Elder R: Browne of his office" (83–84); and Winthrop's own Boston church installs "Mr. Wilson (formerly their teacher)" as now their proper "pastor" and "Oliver [as] a ruling elder," both "by imposition of hands" (Y, 52). Not all these churchly matters show up in the abridged edition of the "Journal," but they are as much a part of its ongoing life as the fact that Oliver's fifteen-year-old son "had his brains beaten out with the fall of a tree which he had felled" (Y, 52); or that an irregular meeting of assistants and "ministers and captains" decides to build a fort at Nantasket in order to prevent the French, with their "divers priests and Jesuits," from gaining a foothold in what was properly called New England; or that the party which went "to view Nantasket" needed to be rescued from extreme cold and hunger "through the Lord's special providence" (Y, 53).

Yet some issues really are more equal, and an intense concern for corporate life and death informs the discovery that "Sir Ferdin. Gorge, & Capt. Mason (upon the instigation of Sir Christ: Gardiner, Morton, & Radcliffe) had preferred a petition to the Lords of the privy Counsel against [them]," and that, in doing so, they had availed themselves of "the letters of some indiscreet persons among [them]." The political danger appears to have been very serious, and yet "through the Lord's good providence, & care of our friends in England, especially Mr. Emll. Downinge (who had married the Governor's sister) & the good testimony given on our behalf by one Capt. Wiggen (who dwelt at Paskat & had been diverse times among us) their malicious practice took not effect" (88). Yet even the favorable outcome cannot alleviate the evident concern. For one thing, Winthrop is here quite willing to name the names of the friends and lovers who effect the Providence; and for another, he is determined to revisit this scene of salvation from political enemies—foreign and domestic—even when the issue is no longer in doubt. Not personal expression but the truth of history appears to demand it.

Several months later, therefore, this same unsettling matter comes in for another, even fuller review. Once again the names are named, with an even more detailed identification:

> Gardiner and Thomas Morton and Philip Ratcliffe (who had been punished here for their misdemeanors) had petitioned to the King and Council against us (being set on by Sir Ferdinando Gorges and Captain Mason who had begun a plantation at Pascataquack and aimed at a general government of New England for their agent there, Captain Neale).

Circumstantial too is the account of the charges made against the Puritan state:

> The petition was of many sheets of paper and contained many false accusations against us . . . accusing us of to intend rebellion, to have cast off our allegiance, and to be wholly separate from the church and laws of England; that our ministers and people did continually rail against the state, church, and bishops there, etc. (Y, 54)

As we have already noticed, certain Tories will repeat these charges in the months leading up to America's moment of *actual* rebellion. Here it is enough to observe that Winthrop's sensitivity about the "separate" status of his quasi-parliamentary government is extremely well founded; and to predict that he will continue to be vigilant in discouraging all local declarations of independence.

And, finally, this second record of catastrophe averted provides a graphic account of how Providence might look when "such of [their] company as were then in England . . . were called before the Council":

> it pleased the Lord our gracious God and protector so to work with the lords and after with the King's Majesty that he said he would have them severely punished who did abuse his governor and the plantation, [and] that the defendants were dismissed with a favorable order for their encouragement. (Y, 54–55)

Blessing following upon blessing, the London contingent is even assured by some members of the council that "his Majesty did not intend to impose the ceremonies of the Church of England" upon them," since it was "the freedom from such things that made people come over to [them]" (Y, 55). This last assurance could hardly be more welcome, even if it expresses only one version of what sovereignty might yet decide. Meanwhile, however, it seems good to have "Sir Richard Saltonstall, Mr. Humfrey, and Mr. Cradock" (Y, 54) in England. And to discover something approaching unanimity in New England; for, to "the answer which was returned to Sir Christopher Gardiner" (94), only the recalcitrant Dudley refuses fully to subscribe.[42]

But even as Winthrop tries to examine the grounds of Dudley's disagreement, other important events press their claim. Confirmed, almost immediately, is the council's sense of why many "people come over to us"; but disconfirmed, at the same time, is the hint that removals in protest of "the ceremonies of the Church of England" might be accepted as a matter of course. For when Cotton, Hooker, and Stone all arrive together (September 4, 1633), along with "many other men of good estates," their story is of having "got out of England with much difficulty"; indeed, Cotton and Hooker have long been "sought for to have been brought into the High Commission" and seem barely to have escaped the "pursuivants" (Y, 55). Yet none of this can quite dim the enthusiasm aroused by these most important new arrivals. Hooker and Stone move on almost immediately to Newtown, where Dudley and other outlanders have been eagerly awaiting the foundation of their own church. Cotton, however, remains in Boston; and Winthrop, with some sense of the significance of the moment he is privileged to witness, bears extended testimony to the exemplary activities of this shining star of international Calvinism.

On Saturday Cotton shows, "out of Canticles 6"—and with the invention that marks his distinctive exegetical imagination—"that some churches [are] as queens, some as concubines, some as damosels, and some as doves, etc."[43] Small wonder, then, if he was immediately "propounded to be admitted a member." Yet this archtheorist of Congregationalism may understand the spirit of its forms better than those who have for several years been living its actual life. Not one to stand upon past reputation or present preaching, "he signif[ies] his desire and readiness to make his confession according to order." His stipulation that it might be sufficient for him to declare "his faith about baptism" might not pass from a lesser man—or from Cotton himself at a later moment in the evolving history of "visible sanctity"[44]—but his admission is exemplary nevertheless. For it includes his reasons for not baptizing the infant "Seaborne" while he was still in danger of an untimely ocean-perishing: "not for want of fresh water," but "because they had no settled congregation there," and "because a minister hath no power to give the seals but in his own congregation." Thus, though Cotton has yet to learn the decorum of a formal profession of experimental saving faith, he is already teaching that a minister is such only in relation to the congregation which has formally called him and that one's entrance into the Church Universal is always and only by way of formal acceptance into some particular manifestation of that invisible body. And if he is moved to give a "modest testimony" on behalf of his wife, requesting "that she not be put to make open confession," a thing not fit for "women's modesty," he nevertheless concedes "that the elders might examine her in private" (Y, 56).

Thus with her consent to "the Confession of Faith made by her husband," both were duly admitted "and their child baptized." And Winthrop does well to savor the moment. For as events unfold, there will be few other scenes of such unanimity. Hooker, could the future be foretold, will drift even further from Cotton's place and position. And what prophetic faith could predict that Cotton's special teachings—plus a violation of the requirements of woman's modesty—will soon enough become the rocks on which the whole enterprise would threaten to split apart?

But as reflection and not prolepsis is the trope of Winthrop's "Journal," the old pace resumes itself. Trading in "Conectecott" and the dissolute behavior of "Capt. Io. Stone" (97) vie for attention with the question of "Mr. Cotton his sitting down": not surprisingly, he has been "desired to diverse places"; still it was "agreed by full consent, that the fittest place for him was Boston" (Y, 57). With a sense of happy climax, therefore, "Mr. Cotton [is] chosen teacher of the congregation of Boston." Winthrop's increasing sense of the complexity of congregational decorum inscribes a detailed account of the multiform exercises of his ordination. In the midst of a curt raising of congregational and then a ceremonious laying on of presbyterial hands, "Mr. Wilson the pastor demanded of him if he did accept" (Y, 58) this call. And while Cotton is answering with the appropriate mixture of personal unworthiness and providential delegation, no one thinks to ask the really important question: will this famous teacher be emphatically teaching the same doctrine as this rather less distinguished pastor will be more routinely preaching?[45] And if not, how will New England's Prime Congregation decide? Ever mindful of suspicion back in England, Winthrop has taught himself to live with the eccentric conscience of his deputy, and he will yet find a way to brave the radical critique of Williams. He might even be able to live with the news that would-be saints at Newtown make a different sort of confession than those at Boston; or with the rumor that Hooker and Stone move to Connecticut to be even farther away from Cotton. But it will strike him between the eyes when Wilson and Cotton, pastor and teacher of his very own congregation, do not seem to share the exact same "faith." And that their differences will amount to a scandal he is bound to record but cannot by himself find a way to dispel. His ecclesiastical subjects are Puritans, after all, and their truth will out.

Yet even with the important arrivals of 1633, the cast of characters for "the most dramatic chapter in the narrative,"[46] is still far from complete: the disputatious Anne Hutchinson is yet to appear, as is the ever-watchful Thomas Shepard; and, though we can easily imagine a scenario in which the colony stands by to watch Cotton and Hooker have it out over the necessity of "preparation,"[47] the story we know as "the Antinomian Controversy" depends absolutely on this remarkable (female) protagonist and her most dedicated (clerical) opponent. Speculation and anticipation aside, however, we need to notice that Winthrop's world has become all at once much less simple and less easy to control, both in fact and in prose. For three full, formative years Winthrop has clearly been the dominant force in the colony—giving, taking, and giving back again, political privileges that might be thought to inhere only in the charter, and even intervening in the affairs of the several churches. And, as Deputy Dudley has had the awkward gift to keep discovering, the reason is only partly that he has been repeatedly elected governor; for that fact itself would have to be explained, on the basis of the charisma of the man or the vision of his "Model." Now—as the drama of the arrival, admission, and ordination of Cotton clearly suggests—someone else seems to be calling the tune; the best Winthrop can do is to try to make his notational prose equal to the task of summarizing developments which, though they seem to go with the territory, could be satisfactorily explained only in a discourse not typical of a journal.

Winthrop never will look back to reevaluate this moment—when his "own" congregation not only admitted but also reveled in the empowerment of a religious thinker whose views of congregational polity might come to seem normative but whose lamblike account of Christian experience never could be made to lie down with the leonine morphologies of the colony's other authorities on the salvation effect. But if his faithful reader were to ask where the mistake was made—where, Bradford fashion, Winthrop might have located the flower of success that contained the seed of failure—the answer might be found just here. For the problem is not only that the pastor and the congregation of Boston have welcomed a teacher whose ideas cannot help but produce cognitive dissonance but also that, more generally, the colony has begun to welcome a class of men whose passion for theological argumentation will make the bold distinctions of Winthrop's "Model" seem primitive indeed. Winthrop's editor rightly observes that "with the arrival of Cotton and Hooker" the opposition to Williams' radicalism would be much "better organized";[48] but it seems just as important to notice that the colony's stake in professional theology has been raised to a new power.

The gain for American literature will be enormous for, given the interests that seem destined to control the notice of British intelligence, Cotton and Hooker would always fail to meet the modest challenge of Donne and Andrews. But the gain will come at considerable expense to Winthrop's vision of social harmony confirmed by a unific account of Christian love. For, where covenant theology is concerned, the Devil is indeed in the details.

For the moment, however, Winthrop's sense of signal success continues pretty much unruffled. Decisive actions are taken to control the effects of an inflation of wages and prices. A first step toward a ministerial "consociation" draws criticism from "Mr. Skelton the Pastor of Salem & Mr. Williams who was removed from Plimouth thither" (102), but Winthrop's dismissal is confident. "The governor and the deputy" fall out again, over taxes to support "the finishing of the fort at Boston," and though Winthrop furnishes us with the details of his refusal of a provocative letter delivered by Mr. Haynes and Mr. Hooker, he lets us know from the outset that the "differences . . . were soon healed" (103–4). A little more solemnly, Winthrop reports the death of "Chikatabut . . . & many of his people" (101) and then, in more detail, that of John Sagamore "and almost all of his people." Winthrop is never completely insensitive to the fate of his Indian friends, but rhetorically at least these deaths are redeemed by John Sagamore's disposition of one of his sons "to be brought up by . . . the pastor of Boston" and his final wish to "go to the Englishman's God," whom many of these dying people "confessed . . . was a good God" (Y, 60).

Meanwhile, at the level of religious "business," "the congregation of Boston met to take order for Mr. Cotton's passage and house, and his and Mr. Wilson's maintenance" (Y, 59–60). And then—though it might have been unseemly to take much comfort in the primitive confessions of a dying race—who could object to the widespread promulgation of conversions of a more serious and elaborate sort? Indeed, only the absence of any prior sense of religion's low ebb could blur the fact that Winthrop's own richly provisioned and famously appointed church was now experiencing something like a revival:

> It pleased the Lord to give special testimony of his presence in the Church of Boston, after Mr. Cotton was called to office there. More were converted and added to the Church than to all the other churches in the Bay. Divers profane and notoriously evil persons came and confessed their sins and were comfortably received into the bosom of the Church. Yea, the Lord gave witness to the exercise of prophecy, so as thereby some were converted and others much edified. (Y, 61)

This triumphant passage stops just short of identifying Cotton with God's own spirit, and we may perhaps forgive this most pious of governors for not recognizing the moment which either began or validated the practice of demanding that one's profession of faith be in fact a particular account of some credible experience of saving grace;[49] but it is impossible to miss the hint of Protestant hubris. For just now, a Jamesian narrator might say, his cup seems full.

Indeed, if Winthrop's often dramatic text were a proper play, we would now begin to look for its "turn" to the darker side. Untroubled by any theology of fate, however, Winthrop rushes on to include the churchly "discipline" of the much-wedded but otherwise hapless Mr. Wilson in the general reception of the Spirit's special gift; and, adding earth to heaven, to sacralize Cotton's timely revelation that "the minister's maintenance" should be "raised out of the weekly contribution" (Y, 61). So it requires some more than ordinary suspension of suspense not to rejoice in the fact that, beginning with his very next entry, Winthrop must now turn his attention to the discouraging words of Roger Williams. For, although the accumulating protest of Williams will materially assist our own wish to disbelieve that Boston's elders, of whom John Cotton has been declared the undisputed paragon, and Boston's citizen-saints, of whom John Winthrop is the repeatedly elected epitome, reflect a marriage made somewhere in the Heaven of Holy History, we may well remind ourselves that Williams is going to lose. Happily, for our literary interests, not all Puritans stand together on all issues. Less happily, perhaps, their combinations may form, dissolve, and re-form in ways that disturb our sense of liberalism's proper logic. Williams will win, if at all, only in the very long run. And for the moment, at least, Winthrop and Cotton will enjoy a victory together.

At issue before all else, perhaps, is Williams' pure-hearted contention that the English, whatever their sanction, "could have no title" to American lands "except they compounded with the Natives" (Y, 61). The reason of this altogether correct belief may lie a little deeper than we usually go when we find our own moral sense confirmed in the Clear Conscience of Past Prophecy. But we need to re-member that it implies an insult to the defunct King James and to his lively son that, within a specifically religious venue, is about the same as saying that nei-ther is wearing any clothes; so that—exactly as with Williams' earlier insistence that Massachusetts declare its full separation from the self-disabled Church of England—the straight-standing Winthrop (if not the far-fleeing Cotton) has got to be concerned about the worldly relation of purity and policy. That is to say: even if the Puritan immigrants had been fully able and freely willing to pay the Indians' price, and even if these Children of the Forest could have been made to grasp the European oxymoron that linked land and ownership, they could hardly do the deal without offending their sovereign.[50] The word would get out: the king of England has no more title to New England than a rabbit; less, even, sup-posing the rabbit were actually living in that disputed place. It could get ugly. Maybe Endicott can get his Salem colleague to retract.

Questioned by a letter from the governor, however, Williams replies, "sub-missively," that his "treatise" had been written "for the private satisfaction of the governor, etc of Plymouth," that it had stirred beyond that sphere only because Winthrop himself had "required a copy"; he even offers "his book or any part of it to be burnt" (Y, 62). Appearing at the next court, Williams "gives satisfac-tion . . . of his loyalty"; and "so it was left," Winthrop concludes, "& nothing done in it." A month later, however, "Mr. Cotton and Mr. Wilson" are advising "the Governor & Council" about the "offensive passages" in Williams' treatise; pour-ing over his "obscure & implicate" prose, they discover that he has not *clearly* said anything indefensible and decide that "upon his retraction & taking an oath of allegiance to the King it should be passed over" (109). And so, for the time being, the matter is allowed to rest. A providential respite, as other issues press.

The murder of Captain Stone—by the "Pequins" (Y, 62), as Winthrop believes[51]—points in a direction the "Journal" would prefer not to pursue, but this unhappy notice is balanced by the fact that one of the few Indian children to survive the more local outbreak of smallpox has been named "Know God," in reference to the Indians' familiar "Me no know God" (Y, 63). The newly insti-tuted Thursday Lecture provides an opportunity for Endicott to debate the rela-tivism of Cotton's doctrine of women's veils. Continuing evidence of "the Lord's gracious presence" is afforded by the exemplary conversion and church accep-tance of Winthrop's son Stephen, "a youth of 14 years of age" (64); and of Satan's opposing power in the "scruple of conscience" (112) by which some members of Charlestown begin to doubt the propriety of their dismissal from the church of Boston. But we do not go for long without encountering an issue that strikes at the root. And so, upon notification of the "General Court to be held the 14 day of the (3) month called May," the deputed representatives of the freemen let it be known that they "desired a sight of the patent"—from which they duly learn that "all their laws would be made," by the freemen themselves, "at the General Court" (Y, 63–64).

Still far from ready to turn on his constituents, Winthrop portrays himself a model of meekness, patiently explaining that "when the patent was granted the number of freemen was supposed to be . . . so few that they might well join in making laws, but now they were grown to so great a body as it was not possible for them to make or execute laws, but they must choose others for the purpose." Furthermore, in his elitist judgment, "they were not [yet] furnished with a sufficient number of men qualified for the business [and] neither could the commonwealth bear the loss of time of so many as must intend it." He offers them, instead, the power to appoint a "certain number of men" who, "upon summons from the Governor," might meet "to review all laws, etc., and to refer what they found amiss" (Y, 65). Refusing this compromise, however, the freemen win back a version of their charter privilege: henceforth there will be four General Courts every year, with the whole body of freemen present "only at the court of election of magistrates"; at the other three, every town should send deputies who shall "assist in making laws, disposing lands, etc." (66). Commentators regularly point out that this "republican" compromise leaves undecided the exact relation between the fully chartered assistants and the newly created deputies of the freemen and that—until 1644, when the assistants finally win their power of veto— the relation between these two legislative bodies will be marked by considerable tension.[52]

For the moment, however, nothing can spoil Winthrop's determination to take things in perfect good humor: "Many good orders were made at this court" which was "carried very peaceably, notwithstanding that some of the assistants were questioned by the freemen for some errors in their government" (Y, 66). What makes this harmonious note especially significant is that at this same court inhabitants of Newtown, complaining of "straitness for want of land, especially meadow," had petitioned the court "to look out either for enlargement or removal" (Y, 65); for when the push of this desire for land comes to the shove of an actual removal, Winthrop will be almost as distressed as Bradford had been in similar circumstances. More significantly still, to Winthrop personally at least, "[t]he Court chose a new Governor, viz. Thomas Dudley, Esq., the former deputy" (Y, 66). Winthrop may feel somewhat reassured by the fact that the freemen—taking the advice of John Cotton's timely instruction that "a magistrate ought not to be turned into the condition of a private man without just cause" (Y, 65–66)—had left him his place among the assistants. But clearly the electorate has meant to send Winthrop a message about their investment in the charter. Which he would have got, no doubt, even if they had not replaced him with his prime political antagonist. And though he will later delete his concluding comment, we may well remark its generous, irenic function at the moment: with the court held in Winthrop's Boston rather than Dudley's Newtown, "the new governor and assistants were together entertained at the house of the old governor, as before" (Y, 66). Truly a Model outcome.

Significant too is the fact that this political revolution does very little to change Winthrop's interest or his tone; not given to sulk in either his tent or his "Journal," he keeps his eye on the fate of a colony which remains "his" in purpose if not in power.[53] New arrivals pour into the Bay almost monthly, as "godly people in England now apprehend a special hand of God in raising this plantation"; on the other hand, "many private letters" reveal that "the departure of so many of the best, both ministers and Christians," has raised the "apprehension of some evil days to come upon England" (Y, 67). Meanwhile, back in England, Mr. Craddock was placed under "strict charge to deliver in the patent"; reliably informed of this order, the (new) governor and his council decide "not to return any answer or excuse" (Y, 68). Faced with a copy of the order itself, the governor and his assistants reply that the charter could be surrendered only by "a general court, which was to be held in September next" (123); and they press on with their fort at "Castle Island" (Y, 68). Clearly the transatlantic plot is becoming more complicated. And the moment is approaching when the leaders of Massachusetts will have to decide whether they do or do not rest the sum of their authority on their precious charter.

Nor is there any rest from internal difficulties: Williams is lying low, but relations with the people of Plymouth are beginning to be strained, particularly over Governor Dudley's interference in their handling of the murder of John Hocking at their outpost in Kennebeck; and the people of Newtown are continuing to "discover Connecticut River, intending to remove their town thither" (Y, 68), where both Plymouth and the Pequots have a competing claim. And this latter question occupies a very long entry for September 1634. The problem might at first seem quite simple: having leave from the last General Court "to look out for some place of enlargement or removal," the representatives of Newtown now ask permission actually "to remove to Connecticut"; yet "this matter was debated divers days, and many reasons alleged pro and con." Even this might look like nothing more than standard Puritan consensus building, but full accord never is reached; and indeed what "unity" could ever be revealed by a decision in favor of physical separation? The men and women of Dudley's new town might still profess a perfect identity of spiritual purpose—"knit together" though "absent . . . many miles"—but were they any less *gone*?[54] And, with a lively spirit of Christian community so expressly the goal, what could Hooker mean by calling it a "fundamental error that towns were set so near each to other"? Economic men might allege, as the principal reasons for their removal, "the want of accommodation for their cattle," the great "fruitfulness and commodiousness of Connecticut," and the "strong bent of their spirits to remove thither" (Y, 70); and commentators might infer a religious leader's wish to be "safer from royal intervention" or to be "independent of [Winthrop's] and Cotton's Boston."[55] But other arguments may have cogency as well.

The first of which we can hardly fail to recognize as Winthrop's own—"that in point of conscience they ought not to depart from us, being knit to us in one body, and bound by oath to seek the welfare of this commonwealth." Winthrop duly adds a multiform argument "in point of state and civil policy" (Y, 70), but the argument quickly shifts from pragmatic substance to political form, as the deputies, who have voted 15 to 10 in favor of the departure, refuse to concede a "negative voice" to the assistants, who fear they will lose the "strength to balance the greater number of deputies" (Y, 71). So they agree to keep "a day of humiliation to seek the Lord" and, before they meet again, they all listen to Mr. Cotton show how "magistracy, ministry, and people" all "had a negative voice . . . and that yet the ultimate resolution ought to be with the whole body of the people" (Y, 71–72). And then, with the "whole body of the people" drowning in this oil upon the waters, "the Court went on cheerfully":

> Although all were not satisfied about the negative voice to be left to the magistrates, yet no man moved aught about it, and the congregation of Newtown came and accepted of such enlargement as had formerly been offered them by Boston and Watertown, and so the fear of their removal to Connecticut was removed. (Y, 72)

The matter will come up again, of course, and the people of Newtown will actually begin their removal to Connecticut in November 1635. For the moment, however, Winthrop takes quite as much pleasure in the rhetorically assisted victory of sweet consensus as he does in the preservation of a veto power among the assistants. And we misread him seriously if we see anything like irony in his admiration of the ministry's power to mystify politics. Having begun the ideology of Massachusetts with the mysterious theology of his very own "Model," he remains a great admirer of the power of distinction to annul difference.

And never more so than just now, when

> there came over a copy of the commission granted to the 2 archbishops and 10 other of the council to regulate all plantations, and power given them or any 5 of them to call in all patents, to make laws, to raise tithes and portions for ministers, to remove and punish governors, and to hear and determine all causes, and inflict all punishments, even death itself. (72)

Winthrop rightly understands that all this is intended specifically for Massachusetts, and the reliable knowledge that

> there were ships & soldiers provided . . . to compel us by force to receive a new governor, and the discipline of the Church of England, and the laws of the Commissioners, occasioned the magistrates and deputies to hasten our fortifications and to discover [their] minds each to other (Y, 72), which grew to this Conclusion, *viz.* . . . (129)

Winthrop's editor points out that the information missing here is filled in by a later entry, in which all agreed "not to accept [a general governor] but to defend [their] lawful possessions (if [they] were able); otherwise to avoid and protract" (Y, 77). But the ellipsis speaks loudly enough in its own right—of the hesitation to admit, on the record, that Massachusetts is ready to resist any direct interference in the providentially assisted evolution of its own "due form of government."

Yet the provocation must not come from the New England side. For when the assistants are informed that "the ensign at Salem was defaced, viz., one part of the red cross taken out," much fear is expressed that "it would be taken as an act of rebellion." The truth, Winthrop insists, is that the attack was upon nothing more than "a relic of Antichrist" (Y, 73), but the matter will vex the "Journal" through a number of future entries: the assistants write to one of their agents in England that they "purpose to punish the offenders," despite their doubts about "the lawful use of the cross in the ensign" (Y, 76); a later meeting of ministers finds them "divided," and so the matter is "deferred . . . to another meeting" (Y, 77); later still, when Endicott is called "to answer for defacing the cross," the court can agree no more than the ministers, and the matter is once again "deferred" (Y, 78). Eventually the defacer of the standard is formally censured and "disabled for one year from bearing any public office." As Winthrop presents the matter, the court declined "any heavier sentence because they were persuaded he [acted] out of tenderness of conscience and not of any evil intent." Yet the censure is portentous enough to indicate just how close to the fault line Endicott's sword had struck: acting rashly and "without discretion" and "taking upon him more authority than he had," he has been guilty of "laying a blemish . . . upon the rest of the magistrates as if they would suffer idolatry" and of "giving occasion to the state of England to think ill of [them]" (Y, 80). Evidently the foreign policy continues to involve no more than de facto separation: speak no evil of Our Old Home, not even symbolically.

In the end, however, Endicott will weather this censure; and he will live out his year of political inability at the same moment when Williams—who appears to have provoked Endicott to a deed of defiance—will be placing himself beyond the pale. Personality matters, perhaps, but so does an important difference of fundamental doctrine: Endicott wants the state which supports his church to join with him, once for all, in some unambiguous renunciation of all former ties with a church that smacks of Antichrist. So it appears does Williams, whose desire for churchly purity, equal to that of any man, seems no longer able to contain itself. But Williams wants not only a formal separation from the corrupted churches of England but also a credible degree of separation of the congregational churches from the civil government of Massachusetts which, under the watch of Winthrop, has not hesitated to intervene when a particular church has threatened to become unruly; and which, in any event, has founded itself on the (unchartered) rock of church-member-franchise. With Williams, therefore, much more is at issue than a prudent foreign policy: nothing less, in fact, than a Puritan "constitution."[56]

For the moment, however, while the public mind is exercised about "the cross in the ensign," it is quite enough that Williams is once again "teaching publicly against the King's patent," naming "our great sin in claiming right thereby to this country," and "terming the churches of England Antichristian" (Y, 76–77). It begins to appear that the men of Massachusetts could solve some of their problems by simply sending back the patent as ordered; but then they would have either to conform to the Church of England or declare that Winthrop's "Model" had been in fact a declaration of independence; and to look to his "Reasons," perhaps, to discover right to claim native lands without purchase.[57] Instead, however, they hope to wait out the order to surrender the charter, silence the rash and simplistic speech of Williams and, in point of ominous fact, go on playing the Pequots off against the Narragansetts, as both these warring groups are sending agents in pursuit of peaceful alliance (Y, 74–76).

Summoned to a meeting of the governor, the assistants, and "all the ministers," Williams is "clearly confuted" in his belief that a magistrate who tenders an
oath to an unregenerate man "thereby [has] communion with a wicked man in
the worship of God." Not his strongest point, it may appear; and perhaps we are
justified in believing that the corrigible Endicott at first agreed with Williams
but at last "gave place to the truth" (Y, 79). But Williams *will* not let it be; and, for
the moment at least, his protests seem even more important than the deputies'
wish for a larger body of "positive laws" (Y, 81). Thus, "at the General Court [of
July 5, 1635], Williams of Salem was summoned and did appear." Evidently he
has accepted the position of teacher at Salem while "being under question before
the magistrates and churches for diverse dangerous opinions, viz."—"1. that the
magistrates ought not to punish the breach of the First Table otherwise than in
such cases as did disturb the civil peace; 2. That he ought not to tender an oath to
an unregenerate man; 3. That a man ought not to pray with such, though wife,
child, etc." (Y, 82). After "much debate," his opinions are "adjudged by all magistrates and ministers (who were desired to be present) to be erroneous and very
dangerous, and the calling of him to office at that time was judged a great contempt of authority." And then, finally, this Court-Augmented-by-Ministers offers
time to both Williams and the Salem church "either to give satisfaction . . . or else
to expect the sentence" (Y, 83).

Asked "for what, precisely," someone in authority might well have
answered—as Winthrop would himself answer Anne Hutchinson a little later—
"The Court knows wherefore and is satisfied." Or, perhaps it seemed self-evident
to (almost) all concerned, given the political climate of 1634–35, that Williams'
teaching about the magistrate and the First Table was, on its face, a disturbance
to the civil peace; for this implied all by itself a rejection of England. True, the
Lord had seemed to frustrate, just now, the design of those who "had built a great
ship to send over the General Governor"—by causing it to break asunder while
"being launched" (Y, 81–82); but godly men knew better than to presume another miracle. And besides, the matter involved far more than foreign policy: the
assembled intelligentsia of New England have just signified that they too wish to
maintain a system of civil penalties for religious crimes. To that extent, as Perry
Miller has patiently explained, their religious revolution remains perfectly loyal
to English (and medieval) precedent.[58]

Still, as if to signify the common sense that political precedent is sometimes
as important as substantial truth, Winthrop adds the following disclaimer:

It being professedly declared by the ministers (at the request of the
Court to give their advice) that he who should obstinately maintain such

opinions (whereby a church might run into heresy, apostasy, or tyranny, and yet the civil magistrate could not intermeddle) were to be removed, and that the other churches ought to request the magistrate to do so. (Y, 83)

One hesitates to attach too much significance to Winthrop's parenthetical syntax, but he appears to be saying, nervously, that several congregations may, in extremis, invite the civil magistrate to intervene on their collective behalf. Which is to say that the ministers have, just now, in the case of Williams, given formal endorsement to a "Way" that has been developing from the first; and that—Miller's "Orthodoxy" notwithstanding—Winthrop is the inventor of that Way. Its intention is not to continue or to reject the example of England but simply to recognize that a truly Christian State will value Loving Consensus above Strict Polity. Now, if only the love will last.

————

Not perfectly, it appears, at least in the immediate aftermath. While the expected sentencing of Williams impends, the court rejects Salem's petition for more land because its church "had chosen Mr. Williams their teacher while he stood under question of authority and so offered contempt to the magistrates." Stung, "the Church of Salem wrote to other churches to admonish the magistrates of this as a heinous sin"; and for this "at the next general court their deputies were not received" (Y, 83). Then—after a long entry dealing with a more literal summer storm (151–53) and a shorter one concerning a French intrusion at Penobscot (153)—Williams sounds his own note of protest: sick and "not able to speak," he writes to the Salem church "that he could not communicate with the churches of the Bay, neither would he communicate with them except they would refuse communion with the rest" (153). Much later, Winthrop will repeat the rumor that this extravagant seeker of purity had got himself to the point where he "refused communion with all, save his own wife" (300), but even now he regards Williams' extremism as insupportable. Thus his only comment is on behalf of the people of Salem: "the whole church was grieved herewith" (Y, 83). And grievance, unless it can be redressed, may be the next thing to banishment.

While yet we wait for the court to issue its ruling, other events will not. Endicott defends "the letter formerly sent from Salem to the other churches against the magistrates & deputies[,] . . . but the same day he came & acknowledged his fault": more "tenderness of conscience," one presumes. At the other end of the social scale, "diverse lewd servants" run away and must be captured and "severely whipped" (154). Plymouth must be aided, modestly, in opposing the French at

Penobscot (155–56). "Great ships" arrive with a number of very important passengers—including Thomas Shepard, soon to replace Hooker at Newtown, a returning "Mr. Wilson Pastor of Boston" (156), "Io. Winthrop the younger with commission . . . to begin a plantation at Conectecott" (157) and, not the least, "one Mr. Henry Vane, son and heir to . . . [the] Controller of the King's house . . . who forsook the honors and preferments of the Court, to enjoy the ordinances of Christ in their purity here" (Y, 84). Clearly Winthrop is reassured to report these significant arrivals. But none of this happy news can lessen the suspense surrounding the open case against Williams.

Unable to guess that he and then "Governor" Vane will be on opposite sides of a controversy even more far reaching than the political one of the present, Winthrop dares to pair him with Williams. On November 1, 1635, "Mr. Vane was admitted a member of the Church of Boston," as if this triumphant conversion of an English Nobleman into an American Saint could in some manner offset the events of the General Court for October 8, when "Mr. Williams, the teacher of Salem, was again convented." Once again, "all the ministers in the Bay [are] desired to be present" with the court; and before this mixed yet tightly "knit" and solemnly consenting "body," Williams is charged with the authorship of two offending letters, one to all the churches, "complaining of the magistrates for injustice, extreme oppression, etc.," and the other to the Salem church seeking "to persuade them to renounce communion with all the churches in the Bay as full of Antichristian pollution." Justifying both letters, which nearly all the members of this civil-religious assembly regard as questionable in theory and dangerous in political tendency, he is offered and eagerly accepts the option of disputing his views on the spot. And so—in a gesture so entirely expressive of an unfolding government by advice and consensus, one that John Cotton will later regard as a paradigm of its policy of instructing a wayward conscience beyond all possibility of persecution—"Mr. Hooker was appointed to dispute with him." Fruitlessly, as it comes to appear; so that, as if it were unthinkable that Williams should persuade Hooker or anybody else who happened to be listening, "the Court sentenced him to depart out of our jurisdiction within 6 weeks, all the ministers save one approving the sentence" (Y, 85).

Williams may not have been given his due, but he certainly has evoked and then enjoyed (so to speak) an extraordinary amount of process. Clearly the leaders of the colony have been making it up as they went along, but surely it is appropriate for us to notice that they do not have much to go on by way of precedent, liberal or otherwise. And if someone should ask what might have happened if the assembled corps of ministers had come to disagree with the authorized body of magistrates and deputies, the answer could only be a denial of the supposition: for these two groups of officials—performing "separate" but complementary functions in a state that was both holier but also much smaller than England—knew each other so well that, given any real chance of a failure of consensus, things would never have come to the present pass. If the ministers had been coming, all along, to agree with Williams, the local deputies to the court would have noticed and reported this fact, and the governor and his trusted assistants would have had to make such explanation to England as seemed possible. But if there had been *any* chance of their coming to agree—that the example of England had to be utterly scorned and execrated, or that their own churches must make no common cause with any form of civil magistracy—they would very likely have become Separatists long ago. In which case nothing like a "great" migration could ever in fact have materialized.

With more than a whimper, perhaps, but considerably less than a bang, the drama falls away from its climax: "[Williams] at his return home refused communion with his own church, who openly disclaimed his errors and wrote an humble submission to the magistrates acknowledging their fault in joining with Mr. Williams in that letter to the churches against them" (Y, 85). Much has been written about the heroism of Roger Williams and the timely importance of some of his provocative ideas; and conversely, of course, about the reactionary nature of the puritanic government which "persecuted" him.[59] Yet exile from a restrictive colonial territory is not the worst thing a person can endure, especially when he has had a fair chance to observe that, upon sober hearing and full review, almost no one in that territory appears to agree with him. The worst we can say about the generality of his official antagonists, perhaps, is that they were unwilling to go on hearing, day after day, ideas that would have canceled their project; and about Winthrop, in particular, that though he cherished the notion of a unity based on holy love, he would teach himself to settle, now and then, for one based on enforced submission to recognized authority.

We do not know if Winthrop actually assisted Williams in his timely escape from the colony of the Massachusetts to the territories that would eventually be chartered as Rhode Island, or what it would mean if in fact he did. All Winthrop will tell us is that, having granted him liberty to stay in their jurisdiction until the spring in exchange for good behavior, "the governor and assistants . . . were credibly informed" that he continued "to entertain company in his house and to preach to them, even of such points as he had been censured for"; that, when summoned, he refused to come down to Boston "to be shipped" to England; and that when a delegation sent "to apprehend him and carry him aboard" a waiting ship "came at his house they found he had been gone 3 days before, but whither they could not learn" (Y, 87). And though Williams will later claim that the "ever honored governor Mr. Winthrop privately wrote to [him] to steer [his] course to Narragansett Bay and Indians,"[60] Winthrop here comments unfavorably on that very prospect:

> he had drawn above 20 persons to his opinion and they were intended to erect a plantation about the Narragansett Bay, from whence the infection would easily spread into these churches (the people being many of them much taken with the apprehension of his godliness). (Y, 87)

He also implies, of course, that the unanimity displayed in the recent judgment of Williams might not last forever, as "the people" (if not the magistrates) were capable of being misled by the appearance—or even perhaps the reality—of extraordinary piety. Indeed, as Winthrop is forced to confess, Williams "had so far prevailed at Salem" that many persons there "(especially . . . devout women) did embrace his opinions and separated from the churches for this cause" (Y, 87). What exactly are we to make of that "devotion"?

It is tempting to speculate that Williams served Winthrop in somewhat the same way as a fiercely independent and incorrigibly pure Bronson Alcott served the better-tempered, less reckless Waldo Emerson—as an example of where idealism might lead if not diluted, occasionally, by a stiff dose of prudence. With an arch-Platonist's disbelief in the body, Alcott could not keep (vegetable) food on his family's table; Puritan in another sense, Williams was in danger of leaving the table whenever anybody else sat down—the communion table, as he himself professed in both word and deed, and even the dinner table, if any natural man or woman thought to ask a grace. Winthrop, we might speculate, would have continued to pray with his scapegrace Henry, if only that unlucky boy had lived through his swimming escapade. More important, perhaps, he would *insist* on administering oaths of loyalty to anyone who meant to make a home in the territory covered by the king's patent; for if saints themselves had to promise, how could one presume the obedience of errant strangers? As for the patent itself, it was, in all likelihood, nothing more than the king's promise not to interfere, so long as all things appeared to go smoothly: why would *any* ocean migrant want to make waves? And—though Williams seems not to have raised the point of restricting the franchise to church members—surely the "Model" implied that something very like that was of the essence. For the elect are those who discover "the image" of Christ in one another, which they "cannot but love" as they necessarily love themselves;[61] and when Winthrop and his Saints left England in order to (re)constitute the visible body of Christ, they hardly meant to subject themselves, once again, to whatever rule a miscellaneous new world should happen to discover.

Winthrop would continue to correspond with Williams, and perhaps it reassured him to observe that a purer and indeed a freer form of religious experiment was not in fact offering the world a more attractive prospect. As the Narragansett area continued to attract persons who found they could not conscientiously conform to the norms of the establishment in Massachusetts—and became a sort of haven for sectaries—probably Winthrop found himself continuing to prefer the image of an increasingly confident state founded on the greatest public consensus to that of a looser union of seekers. Perhaps it was, at last, a matter of temperament: Williams was born to protest or at least to question; Winthrop, to rule. We need to remind ourselves, however, that the theory and even the exercise of that rule are a little more "enthusiastic" than they have often been made to seem; that Winthrop believes in Holy Love—like that of "Adam when Eve was brought to him"[62]—as avidly as in strict conformity; and that eccentric belief troubles him most as a failure of saintly self-replication. In a holy city as in any proper congregation, godly men and women recognized in one another the godliness of each and all. Williams was indeed remarkable for his "godliness": what could it mean if he, in relation to other men trying to be as godly as they knew, repeated thought otherwise?

This question—and others, less poignant if more heavily laden with public significance—will be reprised in the famous "Bloody Tenet" controversy of the 1640s. But much later. Writing from the England of Milton's "Areopagitica," Williams will revisit his experience in New England as another episode in the sad history of "persecution for conscience' sake"; responding for the defense, John Cotton, by then a famously reformed dissenter himself, will strive mightily to put some other name on that and other, similar episodes in the puzzling history of conscientious disagreement.[63] But the controversy is a little less exhilarating than we might anticipate: brilliant (as we shall see) in defense of his "immediatist" theology of the Spirit, Cotton has by then taken up a position only the odd pope might wish to espouse; and Williams, though he attempts the life-giving form of dialogue, is a relentlessly prosaic writer.[64] More significantly, however, if it is all somehow too much, it is also painfully too late: the political character of Massachusetts will long since have been set, if not in stone, at least in the habitual practice of men whose flesh was less weak than that of some others. "The Antinomian Controversy" will, by contrast, provide an utterly full airing of the issue of the style of piety (and hence of profession) that will predictably enable admission to church membership (and hence a vote in General Court elections). But the question of whether a majority of ruling Christians can legislate conscience, or by themselves make up a state, will long since have dropped out of relevance. For Saints are finding a way to make themselves agree. As if to give their ragged tale a proper theme.

———

Thus the "assisted expulsion" of Roger Williams marks an important point in the evolution of Winthrop's "Journal." Serious problems continue, of course, and Winthrop goes on learning to govern them in prose if he can only assist in solving them in fact. Something untoward has indeed happened, but a recognizably "Puritan" challenge has been successfully met: a prime irritant has been removed, more or less peacefully. Moreover, the state machinery has discovered, in the process, how it is supposed to move, even when the problem of moment may seem properly churchly. Now, with Saints united as members of the One Body, surely all will go well. If only magistrates and ministers can keep the peace among themselves.

Brewing up a little separatist activity of his own, "Mr. Batchellor of Sagus" provokes some members of his congregation to complain to the magistrates. "Foreseeing the distraction," they forbid him to undertake any further church re-organization "until the cause were considered by the other ministers." Refusing temporarily to desist, he is called once more before the magistrates who elicit from him a "submission & a promise to remove out of the town within 3: months" (165). But if this church conflict is satisfactorily resolved, by the magistrates, before it can become a constitutional problem, another disagreement, among the magistrates themselves, spreads out over several pages of the "Journal"; and Winthrop's full and frank handling of the interpersonal side of the controversy reminds us, once again, that loving love and hating hate is an even more important consideration than protecting the evolving constitution from disabling critique.

In fact, it takes almost two full pages of Winthrop's entry for January 18, 1636, to discover, amidst an almost unseemly regard for persons and personalities, that the political personages of Massachusetts are going to face up to an important enough political question: is it wiser, in the infancy of a plantation, for magistrates to be more lenient or more strict than they might be in a more well established political condition? Prefacing his account of that question of policy—and even of tone—is a carefully constructed account of a rare but probably essential drama of magisterial decorum. Grown men and seasoned rulers, assuredly capable of keen discernment and shrewd prediction, the magistrates reveal themselves as capable of great politeness and mutual deference as well. With the sort of social discernment one might expect of newcomers, Mr. Vane and Mr. Peter report

> finding some distraction in the commonwealth arising from some difference in judgment, and withal some alienation of affection among the magistrates and some other persons of quality, and that hereby factions began to grow among the people, some adhering more to the old governor Mr. Winthrop, and others to the late governor Mr. Dudley, the former carrying matters with more lenity and the latter with more severity. (Y, 88)

Suitably concerned, they arrange a "meeting at Boson of the governor, deputy, Mr. Cotton, Mr. Hooker, Mr. Wilson," and of course Mr. Winthrop and Mr. Dudley. A paraconstitutional body, it seems evident, but then the real question—of magisterial "affect"—may be metapolitical after all.

This quite literal "meeting" opens with a prayer, of course, and then Mr. Vane—an alienated nobleman without status otherwise—encourages all present to resolve "to deal freely and openly . . . that nothing might be left in their breasts which might break out to any jar or difference hereafter." All agree and Winthrop, expressing puzzlement at Vane's account of the local political climate, solemnly professes "that he knew not of any breach between his brother Dudley and himself since they were reconciled long since." And

> neither did he suspect any alienation of affection in him or others from himself, save that of late he had observed some newcomers had estranged themselves from him since they went to dwell at Newtown, and so desired all the company that if they had seen anything amiss in his government or otherwise they would deal freely and faithfully with him, and for his part he promised to take it in good part and would endeavor by God's grace to amend it. (Y, 88)

It is impossible to know whether Winthrop is merely repeating Vane's crucial phrase or whether his own speech or account first refers to an "alienation of affection," but the overtones, some of them modern enough, accord well with Winthrop's implication in the "Model" that a truly Christian society would amount to a sort of complex marriage;[65] and again we run up against a clear sense that Winthrop thinks of himself as a Holy Lover quite as much as a Magistrate.

Less androgenous, perhaps, and speaking in any event for the party of strictness—both in the constitutional interpretation of the charter and in the punishment of early-colony crimes—Dudley bluntly reaffirms his continuing accord with Mr. Winthrop and leaves it "to others to utter their own complaints" (Y, 89). He leaves it, that is to say, to Governor Haynes, who does indeed have a complaint. Before daring to voice it, however, he carefully stipulates that "Mr. Winthrop and himself had always been on good terms, etc.; therefore he was loath to give any offence to him, and he hoped that considering what the end of this meeting was he would take it in good part if he did deal openly and freely as his manner ever was" (Y, 89). The reader may begin to splutter—yes, we stipulated that ideal decorum would be indeed so stipulated—but none of this impatience mars the steady goodwill of Winthrop's tone. And, finally, just when it begins to appear that butter would not melt in *anyone's* mouth, Haynes mentions a couple of instances "wherein he conceived that [Mr. Winthrop] dealt too remissly in point of justice." Aware that he may be getting in under his head, Winthrop answers not with any allusion to his well-developed theory of a saintly love beyond both justice and mercy but—like a professor accused of grade inflation—

> that it was his judgment that in the infancy of plantations justice should be administered with more lenity than in a settled state, because people were then more apt to transgress, partly of ignorance of new laws and orders, partly through oppression of business and other straits. But it might be made clear to him that it was an error, he would be ready to take up a stricter course. (Y, 89)

At this (probably ingenuous) suggestion, "the ministers were desired to consider of the question by the next morning and to set down a rule in the case."

Assholes with power, as Hawthorne stops just short of calling them in *The Scarlet Letter*,[66] they opine that "strict discipline both in criminal offences and martial affairs was more needful in plantations than in a settled state, as tending to the honor and safety of the gospel." And Winthrop—unaware, as it seems, of the sympathy his writing might be drawing forth from some happily post-Puritan reader—declares himself "convinced that he had failed in overmuch lenity and remissness, and would endeavor (by God's assistance) to take a more strict course hereafter" (Y, 89). Though Winthrop would probably not understand what a modern reader means by irony, that reader may hope for it nevertheless: does it really require "God's assistance" to insist on the letter, even where there may be no positive and well-promulgated law? But even if something in him resists, it remains essential to the Winthrop we are beginning to know that he does not *say* so; for he himself has helped to valorize exactly the sort of ad hoc yet luminous consensus instructing him here. And, in any event, the literary lapse would be only momentary, for it is impossible not to recognize the almost pathetic sincerity in his account of what follows next.

Reconciled, so far as eye can see or word dare say, the entire group enacts a "renewal of love amongst them," articulated in a list of no fewer than ten "articles" (Y, 89). As already decided, "there should be more strictness used in civil government and military discipline"; and, as repeated lessons in the politic of competitive consensus have been teaching, that "magistrates should . . . ripen their consultations beforehand, that their vote in public might be one (as the voice of God)." For if not *vox magistrum,* then someday, sooner or later, *vox populi.* But "if differences [do] fall out among them in public meetings," they shall observe a set of subsidiary rules that sound as if they might be borrowed from Benjamin Franklin. And, moving beyond the sphere of policy,

> the magistrates shall be more familiar and open each to other, and more frequent in visitations, and shall in tenderness and love admonish one another (without reserving any secret grudge), and shall avoid all jealousies and suspicions, each seeking the honor of another and all the Court, not opening the nakedness of one another to private persons, in all things seeking the credit and safety of the Gospel. (Y, 90)

Except for the unmistakable clericalism of the last clause, one might almost think these tough-minded (if also thin-skinned) leaders had been talking to their wives. Or sweetening their mouths, each night, with a morsel of Winthrop's "Model": not only to "love brotherly without dissimulation," but to "entertain each other in brotherly affection."[67]

In the end—but just barely—they somehow manage to conclude on a note worthy of their own accomplished worldliness: "All contempts against the Court . . . shall be noted and punished, and the magistrates shall appear more solemnly in public with attendance, apparel, and open notice of their entrance into the court" (Y, 90–91). Just so, it appears, must the brave new sense of Love make peace with venerable order of Law; and with some small reminder of Old World Ceremony. And just here—had Winthrop known himself to be writing a book—might the first section have ended. Not with the departure of Williams, which Winthrop seems somehow to know had been as much a defeat for rare godliness as a victory for common order. But with a sort of metalegal love feast, issuing in a new set of orders, to be sure, but expressing a hearty renewal of the well-specified and profoundly hoped for Spirit of the Place. See how they love one another: surely New England must express redemption.

The founding of Thomas Shepard's church at Newtown, days later, furnishes an in-streaming population not only with Shepard's own "deep confession of sin" but also with a formalized and fully explicit sense that "such as were to join [a particular church] should make confession of their faith and declare what work of grace the Lord had wrought in them" (Y, 91); and this exemplary event entirely overshadows the news of continuing Separatist "distractions about the churches of Salem and Saugus" (Y, 92). In March 1636 a would-be congregation at Dorchester fails to produce a sufficient number of persons who can make a credible account of the peculiar "work of God's grace in themselves": some appear to have "builded their comfort of salvation upon . . . dreams and ravishments"; others, by evident contrast, upon "the reformation of their lives" or upon "duties and performances" (Y, 93); but this setback—which might have signaled the beginning of something like a "Morphology Controversy"—is quite temporary, as Mr. Richard Mather is successful with his second attempt later the same year. Thomas Hooker, *former* "pastor of the Church of N: town & most of his congregation" (177) depart for Connecticut, but—as John Winthrop Jr. has already become "the governor appointed by the Lords for Connecticut" (Y, 86)—the event is allowed to pass with but a brief mention. And none of this, positive or negative, can match the importance Winthrop has seemed to attach to the "renewal of love" of January 1636. One begins to suspect that all Winthrop's truly originary events are now past.

Volume 1 (of the "Journal") ends with some sobering passages about the unstable relation between Massachusetts and both the Narragansetts and the Pequots, and with some clear indication that Williams is well placed to help the Puritan colonists stay out of war if at all possible. And volume 2 (of the "History")[68] picks up the same matters. Winthrop takes no delight in reporting murders or in detailing the strategy and tactics of retributive justice. He wants to prevail, of course, but he would rather copy out "The Articles" of peace between his people and the Narragansetts than report a body count—or detail the argument between Massachusetts and Plymouth about who is more responsible for deteriorating relations with the Pequots (Y, 104–5). But either way, the reader who comes to Winthrop fresh from the wearing dullness of Bradford's account of the 1630s begins to feel that old déjà vu all over again. What *can* happen now? Dispersal of

population, rethought (perhaps) as the fitting spread of Congregational Civiliza-
tion? Rivalry among the various outspreading agents of New World Puritanism?
Indian Warfare, vaguely misunderstood out of its relation to those native others?
Is this not exactly where we came in?

And then, as if Winthrop's ultimate providence were in fact literary, the
brief introduction of a problem—actually of a person—that will stimulate his
writerly faculty like nothing before:

> One Mrs. Hutchinson, a member of the church of Boston, a woman of
> ready wit and bold spirit, brought over with her two dangerous errors:
> 1. That the person of the Holy Ghost dwells in a justified person. 2. That
> no sanctification can help to evidence to us our justification. (Y, 105)

This initial passage goes on, of course, to mention the existence of further "dangerous errors" growing as so "many branches" from this double root; and other
passages follow in quick succession, clearly indicating that Winthrop has found,
if only in intellectual astonishment, the subject that would make it worth his
while to have gone *on* with his journal, even after it had ceased to be the "Governor's" own log.

Eventually, of course, Winthrop will turn aside from his task of alert, concerned, informed, initiate, theologically literate (if not quite licensed) record
keeping to produce a separate "Story" of the matter here begun. And even in the
"Journal" itself, once the threat of catastrophic internal division has clearly passed,
he will feel the need to keep careful watch on all those who had openly associated
themselves with this bold "Spiritist" challenge: he clearly expects these higher
and holier of the "Hot Protestants" somehow to discredit themselves; and they do
not often disappoint.[69] For the present, however, he is going to have to work it out
as he goes along.

A more retrospective text—Shepard's carefully wrought "Autobiography,"
for example—would know exactly what it had to think before setting pen to
paper and could unroll its entire response in one long sentence of redoubled
parallelism: "begun by Mistress Hutchinson, raised up to a great height by Mr.
Vane, . . . maintained too obscurely by Mr. Cotton, and propagated too boldly by
the members of Boston," the whole astonishing affair had caused "God's name to
be blasphemed, the churches' glory diminished, many godly grieved, many
wretches hardened, deceiving and being deceived, growing worse and worse."[70]
Eventually, of course, Winthrop will demonstrate his agreement with virtually
every premise of this carefully wrought verdict; and already one notices the quasi-
instinctive connection between a woman's "bold spirit" and her "dangerous er-

rors." Yet he is trying his biased best to be empirical: an accepted member of his own church—who happens to live right across the street—appears to hold that Saints are "personally" identified with the Holy Spirit and that works of Christian virtue are no more a consequence of the grace of Protestant salvation than they have ever been its cause; that indeed the Christian has no "other sanctification but the Holy Ghost himself." The results of these destabilizing notions cannot be expected to be good, but who knows exactly how events will play themselves out? Has this woman any important sympathizers? Yes: she is joined in her dangerous opinions by "one Mr. Wheelwright, a silenced minister sometimes in England." Could any such opinions fail to attract official notice? No: "The other ministers in the bay, hearing of these things, came to Boston at the time of a general court, and entered conference" (Y, 106) with the opinionists. They even question John Cotton.

By now we know. No account written up out of close contact with the events of this controversy can possibly arrange its conclusions in advance. Too many astonishingly sensitive issues are involved: divine function, personal autonomy, converting experience, saintly ethics. The odd implications of Williams' perverse piety were crudely political by comparison. And—even if it were only the magisterial John Cotton and not at all the princely Henry Vane—too many important persons. Cotton may have been, from the moment of Thomas Shepard's arrival in the colony, an object of the younger minister's envy and perhaps even suspicion. But Winthrop had welcomed him to the Boston church with a joy bordering on the apocalyptic. And now this: rare but not entirely unfamiliar notions of a saintly union with God so intimate as to cancel the human personality; or else, at all events, to render the ordinary norms of human responsibility entirely irrelevant. As if the Saint were moved, once and for all, beyond good and evil. Clearly this matter—of "One Mrs. Hutchinson" and *possibly* of the unique Mr. Cotton as well—will require of Winthrop a fuller form of analysis and judgment than anything he has attempted so far.

And of us a separate chapter. But only after we take the time it requires to read the doctrinal context of Winthrop's evident alarm—the sermons, that is to say, by which certain "other ministers in the bay" had made the unending contest between sin and virtue seem as perfect a norm for Calvinists as ever it had been for men and women who strove for their salvation without the awesome distraction of their predestination. For men like Shepard and Hooker had already written out, powerfully and at length, if only in the form of pastoral guidance, a subtle and supple theology that made too close a reliance on the immediacy of the Spirit and not enough on the mediation (or the "signs") of saintly good works seem, as they do in Winthrop's very first sentence, clearly wrong and hurtful. As a matter of political record, these men will assist Winthrop in ridding his colony of its most dangerous dissenter; by some accounts they even succeed in persuading her mentor, John Cotton, not only to abandon his disciple, but to profess his doctrine of the primacy of the Spirit with a more circumspect sense of its popular reception and practical consequences.[71]

But they do something else as well: when they question Cotton, repeatedly and with increasing pressure, about his minority view of the place of "sanctification" in the psychological drama of saintly self-discovery—and about the epistemology by which the Spirit may be said to be its own evidence—they draw forth from him a "Rejoinder" that poses a powerful objection to their *most* sincere efforts to keep their "activist" theologies within the world of international Calvinism. Shepard's *Sincere Convert* is as moving a call to the Christian life as ever a persecuted young minister could hope to issue; and his *Sound Believer* goes on, at greater leisure, to complete a powerful and more or less integral theology which regards faith as the choice a person utterly incompetent by sinful nature yet finds himself graciously empowered to make. And the theology of God's determinations and executions in the "preparation" of a soul for a salvation for which he is naturally not quite fit is as fully elaborated and as brilliantly defended in Hooker's *Application of Redemption* as even an older, sterner world might ever require. But Cotton's "Rejoinder"—a contextually provoked reworking of positions Cotton was in the act of "teaching" the Boston congregation he shared with John Wilson—is the most steadily consistent and brilliantly articulated piece of Protestant theology between Calvin and Edwards. It may even be right.

There is, of course, no substitute for John Winthrop's public and largely political account of what followed from the discovery that "One Mistress Hutchinson" was making a stir with her radical opinions. Nor will it do to oppose the "feminist" interpretation of her sensibility and his responses. But we can scarcely appreciate the biased brilliance of that account without some adequate, literary attention to the furious writing by which godly men made the opinions of other equally godly men (and women) seem vital enough to the life of society to be called, in Winthrop's telling word, "dangerous."

PART TWO

DOCTRINE

CHAPTER FIVE

DOUBT'S VENTURE, FAITH'S CALL

Shepard's Activist Calvinism

I. CALVINIST ACTIVITY IN *THE SINCERE CONVERT*

Long before Thomas Shepard heard that certain "Familists" in New England were teaching that a saint knew his salvation "by immediate revelation in an absolute promise"—and that a Christian must not assure himself "by the sight of any graces or conditional evangelical promises to faith or sanctification"[1]—he had developed an emphasis, consistent with the demands of proper Calvinism, as he surely thought, that precluded just these immediatist claims. We cannot be entirely sure of the religious climate Shepard found at Earle's Colne, where he went to preach just out of Emmanuel College: perhaps the local Christians needed to hear that, though salvation was indeed by faith and not by any meritorious works, still this faith was far from being a passive thing; that a divinely *enabled* choice was yet, from the human point of view, a perfectly real choice. More likely, Shepard merely gave the prevailing Calvinism of England, particularly of Cambridge, the emphasis his own religious experience had made seem most profoundly important: he had needed a new heart "to receive Christ with a naked hand, even naked Christ";[2] but that new heart had surely appeared, in the very act of accepting the gift.

Nor was this "Arminianism," which made the gift of salvation depend on a man's own "free" acceptance or rejection. For originally, and of himself, Shepard had been totally unable to accept any such offer; so much so that he would later write of the way his "own experience so sensibly confut[ed] the freedom of the will."[3] He had indeed to make a choice, but he never forgot that it was one he had been graciously enabled to make: for a long, desperate time he could not, and then, somehow, he found he could indeed choose God's way above personal considerations and competing theories.

The main point—in anticipation of 1636, at least—is that the way of salvation is surprising, even mysterious, but a man's experience of it is not at all "mystical": Shepard knew himself a saint the moment he found himself capable of that faith to which the promise of salvation is everywhere in the New Testament attached. Neither Father nor Son nor Holy Spirit had said to him, whether in the body or out of the body, "Do thou know, Thomas Shepard, that thou art a man elected in mystery to salvation in very fact." But equally wonderfully, and to the same end of fair earthly assurance, some rare grace had made him capable of believing in the self-denying premise of salvation from beyond and, as part of that same act, of accepting without at all meriting his own salvation in just those terms. And one certainly *could* put the matter as a syllogism: salvation is promised to faith; Shepard, astonishingly, has been enabled to believe; ergo—unless he is self-deceived somewhere in the subtle process that hides out behind the minor premise—Shepard is a Saint. And now, rather than congratulate himself on this amazing fact, was it not his duty to publish some account of how this active sense of faith was perfectly compatible with what all the truly pious had to accept about the utter freedom of God's predestination decree? Saints are chosen and no doubt but, paradox or not, they discover their chosenness in their enabled ability to accept ("choose") the gift of an utterly free salvation.

One might even go so far as to call upon an assembled Protestant populace, a people of God if ever there was one, to act boldly on the moment and *make* the salvation choice. The skeptical onlooker might press the objection that the minister's call, no matter how meltingly delivered, could hardly be the enabling cause of faith in the hearers: power, as the curiously Calvinistic Emerson might say, "keeps quite another road."[4] And yet, when the alternative seemed to be silence— in which Papists would continue to preach some modified doctrine of merit— why should not the Protestant preacher provide an appropriate human context for God's efficacious work? To be sure, more would be called than had in fact been chosen, but Scripture itself had advertised that very state of affairs; and the God who could have withheld salvation altogether, or have decided to work it in silence, or in total disregard for the consciousness of the saved, appeared to have decided to let the minister's call serve as the ordinary occasion of his own. And was not this ministerial urgency a fit way of teaching that when the moment of unmerited faith occurred, it appeared always in the form of a call and its answer?

Or such at least would seem to be the logic of the sermons Shepard delivered at Earle's Colne (1627–30) and eventually published as *The Sincere Convert* (1641). The enemy is not the privatism of John Cotton but the lazy inattention of most people—some of whom might well be saints. Repeating the call to "labor" (13, 23, 45) or else to "strive" (62),[5] the sermons often sound as if they mean to urge their hearers into the way of salvation all by themselves. But then they remind themselves, repeatedly, that they are contextual merely. And in doing so, they begin a ministerial career bent on demonstrating that predestination need not provoke either fatalism or sloth. Saints are called to an active faith, and the only thing for a would-be saint to do is to try in fact to believe. Without the special assistance of saving grace, of course, he could do no such thing. And the minister was there to identify, in all sorts of trial that ended only in error, the virtually endless array of substitutes for faith which non-native speakers of Protestantism seemed able to generate. On the other hand, no one could believe without *trying* to believe: an offer of salvation was being made, by the Gospel and by its ministers; could one in fact accept it?—accept, that is to say, the counterintuitive suggestion that we cannot save ourselves, and that in accepting salvation at the hands of another, we have to let our selves go entirely.

Truly, there was no other way to know. Private revelations are no part of the Gospel scheme. Its promises are made to those who believe. Do you in fact believe? Are you unsure? Then try—to say *yes* and let go of your misguided hope to save yourself. Can you do this? Really? No residue of self-delusion? Well, then: *if* you do believe, *then* saved you are. QED.[6] And be anathema all who scorn this as a "way of ratiocination" and hence "a way of works."[7] Whenever, wherever they shall appear.

———

But a highly developed rhetoric of urgency is not the only distinguishing feature of Shepard's earliest sermonic literature. A certain structural ambition appears as well: looking almost catechetical—or like Theology 101, for an audience not entirely comfortable with the idioms of Reformed Dogmatics—the six chapters of *The Sincere Convert* cover the matter of Christian theology from the first, common premise, "That there is a God, and this God is most glorious" (9), down to the sorest point of Calvinist difference, namely, that the logic of predestination does not cancel the fact that "The Grand Cause of Man's Eternal Ruin Is from Themselves" (68). The exposition is never "pure," of course, as each of the six sermon-chapters has its own "application"; and this turn toward the practical keeps the audience aware that theology is never quite true unless it is enacted.[8]

But the modern reader cannot miss the sense that this new-fledged Shepard has decided to begin at the beginning and cover the basics; and to suggest that an intimation of salvation is possible at almost any point along the scale of purified theological knowledge.

Recalling his own temptations to atheism, perhaps, Shepard begins by stipulating that very "few thoroughly believe" the fundamental point, that indeed "there is a God"; possibly, he implies, only grace itself can destroy the tendency to linger at this threshold. Still, Shepard cannot proceed without his "main props and pillars"; and so he proceeds—methodically and, as it must have seemed to him, rationally. First, the house of nature, including the "stately theater of heaven," surely indicates that "some wise artificer hath been working here." Replying to the call of poetry, Shepard demands to know, "Who set those candles, those torches of heaven, on the table?" Again, calling on those lights to enact as well as to demonstrate, "Who hung out those lanterns in heaven to enlighten a dark world?" Or: "Who taught the birds to build their nests?" and "What power of man or angels can make the least pile of grass?" (10). Evidently we do indeed "lie in the lap of immense intelligence."[9] Shepard merely takes his own turn to notice the fact.

More problematic, we fear, will be his proof "from the Word of God": surely he cannot take the time to prove that his book is unquestionably a communication from Truth itself. Drawing on Calvin, however—and proving how conservative certain "Liberals" could be in the nineteenth century—Shepard merely issues a dare: given the "majesty stirring" in the sacred books, could any but the "willfully blind" hear them and not "cry out, 'The voice of God, and not the voice of man'"? (10). Subtle too, if a little self-serving, is his third proof, from the observable reality of conversion: given that all men have "hellish hearts," but that "some of this monstrous brood . . . are quite changed," does it not require a work of creation to account for their "new minds, new opinions, new desires, new joys, new sorrows, new speeches, new prayers, new lives?" Then again, do not the "terrors of conscience" predict the existence of a most knowing judge? Never seen in the face but showing everywhere his "back parts," God is the "master in the house" who, though he works mostly by "second causes," forces an honest recognition, now and again, that "Here is the finger of God" (11–12).

As for application, let these considerations serve both as "reproof to all atheists" for all their doubt and denial and as "exhortation" to all who would observe the universe aright: "O, labor to see and behold this God. . . . Pass by all the rivers, till thou come to the prime head; wade through all creatures, until thou art drowned, plunged and swallowed up with God" (13). It may seem curious to be asked to "labor" to accomplish a thing so simple as "seeing," but the paradox takes us close to the heart of Shepard's distinctive emphasis: though the moment of salvation by faith is entirely gracious and can be made to seem utterly simple, still it rarely comes without "preparation";[10] and more to the point, it is never inert. Ideas of color and figure might be passively impressed on an empty mind, as Locke would come along to teach, but meaningful ideas of God required a context of aroused attention. "Labor," here, means something like sit up and take notice. And if one can be called upon to labor, he can also be urged to "make choice of this God as thy God" (14). Even this first of all choices is probably not one an unaided hearer can simply "make"; but evidently the sermonic setting perdures, pretty much unchanged, from its inevitable beginning with the God of Reason to its less predictable conclusion in the Faith of a Saint. And if the natural man can never force the logic of grace, still a divine assistance might be efficacious at any point: choosing "this God" seems but a blessed prolepsis of choosing Christ.

It remains for Shepard the Scholastic to remind his audience that "this God" is "most glorious," in essence, attributes, persons, and works (14–17). But the modern reader may feel the drama has ended with the repeated invitation to "make choice of him alone to be thy God," and with the call to covenantal exchange that so excited the notice of Perry Miller: "give away thyself wholly and forever to him, and he will give away his whole self everlasting unto thee" (14).[11] Do we need to repeat that Shepard does not suppose that his own call and his hearer's unaided response make up the entire causality of this tempting yet severe bargain? If so, we should repeat as well that when the energetic assistance of divine grace is added to the terms of this transaction, the human activity so enabled can only be described as "choice." Try, therefore, to make the choice. And if successful, learn to read that enabled activity not as a paradox of philosophical psychology but as the only supposable outcome of the requisite divine intervention into the realm of human volition. Learn, with love and awe, to interpret the efficacious choice of "this God" not as the originating cause of salvation in some scheme of "freedom" but, much more simply, as the gracious effect of God's determination to save the otherwise unsavable.

With that much premised, Shepard's catechism hastens to explain, in chapter 2, "God Made All Mankind . . . in a Most Glorious and Happy Estate." Intimated already, however, is the grim revelation, in chapter 3, "That All Mankind Is Fallen by Sin from That Glorious Estate . . . into a Most Woeful and Miserable Condition"; and the happier news of chapter 4, of the "Means of Redemption . . . out of This Estate." The compound claim of this theodicy will seem a little basic to the initiate, but in a world where fewer and fewer students can be persuaded to read Milton, they make a fair introduction to the basic premises of Orthodoxy's prime "justification." Which begins with a denial that man's Fall is inherent in his Creation.

When "God made all mankind at first in Adam," he made this epitome of all creatures "in [his] own image"—by which, Shepard thinks, we can only mean that God gave Adam the gift of "holiness" (18). Appearing in his understanding, affections, will, and in his very life, this holiness meant that Original Man thought and felt and chose aright in obedience to nothing more than "his own will, law, and rule"; doing as he would, this Emersonian child enacted godliness, as much as if God himself "had assumed man's nature." Now this initial "integrity"[12] ought to have been our own, by the same sort of "imputation" that makes "Christ's righteousness" that of the believer. Yet if this rare gift were to be lost by Adam—as Shepard begins to anticipate himself—it would be lost to us as well; from which fact we may "see the horrible nature of sin, that plucks man down by the ears from the throne." And while we wonder if this homely language can distract an audience from the difficult question of how a truly divine holiness could manage to lose itself, Shepard continues his emphasis on the evil of sin. Adam pleads for forgiveness and for the life of his children, but *no:* "see [how] one sin weighs him down and all his posterity . . . into eternal ruin" (19). We continue to demur, perhaps, while Shepard hastens to require that we "learn how justly God may require perfect obedience to all the law of every man, and curse him if he cannot perform it, because man was at first made in such a glorious estate" (20). Already, however, there is the hint of the turn to come. For though we clearly see that man, "broke, and in prison," must lie "in hell . . . forever, if he can not pay justice every farthing," we begin to suspect we would be told no such thing if there were not some other, less local and homely way to clear the debt. Nor is Shepard slow to speak an explicit word of "comfort":

> If all Adam's posterity were perfectly righteous in him, then thou that art of the blood royal, and in Christ are perfectly righteous in him much more, inasmuch as the righteousness of the second Adam exceeds the first, so art thou more happy, more holy in the second Adam than ever the first in himself was. (20)

The point, surely, is that just where the modern reader wishes to object to the notion of his *own* sin "in Adam," an emergent Puritan audience was reassured instead by the possibility of their salvation "in Christ."

And the availability of this masterful diversion may tell us more about the genius of Pauline Christianity than about the intellectual honesty of any given

Puritan minister. For though we may blame the problem of Adam on Genesis, and though we do not need Edwards to remind us of the lively sense of some well nigh congenital sinfulness that permeates a fair portion of the Jewish Scriptures, we do not usually think of the original Chosen People as laboring under the sense of a total inability to perform, under the Law, a single act of virtue; and moral visionaries like Isaiah and Jeremiah might be quite surprised to hear their involvement in the sin of Adam described as "imputation." That concept is the inspired invention of Paul, who seemed to see, all at once, that the sinful inheritance of Adam could be "totalized" as long as that of Christ were treated in exactly the same manner. And at exactly the same time.[13] So that neither an exemplary people nor yet a painfully singular person need live out an elongated, as-if permanent period of hopeless moral inability with no hint of reversal or escape. To be sure, the magical ascription might not apply to a given person. But then again it *might*. So that an audience could always be alerted to the possibility of some wonderful redress of what might otherwise become their deepest grievance.

Beyond this common inheritance, however, the distinguishing mark of Shepard's system is its turn to the "urgent." Thus, after pausing to reprove those who resist in any measure the totalizing standard of holiness—which demands what we can of ourselves no way provide—Shepard insists that we "Labor to get this image of God renewed again." He knows, of course, that we ourselves are powerless to renew the righteous integrity of original nature. But as others insist on a sight of sin as so heinous that no human could possibly make reparation,[14] so Shepard urges, as against some preference of the slightly better over the somewhat worse, a recovered fidelity to the standard by which God justly demands perfection. For even our fallen selves can begin to understand the ideal standard of our loss.

Now, with a rumor of salvation blowing in the wind, Shepard settles in for his long chapter on the Fall. Wishing to focus on the "most woeful and miserable condition" that has resulted, Shepard yet feels compelled to set out some of the standard considerations: our perfect willingness to stand with Adam if he indeed had stood; our presence in him, "as a whole country in a parliament man"; or, more metaphysically still, Adam as the "head" of all human "members" and/or the "root" of which we all are the "branches" (24–25). We may require a book on "The Changing Conceptions of Original Sin in New England" to sense that this exhausts the store of available "arguments";[15] but probably we can trust our own suspicions that they explain the matter to just about nobody. Perhaps not even to

Shepard who, by way of admitting the problem is not of his own making, ends his review with an edgy disclaimer: "If these things satisfy not, God hath a day coming wherein he will reveal his own righteous proceedings before men and angels" (25).

The problem, surely, is that the authority of Paul has imposed the idea of "as in Adam, sin, so in Christ, salvation," on an interpretive community with a surprisingly long life; and that community, accepting the premise as normative, has had to do its reasonable best with a "given." But never well enough.[16] The point is not that we require the Fall to be "fortunate"—in its Christic consequences—to be acceptable at all; but that the entire "doctrine" of Adam has to be seen as a back-formation of the Pauline Christ; that no abstruse teaching of our corporate Fall could have presented itself except as a derivative of the doctrine of our representative redemption. And for the moment Shepard has put himself in the position of trying to explain the one without referring to the other. The best he can do in this unfriendly venue is to observe that men do not often lament, as the fountain of their crimes, the aboriginal cause of it all. And then move on, silently, from the reason of universal sin to the rhetoric of its evidence.

Memorably, he elaborates the conceit that every son of Adam is "stark dead in sin." Oh, yes, he concedes, men make a brave show of preaching, of hearing, and even of praying, but none of it proceeds from "any inward principle of life"; and the works of pride and self-deceiving self-love cannot long hide the death beneath:

> First, a dead man cannot stir, nor offer to stir. . . . Secondly, a dead man fears no dangers. . . . Let ministers bring . . . tidings of the approach of the devouring plagues of God denounced, he fears them not. Thirdly, a dead man cannot be drawn to accept of the best offers. Let Christ come out of heaven and fall about the neck of a natural man . . . , he can not receive the offer. Fourthly, a dead man is stark blind, and can see nothing, and stark deaf and hears nothing. (27)

A dead man is "senseless" and "speechless" and "breathless" and "hath lost all beauty" and "hath worms gnawing him" and wants "nothing but casting into the grave." The scandal of Adam aside, Puritan preaching can always do depravity with unembarrassed conviction. So that finally, as the vehicle becomes its own tenor: "O, wonder thou that ever God should let thee live, that hast been rotting in thy sin . . . perhaps sixty years together" (27–28). Confident, now, Shepard hastens to explain that, while dead to every good influence, the natural man lives a perfectly full life of sin—"mind, will, eyes, every limb of his body, every piece of his soul." Not always in explicit, outward act, perhaps, but in the foul play of fantasy that borders on intention, "thy heart is a foul sink of all atheism, sodomy, blasphemy, murder, whoredom, adultery, witchcraft, buggery" (28). And this doctrine of a "lurking" sin that lacks only its proper occasion to break into act may give the lie to those who "comfort themselves in their smooth, honest, civil life" (29). For "such as through education have been washed from all foul sins" would do well to remember "an actual sin is but a little breach made by the sea of sin in thy heart" (30).

Finally, as this lesson in *practical* Calvinism presses closer to its estimate of the moral capacity of every son of Adam, gross and subtle sinners alike must realize that "whatever a natural man doth is sin." Even those deeds which are good as to their "matter" are utterly disqualified—"in the sight of a holy God" (30)—by their failure to proceed from a holy motive. Thus the thoughts, words, civil actions, religious actions, zealous actions, and wisdom of the natural man are all so much sin: "A corrupt tree can not bring forth good fruit." And as every natural man lacks "an inward principle of love to God and Christ," so "All the good things a wicked man doth are for himself, either for self-credit or self-ease, or self-content, or self-safety . . . ; hence, acting always for himself, he committeth the highest degree of idolatry; he plucks God out of his throne, and makes himself a god" (31). Now, if anyone should propose to leave off "praying and hearing" so as to avoid the sin entailed, let them consider that "it is less sin to do them than to omit them"; that one might always prefer to go to hell "in the fairest path" (32) possible; and more seriously, that one might always do, in a world fallen away from holiness, one's own conscientious best. "Venture and try," Shepard therefore instructs; "it may be God may hear, not for thy prayers' sake, but for his name's sake" (32). Who knows, that is to say, when grace will enable a *true* prayer? Its truth will have to be enabled, of course, but no one is going to say it for you.

The rest of chapter 3 turns from "man's misery in regard of sin" itself to a list of those that "follow upon sin." In the present, the Holy God, desperately to be sought, is yet regarded as a "dreadful enemy" (32), by whom man is both "forsaken" and "condemned" (33); and man, being thus condemned, is a "bondslave to Satan" (34), who can expect "every moment to drop into hell." Sounding like a "source" for Edwards, Shepard does not hesitate to trope God as "a consuming fire" and to imagine "but one paper wall of thy body between thy soul and eternal flames" (35). Which brings us to the question of the "future miseries": first a "particular" (37) and then a "general judgment" (38). Fearful in themselves for the exposure certain to be made, they lead on to a punishment easy to imagine but impossible to bear: banishment, God "like a consuming infinite fire against thee" (42), and the painful memory of unrepented sin—personalized as the time when, "almost persuaded," Shepard himself "fell to loose company" and heeded not when the Lord "came unto [his] door and knocked" (43–44).

The conclusion to this inventory of misery begins in a way that seems at first surprising: "do not thou shift it from thyself, and say, God is merciful" because "it is a thousand to one if ever thou be one of that small number whom God hath picked out to escape this wrath" (45). In other rhetorical circumstances Shepard's urgent preaching implies that each one of his hearers could indeed be the one in some thousand, needing only the proper evangelical context to realize that staggering fact in the exercise of efficacious choice. And indeed, in the very next paragraph Shepard will be urging again. For the moment, however, he seems concerned to prevent that premature confidence called "presumption": *surely* God will show mercy to me. Not necessarily, Shepard wishes to emphasize; and not in any event quite so fast. For salvation in mercy comes—predictably, according to the logic of "preparation"—only after the sense of damnation in justice; and Shepard is here imagining an audience still lacking that proper sense:

> If Christ were here, and should say, Here is my blood for thee, if thou wilt but lie down and mourn under the burden of thy misery, and yet for all his speeches, thy dry eyes weep not, thy stout heart yields not, thy hard heart mourns not, . . . dost not think but he would turn away his face from thee, and say, O, thou stony, hard-hearted creature, wouldst thou have me save thee from thy misery, and yet thou wilt not groan, sigh, and mourn for deliverance . . . ? (45)

It *could* happen that way, without a groan or a sigh, but is it not safer to suppose that mercy comes to those who have some fitting sense of their need?

The point of the final peroration, then, is to urge the cultivation of that unhappy but necessary sense: "O, labor to be humbled day and night under thy woeful estate." "Guilty of Adam's grievous sin," "dead in sin, and top-full of all sin," capable only of sin "in this estate," with God as "thine enemy," "condemned to die eternally," "ready every moment to drop into hell," liable to judgment and thence to "God's everlasting, insupportable wrath"—will none of this "break thine hard heart, man?"

> Then farewell Christ forever; never look to see a Christ, until thou dost come to feel thy misery out of Christ. Labor therefore for this, and the Lord will reveal the brazen serpent, when thou art in thine own sense and feeling, stung to death with the fiery serpents. (45–46)

Thus the logic of preparation: not quite a cause, perhaps, the "true sight of sin" is something like a sine qua non. No Good News without the really bad news first.[17]

Possibly the sudden turn to the typology of serpents has the effect of distracting from the hard, "Calvinist" questions raised here: Can the mere "labor" of the natural Anyman cause him to feel this "misery" all on his own? And if so, will Shepard indeed have involved himself, from the outset, in the fateful process Perry Miller calls "Expanding the Limits of Natural Ability"?[18] Certainly this will seem so if he can also be understood to teach that the true sensor of sin may be sure the salvation effect will follow. Puritanic introspection never can force, but can it perhaps predict the will of God? We may agree to postpone these questions, preferring instead to savor the bold rhetoric by which Shepard moves from the body count of irresistible reprobation to the soul's ground of hope among the ruins. But Shepard is bound to face these difficulties when he comes to his full-scale treatment of preparation in the opening sections of *The Sound Believer*. Less vital than the sinner, the scholar can afford to wait.

Convinced, at last, that the state of fallen man is indeed hopeless in itself, the novice Protestant needs now to be confirmed in his mounting suspicion that "Christ is the only means of redemption." And Shepard, eager to get on to the "application" of this redemption, hurries over the more theoretical—one might almost say hypothetical—aspects of this marvelous transaction. To the Israelites in bondage God sent down Moses; in Babylon, he raised up Cyrus; "but when all mankind is under spiritual misery, he sends the Lord Jesus, God and Man, to redeem him." How? By "paying a price," by "assuming the guilt," by "bearing the curse," and by "bringing into the presence of God perfect righteousness" (46). Varying significantly in degree of literalness, each of these points might bear explication. Rather than elaborate, however, Shepard turns almost at once to the "comfort" of those who know themselves as lost, and then to the "terror" (47) of those who are resisting such knowledge: Can they make themselves a Christ for themselves? Or "bear an infinite wrath?" Or bring "perfect righteousness into the presence of God?" (48). Evidently not, once the questions are thus posed. The course remains introductory, to be sure, but the context and debated significance of many of its key terms seem assumed in advance. Shepard's procedure may not be that of continuous exegesis, but his audience had better know their Bible.

And here at any rate they know enough to make a predictable objection: Is not this peculiar means of redemption—this substitutionary atonement— "appointed only for some?" And if not for me, then "how can I reject Christ?" Hovering in the background, perhaps, is Calvin's assurance that reprobates do not know themselves as such:[19] so that the response to the doctrine of predestination must always be from the standpoint of possible salvation. Conceding some modicum of good faith where it may not fairly exist, however, Shepard hastens to admit that Christ did not indeed spend "his breath to pray for all." On the other hand, "though Christ be not intended for all, yet he is offered unto all." Our students begin to worry that Shepard is indeed a closet Arminian: salvation is a gift offered to all, requiring only our own choice. Or else, with Emily Dickinson, that he is some kind of monster, publishing the news of water "[t]o one denied to drink." But Shepard knows the degree of his own difficulty. Carefully, then, he explains: the universal offer is from Christ's kingly and not his priestly office and, as such, it commands all men to do what they ought to do in any case: "stoop unto his scepter and depend upon his free mercy"; and say out loud, with a true sight of their own just deserts, "if ever he save me, I will bless him; if he damn me, his name is righteous in so dealing with me" (49).

Safe in this alabaster Calvinism, Shepard then makes a move absolutely typical of the properly "subjective" reach of Puritan preaching: turning from the logic of the general position to the case of the individual objector, he demands to know why such a person assumes the saving offer will *not* be made to him: are you "ignorant of God, Christ, or his will?" are you "an enemy to God," with a "heart so stubborn and loath to yield"? have you "despised the means of reconciliation"? have you "no strength, no faith, no grace, nor sense of [your] own poverty"? can you "not love, prize, not desire the Lord Jesus"? have you "fallen from God oft"? have you "desire[d] not to have Christ"? do you "fear [the] time is past"? (49–51). Then welcome to the communion of your race. Not to the ranks of the saved, quite yet, but to the universal group of those who are lost and are therefore savable. And if you say, "But if God be so willing to save, and so prodigal of his Christ, why doth he not give me to Christ, or draw me to Christ?" I will answer, "What command dost thou look for to draw thee to Christ but his word, Come?" (51). And here we are, once again, at the prime emphasis of Shepard's salvation system: man is called, not forced, to salvation; its choice depends on a divine assistance, but it has to be *made*.

One may even risk situating that choice within a rhetoric of "conditions." Are you in fact willing (and therefore enabled) to "make an exchange of what thou art or hast with Christ for what Christ is or hath?" Are you willing to "give away thyself to him, head, heart, tongue, body, soul?" to "give away all thy sins?" to "give away thine honor, pleasure, profit, life?" to "give away the "rags" of "thine own righteousness?" If you really *can* do these impossible things, why then you really are a Saint. But do not become one of those idle wishers who merely "flatter themselves" (51–52)—the "slighting unbeliever" who hears only a minister trying to make a buck like everybody else; the "desperate unbeliever" who, at the sight of his sins, flees "from the presence of the Lord"; the "presumptuous unbeliever" who "catcheth at Christ" before coming to see "sin as the greatest evil"; or the "tottering doubtful unbeliever" who sees less good in Christ than in his "pleasure and sinful games" (52–53).

Stepping back from this vernacular portrait of bad faith responses, Shepard turns to the question of the "greatness" of the sin of rejecting Christ—a "most bloody," a "most dishonoring," a "most ungrateful," a "most inexcusable," a "most heavy sin" (53–54). But the momentum of the list cannot distract us from one important instance of objection and response: "O, but I can not take Christ." "O, but Christ can give thee a hand to receive him, as well as give himself away" (53). Obviously, the figurative language predicts the account of Shepard's own conversion experience. We might wonder if this gift of the hands needed to grasp the gift of salvation does not perhaps involve an inelegant reduplication of the order of grace;[20] but Shepard means only to secure his own loyalty to the system of doctrines advertised by the Synod of Dort. Nor will he end this chapter without facing up, once again, to the problem of agency within a system famous for teaching the "limited" nature of Christ's "atonement."

And so one final objection: "But it may be Christ hath not redeemed me; nor shed his blood for me; therefore why should I go to him?" The answer might well be, simply, because Christ-as-King commands you to do so. Instead, however, Shepard returns to the ground of uncertainty, of possibility therefore, and of the need to act in precisely those terms:

> It may be, it is true; may be not; yet do thou venture, as those (Joel ii), "Who knows but the Lord may return?" It is true, God hath elected but few, and so the Son hath shed his blood, and died for but a few; yet this is no excuse for thee to lie down and say, What should seek out of myself for succor? Thou must in this case venture and try. (54)

The point is not that God has promised to reward any decent human effort with the gift of a salvation really available to all; but that salvation cannot be thought of as coming to anyone paralyzed by the thought "maybe not." And if human effort is not to be thought of as the efficient cause of salvation, it cannot be supposed that it will come to anyone who does take the risk of seeking what he does not in fact deserve.

Arriving at about this same point in the logic of salvation and human effort, a would-be saint in a distinctively New England poem will decide to take the gamble because, even if he loses, "Ist not be worser than I be." One degree less poetic, Shepard is satisfied to recommend the typic attitude of "those lepers in Samaria": "If I stay here in my sins, I die; . . . if I go out to Christ, I may get mercy; however, I can but die, and it is better to die at Christ's feet than in [my] own puddle" (54). It is of course not easy to say something like "I will trust him though he slay me," but Calvinism appears to require just such a Joblike attitude. And after doing what he can to make the response seem "proper," Shepard holds it out as necessary in any case. God saves and no doubt. But only from among those who labor to try to venture.

———

Not to be thought more loyal to the wish of his rhetoric than to the terms of God's revealed plan, Shepard opens his next chapter with the emphatic claim that the "Saved Are Very Few." We may suspect that only the second doctrine of chapter 5 will express his full evangelical energy: "Those That Are Saved Are Saved *with Great Difficulty*" (emphasis added). Indeed, it requires a stern principle to keep from suggesting this last phrase as Shepard's bottom-line answer to the question, "How Is Man Saved?" Yet even the first proposition evokes its familiar invitation to make the attempt. Evidently *no* biblical saying is too hard to blunt the force of Shepard's activist preaching.

Again anticipating Edwards, Shepard provides a brief history of the world's rampant iniquity.[21] Beginning with Cain and Abel and not omitting an estimate of "our own church of England"—"flourishing" yet full of "lanterns without light" (57)—Shepard dares the historical witness to discover evidence of godliness on any significant scale. Some imaginary member of the present audience rises up in protest: "I have left my sins I once lived in"; "I pray, and do that often"; "I fast sometimes, as well as pray"; "I hear the word of God, and like the best preachers"; "I read the scriptures often"; "I am grieved and am sorrowful"; "I love good men and their company"; "God hath given more knowledge than others"; "I keep the Lord's day strictly"; "I have very many good desires"; "I am zealous" (59–60). By now we know, however, without ever looking back at the text, that each item in this litany of self-praise will have been met, antiphonally, with a piercing answer. Moralism—as Puritanism should have long ago taught even the refined—is never a match for Piety.[22] Judas also was grieved, with the same "legal repentance for fear of hell"; the five foolish virgins all loved good company; and no one was ever quite so zealous as Paul "when he was a Pharisee" (60). On these evidences, "I will not give a pin point for all thy flattering false hopes" (62). Come back when (in grace) you appear to have got a life.

Meanwhile, "suspect thyself much." And—to repeat the lesson of activity in the narrowest scope of its possible success—"strive . . . to be one of them that shall be saved . . . ; labor to go beyond all those that go so far and yet perish at the last. Do not say that, seeing so few shall be saved, therefore this discourageth me from seeking, because all my labor may be in vain." Consider, for example, Christ's own conclusion: "seeing that 'many shall seek and not enter, therefore,' he saith, 'strive to enter at the strait gate.'" And to this the preacher may add his own voice: "Venture, at least, and try what the Lord will do for thee" (62).

The initiate will know that, more than a century later, pious New Englanders will be debating whether Calvinists can conscientiously call upon an entire assembly of hearers to "strive to enter" in just this manner; and that *some* of them will boldly conclude that the Christ quoted here was not in fact a Calvinist. Nearer to home, we ought perhaps to notice that, as he begins to specify the ways in which "the child of God" must "go beyond these hypocrites that go so far" (62–64), Shepard is already imagining the space for his own monumental sequence of sermons on the wise and foolish "Virgins."[23] But a simpler observation is also to the point. In the face of his own self-cultivated difficulty, Shepard continues to stress the paradox: salvation is all but impossible; therefore, try. Or else, more slowly: salvation is rare and at a premium; the aroused act of self-surrender is the price. No such act is to us naturally possible. But no one can know if that act has been *made* possible for him until he tries to make it. That trial is indeed a sort of gamble. What makes it worth taking, however, is that one has in fact nothing to lose: damned in the attempt is no more damned than damned in the hypothetical consideration. And—can one say it too often?—all successful trials of faith begin as tries. Therefore, try.

With gusto, then, Shepard turns to the question of the difficulty of the trial. Avid readers are warned that "Christ is not got with a wet finger"; nor by "shedding a tear at a sermon, or blubbering now and then in a corner" (64). Nothing quite like this vernacular comedy in Edwards, we may remind ourselves; and who knows how much *more* banal modern Christianity might have become without the strict but still popular example of Shepard? Still, for reasons we find it hard to make out—but in ways he will not repeat in later works—his account positively rushes through the "strait gates" of "humiliation," "faith," "repentance," and "opposition of devils, the world, and a man's own self." An odd list, surely. We get the "preparationist" declaration that "God saveth none but first he humbleth them" (64–65). But we hear precious little about faith; only that men never humbled often "presume" it. And we are not sure it ought to come before repentance.

Nor will Shepard quite settle down to serious business with his "nine easy ways to heaven, . . . all which lead to hell" (65). A nice rehearsal for "The Celestial Rail-road," perhaps, but somehow we seem to know—if only because the same or similar teaching has entered our main stream—that nothing Shepard takes out of the mixed bag of parish, civil education, good wishes, formality, presumption, sloth, carelessness, honest discretion, and self-love (65–68) is going to get it. And so, whatever our resistance to Calvinism, we are a little relieved when Shepard undertakes to show, by way of conclusion, "That the Grand Cause of Man's Eternal Ruin . . . Is from Themselves." Not predestination, that is to say, but individual will. Salvation is a choice saints are enabled to make, but sin is the choice of every natural man as such.

Perhaps we need to absolve Shepard for declining to take on the philosophical problem of "will." Probably he needs to hold, with Edwards, that we are responsible for what we do in fact find ourselves choosing, without regard to abstruse questions about how our particular choosing came about. Most men, observably, do *not* choose to bury their self-serving selves in the tomb of the crucified Christ. Challenged, they may complain that they *can*not; but, on Edwards' theory, this only makes matters worse, proving themselves sinful not only in local fact but also in general and by nature.[24] In any case, what Shepard offers, instead of theory, is a biblical morphology of proximate failure. Whatever else may be true, one can always recognize the presence in the unsuccessful cases of one or more of the following disqualifying conditions: "ignorance" of one's personal estate, carnal refusal to face his "fearful thralldom," carnal confidence in one's "own duties and performances," and "bold presumption" in some "seeming faith" (68). These are the conditions of natural willing, Shepard appears to argue; far from forcing choice against preference—which Edwards will show is an incoherent formula—they are but the stuff of which mentality and its preferences are constituted. We choose as we are.

Externally, the absence of a "faithful minister" (69) might have something to do with men's "ignorance" of their sin; but just as often "people cry out" (70) against such ministers as would aid them in the work of sad self-knowledge. And in the last analysis, "hollow professors cheat and cozen their own souls" (71)—in a number of ways that we might call "Idols of the Understanding." The "understanding's arrogancy" names the fact that "[y]ou shall never see a man mean and vile in his own eyes" (72); its "obstinacy" is its refusal to surrender the "conceit" of its own "good estate" (73); its "obscurity," its failure to discern the "absolute perfection of the law of God" (74), without which sight they admire their own attempts at righteousness. The "understanding's security" consists in men's refusal to "turn [their] eyes inward" (75). "Impiety . . . vilifies the glorious grace of God in another," deluding a man into the belief that "If any be saved, I shall no doubt be one" (76). In its "idolatry," the understanding "bows down to a false image of grace" (77); declining to seek the "rare pearl" of saving grace, "a strange, admirable, almighty work of God upon the soul" (78), it satisfies itself with any "common grace" it seems already to possess.

Finally, the "understanding's error" expands to cover a number of "false conceits": mistaking "some light sorrow for sin to be true repentance" (78); confusing the "striving of conscience against sin" (79) with Paul's sense of "the spirit against the flesh" (80); judging the whole heart by "some good affection" (80); inferring God's love from its "aiming sometimes at the glory of God" (81); and "judging . . . sin to be but infirmity" (81). All this subdividing of lists into further lists puts a certain pressure on the task of thematic summary, to be sure, but it has indeed a literary character of its own. As Shepard begins, in this chapter, to move away from his checklist of essential doctrines and into a full-scale survey of the landscape of the natural man's psychology of resistance, his preaching comes gradually to discover its mature subject and manner. The *differentiae* of Calvinistic theology have been good for openers. And no doubt one would be happy to add, to that consensus of doctrine, some really crushing word on what Scripture and Conversion teach about human "willing." But such "systematic" work does not really express Shepard's genius, nor does it reflect the venue—the genre, one might almost say—of Puritan preaching as such.

A great gulf appears to separate the Converted from All Others on the subject of the place of human activity in the process of salvation. The natural man can never see that predestination does not cancel the need for effort. The Convert appears to have been taught that all his "own" efforts were more or less desperate forms of self-delusion until the moment when some gracious influence enabled a choice he never before had the "will" to make. But the attempt to talk about this problem, across the divide of Grace, could never become a truly "popular" enterprise.[25] The "gnosis" of the converted preacher must always baffle the uninitiate: I know something you don't know, and the color of it is, well, rare and remarkable. The very best the Puritan preacher can do, accordingly, is to remember that he too was once in the condition of his audience and, from the shared knowledge of that moral obtusity, begin to identify the disqualifying conditions a once-born man might be led to discover in himself.

And this is the rhetorical territory into which Shepard's preaching has now moved. The subject, once again, is not the compatibility of predestination with ordinary (or philosophic) ways of conceiving human responsibility but the universality of moral blindness as such. Man as we find him is full of all sorts of "religious" opinions; but these, if we will but analyze them, are part of his natural self-love. Salvation, if needed at all, must certainly be the task of the man himself; or else, if it *must* be accepted somehow from another, surely it is the selfsame self that must be saved. A somewhat suspicious little wisdom, perhaps? It all goes by too fast, to be sure, as if to prove that a first book will have to say everything, just in case there be no second. But as there will be a follow-up to *The Sincere Convert,* perhaps it will be fair to go on with the self-subdividing speed of its final sections.

The second "Grand Cause of Man's Eternal Ruin" divides itself at once: the "bastard peace" in man's conscience is begot "By Satan, By false teachers, By a false spirit, [and] By a false application of true promises" (82–83). Satan works both by "removing" anything which might "trouble the conscience" of even the natural man and by "giving" that hapless creature "all things that may quiet and comfort [him]" (83)—"liberty to recreate itself in any sinful course," a "good diet . . . [of] what dish he likes best," a "cessation sometimes from the act of sin," so that a man is "hardly persuaded" that he lives "in sin," and "fair promises of heaven and eternal life" (84–85). "False teachers" wound no conscience for fear of troubling by implication their own. A "false spirit" parodies every phase of the conversion experience and satisfies a man that a mere "taste" of Christ is sufficient: no impoverishing "purchase" is necessary, and neither need one "work mightily for the Lord" (87) in sanctification. And of course any worldling may catch at some scriptural promise without applying it to his life. Some readers may object to the premise of Satan in this list of causes of groundless self-confidences; others may observe that the use here of "spirit" is far from self-explanatory. But the real problem is the haste: Shepard is briefly identifying things which, to carry full literary conviction, require a more extended and dramatic definition. One begins to fear that Shepard is abusing his gift.

So evident is this sense of haste that one wonders if Shepard's third "Grand Cause"—"corruptions and distempers of the will" (87)—is a meaningful variation of what was promised at the outset of the chapter, namely, man's "carnal confidence" in his "own duties" (68). And when, several pages later, the argument conducts a transition from "the causes why men are ignorant of their . . . miserable estate" to "the second reason of man's carnal security," we may suspect that Shepard's editor was not in possession of a proper text.[26] The effect of this discovery might be liberating, as few readers can be made to attend to the generation of subheadings in the first place; and some even doubt that the *ordo salutis* need be quite so orderly. Yet it seems only fair to notice which of our readerly difficulties can and cannot be blamed on the author; otherwise we are likely to abandon our sense of discrimination and simply resign ourselves to what students think of as more old-fashioned talk about God and sin. More particularly, it may be neces-

sary to recognize "proliferation" as a figure of man's many ways of evading "ultimate concern" and lapse of attention as a comfortable easing of the moral consciousness.

"Will," in this context, names only the familiar tendency to defend or rationalize "a sinful course" or to "extenuate and lessen sin" or to hide from oneself
"the horrible wrath of God" (88–89). And certainly these insights are not *un*-
related to the question of "man's carnal security." For if this condition is possible
partly because God does not now pour out "the full measure of his wrath upon
men," it is the more so because men "put away the evil day" (89); or they "think
they can bear God's wrath" (90); or they feel their woeful condition is inevitable,
like the "prince's child" brought up "in a base house," who "never aspires after a
kingdom or crown" (91). Or they are bewitched by their "recent pleasures" (91),
or they fall under "the strange, strong power of sin," or they "despair"; or, by contrast, they "nourish a blind, false flattering hope of God's mercy," or they "bring
not their hearts under the hammer of God's word" (92), or because they "consider not of God's wrath daily, nor the horrible nature of sin." And because "men
chew not these pills . . . they never come to be affected" (93). The remedy:
"awaken, therefore, all you secure creatures; feel your misery, that so you may get
out of it." Ask "How?" and the answer can only be to "[t]ake a full view of thy
misery" and a "special notice of the Lord's readiness" (93). But before we can
learn much more than that in every sin we not only "fling a dagger at the heart of
God" but also seek to "disthrone" him, the text moves on to "The third reason of
man's ruin"—"that carnal confidence, whereby men seek to save themselves . . .
by their own duties" (94). Once again the method is that of multiplication, as
man's "resting in duties" appears in exactly "eleven degrees" (95). And the effect
is tedious only if we relax our attention. For Shepard's energy reveals itself in his
imagination of the number of ways a man may get it wrong.

Obviously, a "Papist" will rest secure in "superstitious vanities"; or, now, with
these things banished from England, some may "stand upon their titular profession" of reformed religion. Or a vain man may be fooled by the feel of his private
devotions. Or, reminded by conscience that this religion of "the chamber" is a
delusion, a man may "fall upon reformation," leaving off his "whoring, drinking,
cozening, gaming, company-keeping, swearing, and such roaring sins," thus persuading "all the country . . . he is become a new man"; indeed, his smooth behavior may fool even himself (96). Or, being led to suspect these externals, a man
may go in for "humiliations, repentings, tears, sorrows, and confessions"; indeed,
many people have "sick fits and qualms of conscience"; but as Saint is more than
a down payment on Man of Sensibility, so more are driven to Christ by "the burden of a hard, dead, blind, filthy heart than by the sense of sorrows." Or men

grow "very just . . . in their dealings with men, and exceeding strict in the duties of the first table"—good habits, except as men "rest" in such performances. Or they rest in zeal for "good causes" or in "mourning"; or they "dig within themselves" to "work out [of] themselves"; or they "go unto Christ" for help to "save themselves"—much like Papists, "dipping [their] doings in his blood" (97–99). So one is well advised to "take heed of resting in duties." Some men go to hell by "the path of sin, which is the dirty way"; others take "the path of duties, which (rested in) is but a cleaner way" (100).

A timely "objection" leads Shepard to distinguishing between a crass "trusting in" duties to earn salvation and a subtler, more nearly Protestant tendency to "rest in" them, as when a man professes "that only Christ can save him, but in practice he goeth about to save himself" (101); and this latter error is serious enough to merit a sixfold enumeration of "signs" (101–4). Shepard even provides a final reminder that "our best duties are tainted" (104) with self-love; and, even were this not so, no amount of them could outweigh the "debt" (105) of our sin. So insistent is this emphasis on the delusion of duties that we are led to ask—in an objection Shepard will still be answering, years later, in the massive defense of "sanctification" that is *The Ten Virgins*—then why bother? So important is his answer that we may well treat it as the appropriate conclusion of *The Sincere Convert*. Which otherwise breaks off, abruptly, without completing the things it had wanted to say.

———

In some ways the most exciting thing about the end of *The Sincere Convert* is the way it invokes the condition of its own termination: "Other things I should have spoken . . . , but I am forced here to end abruptly; the Lord lay not this sin to their charge who have 'stopped my mouth, laboring to withhold the truth in unrighteousness'" (109). Readers of the "Autobiography" know where we are: Bishop Laud—"fitted by God to be a scourge"—has silenced Shepard for the pains of his preaching. And, given the subtle echo of "other things," readers of Scripture do not need the quote to sense the moment: more important than Shepard's "living" is the life-and-death dependence of Saints upon the preaching of the Word.[27]

Literally, Laud seems only to have foreshortened some remarks on the "bold presumption, whereby men scramble to save themselves," not by their duties, this time, but "by their own seeming faith" (68). But this might well have been a fitting conclusion to a work that has already anatomized so many other ways to mistake the products of one's own fear for the "blessed motions" of enabling grace. Nor need the preacher fear his own "presumption" in setting forth the needful distinctions, or even in issuing the call to take the risk of trying to believe—for Scripture itself demanded no less. And yet *The Sincere Convert* is not without an appropriate ending, just as it stands. For what Shepard's Calvinism needs most to explain—for the clarity of our present understanding and to prevent the future suspicion of a "covenant of works"—is why "duties," so scorned in the pages just completed, are nevertheless of the essence. And it is with a sense of intellectual crisis that Shepard imagines the logic and supplies the vernacular language of his last dramatic protest.

Granting, then, that

> duties are but rotten crutches . . . to rest upon, . . . to what end should we use any duties? Can not a man be saved by his good prayers, nor sorrows, nor repentings? Why should we pray any more then? Let us cast off all duties, if all are of no purpose to save us; as good play for nothing as work for nothing (105).

Students have trouble with the emphasis of the initial "Can not" construction. They figure it out eventually, however, and when they do, they see that it introduces a perfect rendition of what has been all along their very own objection: Predestination? OK, let's party. And sin bravely. Perfectly proof against the answer that duties are in any case required of us by One who has the authority to command, they are daunted only a little to be reminded that the logic here is closely akin to the one that urges us, in ignorance and hope, to "venture." But they will usually stop for Shepard's answer.

Why perform duties? First of all, Shepard replies, "to carry thee to the Lord Jesus, the only Savior." Shepard declines to inquire whether this preparatory performance can be thought of as some sort of participation in the salvation process, but his answer seems implied in his figure of comparison:

> As it is with a poor man that is to go over a great water for a treasure on the other side: though he can not fetch the boat, he calls for it; and though there be no treasure in the boat, yet he useth the boat to carry him over to the treasure. (106)

Evidently the inability to "fetch the boat" is meant to preserve the sense that man can in no way begin the salvation process on his own, while his calling for it is to reinforce the necessity of an enabled human act. A perilous system, one is tempted to conclude, but necessary, it appears, to an activist Calvinism. But given our suspended sense that the events of New England in 1636 are going to make theological niceties seem urgent indeed, the weight of our notice is likelier to fall on Shepard's second argument:

> Use duties as evidences of God's everlasting love to you when you be in Christ; for the graces and duties of God's people, although they be not causes, yet they be tokens and pledges of salvation to one in Christ; they do not save a man, but accompany and follow such a man as shall be saved. (106)

Again, readers of the "Autobiography" will know where we are, for Shepard is here affirming precisely what his "Familists" will deny—that performing the duties of sanctification may be taken as "evidence of God's special grace."[28] And as if to prepare for that moment, Shepard makes his point emphatic: "because duties do not save thee, wilt thou cast [them] away? No; for they are evidences (if thou art in Christ) that the Lord and mercy are thine own" (106–7).

The parenthetical remark betrays the epistemic strain of Shepard's system, no doubt, as duties are true evidences of salvation only if they are *true*. And John Cotton will be entirely up to the task of identifying both the source of and the cure for the pressure Calvinists have put on themselves in placing as much emphasis on duties as evidences as ever a Papist lavished upon them as stipulated causes. But Shepard's understanding of the life of the converted Christian—and of the prophet who would minister to such persons, both before and after the moment of their conversions—falls into confusion without some very central place for the hearty performance which Scripture enjoins upon its faithful reader. It is too soon to decide if Shepard's activism maintains as authentic a sense of Calvinist piety as might some other, less energetic understanding of the way the soul receives and then responds to a salvation it could in no way earn. But evidently Shepard is not a man to surrender the urgent call for moral performance without a struggle.

He hastens to say a word or two against "headstrong presumption," that "false faith" by which "[m]en make a bridge of their own to carry them to Christ" (107). And, on the other hand, he is forced to end before he can contrive to repeat his call to labor or to strive or to venture one more time. But we will hardly be false to the emphasis of Shepard's first sermon sequence if we remember, with finality, his emphatic teaching that

> Christ shed his blood that he might purchase unto himself a people zealous of good works, . . . not to save our souls by them, but to honor him. O, let not the blood of Christ be shed in vain! Grace and good duties are a Christian's crown; it is sin only that makes a man base. (107)

Mindful of this emphasis, we will hardly wonder if Thomas Shepard—or his duty-conscious associate John Winthrop—should take sharp offense at the suggestion that "good works" have no place in a Covenant so New as to abridge effort and embarrass virtue. Or if these men shall insist that all who ventured to New England had better be prepared to labor.

II. THE SPIRITUAL CONTEXT OF *THE SOUND BELIEVER*

We have Shepard's word that *The Sound Believer* (1645) is but a completion of the work begun in *The Sincere Convert* (1640). Together they cover "the nine principles" he had begun at Earle's Colne and "intended to proceed on with in Yorkshire." Hindered from that, and finding the six chapters of the *Convert* already in print, he completed the final three "at Cambridge and so sent them to England."[29] And certainly the reader feels the connection from the very title of the *Believer*'s chapter 1, presenting the seventh of those nine principles: "As the Great Cause of the Eternal Perdition of Men Is of Themselves, So the Only Cause of [Their] Actual Deliverance . . . Is Jesus Christ" (115). The invocation of the sixth principle of *The Sincere Convert* could hardly be more studied, and so the intention simply to go *on* rather than to start up again, as with a different project, is clear from the outset. Other men's thought may be in flux, but Shepard's appears fixed in the heaven of his own conversion: nothing to do but to spell out the necessary implications in the available idiom. A comfortable plan, whether one had meant to publish or not.

On the other hand, however, there are differences, and possibly even problems, as we move from the *Convert* to the *Believer*. First of all, the second book is longer: the first six principles could be covered in about a hundred pages; the final three require more than half again as much. And this simple fact means that the texture—the specific literary density—will be different. The division of chapters into numbered sections will help to control the multiplication of numbers within numbers; it may even ease the strain of ongoing argument; but it cannot disguise that fact, for the long first chapter at least, more is being said about less. This "scholastic" increase might signal no more than Shepard's awareness that his audience now includes readers as well as listeners. Or, inferring that some form of the material of the *Believer* was indeed preached at Cambridge before being sent off to the English publisher, it could reveal the presence of a more competent set of listeners; and indeed it makes some sense to think of the *Convert* as covering the basics for a decidedly mixed English audience and of the *Believer* as firing the hard stuff, full bore, at an audience already venturing to be Saints. Or it may be that, having flexed his supple rhetorical muscles in the *Convert,* Shepard himself is ready for some heavier lifting. However we assign the cause, the literary effect is going to be different: fewer glowing appeals, more careful definition and distinction.

One way to register the new range of *The Sound Believer* is to notice that its first chapter—on Christ as the "only cause" of man's deliverance—represents a return to the ground already covered in chapter 4 of *The Sincere Convert,* where the same Christ was the "only means" of precisely that deliverance: 9 pages then, 122 pages now. One explanation of this massively differential repetition is that, though the earlier treatment allowed for the Spirit's "application" as well as the Son's "purchase" of redemption, it did not pretend to set out anything like a full sense of what the experience of that spiritual application would feel like. What might be its beginning, what its morphological steps or stages, what its moment of consummation? Here, by powerful contrast, Shepard gives not only 47 pages on the nature of that mysterious Faith which unbreakably seals the connection between the saving God and the soul of man, but a full 75 pages on the parts of man's preparation for that faith and on the peculiar affect of each distinct part. Nothing truly difficult is ever easy.

It is, of course, precisely the first seventy pages of chapter 1 of *The Sound Believer* that mark Shepard as a prime preparationist, second in this emphasis behind only Thomas Hooker, from whom he may have learned the tricks of that arduous trade.[30] But that is neither Shepard's most significant literary identity nor yet the most important revelation of *The Sound Believer.* For Shepard does indeed go on—to Faith, at some length, at this lengthy chapter's end, and to the subsequent matters of Justification, Reconciliation, Adoption, Sanctification, Audience, and Glorification in chapter 2; and, finally, and as if to remind us of the *Convert*'s concluding emphasis on "duties," to a separate peroration on the Saint's signal commitment to loving obedience. One still goes to Ames's *Medulla* for the best adult "catechism" of Puritan doctrine. Hooker remains the standard on preparation, Bulkeley on covenant, and Cotton on the Spirit. But for a balanced account of the various stages along the Saint's way—which the Antinomians would dismiss—one simply has to read *The Sound Believer.*[31] All of it.

————

Shepard's first section makes it clear that his venue is now the "application" and not the "purchase" of redemption: Christ having paid the "price" of God's justice, the Spirit must exercise the "power" (115) of putting the human person in touch with the result of that sacrifice. Socinians deny "price" by refusing Jesus his proper divinity; "power" is denied by the Arminian emphasis on the "liberty of the will of man." Apropos of this latter sign of an "adulterous generation," we need to ask, "what is the way for us to seek, and so to find and feel deliverance by the hand of Christ's power?" (116). Shepard might have asked how the Spirit may be thought to apply the sacrifice of Christ; but, as we now expect, he will—with the Arminian pitfall always in mind—always choose the more *active* formula. And, since the seeking is linked here to a successful finding, we may be sure that he has not placed us on a slippery slope. Not all seekers may find; but no one finds apart from a fairly arduous search.

Now, as there were four principal "ways whereby man ruins himself," so there is a "fourfold act of Christ's power, whereby he . . . delivers all his [saints] out of their miserable estate": "conviction of sin," "compunction for sin," "humiliation or self-abasement," and "faith" (116–17). Equipped with flexible categories like "bummer," students often dare Shepard, at just this point, to maintain the distinction of conviction, compunction, and humiliation—so *many* ways to feel bad about sin, little man? Perhaps they have a point. A few have the wit to wonder if "faith" can afford to be part of a perfect continuity with its preparatory phases. But it usually requires the reading of a book on "The Holy Spirit in Puritan Faith and Experience" to notice the slippage by which the "power of the Spirit of Christ" (115) has become simply "Christ's power" (116); and to wonder if the refusal to invoke the Spirit as a separate agency may not betray a certain "Christifying of the Spirit."[32] Or to wonder if a Spiritist like John Cotton might be expected to wonder. For the slippage continues to occur: section 1 ends with the decision to press ahead with "the manner of the Spirit's work"; but section 2 announces its subject as "The First Act of Christ's Power" (117). Perhaps it is enough to observe that Shepard does not always maintain an available separation of Trinitarian function.[33]

As if to announce that he is, in any case, more interested in observable effects than in abstruse causes, Shepard devotes some twenty pages to his understanding of the "Conviction of Sin." Eager to make all the stops, he first stipulates that as there can be "no faith without sense of sin and misery," so there is "no sense of sin without a precedent sight or conviction of sin" (118). Satan works to obscure the idea of sin, but the "Lord Jesus by his Spirit" works to emphasize and to specify: in these Reformed Times all men are heard to confess that they are sinners in some generalized sense, "but that which the Spirit principally convinceth of is some sin . . . in particular" (119). The first discovery will vary with the bias of the individual sinner, but other notes are bound to follow: the "woman of Samaria" was first put in mind of her "secret whoredom," but "upon this discovery, she saw many more sins" (120); Paul was first convinced "of his persecution," but then "many secret sins of his heart were discovered" (121). Next, after this discovery of the facts, comes the knowledge of "the great evil of those particular sins" (122) and "the just punishment which doth follow sin" (123). At a conscientious minimum, then: "I am the man," the sole author of acts of the greatest evil there can be; for which Christ himself will come against me in a "flaming fire"; and then I must face the "bottomless pit" (124–25).

Students love to talk about the bogey of hellfire, but the real energy of this section begins to appear with the discovery that not "all confession of sin" is identically "conviction." Competing with Hooker's famous passage on "The True Sight of Sin," and furnishing language to Edwards' "Divine and Supernatural Light,"[34] Shepard insists on a sight of sin that is so demonstrative that "a man's mouth is stopped" (126) from protest or exculpation; that is intuitive rather than discursive, as a man is more afraid of a real than of a painted lion (127–28); that is constant and unwavering, so that "God's arrows" may be said to "stick fast in the soul" (129). Especially memorable is Shepard's evocation of the "excuses and extenuations" which mark the familiar evasion of conviction:

> One saith, I was drawn unto it (the woman that thou gavest me), and so lays the blame on others: another saith, It is my nature: others say, All are sinners; the godly sin as well as others, and yet are saved at last, and so I hope shall I: others profess they can not part with sin; they would be better, but they can not, and God requires no more than they are able to perform: ... others say, We are sinners, but yet God is merciful and will forgive it: another saith, Though I have sinned, yet I have some good, and am not so bad as other men. (126)

"Endless," that is to say, "are these excuses for sin." It remains for Hooker to remark that "all this wind shakes no corn."[35] But Shepard is sure enough of his own vernacular to predict that "when the Spirit comes to convince, he ... pulls down all these fences [and] tears off all these fig leaves," forcing the soul to stand "before God, crying ... guilty, guilty" (126); and reminding us, once again, that if the Puritan cannot quite justify God's ways, he certainly can embarrass most of our own self-justifications.

The final "doctrine" of Shepard's little treatise on the sight of sin raises the question of the "measure of spiritual conviction" that may be found "in all the elect." Hell's own supply, we may be expecting to hear. More subtly, however, Shepard answers, with what will become a refrain, "so much [as] is necessary, and no more": "so much conviction of sin as may bring in and work compunction for sin"; or, in the language of the faculties, "so much sight of sin as may bring in sense of sin." His point, it appears, is to allow for some variety, particularly in New England, now, where so much depends upon the narrative of conversion: "Everyone hath not the same measure of conviction" (130). Be not discouraged, therefore, if you "have not such a . . . constant light to see sin and death as others" (131): as long as compunction shall follow conviction, and humiliation next, the progress will be keeping its course. And who would linger at the threshold?

With this transition, Shepard moves to "a word of application." Ministers of the Word, aware that "other doctrines are sweet and necessary," must yet begin "with conviction of sin" (131). Hearers of that Word, moreover, must be warned against their tendency to "stand it out against" the sight of sin (132); let them learn instead to "look upon every conviction . . . as an arrest . . . given from the Lord himself" (134). Finally, as to those already convicted, let them say, "Blessed be the minister of the Lord . . . that gave me that counsel." But while we pause to estimate the precise degree of self-service implied by the difference between this response and David's "O blessed be the Lord," Shepard goes on to introduce a very sensitive point: do not undervalue conviction, he warns, just because it may be a "common" work of the Spirit.

Willing to concede that "some reprobates do see sin," Shepard wishes to stress the opposite point, that proper conviction is "a favor the Lord shows not to all mankind" (135–36). What the more guarded logic of preparationism intends, perhaps, is that while conviction is not by itself an evidence of election, still the saved are hardly found to be without this act of self-discovery: for what sense could "faith" in some vicarious rescue from sin possibly make without knowledge of the sin from which? What Shepard actually says, however, is more curiously interesting than would be the flat identification of conviction as a condition sine qua non. Conviction may be a "common" work, but it remains "the first fundamental work of the spirit, and is seminally all"; exactly as "ignorance of sin is seminally all sin." The process of salvation, Shepard seems to argue, not only begins, but finds its entire meaning implied, just here, with the mind's grasp of the fact that its own self is a sinner as such.[36]

We might begin to wonder if all witnesses would agree that a common work of the Spirit can really serve as an epitome of its entire saving function. But Shepard's confidence provides its own transition—"sense of sin begins here," with sight—and provides him with an analogy to which he may have felt particularly entitled:

Remember that the discovery of Faux in the vault was the preservation of England: we use to remember the day and hour of some great . . .

deliverance: O, remember this time, wherein the love of Christ first brake out in convincing thee of thy sin, who else had certainly perished in it. (136)[37]

Treasure conviction, therefore, not only because "Christ by his Spirit begins the actual deliverance of his elect here" (117), but because the chances are that all such knowledge is already instinct with salvation. Certainly no *system* could teach otherwise—as if the Soul might wait and wait, for the ultimate grace of faith, by itself, alone.

Eager to get on with what his unction wishes to make a smooth and continuous process, Shepard opens his next section with the assurance that though "Compunction, pricking at the heart, or sense and feeling of sin," is indeed "different from conviction of sin"; and though "a man may have sight of sin without sorrow and sense of it," still, the "conviction which the Spirit works in the elect" is eventually "accompanied with compunction" (136). Scholastically stated, conviction differs from compunction as understanding from feeling or will; and impatience with that distinction will increase the resistance at just this point: why proliferate in nature what will become reconciled in grace? Unless that were the point of another venerable distinction—namely, that grace works to reestablish the integrity of fractured and fractious nature. And, to the objection that, having already distinguished between the "spiritual conviction" and some merely "notional" knowledge, Shepard has less room left than he imagines, the answer might be that his genius is all along for coordination, not discrimination: can things that pass so well into other things be all that different? Shepard's main "argument" for such an inevitable continuity here is simply to ask, what else might we suppose? "Why doth the Lord let in the light of the knowledge of Christ and his will?" that it should "like froth, float in the understanding . . . ? No, verily, but that the heart might be thoroughly and deeply affected therewith" (137). At risk here, perhaps, is the credibility of the case of the reprobate who gets the sight but not the sense of sin: how *not* move on from head to heart? But rather than preempt Hawthorne and Kierkegaard on the strange half-life of intellectualization,[38] Shepard insists only that conviction is more likely to force compunction, most immediately, than "to drive the soul to Christ" all at once.

The serious matter of the long section 3 begins with his discussion of the "necessity of this compunction to succeed conviction": does one really need to feel that bad? Conceding, finally, that there may be exceptional cases in which Christ uses "neither law nor gospel" to work his saving effect, Shepard prefers to discuss only the "ordinary dispensation," which is what grumblers would be questioning:

What need is there of sorrow and compunction of heart? A man may be converted only by the gospel, and God may let in sweetness and joy without any sense of sin or misery, and in my experience I have found it so; others . . . also feel it so; why, therefore, do any press such a necessity of coming in by a back door unto Christ?

To this unsettling proposal—of the availability of faith without its preparation, the New Testament without the Old, the good news of grace without the bad news of sin—Shepard responds with conscious caution: a "weighty point," to be handled with "much tenderness" (138). Evidently he is beginning to notice that there are at least two "Orthodoxies" in Massachusetts.[39]

One mark of his caution is his clearing away of possible misunderstandings: all need not have the same "measure" (138) of compunction; nor need one be able to tell—in a formal profession—the time of its "first beginning" (139). Further, compunction may begin in a wide variety of circumstances, different for Paul, obviously, than for "Lydia or Apollos." Mention of Lydia recalls the claim that "many in Scripture are converted . . . without any sorrow for sin" (140); but Shepard suggests that her preparation probably occurred in an unrecorded portion of her life. And, turning to his own preacherly problem, he dares his objector to think of Paul or his cohort as ever preaching Christ "without preaching the need men had of him"; or preaching that need "without preaching man's undone and sinful state" (141). Thus after allowing for atypical cases, Shepard more urgently suggests that the faithful minister must stick to the norm. Surely compunction must follow conviction; otherwise, "a sinner will never part with his sin." Conviction may "light the candle to see sin," but "compunction burns [the] fingers, and that only makes [a man] dread the fire." Are men not amply instructed, "'Be afflicted, and mourn, and weep'"? And, elsewhere, "'Rend your hearts, and not your garments.'" "Not that they were able to do this" (142), the Calvinist in Shepard hastens to add; but he who offers faith to the elect must first work sorrow. And those softer-minded souls who continue to imagine that "the sweetness of Christ in the Gospel . . . [may] separate from sin, without any compunction," need to consider that "Christ's sweetness" draws "the soul unto Christ" only after compunction has worked "to turn the soul from sin." In a word, "Aversion from sin is distinct from, and in order goes before, our conversion unto God" (143).

So telling a maxim might well end the discussion, but Shepard adds a flourish of biblical support: words "in season" are spoken "unto the weary"; invited guests strayed from the supper because "they felt no need of coming"; "the prodigal cares not for father nor father's house, until he comes to see, Here I die." "The gospel draws men unto Christ," true enough, but that gospel reveals no grace but with respect and with reference unto sinners, and men in extreme misery; the gospel saith not that Christ is come to save, but to save sinners. . . . It reveals not . . . that God justifies men, but he justifies the ungodly; it reveals not . . . that Christ died for us, but that he died for them that were weak, for sinners, for enemies. (144–45)

And when the Redeemer stipulates that he "came not to call the righteous, but sinners," he evidently means, on the one hand, those who *consider* themselves to be righteous and, on the other, those who *know* themselves to be sinners. Just so, the Lord "leaves the ninety-nine sheep" who seem not to need repentance for "the one lost sheep that feels itself" so.

Indeed—as Shepard crowns his argument for the necessity of compunction—what other sense can the whole story of sin and redemption be thought to make?

Why did the Lord suffer the fall of man? What was his great plot in it? It is apparent[ly] this, that thereby way might be made for the greater manifestation of God's grace in Christ. The serpent poisons all mankind, that the seed of the woman might have the glory of recovering some. . . . Surely Adam might have glorified grace if he had stood. . . . But the Lord saw grace should not be . . . advanced to its highest dignity by this, and therefore suffers him actually to fall. (145)

So far, so very familiar: the happy Fall, that brought forth such a redeemer. Now, however, Shepard's plot summary attempts a noteworthy amplification of the venerable paradigm: consider that man's Fall *in itself* actually "obscures all the glory of God"; which can be restored only if men "see and feel their fall and misery" (146). Thus, Shepard seems to insist, Paul's metahistory of Sin and Grace makes insufficient sense without the Baptist's premise of preparation: What if they gave a Redeemer and no one noticed the need?

Anticlimactically—given this elevation of John the Baptist to the status of Adam and Christ—Shepard now turns to the task of defining compunction, this "pricking of the heart." It contains three elements. First, "a marvelous fear . . . of the direful displeasure of God, of death, and hell, the punishment of sin" (146). And as these fears are as "arrows shot into the conscience by the arm of the Spirit," they are clear, strong, and well directed; the ignorant may slumber, but those who know the "house is on fire" are likely to be "full of fear" (148–49). Then, "as fear plucks the soul from security in seeing no evil to come, so sorrow takes off the present pleasure and delight in sin" (150): not a "summer cloud, or an April shower," this mourning for the "greatest evils" (151) is a "constant mourning," aptly called a "spirit of heaviness" (153). Finally, compunction implies *some* sort of "separation from sin": a difficult point, Shepard observes more than once, since "sin in the will" is mortified only "by a spirit of holiness," which comes "after the soul is implanted into Christ" (154). On the other hand, what use were fear and sorrow if they left the sinner's relation to his sin unchanged? Evidently one needs to ask about the "measure of compunction" (155) in just this context.

"So much compunction or sense of sin," Shepard stipulates, "as attains the end of it." And if one asks about that end, the answer can only be "No other but that the soul, being humbled, might go to Christ (by faith) to take away his sin." Or—not to get too far too fast—"the *finis proximus* or next end of compunction is humiliation, that the soul may be so severed from sin as to renounce itself for it; the *finis remotus,* or last end, is, that, being thus humbled, it might go unto Christ to take away sin" (155). The Schoolboy Latin may seem a (transparent) covering for the fact that, even in the best-motivated systems, not all entities of reason can be made to lie down with all other such entities; but the primitive distinction gives Shepard the opportunity to instruct his audience that Christ's condemnation touches not so much our sin as our "being unwilling the Lord Jesus should take it away" (155). The greatest sin of all, so to speak, is the attempt of the sinner to free *himself* from his sin—which would seem to imply that even a reprobate might experience compunction. What Shepard wishes to emphasize, however, is that "sense of sin," unlike the mere sight, causes the soul to look ahead to liberation; and, to do this validly, it must look through the glass of "humiliation," which reveals that soul's helplessness to help itself.

Before moving on to this humiliation, however, Shepard turns aside to certain explanations and applications. First of all, the "loosening from sin" involved in the work of the genuine, forward-looking compunction is supernatural as well as moral: the Spirit not only affects "the heart with fear and sorrow," but actually "puts forth its own hand physically or immediately, and his own arm brings salvation to us, by a further, secret, immediate stroke, turning the iron neck [and] cutting the iron sinews of sin" (157). Granting that the hand and the arm are metaphoric—whether "its" or truly "his"—we may yet wonder what Shepard may precisely mean by asserting that the Spirit acts "physically." "Immediately" would be enough to signify that there can be no second-cause reduction of this well nigh miraculous activity of the Spirit. Perhaps Shepard means "only" that, going far beyond the work of moral suasion, the Spirit actually begins to "convert" the will itself, from the sort of faculty that can choose only its own loves and lusts to one that can will beyond itself. At very least it is his emphatic way of saying that the change from love to hatred of sin involves a divine operation of the first order: men may "think it is easy to be willing that Christ should come and take away all your sins," but Shepard insists that it requires "the omnipotent arm of the Lord" (157–58). Just here, at any rate, do men begin to be enabled to make the required choices.

Not yet in favor of Christ as the only remedy, but only against sin "as the greatest evil" (158). "Torment and anguish" may affect reprobates, as Saul and Judas; only those "actually justified, called and sanctified" can lament sin as an injury to God. In between, so to speak, the elect feel, at the "first stroke and wound . . . the Spirit gives them," a keen sense of the "separation of the[ir] soul[s] from God" (158–59). "Seeking" but not as yet finding, the soul wanders in search of "fellowship with God, the only blessedness of man." Nor is this "Augustinian" condition avoidable;[40] for "if the soul ordained and made for this end should not feel its present separation from God by sin, . . . it would never seek to return again to him as to his greatest good" (159). Evidently our original hearts were *not* made for sin; and possibly compunction can be thought of as a recognition of just this fact. Certain it is, in any case, that "the souls . . . God saves are never quiet until they . . . have communion with him" (160). Which may reprove those who "think there is no necessity of . . . misery before the application of the remedy" and who would, therefore, "not have the law first preached in these days." Possibly "these days" mark the beginnings of the Antinomian protest against all emphasis on sin and the law as smacking of a covenant of works. Certainly Shepard is working hard, in his first application, to stress the necessity of just such preaching: the doctrine of "seeing and feeling our misery before the remedy" is, he claims, "universally received by all solid divines, both at home and abroad"; further, at the level of practice, just this sort of preaching has been widely sealed as "God's own way by his rich blessings on the labors of his servants faithful to him herein" (160). Nor will it help to valorize a preaching of the New Testament before the Old; for Paul clearly "proves Jews and Gentiles to be under sin . . . before he opens the doctrine of justification" (160–61). And Shepard himself has not read "in Moses, or in all the prophets, such full and plain expressions of our misery as in the New Testament." Evidently, therefore, conviction and compunction are no mere "back door." Backward, rather, is the idea that "a man must first have Christ . . . before he can feel any spiritual misery"; for that is "to say that a Christian must first be healed that he may be sick" (161).

The name of that tune—we may be tempted to conclude, before we discover whether any person with serious claim on our attention may have something to say on the other side.[41] The limits of that particular metaphor, in any case, as Shepard ends his first application on a more ironical note: "Are we troubled with too many wounded consciences in these times," he wryly inquires, "that we are so solicitous of coining new principles of peace?" Is it not still the common case, rather, that omnivorously sinful men still hold out against being "cast down"? And can we seriously imagine that the sinful can "prize" (or "taste") Christ "without any casting down"? Rhetorical questions are always dangerous, and never more so than from the tongue of a Puritan. Perhaps we ought to withhold our answer. Indeed, Shepard himself sounds a note of caution in the second of his two applications, a carefully worded warning to those who admit that there is "a necessity of a sense of misery by the work of the law, before Christ can be received"; but who also hold that "there is no such feeling of misery as hath been mentioned, but that it is common to the reprobate as to the elect, and consequently that in sense of sin there is no such special work of the Spirit as separates the soul from sin before it comes unto Christ" (162). Willing earlier to invoke the authority of "all solid divines," Shepard is here constrained to admit—in deference to the nearby presence of John Cotton, one dares to infer—that such "is the judgment of many and holy and learned." Yet Shepard requests persons so convinced to measure their doctrine against "the truth of Christ" and in Latin admonishes not to make too much of a small difference. In the end he resigns himself to this divergence from Orthodoxy on the condition that there be "no disagreement in the substance" (162): some may say compunction is but a common work of the Spirit, but all must hold its necessity in any case.

Or what?—one wonders, in a Congregationalist colony. But while we are wondering, whether the first great doctrinal debate in Winthrop's holy state *might* have concerned preparation rather than sanctification,[42] the third section of the first chapter of Shepard's *Sound Believer* disturbs its own sense of structure by going on well beyond its promised scope. Suddenly more embattled and more technical, this second application expands to the length of a sermon in itself, pulling out all the stops of academic distinction and pressing to the limit both its types and its tropes. The scene is New England, of course, so that Shepard is in no particular danger. Yet we get a clear sense that the pressure of current events is once more deforming the best-devised emplotment of normative religious experience.

———

A book on the (acquired) taste for the (rarified) pleasures of the (not quite canonical) books of New England's first Puritan generation is sorely tempted to skip over Shepard's twelve-page afterword on compunction: Shepard is driving toward "humiliation," we gather, and we are anxious to see how he will define that step, which takes us from some sort of "separation from sin," together with a sense of seeking and not finding, to the inspired knowledge that, as our hearts were made for God alone, our souls can be saved by no one but Christ. Can't we now, in all decency, just *go* there? To linger here is to sense that something further *needs* to be added, something his own refined theological taste and emergent idea of literary construction would avoid if they could. With others unable to hold their tongues on the subject of grief and the Spirit, Shepard *must* be allowed to speak his own further word—more technical than his "popular" form would encourage but more passionate as well; and more personal, as if his own words were being disputed. An interesting mood, whether or not we can fix its precise polemic moment.[43]

At the outset Shepard stipulates somewhat more than he has explicitly emphasized so far: that "there must be some sense of misery before the application of the remedy" he takes from his own demonstration; but he has been a little less overt in his teaching that this "sense of misery is wrought by the Spirit of Christ, not the power of man"; and, given the sense of his foregoing paragraph, on those who hold that misery is "common to the reprobate as to the elect," it is a little surprising to hear him concede as "agreed on all hands" that the "terrors and sorrows of the elect do virtually differ from those in the reprobate, the one driving the soul to Christ, the other not." At issue is whether "there is not a special work of the Spirit, turning (at least in order of nature) the soul from sin, before the soul returns by faith unto Christ" (162). This, of course, is the "stroke" Shepard had dared call "physical," and to its necessity, prior to faith, he remains entirely committed.

With Ferrius he holds that an "actual grace" can drive out sin as well as can the saving and "habitual" sort; and—less scholastically—he argues that this must indeed be the case: "Christ . . . must first bind the strong man, and cast him out by this working or actual grace, before he dwells in the house of man's heart" (162). Original Adam might have been a subject for the immediate reception of God's habitual grace, but fallen man harbors a "resistance [which] must first be taken away, before the Lord introduce his image again." Were this not so, a natural man might dispose himself unto grace, and this was "Pelagianism in Aquinas' time." Fallen nature resists not only the state of grace, entirely opposite to his prevailing state of sin, but also the "God of grace himself when he comes to work it" (163); how necessary, therefore, is some active stroke against this active opposition, some "cutting off from the old olive tree, the old Adam," before the "implanting into the good olive tree, the second Adam"? Or—outside this over-planted forest of biblical tropes—how can a man "wholly resist God and Christ, and yet be united to him at the same instant"? *Simul justus et peccator,* in good faith; but this is only to say that one's sanctification is never perfect.[44] The present question is whether a man can prove his "union to Christ and to his lust" as well. As if one could serve both "God and Mammon" (164).

Technicalities continue, alternating as we sense with the furious attempt to assemble all the relevant tropes and make them express an Augustinian experience and articulate a late medieval education. No surprise if it cannot quite be done. Yet our very skepticism owes something to the unflagging efforts of just such Protestant dedication; for it was not from the first evident that no reformation of categories could ever make Hebrew poetry underwrite the self-hatred needed to guarantee the half-life of early modern repression. And—though we have our own books to express the conclusion—surely Puritanism has raised this "discontent" to the highest point of dialogic art. *Plymouth* might subdue *Canaan* with form and with tone. But somewhat more was required when the very godly learned to say, "Screw guilt."

Terms proliferate, but the moral outrage remains the same: that "vocation" must come before "justification" is proved from the fact that the soul "effectually called" is called "first from darkness, then unto light" (164). Those who think otherwise—that God's notice of man's justification can come first, joyfully and all at once—are simply deluded: they are those who would "cut off John Baptist's head"; less graphically, they think they can "clasp about Christ" though yet "enemies to the cross" (165). Surely the "blessed and learned Pemble" is right to teach "that actual faith is never wrought in the soul, till . . . the will be . . . freed in part from its natural perverseness" (166).[45] Further, to place justification before faith is to deny "the whole current of Scripture, which saith, 'We are justified by faith,' and therefore not before faith" (166–67). Worse, perhaps, to place sanctification before justification is to say that a "Christian's communion with Christ goes before his union to him" (168). Too *many* terms, clearly enough, from the moment Paul's exasperated list of all the things a redeemer could gratuitously do became a morphological table of stages along the way of reified grace. Believing he needs them all, and in a certain order, Shepard moves from the mild manner of his confident tuition toward something like polemic hysteria. The challenge of the moment must have seemed serious indeed.

All talk of the legal fiction of our being "justified declaratively by faith, or . . . *in foro conscientiae*[,] is a mere device": our justification is every bit as "real" (167) as our guilt and condemnation; and in Shepard's New World congregation, at least, the guilt must be known and confessed before its cancellation can credibly be claimed. Again: "Let none say here . . . that we have union to Christ, first by the Spirit, without faith, in order going before faith," for that is only to recall that "the Godhead is everywhere, in whom we live and move"; and salvation theory must concern itself with "some act of the Spirit peculiar to the elect, . . .

working some real change in the soul" (168). Intriguing, perhaps, is the question of what exactly Shepard means by "here": In this logical or local place? And if the latter, in New England merely? Or in his own audience?

But Shepard, as if to call us back to more strictly literary questions, moves on to apologize for his outburst. "I am sorry," he assures an audience as surprised as ourselves, "to be thus large in less practical matters," but

> I have thought it not unuseful, but very comfortable, to a poor passenger, not only to know his journey's end and the way in general to it, but also the several stadia or towns he is orderly to pass through; there is much wisdom of God to be seen not only in his work, but in his manner and order of working; for want of which . . . many Christians in these days fall . . . into erroneous apprehensions in their judgments, the immediate ground of many errors in practice. (170)

No less a prediction of Melville than an approximation of Bunyan, the text of Shepard's intruded subtext not only assures us of the usefulness of theory but also reminds us that even the Calvinist elect may require lessons in spiritual geography precisely as such.[46] No *very* big deal, it seems to say. And yet the apology concedes that something uncustomary has indeed occurred, even in a venue where the line between popular and intellectual culture is unusually difficult to draw.

Nor does it signify vernacular business as usual when Shepard attempts to epitomize the teaching and express the mood which has provoked him to venture beyond his customary, well-controlled literary self: "Look narrowly to your union," first of all; if not "cut off from your sin," a "resistance of Christ" will surely remain, disqualifying compunction and preventing salvation thereby. And also, more rhetorically: "Trouble me no more . . . in asking whether a Christian is in a state of happiness or misery in this condition [of compunction.] He is preparatively happy; he is now passing from death to life, though as yet not wholly passed" (170). No generation so therapeutically convinced of the need to "feel its feelings" can be asked to make sense out of the concept of "preparative happiness"; and even here, the world predicted by Shepard's tone is evidently having difficulties of its own. A man or woman who endures the agony of running a marathon, say, may be preparatively happy all the while if certain he or she will win (or even finish); and Shepard means to argue that the killing pains of compunction are already a trustworthy sign of victory. The problem, however, is not in rule but in fact: are these present agonies indeed owing to the Spirit's "physical" stroke? Or is it all just another orgy of "prayers, tears, fears, [and] sorrows," in which a man may perish as easily as in the prosecution of some lust? They seem indeed to be asking. They seem indeed to have heard, somewhere, a rumor that it need not be *this* hard. Not so hard "psychologically," though they scarcely have the concept, and though the majority might themselves resist a way that seemed too "faire and easy." And not so very difficult as a problem in knowledge, for faith has its own epistemology, whether early modern saints can say the word or not.

Shepard, of course, has already passed through the exquisite pain of compunction and on to whatever else the Pauline program predicts this side of the grave. To him and to his ilk, therefore, the preparative happiness is largely the afterglow with which a successful outcome may suffuse the suffering of any process whatsoever. What can this successful person say to those who do not yet succeed? Augustine can write the master text of his *Confessions* and, down the centuries, Shepard may force his footnote into the canon of something or other. But what can he say in his service? Check with me when you're certain? Write if you get Word? Clearly he has to say something. And evidently something like conviction, compunction, humiliation, and faith had seemed about right, to extend the system begun back in England, and to fill in the dark patches of those who *also* sought a purer way. But did they come all this way for godly sorrow? Or to make their sorrow look like happiness? OK, if you say so. But even those whose time and place forbid them to shop around for words they love to hear at Sunday service will sooner or later get wind of other doctrine. What if one should overhear that Protestant Salvation—"free" as such a thing could ever be—does *not* require any "special change in himself," and that it comes indeed "by immediate revelation in an absolute promise"? Would the case of him and all his kind require a "synod"? Or might it be enough if some faithful shepherd turn his second "use" into a sermon of its own?

Complete with its very own uses. Of lamentation—"for the hardness of men's hearts in these times," when men imagine "you come to pull away their limbs when you come to pluck away their sins" (171). And of exhortation as well. For, just as in *The Sincere Convert,* we must be reminded to "Labor for this sense of misery, for this spirit of compunction";[47] and by a man who remains quick with his Calvinist disclaimer: "I know it is not in your power to break your own hearts, no more than to make the rocks to bleed." But if "He only can do it for thee," remember what rough, heartbreaking work it is that must be done; and remember too that "he can break thine [heart] much more when thou art desiring him to do it for thee" (173). Or if this fusing of context into cause be too daring, remember to respond with "abundant thankfulness" for the "rich grace" revealed in "any sense of thy sin and danger by it" (173–74). And, for a final use within a use, weary not of the strange burden of a happiness that is merely preparative:

> O, consider that this is the hand of the Lord Jesus, and that he is now about to save thee, when he comes to work any compunction in thee—especially such as whereby he doth not only cut thy heart with fears and sorrows, but cut thee off from thy sin, so far only as drives thee to the Lord Christ to take them away. (174)

For this sorrow really will lead on "to the third particular, of humiliation." If any can follow it, that is, in life as in logic, in spite of distractions that threaten the process. No doubt Shepard really will "trouble" himself to go over it all again and again, with reference to this or that particular soul itself. But the cycle of salvation can spin its wheels for just so long.

By this point we probably feel the full force of Shepard's preparationist logic: the ways of God in salvation *might* have been as strange as any theosophist might suppose but, given the sort of revelation the Christian community believes fallen man to have received, nothing significant can be *expected* to happen to a person not convinced in his mind that he is indeed a sinner and stricken in his heart with the enormity of that fact. Wherever we mark the end of the Spirit's common and the beginning of its saving work, this much seems demanded by a norm we might call adequate spiritual consciousness. And though we might wish to argue that the Puritan's sight of sin—as infecting every voluntary action of the natural man and offering infinite insult to a God understood as "holy" by nature—is a back-formation of its theory of salvation, Shepard's own treatise must move forward: only the man touched by the true outline of his Adamic problem can begin to appreciate the inspired necessity of its Christ-ian solution. "Humiliation," the recognition that there is no hope from ourselves, is the predictable state of the soul in extremis.

Of course, there will be some overlap for, "in a large sense, a wounded, contrite sinner is a humble sinner" (174). Yet a crucial difference exists: the Lord may so wound a man that "he will resist no more; yet he will rather fly to his duties to heal him" for such self-trust is, it appears, the universal way of "pride." Humiliation, *per contra,* is "that work . . . whereby the soul, being broken off from self-conceit and self-confidence in any good it hath or doth, submitteth unto, or lieth under, God, to be disposed of as he pleaseth" (175). A "willingness to be damned," the future will say. And its need seems readily apparent for, stricken with the knowledge of their own ruin, men practice all sorts of homemade self-repair:

What shall I do? Do? saith the conscience; leave thy sins, do as well as others do, do with all thy might . . . , pray, hear, and confer; God accepts of good desires, and requires no more of any man but to do what he can. Hence the soul plies both oars, though against the wind and tide, and strives, and wrestles . . . , and hopes one day to do better; and here he rests.

Not that Shepard would teach *against* "striving." But there are ends and ends, and surely the pleasure of "the casting away of sins" is less than ultimate; for while the soul is thus occupied, it is utterly "incapable of Christ" (176). Strive, rather, to know the limits of all *such* strife.

As to the means, let it be understood that they involve the Spirit's "immediately acting upon the soul." Later, to be sure, the soul "in Christ" will have "some power to humble himself." At this point, however, "the Spirit of Christ doth it immediately by his own omnipotent hand"; for natural men will "never come to Christ if they can make anything else serve." Once again Shepard is making a place for the Spirit to work in a way for which private effort is no substitute. Just so, perhaps, he sought to protect himself from someone's metalegal critique. And yet, as he goes on to explain, the Spirit's activity is not at all "without the word"; and, pointedly, "the word it works chiefly by is the law" (177). At this stage at least, the Spirit's task is to force a perfect grasp of man's utter loss in the face of the Law. And we should not be surprised if other saints can think of ways for its operation to be somewhat more "immediate"—more direct and more swiftly efficacious—than that. Undaunted, however, Shepard goes on to elaborate a "fourfold act" by which the Spirit uses the law. "By discovering," first, "the secret corruption of the soul in every duty"; by letting the soul see "that all its righteousness is a menstruous cloth" (177–78). Next, by making more of "original corruption" to appear "than ever before": not only are one's duties "defiled with sin," but the heart itself is the very "dunghill" (178) source. Third, by wearing the soul out, "not only [with] its sin, but [with] its work"—until it cry, "I can do nothing for God or myself: only I can sin and destroy myself" and place itself, thereby, in range of a call that says "Come to me" all "ye that labor" (179). And finally, by clearing the "justice of God" in showing "neither pity nor pardon" to those toiling in the ways of the law. For despair of the law is not despair in very fact; and the work-weary soul is not to infer, just here, that "the Lord's eternal purpose is to exclude him" but simply "to fall down prostrate in the dust before the Lord, as worthy of nothing but shame and confusion" (180). What but faith could follow such a moment? Indeed, this fine a humiliation might almost be considered faith already, in the negative case; for there is now, besides some miraculous salvation *ab extra,* nothing else to expect.

Yet Shepard's argument is less that salvation *must* certainly follow this moment of exquisite suffering than that the end point of preparation can be nothing but the renunciation of all expectations of reward for effort. A logic of honesty and not of prediction, Shepard's preparation amounts to little more than a grasp of the Pauline facts: preparation ends only when, in "just" humiliation, the soul "submits to be disposed of as God pleaseth" (180). Man is sinful and no doubt. More important, perhaps, God is God. His will be done. He can save a sinner if he wishes. Or not.[48]

But even here, in a negative ultimate that might seem to admit of no degrees, we pause to ask, "What measure?" (181). Enough humiliation to make us earnest in the wish to lie low. But not so much as to inspire the thought that one's vileness is beyond redemption. For that mood—an affectation, surely—can barely conceal its intention to reject the terms of salvation and to "quarrel with God." And faith, which can very intelligibly come to a person who has seen the impossibility of any other means, cannot easily be thought to occur in a mood of resentment. Accordingly, the same Spirit which earlier had to remove "a secret unwillingness that the Lord should work grace," must here act against "a secret quarreling . . . , in case the soul imagines [God] will not come to . . . manifest grace" (182). At first glance it may appear that Shepard is assigning to the Spirit's "supernatural" operation too many local duties in a salvation at the hands of a God whose very will constitutes justice. Yet this very proliferation is Shepard's way of emphasizing that the God who could just *declare* salvation has revealed himself to work in quite another way: no salvation without faith; and no faith without the appropriate human context of call and answer.

To say that "the next end of humiliation is faith" (182) is to suggest that, though indeed "irresistible," the grace of salvation should not be thought of as a violation of the ordinary sense of human volition. Faith is, as we shall see, a call that must be answered, an offer which must be accepted; but the graciousness of that offer consists precisely in the Spirit's "omnipotent" but mostly gradual reconstruction of the human personality to the point where faith becomes what we might call a meaningful option. Otherwise God might well "save geese." But it is also to say that, given the revelation of God's contextual plan, the pain of humiliation can be "of unspeakable . . . consolation to every poor empty nothing that feels itself unable to believe" (183); for without this endgame of humanism, "the Lord should not advance the riches of his grace." And also, come to think of it, he "should not be Lord and Disposer of his own grace"; for, without this realization of utter helplessness, man would still be having salvation on his own terms. As if the "beggar" should quarrel with the "master." And just so does Shepard turn from his careful elaboration of the "psychological" context of salvation, which Scripture reveals to be fitting and reasonable, to the (equally revealed) reminder that, reasonable or not, the proper agent of salvation is God's alone: "I will be merciful to whom I will be merciful" (183–84).

Only thus, perhaps, can Preparation and Calvin (not to say Reason and Revelation) be made to agree: God saves whomever he will. But, against those who think nothing more can be said, God has uniformly associated salvation with the realization of its utter need—its perfect unreachability by the human will as such, and the unquestionable justice of its dependence on the grace of God alone. As Shepard emphasizes elsewhere, in regard to the "covenant," this Calvinist God need not have saved *any*body; or he might have saved them in any way at all, with or without promulgation of the terms and method. Yet he has, by his own revealed admission, decided to save precisely those who—with the aid of the Spirit—come to see their plight exactly as it is.[49] And if this should amount to a limitation of the divine freedom, the limitation is one the Deity has imposed upon itself. Unless one were to protest truth as a limitation on error. Or to regard Scripture as at the mercy, always, of a Spirit who is beyond the bounds, and bound to upset the certainties, of that selfsame Word. The way of preparation may seem operose to some, requiring repeated irruptions of divine power within the terrain of man's spiritual incompetence, but Shepard assures us it is God's own way. We need to learn of God's own revelation, therefore, that "if the lord doth not sever your sin in compunction, and empty you of yourself in humiliation, you cannot receive Christ" (184). Difficult as it may be to leave off sinning, it is harder still to abandon a natural reliance on our own efforts; and yet "trusting to one's own righteousness, and committing iniquity, are couples." Nor is this to flatter the Familist denial of "inherent graces" in those whose nature is regenerate; or their rejection of "sanctification" as evidence of justifying faith, or their impudent casting off of "all duties, because they cannot save themselves by them" (185). For here, again, rash logic would rush in to cancel the plain sense of Scripture. "Foolish virgins" must one day learn, if only from Shepard's own opening of their parable, that faith motivates virtue exactly as the renouncing of all "reliance" on righteousness enables faith.

And so, let those who can grasp more than one idea at a time "be exhorted . . . to lie down in the dust before the Lord" (185); and, if left there for a time, not to "quarrel with God for withdrawing his hand" (186). For "the potter . . . may do" with his clay exactly "what he will" (188). And if there are those who fear, with the poet of their condition, that their solace might prove *too* long withheld, that death might interrupt this game of hide-and-seek, let them ask what mood their "quarrel" in fact bespeaks; for as the Lord intends "to bestow his favor only upon a humbled sinner, he will therefore hide his face until they lie low, and acknowledge themselves worthy of nothing but extremity of misery" (189). Perhaps the "look of agony" is not entirely "true."[50] Perhaps, in Shepard's view, it never is until the suffering lapses into faith.

———

To Shepard, of course, faith is the very opposite of a lapse. Yet it is, at the first moment of its introduction, a notable form of self-relief:

> The Lord having wounded and humbled his elect, and laid them down dead at his feet, they are now as unable to believe as they were to humble their own souls; and therefore now the Lord takes them up into his own arms, that they lean and rest on the bosom of their beloved by faith. (190)

"Metaphor!"—one might object, if the context were postmodernism and the play of rhetoric. "Using the term to define itself!"—if the audience were more scholastic than pious. But Shepard also knows he has now broached a subject of "great difficulty"—of paramount importance yet "very little known." More than a poet, he knows that salvation is only *somewhat* like a child being lifted up from a playground mishap. So he tries again, more technically: "Faith is that gracious work of the Spirit, whereby a humbled sinner receiveth Christ." And again, as if to say the thing most carefully at last: faith is the moment when "the whole soul cometh out of itself to Christ, for Christ and all of his benefits, upon the call of Christ in his word" (190).

What the reader notices in Shepard's various formulations, however, is not identity but significant variation, from a perfect passivity to a significantly human act. As good as dead, the elect are first said to be lifted up: volition is irrelevant. Receiving Christ, in the second formula, is much more nearly a voluntary act, since (most) offers can be refused as well as accepted. In the final version, the elect finally get a move on, coming forth from the shards of their old identity, on purpose to get whatever is to be got: they are responding to a call, to be sure, but when called they do indeed *come*. And surely this final definition is the one Shepard wishes to make emphatic. For, when all else is said and done, in honor of Calvin and in deference to Dort, the Saint has to *act:* "Faith is the complement of effectual vocation, which begins in God's call, and ends in this answer to that call." Coming before one is called is indeed "presumption"; and no doubt the call—as issued to a soul inured by humiliation to the awful sound of silence—

may be thought to enable the response; and yet what is "properly and formally" called faith can be nothing but "to come and receive when called" (191).

Excluded as trivial, clearly, is the Papist's "supernatural assent to a divine truth, because of a divine testimony" (191). And also, at the other extreme, that "faith of assurance" by which Arminians, certain that Christ died for all, happily infer that "Christ died for me in particular"; or by which certain "holy men of ours" have sought to describe not "what faith is in itself" but "of what degree and extent it may be, and should be, in us" (193). An important tale hangs by the thread of this last concession, but not the one that forces Shepard into battle with John Cotton, for the body of Calvin and, more significantly, for the theme of confession narrative and the morale of saintly life in New England.[51] Aware of the problem, but unwilling himself to force the confrontation, Shepard goes on, more or less academically, with the mainline Calvinist things he can say about faith without fear of local contradiction.

The "efficient cause of faith" is of course "the Spirit": "the Spirit doth not believe"—that must be our own human act—but it "causeth us to believe." And its operation here is "creating," therefore "irresistible" (193–94): the truly called are enabled to do that thing without which their humiliation would leave them the most miserable of men. And is this not a great consolation to "all those who feel themselves utterly unable to believe"? For they are to "consider the Lord hath [under]taken in the covenant of grace to work in all his the condition of the covenant, as well as to convert thee [to the] good of it." In one act of grace, that is to say, God stipulates the terms on which salvation—free to offer and free to withhold—may in fact be had; and then, in a second moment—redundant except under the regime of Calvinist thought—he directly enables the human performance of those very terms. And consider, further, poor unbelieving but would-be Christian:

> if the Lord had put it over unto thee to believe, it is certain thou shouldst never have believed; but now the work is put into the hand of Christ; that which is impossible to thee is possible, nay easy, with him; he can comprehend thee when thou canst not apprehend him. (195)

Few enough may worry that the order of grace not be reduplicated unless absolutely necessary; and the slightest intimation of "a life" will surely annul the question of whether Perry Miller made too much of such a (rare) moment of covenant-thinking in Shepard; but, granting criticism, must we not notice the theology of Shepard's prefixes? Unable to grasp Christ because spiritually "unhanded," man may be saved only if his identity is somehow subsumed.

Yet not entirely obliterated, for faith remains an answer to a call, and no active theology, not even one preaching chiefly to the choir, dare risk the implication that salvation is an affair in which Christ talks chiefly to himself. Man is not to insist on his natural identity, to be sure: the New Adam is no longer a "simple separate self." But he must remain distinct enough, in the midst of his spiritual identity with Christ, to maintain an interest in what grace shall enable. Nor, when addressing his Saints—"all you whose hearts the Lord hath drawn and overcome" (196)—would Shepard confuse these human subjects with the object of prayer. A renewed man is still man; and only the badly motivated would dare suggest that the Saint is merged, somehow, in the "person" of the Spirit. And to the doubtful, "afraid [their] faith hath been rather presumption, a work of [their] own power," Shepard boldly advises the test of "covenant": "if any promise be actually yours, it is no presumption to take possession by faith of what is your own." If you really do, for example, "thirst after Christ," then read on and rejoice: "If any man thirst, let him come unto me and drink" (196–97). Cotton will be arguing that the *satisfaction* of thirst, not the thirst itself, is the test for doubting Christians to apply; but Shepard is sure it is a mistake for persons to imagine "the Lord should first make them feel, and then they will believe." Further—to those without the sense of having been enabled to fulfill any of the promises to which salvation is (in covenant) attached but have "only . . . the Lord's call and command to believe"—"do you now, in conscience and obedience to this command, or to God's invitation and entreaty in the gospel, believe" (197). As a woman "overcome with the loving words of her suitor" finds it "no presumption now, but duty to give her consent," so here, with a Christ who is "precious in his words." With this one backward-looking proviso: "If repentance accompanies faith, it is no presumption to believe" (197–98); for, as we are reminded by Shepard's second academic point, the "subject or matter of faith" is precisely "the *humbled* sinner" (199; emphasis added).

As to the "form" of faith, it is "the coming of the whole soul out of itself unto Christ." The coming must be pure, a nearly unmotivated answer to the loveliness of the call (and perhaps the caller), for to come to Christ "for life" (201) is to wrap oneself up in another covenant of works. Negatively, the elect "forsake and renounce themselves." At a loss, thenceforth, they are wont to ask, "Whither shall I go?" In prayer they plead, with Augustine perhaps, "turn me, Lord, and then I shall be turned." And then, at last, when the theology of grammar has done all it can, "Lord, behold, I come" (202). And just this motiveless benignity is faith—an enabled response to an unmerited offer, a "being taken up" in a metaphor of infancy, but a voluntary coming forth when all is said and done. And, as unreserved as it is untainted, it is coming forth of "the whole soul" (203). If the connoisseur of ambivalence—a certain "double-minded man"—shall ask how he shall know "when the whole soul comes to Christ," the answer can only be when it "resteth in Christ, as in its portion and all-sufficient good" (207); for if there is truly "an unregenerate and a regenerate part in a godly man," still there is "not a heart and a heart." And so, if unicity, or "rest," is not a given of nature, it surely must be thought the end of grace. Or else "our hearts were made for" nothing in particular.

A long section on the "end of faith" assures us that the extraordinary "bene-fits" of Christ, not to be sought in the first faithful coming, are indeed entailed in that most pure of acts. "Union to Christ," which names the fact of human salva-tion as such, is the sole end of our first coming; but "communion" (212) with him is certain to follow, and it is from hence that the benefits proceed. Easy to reprove, therefore, are all those who find themselves "catching at promises"—of peace or comfort or even holiness—"without seeking first to have the person of Christ." Equally censurable, however, and far more dangerous in local context, are those found to be "despising the benefits of Christ, especially grace [and] holiness," be-cause, they say, "Christ is all in all to them. Ask them, have you any grace, change of heart, etc.? Tush! what do you tell them of repentance, and faith, and holi-ness? They have Christ, and that is sufficient" (213). A nice characterization of the Christ-without-his-benefits position, even if it should turn out to be done in parody. For Cotton, even before he left England, was already preaching that those who would have Christ "and life in him" might have to have him "in justification, but not in growth of sanctification."[52] And some such position—of saving grace without any attendant regeneration of nature—is precisely at issue here.

In Shepard's pungent formula, Christ came "to save men from their sins, not to save men and their sins." As faith involves, in his view, an active response to a call, so it has to entail, if only in its second moment, a commitment to the holiness as well as to the lovely person of Christ. "Naked" in his initial offer—as Cotton's "bare man," whom the woman must choose without sight of his gifts—Shepard's Christ offers but also demands acceptance of a life of virtue, possible now, for the first time, as a result of the Spirit's working of faith. Not just Salvation: Ah, thank you; but holy duties, now, as the only possible form of thanks. For he that "wraps you up in the covenant, will write his law in your hearts also." Thus Shepard's Familists who, "in advancing Christ himself, and free grace, abolish and despise those heavenly benefits which flow from him unto all the elect," are dangerously "deluded." And, mindful of Augustine's distinction between having Christ and following him, and aware that "to close with Christ's person is sweet to many" who yet resist closing with "his will," the exhortation of the moment is carefully compounded: "O, come, come therefore unto the Lord Jesus for Christ himself, and for all his benefits" (213–14).

Finally, in Shepard's table of scholastic topics, there is "the special ground of faith": if faith is a spiritually enabled coming of "the whole soul . . . out of itself to Christ, for Christ and all his benefits, upon the call of Christ" (190), it remains to explain that this call comes, in ordinary circumstances, from "Christ in his word" (219). Unlike Adam, who was immediately sanctified, fallen (and humiliated) man, expecting nothing but misery, requires some special "vocation"; and unlike Abraham, who enjoyed "dreams and visions . . . before the Scriptures were penned," he is to expect it "by some word or voice," usually that of "God in Christ[,] . . . although dispensed by men, who are weak instruments for this mighty work" (220–21). And though Scripture makes "a general . . . offer of grace to every one" (222), effectual calling is always in some sense "particular"; thus no man should come without a sense of personal involvement. And, as Shepard appears to thicken his own plot, hearing and responding to a call to "come" is more essential to the act of faith than identifying with some "promise" (224).

Other difficulties also press, some close at hand. Questioning the elaborate, inferential indirection of Shepard's multiform way, some suppose "an absolute testimony of actual favor and justification" to be "the first ground of faith." But this way of immediate assurance amounts to saying that "a Christian must be justified before he believe" (225), and Shepard finds this opposed by both plain Scripture and Protestant precedent, in which one is, emphatically, justified "by faith." In Shepard's carefully constructed model, the elect, in a state of appropriate humiliation, are enabled to respond to a call; and only then, by this fact, are they declared to be and accepted as justified or forgiven or made righteous again. The call is personal enough to permit Shepard to risk quoting John's "I have called thee by name" (223), but it is significantly a call and not a mere notification: "P.S., I love you"; and the work of the Spirit is more properly that of enabling a new dimension of religious activity and not merely revealing—in a way Scripture knows nothing of—the accomplished fact of one's redeemed status. God saves his elect, entirely and without exception, and he knows them in advance of any action they may perform; but the method of their salvation is public and, from Scripture, entirely predictable. The saved are those self-known sinners whom the Spirit has enabled to answer a call to come out of themselves, in love, and for the pursuit of holiness. And no otherwise, Shepard was convinced, with or without John Calvin, could Scripture's mysterious discourse of predestination and free grace be reconciled with its more worldly idiom of necessary repentance and active faith.

And no otherwise, if we care to notice the fact, could churches of professed Saints discipline their membership or present their orderly selves as the conscience of a nation. Bounded by the Word—and also by the faithful and the sanctified Work—the Spirit was a necessary premise in all schemes of Christian "Application." Unbound, however, that same Spirit might turn the world upside down by revealing salvation to absolutely anyone at any time. Perhaps this is why Shepard insists on calling Him/It "the Spirit of Christ," whose faithful work enabled a justification by nothing more than faith, but whose call required a loving answer more essentially than it guaranteed the gift of wonderful Life.

———

The two remaining chapters of *The Sound Believer* are brief. Chapter 2 fills out the list of things which come after faith, completing a well-made system but not always advancing Shepard's argument-at-a-distance with his "Familists." And the seven pages of chapter 3 are really a sort of postscripted application of the whole—issuing a call to action which is inspirational in the moment but predictable from the course of Shepard's thought so far and amounting, in the long view of his career, to a modest down payment on the massive emphasis of the *Parable of the Ten Virgins*. For, as it turns out, once Shepard got to the end of his activist system, he settled in to compose, from week to week, a work that in its dedication as well as its sheer length might stand for all the saintly life that might ever follow "after the surprising conversions." Haste now, but incredible endurance next time.

Justification, as we have already been prepared to understand, is "the first benefit which immediately follows our union unto Christ by faith" (237). Although it might be possible to conceive of faith as our personal reception of the spiritually communicated news of the (eternal) decree of our justification, Shepard is adamantly convinced that we are justified, by "imputation" of the righteousness of Christ, only *after* we have answered God's call. In his emphatic formulation, "our justification is not God's eternal purpose to forgive, but it is God's sentence published; a sinner is justified intentionally in election, but not actually until the sentence is past and published." As the injured party, it is "the Father" who "hath chief power to forgive," but this he *cannot* "in justice" do until "the Son step in and satisfy"; nor *will* he do any such thing until, the Spirit assisting, the elect person accepts the particular offer of just such a vicarious satisfaction. Thus "justification is wholly out of ourselves, and we are merely passive in it" (238); yet this declaration of divine forgiveness is never made unless and until an enabled person shall have heard and answered the call to come to Christ in faith.

Other considerations seem ancillary: God the Father justifies "merely . . . out of his grace" (239) and not because any have been "less sinners than others"; further, as Christ is the price of our redemption, so "neither works before conversion . . . nor works of grace in us after conversion can be causes of our justification" (240); "the persons the Lord doth justify" are, as if the point could not be repeated too often, "believers" (242); those believers are accounted "perfectly righteous" (243), and have a "continual" (244), indeed an "eternal righteousness, that never can be lost" (245). Daring to challenge the unbelief of a later generation, Shepard ventures to assert that, by their imputed righteousness, the elect are "more amiable" (245) before God than if they had a righteousness all their own. Only one discouraging word disturbs the otherwise perfect composure of Shepard's celebration of the system which saves with faith alone and in spite of all sin, both before and after: anyone thinking with presumption to say—in any one of a number of perverse formulations—"Let us sin that grace may abound"—had better "tremble"; for such a one has "never yet come to Christ"; all his sins are yet upon him and will meet him "in the day of the Lord's fierce wrath" (247).

Determined to accentuate the positive, however, Shepard goes on to luxuriate in "Reconciliation." This "second benefit which in order of nature follows our justification" (247) names the fact that God's former "enmity" now turns to a "love of complacency and delight" (248), the sort of thing that might inspire a poem: "Peace, Peace, my Honey, do not cry."[53] Or, if not quite yet, then certainly in "Adoption," where lovers turn in fact to sons. Threatening to spoil both the peace and the parallelism is Shepard's awareness that the experience of a "Spirit of adoption" is sometimes taken, out of context and too simply, as a "Noetic testimony" (254) of salvation all by itself. Shepard "will not now dispute it" for, as he looks toward the completion of his Pauline list, he knows he will have to meet the claims of those he will never call anything but "Familists" in his very next section. Indeed he seems already to know that "Sanctification"—the virtue which regenerated human personality really is able to perform—will become the issue over which the battle for the Spirit of New England will inevitably be fought.

Modern suspicion might tend to regard sanctification as a burden—the duty of holy living imposed on the Saints in the wake of their gratuitous justification. And no doubt it might function this way in the economy of social control: those claiming to be justified by faith could be asked to validate their justification by the hearty performance of all acceptable deeds. In Shepard's scheme, however, sanctification is emphatically a "benefit" and, before any mention is made of its expression in or as "works," we are assured that it involves a witnessing of "the image of our Father by the same Spirit" that witnessed "the love of a Father" in adoption. Clearly that man who used to be Saul of Tarsus has a lot to answer for; so does Emmanuel College. And so too may certain local sponsors of a theology of the Spirit, for Shepard is talking to persons other than his own "beloved" audience when he proposes, "with submission," that sanctification itself is "the seal of the Spirit" (255) and not some subtle gnosis. Above all else, however, Shepard is careful to emphasize that sanctification is a restoration to fallen man of "the image of God" (256). If the Saint can be, for the first time, truly virtuous, the reason is simply that he has regained the holiness that Adam lost.

And just as *really* regained as it was really lost; so that sanctification involves not "the immediate operation of the Spirit" but certain "created habits of grace abiding in us." Justification may be a transaction that goes on above the heads of those who have, in faith, responded to the divine call, but sanctification is inherent: "it renews you unto the image of God himself."

> And therefore let all those dreams of the Familists (denying all inherent graces, but only those which are in Christ, to be in the saints) let them vanish and perish from under the sun, and the good Lord reduce all such who in simplicity are misled from this blessed truth of God. (257)

And let all "blessed souls" forever prize the "privilege" of sanctification. For though they may justly mourn the endurance of a heart not fully subdued "unto the will of Christ," yet they are to remember that, as "the Lord hath given [them] another nature, a new nature," there is something now within them which makes them "wrestle against sin, and shall in time prevail over all sin" (258). Thus, where the fallen man strove for faith—or else, at very least, for a true sight of sin—in response to the commandment, and as the least sinful expression of a corrupted nature, the convert will strive to make the new life of grace prevail. Formerly impossible, and never really easy, true virtue becomes now a meaningful and necessary project.

Which we should not fail to recognize as "a most sweet and comfortable evidence of [our] justification and favor with God," should the reality of our faith ever become obscure to our searching inward notice. To deny this use is to "abolish [the] many places in Scripture" (258) where we are challenged to prove our faithful words by our virtuous deeds. And as failure here proves the negative, so some measure of success is explicitly said to mark out the positive: "Hereby we know that we know him, if we keep his commandments." Faithfully, that is, and lovingly, since anyone might make a show of superficial obedience. This being understood,

What a vanity is this, to say that this is running upon a covenant of works! Is not sanctification, the writing of the law in our hearts, [as much] a special benefit of the covenant of grace as . . . justification? And can the evidencing, then, of one benefit of such a covenant, by another, be running upon the covenant of works? (259)

Granted, on all hands, works never *merit* faith, as their perfect performance might have won "life" for original Adam. But is it such bad Protestantism to think they may *ratify* it? Probably not, we are tempted to think, until such a time as those who reason otherwise shall have the chance to recast the problem with their own peculiar overdetermination. And even then the position sponsored here may retain some of its cogency, for when he asks if the same Spirit that witnesses justification cannot "shine on your graces" and witness sanctification as well, Shepard is cutting very close to Cotton's own prime position.

Nor will it satisfy Shepard to hear that "sanctification may possibly be an evidence." As soon question the universal certainty of "God's own promises of favor" (259). For sanctification is exactly the same thing as the fulfilling of those (covenantal) conditions to which the promises of salvation are so solemnly made. What curious sort of religious experience—Shepard can only wonder, explicitly, repeatedly—can possibly motivate this hesitancy to embrace the obvious significance of regenerate holiness? And what will such persons say to themselves on their "death bed"? Will they be willing to maintain their justification then, do they think, in the face of the evidence of a life devoid of holiness? He cannot see how. And so, to his own congregation, he proposes that sanctification is their "glorification" begun here and now, that it is the source of an "abundance of sweet peace," and that it alone makes a person "fit for God's use" (261–62). And finally, as "a little holiness is eminently all," one is not to "despise it because it is but little." Properly prized, "it shall at last prevail." Not without some serious effort of cultivation, of course, but that thought may well be lost in the glowing vision of a "soul perfected in the day of the Lord" (262–63).

What wonder, now, if the next "benefit," of an "Audience of all Prayers" (263), comes to seem a little anticlimactic? And what matter if the glories of (heavenly) "Glorification" sound a little too familiar to be quite spiritual? The "glorious body" will be a "powerful, strong body" (269), but one was hardly expecting to arm-wrestle the "Angels" and "Saints" (271) one had hoped to meet on the other side. And yet, as we would indeed "choose life," perhaps even we may be permitted to "despise this world" of death by contrast. Nor would criticism deny Shepard the conclusion of his list, however devised. But *The Sound Believer*— and, by implication, of *The Sincere Convert,* devised and delivered a number of years before and half-a-world away—ends not, beatifically, with a vision of re-deemed man "nearer to God than angels are" (273), but with the more sober, this-worldly reminder that "All Those That Are Translated into the Blessed Estate Are Bound to Live the Life of Love, in Fruitful and Thankful Obedience unto Him That Hath Called Them, according to the Rule of the Moral Law" (275). Just in case the thought of effort had indeed been lost. And in spite of whatever anyone might want to say about the paradox of being "bound" to "love." Far too important in the New England context to be left to inference, the duty of sancti-fied obedience becomes the explicit conclusion of Shepard's extended account of Calvinist affect and activity.

Still hesitant to identify sanctification with obedience simply considered, Shepard begins with something like a "psychological" account, as of divine stimu-lus and human response: the Lord has no sooner "crowned" his people with all "these glorious privileges" than "they immediately cry out, O Lord, what shall I now do for thee?" (275). Sanctification enables holy behavior, to be sure, but the motive to that behavior appears to be understood as the grateful response to *all* the benefits that follow saving faith. And Shepard is swift to concede—again in the context of the cry of "covenant of works!"—that "obedience to the law is not required of us, as it was of Adam," "as a condition antecedent to life"; but only "as a duty consequent to life, or as a rule of life." At the same time, however, "It is a vain thing to imagine that our obedience is to have no other rule but the Spirit." The Spirit is, remotely at least, "the efficient cause of our obedience,"

> but the will of God revealed in his word, especially in the law, is the rule. The Spirit is the wind that drives us in our obedience; the law is our com-pass, according to which it steers our course for us. The Spirit and the law, the wind and the compass, can stand well together. (276)

Or, in a less obviously metaphoric version: "Obedience is our debt we owe to Christ . . . , though we are to go to Christ . . . to enable us to pay" (277). On no ac-count, however, is salvation to be thought a "moral holiday." We can, now, faith-fully obey; and it is no less than common gratitude for us, now, lovingly to do so.

So certain is Shepard that this "life of obedience" can be lived "out of love" that we might dare to call it "the life of love" (279), expressing itself in "musing much on Christ and upon his love," in openly "commending" (280) that love, in seeking a more "familiar" acquaintance with the object of that love, "in doing much for him and that willingly," and in "enduring any evil for his sake" (281). For evidently the assurance of salvation, such as one might have from the fact of acceptance into a properly purified church such as Shepard's, is but the beginning of the Christian life properly considered: what *now* shall one do to express one's thanks? Young men he urges to look forward to a "fair time before you to do much for Christ." "Aged men" with "one foot in your grave" already had better "awaken now at last before you awake when it is too late"; like those very foolish virgins. And as for the reformed population at large, let everyone understand that, "if you are not good in your places, you are not good at all" (282). Not a thrilling message, perhaps, especially to those who may have crossed a furious ocean in pursuit of something more climactic—a personal transfiguration if not an historical denouement.[54] But somebody has to preach to the condition of those who live on, past the moment of lively personal and historical excitement, into the odd times that follow the surprising conversions.

Feeling the drag of "lukewarm times" himself, perhaps, Shepard predicts the proximity of the time when "the Lord will come for fruits of his vineyard." But the mood is one of solemn warning and not at all of triumphant zeal: better not "drink, and whore, and scoff, and blaspheme"; nor offer a profession that is "mere paint" (283). For not law but only *love* of the law will serve. So much so that Shepard's last paragraph feels tempted to revise its biblical text:

> I can never think enough of David's expression . . . , "I have kept thy commandments, and I love them exceedingly": should he not have said first, "I have loved thy commandments, and so have kept them"? Doubtless he did so, but he ran here in a holy and most heavenly circle: I have kept them and loved them; and loved them and kept them. (284)

Whatever!—as we give in to our own temptation. But Shepard knows what he is about, and he can draw his bottom line whether taught everywhere in Scripture or not: "If we love Christ, we shall live such a life of love in our measure, and his commandments will be most dear, when himself is most precious" (284). Others might confess a Spirit whose byword is freedom from the law. Shepard began by preaching a regimen the natural man was not really free to adopt. And he ends, for the moment at least, by challenging some newfound freedom to seek expression in obedience to the law it is now, finally, empowered to obey. A challenge we ought to notice, somewhere in the history of thoughts required to make a book.

———

Or two. For when Shepard goes on, or starts up again, with the preaching Bishop Laud never could shut down, it will be from this very moment: grateful Saints are waiting for the end. And all of them in New England's own "virgin churches."

All have heard of the need to live as if the end were near, even at the door. But many, aware that their own deaths might come at any moment, and that the Bridegroom's Return could come upon them as a great surprise, seem let down, nevertheless, by the ordinariness of their ongoing life: pure churches, to be sure, with the pure ordinances after which their souls were said to be "panting"; but a less varied life than the one that could be lived in Old England, and those Ten Commandments still. The passage from loss to salvation, through all the stages of preparation and then, by faith, into the domain of Christian "benefits," could be, in its way, as exhilarating as a sea voyage itself. But "the life of love" might grow as stale as any other marriage. Particularly when the Bridegroom came only once, in the form of his "Spirit," and never would seem to come again in very flesh.

It will be the mark of *Parable of the Ten Virgins* that it takes up—and, for more than six hundred pages, sticks to—that precise problem. For that is where, in Shepard's instructed view, the saintly population of New England appeared to be stuck. For the moment, however, it is enough to remember the accomplishment so far. Calling those who could hear to a religious activity that nowhere ceded the field to Arminian freedom, and then guiding them, in their New World setting, past the temptation to seize hold of the Spirit and disregard the law, Shepard's "nine principles" epitomize, and express at a very high level, all the intellectual and literary energy the world once devoted to the project of keeping God's sovereignty in proper relation to man's choices and society's good order. Dauntingly sustained, the effort of Shepard's *Convert* and his *Believer* is only one effort among many such. We need not even agree it is the most cogent or attractive of the efforts his world has to offer. But without that effort, it is all but impossible to understand why that world was as distracted as it was, by efforts to streamline—if also, in no trivial sense, to spiritualize—the account of how latter-day Calvinists could expect to be saved. With it, on the other hand, it begins to be possible to grasp what it meant for a few jargon-bound religious propositions, maddening like others they are set out fiercely to oppose. Interpretation was clearly at stake; perhaps the act of reading itself. And so, in some relation to that, was the way one construed the significance of his life so far: you mean to say it might all happen some *other* way?

Shepard or Cotton may sound to us a little like "clam or cod." Truth to us wears another dress. But literary history must attend most strictly to just such changes in intellectual fashion. And to say of a book that its determination and its energy "explain an age" is not far from claiming that it is something like "good." If it should happen to convert anyone along the way, it will have to share that liability with many another book we teach in "English."

CHAPTER SIX

REGENERATION THROUGH VIOLENCE

Hooker and the Morale of Preparation

I. "SUFFER THE WORDS"

We do not know exactly why, in May 1636, Thomas Hooker and most of his congregation left Newtown for the territories of Connecticut. Perhaps, quite simply, the desire for more land. Perhaps too, as knowledgeable observers long ago suggested, Hooker sensed that the heaven of Boston was not large enough to contain two stars as bright as himself *and* John Cotton: quite possibly Cotton's brand of Calvinism had already begun to embarrass the relentless preparationist emphasis of Hooker's own pulpit instructions.[1] Certainly Hooker did not move to make a comfortable place for Thomas Shepard and other recent arrivals loyal to his particular ministry. Or to leave it to Shepard to lead Harvard College. Or to instigate the inquisition of Anne Hutchinson. Or to guide the more polite questioning of Cotton himself, whom an anxious consensus first identified as the source of the theology casting a shadow on an assurance of salvation that had mainly to do with sanctification.[2] Such were the results, in point of fact, but they could hardly have been the purpose of Hooker's deliberate self-rustication.

But perhaps Hooker was indeed interested in going his own way, just a little. He may not have wished to make Connecticut a "democracy," in any meaningful sense; and there is no reason to suppose that the tests for admission to his congregation were not strenuous enough, in their own way. But they may have been different, just as his version of the New England Way was significantly his own.[3] Cotton was determined to emphasize faith, first and last, and he was virtually constant in his emphasis on the Spirit as the only worker of significant works. Shepard respected the point about *sola fides,* but he wished to emphasize that the works the Spirit enabled were in a significant sense our own—especially in sanctification, toward which his whole system drives and in which his *Parable* would luxuriate. Hooker's emphasis rests upon the point prior to both of these: long before faith did (or did not) lead on to some meaningful sanctification of the justified Saint, the work of preparation demanded to be carried out, in painful good faith, by God as the principal worker of the necessary process, by man as the not altogether inert subject, and by the minister as the ordinary mediator.[4]

Thomas Shepard certainly deserves to be called a preparationist, on the strength of the first three sections in the opening chapter of *The Sound Believer.* And, on the other hand, it would be false to say that preparation is Hooker's only theme; for the sequence of sermons he delivered in the days before New England resulted in published works on the Soul's "Vocation" (or "Effectual Calling"), its "Ingrafting" (or "Implantation") into Christ, and even its eventual "Exaltation." Indeed, the most determined modern study of Hooker's theology uses these works to fill in the outline of a salvation process that is not noticeably incomplete.[5] And yet when Hooker settles down, in the New England context, to go back over his system, in the name of fullness and finality, he never does seem to get beyond preparation. The front matter of the 1656 edition of *The Application of Redemption* announces itself as consisting of "Eleven Books made in New England," and goes on to promise that "There are Six more Books of Mr. Hooker's, now printing in two volumes."[6] In fact, only ten "Books" actually appear, eight in a first volume and two more in a second. Preparation we get, emphatically and to a point near its limit. But nothing further.

A sustained situating and defense of preparationist activity occupies the four hundred fifty pages of the first eight books of this *Application*; the ninth and tenth books devote more than six hundred pages to an actual preaching of the "contrition" in which (along with "humiliation") Hooker believes preparation humanly to consist. It is easy enough to imagine the topics left uncovered—and even to name them, from the titles of Hooker's earlier publications.[7] But when we examine the careful—"Ramist"—structure of the work that does get published, we notice a space for only one more really essential book: ineluctably paired with Preparation is the crucial topic of Implantation, the beginning of such salvation as may lie beyond everything that necessarily went before.

$$\text{Redemption divides as}\begin{cases}\text{Christ's Purchase}\\ \&\\ \text{Spirit's Application; Application in turn as}\end{cases}\begin{cases}\text{Preparation for}\\ \&\\ \text{Implantation of}\end{cases}$$

One readily understands how, for Hooker, the concept of preparation may further subdivide and so proliferate its own analysis, but we really do feel a little cheated if we do not get back to the place where the Soul's actual realization of Grace has been left hanging.[8]

Thus a book on the implantation of the prepared soul into Christ is what we feel essentially to be missing.[9] After more than a thousand pages of preparation, what? Will there be a way to keep the crucial event, the arrival of salvation in very fact, from seeming a little like an anticlimax? Nor, as we learn from the earlier work on "Implantation," are our suspicions entirely misplaced. There, in the earlier work on the Thing Itself, the best answer Hooker can make to the tortured question "Now?" or "If not now, when?" from the soul already far along in preparation is something like "Probably already." And then, while we are wondering if this is an adequate answer to the question of whether this *most* ardent preparationist is guilty of limiting God's freedom in the bestowing of the gift of salvation, Hooker proceeds to explain how saving grace could have come on us unawares. A thing Cotton and his followers might find hard to imagine. Maybe someone *did* have to move.

But if Hooker did the moving, he also did the coming back—to serve "from August 30 to September 22, 1637[,] . . . with Peter Bulkeley of Concord as one of the two moderators of the three-week-long formal inquiry into the spread of Antinomian opinions."[10] And doubtlessly he had left a long shadow behind him. Thus, whatever we may conclude about the contemporary bearing and local influence of the anti-Antinomian sermons posthumously published as *The Saints Dignity and Duty,*[11] it seems necessary to imagine that this predecessor of Thomas Shepard made his own contribution to the spiritual climate in which first John Cotton and then some less well credentialed associates were called to explain the grounds of their dissent from the local norm. The ministers of the Bay meant to be Calvinist, but they also stressed the importance of an active use of all available "means" both before and after the moment of the irresistible and "inammissable" grace of salvation. If the truth were known, they were a little vague on what, between the arduous process of preparation and the lengthening life of sanctification, the moment of faith was supposed to feel like. And they got testy if anyone found this local consensus just a little worksy.

Clearly Cotton will be up against Hooker as well as Shepard. Against them personally, in the short run of colonial politics and, in the longer run, against their bravest books. Shepard's *Parable* will be preached back against Cotton's Spiritist position: adjusted learning, in the kindest view; co-optation of the enemy's metaphors, to the recklessly judgmental. But like Shepard's *Sincere Convert* and *Sound Believer,* Hooker's *Application of Redemption* reads best as one more indication of the word-world Cotton would have to face.[12] A "Calvinist" world, to be sure, but one in which the zeal required to make a book appeared to be running in favor of the necessary moods (if not quite the needful works) which ran before and followed after the free gift of faith. To the point where it got a little hard to tell the graceful discovery from the arduous search. As if the subtext of Hooker's work on preparation were to read, "Truly seek and you have surely found."

The publishers of *The Application of Redemption* had wished to assure their public that the chapters which take us beyond Hooker's lengthy treatment of everything up to and including the soul's "humiliation" were all in hand and even in production. But Goodwin and Nye, those distinguished independents who wrote a preface for the 1656 edition, evidently knew better.[13] Based on their familiarity with Hooker's first and second run-through of his entire salvation system, they confidently assert that Hooker was most "able for" the explication of the latter and the last of the "Great Points" of evangelical religion—such "as Union with Christ, Justification, Adoption, Sanctification, and Glory"—and that "his heart was most in" these ultimate topics; but they are forced to admit that, so far as a final revision was concerned, "he hath left them unfinished." And thus his most considered account of "those higher Subjects, as the Close, and Center, and Crown of what forewent, as preparative thereto, are now perished, and laid in the dust with him."[14] Perhaps the publisher had been intending merely to reprint earlier versions of works needed to get the reader *on,* beyond preparation, to the acts and monuments of salvation itself. But bibliography and bookselling are only one part of the problem. Also worthy of notice, surely, is the force of the claim that Hooker really was every bit as interested in the saintly and then the heavenly end of the salvation process as he was in its lawful, sorrowful beginning. But *was* he?

Scholars know what it is like to hope they will live to finish the important work on which they are presently engaged—their very masterwork, no doubt. Though still a fairly young man, Shepard thanks God for letting him live to add his *Believer* to his *Convert* and, for the good of the souls in need, to have them published together. So perhaps we should say, simply, with Goodwin and Nye, that "None but Christ was ever able to finish all that Work which was in [Hooker's] Heart to do." But it is worth wondering: if Hooker was *so* interested in coming to the end of his process, why did he not stir himself a little? One thousand fifty pages looks a lot like emphasis.[15]

―――――

The beginnings of the *Application* are, at all events, decidedly unhurried. The table of contents, of the volume that contains the first eight "Books," gives every indication of having been set with method. And Book 1—on the "Purchase" of Redemption, by Christ, from a Father whose justice insists that man's original sin cannot be forgiven without the payment of some (infinite) atoning price—turns out to be a little longer than we might anticipate from a book which takes its title from the *other* half of a foundational dichotomy. But opposites do attract and, in the Ramist system, they imply one another in a relation both exclusive and mutually referential.[16] And, a less strict binarism might think to add, Hooker evidently wishes to find a place to answer in advance a style of Protestant emphasis that would prejudice the cause of preparation most severely. Once fairly launched, Hooker's treatment of the reason, parts, and the affect of preparation moves with a wondrous energy of its own. At the outset, however, he wishes to rebuke the Antinomians.[17]

In Adam's fall we sinned all—with two important consequences: first, as nearly all admit, "There must be a *Redemption* . . . that God's justice and holiness which were wronged might be satisfied"; and second, with a little more acumen, "There must be an *Application* of this Redemption unto the Souls of such for whom it was paid" (4). To be recovered, at very least, is all the "grace and happiness" Adam had and lost; and this recovery, as Anselm had long ago taught the orthodox to reason, involves an infinite price which only some "God-man" could possibly be thought able to pay.[18] Happily, therefore, "Christ hath purchased all spiritual good" (5), fully paying the "price laid down" (6); but in the wake of Calvin we need to ask, "For whom?" For sinners!—the students in the front will wave their arms to answer. But simple zeal must learn the deed was not for them *as such*: "this precious blood of Christ was shed for Sinners, BUT NOT AS SINNERS" (11). Denied here, of course, is any doctrine of universal salvation: "if our Savior should die for sinners *as sinners,* then he should die for all sinners, and therefore for all men, because all are sinners."[19] Clearly, however, the Scripture's offer of salvation is *not* made to "such sinners as are secure and carnally confident in their own righteousness" (12). Which is to imply, in advance of the specific teaching, that salvation has been purchased for such sinners as are by sad self-knowledge well prepared.

One could say that "Christ died for none but the Elect" (12) and go on to insist, properly enough, that as election is out of God's "mere good will and pleasure" (13) it operates "before or without" respect to any condition. But Scripture's omnipresent language of Covenant invites one to say also that salvation has been purchased for sinners who "shall believe" (12). Not in the Arminian sense, to be sure, as if this belief were a subtle work that a carefully instructed man might learn to will; for it remains to natural man "as impossible to believe as to fulfill the law" (14); but only to indicate—as Perry Miller suffered to reveal—that Decree is not in every sense unintelligible.[20] God might in theory have offered salvation to no one; or to just anyone, with no distinguishing mark. But he has in fact arranged for saints to discover themselves in the act of (enabled) believing. Evidently, as we may see in the logic of Shepard, the Puritan loyalty to Calvin and to Covenant is about equal. And so our readings will have to learn to live with a system whose God both offers the covenant and, if only in the "person" of his Son, engages to "perform the condition" (23) as well.

That Hooker's anxieties are the very reverse of our own becomes evident in the Cases of Conscience which follow his delimitation of the divine purchase: not power to perform the act of faith but freedom from its stern condition is at the center of Hooker's embattled resistance; and though very much of the *Application* is written with the energy of self-proliferation, Shuffelton is certainly right to discern the specter of Antinomianism at just this early point.[21] Accordingly, no acceptable theory of election allows a man to "challenge any interest in . . . Christ" or to claim "any Spiritual Good received" before he in fact believes; if, as already argued, "Christ purchased all for believers as such, then they must be such before they can . . . take this purchase as their own" (23–24). The Covenant of Grace, that is to say, is indeed a covenant, and its sole condition is faith: possess that, however mysteriously, and *only then* may God be challenged to provide all the rest. So too, in a specific case, the Spirit of God must not be thought by any "special and immediate revelation" to witness "pardon of sin, adoption, [or] justification" (27) before a man shall believe.

Before and after are tricky notions when dealing with God, and surely the instructed soul will know what follows, by promise, after faith, so it may be appropriate to state the matter as an inferential all-at-once: for God to make known a man's election is just the same as to enable his faith in a system of salvation beyond the capacity of his own natural will. Not God's private "You're it, and don't ask" but a man's own (enabled) "Now I see and do believe (which makes the promises altogether mine)." Let no one suppose, therefore, that "Christ may be united to the soul, and so he be justified and adopted before he have any faith." More than a "dangerous opinion," this "desperate delusion" furnishes "the plot of all profaneness" and indeed "the ground of all looseness and Familism." It seems to imply that a man deep in sin may simply invoke the "witness of the spirit" (29) and then deny that anything more can possibly be required, and clearly it makes nonsense out of the "promises" expressly made to "them that do believe" (30).

The subtext here may well be the sort of profession one was to make in order to enter a church of Visible Saints. In this context the practical import of this difference of opinion becomes immediately obvious: in theory at least, the Spiritist might be able to claim, without regard to anything else in his life, that God had revealed to him, privately, the rare fact of his own election; the Covenant Conditionalist, by contrast, must confess, in some detail, the specific scriptural condition he has been enabled to accept or fulfill or perform. The latter case makes of faith something slightly more "objective" than the unopposable belief that one is indeed an elected saint. Further, it can be expected to generate a narrative that situates faith in the context of a life whose moral shape makes approximate human sense. The former, as Hooker seems to know, might rest in some flat fiat: God has revealed my election: "I must believe it, and you must believe me" (30). Such a declaration could be dramatic, no doubt, but it takes somewhat more to generate a tone; and that no doubt is what established saints were asked to judge.

The Immediatist is permitted to object—with a show of high-minded concern for the purest form of Protestant piety—that as "the covenant of grace is free," so "the Lord hath not in it any respect to any thing we have or do" (32). Only so, this argument would go, even from the pen of Cotton, can we be absolutely sure we are not falling back into a Romanist position. Unwilling to concede an inch of this very high ground, Hooker hastens to confess the theoretical point but to deny that his regard for God's perfect freedom is any less careful or pure: "Free grace is the fountain of all: it makes the condition, it works the condition, it maintains the condition which is wrought" (33). The difference between the studied repetition of Hooker's elaborated version of a "Conditional Calvinism" and the relative insouciance of the biblical text is too apparent to require comment, and somewhere someone is going to have to face the question of whether "Calvin" and "Covenant" are idioms that seek out or repel one another.[22] For the moment, however, it is enough to suspect that if Hooker's best emphasis sponsors a system requiring God to work his own arbitrary yet required condition, the stakes must be high indeed.

Thus a "Third Case of Conscience," which grants that "Faith is there" and still wishes for the Spirit to reveal salvation without respect to it or to "any gracious qualification in the soul," calls forth first an admission that "the dispensations of the Spirit" are indeed "unsearchable" (33–34) and then a somewhat scholastic response to that seemingly unhappy fact. It also confirms our sense of how easily Hooker's discourse of purchase slides over into application: how may the individual know if Christ's sacrifice was meant for *him*? By an immediate revelation? Or by the recognition of some condition realized? And no matter how many times the question is asked, the answer remains unswervingly the same: The Spirit never witnesses "that we are made partakers of any benefit from Christ without respect to some qualification, gracious disposition, or condition" (34). "Election" is "without any eye to works," but "consolation" is not entirely so. The "decree of God" is indeed "independent" of all such considerations but not its "execution" (40). Elected for no "reason," we yet discover election in the act of faith.

"Arguments" follow, in profusion, many of them centering on the proposition that "the Spirit never evidenceth without the Word" (43), but they add little to the cogency of the insight at the center of Hooker's analysis: Scripture's New Covenant offers salvation on the condition of faith—by which it means something more than the belief in one's own salvation. It is easy enough, Hooker knows, to give inference a bad name when dealing with matters spiritual, yet he has Scripture to confirm his sense that there must be, somehow, more terms than just one. Why else have a *verbal* revelation at all? Or else, just less drastically, why not have a revelation which says merely that the one magic Word will be given to all those for whom that Word is true? All others hold their peace. Strictly speaking, of course, it is as easy to be mistaken about the sincerity of one's Saving Faith as about the authority of the Voice that speaks the Word. And yet the conditional, inferential system is inherently more public than the one more immediately inspirational: one's expression of faith, in word and in deed, can be referred back to its extended Scripture definition; the "special Word appointed, appropriated to me alone" (44), can only announce and then repeat itself. A kind of verbal solipsism, truly. And so Hooker struggles to vary and to repeat.

Book 1 begins to wind down with a return to the question of universal salvation, said to make way for "universality of corruption" (58) but not particularly in vogue in New England; one begins to suspect that the anti-immediatist sections of this first book have been interpolated, at need, into some more familiar beginning. Objections force both a restatement of Anselm—"The Divinity cannot suffer, the Humanity cannot satisfy" (60)—and also a latter-day Calvinist deferral of the problem of freedom—the Gospel requires only that a man "should be willing and content to be made able to believe" (61)—but the fire seems to have died down. Then, abruptly, a "Use" of "Exhortation," where only arguments, objections, and answers had gone before: "To provoke our hearts to get faith," as if the seeking made the finding sure. Indeed, "since there is all good purchased by Christ, and all for those that shall believe, who would not now be a believer?" (66). Well, somebody *else,* we are left to infer; for here, in Master Hooker as in Disciple Shepard, the authentic, "subjective" response can only be to labor or to try. Ministers may explain and defend before they exhort. But when in fact they issue God's appeal, to cavil then is simply to mark oneself: defensive distinction as bad faith. Have you not indeed been called? Then why not come?

Thus the ending of Book 1 is fairly conventional: uncommon energy of argument has been brought against the claim that assurance may come without some act of faith, but no one protests the call to *get* that faith. Eventually, of course, when fully set upon the course of preparation, the soul may wish to know not only the reason of the process but also the proper sense of end and means. But here, where faith is nothing like a pure reception, one is ill advised to wait around.

The second "Book" of the *Application,* more neatly wrought than the first, increases our suspicion that Hooker's introductory performance—not well prefigured in his earlier works—may have been subject to interruption by the controversy of 1636–38. Clear in outline and emphatic in execution, Book 2 fully treats the theory of application, whose difficulties could not keep themselves from intruding on the domain of purchase itself. The "Doctrine" that "Christ puts all his into possession of all that good he hath purchased" is divided into two "Branches": first, with some repetition, that "Redemption and Application are of equal extent"; and second, as Hooker moves toward his special subject, "the manner how this Application is wrought." And, as if to prevent the suspicion that preparation is a threat to strict Calvinism, Hooker emphasizes that Christ must be seen "not only to offer salvation and redemption" to his own, "but to make it good to their hearts and consciences" (72). The scandal of "natural ability" has been taken, by Miller and others, but Hooker has no intention of giving it.[23]

To emphasize that "Redemption and Application are of equal extent" (76) is to avoid the implication that God's scheme of salvation is somehow imperfect. It may sound more kindly to hold that Christ has in some sense died for all; but this is to concede that the efficacy of application "depends . . . upon man's will." The issue, that is to say, is sovereignty: God wills only what he wills, and his means are always equal to his ends; to deny this—"to make God's saving grace serve men's wills and humors" (77)—is to abandon Calvinism at a stroke. Some mystery, it appears, must always pertain to the question of actual salvation. Arminians refer that mystery to the individual will, avoiding thereby the implication that in the last analysis it is God who bears the blame for reprobation. Unable to ignore this difficulty, Calvinists regularly try to show that decree does no violence to the human will. When push comes to shove, however, they dare not deny that God is God and that, as Calvin himself had taught, his will is the only standard of good and evil.[24]

Then too, removing human will as the cause of individual salvation makes it possible to appreciate "the wonderful mysteriousness of that work; that it prevails most powerfully for the good of sinners when they do most of all oppose it" (77). Cotton, as we shall see, can make more emphatic use of this paradox, but it is a clear sign of Hooker's Calvinism that he can advise, if only rarely, a sort of wise passiveness: "Learn we to sit down in silence, and look at the prevailing power of the purchase of Jesus" (78). For it always does accomplish its end: the Father having designated those to be saved, "our savior undertakes to purchase and perfect redemption for them, and it therefore proceeds, he gives them his word and gives them a heart to keep it" (78–79). Elsewhere, in the moment of address to a man whose will cannot be forced, the work is the work of a heart prepared; but when called forth by the thought of a sovereign plan, the logic is that of Dort.[25] And of Calvin himself, who taught his followers not to "pry into God's counsels, nor suffer thy self to be bewildered in such curious speculations as to search the depths of God's everlasting decrees whether thou were elected or no." For, as Hooker learned from the case of the tormented Joanna Drake, it is all too easy to lose oneself in such "secret things."[26] A man may cry out that he needs to *know* if salvation is "purchased for me," but his duty is simply to make use of the means, and to say, with the Leper, "if thou wilt thou canst make me clean." He is to recall that "whether God will do it" is "his prerogative[;] if he give thee nothing he owes thee nothing"; to remember, that is to say, the wide difference between "his will and my duty" (81).

Accordingly, as Hooker comes to the second branch of his doctrine—"the manner" in which the application of redemption is wrought—he establishes the orthodoxy of his emphasis at the outset: salvation is "made theirs": "they cannot make it their own themselves; they cannot put themselves into possession" (81–82). Unable to claim it in justice, those to be saved are, as natural men, not even capable of accepting it, "though provided and freely offered" (82), for men do not by nature wish to "receive that grace which being received" (83) would utterly change their cherished if distempered selves. Away with such as think to save themselves; and take heed all those who claim themselves the site of honest application. "You take Christ," you say? "You hang upon free mercy?" Well,

"How came you by the power so to do? You say, you took the promises, but who gave them you, or gave you a hand to lay hold upon them?" The Cynic will notice the "regress," but the Puritan makes all the stops along the way: "Unless he who . . . gave thee promises, do . . . give thee a heart also to take them, thou wilt never take possession of them; unless Christ comprehend thee, thou wilt never apprehend him" (88). The mistake of imagining that *we* make the application may be encouraged by the "tenderness" of Scripture, or it may spring from our own "legal terrors"; yet the Lord "must apply himself to us, before we can apply him to our own hearts" (90).

So it makes sense to inquire how the good of salvation "*is made* ours" (93; emphasis added). As to the order, the soul is first "made capable of all . . . those precious blessings"; then comes "a right and title thereunto"; only then is the soul "actually estated in all these spiritual good things"; and only then has the soul a "liberty to use and improve Christ" (93–95) in the way of sanctification. So enunciated, this bare-bones "order of application" (95) finds its literary release in a profusion of Uses. Of admiration, as one recognizes that God "not only provides a gift, but a hand to take it" (96). Of humiliation, in the allied recognition that we have it in ourselves "to oppose all good" (99). Of encouragement, as nature's inability is matched by the power of one "who can do what he will in heaven and earth" (102). Of direction, to show us how "to set forward the great work of application on our souls when ever the Lord is striving with us in the ministry" (104); and of "exhortation," to use the gifts from Christ as our own (106). Preparation and sanctification being equally gifts, denial is a poor way to express gratitude.[27]

Not to be distracted by the logic of meritorious action, on the one hand, or the claim of spiritual union, on the other, Hooker carries on to "the causes of application" with systematic determination. Calvinist loyalty remains: "God himself is the principal cause of application" (111). The Father, first of all, as the one "directly offended" and "now appeased," is now required by his very justice to put the saints "into possession" of all that was "purchased in their behalf." And given this primacy, it makes some sense to attribute "the works of application . . . unto the Father" (112). More appropriately, however, "Christ is said to make all spiritual good ours, as mediator, God and man," as the "head of the second covenant," and as "the root from whom the sap of saving grace issues to all his branches" (113). The climax of "the Spirit" is sure to come, we feel, but Hooker takes his own scholastic time to explain that, though Christ's resurrection is "no part of that payment by imputation whereof we are pronounced just" (114), yet it serves as a "powerful cause to make application of the merits of Christ to us" (116). Delayed by theory but not distracted from purpose, Hooker resumes the overstaid fraction—weakly, at first, with the recollection that "The Spirit of God also hath a hand in this great work of application" (123). Yet things come out even in the end: application is in a special manner attributed to the Spirit, as creation to the Father and redemption to the Son.

Then, as if to compensate for a lapse into professionalism, Hooker composes the use of his first proposition on the "causes" in the form of a homely analogy: the Savior himself appears to the sinful soul in the person of a "high sheriff"; confusion and resistance ensue, as the soul—"a prisoner to divine justice," with "sin [as] the prison, and the Devil [as] the jailer" (124)—cannot imagine that "those sins of [his] should be pardoned" (125). In this mood, however, one must not look to "the justice of God," which can only "condemn," but to fasten instead on "the operation of a God that can quicken and raise up the dead heart, as he did raise up Jesus Christ" (127–28). Thus is the resurrection, not at all "required" to satisfy "the law," redeemed on the level of vernacular allegory. A trick which Cotton himself might learn to admire, even if Hooker's Spirit has once more receded into the logical background.

In the last analysis, however, Hooker is not much concerned with the divine separation of powers. Climactic in his treatment of the causes of application, instead, is the Calvinist proposition that the "power by which the Lord works in application is an almighty power," so that "this work of application looks to God as the author of it, not in regard of any common concourse of providence" (128–29). There may be moments when Hooker seems to imply a causal role for human ability, but not *here*—where his ardor expresses itself as a love of truth rather than a desire for converts. And even in his most evangelical moment, it should be possible to recall the bearing of clear theory on ambiguous practice: the God who alone saves souls has elected his ministers to speak on his behalf; and the Word he commanded them to speak is an urgent call, not a feckless wish—Well, shucks, I hope you all are mostly elect. We need to think of a way to remember that a "mass of miracles [is] met together when a sinner is converted" (129).

Consider the "hellish opposition" a man "hath naturally against good" (129). Consider too that the good of conversion is a "supernatural good": "that which must lift nature to act above itself, must be something above nature." Furthermore, given man's opposition, conversion is "harder than the work of creation itself," for though God had at first "nothing . . . to help him," he had at least "nothing to hinder" (131). Hence the need for almighty power. An objection wonders, "Why then are commands so frequent in Scripture?" "If a man have no power to turn himself, to what purpose are these commands?" But the answer is full enough to cover the cases of conscience we are yet to encounter. First, the commands of God in Scripture indicate "not what our ability is but what our duty is, and what would be acceptable to the Lord." Then too, the same Lord who commands also "gives a power unto all his elect to enable them to obey." So that, finally, the novice of salvation should hear himself precisely commanded to "be content that the Lord should work in [him] what he requires" (132). Not in such a way as to force God's hand, but only with the resignation that says, "Lord, if *thou* wilt," remembering that "he owes thee nothing." Such protestations ought to be enough to establish Hooker's intention to remain loyal, if not to the system of John Calvin, at least to the piety that framed the answer to Arminius. Preachers must be willing to preach that men must be willing to be prepared, but God alone can do the work. Or not.

That said, the orthodoxy of a "third proposition," concerning "those means which the Lord is pleased to appoint," ought to be safe enough; for these means can be nothing more than "the instrumental causes of application" (132–33). And yet these means are not negligible, for it is but a "vain conceit of the Familists" that "there is nothing for us to do." Efficiency lies elsewhere, to be sure, with the power of God, but God himself has chosen to work with human instruments—"the Word," principally, accompanied "by the presence and operation of the Spirit" and "published" by a faithful ministry. Nor is the practical point allowed to pass without emphasis: "Word, prayer, preaching, sacraments . . . are but weak in themselves, yet they are mighty through God" (135). Suitably informed that God's work "upon the souls of his servants is not done by moral persuasion" but by the same "irresistible . . . power that raised Christ from the dead" (135–36), we must make certain that our conversion is "from the almighty power of God," even if we fail to see *how* the impression is made. If so, then comfort may be had, even in the face of the "disproportion" there is between one's soul and the "blessed work" (137). Yet only so long as we remain "tremblingly fearful not to slight any ordinance God hath appointed" (138).

God alone works Protestant salvation, but he works it here and now and, as Hooker concludes his treatment of "application in general," he cannot let go of either emphasis:

Be also tremblingly fearful when the Lord works by any ordinance, lest you should . . . withdraw yourself from the power of it when you find and feel something more than man, and means, and ordinances, Oh let it not slip away; the Lord was in that Word, do not suffer that stroke to go away. (139)

Were this a use of information and not a climactic exhortation—analysis rather than enactment—we might justly emphasize the slippage, which the excitement of a run-on syntax can blur but not conceal: can one really "slip away" from an "irresistible" power? On the premise that it is indeed "the Lord now . . . working," how could one *not* persevere unto "the effectual working of his Word and Spirit"? (139). In context, however, we are supposed to respond, not quibble.

Not that the heat of oratory should carry one beyond the limits of logic but that Puritan logic itself requires just such calls to be made. God does the work. But he does it, we observe, just when the preacher gives the Word.[28] In this overdetermined context, "Do not resist" is clearly a prayer; and also a performative. It means: share with me the gladness of nonresistance. Or else: notice how you *will* have to cease to duck "the blow." And learn to recognize almighty power just when you come to realize the thing you never could but always ought to will. Oh, that you might will it *now*. If not, then soon, God willing. For in the tactic of rhetoric as in the strategy of grace, there are more blows where that one came from.

———

Book 3 of the *Application* arrives at Hooker's very own subject, as the scriptural derivation, the rational defense, and indeed the ministerial enactment of preparation will occupy him for the 850 pages of his remaining eight books. Hooker's care reminds us that, "having dispatched the nature of application in the general," we now come to consider "the parts thereof"; and we can easily imagine the scheme:

Redemption
{ Purchase (Bk. 1)
or
Application }
{ In General (Bk. 2)
or
In Its Parts }
{ Preparation
or
Implantation }
{ In General (Bk. 3)
or
In Particulars . . . }

Accordingly, Book 3 will treat preparation as the first of the two "parts" of application, but it will treat it in some "general" way. Particulars are bound to follow, we presume, but what will happen to the bypassed topic of implantation is anybody's guess.

Having reached preparation itself, however, Hooker's emphasis is anything but proleptic. What we need to know is that "before the Soul can be engrafted into the true vine Christ Jesus, it must be . . . fitted thereunto by the powerful work of the Spirit" (141). The grafting metaphor must come to count for something, but so long as the question is doctrine straight and strict, Calvin rules. And also, in another sense, "John the Baptist," whose task it was, antitype of Elias, "[t]o prepare a people fitted for the Lord" (142). Hooker even quotes the *Institutes* on John's necessary intermediation.[29] What he means to suggest is that the need for something or other to come along before the moment of salvation itself is built into the drama of Scripture, and that it requires no great interpretive skill to notice this obvious fact.

Hence this "doctrine": "The soul must be fitted for Christ before it can receive him." Indeed we are to take it as a maxim that "where there is no preparation made, there is no expectation of a Savior." This coming may be sudden, but it cannot be in defiance of context: someone has to say "repent" and "prepare" until the soul shall understand that "repenting is preparing" (144). Technically understood, preparation is both a "fitting of the soul for faith" and, before that, "a renouncing of whatsoever might cross the coming and entertaining of our Savior." From the tyrannical rule of "bosom corruptions" (145), first of all, the soul must withdraw all allegiance, whether it can yet "wage war" with them or not. One may think of the first act of preparation, negatively, as a "leveling" but not yet a "paving." Or as a preliminary emptying out—as "a rusty vessel is not worthy of precious liquor: a dusty cabinet not worthy to [hold] a diamond" (146). Further, but negatively still, "the soul must be emptied" not only of its corruptions but also of confidence in its own "spiritual sufficiency or service"—as if the Purchaser of Redemption were "not either able or willing to be the author and the finisher of our Faith himself" (147). Again, intensely, the soul must renounce all sense of its own "worthiness" to receive the "grace and mercy" it surely needs, being sunk, rather, with a lively sense of its own wretchedness (147–48). Only now will grace bear expectation.

Not yet "able to kill sin," the soul is at least "empty," and "the coast is clear," so that "the soul stands ready" for Christ to "come and take possession of it." Not emboldened to challenge the promises of the covenant on this account, but possessed only of a hard-won emptiness, "the soul is content that Christ should do all." The moment has the monument of a small military allegory of citizens who cannot evict the enemies from their town but only beg a famous general to come and drive them out. And also a prayer: "I cannot subdue my sins my self, but let Christ do what is good in his eyes" (149). From which it fairly appears that "The soul of a sinner is merely patient herein; it's wrought upon him, not wrought by him" (149–50). "And therefore"—as Hooker rises to someone's challenge—"it's no work of sanctification." Not yet in possession of any "principle of life whereby he comes to be active," the soul has nothing of its own to offer. Preparation pleases God, no doubt, but "these saving preparations are no acts of mine" (150–51). Problems of emphasis remain, but it is hard to imagine how Hooker could have made his orthodoxy any more explicit.

R. T. Kendall is probably right to assert that preparation is Hooker's prime form of assurance, if only as a sign predictive. And certainly it is a mistake to look for an expansion of natural ability at this point: preparation pleases God because it is a work of the Spirit. And besides—as Hooker tries his hand at a favorite system of Puritan metaphor—though the soul may be thought of as suing for a divorce from Satan, removing thereby all "claim of marriage" to sin, still this "divorce is neither marriage nor matrimonial love" but only a "making room for the right and possession of the spirit by faith" (151). An embattled position, it may be, whether "misliked" by Anne Hutchinson or not. But clearly an orthodox position still.

And even the predictive value of preparation is carefully protected from naughty misunderstanding: "When this preparation is fully wrought, faith . . . will undoubtedly be infused, and cannot be hindered"; but only, to repeat, when it has "come to its full period *in ultima dispositione.*" This perfect course of "evangelical preparation" must be distinguished from that "legal preparation which may befall reprobates" (152). And these considered distinctions should stop the mouths of those who wonder about the fate of a soul who dies in preparation. The answer is that such a man "is in a state of salvation preparatively, and shall certainly possess it" (153). It might be possible to object that Hooker has made assurance of salvation possible before the moment of faith. But more so in theory than in practice, for the infusion of faith would appear to come—suddenly—in the very moment when an elaborate and lengthy preparation is in fact complete. As true preparation can only end in faith, so nothing but faith can mark the end of preparation. Otherwise, how could anyone affirm he had undergone preparation in its last degree?

Quibbles aside, the first doctrine of Book 3 finds its energetic center in a section on the "Reasons why there must be such a preparation," including—in the midst of its energetic uses—a specially titled set of "reasons" why Christ "cannot be united to the soul . . . in its natural condition." First, "[t]he Scriptures are pregnant" on this point (153). Besides the "structural" example of the Baptist, Hooker emphasizes two texts from Matthew: "If any man will be my disciple let him deny himself and follow me" (16.24) announces that "Where there is no denying of a man's self, there can be no following of Christ" (154); and, even more friendly to Hooker's love of vernacular allegory, the revelation that "No man can enter a strong man's house before he first bind the strong man" (12.29) appears to prove that the preparatory work of binding Satan must go before all thought of Christ's entry into the soul (155–56). Further, scholastic reason suggests that "if there be not preparation before implantation," then the soul would be "the kingdom of light and darkness together" (156). And before we ask why cannot the light be allowed to oust the darkness—of itself and all at once?—the voice of reason speaks again, in paraphrase of Romans: as "cutting . . . must be before engrafting," so "preparing is before implanting" (157).

Objection here could only mean deconstruction: you mean cutting and grafting are merely tropes—metaphor in the body of Revelation?[30] Hence the lucky pun: whenever Hooker says "pre-pared," he may well be thinking "pre-cut"—pared in advance for the express purpose of being engrafted. But while criticism is stunned by its own verbal play, faith must sit still for the uses.

Instruction might seem to require little more than repetition: "the sinner must be prepared and cut off from his natural condition, before his implantation," for "while he is in his natural and corrupt estate, there can be no union . . . with the Lord Jesus" (157). But then, as if unruly local resistance had begun to alter the course of patient exposition once again, a long coda separates this first Use from another four. We need to be warned, first of all, that "the contrary opinion . . . that Christ may be united to the soul remaining in the state of corruption is a brooding error" which will bring "a whole nest and company of delusions with it." Leaving the reader no time to determine whether his "contrary" is logically perfect—and barely enough to recall Luther's paradox of *justus et peccator*—Hooker numbers the errors generated by this doctrine. Beyond maintaining the sinner in a "remorseless security," it makes him "bold to adventure upon the . . . grossest evil" (158). It also makes a man "sleepy" and "heartless": "sure of a Christ, that will answer all, . . . he troubles not himself with holy duties" (158–59). Worst of all, perhaps—in terms of the idea Hooker and Shepard have sworn on the altar of God to defend—the doctrine of faith without preparation permits a man to "have evidence of his good estate without the sight of any saving qualification." How "easie" this formula of assurance: a life of sin as usual plus "an immediate revelation" of union with Christ. No "gracious actions" to validate the claim and no chance for "the want of them [to] infer the denial of a good estate" (159). A delusion, surely.

So desperate is this misconception that, like Shepard at the comparable moment, Hooker cannot refrain from a display of rhetoric as such:

> this one delusion like an Egyptian fog, darkens the whole heavens, even the bright beams of the sun of the Gospel, and the everlasting covenant of God's free grace; cuts the sinews of sincerity, and eats out the blood and spirits of the power and presence and life of grace; and under the pretence of advancing Christ and free grace, destroys his kingdom. (159–60)

This outburst, unleashed at the Antinomian moment or not, is a fair indication of the depth of conviction any "anti-inferential" teachings are going to encounter.

Cotton will dare to imply that the "elders" who address him their "questions" are not strict *enough* in their Calvinism. And Hooker himself plainly recognizes that the position he opposes—antipreparationist as well as antisanctificationist—goes about under the sign of a finer, more Protestant sense of grace.[31] By the terms promulgated here, however, Cotton and his cohort can seem only a sort of Antichrist.

Nor will Hooker give his rhetoric a rest: we are to regard "these so desperate delusions, not as rocks and sands where men may suffer shipwreck and yet be recovered; but [as] a devouring gulf, or whirlpool" from which "there is no hope or help to come out." And he only increases our suspicion of local distraction when he further postpones the rest of his uses in order to add some further "reasons" why Christ "cannot be united to the soul while it is in its natural condition" (160). Five in number, they tend to vary only slightly the earlier arguments, but their disruptive presence alone suggests an irruption of controversy. Out of John 14.17 comes the premise that "the world cannot receive" the "Comforter" whom Christ had promised to send; a fortiori then, as it seems to Hooker, those worldlings who "cannot receive the Spirit, cannot receive the Lord Jesus," until they are "called out . . . from the power of Satan." Those who object that "conversion [is] a creating work" and hence "needs no preparation" need to be reminded that, though God needs no "help in the execution of his holy will," yet his wisdom seldom violates the order of things. "God can turn water into wine, but in reason he must destroy the nature of water, and then make wine" (161). So with the soul: God "can change a proud and unbelieving heart into a believing heart, but he must first destroy the power of unbelief" (162).

Nowhere, it appears, can Hooker regard change of phase as a simple phenomenon. Preparation is virtually a physics: resistance exists, everywhere, and needs to be destroyed before consent can rule. Other reasons sound less scholastic, but they partake of the same principle: a person in the state of nature is "in the state of condemnation," and no one can be in the state of "condemnation and acceptation together." "Opposition and resistance" preclude the possibility of union, and every man in the state of unbelief is "wholly opposite to Christ" (162). No one can be under two covenants at once: those "under grace" are no longer under the "dominion" of sin; but those in the state of unbelief "are under the power and dominion of sin" and are therefore "not under Christ" (163–64). Sin and grace are simply contraries; they can neither interpenetrate nor lie in proximity to one another. Natural man is sinful in every part and aspect. Preparation must drive that sin out before faith can, without mental outrage, possibly be thought to enter.

Some such doctrine is required (in a second use) to dash the "fond conceit" of men who imagine "a speedy way to heaven" (164). As if the Lord had agreed to "carry the drunkard and his cups, the adulterer and his harlots also, the riotous gamester his cards and dice, hawks and hounds, and all to heaven together." In fact, the way revealed is altogether otherwise:

> No Harbinger before, no King follows after[;] where the heart is not fitted for a Savior, there is no hope to enjoy the presence of a Savior: It's the condition upon which his coming is promised and can be expected on any sure ground. It's the order and connection of things which God hath set in the work of grace. (165)

Preserved here, implicitly at least, is the sense that God *might* somehow have violated the physics of opposition and of transition but that his revealed way is in fact the reasonable one: only when we are "made meek and tractable," only then is there "some hope that salvation will appear." Otherwise—as Hooker presses his worst-case scenario of sin and grace together—it is as if "the King should lie in the truckle-bed under a company of traitors" (165). How much more fitting to suppose that salvation begins only when "the wicked man [shall] forsake his way" (166).

Hence (in a third use) a way to gain "certain evidence whether . . . Christ is come or that we have any grounded hope that he will come unto our souls." The negative we already know: no Baptist, no Savior. The positive is the more treacherous case, but Hooker announces it with a certain clarity and confidence: "If Christ fit the soul, he will certainly never loose the soul[;] if he prepare it for himself he will undoubtedly possess it by his spirit and grace"; for he is not so weak "that he cannot accomplish his work and intended end," nor yet so unwise that he will "lose his labor or leave his work without success." Reluctant to take even the first step down the road that leads to the scandal called "temporary faith,"[32] Hooker risks again the implication that assurance may be had before faith. Then, characteristically, he tries to protect his belief in the predictive value of a perfect preparation by distinguishing it from other, confusable cases. Warily, therefore, we are to observe the difference between "restraining and preparing grace" (166). For the latter there can be only one use: redemption. For the former, however, there may be other uses.

Indeed, there appear to be a number of "other ends for which the Lord in his wisdom sees fit to curb . . . the corruptions of the wicked": to show, for example, the "absolute sovereignty he hath over the worst men" (166); or "to provide for the subsistence and continuance of the society of men"; or to "put his servants to a more narrow search," realizing that "something like preparation" has brought

them no further than many a hypocrite. In the case of the hypocrite, this temporary restraint by "legal terrors" is often no more than a "preparation for sin"
(167–68). For the Lord needs to do more than merely "curb a sinner, or hack and
rough hew him a little" (169). But if, on the other hand, he will go so far as to "cut
him off, as a branch or scion fit for a savior he will never let him die or wither"
(169). And this distinction should warn those "who as yet never came into the
suburbs of salvation" because they regard the work of preparation as "merely su-
perfluous." Some "conclude their condition good, because they never knew what
a good condition meant" (170); some hold out against preparation with the "presumptuous" claim that God "will take less" (171–72). Others, imagining a "more
easy" way, will "catch after Christ . . . before there be any breach of league with
their lusts" (172); like "travelers" who fancy a shortcut, they forget that sinners
must hear "the Word with sorrow first, and afterwards with joy" (173). To the objection that we are commanded to believe "at all times" and not hold back,
Hooker replies—Shepardlike—that man's duty is always to "believe if he can."
But, his conviction quickly adds, one simply cannot do this while "under the
power of corruption" (174).

Still others, beginning well enough, feel "the terror and trouble and heart-
smart which sin has wrought in them" and turn busily to the "amendment of it"
but find themselves involved in "legal reformation" merely, aiming at their own
"honor and quiet" and revealing "a deep silence about a Christ" (174–95, *sic*).[33]
Others, aware they need Christ, imagine their long suffering has already entitled
them; "they cannot endure with patience to think they should miss" (196). These
misunderstanders of that selfless preparation which really is predictive may know
themselves if they "secretly snarl at Gods dealings . . . and privily grudge and re-
pine" at the spiritual fortune of others; or if, "wearied with delays," they sit "down
in a forlorn condition," imagining their "worthiness is not attended" or that "the
Lord hath forgot himself" (196–97). Thus we have been made as wary of the
dangers of gratuitous dreariness as of cheery avoidance. Again, as it readily appears, a man may adopt all sorts of affective poses, but only God can cut to the
quick. No cut, no grafting. And—if only men might receive the doctrine without
cavil—blessed are those who are cut for they shall be engrafted.

A fourth use aims at the "encouragement" of a "poor distressed sinner," pitied by family and friends but now finally "in God's way"; for "as in childbed,
when throws come thick and strong, there is most hope of a speedy and happy
delivery," so in this "new birth" (198). Finally, and in fitting preparation for this
long book's second doctrine (on the "plain and powerful ministry"), a fifth use
encourages all would-be believers to "suffer . . . the exhortation of the Baptist"

and to stir their "souls in the use of all means." And just here—at a stroke but according to a logic for which we are well prepared—the rhetoric drops all trace of embattled distinction and simply exhorts us to "bestir our souls," for "then we may undoubtedly expect him, and we shall not miss of our expectation. . . . If the door was open, he would come in without question" (199). Our ear, perhaps, must still hear the distinctions: He comes, infallibly, only when preparation has been made perfect, and that by the work of his own Spirit, so that much more is at issue here than in many an ordinary invitation. Only those called *will* come, and they only when prepared. But they are to be called, by the minister in close and faithful imitation of Scripture, and—as it became Shepard's mission to emphasize—they do need to hear and answer the call.

The problem, it plainly appears, is not between Calvin and Covenant or yet between Grace and Nature but simply between analysis and exhortation. At some point the Puritan stops explaining the reason and simply issues the call. At that moment his problem is one not of the logic but of the pain of a salvation that must always begin in sorrow: "I know this manner of entertainment seems hard to flesh and blood"; and no wonder therefore that so "many are content the King would go another way." Is he "come to torment us before the time?" (199–200). Hooker will not move on to his own preacherly concern before reminding us that we are in fact "a company of poor, miserable, sinful and damned creatures," "dust and ashes" in one lingo, "dead dogs" (200) in another. Are we, do we think—any more than the centurion in the Gospel—worthy that the Lord should come under our roof? Can we not feel the force of the simple, almost predoctrinal point?—that "the baser the place is that should entertain him, the greater the preparation should be." If we mean to "entertain his majesty," ought we not then "sweep [our] hearts, and cleanse those rooms, cleanse every sink, and brush down every cobweb"? And if all this, in common sense, for some local eminence, how much more for "the King of Kings" (201), who brings in his train "all the good we need or can desire" (202), who comes not "in judgment to condemn us, but in mercy to save us," who "entreats" and "beseeches" (203) our acceptance?

Indeed we are to picture the Savior who "hath taken a great journey from heaven to earth to save us," knocking at our hearts, it may well be, for the very last time. Picture him there, with "streams of blood trickling down his cheeks"; or "upon the cross," his hands "thrust through with nails, and his side pierced with a spear, enduring the wrath of God for our sins." Imagine you saw *this* Christ "knocking at the door of your hearts . . . : Will not this move you to prepare your hearts for him? . . . Will you suffer Christ to stand thus, knocking at the door of your hearts and not let him in?" (203–4). The moment is passed, finally, when the minister needs to say he *knows* you cannot open your heart of yourself. When analysis lapses at last to exhortation, he must simply preach the word he has been given. Trusting in the force of his prior explanations. And trusting too that the plain and powerful preaching of God's very Word is fit occasion to perform his own most gracious work. For who would quibble when such a One should knock?

———

No one would charge incompletion, surely, if the third book of Hooker's *Application* had decided to end just there, with preparation justified to the household sense and then preached with richly imitative passion. Indeed, a lesser theorist— or one with a less patient audience—might have thought to conclude an entire treatise, in lively voice or enduring print, at just about this point. But life goes on and, in New England at least, the preaching in about the same degree; nor, as certain subjects appear to generate their own unfolding, should the test of godly letters look more to the height of passion than to the breadth of the subject. Then too, revivals to the contrary notwithstanding, souls are saved one at a time, and one soul's triumph may be another soul's terror. Anticlimax, accordingly, is a prime fact of Puritan literary life. The trick to be learned is that of starting up again with more of anticipation than of memory.

So here: the third book has a complementary second doctrine: as the heart of man *must* be prepared, so "a plain and powerful ministry is the only ordinary means to prepare the heart soundly for Christ" (205). The institution of Calvinist preaching—to the "choir" of those elect—will surely bear some explicit justification, and it is possible to feel that Hooker's concerns here are significantly "professional." But the work of public justification has been done before, by William Perkins most notably, and Hooker's brief exposition adds little to the general store of neo-Calvinist Professionalism.[34] And not much to what his less self-justifying analysis has managed to imply so far. Indeed, this would be a *bad* place to introduce a skeptical response to the question of why the power of divine decree requires, in curious supplement, the weak addition of a human ministry.

The issue of moment, perhaps, is the problem of Calvinist audience. And also, more specifically, the frame of mind in which one is to accept the heavy news of the necessity of preparation. That God saves some and refuses others is not open to question. At issue, rather, in Hooker's most strenuous version of "Application," is why God has also decreed that virtually all the elect, on their way to spiritual assurance, should suffer the terrors of the damned. And this, almost always, at the hands of some minister who, trusting his own salvation, can only hope his audience contains a quorum of persons whose path would be somewhat like his own. Implied, of course, is the question of how assurance shall address itself to anxiety—how faith shall conduct its arguments to those whose hope looks a lot like doubt. Equally unavoidable, however, is the question of how to get an audience past its inevitable resistance, not to salvation, which only the proud would find too fine, but to the bad news of sin by nature before the good news of salvation by grace. It had to be said. It was certain to be resisted. What then was a minister to do?

One answer was to explain again, to those who have already been heard to say (to Christ), "Art thou come to torment us before the time?" (199–200), that it is better to suffer the torment now, on the way to assurance, than to rest secure in tainted good deeds or in the hope that fate will yet prove kind, only to find out later, *in illo die,* that damnation is in fact the just desert of those never brought to suffer repentance. The logic, of course, was never quite simple, for some would always blame their nonrepentance on predestination. But the question could also be put another way: decree in fact includes the experience of a profound, painful sorrow for sin; do not resist the pain. The pain may seem to issue from the personal style of the local preacher, but it comes in fact from God. Do not resist the "plain and powerful" message the minister is bound to deliver: it is "the Lord's, and not [his] own." As Perkins explained, the faithful minister will speak "not only the word of God, but as the word of God."[35] There is some self-service here and perhaps a certain mystification as well. But we have it on the authority of no less an observer than Emerson that teachers who aspire to be prophets must always point to the authority of some Truth beyond the scope of personality. And, as we may easily realize, Puritan Reformation is hardly the place to look for skepticism about the link between authority and the Word.

So Hooker will do what he must—and then do his best to prepare the way for a patient reception of his insistence on the necessity of pain and terror. For on his account, the same God who decided that salvation was to be realized in the context of godly sorrow also saw fit to prepare "workmen" for the task of its human cultivation. The typic Elias was such a one, and the antitypic Baptist as well: neither had much talent for ingratiating speech; rather, both were fitted to wield the Word "like an axe" so as to "take off the knotty untowardness in the soul" before it could settle upon the Lord as a "corner stone." Or, in another figure of the rugged before the smooth, the "powerful humbling ministry" is "like the plow" which must work its rough magic before the soul may receive "the immortal seed of the Word" (205). Enacted here, however, intentionally or not, is the paradox of Hooker's preaching considered as "style": sometimes in advance and sometimes after the fact of doctrine, God's undisputed words are never far from Hooker's tropic justification. As if "plainness" required the sacred types to pass the test of homely troping.[36] As if the truth were not itself unless it could be spoken in "the language really used by men." Unless, that is to say, the minister were a manly poet no less than a godly prophet.

Not self-confessed, of course, as Hooker's plainness offers itself chiefly as a matter of such words "as those of the meanest capacity have some acquaintance with," even as it resists that "eloquence" which consists either of "the frothy tinkling of quaint and farfetched phrases" or—more metaphysically—of that "pompous gaudiness . . . which . . . steals away the mind and affection from the truth, and stays it with itself" (206). The prime concern is clarity, for what "the mind conceives not, the heart affects not"; but such clarity is often enhanced by figures and, though Scripture itself may be thanked for outlawing the offer of "dry crust or stones" to the hunger of a child, it requires a wit more liberated to evoke the ministry as "nurses" who shall "prepare milk for the meanest and weakest, and meat for all" (208). Evidently Scripture is richly to model but not rigidly to constrain the language of spiritual urgency.

But as "plainness of preaching" is to appear in the matter as well as the manner of what is spoken, so it becomes necessary to call things by their proper names: a "drunkard is a drunkard" and—with no rule of correctness to complicate the issue of "native and natural colors"—a "spade is a spade." Satan's policy is to "smut and disfigure" the ways of grace with the "dirt of reproaches," naming "sincerity" as "singularity" and "exactness" as "Puritanism and hypocrisy" (210–11); but somehow the eventual message seems less noteworthy than the figures. Or if that is the effect of latter-day criticism, we must notice that Hooker is seldom at a loss for colorful words and suppose that his original audience was surely edified all the better for the resources of his homely gift. Satan, plainly, is cavalier (that is, English) with the Truth about sin. Puritans, in destiny if not in express confession, are the sort of American writers who can expose the charade in which "covetousness comes masked under the vizard of frugality and moderation" and "cowardice is . . . decked up in the robes of discretion, and wariness" (211). Much is still to be written about the way Puritan preaching performed many of the same functions as Jacobean drama, but Hooker is doing more than professing literary tradition when he imagines the minister not as a prophet but as "a jester" and the pulpit not as a scene of insight but as "a stage to play with sin" (211). He is in fact enacting the terms of Puritan transaction with rhetoric: to instruct and to exhort; to try and to warn and to comfort; and if to please at all, then only with the grim pleasure which comes with the recognition that, when Scripture talks sin, it speaks the vernacular; and that its plainest speech is often metaphoric. Even to the plainest understanding.

Plainness so understood, power has only a little to add: "undeniable evidence of reason out of the Word, which is able to command the conscience" (212)—"meter-making argument," that is to say, whether or not the minister be tuned as well as "fit." And withal a certain "inward spiritual heat." Conventionally, "he that mourns in speaking of sin, makes another mourn for sin committed" (213)[37] because, more generally, and with a little more élan, "an exhortation that proceeds from the heart carries an authority and commission with it," whereas "brainish discourses talk only with the understanding" (213–14). Here, as elsewhere in early modern psychology, the heart is the root of human behavior,[38] so that God's Word must soak "deeply" to the "heart root of him that with meekness will receive it" (214). As the sinner is told to pray as if it all depended on prayer, so the minister must preach as if it all depended on rhetoric.

What this will mean, less formally, is that an effective ministry will always discover "the secrets of sin" and make known "the close passages of the soul to itself": "killing me softly," as the students can be taught to say—"as if he'd found my letters / And read each one out loud." Or else, less softly, "Was not Paul in your bosom? Did he not ransack every corner of your consciences?" (214). Against predictable opposition, the minister begins with a sort of paradigmatic exposé, revealing sinfulness in its true color and trusting that its qualities are roughly the same in all. Reception will vary, no doubt, but in the hearts of "such to whom the Word is spoken and blessed . . . a lively ministry over-powers the corruption" (214–15).[39] Of course, the Word must be *blessed;* otherwise, contrary to fact, the experience of salvation would be identical to audience. But in context the emphasis falls on *spoken,* to remind the audience that the fact of their own sin will indeed find lively voice, that their moral sensibility will indeed be assaulted, as plainly as possible and as often as necessary. To explain what the minister must do, that is to say, is also to announce what an audience had better learn to expect. To be sure, no masochism can alter the outcome of decree, but resistance to the needful insult is surely a sign that a man's heart and God's plan are not (yet) in harmony.

As "strong physic either cures or kills," so the Word, which is "but an instrument in the hand of Christ," either "humbles or hardens." Expect, therefore, not a "sleepy tale, a toothless, sapless discourse" (215). Prepare, instead, for a cadre of ministers trained up to "speak with authority"—keenly conscious that their authority is not themselves, but firmly persuaded that God has determined to make their heartbreaking rehearsal of the sin-exposing Word "the only ordinary means" of preparation. So essential is this ordinary dispensation that ministers are at fault if "not one poor soul [is] prepared for Christ" (216). Surely "God is as merciful as ever," but "ministers do not deliver the Word with a heavenly, hearty, violent affection" (217). Implied, perhaps, is the charge that "heartless" ministers may not be themselves converted. Equally important, however, is the prescription of style: do not send "a child" to deliver a message "to a man." Too easily will the weak and deferential minor be put off with flimsy excuses and deferrals; the man, in the same place, "will not be dallied withal, he will take no denial but will have what he came for" (218).

This instruction—in the art of manliness—is explicitly for ministers, yet we have no trouble imagining the mutuality involved in the transaction of preaching. Here and there, no doubt, some hapless practitioner may not have realized that in the matter of preparation, as elsewhere, the ways of Providence are a little rough. More likely, however, is a certain predictable inhibition: as teachers surely know, students do not like to be taught what they do not already know; and here, where the stakes are higher, not all members of a congregation may wish to reward the preacher according to the violence of his assault. Puritans are Puritans, but nature is nature, and small wonder if a minister should temper his message of sin with a word about grace and mercy—"in season," as they might think, but a little previous in the logic of preparation. The problem is circular, of course, like all those involving more than one literary intelligence: preachers are timid because congregations resist; and congregations resist so long as ministers hesitate to speak the word that shall "over-power" their corruption. The way to break the impasse is to persuade ministers that God's occasional causality is vastly more important than the Sabbath's steady decorum.

Still, we are hardly surprised when Hooker moves from speaker to audience without missing a beat, or that his treatise of the ministry of preparation ends with two Uses addressed to the subjects of that violent work. More vital than the rebuke to a decorous ministry lies the discovery of the "miserable condition of those that [have] lived a long time" under a "plain and powerful ministry, and yet their hearts have not been fitted and prepared" (218). Perhaps the season of redemption has passed; the minister has "hewed" the living wood of the soul, yet he finds "one piece broken, and another crackt, and another knotty," fit in the end "for nothing but for burning" (219). So the use of warning is one of exhortation as well: since "he that will not be fitted for grace shall be made a firebrand in Hell" (219), it only makes sense to welcome and indeed abet the disruptive preaching which nature hates so much. Again the minister aims not at what he himself can *cause* to happen but says the thing God wants said at just this moment, the thing which *will* happen in every successful case. Since a plain and powerful ministry is indeed "the means of preparing the soul of a poor sinner for the Lord Jesus, why then . . . labor that the Word may be so unto you as it is in it self: It is a preparing Word, labor you that it may prepare your hearts." Labor, also—as the embarrassment of preaching to the predestined is overcome by the confidence in the revealed necessity of preaching—"to save the soul of another." Let every home become a site of application, where the Word is repeated and abetted rather than resisted or assuaged. Let us all be prepared, Lord, "if not this sermon, then at the next" (220). Let preparation become a social scene, even as resistance to violent preaching could never be blamed on a single individual. "Suffer your souls to be wrought upon": it may seem more the performance of rhetorical man than the ordinance of electing God, but "the word is powerful to prepare your hearts" (220).

Above all, perhaps, remember that preparatory address is far from arbitrary: "the minister must hew and square your hearts," and so you must suffer the words of exhortation. Thus, as the logic of preaching resolves itself into the psychology of audience, Hooker's final word of exhortation is to suffer exhortation. Suffer too, he hastens to add, "the words of conviction, of reproof, of admonition" (221). But even as we measure the relief gained from tautology, we realize that the real emphasis is on "suffer." Emerson, at a similar moment of apologia, will ask his audience to "tolerate one or two solitary voices in the land" speaking a language men do not eagerly relish; and the reference to the voices as "solitary" suggests that Emerson too is thinking of the Baptist.[40] But Hooker, though he too would plead for a certain tolerance, is quite clear that this tolerance will entail suffering. The bad news comes first, always. And the response to this upsetting news is, predictably, so adverse and determined that the first assaults on its embattled self-defense can hardly be less than violent.

As not even Adam could earn salvation, some "application" there must always be. Moreover, because there has been a fall, this application is of "redemption": an offended God has had to be compensated, and a fallen man, now much less than able to merit with God, has had to be made the beneficiary of the redemptive act. So far, the familiar Christian construct. Just here, however, all Calvinists have the additional problem of deciding how the disposition of redemption is to be communicated to those predestined to receive it. Perhaps not at all: "the court knows . . . and is satisfied." Perhaps by personal revelation: "Peace, Peace, My Honey, do not Cry."[41] Or perhaps—in deference to a set of books that speak more than Isaac and Ishmael—in a "moral" way. Nowhere can there be men and women who actually earn salvation; yet perhaps the saints are those empowered to perform what God is pleased to command, namely, to believe in a counterintuitive scheme of vicarious atonement. For some. Possibly too, these same saints begin to know themselves in the moment they begin to know themselves as sinners. Not formally or in fictions of reason but really and as such. Resist they will, but hammered they must be. Until they cry, "Batter my heart, three-personed God."[42]

No wonder, of course, if not all forms of pious intelligence have been willing to follow this scheme from beginning to end. A wonder of history—of Scripture and interpretation, that is to say—that anyone ever managed to internalize the whole of it. But Thomas Hooker is one such man. And his *Application* is only just now well begun. Calvinist but not *only* that, perhaps the schema will acquire credibility from the energy of its further elaboration. Or, in the last supposable case, from its full enactment.

II. "A Holy Kind of Violence"

Only a fairly ample account of Hooker's *Application* can afford to pause long over Books 4 and 5. We begin to sense, first of all, the pressure of an unfolding schema which, though perfect in its own Ramistic way, does not always correspond to Hooker's most penetrating insights. Then too, when Hooker moves from the need of preparation "In General" to certain "Particulars," we quickly discern that some parts of a dichotomy are more equal. It looks perfect—

$$
\text{Preparation}
\begin{cases}
\text{In General (Bk. 3)} \\
\\
\text{Particulars}
\begin{cases}
\text{Quality}
\begin{cases}
\text{Free (Bk. 4)} \\
\\
\text{Fit (Bk. 5)}
\end{cases} \\
\\
\text{Parts}
\begin{cases}
\text{God's Dispensation (Bks. 6–8)} \\
\\
\text{Our disposition (Bks. 9, 10)—}
\end{cases}
\end{cases}
\end{cases}
$$

but the discussion of the "freedom" of God's work is twice as long as the complementary account of its "fitness." And the longer essay, brilliant in places, is sometimes a little doctrinaire. Yet part of the effect of the *Application* comes from an evident determination to be complete. If God grant life.

Book 4, on "the freeness of the work," lingers over its "opening" of a text on salvation in "an acceptable time" (221). "Salvation presumes always danger and evil" (227), of course, and so the need for preparation: without an awakening to the danger of sin, what sense could it possibly make to be saved? A learned account of a Scripture "day" leads to the hopeful conclusion that "to a man his day is his life, so long as he breathes in the air and sees this sun, that's the time allotted to . . . trade for his everlasting state" (226). Along the way, Hooker's Corinthians make the objection that "It is not in our power to receive the spiritual good of this word, nor sufficiency in you that are Apostles to work it," but Hooker is ready with an answer already in part familiar: "True, the blessing is the Lord's, but the endeavor must be ours" (224). The point, surely, is that the issue of time in no way increases the force of the objection of human inability: one simply has to try, always, and "now" is the acceptable time. The opposite of timely endeavor is not humility but evasion, avoidance, denial. And these three abide.

What this book settles in to argue, as the first of two doctrines, is that "the work of God is altogether free"—in preparation as ever in decree. It is simply "not in our liberty nor ability to take hold of the offer of his mercy" and, though we might come to feel a mighty thirst after salvation, we have it in the Word that "to him that thirsts I will give the water of life freely" (229). An innocent reading of the text might take the word *freely* to mean "liberally," but Hooker's orthodoxy discovers here a denial that human longing creates any obligation in God. Elsewhere Hooker will be at pains to emphasize that thirst is a necessary condition of the dispensation of water; and Cotton will accuse him of allowing the soul to derive a certain comfort from the mere condition of thirst.[43] But though Hooker may indeed hold that a certain kind of longing faithfully predicts a certain kind of satisfaction, his orthodoxy is guaranteed by the fact that this longing is itself a creation of grace. Some sense of absence makes the experience of satisfaction intelligible; but drought alone can scarcely *cause* the clouds to rain.

With unabated enthusiasm, therefore, Hooker notes that "free it was for God . . . whether he would appoint another covenant, when the first was broken and made void" (229). Equally dependent on "his good pleasure" is his decision "to reveal and make known the means of grace": no one can explain "why the dew of heaven . . . is sent to one people and not to another" (230). Free as well is the efficacy of those means, for "it is only from God's good pleasure to give good success to some, which he denies to others." No "inferior causes" can explain why Paul, in the midst of "rebellion," should have the Lord "revealed to him" (231); or why, on the other hand, the "doctors of the law . . . should despise the counsel of God" (232). The case of Paul might seem to argue against the inevitability of preparation, but its inclusion expresses the wish to spare no effort in recognizing the sovereignty of God's decree. Reasoning solely on the issue of freedom, therefore, Hooker stresses only that "nothing man hath" (232) can purchase redemption: "nothing a man can do" can "procure and obtain this spiritual good"; and, crucially, that "there is no promise made to any natural man whereby he can challenge [grace] at the hands of the Lord" (233).

This last assertion is one Miller might have regarded more closely for, in Calvinist context, the New Covenant exists to guarantee that God will promulgate and then stick to his own terms. Others, agreeing that God can freely attach salvation to anything-at-all, might hold that it has been freely offered as man's stupendous reward for trying really hard; and in these terms the covenant would have the effect of compensating for the difference between the "condign" and the "congruous" merit of Catholic tradition. But the original covenant is made between God and Christ, so that a man may challenge God to keep his promises only after the miracle of his new birth into Christ. The point to be made about the Puritans is not that their covenant idiom tends to dilute their predestinarian theology but simply that they celebrate the fact that God has publicly agreed to keep certain promises, which he need not have made at all. Hooker may indeed differ from some important consensus but not on this prime point.[44]

Here, predictably, the first use is of thanksgiving: why, out of so many, is "my heart touched"? The answer can only be that "it's thy grace"; and though Hooker goes on into the redundancy of emphasis—"It's thy free grace"—we already learn, perhaps, not always to read "grace" physically, so to speak, as an aid to or a perfection of nature, but in its simpler sense of favor freely conferred. For "what am I that thou shouldst be mindful of me? . . . Was I not as blind as any, and knew not?" (234–35). Only after this astonished response to the gratuitousness of the divine plan does Hooker modulate from God to minister: "gainsaid I not, yea, rejected thy compassions so often tendered in the ministry of the Word, and forced upon me by . . . thy faithful ministers?" (235). The mood of salvation, it appears, is thanksgiving, now, for exhortation resisted then.

A use of encouragement reminds all "disconsolate sinners" that even *their* hearts "may be quickened"; for "as there is no worth on our parts that can move the Lord, so there is no vileness so great that can hinder him." Assailed, again, is the notion that unless men have their own spiritual funds "they . . . shall not be able to purchase God's . . . graces and comforts" (236). Rather—purchase already accomplished—God "intends not to sell [his] graces and comforts, but to bestow them freely upon such as have an open hand to take them, and an empty heart to carry them away" (237). We recall, of course, that hand and heart have been emptied by preparation; and those who ask if emptiness is not itself a sort of qualification need to remind themselves that it too has been a work of the Spirit. A more legitimate objection will protest that this is all a small comfort; "for if the dispensation of grace depend on God's free will, he may . . . deny it, as well as give it." And the answer indicates that Hooker has no intention of weakening the backbone of New England: "He may give it as well as deny it, and that's argument enough to sustain our hopes, and to quicken out endeavors." He even sounds the note he taught to Thomas Shepard: put it to the "adventure" (238). Finally—though patience is not the same as sloth—some souls need to "stay God's time, and to wait his pleasure." "Beggars must not be choosers," and he that "may give what he will . . . may give when it seems most fit to himself." God being God, "just cause we have to wait, no reason at all to murmur against him: Hast thou then endeavored after this work of grace, and canst not attain it? Endeavor still" (239). Waiting implies a continued attendance upon the means. Not activity is being prevented here, but only despair, the impatient wish to have the affair of salvation settled at once. One is to endeavor, now, but to leave the issue open throughout the whole season of life. Why be in such haste to infer reprobation? "You may go to Hell time enough" (240).

Which serves perfectly to introduce the second doctrine of Hooker's treatise of freedom: "while this life lasts, and the Gospel is continued," that is the season "wherein the Lord expresseth his good pleasure." Seamless to us, the text generates two separate doctrines to the perspicacious notice of the professional. Obviously, "grace is only to be gained in this life." And more urgently, perhaps, the "season which the Lord usually takes to work upon . . . those that belong to him" is while "the means of salvation are continued"; for a preparationist preacher might not stay forever, in Chelmsford, at Newtown, or on Earth. That "preparation . . . must be made in this life" is simply a matter of doctrine: "after the parting of the Soul from the body . . . God's peremptory sentence is passed"; a bodily resurrection awaits, but at the very moment of death "the soul of him that is wicked . . . is dragged by the Devils into torment" (241–42). Then too, morally, "the wicked after death are wholly delivered up to . . . their corruptions"; no more "common graces," now, to prevent their "notorious outrages" (243). This last thought prompts a moment of something between sympathy and vengeance—there is now "no heart to pity the damned sinner, no friend to pray for him, no counsel to advise, [no] reproof to stop, no exhortation to persuade any more" (244)—but Hooker has more important work than to invent Wigglesworth. One is to suggest that the "season of God's acceptation" is whenever "he puts forth the power of his grace to prepare the heart" (244–45). God's favor might be revealed at any time. But the time to prepare is now—when, in the marketplace vernacular, God "sets open the stall of the Gospel before our eyes, cries his commodities in our streets, and proclaims . . . Ho, every one that will, let him come" (245).

Largely a literary creation, this "now" is better experienced than described: it is any moment when the Scripture call is heard—privately, where no minister shall appear, or proclaimed aloud and in the public space of a congregation wherever the paradigm shall find its expression pure. While "wisdom cries and ministers call," now is the time "for God to work it, for us to endeavor it" (245–46).

Something like this is what is meant by hearing the Gospel, as opposed to listening to the theory of salvation: "behold all is ready, only come." *Come,* that is to say, and quibble not the theory of coming. Time enough for that "when the feast is over" (246). Success, on this account, is always the result of eager pursuit; theory, the bad-faith residue of refusal. Nor is present unworthiness any reason to resist: "you cannot snatch Christ," but you do have to start somewhere; and it often is the Lord's way to take "the sinner in the . . . most desperate condition." Only so can saving grace "be set forth to the wonder of the world, and to the encouragement of those who should come to like straights" (247). From which we learn not only the "blessing" of a "long life" (249), but also, a fortiori, of the "hellish distemper of self-murder," even for one who says his constant sight of sin and Hell has made him "weary of my life." "Bless God for your life," Hooker responds; for "while your life lasts, you are in the way to mercy" (250). And only then. Which is another way of saying "now."

Finally, however, in an instruction which ought to be settled on "the consciences of us all," Hooker comes back to the level of his previous enactment of the "gospel present." Since the Lord "usually" accepts the soul "while he . . . continues the means," what then remains but to improve them "to the uttermost?" (251). "Now is the season" is less an Edwards-like observation on the history of redemption than a Thoreau-like call to redeem the present. And to a voice that questions whether a "season" is indeed offered, Hooker replies with an "invitation" worthy of being imitated in almost anyone's "Address": "Behold now: while I am speaking, and you are hearing, while the doors of the sanctuary are yet opened, while we are in the land of the living, behold now is the acceptable time" (252).[45] And, to suggest that such a moment might transport the preacher as well as the audience, he even risks a rare deviation from his customary rhetoric of the rough and ready to the poetry of sexual request: "Arise my Love, my Dove, and come away."

Immediately, as if to prove that Canticles is no literal invitation to rapture, the lover's reason—"for the winter has gone"—reminds Hooker the allegorical historian that the "mists of popery and . . . superstition" are indeed "passed away." He even permits himself to say that "the voice of the turtle is heard in *our* land." For this quondam victim of Laudian persecution is acutely aware that, though not quite a Gospel, New England is itself an opportunity. Recovered from a close brush with oriental sexuality now, and mindful once again that all salvation is local, he returns to the sensibilities of the audience before him:

Arise, arise, therefore ye secure and dead hearted sinners, and come away.
Arise ye drunkards, come away from your cups. . . . Arise, ye adulterous

wretches, come away from your base haunts, and beds of dalliance; come to him who . . . promises to accept you, who is willing and able to save you. (252–53)

But if the audience is now New England, the season is Gospel-present once again. And the happy fact that the Lord, having "seen other countries," has "settled his abode amongst us" is less a fulfillment of biblical prediction about "America" than an acute reminder that New England is the place where the season of *now* has fled to enact itself. Elsewhere, the Mass or its Prayer Book remnants; here, the living Word. Wonder ye then at the "original relation"?

Trivializers of the present need to hear that a day in any sense is "very short" and "who knows how soon it may end?" Young America quotes Old Ecclesiastes in support of "present pleasures," but Luke knows that "this night may thy soul be taken" (255). And even if we grant that "the day of thy life continue," it seems not at all certain that the "day of salvation" shall last. What if the Lord "remove his candlestick"? Hooker could die; or the forces of Laud could invade. Better listen when "the Lord raps at the door of thy heart," even if his rapper be the rough "hammer of the law." Resist not the preparation of the day, but suffer the "ordinance of God to have its full blow upon thy soul" (256). Learn of Augustine the fallacy of "tomorrow, tomorrow": dallying with familiar pleasure, the proto-Protestant cries out in a "holy kind of violence": "Why not today?" And from that day "the Lord gave him victory" (257). And so, as the lesson of an experience that absorbs the subject in an act of hearing and responding *now,* "dispute no more." But say without the mediation of indirect discourse, "while therefore the Spirit speaks to my soul, seek thou my face; give me a heart to echo back again, thy face Lord will I seek this day" (258).

Thus an essay on God's freedom in the work of preparation has turned into an enactment of man's response to God's invitation. Well advertised, we could say, is the happy case of actual conversion, for God's call is always present to the moment of man's response. He may walk away from many a sermon, but the memory of its Gospel-presence defines the moment of later choice as its very own "now." But it is more correct to say that Hooker has defined the moment of forced option as such: when we agree that this life and the next both turn on one's present *yes* or *no,* it is clear bad faith to raise the question of "free will"; and to say "I'll think about that tomorrow" is simply to postpone the moment, in the hope that something other than subjectivity will intervene. A way to get past a rough place, perhaps, but a frank deferral of "ultimate concern."[46] Academic structures encourage us to teach the history of religion—or to sponsor the Bible as Literature—but here and there our godly letters insist on reenacting the demand of the Gospel-present. Maybe we should be forbidden to *teach* such works.

Book 5 of the *Application* seems, by contrast, a little pedestrian, as Hooker backs down from a philosophical discovery of the way faith must be to a more or less sociological account of the way religion usually operates. Grace may begin to work at any time, nor does the decision to work in the time of a faithful ministry lessen the divine freedom; but, in the complementary human fact, the season of salvation usually comes earlier rather than later in the life of a man. In the form of a doctrine, derived from the "Parable of the Vineyard" (262), "God calls his elect at any age but the most of his, he converts before old age" (264)—before they are "in the crazy and decayed estate of fainting age, when the whole frame begins to shake and go to ruin" (270–71). Hooker is trying to have it both ways, of course, but by now we understand that this comes with the territory—of a Calvinism that refuses to compromise the sovereignty of God's will but is also bent on maintaining that his revealed ways exhibit sound wisdom. Then too, this yoking of the dangerously unpredictable with the reassuringly plausible gives Hooker the chance to sound a note not entirely characteristic of Puritan tradition: as "grace destroys not" but merely "perfects" (269) the faculties of nature, so all the luminous "courage and resolution" which may be found in the character of a natural man, however sinful, will shine the brighter when these powers have been redeemed for the service of God. At risk here, perhaps, is Hooker's earlier emphasis on the need for the Spirit to destroy sin before God can enter into the soul in a special, redeeming way; but his point is simply that grace drives the habit of sin out of the faculties, returning them to their uncorrupted state, in which they undergo a marvelous perfection when their habits are founded in grace. And in no event will Hooker befriend the Scholastics at the risk of his Calvinism.[47]

Avoiding such professional difficulties, Hooker devotes more than half of Book 5 to the uses of his paradox of fit though free. No one, first of all, is competent to predict "the final estate of any in this life" (271). Though it is certainly no violation of the judgment "in charity" to distinguish "the children of God" from "the children of the Devil" (273), the worst that can be said of any man, in this life, is that his conversion is "not yet" (271). And this same principle of timely uncertainty may provide "a cordial to . . . the fainting hearts of decrepit and aged sinners": the case is desperate, to be sure, when "the great work of everlasting life" comes down to the last hour; and yet the thing is possible, and "this hope it is which keeps the head above water," that it is "never too late to forsake our corruptions" (274–75). Satan, whose song had always been "tomorrow," now declares it "vain . . . to begin so great a work of preparation." Wisdom now is all a discouragement, but power remains a hope: truly, "thou hast one foot in the grave, but the arm of the Lord is not shortened that he cannot help" (275). Now is (still) the hour. And yet, as the pendulum swings back at last to fitness, all those "whose breasts run full of milk, and their bones full of marrow" (276) had better take heed: now is your hour. Demographics may not recapitulate Decree, but probability certainly does nothing to weaken the way of the Word. God decrees. And he works his will whenever. The minister marshals arguments as the Word instructs. Now: decide.

———

Book 6 of the *Application* is also very short, but this single-sermon work is designed to introduce the first half of Hooker's final dichotomy. Having moved on from the "quality" to the "substantial parts" (283) of preparation, Hooker devotes Books 6, 7, and 8 to the "the dispensation of [preparation] as it comes from God"; and Books 9 and 10—602 pages in a separate volume—advertise and imitate "the frame and disposition which is wrought in the soul thereby" (284). The present matter arranges itself as follows: because "[t]he soul is naturally settled in a sinful security" (Bk. 6) and is "unwilling to be severed therefrom" (Bk. 7), it requires "a holy kind of violence" to drive it "out of this condition and . . . into Christ" (Bk. 8). The "dispensation" at issue, then, is some "holy kind of violence," and this is the point Hooker announces he will emphasize; but not without a sense of the opposing condition of natural will that explains the "necessity and mysterious depth" of God's violent intervention (285).

For a type of the natural condition Hooker takes the infamous "Church of Laodicea": "they need nothing in their own apprehension though indeed they have nothing" (285–86). All goes smoothly as long as Satan is in charge: if some "require . . . a higher strain of holiness," the reason is given as their own "pride and singularity" (286). Only a jolting dose of "the law" can provide the needed insult. And so with the natural man: "before the Lord come to seize on him, he sees no danger in his estate" (287). So long as the Lord hesitates to task them for their "grievous offenses, they feel no evil." Seeing that "other men as vile as themselves, fare like themselves," they conclude "there is no danger" (288). In just such a "deluded" condition, the sinner puts his safety "beyond all question": unable to "give any . . . sound evidence of his spiritual welfare," he simply "takes it for granted" (289). "Let men speak what they will, preach as they please, he promiseth himself comfort and success in his way." Because the ways of grace are beyond their "carnal and formal course," sinners regard them "with disdain, and cast the name of giddiness and folly upon them" (290). Each of these propositions has its own supply of texts, but surely Hooker is simply singing, from his own English experience, a song called "The Puritan in the Parish."

Pressing hard to prove that things must be different in the congregations of New England, Hooker is yet forced to summarize the law of opposition as he reads it from the face of nature: "If his ways of exactness be pressed and practiced with zeal," even the man "most inoffensive in his carriage will count it a matter of conscience to proceed to fierce opposition" against these zealots; the resisters all conclude "they are as good as men should be" (291). Indeed, Hooker is content to provide a universal rule: any man so opposed to anything that shall "blemish" his present condition is evidently "settled immovably in the security of his carnal estate." For this more than impish perversity Hooker offers three Reasons: the "subtlety of sin" which promises "content" (292); the "sensuality of the soul" which naturally can "taste nothing but that which answers their palate" (293); and that ever-present "self-love" which will "not suffer the sinner to hear of anything that may disquiet" (294). Well founded here is the claim that God's initial approach might *have* to be violent: the beast is tractable, but you have to gets its attention. Just so, at the comparable moment in the "Meditations" of Edward Taylor, the soul has reason to suspect that, like a "Box of Ointments," God's favor is "sweetness most sweet," and yet it appears that the same God might have to "break [that] box" on the sinner's hardened head.[48]

Yet Hooker is in no hurry to produce his own account of regenerating violence: uses accumulate, and all of Book 7 is devoted to the same task of preparing the way for an account of a holiness whose first approach can seem a little destructive. We understand immediately why "sharp and soul-saving preaching seems so grievous": nothing worse to those in a "sleepy security" than to be shown "the candle of the law"; and, as there is no one here to suggest you don't *need* that "candle to see the sun rise," we get instead the moral that "rough dealing evermore finds harsh entertainment here." Men may favor preachers who imply that "they and their sins may all go to heaven together" (295), but they should learn, to their "terror," that "the heaviest plague that can befall a man [is] that God should suffer him to sleep in his sins" (296). From which we may derive important evidence: "if Christ never awaken thee, he will never give thee light" (298). Even so, Hooker remains conscious that his compound formula covers the problem of preparation "only negatively" (297), explicitly deferring the question of "how far God may awaken a man, and yet not communicate his saving grace" (299). For the present he concludes with an exhortation quite certain of its comprehension: to all you secure sinners "that have been carried on a calm all your days: Oh! Know it, . . . a man becalmed is drowned." And then, as figure lapses to the plain language for which Book 10 has become famous, he offers this precise instruction: "call for the sight of sin, and sorrow for sin, for conviction, and humiliation, as you love your lives and souls" (299).

The literal continues: all those who "cannot say they have anything more than they brought with them into the world" must expect to hear nothing but "humiliation." Those whose condition is no more than the natural one must, for the time being, expect of religion only a flat refusal of all "carnal reasons" and, in their stead, a steady emphasis on the need to discover that "I am a miserable damned Creature" (300). Hold that thought, Hooker insists: "think so, and sleep so, and eat so, if you can. And when it's come to this, you may happily be prepared for the glad tidings of the Gospel" (301). The curious will wish to scrutinize the ambiguity of the last sentence: are we now in fact prepared or merely ready to be prepared? But as it is the mark of Hooker's preparation to go *on*, the best answer is simply *yes*. A strange happiness, to be sure—violent in the onset and self-denying in the continuance. But easier to hold, perhaps, than the exquisite sense that the God of the Universe is thinking of one's self with thoughts of peace.

And as if deferral of "the positive" were becoming the law of Hooker's *Application*, Book 7 delays the advent of God's holy violence with a further account of the reason of its necessity; for, as Hooker repeats his plan, the soul is not only habitually "settled in the security of a sinful estate," it is actively "unwilling to be severed" (302). Except that this second preliminary forces Hooker to face the question of "will," one almost imagines that Books 6 and 7 are trying to say much the same thing: the Fall has made salvation possible only *ab extra* and with great difficulty. But evidently Hooker means to deepen his analysis of this difficulty. And so he warns us that "the discovery of this second divine truth"—of human unwillingness—helps to make way for the "mysterious manner of God's dealing with the sinner when he would bring him [out] from under the power of his lusts" (302–3).

Proceeding to unpack the burden of Romans 8.7, Hooker explains that "the wisdom of the flesh" comprehends "the frame of the reasonable faculties, the understanding and will, in the extent of their full work" (303); nothing human, that is to say, escapes the condition of "enmity" to God and to the law (304). Thus the full reach of the doctrine at issue: "the frame of the whole heart of a natural man is wholly unwilling to submit to the work of the Lord" (305); not ambivalence but contrariness is the story of natural man—"unable to follow the direction of the law" and "not willing to bear the power thereof" (306). A text from Matthew supports this emphasis on man's "desperate unteachableness," and Genesis itself is made to cross the *T* in Total Depravity: "the frame of the imagination of our hearts is evil, and only evil, and that continually" (306–7). No prior references to the perfection of nature by grace (cp. 269–70) can soften—and no subsequent reference to the "leprosy" (316) of the whole man can do much to intensify—this emphasis: flesh being flesh, "it can do nothing but oppose the Spirit" (304).

And as texts certify the totality of human unwillingness, so do present observations register its "several degrees": unwilling to seek the truth, carnal hearts are, "like bats, . . . most at ease when they have least light" (307); or if the Lord will continue the truth, the sinner will devise ways to "break . . . the strength of the blow" (308), like the man who tells his servant, "draw the curtain, there the sun comes full in mine eyes" (309). And so on, by degrees, until in the last case the natural opposition requires, Poe-like, the sealing up or the starving out of conscience itself. Some injured objector might ask if wicked men are not "many times willing to part with their corruptions." Oh, yes, comes the reply, natural men may *profess* "subjection to the law," but notice that "they neither do, nor can, nor will do what they say" (313). A "corrupt heart" may "reform sin outwardly"; but when it comes to parting with the bosom sin, such a man will "discover his falseness." And then, in response to the protest that "the servants of the Lord" appear, many times, "unwilling to bid adieu to their special and ancient distempers," we make the more knowing discovery that it is only "a regenerate man" who may be said to be "two men," to have "a heart and a heart, a will and a will" (314)—a regenerate gift in powerful opposition to but not in total mastery of the fallen remnant. Only a *regenerate* Paul can complain of not doing the good "he would." The natural man, by contrast, wills nothing but himself. And to oppose anything cross to the short-term pleasure of that shortsighted persona.

Still skirting the punning project of "will," Hooker rehearses instead the reasons for his commitment to Pessimism. Holding with Calvinist tradition that, since the Fall, the will of man is infected with corruption which "universally overspreads the whole man" (315), Hooker blames the sin of Adam for "the deordination of the whole nature of man, and that against the whole law of God" (316), and he will hear no appeal to certain "reliques" of the "glorious Image of God": there may be "something left of the law, but nothing left whereby a man can do anything as an act of spiritual life that may be acceptable to God" (318). Taking "the poor Indians" as unhappy example, Hooker permits the observation that man was made "for a better" end than he now pursues and that "he ought to yield obedience to that other, and better"; but he quickly adds that "to know the will of God and do it, to be able to close with God, and to do that which is acceptable to him, this is far estranged from the sons of men by nature" (318). Such seems to Hooker the strong testimony of Scripture and also the steady tendency of human experience. And if the penalty of the Fall seems harsh, we are to remember that "the revenging justice of God," infinitely dishonored by the "apostasy of Adam," has but "delivered up the soul" to the life it seemed to prefer.

"Adam turned from God," so "God also turned from him," leaving him with "the deluded conceit of his own sufficiency" (319).

Already implicated in Hooker's language of *versio* and *conversio,* Augustine is allowed by name to authorize a "deep and sweet speculation" on freedom and its loss: "It was in the power of the mutability of Adam's will, to have used his will either well or ill . . . ; and because he did use this liberty . . . ill, therefore God put him under the power of that perverted mutability that he never should nor could do anything but evil" (320). Armed with this conclusion, Hooker denies that "Original Sin" is a "mere privation . . . of original righteousness": rather, it is an "exorbitation, or running wrong of all . . . the faculties," and this because "God doth not only take away his image, but delivers up the soul to the power of corruption" (322–23).[49]

Other conclusions follow as well, now Scholastic, now Pauline in diction. But their upshot is clear: "there is no possibility that a sinner should be recovered by any power he hath," for "the curse of the breach of the covenant is forever to be acted by the power of sin" (324). From which it plainly follows, as the first of a number of uses, that "it is the heaviest plague in the world for a natural man to have his own will"; indeed, it is the "vengeance of the Lord when he delivers a man up to the distemper of his own heart" (326–27). Earlier the heaviest plague was that God should suffer a natural man "to sleep" (296), but one sees the nexus: to sleep is simply not to realize the disordination of one's perverse will. And here we are to realize that "the will of a natural man is the worst part about him" (327). Men often do ill and yet claim "my heart is good": they need to recognize that "a man's carriage is but the shop" of his corruption, for which the "heart is the store-house" (328). So that the desire to be left to one's natural will is a sort of "madness"—as if a "malefactor *will* lie in a dungeon, when . . . deliverance is afforded" (329).

And because men will not come to Christ, when they "may have life and happiness for the coming," the matter of the will furnishes an important "ground of trial":

> We need not send up to heaven to look into the cabinet counsels of God's everlasting decrees. . . . Thou hast that in thy bosom [that] will be the best discovery of thy condition. Ask but honestly . . . thy own heart, and that will cast the balance. . . . Such as thy will is, such is thy condition. (331–32)

Boldly put, for a man who has just disqualified the entire *natural* will. Yet the "psychological" point of Calvinist analysis is perfectly clear: you are as you will. No one but God can enable you to will God's law above all else; but if you do indeed so will, there are no other questions to be asked. Mysteriously enough, a woman expresses her character in the choice between suitors. Just so here, look-ing at the fact and not at the theory of its possibility: "art thou to be matched to thy sin, or to thy Savior? to thy lusts, or to the Lord?" (333). How do you choose? Would you choose Christ? Then do so. Or—to insist on the deconstructive clarity of Edwards—if you *would,* then so you *do,* for there can be no such thing as willing to will.[50]

Someone—well instructed in the fact that "our natures are naught" and taught to notice that we are too frequently "snatched aside and surprised by our corruptions"—is sure to protest: "the Lord knows . . . we would be other, we want power against our distempers, yet we want not will to be severed from them." But if so, Hooker will promptly reply, then you are already in the condi-tion of Paul's regenerate ambivalence. Only be sure of the fact: *would* you be sev-ered from your sins? Are you, that is to say, indeed *willing?* Then "so said and so done." For "this is the very door of grace . . . , to be willing to be severed from sin: God never wrought upon you for good, unless this be wrought in you" (335). If willing is a great mystery, a priori, it is also a plain fact in the outcome. And to this fact Puritan preaching always looks: love of God is observable as an effect; so is hatred of sin which, in Hooker's account, may amount to the same thing. And in New England at least, the person who loves to echo Paul in the cry that "I cannot do as my duty is, but Oh that I could do so" (336), had better be ready with an offer of proof. For "he that is willing to part with his sin" is, identically, he who "takes greatest delight" in the means which "discover his sin most fully" and are most "powerful to remove it" (338). Repugnant to nature, these means work most "kindly on the heart" (338) of the man God is saving; and, though it may seem to blunt his (still deferred) emphasis on violence, Hooker makes the most of this killing comfort: "When a reproof stabs him to the quick, Oh more of that Lord" (339).

A final use offers "exhortation and direction" together. The first insists on a completely honest reception of the doctrine of the will to severance:

> Never leave thy prayers, and tears, and sorrows . . . until thou come to thy very heart; thy tongue professeth fair, and thy hand forbears the practice of evil, but ask thy heart, Heart what sayest thou? Shame may prevail with thee, authority . . . may constrain thee, and conscience may force thee to abstain from evil; but what says thy heart, art thou willing to part with sin? (343)

Easily figured as heart, will has come to mean something like fixed and settled loyalty, but the stakes remain fairly high nevertheless. Men to Hooker are all sinners, and they really seem to love their sins. All he asks of them is to hate the sin they find in grain. "They" cannot, as critique seems bound always to recall. Or perhaps they find in fact they do. Then QED. For it seems the prime implication of Hooker's system: only grace can hate sin enough.

Unaware of the anticlimax we have created, however, Hooker himself ends Book 7 with a last direction—aimed, perhaps, at those who find his doctrine of will too philosophical or too easy: "[W]hen thy heart is so besieged that it finds no relief, then Brethren look often up to heaven. He only that made the heart can frame the heart to the blessed obedience"; all we can do is "lie under the ordinances that God may do that for us which he requires of us." We, who may be enabled to choose God, must expect to suffer the pain of sinful self-knowledge along the way. We certainly should "cry to heaven" for God to give us "a heart to hate sin" and—who knows?—"he may do that for us which we cannot do for ourselves." Here and there some "I" may lose its sense of who is who. But "if I think it's easy I never knew what it was" (347).

———

Whatever it may imply about Hooker's preaching life in New England—or about the way the pages of the *Application* were prepared and assembled—Book 8 returns to Hooker's long form, in which we cannot discern the shape of several distinct sermons. After reminding us where we are in a three-chapter sequence, Book 8 offers but a single doctrine: because the sinner is "settled" in his condition and is "wholly unwilling to be severed" from it, "God the Father by a holy kind of violence as it were, plucks his [own] out of their corruptions, and draws them to believe in Christ" (349). Nor does Hooker take much time to worry the distinction between plucking and drawing: both are indeed "required before a man can receive the grace he stands in need of"; but because both are performed "by the same motion at the same instant" (350), it is perfectly proper to handle them together. What fills out the first sixty pages of this book of violence, rather, is the fact that Hooker divides his single doctrine into six topical sections. After that, three uses occupy the space (but do not exhibit the shape) of about two ordinary sermons. All the signs agree, therefore, that we have come to a distinctive place in Hooker's system.

Hooker's first task is to explain that neither plucking nor drawing is to be thought of as "moral suasion" (351); Jesuits hold that God "opens the eye and stirs up the will, by propounding objects of worth and . . . excellency," but this theory will not satisfy Hooker's sense of his text: the Pharisees fail because "none can come to Me, except my Father draw them" (352). Many men subject to the Gospel's "outward suasions" do not come, and therefore these "mere offers are not the drawing meant here." Instead this irresistible influence—which some divines call "physical" but which Hooker prefers to think of as "internal"—involves a "spiritual and divine power, a divine inspiration [that] falls powerfully upon the will," by which "the will is determined, and undoubtedly carried to its object" (353). More familiarly, "plucking implies a breach of the union between sin and soul," and this is inevitably accompanied by a "turning of the heart the right way"; and, to speak properly, "the will puts not forth a deliberate act, but is acted by another" (353–54). Like Lazarus raised from the grave: "noisome distempers" had to be removed and wholesome life restored.

What this lacks in elegance it more than makes up for in Calvinism: it is the "powerful impression of the Spirit . . . upon the soul, not any habit of grace in it, nor any act of the soul which concurs with the work of God in this first stroke of preparation." This emphasis must be maintained because a soul "wholly possessed by the habits of Sin is not yet capable of the habit of grace"; indeed, it is "the aim of this work to make . . . room for the habit of grace to be received." Again, "God first turns [men] from darkness, and then to light"; and as it is this light which will enable "supernatural works in future times" (354), its admission cannot be the present act of natural will. Scholastic science will demand to know "whether nature or grace be the first subject of grace." It cannot be nature "For, I Cor. 2.14, the natural man receives not the things of God"; but not grace either "for then there should be grace before the FIRST grace." But Hooker is ready with an apt "distinguo": "grace is attended in a double respect, 1, as it is a habit or gracious quality received into the soul; 2, as it is a gracious impression upon the soul." Which he then immediately applies:

> The heart must be prepared before any habit of grace can be received: but there needs no disposition in the soul to receive the work of the Spirit that must dispose; there needs no preparation to make way for the work of preparation, but there needs preparation to make way for the habit. (355)

Somewhere, perhaps, Zeno is still smoking his last cigarette. But not here. The work of grace has to start somewhere. It starts, for Hooker, exactly where some holy violence drives out the enduring reality (*habitus*) of sin, which allows the softer reign of habitual grace efficaciously to begin.

Now, what are the "cords" by which God "draws"? First there is an enlightenment: "this is not the right way to life and salvation." This sudden revelation surprises "the poor deluded, blinded creature" into "second thoughts" (355–56) about his condition: "I never doubted my estate, nor ever dreamed of any necessity to be other." This "cord" of "light" may also be called a "knock at the door," but in no case is the influence very subtle; in the first act of preparation, God "dazzles the apprehension by some mighty flash of truth, like lightning darted in." As light, no dim reflection; as a knock, no light tapping. Well may the soul ask, "Who is there?" (356). And though the soul will try to "shut its eyes against the . . . truth," yet preparing grace will "fasten it upon the soul so that it shall not avoid it." The truth will *in*—as "the sun rising will break through the least crevice" (357).

Having taken the soul "by the hook of instruction," God then "encloseth him with the cords of mercy," encompassing him "with the tender of his compassions." Only so can the awakening sinner be freed from the "discouragements" that would "split [his] hopes": "What? Is Christ at the door? Is it not that Christ whose grace I have refused . . . ? He certainly comes to destroy me" (357–58). Beginning to know himself, that sinner needs to know as well that mercy has a number of cords. He needs to hear, first of all, of that "plentiful redemption . . . laid up in Christ" (358). And should he yet "stand murmuring," he needs to hear not only of the "sufficiency" of the salvation purchased by Christ, but that he "freely and frankly offers it to all that will have it" (359); unlike the offended "husband," God will always take the sinner back. Indeed, so heartily does he intend his offer that he "not only commands the sinner to come, but if he go away, mercy pursues him"; as if a king should "entreat a traitor to be pardoned" (360). And though this vision of mercy is nearly attached to the affront of presumption, it remains true that the Lord who "waits to be gracious" will wait for a sinner's repentance, "pulling at him . . . with these cords of his compassions" (361).

But just when we imagine that the holy violence was nothing but an opening shot, the tough side of love reappears; for if the softening cords of mercy cannot hold the recalcitrant sinner, God has "iron chains which will either pluck you from your evil ways, or they will pull you all in pieces." The essay on this iron "cord of conscience" (363) occupies almost twice the space of the two preceding, leaving only one paragraph to "the hand of the Spirit himself." The disproportion seems significant, for though Hooker certainly regards an awakened conscience as itself a spiritual work, he seems more comfortable if he can avoid the question of "the Spirit himself."[51] And, in any event, the rhetorical energy invested in the rough work of a "plucky" conscience seems distinctive of the honest pleasure Hooker takes in the committed practice of godly letters.

There are, we learn, three "hooks whereby conscience . . . tears the heart away from [its] wretched distempers" (363). Armed "with authority," conscience is first of all "to be a forewarner, and to . . . give uncontrollable commands against sin."

It fares in this case with conscience as with a high sheriff ... in the absence of the king[:] while he is gone aside there ariseth a mutiny and tumult of unruly persons, which tear his commission ... and offer in an outrageous manner to lay violent hands on his person; so that he can do nothing. (364)

Ah, but when "the king returns, renews his commission, and gives [his agent] more power than ever ... , then the sheriff lifts up his head [and] comes with more undaunted courage and resolution" to let the disorderly resisters know that "they are all to be ... commanded in the king's name ... to lay down all weapons" (364–65). So with conscience: command, shameless resistance, stronger renewal of forewarnings—"upon pain of everlasting damnation" (365)—which at last make the soul "shy of stirring out unto such ungodly courses" (366). The World, the Flesh, and the Devil respond, of course, protesting that all "this wind" is but "in way of policy to scare men." But as these assurances begin to draw the soul back to his "sinful courses," conscience "makes after him, lays violent hands upon him, and holds him faster than ever." Failed as a "herald" in proclaiming "what should be done," conscience now becomes "God's pursuivant to summon, his sergeant to arrest him for what he hath done." That is to say: though the awakening sinner "could avoid or neglect the command of conscience, he cannot avoid the stroke of conscience" (367).

An ungracious audience might not be converted by such talk, but it could scarcely pretend not to understand. Or even to appreciate: Old Tommy Hooker's in his element now. Not that he means to entertain in any ordinary sense, but when he transposes his own experiences in England, at the hands of a worldly king and his cunning sheriffs, into the register of sin and grace in New England, it requires a dull boy indeed to miss the play of words amidst the work of grace. In no way "conceited," in the manner of the metaphysicals, and not much typological, except here and there, and almost by an accidental concourse of a heavenly type with a homely trope that gave it force in the first place, Hooker's prose rejoices in its own vernacular conviction. *The Application of Redemption* is a long and serious book, worthy of much more commentary than it currently receives. But there are considerable stretches where it reads itself.

"After his commands have been slighted," conscience, not unlike John Endicott, "surpriseth the sinner in the midst of his mirth and greatest jollity," and the play takes a sudden turn for the somber: "you shall answer these sins before the Judge of the World"; and in this somber mood, he follows the sinner "home to his house, and to his bed" (368). Until—with "all his friends, delights, comforts, companions, corruptions," unable to "pluck this hook of horror out of his heart"—

he falls to "bewailing, repenting, reforming, promising, yea, engaging himself to his conscience, and that as in God's sight, that if he will abate his accusations, he will . . . yield unto whatever . . . it shall . . . require of him." It's fake, of course, because when the "accursed crew" of his lusts notices that the sinner is "out of prison again" (369), the cycle starts up once more, until (finally) "conscience lays the last hook upon him, and rends him all in pieces":

> As it forewarned him of sin that it might not be committed, and accused him of sin when it was committed, so now it becomes an executioner of the final doom and judgment which belongs unto him; because against all means of redress he still continues in his sin, . . . he drags him to execution. (370).

And now, faced with evidence of both law broken and Gospel despised, "the sinner conceives himself in the possession of the Devil really, and irrecoverably in Hell" (371).

Our students are, most of them, born too late to feel the force of this story firsthand; and we, who have been duly warned of the danger of clinical depression, are mostly loath to wear our black veil to class; but where is it written that this is a kind of "otherness" whose knowledge we can do without? That our history of Surveillance may begin with the Superego? And that in the list of subjects which have driven members of our common kind to write with passionate conviction, the guilty conscience is one we do well to spare? Our caution might be enlightenment, or it could be embarrassment merely, but would it take a Hawthornean intelligence to suspect repression? Once aroused, catholicity of interest might even permit Hooker his turn toward a hopeful conclusion. "Panting upon his sick-bed," the sick soul awakes from terrifying dreams and raves: "Oh my stubbornness, my carelessness, my contempt of the Lord." Justly condemned, "with what face can I beg mercy who have abused it? Crave grace who have opposed it?" (371). And still the thought of preparation: you, who have taken "the greatest delight" in sin, what think you now?

> "Would you give yourself the like liberty? Or can you take the same comfort in the same ways now?"
> "Oh no: I now see how [my sins] hath deceived me."
> "But would you be content to part with these, and take grace and mercy in the room of them?"
> "Oh that I might: but there is no reason that I should expect it."
> "Why, if you would have mercy, God will show you mercy." (372)

Only now does Hooker tilt his little drama toward the doctrinal: "Then Lord give me a will." And even that paradox—the want of a will to wish for a will—will have to wait its turn.

All we need to know here is that "by this time the heart and corruption are almost pulled asunder," and so the "last cord": "The Lord by the hand of his almighty Spirit doth pluck it quite asunder, that the will of the sinner may never *solder* again with his corruption, nor suit any more with them." Why the Spirit is a hand and why "solder" rates italics but "suit" does not are questions for insomnia absolute. But we are to recall, from an earlier chapter, that the power at issue here is "the same power that raised Christ from the dead." A creative power, commanding sin as Christ sometimes commands Satan, violently, "Come out of him." A miraculous power, that is to say: "That which all the disciples did not, could not, Christ did there in the possession bodily, so here spiritually" (372). Rousing his own dramatic element, evidently Hooker knows exactly where his own powers surely stop.

———

And where they begin again, as Hooker is full of "conclusions" about "how this holy kind of violence may best be discerned." Skirting the subject of the Spirit and facing instead certain problems of will, these highly academic conclusions make it clear that homely allegory is not Hooker's only venue. The doctrine that "the will of a man is . . . in its own nature, a capable subject of sin and grace" is made to resemble the less obscure fact that "the same vessel is capable of puddle and pure water." But scholastic language is also ready to hand: "though there be not the *next passive power* in a soul possessed with sin to receive the things of God, . . . —it being impossible that two contraries should be in the same subject at the same time"; yet drive out the corruption and grace can surely enter in, for "the soul hath ever in it a *remote power* to partake of grace" (373), and this remote capacity grounds Hooker's repeated (Augustinian) observation that the soul "was made for the better." It also ends the multiplication of certain entities: no need to invent some "obediential power," and even less for God to make a "new faculty": "a wheel that runs wrong" needs not "another wheel" but only a "right setting of it" (374). Evidently Hooker is still thinking of the will as a reified "faculty," from which some fairly substantialized sin must be drained or driven; but he clearly understands that the "new will" is not a new thing. And in a discursive world where a limit issue of a many-handed religious poem is being referred to a constitutive mental operation on which our reflection seems inherently imperfect—where, that is to say, anything might be true—Hooker has about as much right as anybody.

Which he continues to assert: "the faculty of the will attended only in its natural being and ability cannot will a spiritual or supernatural good, it must have a spiritual and supernatural power put into it" (374); but "the corruption that takes possession of the will and rules in it . . . utterly indisposeth the soul to receive any [such] spiritual power from God" (375); and "though there be no force afforded to the faculty of the will, yet the power of corruption must by a holy kind of violence be removed, before any spiritual power" (376) can enter in. A simple enough plot, it would seem: sin, its violent ouster, then the rich gift of a supernatural ability which the will, emptied of sin, is now in a position to receive. The difficulty Hooker fears most is the idea of violence offered to the will: no spiritual rape occurs; no person and no pseudopersonal human faculty is dragged to salvation, kicking and screaming, against its very own "will." And yet, clearly, not everybody can will just any thing at any time. Entirely in the grip of sin, the will of fallen man must be liberated and, again clearly, sin is not just going to get up and go away. It must be driven out: "by constraint it must be forced away" (377). Yet the violence must be understood as done to *sin* and not to *the will*. The crucial "opposition," the deadly feud, is not between God and the will—God's natural creature, after all, though it hurled itself away—but between "the Spirit of grace that doth remove the corruption, and the corruption itself that is removed." Originally, or in itself, an adequate "subject" of both sin and grace, the will is now a scene of opposition: "one contrary drives [out] another . . . by constraint and violence" (378).

It would be wrong to slight this scholastic emphasis on will and willing, but Hooker's deeper interest is in the power of irrational resistance in the human personality. Whether we regard God's preparatory work as a matter of sin to be "subdued" or of Satan to be "vanquished," the need for violence is just about the same: one "sovereignty and supremacy" (380) is to be replaced by another; and the available personification, like the tendency to reification, is chiefly a way of saying that the power of sin is "substantial." Even the loyalty to Calvin chiefly subserves this point: in the master's honored words, "the works of the Devil will never destroy themselves"; and in the disciple's strong extrapolation, therefore Christ "must destroy them with a strong hand."[52] Moral suasion, therefore, is but a "sleepy dotage and a deluded dream" (381), a "kind of silliness" (382)—the rough equivalent, perhaps, of saying that God died on the cross to get our attention. Christ suffered to atone, and somewhere down the line the Spirit has to kick butt and take names. Oh, the hypocrite may have his lusts temporarily curbed by a "restraining grace," as one may keep "a fox in a chain," but the figure of "effectually converting grace" is "war": armies clash, in a contest of sovereignty, and when the battle is over, "the forces of the enemy [lie] not only defeated and scattered, but slain and cut in pieces" (383). Perhaps we will yet discover something feminine in the faith of John Cotton, but it would be hard to deny that the morale of Hooker's preparation sounds a little macho.[53]

Yet it cannot all be done with figures. Force ousts force, plainly enough, but as Hooker returns to another necessary idiom, the problem is not Satan's power but man's resistance—the life itself and not "the life within the life"[54]—which must be overcome; and this without "offering violence to the will" itself. And here Hooker can only repeat Augustine: "God makes of an unwilling will, a willing will" (384). And then worry the pun into numbered propositions:

1. The will is wholly unwilling to receive any spiritual good (384).
2. Willingness must be wrought where this unwillingness is.
3. The will must cease to be unwilling . . . ; aversion can not will conversion.
4. . . . It's impossible it self should remove or destroy it self, . . . therefore there must be an almighty constraining power that must [do so] by a holy kind of violence. (385)

But, comes the objection, "if the will do not freely will the removal of corruption, then it is compelled contrary to the nature of the will." Aware that he may hold *neither* that the "will freely wills the removing of sin" *nor* that "it is compelled thereunto," Hooker proposes simply that "A sinner hath no will at all to it."

Famously in Locke, but repeatedly, in the history of Will in the West—in Sartre no less than Augustine—the negative has a way of coming along to rescue, by its very nonbeing, all sorts of painful reifications.[55] So why not here? Not "to will freely," which is Arminianism. Nor "to will by constraint," which is nonsense. But "not to will at all," "to have the work done only from the will of another" (385). Time enough, no doubt, for the *enabled* will of Thomas Shepard to perform its part at some later moment. But here, in an event just violent enough to be called "physical," the power of sin is driven out but not at all by us. The objection reformulates itself, as do the refining distinctions, but the outcome is about the same: "Where the will hath no power to put forth any act upon any object, there is no will properly to speak, and there can be no violence or compulsion" (388). Nor is one surprised that the final reason (of the fourth conclusion) returns from rough landscape of mental philosophy to the friendly terrain of biblical myth: surely Satan, who "will not, nay in truth cannot be entreated, must be compelled to lay down his jurisdiction" (389). And though it pains the critic to say so, it seems perfectly expressive of Hooker's epistemology—or at all events his genre—that he ends his most embattled section with a syllogism that finds its test not in the dismal half-world of Protestant Scholasticism but in Scripture's power to tell the tale of moral experience:

> The power and rule of Satan cannot be destroyed without violence[;] but in this work Satan his power is destroyed, and himself bound and conquered; therefore it's done by violence. (389)

By violence, as the central fact of Hooker's conversion psychology. And not by our will, as the lesson of his own life confirmed the steady tendency of Calvinist interpretation.

When Hooker's "fifth particular" invites us to inquire "how the plucking of the soul from sin . . . is accomplished by this holy violence," we begin to suspect that his fourth may have been mistitled: for it seems, in retrospect, more an account of how "possible" than how "discerned." But we sense a profound change of emphasis, nevertheless, as the difficulties of this new section are scriptural. Generally speaking, once the authority of "sin & Satan" is removed, "the Lord now comes to manifest" his own claim: "they are mine, I have died for them . . . ; hands off sin, hands off Satan" (390). More particularly, however, the Lord first calls in that "commission" which formerly permitted Satan "to lay hold of the heart of a sinner," for that jailer "is but the keeper or under officer," whereas "the Lord is the sole commander" (391). Next, when sin and Satan continue to press "the claim they can make yet unto the sinner" (393)—exactly as they will in Edward Taylor: he still looks a lot like a sinner to us—it falls to the Father to explain the Protestant scheme of purchase, including the now-familiar fact that the Son will even "work in them what may be answerable to the covenant and the condition of it" (394). Before moving to his third and fourth particulars, however, Hooker immerses himself in the explication and cross-referencing of some of Paul's least lucid formulations, so to insist that, though "the righteousness for which we are justified is fulfilled for us by Christ and is in him, it's not fulfilled in us" (395), we are, nevertheless, in another idiom entirely, already freed from "the marriage covenant between sin and the soul" (397).

It is hard not to sympathize with Hooker's sense that violence must drive out the power of Satan, even if the object of attack seems at times our very own nature. But it would be even harder to argue that Hooker's lapses from vernacular Protestantism to embattled Calvinism do anything but intensify the more general problem that a latter-day theology has availed itself of too many terms, and that quoting Paul in the Greek can raise our sense of the stakes without sharpening our grasp of real entities. So that only the most technical readers will be disappointed when Hooker returns to the simpler outline of his stronger emphases.

Even his repetitions, disguising themselves as short but necessary steps in a full description of a complex process, seem friendly to the flesh: "As sin and Satan can [now] make no claim to the Soul, so neither can they keep possession of it; but they are outed there also by Christ." As the original "breach of the covenant of the law" had doomed us to a covenant of sin, so now, when the Lord comes, intending "to bring the soul under the covenant of grace," he first "casts out . . . Satan"; he can still cause trouble but never again say "I will return to my house . . . and enjoy [my] habitation as in former times" (398).

Hooker hastens to explain that the sense of his little domestic allegory is exactly the same as the "place" in Scripture where "the prince of this world" (399) is cast out. But would it be *so* wicked to imagine an audience that might come to prefer the play of the literary figure to the convoluted intensity of the doctrinal gloss, or even to prefer the tropological tales which Scripture provokes, to the inspired text itself? The thing appears to happen every time we read Edward Taylor, who has learned as much from Thomas Hooker as from George Herbert. At the very least we are to notice that Hooker's vernacular aftereffects, however "plain," are literary causes in their own right and need to be judged as such. And to remind ourselves that Hooker's American style has never been entirely willing to exchange the "vivacity" of his own word for "intense grumbling enunciation of the Cambridge sort, and for Scripture phraseology."[56] Scripture "itself" might be forced to deliver up the doctrine that there is some point in preparation where, though sin and Satan may now and then "jostle it . . . out of its intended course," yet "the set, and face, and frame of the soul will be towards God"; but its inspiration stops short of knowing how easily this fact might remind one of the path of the "bowl [in lawn bowling] that is strongly biased one way and so carried to the mark," whatever the "rubs and ruggedness of the way" (400).

Hooker's last particular explains why the work of preparatory "attraction [is] given to the Father." The preliminary assurance that "this work as all actions which pass upon the creature and leave some change there are equally and indifferently wrought by all the persons in the . . . Trinity" (401) expresses Hooker's loyalty to the dogma that the divine "persons differ each from other only in some internal and incommunicable relative property" (403). But it also provides an occasion to teach against the "dangerous deceit" that there are "several ranks and conditions of Christians," some being "under the Father's work," others "under the Son's," but either or both "not yet attained to the work of the Holy Ghost" (403). All the elect are under all the works of all the divine persons, and no one's salvation is any more highly authorized than anyone else's. Still, Hooker argues, Scripture's division of function makes a kind of experimental sense: as we think of original sin as "committed directly against" the creative work of the Father, and of Christ as "an advocate . . . to plead with the party offended" (405), so we may think of the Father both as sending Christ and as drawing the sinner to him in a way of repentance.

All but displaced in this is any reference to the experimental work of the Spirit, and we can tell from the reference to those who wish specially "to be sealed" (403) by that mysterious agency that the slight is deliberate; for Hooker's system is designed to be as public as it is rough. Elsewhere, at the crucial moment, the Spirit seals a union between Christ and the soul, but here, well in advance of any mystical marriage, the needful act is for the Father to attract the soul to the Son—after hitting sin with a knockout blow.

———

The Uses of Book 8 reveal, in their range of materials and styles, a work which began as a series of sermons—to an audience which, though significantly self-selected for literacy and for interest, must nevertheless be counted as "popular"— and then lived on to undergo revisions for publication in a form open to examination by professionals, who might quarrel with one's theology, whether they relished one's tropes or not. Use 2, of "consolation" (435–44), and 3, of "exhortation" (444–51), both suggest the kind of work regularly done as the conclusion of a Sunday performance; and both are short enough to function as the appropriate conclusion of an actual sermon. Use 1, by contrast, offering "instruction" with a vengeance, spreads out to an uncustomary length and, dividing itself into six "collections," gives the clear impression of having been *written*. And, significantly, this nearly concluding section provides a massive defense of Hooker's orthodoxy. As if the prime purpose of his "professional" writing were to deny that preparationism is anything *like* an oblique compliment to natural ability.

Know, therefore, in a first collection of doctrine, that the "work of attraction . . . proceeds from God as the only cause thereof, and depends wholly on his good pleasure, and that he works in us without us" (408); for, surely, "That which is done by a holy kind of violence against the natural inclination of the heart . . . must needs be done upon us, but not by us." The factitious complexity of this formulation could hardly be more evident, and yet Hooker dares offer a reason out of Romans: "It is not in him that willeth, or in him that runneth, but in God that shows mercy." "Pelagians" had wished to say that the willing and the running avail not "without mercy pitying" and "grace assisting," but this cooperative theory is no more acceptable now than before: "it's . . . only in him that shows mercy" (409). Aroused, Hooker waxes scholastic: the ability which God gives to enable the human will to act in the matter of salvation "must be before the ability of the will and act of it, and so cannot be caused by it"; indeed, it is the work of preparation—done *upon* us—"to make way for a spiritual ability to be given to the will for the work, and therefore it is before the will and work" (410). Jesuit genius to the contrary, "the Lord gives a power spiritual to the work, which it had not before he concurs with the act of that power when it is put forth" (411). That theory may entertain fewer occult entities, but Hooker serves the passionate interest of protecting the sovereignty of God at all costs. And also, perhaps, the reputation of Paul.

Accordingly, the second collection stipulates, against those interested in assigning some role to individual choice at the nodal point in the application of redemption, that "the conversion of a sinner depends not upon, nor is lastly resolved into the liberty of man's will" (412). For—to put the question in its baldest form—"why doth Peter receive Christ, and Judas reject him?" As to the means, both were "trained up under the wing of Christ, and received the droppings of his daily counsels alike," and yet the stunning difference between Founder and Traitor. Clearly there is a mystery somewhere: the Arminians place it "in the liberty of their own wills," which did in the triumphant and did not in the scandalous case accept the gracious assistance freely offered to enable their damaged wills to take hold of a salvation God need not have offered at all. Enough of grace, already. But "orthodox divines" answer that the Lord "gives a heart of flesh to Peter . . . which he denies unto Judas, as he justly may, and Judas justly deserved he should" (413).

Students may wish to pursue the reason why Judas might "justly" be denied: how, again, am I implicated in the sin of Adam? And once every six or eight years a displaced creative writer will note that "flesh" suddenly changes sides. But Hooker turns to arguments already familiar: since "the will of itself hath not the next passive power to receive grace and Christ, then it is not in its liberty to choose or refuse" that wondrous option. Or, if it *were* in the liberty of our will to choose or refuse Christ, then it would be in a man's own power "to make himself differ from another" (413)—which Paul denies. Largely, we gather, because "that which exalts the will of man above the power and will of God," making it the "principal cause of our conversion," is injurious to "the glory of God's grace." Indeed, the "delusion" of the human power in the matter of salvation is "exceedingly derogatory to the glory of God," depriving him of "that praise and thanksgiving which is due to his name" (414). And there it all is: Calvinists protect the divine *gloria* above all else and go on to encourage salvation with whatever logic may be left; Arminians go down the road of free grace as far as they can but pull back when their understanding of will (and the logic of preaching) begins to oscillate. Scripture feels very strongly both ways. And, as no one understands either God or freedom, you takes your choice (though you no longer has to pay your money).

Yet Hooker can think of at least one more powerful, empirical way to bias this foundational choice of freedom or *gloria:* "the Saints when they come to acknowledge the Son of God" all profess "it was not their prayers, their tears, . . . nor resolutions, nor performances," which took away their guilt, "for they see the spawn of all sin in their hearts" (414–15). This too is about as good as it gets, before William James at any rate. Arminians, on behalf of the "once-born," try to make a place for good sense and a favorable disposition toward the things of God. But saints—the "twice-born," for whom Augustine writes the rules—all know it works some other way: God does not gently coax, he violently intervenes; if one "turns" to God it is only because he has "been turned," at a time and in a direction when total reorientation was the least thought in mind. The problem is not the decree of Hooker's faithfulness to the theology of Calvin but the extent to which any church can succeed in popularizing the piety of saints.[57]

For the moment, however, Hooker continues mindful of the professionals. The third collection denies, at considerable length, that "our conversion" can possibly depend on anything like a magical "congruity" (415) between the just-right religious means and the just-right moment of human sensitivity and interest. On the contrary, he argues, the saints all testify that God "takes sinners at the worst, and overpowers the perverseness of their hearts" (418–19) with the holy violence that is their necessary preparation—for some holy willing, perhaps, that may be yet a ways off. For a purer sort of argument, consider that to resolve "the conversion . . . of a sinner . . . into the congruity and suitableness of moral persuasions" is to reduce our "supernatural call into a natural cause against rule and reason" (421); for, as we are supposed to know, no cause can produce an effect beyond its own nature. Consider also those cases in which "the greatest congruity . . . of all moral Persuasions" must be thought precisely to fail, for what else are we to make of those who "sin the sin against the Holy Ghost"? (422). And since there can be *no* congruity between God and corruption, it makes better sense to insist on the "wholly incongruous" (424) nature of the salvation event: offering pretty motives to the depraved seems at last a little "silly," like playing the "choicest music to delight a deaf man" (425). Anglican service may sound the tinkling symbol, but Puritans play a heavier metal.

More briefly, now, the fourth collection insists that "the power of grace put forth in the work of conversion is," in the word of the Synod of Dort, "irresistible." We do, of course, resist. How could we not, struggling to preserve the only life we know? But nothing in the end can "frustrate God's intent" (426). From which it will follow, in the fifth collection, that "wheresoever there is spiritual sufficiency of grace, there is also spiritual efficacy put forth in the work of conversion" (427). With power of this order, *sufficiens* and *efficax* (428) are *idem per idem*. The doctrine here denied might have made converting grace *sufficiens sed non necessitans*, trying its Fearful Jesuit best not to convict God of forcing the human will; but Hooker, without benefit of Edwards, dares not risk the nasty association. Furious distinctions follow, but Hooker's curious position is long since clear: apart from our will God destroys our will to fight the good. And so the sixth collection is left to rationalize the sad remainder: reprobates are not simply those whose free will failed to "improve the help" of a "preventing grace" (433) offered to all; they are, in somber fact, all those "not given" (434) to Christ by the Father. For the erosion of Calvinism, look elsewhere.

Turning to face the local need, then, "forlorn sinners" will find it a "ground of incomparable . . . comfort" (435) to recall that it is not for them to accomplish the astonishing work of their own salvation: "thou art not able . . . yet God is able, and it's his work[;] here stay thy heart, God can do it, and who knows but he may." Satan will protest that, given so many sins, "Hell is too little for such a rebel" (436), but he can be met with the thought that "though my soul cannot leave my sin, . . . yet God can force away my sin from my soul" (437). Or the world will catch the soul up, again and again, in all its "licentious courses" until it realizes it is "not able to get from under these sins" (438–39). A true sight indeed and, whatever the sequel, enough to force the speaker into the first person: "Here's all the hope I can give you: It is in God's hand yet to pluck off thy soul. . . . If I should tell you, it is in the power of means and mercies, and any congruity of means, or liberty of your own wills, your souls might be deceived, but would never be comforted" (439). And the same consideration—that salvation comes *to* us, and does not arise from the action of our own will—may console the faithful as well. Whatever their "discouragements," let them reflect: "he that plucked me away from my sin with a holy kind of violence, [and] . . . forced his mercy upon me when I resisted, . . . will he deny me mercy when he hath given me a heart to beg and prize it?" (441–42). Will God knock down and not pick up? Will he prepare a man, that is to say, for just nothing at all? We hardly dare to think it.

Thus assurance in Hooker's system comes not from the holy works an enabled will has been empowered to accomplish—and certainly not from the seal of the Spirit—but from the prior fact of forcible separation from the bias of sin. Exhortation may complicate, but it cannot unseat this emphasis. The converted are to follow the divine example: if God is seen to draw men "from their sins," the saints are instructed to do "likewise"; to express their election in showing "compassion to others," endeavoring "even by a holy kind of violence to pluck sinners away from their sins" (444). Cotton Mather will be more socially conscious, in his moral instructions, but he will hardly improve Hooker's sense that the Christian should be "as busy as a bee" in seeking the "occasion of doing good." Laboring to bring sinners to the "means of grace" (446), the elect become themselves a means. God saves, but men must do whatever they can.

Which goes for the "unconverted" as well: "this work of drawing is God's proper work, come therefore under his hand" (447). Defying the implication of the hard-won "therefore," a still-active objection seeks to set the proposition asunder: since "it is only God that doth this work in us, . . . why should we endeavor what we can never do?" Patiently still, the familiar answer:

> I do not say thou canst do the work, but do thou go to him that can do it. Thou sayest thou canst not go; I confess thou canst not go as a Christian, but [what] I exhort unto is, do what thou canst as a man, improve those . . . gifts that are yet left in thee; and come under, and keep under the call of God. (448)

To which *we* might query: is that not exactly what an Instituted Church might be expected to answer, however the precision of its divinity shall have compromised the logic of sacrament? But Hooker would rally himself on Scripture all the same. Those who think that to go to church is to begin "the work" for oneself— and so to compromise the freedom of God in the application of redemption— need to remember what Scripture itself commands. Cavils about nature and grace go on forever, but in God's own letters the buck has to stop: "God meets his people in the place of his worship." And again, "I do not say thou canst pray so as to please God, but pray still, who knows but God may help thee[?]" (448). As Taylor might put the case, You'st not be worser than you be.[58]

As for specific directions, take two: "present thy self before God in the use of the means . . . , and when thou art there renounce thy own abilities" (448); and then, more boldly, do not leave these ordinances "before you find some power beyond the power of ordinances, and man, and means." Especially you, in New England, that "are in the crowd of means," cry out, like the woman of bloody issue, hoping that "power may come from Jesus Christ" to work upon your soul. Which you will know when you find an ordinance as powerful "upon your heart" as ever in your mind; and "then you shall find the work really done" (450). Elided in this transition from hope to discovery, from an indefinite future to an instant just past, is the moment of change itself. Burn with desire, continuously, and some day perhaps it will *have happened*. Not by any transaction of your will, yet the power of God may cause the passion of the heart to have become one with the design of the ordinance. Or not—as the Calvinist motive asserts itself again, this time personally: "Let me leave this upon the record for ever amongst you. This effectual drawing and quickening of the heart is alone the work of God. It is not in him that wills . . . but in God that shows mercy" (450–51). And yet the lesson is never just to wait and see. It is, rather, to do as God commands in any case— to seize the means with as much ardor as Nature can show. And for as long as it takes.

> When you have run what you can run, and willed what you are able, then look up to the Lord to show you Mercy: the minister hath spoken what he can, and I have heard what I can, but Lord show Mercy. And never leave until you have found that the Lord hath showed you Mercy. (451)

"Never leave until you have found" may mean that all who *truly* seek are surely those whose fate it is to find. But it also means that there can be no giving up.

Modern acumen will suspect that a conscientious following of these instructions will surely produce the desired result: wishes this intense seldom go unfulfilled. And the Cynic will say the "psychological" result is quite enough: where God only knows, the *thought* of sainthood is as good as it gets. But we should not write our "Conclusion" to the first eight books of Hooker's *Application* without noticing a certain purity of intention and precision of demand. Hooker wanted saints, but he wanted them on a Calvinist model. He could not take what God would not give.

III. "Hammering a Truth"

Thus far, the chapters of this long work have simply pursued the meaning of their several texts straight through. The Puritans wrote extended compositions— books, in our usage—and we should learn to read them.[59] Some compiler of sermons might have stopped after Book 3 of the *Application,* but Hooker went right on. His publishers wrote "FINIS" at the end of Book 8, even though they meant in 1656 to go right on, even to the ideal end of a sixteen- or seventeen-book opus. We do not know just how far Hooker himself, who died in 1649, may have been "intending" his summa to go, but we easily notice that Books 9 and 10, which were indeed published, in a separate volume, the same year as Books 1 through 8, are an integral part of the Ramist design of the *Application* "itself": "God's Dispensation" in the matter of preparation involves the driving out of sin by a "holy kind of violence"; "Man's Disposition" is, relationally, an affair of contrition and humiliation. And even a treatment of implantation—the inevitable "relative" of preparation—seems entailed by the structure that Hooker's small diagrams have led us to expect.

Accordingly, a whole book on Hooker's *Application* would have to march ahead, explicating the slender single sermon of Book 9 and the nearly six-hundred-page elaborations of Book 10, then doing whatever is necessary to compensate for the material that appears to be absent. Honoring a weakness in the flesh, however, the rest of this chapter merely sketches an outline of what remains. Beginning with an odd problem of its partial "familiarity": Books 1 through 8 of the *Application* have been available (in facsimile) since 1972 but, so far as I have been able to determine, no portion of its text has been reprinted in any classroom anthology. Instead, the books that represent seventeenth-century religious literature at all appear to follow Perry Miller in offering samples from Book 10, which exists only in rare book libraries and on microfilm. One might infer, perhaps, that Miller and his imitators preferred the preacherly enactment of preparation to its theoretical description and professional defense; yet it seems curious that students know Hooker from the portion of his text the modern age has never reprinted in full.

There is also the larger problem of having students read—and often go on to teach—a few passages selected by someone else, from a work they have never read in its entirety or even held in their hands. There are worse fears, of course, but one is occasionally left to wonder how many survey courses have left their students with the impression that Hooker published a short work entitled "The True Sight of Sin." So it might be worthwhile, as part of an attempt to project the long remainder of Hooker's *Application,* to contextualize the famous passages from its last completed segment. If we cannot quite answer the question of why Book 10 is fifty times as long as Book 11, or account for the deployment of Book 10 into its eighteen separate doctrines, we may at least notice the problem of representing a system that knows the way to its own salvific end but whose energy is clearly a function of its ability to stay where the way is most difficult. Not to intimate the lovely influence that sanctifies and points beyond itself to glory, but to hammer home that rougher grace which breaks the sinner's heart. A bias of doctrine, perhaps, but certainly a bent of genius.[60]

Book 9 of the *Application* is well aware of what has gone before: "preparation having two parts, first, the Lord's manner of dispensation" whereby, "with a holy kind of violence he plucks the sinner from his sins and unto himself" (1–2); and this matter having been "dispatched already in the former discourse," it remains to discuss the second part, "the frame and disposition which is wrought in the hearts of such as the Lord hath purposed to save." And "this disposition consists especially in . . . contrition & humiliation." As the text announces the Lord's intention to "dwell" with him "that is of a . . . humble spirit" (2), Hooker opens the notion of "dwelling," concluding of the person "to whom the Lord vouchsafes acceptance, special presence and abode, and particular guidance [that] he owns him, abides with him, and rules in him for ever" (4). True enough, Hooker concedes, "Christ dwells in our hearts by faith," but we are to trust that while the soul is "breaking and humbling, faith also is coming in a right sense," and that the ambiguities of preparation and faith will be removed "if the Lord give us leave to come to that place" (5).

First things first, however, for "the heart must be broken and humbled, before the Lord will own it as his, take up his abode with it." In all common sense, "the house must be aired and fitted before it comes to be inhabited." Or, in a familiar type, the Children of Israel must pass through a "vast and roaring wilderness" (5) before they find their Promised Land. Reasoning on the matter, we will recall—literally, if we have read the first eight books—that our hearts are full of "lets and impediments" which present faith with "a kind of incapability, yea, an impossibility" (7): either the soul is content with its condition, so that to seek another condition would be "contradictory" (8); or, if it indeed "finds sin as a plague," it naturally expects the remedy "from its own sufficiency" (9), whereas faith involves "a going out of the self to fetch all life and power from another." Nor will God himself deign to enter until "in contrition we are cut off" from the power of sin and "in humiliation pared, and so fit to be implanted into Christ by faith" (10). It *still* remains for Hooker to make good on his horticultural metaphor, and to make it agree with other languages appropriate to the problem of going out of oneself and relying on the sufficiency of another; but there seems to be no hurry. The doctrine and the reasons of Book 9 are familiar; nor do the uses do much to counter an accumulating sense that, in hearts truly prepared, the problem of faith will solve itself.

Terror to those that "were never broken-hearted for [their] abominations" (11): "thou are the mark of God's direful indignation and vengeance." Will they plead their many "girds and galls of conscience"? Well enough, if they do go on to "*yield*" (12). But bear in mind the likely case: "the heart may be battered, but it was never broken, it may be overpowered and awed, but it was never humbled." Others, less "frampful and froward," must learn to delight in the society of "contrite and humble men" (13). And all may be exhorted to "take the right way to enjoy God's presence, not only to seek for mercy, but seek it in God's order."

> Labor to be humble and broken-hearted Christians: then expect . . . the
> presence of . . . grace and Spirit. . . . Every man catcheth at Christ . . . , but
> not in a right method, and therefore they lose him, and their labor also.
> This is God's order: first be humbled and broken, and then he will revive
> your spirits with his presence. (14)

This emphasis on method and order—on the need for preparation to destroy the
habit of sin and so to clear a suitable space for faith—makes Book 9 a pithy summary of Hooker's general theory. But it cannot quite prepare the unsuspecting
reader for the heavy work that is to follow.

Book 10 sets out its text plainly enough—"when they heard this, they were
pricked in their hearts, and said unto them, men and brethren, what shall we
do?"—but there is nothing to indicate that the scene from Acts will sponsor eighteen separate doctrines; or that the treatment of these doctrines will vary from
several pages to more than one hundred fifty. We are reminded that "contrition
and humiliation" are the two things "which the Lord requires in those he will
draw to Christ"; and the assertion that contrition "loosens a man from sin" and
humiliation loosens him "from himself" (15) recalls Book 9's account of these
twin impediments. But there is no indication of whether the analysis will pass
from contrition to humiliation, or whether, after many pages on contrition, we
are to look elsewhere for its correlative.

Instead, without further preview, we are given a definition: "contrition is
that preparative disposition of heart, when by the sight of sin, and the punishment due to the same, the soul is brought to sound sorrow for it, and so brought
to detest it, and so to sequester itself from it"—and informed that both the
"causes which bring in this contrition" and "effects which nextly discover" it
admit of a twofold subdivision. And, just in case we are still on the lookout for
some shift in the winds of doctrine, Hooker makes it emphatic that Calvinism
still rules: "here I desire that still it may be remembered . . . that all these are
things rather wrought upon us by the impression and motion of the Spirit, than
performed by any inward principle." Thus the definitive use of the passive voice:
"The soul [is] *brought* to see his sins, *brought* to sorrow for them, *brought* to detest
them, and sequester itself from them" (16). Sinful nature *still* has no power to detest itself, and Hooker is not going to concede in practice what he has so elaborately denied in theory.

The single, all-purpose text inspires the reflection that no "bare hearing
would serve the turn" (17) but that a "serious meditation" is implied, and that the
pricking was "not in the eyes only . . . but in their hearts" (19); and an apt "consideration of the parties to whom Peter here speaks" forces the astonishing con-

clusion that mercy may be extended even to "such as had rejected, blasphemed, crucified the Lord of Glory." Hence a doctrine: "stubborn and bloody sinners may be made broken-hearted sinners" (20). For reasons we have heard before: the "largeness of . . . mercy" (22); the infinite "merits of our Savior" (23); and the "power of the Spirit" (24). The uses, which conclude this first, sermon-length section of Book 10, are familiar as well. "Admiration . . . at the riches of God's mercy and grace" (25). "Encouragement to sustain the hearts of such forlorn creatures as are sunk down in desperate discouragements": your condition is indeed "desolate and dangerous," yet "there is a peep-hole of hope" (26–27). And timely instruction in the "heinousness of the sin of despair," which tramples mercy "under feet of contempt" (30).

Coming now to "the particulars" of contrition, we discover a second doctrine: "there must be a true sight of sin, before the heart can be truly broken" (35). And those who have read Hooker in either of Miller's anthologies may begin to gather their bearings. For at the heart of this 157-page essay on his foundational premise, Hooker will furnish his anthologizer with a little section of vernacular preaching worthy to be entitled "The True Sight of Sin" and to stand, so titled, as a truthful advertisement for the mentality of preparation: harbinger before king, sorrow before grace. But first the psychological proviso: "that which the eye sees not the heart rues not" (36). Then the "means" by which "God works this sight of sin," in a series of conclusions: "the righteous law of God . . . is the discoverer of our sins" (37), yet not effectively so "unless the Lord put a new light into our minds" (38). And even this light requires that the fallen understanding be turned away from the darkness and receive a certain "set" toward the light (42). Then too, past this demonstration of how poetry may force theology to multiply entities, the Calvinist will need to ask "how far the sinner may be said to be active in this sight of sin" (43), and to answer that, though natural conscience may see the "loathsomeness" of melodramatic murders, it does not realize that "every blasphemer stabs the Lord" (45). Indeed, we resist "the spiritual light" that would discover "our corruptions" (46); for we are, as the Apostle says, "strangers to the life of God" (47). Hence the need for that violence by which God "forceth the understanding" and destroys "the sovereignty of carnal reason" (48).

By now the point is familiar, but the energy of Hooker's rhetoric of violence is never lacking, and it is worth noticing that what passes just before Miller's vibrant passage on the "true sight and apprehension of sin" is a positive tour de force. To destroy the "over-swaying authority of carnal reason" is to reverse "Satan's policy to turn the understanding from the Lord" (48); beginning now "where Satan ended," he turns the soul "from darkness" back into light. Having ever "one oar in the boat," carnal reason is the name for the fact that every sinner has some self-deceiving "pretense," and therefore it is called the "stronghold of Satan" (48–49); and so the Lord "forceth" this fort, demolishing "the frame of it"; so that, "though there be some remainders . . . yet it's never made a place of retreat . . . , wherein [Satan] can fortify himself, and stand it out against any Truth." And though it is perfectly clear that "nothing but the power of God can do this," the reader is likely to imagine a standing out against Hooker, who also "forceth the understanding to submit" (49), even as he protests that "no liberty is prejudiced." The forcible retooling of the understanding may begin with "common" things, such as the historical "truth of the scripture," but it never ends without a proper sight of "follies and delusions" that we cannot give ourselves. So that the soul "behaves itself passively, and is wrought upon . . . by an over-ruling power" (50).

A further operation of the Spirit, which "follows without fail," is also passive: "there is room made for the ready entertainment of light" which, when it does (irresistibly) arrive, will be "like the sun-rising," whose beams so spread themselves that no "secret corner or crevice of our corrupt hearts" (50–51) can escape its bright illumination. And yet the constant reminder: overcome "by the power of this light," the understanding "doth move again" yet not from any "habitual principle of grace" (51–52). Best to say, even now, that the human understanding but "reflects the light" (52).

And only now—after a strong shot of the rhetoric of force, followed by the necessary chaser of neo-Calvinist distinction—does Hooker propose to reveal "wherein this true sight . . . of sin properly discovers itself": God's reflected light enables us to see sin "(1) clearly, (2) convictingly, what it is in itself, and what it is to us, not in the appearance and paint of it, but in the power of it; not to fathom it in the notion and conceit only, but to see it with application" (52–53). What follows is almost too famous to repeat, except that even the students who come to lecture misread its import:

> It's not every slight conceit, not every . . . confused thought or careless
> consideration that will serve the turn or do the work here, we are all sinners; it is my infirmity, I cannot help it; my weakness, I cannot be rid of
> it; no man lives without faults and follies, the best have their failings, in
> many things we offend all. But alas all this wind shakes no corn, it costs
> more to see sin aright than a few words of course. . . . We must look
> wisely and steadily upon our distempers, look sin in the face, and discern
> it to the full. (53)

Given the limits of modern literacy, only the born-again can feel the force of Hooker's indirect discourse: "my infirmity," indeed! As if that were the worst one could say about human depravity.

The "goldsmith" is not casual about the difference between the gold and the dross: "he must search the very bowels of the metal, and try it by touch, by taste, by hammer, and by fire; and then he will be able to speak by proof what it is" (53). So with us. And, to change the figure, learn to see sin like a man who has lived a long and painful time in the country of his own soul, not like the amateur geographer who has merely looked over the map. Consider that sin "would dispossess God of that absolute supremacy which is indeed his prerogative royal" (55), that "by sin we jostle the law out of its place, and the Lord out of his glorious sovereignty," plucking the "crown from his head, and the scepter out of his hand" (56). Learn also that as sin "smites at" the very essence of the Almighty, it is the sinner's de facto desire "not only that God should not be supreme but indeed that he should not be at all"; appropriately, therefore, does Scripture call sinners "the haters of the Lord." For he that hates "endeavors . . . the annihilation of the thing hated";

> and it's most certain were it in their power, they would pluck God out of heaven, the light of his truth out of their consciences, and the law out of the societies and assemblies where they live, that they might have elbow room to live as they list. (58)

The insistent literariness of this and similar luminous passages is such that, read aloud, they threaten to turn the most secular of teachers back into the preacher from whom his kind appears to have devolved. To which threat our resistance proves an important point: bespeaking a world quite other, works written on purpose to convert may succeed even when they fail of their primary end.

Nor is Hooker less forceful when he turns to the sight of sin "in regard to ourselves." Armed with Augustine's famous comment on the problem of "desire"—of hearts that "rest" only in God[61]—Hooker observes that the thing which "deprives me of my greatest good for which I came into the world" (60) cannot possibly be worth pursuing, that it brings in its train "all other evils . . . into the world" and surely "blasts all our blessings" (62). If there is always the danger that the range of Hooker's interest will betray him into a list, there is also some point in noticing that, beyond the limit of Miller's selection, his questioning mind must try to explain why, "if sin be thus vile in its own nature" (66), men do not discern it so; and that, between the "delusion of Satan" (66) and the "want of . . . spiritual knowledge" (71), Hooker creates a fairly subtle morphology of rationalizing self-deception. And if he urges us to "labor" for the necessary spiritual insight and to "strive mightily to attain a clear sight of God himself" (73), it is with the reminder that this sight is truly a gift, without which nothing else will really do the work. Men sin, it appears, in precisely the space where God himself is absent.

But while we pause, to savor and to discriminate, Book 10 pushes ahead through another month of Sundays. Doctrine 2 continues for more than 115 pages. It will not do to say *simply* that Hooker has now passed from description to enactment, for—owing partly to a great respect for learning and partly to a certain anxiety of Calvinist causation—Puritan preaching is never purely a call to conversion; always there is intellectual work to do. And yet as Hooker is now well launched on the question of "our disposition" in preparation, it comes as no surprise that the work of sinful self-analysis should be permitted to find expression in full measure. Accordingly, the "sight of sin" must be subjectively "convicting" as well as objectively "clear": "We must apply sin particularly to our selves" and settle it "with an over-powering strength" (75). Leaving aside our readiness "to be eagle-eyed into other men's occasions," we must learn to say, "What have I done?" (76), passing sentence "impartially," without "any private end" (78); and the certainty of this heart knowledge must be "undeniable, immoveable, victorious and invincible" (80). Two reasons for this emphasis on a "true sight" present themselves as the last "particular": what "the eye sees not the heart rues not" (87) and "ignorance frustrates wholly the end of all the means we use" (88).

Finally—if only in a formal way—five uses confirm our sense that a single sermon has grown up to be something like a book in itself and that Hooker's preparationist instinct can always find or make a form. Instructions warn that "he that never saw his sin aright, he never saw a good day" (91), so that "to be hard to be convinced" (94) is a very bad sign. More sobering is the warning that "men of the greatest . . . depth of brain . . . are most hardly brought to brokenness of heart" (98). Things get still more tense when Hooker offers an examination by which "we may gain certain evidence" whether the Lord has yet begun "work of preparation *and so* any expression of his purpose to call us to himself" (emphasis added). If he has "knocked hard at thy door," then fine: "conclude thou mayest, thou art in the right way, and the Lord begins to deal with thee as he does with those he intends good unto" (101). If not, not. Which may be known from any "careless adventuring upon the commission of sin" (102), particularly when this involves "something a man prizeth as his chief good" (103). But, as his editors seem to realize, Hooker seems most effectively himself when a "privy search" reveals four sorts of persons who fail to "see sin convictingly" (105). Some resist discovery of their particular corruptions, like the English knight who "once professed . . . he would not come to the assembly until the minister had made an end to such a text" (106). Others, on whom the truth has indeed burst in, will try their best to "darken the evidence," as do "subtle Lawyers" (107). Others raise "brabbles" (109); or flatly "stand against the truth" (110). Clever and self-reliant men, beware.

Still it is Hooker's fifth use, of exhortation, that threatens to run doctrine 2 of Book 10 from here to eternity. The exhortation—to "get this true sight of sin"—warns us not to dream of devising "a shorter cut to grace and glory" (111) but to "begin where the Holy Spirit begins" and propounds first "some means to help" and then "some motives to quicken." The table of contents allows that "the means are six," and so they are; but some are more equal. Conventionally, we are to "labor" to see the "excellency of holiness that is in the Lord" (114), and also to second the motion of "conscience" when it "shall come in as a witness to accuse" (117). But then, after we are urged to "labor" against all those "wily . . . devices" by which carnal reason attempts to defeat "the authority of truth" (118)—and while we are estimating Hooker's attempt to range these evasions under "three heads"—suddenly all literature breaks loose, in the form of a dramatic survey of the ways men avoid self-knowledge. "To lighten the evil of sin" they have no fewer than eight "shifts," which to evoke and answer takes about fifty pages: sin is so common (119), so natural (122), so easy to blame on "companions" (125), on "provocations" (131), on forgetfulness (134), on the "hazards" (139) of virtue, on the strength of our "original corruption" (141); or, in a shift calculated to renew the cardinal point, on the claim that "the sins themselves are slight" (145).

And yet the same Hooker who will explode—look at your sins "in their own nature absolutely" (146)—will also stay to detail the question of sin in "words," "thoughts," and "matter[s] of practice," concluding with the inverse discovery that "the less the things are [the] more heinous thy fault," who were willing to "break with [God] for a trifle" (168). And to return to the four shifts of those who "cannot but confess the danger" of sin yet "vainly hope [to] prevent it" (174), and to a series of sharp rebukes to the man who, confessing the danger of God's wrath, says simply, "I will bear it, if I be damned I will suffer it as I may if it come to the hardest" (180). Nor will he forget, after long self-interruption, his last three means to abet the divine work of producing in the soul the true, indeed saving sight of sin: "yield unto the evidence" (182); "take home" whatever we read or hear of "corruption[s] of which we stand guilty" (185); and "keep the evil of sin present in [our] apprehension" (186). He even remembers to end his exhortation (and so his second doctrine) with the promised offering of motives for welcoming the unpleasant work of sinful self-discovery—down to the conclusion that the way of preparation, painful as it is, is yet the "safest and surest way":

> See our sins we must, first or last; either here to our humiliation or hereafter to our confusion; and we had better see them by the light of the Gospel while we are within the sight of mercy . . . than to see them by the flames of Hell when there is no remedy. (192)

Bitter medicine but necessary; for who would not "see his sins now . . . that he may never have them then laid to his charge?" (192). Even if the sinner were to remain unsure whether this "humiliation" is already implied in his own present sight of sin or is entirely a matter of Hooker's secure prolepsis.

———

Seizing on the first four words of its single text—"when they heard this"—the third doctrine of Book 10 takes us back, briefly, to the matter of Book 3 where, in a sort of coda on the need for preparation "in general," Hooker set out his view of the function of the ministry. And it is worth noting that here, in the midst of his attempt to dismantle as many cases as his fertile imagination of resistance can invent, Hooker thinks to narrow the focus of his Scripture warrant: a "plain and powerful ministry" had been "the only means to prepare the heart"; here "a plain and particular application of special sins by the ministry of the word is a special means to bring the soul to the sight of, and sorrow for them" (193). More precisely now, the application of redemption appears to begin with the *particularizing* work of the minister: "you are the men I mean, this is your sin" (194). No "daubing discourses and roving reproofs, toothless, powerless dispensations, like arrows shot a cock-height" (199). Men and ministers had better realize that, "though squeamish stomachs had rather take sugar-sops a whole week together than a bitter potion one day" (201), still it's the duty of a minister to take "aim at the sins of the persons . . . to whom he speaks" (202).

The energy of professional self-defense continues to run high and yet, as Miller realized, the next proximate *human* cause of the true sight of sin is not faithful preaching so much as the self-searching afterthought that preaching was supposed to provoke. Thus the same brief text sponsors also a doctrine of hearing closer home: "meditation of sins applied is a special means to break the heart of sinners" (208). And it seems only just that, along with well-known sponsors of Counter-Reformation piety such as Loyola and de Sales,[62] this Puritan Saint

Thomas has been allowed to have his say. Even if he insists on some more than ordinary aid to reflection.

Elsewhere eager to advertise his scholastic doctrine that there is nothing in the will that was not first in the intellect, Hooker is here only nominally concerned with the "faculties." Meditation is defined as "a serious intention of the mind whereby we come to search out a truth and settle it effectually upon the heart" (210), and although "mind" and "heart" get about equal space, Hooker's concern with the vital importance of the "sight" of sin keeps his account from becoming affect oriented. Yet as the conceptual for Hooker is never merely cerebral—as his vernacular head covers such a multitude of evasions and discoveries—so his intellectual sightings are often most heartily expressed. Meditation's "intention of the mind," for example, is "not a flourishing of a man's wit, but hath a set bout at the search of the truth," in which a man "beats his brain as we use to say, hammers out a business." Like the familiar goldsmith, meditation takes a thought and "heats it and beats it [and] turns it on this side and then on that"; indeed, "meditation is hammering of a truth or point propounded that [a man] may carry and conceive the frame and compass in his mind" (210–11). Like preventing grace and the preparing sermon, it appears, meditation works on the *mind*.

In as many homely figures as you please: in meditation we do "not salute a truth as we pass by occasionally but solemnly entertain it into our thoughts"; nor does it look on things as a "spectator or passenger that goes by" but seizes some "employment for the present to take up our minds."

> It's one thing in our diet to take a snatch and away, another thing to make a meal, and sit as if on purpose until we have seen all before us and taken our fill of all, so we must not cast an eye or glimpse at the truth by some sudden or slighty apprehension, a snatch and away, but we must make a meal of musing. (211)

Is this the place to propose that, where Cotton will establish himself as New England's great Connoisseur of Grace, Hooker identifies himself as its Gourmand of Sin? Or is it just that he never met a homely trope he couldn't turn to sacred use? From the past, meditation "revives the fresh apprehension of things done long before, marshals them all in rank together" (212), that we may read the "pedigree of our lusts" (212–13). For the present, meditation eschews the view from "crevice or key-hole" but rather "lifts up the latch and goes into each room, pries into every corner of the house" (213): or, like some Hawthornean "searcher at the . . . custom-house," meditation satisfies itself "not to over-look carelessly in a sudden view, but unlocks every chest, rummages every corner, takes a light to discover the darkest passages" (214).

It would be unjust to suggest that Hooker has turned meditation's necessary prosecution of the true sight of sin into some rare form of language game. But it might be even worse to overlook the fact that there is almost no subject sober enough to daunt Hooker's verbal genius or displace his sense that his Puritanism has made the moral life a drama. Nor does this curious form of play abate when he moves from the witty head to the vulnerable heart. Meditation settles some important matter "effectually upon the heart" *because* (so to speak) "it's not the pashing of the water at a sudden push, but the standing and soaking to the root, that loosens the weeds and thorns" (214). In meditation as elsewhere, "it is not the laying of the fire, but the blowing of it that melts the metal." Meditation makes a truth "really sink and soak into the soul" (215); it "keeps the conscience under an arrest, so that it cannot make an escape from the evidence and authority of the truth" (215–16); it even sets open the "flood-gates, which carries the soul with a kind of force and violence to the performance of what [a man] so bestows his mind upon; as a mighty stream let out turns the mill" (216). Definitions pass over into reasons—and Miller signs off at just this point—but the barrage continues as if Hooker somehow knew it was tropes all the way down. Or else, at very least, that in the *ordo salutis*, meditation was the last stand of rhetoric.

Meditation "sharpens the sting" of our corruption, drawing out its essence like a man practiced in "chemistry and distillation" (217). It not only "pinch[es] the heart with the present apprehension of sin," but it "holds the heart upon the rack" (219). And, just before Hooker passes on to his uses, his meditation "increases the weight of the evil of sin, and presseth it down upon the conscience" (221), reminding us of what we learned at the outset: the daily practice of sober self-reflection continues to add weight until the "bones" of nature break and the life of sinners fails "under the overbearing pressure" (208). Evasion is still possible of course: "You say it was your infirmity, you were ignorant and knew it not, it was a temptation that surprised you, you were not aware of it, the matter was not great and therefore you hope there is a place for pardon." Well, "think it over again" (222) and find, just here, "matter of humiliation to every soul in the sight of God" (223). Remember, that is to say, that meditation asks the soul to see itself not just anyhow but precisely as it appears to the view of Holiness Itself.

So insistent is the literariness of this account that we almost miss one of Hooker's most curious formulations: "the Lord *usually never* works upon the soul by the ministry of the Word to make it effectual, but he drives the sinner to said thought of heart, and makes him keep an audit in his own soul" (215; emphasis added). Clearly Hooker (or some scribe) means "almost never," but the locution remains striking nevertheless. As if Hooker had said that the Lord never, well almost never, and not in any case the ministry needs to regard, ever speaks peace to a man without first serving notice, to his awakened conscience, that a state of war has indeed been in effect. Salvation remains free, of course, but would it not take some nerve to ignore the order set forth in revelation?

Recovering himself, Hooker offers uses of terror and counsel to such persons as think to avoid meditation, distracting themselves with holy talk, or slighting its need, but especially to those who complain of "the unsteadiness of their own thoughts" (229). A curse indeed, Hooker admits, a "giddiness of mind" (230) coming down from the sin of Adam, and so what Miller anthologized as "Wandering Thoughts"[63] is no trivial matter. Incurable absolutely, perhaps, this deficit of adult attention is to be opposed as often as it appears, most effectively by possessing the heart "with an actual consideration and a holy dread of the glorious presence of the Almighty" (235), a cure for more disorders than just one. And if anyone were to plead his "unhandiness to this service" (238), the answer is "the more thou hast need to learn" (239). Useful also is the caution to avoid "loose company" (240); and the exhortation—to "follow the counsel of the Lord" so far as to "try our ways" (242)—comes complete with several "provocations" but also a series of "directions" that grow to a thirty-three-page treatment on the "art of meditation" (249). Not a general account of the several faculties and various devices appropriate to the affecting of each, it is focused instead on the question of how to think about the subject of sin; or, more precisely, how to discover ourselves under that unique and demanding aspect. A gift we now lack, clearly, but one that had to be learned, even then, and which may call for a study of its own.[64]

———

With its fifth doctrine, Book 10 turns from the "means" by which God works contrition to "the work itself." A few pages are sufficient to remind us that as the "pricking" in question "was not of all but some only who heard the word," so "the same dispensation of the Word which is . . . profitable to some is unprofitable to others" (283); only so, we are to recall, may God express the "sovereignty of his good will and pleasure" (284). From which we learn a certain fear amidst "the enjoyment of the greatest means" because in fact "the prevailing fruit of the means is not in the means" (285); but fear coupled with an eagerness "to use all means" and to return proper "thanksgiving to the Lord for what [we do] receive." The point becomes emphatic when, mindful of the "crew and company of refuse wretches" (286) who were "pricked" (287) by Peter's sermon, we notice that, in the words of doctrine 6, God often "makes the Word . . . prevail most powerfully in the hearts of sinners" (287) precisely when they are most opposed.

We may, for a moment, think we are reading Cotton on the incongruity of God's saving intervention. Except for the diction: it may happen "when men lie snorting in their sins" (289), in the "ruff and height of their wretchedness" (291). And except for the fact that what breaks in is not faith or the certainty of justification, but merely the dramatic beginning of preparation's true sight, which Hooker repeatedly insists is the lesson of Paul struck down. Rejected in any case is "that heretical doctrine of the Arminians, so deeply dangerous to the salvation of man's souls and so exceedingly derogatory to the glory of God's free grace," which Hooker sets out with alarming simplicity: "if we do what we can . . . , God will not deny to give us the grace . . . we want" (299–300). So represented, they now make "the Jesuits themselves" look pious and subtle by comparison. And the truth demands repetition: improving our natural abilities can neither "deserve grace" nor "dispose the soul . . . to receive grace" (303); nor is there a single Scripture "promise of giving saving grace" (304) to such as do their best. It's pretty lively, but it's also a story we have heard before—including the objection, "why should I endeavor any further?" (305), and also the answer: the divine command to obey. Evidently Hooker's *Application* is a text which, for the sake of the "turnover" in its original audience, or the changing pace of its spiritual need, is conscientious in its desire to anticipate and recollect.

Doctrine 7 offers whatever comfort or terror we can take from the fact that in preparation one can expect that "sins un-repented of, and continued in, [will] make way for piercing and perplexing terrors" (325). Briefer still, doctrine 8 pauses just long enough to play upon the single word "pierced": "The truth is terrible to a guilty conscience"; indeed, "it's a hammer that breaks, a fire that scorcheth, an axe sharp and keen that cuts and wounds the soul" (332). And to remind the curious that, though even "the best" can afford to tremble at the truth, still "the saints of God ever find sweetness in the . . . most keen threatenings" (333). Doctrine 9, by contrast, is identified as the first part of a "main observation"; and indeed Hooker devotes a sermon-length treatment to the claim that in preparation "gross and scandalous sinners" are usually exercised with "heavy breakings of heart" (334). Not that God might not deal heavily with any man, sin being (in itself) an infinite offense; and one should not overlook the cases of *heavy preparation* where God means to prepare "choice instruments" or where it is his purpose eventually to "manifest himself with some ravishing sweetness" (336). But the usual way is, in God's "good pleasure" (337), the usual way. Nor, in truth, is attention to "the incongruous" a peculiar mark of Hooker's system of rough justice before smooth mercy.

And, at all events, it is only with doctrine 10, an energetic treatise of more than ninety pages, that we discover the second epicenter of Hooker's monumental Book 10; for what *must* follow the "sight of sin," in its own essential nature, can only be evoked as a "sorrow for sin" which "pierceth the heart of the sinner through" (358). Agreeing with Cotton that the Gospel's pricking involved more than the eyes, the tongue, and the hands—but declining to reproduce the conceit of a natural heart pierced through[65]—Hooker emphasizes first that more was involved than a "rippling of the skin, . . . a sudden pang, a sigh and away," and then that this piercing to the "bottom of their hearts . . . proceeded not from any power of their own" (358). These "patients" were worked on "against the heart and hair"; they "*were pricked* [and] did not prick themselves" (359; original emphasis). God's way of producing this wounding may be various: "by degrees," beginning with "some unexpected flashes of spiritual truth" (363), followed by more particular seizures of fear and arrests of conscience, until the knowledge of one's sin becomes unbearable; or suddenly the Lord may "pierce the soul through at one thrust" (372); or, more rarely, his way may be "sweet and secret" (374), "sanctify[ing] the soul in the womb" (375) or providing the "common graces" which prevent "scandalous evils." But "though the manner of God's dealing be diverse," and though the "degrees of contrition" (375) may differ, the "substance of the work or preparation"—the piercing—is "truly wrought in all that are effectually called." A man may not be able to "tell the time of his conversion," yet every saint must be able to give "proper and special evidence" that "the Lord hath broken his heart kindly" (376).

In Connecticut, that is to say, one had better not approach the elders of the congregation without an enhanced sorrow, well beyond the sort the sinful self might itself produce. For again it appears that only God can make the "soul to feel sin as its greatest evil, when naturally it finds greatest content in it" (379). Not God in us by gracious habit; and not God enabling our will; but God "countermand[ing] the authority of sin" (383). And in the "overpowering of this opposition that a carnal heart naturally carries against God and his grace, the will of the sinner itself is a mere patient." Again, it makes no sense to say that the will is compelled, but Hooker feels bound to argue that "it may be constrained to suffer without the least prejudice to its liberty" (392–93). The significance of this insistence is worth repeating: rather than clear a field for increased human agency in the salvation event, Hooker's preparation emphatically extends the range— and the style, so to speak—of divine participation in the process; before the liberated sinner can realize faith or the power of infused habit can enact virtue, a deeply recalcitrant will must be overrun by the power of divine grace operating efficaciously—irresistibly—*ab extra*. Again, orthodoxy over elegance.

And Hooker returns to it, with relief, in a consideration of the "behavior of the heart under this [piercing] stroke" (396). Once oblivious, the stricken sinner will now "see nothing but sin" (397). Once resistant to self-knowledge, he is now become "marvelous tender" and "of a yielding disposition" (399). Now truly affected, "he loathes himself and his soul for it," sees that shame is what "his sin hath deserved, and therefore is willing to take . . . his due and desert" (404). Far from eccentricity, such is the "behavior of all those whom the Lord doth kindly and really break off from their sins," and this sensitivity goes far beyond a man's instinctive distaste for "murders, adulteries, incest, and sodomy" (404–5). The stricken man "fears all sin, and all provocations to sin, because he hath felt the evil [and] the danger of all" (406).

Willing to endorse all means, Hooker places most value upon those that work most "thoroughly for the discovery and removal of corruption" (407)— upon confession, for example, which offers a stress the "perverse heart is wholly unable to undergo" (410). And he is "restlessly importunate in seeking relief from God against his sin" (411)—so much so that should the Lord release him from all his ordinary "miseries, troubles, inconveniencies, punishments" (412), he would continue to press for "deliverance from sin by Christ" (413). For as sin smites God and separates the soul, so only this "true" sorrow will move the alienated heart back toward its source and end. Thus he feels entitled to complain against a "secure age" which can show so "little saving sorrow." "Fearless professors" abound, pretending a "care to God's command" (417), yet slighting their duties and excusing their faults as "petty things," just where the man truly pierced fears "all sin as such" (419). Abundant also are those "formalists" who follow Christ for the loaves and go away sorrowing at the "hard saying" (420). Count in "your self-conceited Pharisee" whose sense of self-worth precludes anything like "shame" (423); and "your complaining hypocrite" (425), lamenting his inability to bear God's stroke, but keeping his sins along with his complaint; and the "discouraged hypocrite" who, rather than become "importunate in seeking the Lord," concludes he should "as good sit still as rise and fall" (427). Justly too may one denounce terror upon all those "drowned in a senseless security" (429) and, more fearfully still, those who have been "exercised under the displeasure of the Almighty" but who "at last . . . have shook off their terror" (434–35).

Comfort may also be had, in the midst of piercing sorrow, for contrition, once again, carries its own sort of hope: the "anguish" of knowing oneself under the aspect of sin is not a way "unto death" but is in fact the only "means to deliver from death" (439). Objections express the overwhelming sense of guilt of the truly contrite, but answers only press the paradox: the worse the suffering, the more certain the cure. Cotton will object to a theology that seeks to infer salvation from the pain of its absence, and he well may have in mind Hooker—who seems only too willing to "learn the transport by the pain": when sin becomes "unsupportable, then lift up thy head, know this is the right way to Christ, and thou art near home, even within the ken of the promise" (440). Indeed, if this pain implies a separation from sin, he will even leap ahead to the outcome: "be divorced from thy lusts, [and] Oh welcome"; though "weary and tired, no sooner there arrived but the Spirit of comfort shall pour peace into thy conscience" (441). So friends are to rejoice at the sight of this familiar pain, and its incorrigible subject must be willing to be "pierced through" until—the plural seeking to publicize the privacy—"we see our lusts bleeding out their heart blood" (448).

"Resistance" there will be; but just in case the reader should miss the sense of the near-presence of mystery, Hooker adds the appropriate warning: "Do not tug with this resistance in thine own power" (449); bring thy soul "into God's presence" where one need not fear "the terror of the truth" (450). God alone will do the saving, even at the point thus early in his process. And—in or out of an "open boat"—how could he bring a man this far without meaning to save him in the end?

———

After this extended treatment of the affect of the true sight of sin, subsequent matters move apace. The fact that those whose hearts are indeed "pierced by the Word are carried with love and respect to the ministers of it" (453) reminds us of the "professional" importance of preparation, and perhaps Miller was not wrong to reprint, under the title of "Repentant Sinners and Their Ministers," the entirety of this eleventh doctrine.[66] For, along with the needful self-service, it gives Hooker the chance to evoke the reversal of values involved in a conversion experience:

> contrition and brokenness of heart brings a strange and sudden alteration into the world, varies the price and value of things and persons beyond imagination, turns the market upside down. . . . Those who were mocked as men full of new wine are now the precious servants of the Lord; flouted to their faces not long since, now they . . . honor and reverence them, yea fall at their very feet. It was before men and drunkards, now men and brethren[;] the world you see is well amended but strangely altered. (557)

And this same conversion-that-is-preparation makes the all-but-new man "busy"—in the language of doctrine 12—"to enquire and ready to submit to the ministers of God" (560).

Yet those who wish to begin the New England Jeremiad at the earliest possible date will take comfort from Hooker's very discouragement in this regard:

> Walk we from one plantation to another, . . . nay . . . from one assembly to another, all the earth sits still and is at rest; there is no stirring, no trading in Christianity; men . . . enquire not after the purchase of the precious things of the Gospel. . . . As though Christ were taking the charter of the Gospel from the present generation, and were removing the market; there is no stirring, trade is dead. (565)

A bad sign indeed, for although sinners in distress are "unable to help themselves" (576; doctrine 13), they also see "an absolute necessity to come out of the[ir] sinful condition" (583; doctrine 14); so this doctrine of distressed seeking is plainly a "bill of indictment" against such "neuters who study to compose their course with prudence and conveniency" (592–93) and such "formal professors" who swear they will "go far to accommodate the Lord Jesus" but with a "reservation they make to themselves" (594), like a man who rents his house but reserves a room of his own.

Back in the positive case, the truly pierced are the subject of a "secret hope wherewith the Lord supports the[ir] hearts" (596; doctrine 15). Indeed, their very question—"What shall we do?"—reveals that, though they know their "case be dangerous and their condition miserable," they by no means conclude that "there is nothing that will or can do any good" (596–97). And buried in this hope is a doctrine of value: "They who are truly pierced for their sins do in an especial manner prize and covet deliverance from them" (608; doctrine 16). Their hopeful question, that is to say, is not "what shall I do to be eased of my distraction"? but, the sight on premise being "true, "what shall I do to be saved from my sin?" (609). Such freedom alone will now content him, and this "though he want all the rest" (611). And now, as if to show the difference between imagining and enacting this untainted form of contrition, Hooker proposes, with distinction and emphasis sufficient to have invented the premise of *The Scarlet Letter*,[67] his own arch-Protestant decorum of confession. "They who are truly pierced with Godly sorrow for their sins are willing openly to confess them" (619; doctrine 17); and after we have heard when a sinner is in fact "called" to confession" (620–30) and learned how to tell "when confession is serious and hearty" (630–41), Hooker moves toward the logical conclusion of his understanding of preparation.

Once we understand "how . . . contrition bring[s] in this confession" (641–46)—and make our way through uses, complete with questions and answers and provided with motives (646–70)—we are ready to see, in "the last doctrine" implied by the Pentecostal piercing, how a "soul that is truly pierced with Godly sorrow for sin" not only is "carried with a restless dislike against it" but also is ready to make a "separation from it" (670). For when the heart of the sinner is so wrought upon by God that he is "no longer able to brook or bear" his sins, but "vomits them out with vehement distaste" (641) in confession, what remains but to sound the depths of this "detestation" and to watch it enforce that "sequestration from sin" (672) which, except for the rumor of humiliation, might well be accounted the very "end" of preparation.

Aware that he might well be accused of making his preparatory separation from sin too perfect and complete—of making men "better Christians before they are in Christ than many are afterwards"[68]—Hooker is anxious "to difference this work of hatred" from that which is "expressed by the saints" (672); and, as often when he finds his theology in extremis, Hooker presents his position as a series of academic conclusions. First, as the sons of Adam are all turned from God, "there must be an aversion . . . from the creature, before there can be a conversion unto God" (673); second, as "[t]here is [now] nothing in the soul that can turn the soul from sin," so "this first aversion from sin" must be wrought by God directly and *ad hoc,* and not by any "gracious habit" (674); third, this means that the "spirit of contrition" works its irresistible effect not within but rather "upon the Soul" (675), making way for gracious habits in the soul but not yet residing there inherently. The right to force this radical reorientation has been won by Christ, whose death "brings a release from under the hand of divine justice" (676), and it always begins with the soul being forced "to feel sin as sin" (677). One hesitates to imagine the maze of "sources" that lie behind this assemblage of propositions,[69] but its motive seems perfectly clear. A plain Calvinist in his refusal to grant man *any* part in the first movement of conversion, Hooker is also quite anxious to differentiate the "assisted" loves and hates of preparation from the "habitual" acts of sanctification: in the one case the soul is "acted wholly by the power and impression of the Spirit"; in the other, "we apply the power of Christ's death to this end with him" (678).

Hooker even tries again a favorite figure: a city which has no strength effectively to oppose its alien rulers may yet have the power to withdraw allegiance. And here as elsewhere he seems more comfortable when his tropes can subdue a system built to serve too many discursive masters. Would you know the extent of God's "first work" in turning the soul? Then know this:

Fear stops him, sorrow tires him, hatred turns him. Fear troubles his sin, sorrow loosens it, hatred abandons it. Fear finds the knot, grief unties it, hatred dissolves and breaks it off. Fear questions the lawfulness of the match between sin and the soul, sorrow gives in proof and evidence out of sense of the evil of it, hatred dis-annuls the league and sues for an everlasting divorce betwixt sin and the soul. (678)

There you have the thing itself—a hatred "of preparation" and not "of sanctification," a hatred from the Spirit "assisting" but not yet "inhabiting." "Take the wheels of a watch out of place"; or take "a member out of joint" (678–79). Take the A Train. Take my wife. Please.

But if there is impatience here—exasperation verging on deconstruction—the problem is clearly not that of "Calvinism" simply understood. We seem on the alert, always, to detect the first stirrings of our own profound resentment of predestination, but such hatred nowhere enters the all-but-meter-making argument of early American Puritanism. The interest is more complicated and indeed more intellectual. The first discovery we make in studying Hooker and Shepard, standing against John Cotton, or in considering the trinity of them together, is that all of them are trying, in the name not only of Calvin but of the consortium of All Saints, to glorify God in man's dependence.[70] What turns out to be true as well, however, especially in the congregations of New England, is that a number of strong and liberated readers of Scripture were unable to force their academic tools to carve, out of a set of poems too various for even Paul to epitomize, a single sense of salvation peculiar to every one of God's elect. God hates sin. Hooker hates sin. Somewhere, presumably, even Fala hates sin. But how? All at once and in one way only? Or one way now and another way later? And if a preparatory hatred is a good sign, of the first beginnings of God's irreversible process, would not a sanctified hatred be somewhat better? Infallible evidence not of process but of fate now accomplished? But what if the first were, for some good long time, the only hatred a body of mobile men and women could conscientiously confess? An assisted but not yet an infused hatred? Might that be enough to prove the needful point? Might it populate Connecticut?

Happily, in any case, the marks of this assisted hatred of sin are easier to discover than those of its infused counterpart: "Continual fear of the presence . . . of sin" (680) and a quenchless seeking for "the destruction of sin" (684) as the "common enemy" (688); and, more philosophically, since "sin is the only enemy of the soul" it is indeed "the only proper object of our hatred." So we do well to complain "how few there be in the world who ever knew . . . this hatred of sin" and to use the presence of this hatred as "a touch-stone of the truth of this work of contrition" (691). For there seem to be whole classes of persons, transplanted from England and enduring in their resistance, who want the transport without the conviction, and whose ranks have been surveyed before—principally, it appears, those "careless Christians" (693) who can speak of sin without fear. And then, in a couple of brief but unhurried pages, a few words on the last note of preparation's "contrition," namely, that "sequestration from sin" which might look even more like an act of sanctification than did the hatred, but which Hooker uses to draw the line between those made preparatively holy and those "never cut off from their corruptions" (701). The strategic reference to cutting reminds us that somewhere, beyond a printer's finis, Hooker's system must again make a space for the implantation of the soul cut off from its sin into the true vine which is Christ and do its best, wearily or with ravished expectation, to make horticulture complement hatred. Supplement it cannot be, for then preparation would have frankly usurped the place of salvation itself. For surely Hooker *intends* no more than to suggest that the link between true preparation and authentic faith is one unbreakably forged in Scripture.

Not Arminianism, therefore, but only a proper relish for God's own means and ends prompts him to conclude, with Jeremiah, "If thou wilt part with thy sins the Lord will set his love upon thee." In Hooker's system the man who cries out "unto the Lord, turn me, and I shall be turned" (702) has got to know the Lord may turn him or not. But he may also know, with equal certainty, that those whom God does turn from sin, with a violence acting apart from themselves, shall in time be turned all the way back to God himself.

IV. "I See Not a Savior"

Inclusive as Hooker may have intended his summa to be, and long as even this summary analysis has discovered it, *The Application of Redemption* is radically incomplete. Leaving aside all those well-titled "Books" which the printer confidently announces and the prefacers consign to the care of God alone, there is quite obviously the matter of the soul's "humiliation"; for, as Hooker's own schematic reveals, "man's disposition" in the work of preparation involves not only a contrite hatred of and sequestration from sin, but the truly humbling realization that the truest contrition in the world leaves him still unable to help himself to the grace of faith. And—back a few branches on the relevant structural diagram— the logic of preparation implies, as its necessary correlative, the numinous event for which this preparation has on premise been preparing, which Hooker's idiom consistently identifies as the "implantation" of the soul into Christ.

Having noted the obvious, however, patient criticism might still wish to ask about the exact degree of self-misrepresentation implied in Hooker's failure to finish. Absent "implantation," are we indeed left on the steps of the temple? Or is the connection between salvation and the church porch of preparation so fair and firm that we can rest assured in just what has in the positive been accomplished? Could we, that is to say, die assured in a state of true contrition? Clearly our "humiliation" would add only a *degree* of security, for it is nothing more than the other half of the "disposition" that God's "dispensation" of holy violence creates in the heart prepared. We linger on the threshold still. And though Hooker's earlier treatise, *The Soul's Humiliation* (1640), gives the subject far more space than it enjoys as part of Shepard's triad of conviction, compunction, and humiliation,[71] it is hard to feel that Hooker has as much invested in the recognition of inability as in the sight of sin. Someone, surely—Cotton, perhaps—might feel that so much talk about hatred of sin might, despite the best intention, in fact throw the emphasis away from the operation of the Spirit and onto the self and its affect, but evidently Hooker is not the man to make that precise point. The *Humiliation* patiently anatomizes the conditions of and the tests for a sufficiently humbled recognition of one's utter inability to help himself out of the state of sin and loss—and, indeed, of his need to rest content in the workings of the will of God—but compared to the *Application* its emphasis is extremely "psychological." God's own stroke having already been made, in piercing the heart unto contrition, the soul is left to pick at itself. And if it has been, on premise, already turned away from sin, we feel pretty sure it will yet find the prime truth of Protestant salvation.[72]

To *The Soul's Implantation* (1640) we must go, therefore, if we wish to confirm our sense that the link between the enforced sight of sin and the free salvation of the soul is sufficiently strong that Hooker has indeed given us, already, the fullest force of his religious thought; that a full and true preparation—could we but know it as such—makes union with Christ a foregone conclusion. Nor do we require the entire volume, for the relevant remarks are pressed between the pages of a text of "preparation" on one side and one of "love and joy" on the other; only the middle eighty pages or so are specifically entitled "Ingrafting," and even here a number of pages are taken up with a review of matters preparatory. Only after another careful buildup, that is to say, do we arrive at the place where we feel the climax ought to be.

————

Asking us to "remember" that he has "the last day . . . finished the doctrine of humiliation of soul" (67),[73] Hooker nevertheless begs leave to preface his present remarks with a review of the appropriate context: remember that there must indeed be a preparation "before the sinner can come to receive Christ" (68) and that this preparatory work must be considered both as a "dispensation . . . on God's part" and as a "disposition which God works upon the hearts of all those he will prepare for Christ," this latter consisting first in contrition and next in humiliation. Contrition "pierceth the heart through" (69) with an appropriate sense of guilt and necessary punishment; humiliation brings the soul to despair "of all help in himself," causing him to fall down "at the foot of the Lord, . . . content to be at God's dispose." And all this while the "poor sinner is like the children of Israel traveling in the wilderness," not coming "immediately . . . into the land of Canaan, but . . . wandering under the hands of Moses, which was a type of the law." Now, finally, we who have wandered so long in the way of reading are almost *there*—"just upon the coasts of Canaan, and hard by all those spiritual good things Christ hath purchased for us" (71).

Ironic, we may think, if Hooker, who made it from England to Holland and back again, then all the way to Newtown and on to Hartford, never got back to this climactic point in his New World redaction of the long, long journey to this one great end. Ironic in a less obvious way, however, if at the climax of his account of the soul's spiritual journey—which wandering around the backwater of the seventeenth century could only type again in lowercase—there should turn out to be almost no "there" there. What if there is no "moment," that is to say, when the heart shall be sufficiently prepared to *do* something, like make an act of saving faith? Or if it turns out, in Hooker's quite high form of Calvinism, that *no* preparation can enable so rare a saving act, what if there is not even a moment when the Soul says, with fair assurance, *yes,* this is Christ, truly come and no mistake; now do I recognize the end for which the Lord has made my heart prepared? What are we to say if, after so long and arduous a journey, well symbolized by the length and difficulty of its prose equivalent in Hooker's *Application*—after a rough process rudely conducted, like our reading of the *Application*—we suddenly find ourselves to have passed *by* the point so ardently sought? Too bad you blinked? Or do we need to ask again: what did you indeed go out to seek? The seeking itself? Blessed are the seekers for they shall seek seeking.

Now, while we are thus ready to "lay hold upon Christ"—or, for the more literal minded, to "enter into the good land"—we are asked instead to consider that the "soul is like a graft, cut off from the old stock by contrition and also pared and fitted by humiliation" (71): and to sit still for the explanation that ingrafting "is a work of the spirit of God, whereby the humbled sinner stands possessed of Christ." Yes, yes, yes: the language says that a man "stands possessed of Christ, rather than that he possesseth Christ"; and this because "the work lies on

Christ's part" (72). And yes, the same man who stands possessed of Christ "is made partaker of all the spiritual good things that are in Christ" (73). But who Christ, what Christ, how Christ? And most of all *when* Christ? All preparation long we have waited to know the thing we know we need to know, and now, suddenly, without so much as a by-your-leave we are made partakers of God-knows-what-all. How was that again? You say he comes "suddenly" (79), like a king, when royal preparations have all been made? Too suddenly, by half: could you slow that thing down? You say he "will not delay to come into the heart that is truly humbled and broken" (78). Well, that's worth something, I suppose, but largely before the fact. Are you truly humbled? Then expect the Lord soon. This very year, month, week, day, hour, instant—which? Oh, speak not of "reasons why the Lord will not delay" (81): have I not agreed that, on premise, "all hindrances are now taken away"? (84). Talk not of uses or of motives. Show me. Now.

But there *is* no now, just now. The preparationist could well enact the scene in which his call to contrition should accord—by grace and not by congruity—with the Lord's violent but involuntary blow to the consciousness of sin and self, but he evidently declines to mimic the moment when a long awaited and well prepared for salvation is known as such. Having been humbled, we have also, somehow, been made to stand ready. No reason *not* to be by love possessed, for nothing now withstands. But Hooker has no text to speak for any such transcendent possession. And he appears to know exactly what he has elided.

The crucial objection is a little self-defensive and, at the outset, a little too wordy for perfect emphasis: "I hope nothing shall be too hard for me, that I may gain a Lord Jesus Christ, if I know mine own heart, and if I know it not, let the Lord make it known to me." But it does come finally to its point: "I see no sufficiency in my self over my sin to succor me, and I have a care to be burdened, yet I see not a savior." And, in any case, Hooker's answer takes up the logic of his cardinal objection with perfect acuity:

> Is this true? And is thy heart humbled as thou sayest? Then, I say, the Lord Jesus Christ is come, and hath come many a day though thou perceivest it not. So soon as thy soul is thus disposed, the Lord Jesus comes, and that suddenly too, though thou knowest not at what time. (101)

Unspoken but well implied is the possibility that the objector is simply wrong about his premise, that his heart is not in fact *entirely* humbled, and in this (not unlikely) case he must simply go back and look again. And again, perhaps, to the length of the *Application* and then some. Sooner or later, however, some objector will stick with his story and make his own acute response to Hooker's actual answer: "But can this be, that the soul should be possessed of Christ and not apprehend a Christ?" (102). Is it really possible that Christ in the soul is one of those things with or without which everything else feels pretty much the same? Perhaps so, we permit ourselves to editorialize, but we shall not be surprised if not everyone can be got to think just so.

The preparationist, however, is quick to reassure: "Yes, it is not only possible"—for Christ to be present all unknown—"but it is too ordinary," for there are a number of "hindrances which keep a soul from seeing" (102). The most intriguing of these seems to be our tendency to "judge Christ's presence by our own sense, and by some extraordinary sweetness that the soul imagines should be with him if Christ were there." Worst with the incautious readers of Canticles, perhaps, it yet appears to be the "nature of every poor creature" to set up "a kind of imagination in his own head, and thinks if Christ were come once there would be extraordinary sweetness and joy" (106). Perhaps they fall into thinking, with John Cotton, that some of those who labor really *are* to know refreshment as such. Here, however, they ought to learn to recognize Christ not in some rapturous transport but in their (Pauline) struggle against sin—not in any sweet "overcoming," perhaps, but in the more or less settled "opposition" (107).

Perhaps, as earlier suggested, we should be looking *back,* and not to some moment, but to the process of our hatred of sin. "Thou sayest, it is many a day since the Lord Jesus . . . made my sins loathsome to myself." Well spoken. Now consider:

> Whence comes it that thou art content to see thy sin? And whence is it that thou art burdened with it, and that thou art content to be rid of thyself, and sin, and all? Is it not from Christ thy Savior? Whence is it that thou art content to lie under the Word of God, and to be disposed by it? Is it not from Christ? (103)

No objector rises to ask whether such a disposition might not be the effect of some extrinsic grace, but we can be confident that Hooker's power to manufacture distinction would be equal to any such challenge. If indeed he cared to make one. If, that is to say, he had any strong interest in distinguishing the moment when assisted contrition and humiliation became in fact habitual. Evidently he does not. Evidently the force of Hooker's theology of conversion—including its interest in the unavoidable question of assurance—depends most essentially on the moment when, with "a holy kind of violence," God turns the savor of self-seeking to the true sight of sin. Evidently his system is willing to live with—even perhaps to trade upon—a certain amount of ambiguity after that.

Perhaps the simple fact that this strange content to be disposed as God shall see fit has endured for "many a day" is the sign that grace has become at last inherent or at least habitual. What is clear, in any case, is that Hooker has no interest in the idea that the Christ who broke the back of sin without the sinner's quite willing it must also personally testify to his presence as a permanent, live-in guest. Certain it is that "wheresoever Christ is, there is sight of sin; yet this extraordinary sweetness does not follow." It is just "as if some gentleman should receive the king into his house, and yet he would not be persuaded the king was come, because he would not presently send for him into the presence chamber, and advance him to some great place of honor" (108). There must be *some* sign, of course: even deconstructionists admit that the illusion of presence does not feel exactly like the reality of absence; and Hooker's theology of visible sanctity is at least as perspicacious as that. Contrition and humiliation infallibly reveal Christ irresistibly at work; perhaps their significant continuation reveals him to be at last at home. And perhaps that is as far as we get. Perhaps it is a failure of humiliation to think otherwise.

Certainly this is as far as our present effort can fairly go: preparation implies implantation in the perfect structural plan of Hooker's *Application*; but when we go looking for this perfect completion, beyond the limits of that plan's final manifestation, we are somehow thrown back upon things we already know. Hatred of sin and willingness to be disposed—to be damned, if the push of decree comes to the shove of refusal—this, it fairly appears, is all ye know on earth. And all ye need to know, were it not for the curious demand of the New World churches. Then set down this: here (in Connecticut) one speaks contrition. And that enduring for "many a day." Elsewhere they might require more, some sight of Christ which satire will call "an immediate revelation in an absolute promise": "Arise my Love and come away." Here, however, where a man's thoughts are "busied . . . about the guilt of sin" and about how "temptation . . . may be removed" we can well understand how we may have "no leisure to see Christ" (110). Consider how the disciples that were going to Emmaus did not recognize the risen Christ who walked the way with them. Of themselves they might say—and we with them, though walking a remoter path—"We had pregnant testimony enough of the divine presence, but we had no eyes to see it: the burning of our hearts was argument enough that it was Christ that spake to us" (111). Must we conclude that, for now at least, we have not in fact "seen" our redemption? Then write us down as those who continue to be consumed with the hatred and obsessed with the sequestration of sin.

————

Enough. Hooker must add to his list of self-hindrances a set of reasons why the Lord, really present, will sometimes hide himself from an anxiously inquiring view. A second doctrine assures us that "When the Lord Jesus comes to a soul truly humbled, he taketh possession of it as his own," but this is only to say that when he comes, "he rules" (122); and though our sense of being overruled adds some weight to the assurance we have been seeking, we have now moved to a point beyond the (absent) moment when the preparatory shall have become the real. The remaining movements of the general story—"vocation, justification, adoption, sanctification, and the like" (122)—are all predicted to come along in after-dependence on the crucial work of ingrafting, but they too are after the great fact of closure. In time to assure us, perhaps, that Hooker never meant to theorize the broken heart and let it go at that. But too late to tell us what it might feel like to mark the entrance of Christ into the heart broken just so.

Perhaps—says the sleepless voice of scholarly conscience, tempting the reader of a vital book to become the master of a complex and multiform oeuvre— perhaps the sought-for moment lies elsewhere still, in Hooker's account of "vocation," perhaps. But no: beyond the (psychologically) missing moment of closure, we find ourselves engaged in a process which Hooker's most scrupulous modern apologist has called not "finding faith" but "Becoming Faithful," which must be discussed not as the climax of a drama but as a set of concepts—"Hope," "Desire," "Love and Joy," "The Will." After that, in still other unrewritten books, we find that the topoi of "Union, Justification, Adoption, Sanctification" are scholastic indeed and are well handled together as a "Going Beyond Faith."[74] So we have moved from one process to another; or more critically, we have abandoned the experimental for the categorical. So that our "literary" conclusion survives: the life of Hooker's system depends on its power to philosophize the preparatory work of the true sight of sin, even as Perry Miller seemed to imply.[75] Thus if our reasons for continuing to maintain for Thomas Hooker a small but honorable place in our shifting and expanding canon have been the sort we call psychological, we probably need to remind ourselves that Hooker's forte is indeed the affect of sin and not of grace. Or of sin repented, at any rate, which is to say, contrition.

If preparation for salvation was for Hooker a matter of the most intense personal concern, the experience of salvation itself was something else entirely, something he has almost the nerve to call a figment. The application of redemption was his subject, not its purchase by Christ and not what we might dare to call its consumption by individual Christians. In the church, under a godly ministry, men and women must learn to hate sin—utterly—and after that who knows what transport of grace or graces might ensue? But that may be to say that what distinguishes Hooker's system is his sense of just how much grace it takes to hate sin enough. An assistive grace, at the outset, but a strong, even violent one nevertheless; indeed a *converting* grace, even if not as yet habitual. Elsewhere Cotton will essay to prove, in self-conscious answer to the probing (if also impertinent) questions of an assembly of congregational "elders," that their chosen brand of Protestantism forces them all to identify a saint as one who can confess, however awkwardly, that he has seen or felt the presence of God's own Spirit. It requires, on this account, nothing less than God to recognize salvation. He may be right. And exhilarating it will be, in any case, to watch him prosecute his case out of precisely the premises his questioners suppose they all must share. Hooker's achievement is of another order. Its genius takes longer to elaborate and, in an important sense, it agrees to settle for less. Not for a less effective assurance of salvation, perhaps, if there is indeed a calculus of so rare a mental poise; but less in the way of ontological claim required.

If for Cotton it will require God's Spirit to recognize God's presence, for Hooker it requires some definitive form of divine assistance to hate sin properly. And that may be quite enough: if one is sure about this proper hatred, then surely one is sure enough. The God who merely hovers about, near enough to force this revolution in human knowledge and affect, will surely not hesitate to follow up this purposive *coup de mentalité*. Not "if you build it he will come," to be sure; not in Connecticut and not anywhere in this terrain of godly letters. But if you have truly undergone God's deconstructive preparation, then you may safely expect. How soon? Soon. And if it should become, conscientiously, too late to be any longer soon, why then he who will not delay must indeed be already come—"and hath come many a day, though thou perceivest it not." We may protest that the system lacks a center, which can only be an encounter with the divine, without which there must remain some fundamental question: which side of saving faith am I on, exactly? Is this hatred of sin preparative merely? Or is what I feel the real McCoy?—the settled hatred that proceeds from a saintly grace? But Hooker, dismayed by our need to be so knowing, may rest content in his knowledge that salvation effectively entails not a sweet vision of Christ but a violent awakening to the sight of sin. And that its assurance will continue pretty much the same.

CHAPTER SEVEN

PRIMITIVE COMFORT

The Spiritual Witness of John Cotton

Though John Cotton's life as a professional Puritan was somewhat less unsettled than that of either Thomas Shepard or Thomas Hooker, it too afforded the opportunity to adapt his message to different scenes and conditions: England before the Laudian crackdown, serving a decidedly mixed audience; England during the Puritan suppression, when earnest souls might be led to seek out a more gracious message; New England, in the awakening that seemed to mark the arrival of a number of famous ministers; and the public controversy which the enthusiasm of this moment clearly encouraged; the years that led away from that early climax of Puritan self-attention, toward an imminent apocalypse, perhaps, or merely toward the next developments in the history of aroused religion in a World Without End. Unlike Shepard, however, whose whole career tends toward the monumental *Parable of the Ten Virgins,* and Hooker, who prepared his *Application of Redemption* as a sort of summa of his life as a preacher of preparation, Cotton's oeuvre is rather hard to epitomize.[1]

The Way of Life has some claim to the scope of its title and has been well represented in modern collections. Noticed by Everett Emerson for its "gentleness," praised by Phyllis and Nicholas Jones for its "broad applicability," and mined by Ann Kibbey for the political implications of its rhetoric, this pre-American work appears to offer Cotton's fullest account of the whole life of the Protestant saint.[2] The first section evokes the possibility of a nation coming to experience such a "pouring out" of God's Spirit that one might imagine an entire generation learning not only to "wade" but also in the end to "swim" in grace, "as fish in the water, with all readiness and dexterity, gliding an-end, as if he had water enough to swim in" (105); nor did Perry Miller hesitate to imply that one page of this spiritual exercise might convey enough about the assurance of Cotton's intellectual style.[3] To be sure, no such expression of sanctification could be expected unless "the very life of nature" should run out, "trickling and bleeding," from a heart most suitably "pricked" (126–27); and other anthologizers have thought to represent Cotton's subtle but not contentious mentality with something from the second section.[4] Melville need not have had Cotton in mind when he counseled Clarel, with the motto of the third section of Cotton's *Life,* "Keep thy heart"; and the Jones anthology reprints the first of the three sermons that make up the "The Christian Charge" merely to stress that the heart "alone is the meeting place of the sanctified motives of faith and the actual practices of the natural world."[5]

In something of that same spirit, Miller's second anthology of the Puritans represents Cotton by nothing more than his sermon on "living by faith in [the] outward and temporal life" of our worldly "calling," from late in the *Way*'s last section, entitled "The Life of Faith." Students who have heard of Weber and Tawney are quick to notice the worldliness of this sermon—"as soon as ever a man begins to look towards God, he will not rest until he find out some warrantable calling" (437)[6]—and are with difficulty brought to see that faith may redeem worldly work more cogently than success can validate grace. Actually, the distinctive note of this last section is the sense of how much of Cotton's message can comfortably be included under the single heading of faith. Indeed, Cotton's confidence is such that his whole sequence seems addressed to an audience for whom available sainthood and not uncertain anticipation is the norm, even amidst the parishes of England. His continuous account of the "way" to the "life" is broken, here and there, with an objection aimed at clarity, but no one *ever* forces Cotton to say out loud that (of course) only grace can enable the activities being described; as if he spoke to those whom grace itself would now or soon instruct. An audience, we need to recall, is always in some sense a creation of the speaker's own rhetoric; and in this context we easily recognize Cotton as a man who loves to address the saints.

Closer to the problems of New England, *Christ the Fountain of Life*[7] provides an introduction to the Cotton who attracted followers from outside his own locale and inspired some of them to make an ocean crossing in his name. Distinguishing its style, perhaps, is its extended conceit of a spiritual "life" which, quite like the natural, is the cause of "motion," of "feeding" (including the power to keep food down and to be nourished by it), of "growth," "expulsion" and "propagation" (127–42) and which is marked by "warmth," "pliableness," and "sweetness" (145–60). Clearly Cotton feels that the "fullness" of Scripture entitles him to subject any of its key terms to all the pressure the valid scientific learning of later generations might supply.[8] Or one might also notice that, for Cotton, life in the Spirit is characterized by "a certain variety of graces of God in themselves so different and opposite" (109): most obviously, "no small measure of joy" in one's redemption will be mixed with a "full grief of heart" (110) for sin; but joy will also mix with fear and with affliction (111–13), and the gracious habit of patience with men will never cancel anger at all sin; meekness will mix with strictness, modesty with magnanimity, and diligence in business with deadness to the world (113–19). These ambivalent experiences are never sought for as such, of course, for faith aims at Christ himself, as the "woman in true conjugal affection" must look at "the very bare man" (53); they are simply "the comfortable signs of our life of sanctification" (126).

Yet this complex fact is never to be used as primary evidence of "justification," our free forgiveness by God the Father in the name of his atoning Son. For the last point of the second sermon of Cotton's *Fountain* provides a perfect anticipation of the very issue which the New England elders will wish most earnestly to debate—namely, the relation between justification and sanctification. Indeed, one hardly understands how Miller's original anthology selection could stop just short of this precise point. The subtle student may see the implication of Cotton's prior teaching—that Christ may require the surrender of "all the good common gifts of grace, which are sometimes found in nature and sometimes in the children of the church" (25), and that religious competence is by itself no sure sign of saving grace. But the touchy point is explicitly touched when Cotton goes on to suggest that we might well "have [Christ] in justification, but not in growth of sanctification" (27).[9] The saint may go about in the world as a fool and even, shockingly, as a sinner, for "the life of Christianity is not a life of wisdom and graces, but of faith" (29). A dangerous slighting of Christian virtue here, the New England elders will surely think. And for the sake of public morality, at the very least, they will call for a stronger link between the Grace that saves and the graces that then appear. In full confidence, it seems, that no slight can possibly be done to the purity of their Calvinist doctrine by making real good works the inevitable effect of real redemption.

Or one might choose to emphasize *A Treatise of the Covenant of Grace,* some version of which Cotton seems to have been preaching in New England, in 1636, when the lurking difference about justification and sanctification, about conditional and absolute promises, and indeed about Law and Spirit in the Protestant sense of salvation erupted into controversy.[10] This sequence, clearly, is the one Cotton mines most frequently for language to meet the objection of his questioners, often adding only a tone of argumentation to explications already very well made. To be sure, it takes him long enough explicitly to deny the charge of

"Antinomianism" (97), but he refers to an "agitation" over doctrines "taught amongst us" (43) fairly early on; and disputable propositions appear from the outset. God, obviously, is the first giver in any covenant to which he is a party, but not all would agree that his gift is "not of obedience first, nor faith first, . . . but Himself is *Donum primum*" (12); or that, like a great prince adopting a "neighbornation" without telling them of that fact, God simply "maketh a covenant with Christ and taketh us into that covenant" (13). Nor would all of New England be eager to define faith as "the Spirit of God taking possession in our hearts"; or to stress that this faith always proceeds from an "absolute free promise of God unto the soul" (22).[11]

It might be instructive if our chronological science were exact enough to tell us precisely where Cotton was in his exploration of the Covenant the day it began to dawn on the outspreading but richly intercommunicative community of New England that their well-trained and duly chosen ministers were not all saying the same thing about the order or indeed the *affect* of salvation. We should like to know, as well, where, at the same moment, we might find Peter Bulkeley in his more scholastic version of the same topic; and Shepard in his unfolding of the latter stages of the Christian life in the "Sound Believer"; and Hooker, down in Hartford, in his final elaboration of the necessary and perhaps even sufficient condition of preparation. But the local problem might come down to the relation—and the perceived difference—between Cotton, the new teacher of the Boston church, and John Wilson, its established pastor. Just here, where comparisons were certain to be made, the cognitive dissonance must have been pronounced. If only Wilson had thought to publish.[12]

But if, in any event, we ask where Cotton was driven to explicate and defend the logic of his eccentric but hardly egregious position with the greatest clarity and force, the answer can only be in the famous *Rejoinder* to such "elders" as had inquired of his orthodoxy and then commented adversely on his itemized but terse replies. It really is quite a remarkable work: written in haste, under considerable public pressure, and in terms he has allowed others to set, it not only manages to defend the internal cogency of his own theological position but to explain, in language only rarely given to the rhetoric of insult, why the position that seems to be growing widespread but without conspiracy into a dominant system in New England is not nearly so secure an orthodoxy as his critics seem comfortably to be assuming. There is, of course, something to be said on both sides: much, if one has the appetite for intellectual controversy once vital; less, if one prefers the terms of theory's new cuisine. But an odd selection of Puritan sentences inhabits all our survey books, pointing to works it took genius and passion as well as

emergent occasion to produce. And here and there, in a moment of luminous intelligence, local distinctions remove the veil from a law of thought.

———

Though Cotton by no means shunned opportunities to teach beyond the realm of
the single congregation, and though he had already exchanged polite letters with
Shepard and Bulkeley,[13] his reply to these "Sixteen Questions of Serious and Necessary Consequence" is prefaced by a protest: he might well refuse to answer *any*
questions so put and, like Jesus before the High Priest, simply remind them that
he has "ever taught and spoken openly to the world." Declining to claim the independence implied by New England's congregational structure, he answers only
because his questioners are so "dear and precious."[14] It is not clear how answers of
duty might have differed from those of love, but it is worth noting that the social
and intellectual history of New England might have been much different if an
insider of Cotton's stature had clung to his right of refusal: the politics of loving
consensus would have been dealt a keen blow very near the moment of its first
full flowering. Local "synods" might not so easily have claimed their authority
was merely "advisory"; or, if that were too frankly "Presbyterian" an effect, the
Winthrop government might have had to become a little more frank about the
role it was learning to play in a world where love is only *almost* the equal of law.
But as Cotton in fact agreed to answer, no road diverged.

Plainness is probably a matter of opinion, but Cotton certainly kept his answers "short"—ten pages, in the modern anthology of the "Controversy." First,
he explains, the "Seal of the Spirit" is often used to signify "sanctification," but
others identify it with the "Witness of the Spirit in itself"; and, in an answer destined to raise more questions than it resolves, no, not every believer is sealed with
the "Witness of the Spirit in itself" (48). "Broad seal" is no term of his own, and
to Question IV, yes, a true believer may see some "work of Christ in himself . . .
before he be sealed with the Witness of the Spirit in itself," yet "full settled comfort he cannot take" until he receive that very witness; and though its strength
may not endure, it is clear enough to assure salvation "without respect unto [any]
work" (49). Gross sins may indeed weaken Christian comfort, yet assurance may
be maintained even then. And yes, the soul waiting for grace may, without the
Spirit's Spirit, apply some promise to himself—precisely as to one who waits.
Deep difficulties lurk in these brusque, professional replies, especially in the language about "the Spirit in itself," but Cotton is not looking for trouble.

Yet even in this preliminary attempt to avoid irreconcilable differences Cotton will sometimes advertise his power to distinguish: asked "whether a Christian must . . . have first assurance from an absolute, and not from a conditional promise," he answers that the

> first assurance doth arise from the Spirit of God, applying God's free grace in an absolute promise. Or if in a conditional promise, it is not to works but to faith, and to faith not as a work, but as it revealeth the free grace of God offered, and applied in Jesus Christ. (50–51)

Indeed, he had said the same thing before in public: "our first coming on to Christ" must be upon an "absolute promise." When the Lord bears "witness to justification, it is either absolute or to faith," and the Spirit's working of faith must be experienced in itself and not inferred from some act it appears to have enabled. To think otherwise, he had warned, is to invite a certain "misprision of sanctification."[15]

Next, coming straight to what became the crucial case, how does this insult to conditionality affect men's use of sanctification?—the saint's hearty devotion to Christian virtue—as a sign from which may be inferred the fact that a person has indeed been justified—forgiven, that is to say, adopted, accepted as a person elect of God? First, though sanctification can be said to proceed from an "infused habit," it makes better sense to say that Christian holiness proceeds from "the indwelling power of the Spirit," an advantage unfallen Adam himself never had. And now, about this special form of human experience and behavior as evidence: "evidently discerned," sanctification is indeed "a true evidence of justification, *a posteriori*": even as "justification is likewise a true evidence of sanctification, *a priori*" (51). We suspect the elders will find this an academic evasion; but for the moment Cotton can only go on with the game of innocent Answers to loaded Questions. Accordingly, he denies that sanctification is a proper "ground of our primitive comfort": the fact of our "faith depending on Christ" is sooner discerned than our "sanctification by Christ"; and so, by implication, "if my justification lieth prostrate . . . I cannot prove myself in a state of grace by my sanctification" (52). By now, clearly, the strictures on the evidentiary use of sanctification are severe; we feel certain that Cotton's sleek and stylish answers are not going to end the confrontation.

And with Question XIII—"Whether evidencing justification by sanctification" is an entirely safe practice—Cotton himself is overtaken with a sense that no one is going to be satisfied with perfunctory answers. Thus his reply takes the form of seven propositions, discovering increasingly subtle cases of a "going aside unto" a covenant of works. Obviously, no Protestant will regard sanctification as the "cause" of justification, for this is but another way of saying that man earns his own salvation. But neither may a man rest the entire judgment of his estate on the sight of his sanctification; indeed, as the rest of Cotton's propositions insist, a saint must at some point have experience of something *other* than sanctification, with the *spirit* of which that sanctification must be seen to agree. Holy activity is clearly dependent on justification; and though there is no human experience of God's decision to forgive (some) men, in the light of Christ's atoning sacrifice, yet the soul's best knowledge of this amazing fact comes from a spiritual conviction of its foundational reality. For—as he has heard both Hooker and Rogers soundly teach—"there be saving graces which are not yet sanctifying" (54–55); and in his own words, sufficient assurance comes only when "the Spirit of God" provides the doubtful soul a "clear sight of his estate in a free promise of grace in Christ" (57). After which, justification and sanctification happily witness one another.

This much premised, Cotton's answers to Questions XIV, XV, and XVI return to their original pace. Obviously, "a Christian is more active after regeneration than before": before regeneration "we are not active at all" in any spiritual sense. Yes, a man may establish his "safe estate" by "practical reasoning" if "the reason be not carnal but spiritual"; even so, "a good conscience will not satisfy itself in this way, till it be established by the Witness of the Spirit" (58). And finally, a Christian *may* press the Lord for spiritual mercies with arguments drawn from the graces of Christ in himself but ought much more properly to press the Lord with "arguments drawn from his own spiritual miseries and infirmities than from the graces of Christ in himself" (59). Nor can modern idiom resist the point: It's about Faith, Stupid. Early and late, men love to regard their works, but the Spirit wants to witness only God's free gift.

Yet the elders were not *that* stupid. They immediately saw, in Winthrop's words, that "some doubts" had been "well cleared" but that in other things Cotton "gave not satisfaction."[16] They saw, for example, that Cotton's answer to the very first question had not been explicit about his *own* position on the Seal of the Spirit (63); and they had hoped his answer to their fourth question would have involved some reproof of those who say "a man must see nothing in himself until sealed with the Spirit" (64). So they felt the need to write a considered "Reply": running to about sixteen pages in its only printed version, it argues for both the orthodoxy and the prudence of their use of sanctification as an evidence of Christian identity. Nor does it avoid the personal. Appealing to "the Searcher of all hearts" to witness their purity of motive—and utterly refusing the role of "high-priest-like interrogatories" (62)—they preface their "Reply" with the "tender" suggestion that Cotton appears to have stepped aside from the main "stream of most divines" (61); or if not, then he should welcome the present opportunity to clear up the sense of things he has "publicly uttered" but which were "darkly and doubtfully delivered" (62). A little friendly advice, they dare to imply, from persons more keenly aware of the problems of a popular audience.

Further, in expressing a hope that Cotton's fifth answer does not mean that "the testimony of the Spirit is or must be the only or usually immediate without respect to a work," they warily predict that "such an opinion may be a seed of much hypocrisy and delusion." Does Cotton really wish to "train up a people to a plain forsaking of the Scriptures" (65)? They also fear that any doctrine of assurance without reference to sanctification will "open a wide door to temptation, as into sin with less fear, so into a bold continuance and slight healing of sin" (66). And, on the other hand—though their rhetoric does not concede the opposition—they have a great concern for the blindness caused by the enduring reality of "ignorance, weakness and sin" (73); so they also refer their trust in sanctification to the needs of many a troubled soul for whom a dauntless love of virtue is the only consolation. Surely the dangers are clear: on the one side, the "Bold Libertine"; on the other, the "Poor Doubting Christian." What the elders imply, in a tone that takes collegial concern to the point of condescension, is that Cotton's steady invocation of the Spirit—in the place where they are used to look for the works of valorized virtue—is more than a little out of touch.[17]

Yet the arguments of the elders are not all pragmatic: the requirement that a man take "first assurance . . . from the Spirit only" will certainly destroy "the comfort of many" (66–67), but it may also limit the ways of God in salvation, for his "free grace may be revealed and received in a conditional (where the condition is first wrought by God's free grace and not trusted to, as we desire ever to be understood when we mention conditional promises) as in an absolute promise." Hearing the redundancy, in a parenthesis that appears both structural and constitutive, we sense the strain of pious inelegance: given the utterly unequal relation between God and man, only grace can make the condition; and, given the Fall—or is it just the fact of God's decree?—only grace can perform the condition. But we feel as well the force of a consensus repeated into the familiarity of truth: "it is grace that works the condition, it is grace that reveals the condition, it is grace that makes the promise, it is grace that sets on the promise" (67). There can be, the elders feel sure, no going back to the (Thomist) logic of "fitness": no God worth his pillar of salt would attach salvation to a work of depravity. And who could cavil with a theory so careful to exclude every human claim?

Confident as well is their response to Cotton's tenth answer, avowing a sort of mutual witness—of justification forward to a sanctification to follow, and of sanctification backward to its only possible justification. So assured is their reply, in fact, that students who can read for tone are hardly persuaded to read any further. Does Cotton really maintain that "sanctification cannot be evident unless a man see his justification first"? If so, "If this true sanctification be evidently discerned by seeing our justification first," then it seems "a man shall evidence by sanctification only that which was evident before; and thus upon point it's no more an evidence than a candle to the sun" (67). Emerson, faced with a similar problem of evidence in relation to intuitional certainty, and convinced that the intuition is *indeed* available, will more felicitously exclaim, "You don't get a candle to see the sun rise." But the elders' rhetoric has its own sting: you don't say "upon point" unless you think the argument is just about won. And indeed, how could Cotton be missing this crucial point? If the multitudes of the saintly minded could indeed testify to some moment in which their faith contained the knowledge of their Justification as such, then all this fuss about sanctification were, in Emerson's perfect word, "operose." Clumsy, that is to say, but also "worksy."[18]

Evidently the practice of inferring justification from something else—from the lucid realization or perfect enactment of some condition to which the Scripture attaches salvation or, more generally, from a swelling love and increasingly competent practice of virtue—was much more a derivative of experience than an invention of doctrine. Who indeed would choose the low, "moral" road for its own sake? Not Shepard, we feel pretty sure, who made up his assurance out of his anxieties; and hardly Hooker, who flatly rejects the expectation of some assuaging "sweetness."[19] Or, as Edward Taylor would figure the question, who would consult the wracking demands of contrition if he could report the voice of God speaking to him as to a "Little Darling"? Would that there could *be* as many as two orthodoxies in Massachusetts; but—dammit, Cotton—what are we going to do about those who do not know "the kisses of his mouth"?[20] Including, perhaps, our own Elderly Selves?

For exactly the same reason the elders protest that a man's "primitive consolation" may *have* to "arise from his sanctification" (68), that virtue may be a man's only comfort when "the Lord seems to forsake him" (69). They agree that a "person is accepted before [his] work" but staunchly insist that "what first is" is not necessarily "first seen" (70). Agreeing with Cotton that it is easy for men to fall into all sorts of un-Protestant habits of thought, they yet beg that ordinary (i.e., "doubting") Christians be better instructed in the ways of faith and not "be condemned as going aside to a covenant of works." And, after branding his reading of Abraham and Hagar as "allegory" (73), they conclude their extended reply to Cotton's answer to their thirteenth question by accusing him of reducing the entire question of assurance to that one rare thing called "the immediate witness of the Spirit itself" (75).

Then, leaving the modern reader awash in a sea of terms, they end their "Reply" with the pious—Winthrop-like—hope that they "may all think and speak and preach the very same thing" (77). Yet how, we wonder, can this thing end? Can't someone just say they won the war and go home to their own congregation? There will be no answer, let it be: like the man said, a Pope in every Parish. Or, if the church of Boston itself shall divide on the issues involved, then take up your pen and write *two* such churches: there must be fifty ways to leave your pastor. Or might it just be possible for someone to say what latter-day Calvinists may *have* to hold to keep from lapsing back toward the common lot of more or less Reformed Christians, Protestant and otherwise, none of whom want to take *much* credit for their own salvation? If not, of course, no surprise; for where is it written that fools cannot raise more questions than other fools can answer? But what if someone *could*? Would not the weary scholar wish to read his book?

———

Making that book available for the first time, David Hall suggests that Cotton's task is to convince his critics that only a *mistranslation* of Paul to the Ephesians could support their contention that "faith was somehow prior to, and a condition of, receiving the Holy Spirit." Actually, Cotton argues, "in the order of causes, the Spirit came first." But more than this, Hall curtly announces, "Cotton's major concern was to rebut the logical distinctions the ministers were employing to explain the role of faith."[21] Rebuttal there certainly is, and indeed Cotton can be as academic as anyone might wish. Yet clearly he is a scholastic of a different sort—more Platonist than Aristotelean, more interested in the feel of coherence than the test of logic. He will school the scholars on the text and on the order of causes; but his subtler interest is to show just where a religion dedicated to the divine *gloria* had better learn to hold its tongue on the subject of works.

Politely, yet with more zeal this time, the "Rejoinder" begins exactly where the Questions, the Answers, and the Reply had all begun. Indeed, Cotton had *not* said what he himself means by "the Seal" (or "Witness") of "the Spirit." What he means is simply "the Spirit himself." Sticking hard by Scripture language—avoiding thereby any reification of the notion of seal—Cotton reminds his colleagues that Scripture's word is a verb and not a noun: "we are said to be sealed by the Spirit," from which we learn that when God marks us as his own he does so "by giving the earnest of his Spirit in our hearts" (79). Plainly, God "seals" us by giving us his own Spirit—a fact quite intelligible in its own terms, even if we take "Spirit" to mean nothing but God's own mood or bent of mind. Holy works might follow from this holy mood, of course, but by their spirit alone shall you know them. Seek first, therefore, the Spirit of God, and other (discursive) entities need not apply.

Without God's Spirit, after all, we do not even accept God's Word in any meaningful sense. And though "Translators" have made it seem as if "believing went before, and sealing by the Spirit followed after faith," yet Calvin and Piscator have set the record straight:

> in time faith and the sealing of the Spirit go together, and [moreover] in order of causes the sealing of the Spirit goes before faith, as being the efficient cause of it. And so indeed may the word be better translated . . . in believing you were sealed, or, having believed you have been sealed with the Holy Spirit. (79–80)

Consenting with these predecessors, Cotton thus refuses to make the witness of the Spirit something extra, a supplementary something that may come along later and swear to the validity of some prior transaction. Faith is simply the Spirit-assisted recognition of Christ as the only way of salvation. The "proper and effectual cause of faith," the Spirit is thus appropriately referred to as "the Spirit of faith," working "with his own immediate power" not always without but in every case "above the power which either the word hath of itself, or the work of any creature" (80).

Beyond this irreducible minimum, it is possible to mean by the "witness of the Spirit itself" some *ultimate* assurance—the affective certainty of one's very own place in God's redemptive plan. And here it must be confessed that not "every believer is . . . sealed with the Spirit expressing his own proper and peculiar witness and work"; for, clearly enough, not "every believer hath received the fullness of joy of the Holy Ghost" (81). Transcendence need not become the sine qua non of New English Sainthood. Yet surely every saint must be able to confess, as the essence of his faith, "the Spirit's manifestation and impression of the work of the Father and the Son upon the soul" (82). Does the Father indeed elect saints from the ranks of sinners, and does the Son in truth enact the price of their redemption, as the Word seems wondrously to hold forth? In fact they do, the Spirit to the man must swear and, so swearing, make the faith that saves, distinct from the rehearsal of doctrine. More than this there may be, in the infinite life of the Spirit, but less is always something man's own desire has cooked up in the name of moral plausibility: see how I just love the law.

With any lesser sense of public pressure Cotton might well have declined to pursue the task of explaining the reason of his differences with the elders much further than this. You well perceive, he might have concluded, we differ not only in our sense of the number and order of events that mark a man's conversion but also and more fundamentally in our understanding of the Spirit. For you he is a witness on whose testimony certain lucky ones may come to rely in supplement to the evidence of their fulfilling a Gospel promise; for me he is the work itself. You talk of his providing some sort of "seal" of a complex and multiform process; I speak of his active presence as the very event. Would you have me, like some confidence man, call upon the Spirit to witness himself? Or will you cry "Transcendentalism" if I teach that God's Spirit must always be its own evidence?

With some mix of political exasperation and moral duty, however, Cotton goes on—with an argument aimed at the tone of congregational practice.[22] Accordingly: a man may confess a "work of Christ that accompanieth salvation" before the Spirit shall have offered him "his own proper and peculiar work in the fullness of comfort and power" (83), but it remains true that we cannot "gather any evidence to our faith of our safe estate" without the original spiritual testimony that constitutes faith itself, for "the work without the Spirit" is as powerless as is the Word thus unassisted. In no case, therefore—even if reproof were indeed the part of a teacher—can he be asked to reprove those who say "a man must see nothing in himself until he be sealed by the spirit" (84) for such, rightly understood, is his very own doctrine. Cotton promises to show "hereafter" why "in the evidencing of justification [the Spirit] beareth witness in the word of free grace only," but for the moment he must oppose those who would "see a work before the . . . witness of the Spirit . . . and then to see a promise made to that work; and then from both to gather a faith of [his] justified estate" (85).

The same for those who would assure themselves from the strength of their desires after what they take to be godliness. "Can any man take as much comfort"?—he asks, in epitome of a question developed at large in *The New Covenant*—"can any man take as much comfort in thirsting after the water of life, as in drinking of it" (85)? Surely Protestant faith is more than an anxious hope. And to the accusation that the doctrine of Spirit-first is sundering things God has joined together, Cotton insists on a proper *ordering* of those things: "In the comfort of sanctification, let the object or ground of our comfort go before, to wit our union with Christ, and it revealed to faith . . . , then let the works of sanctification follow according to the commandment of the word." In the order of our confessions, that is to say, let the works of virtue always appear second and always as an effect, less the evidence than the simple consequence of our salvation. Never the cause of our salvation, they should not even figure as the prime reason of our coming to believe that salvation is indeed our own. Lovers of Christ keep his commandments, well enough, but "no man can love Christ except he first believe in Christ, and by believing be united to him, and know the love that Christ hath towards him." The true ground of our comfort, in short, is this "knowledge of his love towards us; thence follows our love of him," the fruit of which is that "we keep his commandments." Thus, in this most circumspect form of neo-Calvinism, neither the granting of salvation nor the reception of its comforting knowledge is "laid up in the work" (86).

It gradually becomes the work of the "Rejoinder" to demonstrate that this secondary, "affective" rejection of works is the only safe ground for New England men to hold. Safe from "fear of delusions" (87), in the personal cases that worry Cotton's pastoral critics; and safe from collapse back into the position of Reformed Catholicism. Patiently, however, Cotton continues to press for clarification—content to wait for a place where his argument can break free from the scholastic structure the elders have imposed.

Eager to emphasize the necessity of spiritual witness, Cotton's fifth rejoinder contends that "delusion in the Churches" is to be feared only if any should teach that the Spirit's witness in the soul ever left it just "as barren of good works" (87) as it had surely been the moment before. Ever a lover of Christian virtue, Cotton thinks of it, lovingly, as a "way of life" and not as an evidence. On the way to his counterassurance, however, his teaching that the Spirit may work with or without sight of a work begins to reveal that his sense of witness is quite different from that of the elders. They wish to allow the relatively public fact of works, done for a godly motive, to imply the mysterious fact of God's acceptance. Convinced, on the other hand, that "godly motive" is itself an arcane entity, Cotton wishes to invoke the premise of spiritual witness at every point: salvation is the imputation of Christ's righteousness, sanctification a consequent moral empowerment; and it requires an act of God's own spirit to "believe" either one. Cotton may seem to be invoking two mysteries where the elders honor but one; but it could also be observed that, in refusing to focus on the difference between godly works and their trashy imitation, they may be eliminating the element of mystery altogether—citing Scripture and confessing Calvin, but featuring works all the same.

The sixth rejoinder continues the reassurance. Loving virtue above everything except God's own Spirit, Cotton almost humorously rejects the contention that his strictures on the virtue test amount to something "dark and dangerous." "Modal propositions expressing possibility" imply nothing at all about likelihood; so the elders must understand him to mean only that one must admit the possibility that assurance may remain firm despite a fall into sin. But if he *must* address the case of conscience, then this: if a man

> know the riches of God's grace in Christ, he ordinarily both may and . . . ought to believe that his justified estate doth still remain unshaken,

notwithstanding his grievous sin. For as justification and the faith of it doth not stand upon his good works, so neither doth it fall or fail upon his evil works. (88)

In practice we all assume that the Lord will carry on "all his works both of faith and holiness in some near symmetry and proportion," that "the stronger faith" will bring forth "the purer holiness"; and yet great saints may have their great lapses—teaching them to live in Christ and not their own gifts. Surely New England can be trusted with this *essential* Protestant paradox. Fear not the "wide door to fall into sin with less fear" but anticipate instead the voice of the sincere convert: "How should I commit . . . this great wickedness and sin against the father of mercies, the god of all grace" (88–89)? Why always expect the worst?

All this may be a little idealistic, but surely Cotton felt entitled: if not here—where we have dared believe saints can appear in truth and learn to rule—then where in the world? Is Protestant logic but a loophole in the Law? Is the saint to be understood as the man just *looking* for a reason to sin with impunity? And so, in the same mood which trusts that our assurance ought to be "perpetual" (90), like the act of justification itself, Cotton pleads for a doctrine of spiritual waiting: cannot a man "come to conclude that peace is provided and laid up for him in Christ on whom he waiteth, and still wait till he hath found him more fully, and peace in him"? And to realize, "in the midst of his waiting," that his faith "is not built on his own waiting but on Christ." Spiritual prolepsis, that is to say, is different from anticipatory anxiety. And the spirit of quiet waiting for "the Spirit in his own proper work" to provide "full assurance" (91) is quite different from the mood of preparation.

Surely the rhetoric of good faith can go no further. Cannot we trust, Cotton seems to be asking, that those who love God's Word enough to take the point that salvation is in every sense through Christ and that God is glorified by this cardinal case of man's dependence will also be those whose gratitude will express itself as a desire first to walk and then to "run the ways of God's commandments"?[23] That to refuse to see works as originary evidence or primitive comfort is not to discredit their performance or to banish them forever from the world? All we are saying, Cotton seems to plead, is give faith a chance. What saint would we really exclude if we listened not for a convincing account of the heartfelt enactment of some holy work but for the sense that a person really had come to grasp and rejoice in the counterintuitive plan of vicarious atonement? The rare and remarkable sense of which, by all accounts, only the Spirit of God can enable, and which might precipitate the thought of divine election all by itself. Ask then, if you wish, what's next? and worry if gratitude express no gracious wish to embrace the Christian way of life. But why cannot we all learn to name the name and confess the noetic effect of the Spirit of God from the first?

———

With the rejoinder to the reply to the answer to the eighth question, however, the mood begins to change—from an ideal of trust, all around, that the highest explanation will always be accepted as the truest, to the unhappy recognition that some entrenched opinions really are errors. Nothing runs before to advertise the turn: no more nice guy. But Cotton can hardly set out to write a critique of the logic of the conditional promise without a sense that he is taking his campaign inside the enemy heartland. Secure in their accumulated conviction that conditionality *cannot* threaten free grace so long as "it is grace that works the condition, it is grace that reveals the condition, it is grace that makes the promise, it is grace that sets on the promise" (67), the elders expect the pious redundancy to overwhelm (and to intimidate) the otherwise agile and active Puritan will to oppose and to pursue. But logic is not less potent than rhetoric, and not those who cry "grace, grace" are fit to "break the green damp mould with the unfathomably wondrous" Calvin but only those who see that "we must first assuredly discern our union with Christ before we can assuredly discern that the right of such a conditional promise belongs to us" (92).

Shepard has taught that a man may test his faith—and thus know his salvation—in the performance of some act or, more generally, in the satisfaction of some condition which certain Scriptures identify as predictive: "Blessed are the poor in spirit," for example; "they shall see God"; and pay heed, now, to the richness of my poverty. So long as the man admit that this humility has been graciously enabled, what possible going aside to works? Grace makes and reveals the promise, of salvation for true humility, neither of which it was on premise at all required to do; and Grace *also*—or some *other* Grace, strictly speaking—comes along just in time to make us humble. Praised be the name of Grace. Surely God alone is glorified in so dependent a redemption. And yet one could always ask how one knows his humility is quite *true,* the spurious sort of self-deprecation being about as common an expression of self-regard as any other social face our self-love contrives to arrange. Would not this new humility have to derive from and to express a certain "spirit" not our own? Would not this spirit be the same one in which one came really to accept and positively to rejoice in the fact of salvation from without? From the gift of faith, that is to say. And would it not sound better—more properly Protestant—to talk about that needful fact in and of itself? Elders can be cautious men, but should Reformed Religion not aspire to a certain precision of language, including a perfect propriety of tone? For errors lie all about.

For example, if God ever does work faith in a conditional promise, it must surely be "without respect to any such condition as pre-existent in the soul, though by the promise the condition will be wrought in us" (91). Clearly, some gracious thing must come before our satisfaction of any condition, and Cotton appears to be insisting that this first in the order of being must also be first in the order of appearing. In their established grace-to-fulfill-the-gracious-condition model, the elders have elaborated a system in which God enables the satisfaction of some specific command—from which justification may surely be inferred. Cotton, on the other hand, sees grace as that which works the conviction that salvation is indeed offered, freely and without condition, to men who can do no more than see and appreciate the way things have to be. By and large and on the whole and in the end, Saints will indeed fill up the biblical outline of the saintly life, but inceptively and definitionally they are those who accept the fact that salvation is quite free. Including their own, if they happen to think in "personal" terms at all.

Conceding a supplementary use for an absolute promise, the elders have yet judged that "to take our first assurance . . . from an absolute promise only" seems "not only difficult to believe but dangerous to maintain" (91). Much less fraught with peril, they think, to ask a man to confess that he has been enabled to do a certain thing or to be or feel a certain way that Scripture has linked to salvation; much more dangerous to ask for a show of faith, all by itself, in its very own terms. God saves those who believe; I believe; QED. Or, if that bald formula were itself too conditional, I do indeed believe that God alone will save whomever he will. And you are to help me judge the sincerity of that belief not by my subsequent behaviors but by the spirit in which I hold forth the text itself: God saves, I come at last to see, for no human reason; if *me,* then surely for nothing of my own; if not—for I do not yet enjoy a "full assurance with comfort and power" (91)—then no matter. For God must surely be God. (Of course, the "I" who says these things, in the mock inspiration of academic composition, may not really *believe.* Literary competence can go just so far. But surely the discerning Puritan pastor might judge of this matter no less well than a distracted academic reader.)

At bottom, it appears, the difference concerns the human moment of faith: is it an activity or an insight? Shepard has been defining it as an enabled response to a call, the result of which is one's justification. And gracious it is said to be at every point: most freely, God attaches justification to faith; and most freely still, he enables some men to respond to an unswerving demand for belief. And all other conditionals are in strict imitation of this: if I have been enabled to do such and such a saintly thing, then I must indeed be a saint. Cotton does not quite insist that faith is "passive," but clearly it is for him more an insight than a volition: justification is not given as the result of an (enabled) activity, but its efficacious reality is implied in the Spirit's witness to the way of salvation itself; and to enjoy this witness, to the impossibility of salvation except in Christ, is not different from a certain "union with Christ," outside of which, Cotton insists, "all conditions . . . are corrupt and unsavory." Cotton takes it as granted that all Scripture promises "are first made and fulfilled in Christ, so that we have no right unto any of them by right of any condition or qualification or work in ourselves" (92); and, rather than infer our "union with Christ" from something it may enable, he insists that such union can and must be known in and of itself. It is to this very union that the Spirit testifies in making elective salvation and vicarious atonement appear. A complex insight, but one miracle only: it requires God's presence to accept God's way.

Reformed theologian Pareus freely concedes, Cotton instructs the elders—and to no less an adversary than the Jesuit Robert Bellarmine—that our assurance is indeed "before works," that it comes "from the testimony of the Spirit bearing witness to our spirits that we are sound." And surely it will not weaken the case to cite the authority of Calvin, who instructs us to support our faith with "such a promise of salvation [as] is offered freely and liberally of the Lord, and hath rather respect to our misery than [to our] worth" (93).[24] In this context the crucial distinction bears repeating: if salvation be offered in a conditional promise, "it is not to works but to faith, and to faith not as it is a work but as it receiveth the free grace of God offered in Jesus Christ." Not even to faith as a grace-assisted work: "In a man's first conversion the conditional promise is not to faith at all as . . . pre-existent in the soul, but as to be wrought and to be begotten in us by the power of the Spirit who breatheth in the promise of grace" (94). Men hesitate to discover salvation in God's bare "I promise," but they must avoid the delusion of supposing that anything is promised in exchange for faith. The promise is made "in faith," and not at all "for faith," no matter how this condition is wrought. Just so, when Peter "promised remission of sin to every believer, he did not presuppose faith in all his hearers that so they might apply Christ . . . unto themselves" but only that "the Holy Ghost going along with the word and coming down upon their hearts with it [to] beget faith in them and assurance thereof." And if faith first come this way, and some assurance by that very fact, may not God build a man up "to full assurance by giving him a fuller . . . measure of his Spirit in a like absolute promise"? Thus, where the elders contend that God's freedom is expressed in *both* absolute and conditional promises, Cotton contends that in any "condition presupposed in us" the thought of grace is to some extent "veiled and obscured" (95).

Nor will this purification prejudice the cause of them that hunger and thirst for justice; for such longings are meaningful only in those who know "by a former assurance" that their spiritual satisfaction is "wholly and absolutely laid up in Christ"; and, as Cotton paraphrases one of his emphatic public teachings,[25] Scripture clearly points to the *satisfaction* of these longings. The Savior himself instructs men that "be athirst" simply to "come unto [him] and drink." Neither ironic nor gratuitously cruel, God

> does not send men that are thirsty to consider of their thirst, what a gracious disposition it is, and to drink well of their thirsting till they be filled with it . . . ; No, no but let them come (saith he) to me . . . and drink; not drink their consolation out of their thirst, but out of Christ. (96)

Men's first qualification—of being poor and mourning and hungry—can come from nothing but "the revelation of free grace in Christ," which they ought to be able to confess as such. And their assurance must come not from (grace-enabled) qualifications but from "the same free promise of grace," which brings them again to Christ, "to drink again of him" (96–97).

Once more, in some other venue the argument could stop just here: Cotton takes Scripture to reveal some illuminating and then assuring experience of God's own Spirit in the positive, the actual, the real—some "Divine and Supernatural Light," as Edwards will have it. The elders are doing the best they can for those terribly earnest persons who cannot conscientiously discover any such experience. The difference is fundamental. Hooker chose rustication in Hartford rather than the need to explain, to an increasingly competent audience, how the Spirit can arrive, in the soul aroused by preparation to unwonted perspicacity, all undetected until well after the momentous fact. To Shepard, principally, has fallen the task of defending the proposition that the presence of God's Spirit may be detected as a valid inference, from the performance of a condition only he may authorize. And of trying to convince friend and foe alike that the inferential system does nothing to impugn or to obscure the absolutely free ("gracious") nature of salvation, or to give to lost and needy man any reason to link salvation with any fact proper to his own natural self. And for his pains—continued as they will be in his tireless *Parable of the Ten Virgins*—Shepard will survive as the only Puritan founder to enjoy republication in the nineteenth and twentieth centuries.[26]

But Cotton is not impressed. And there seems now no place to go, except on with the disagreement. The elders defend the "free grace" of a "conditional promise" so long as "the condition is first wrought by God's free grace and not trusted to." "Ingenuously," Cotton professes, he cannot understand how a work that, by fulfilling a stipulated condition, thereby assures a person of his salvation cannot in some important sense be "trusted to."

> Yea, so much do I trust to that work that if I see not that work in myself I dare not trust a promise . . . to belong to me; but if I take the promise to belong to that work (though given of grace) and find that work . . . in me, then upon the sight of that work I may claim my right to the promise . . . pronounced in it. (97)

Had they the heart to remonstrate against Cotton's rejoinder, the elders might hope to shift the emphasis back from "not trusted to" to "first wrought by God's free grace"; they had meant, they might urge, not trusted to as "our own." And the modern reader may wish Cotton had known to call the elders' reduplicative theory of the grace-required-to-perform-grace's-own-condition simply inelegant. But he does pretty well nevertheless. For he has seen the grace-and-grace position before. And not in a place the elders might like to turn for help.

The tone may be earnest, but the irony is evident: the elders have come very close to replicating the position of Reformed Catholicism.

> Be not deceived . . . that because you profess to take all from grace—condition, promise, and the revealing of both—that herein you do not derogate from grace. It was that which deceived Bellarmine to plead that justification by works doth not derogate from justification by Grace, "For the works themselves (saith he) are not works of nature but of Grace, and therefore though we be justified by them, still we be justified by Grace, unless we make Grace to fight against Grace." (97–98)

Cotton's "teacherly" inclusion of the reference (Bellarmine *de Justif.* I. i. c. 21) may suggest that the elders have not done their homework. And we may wish to defend them by protesting that their work-enabling grace is a more special (elective) thing than the Fearful Jesuit had in mind.[27] But Cotton does more than enough to indicate how the argument has got to go: "our divines" see the need to emphasize that grace and works are, "in the whole course of our salvation . . . not subordinate one to another, but opposite." Accordingly, salvation inferred from a work simply does not *sound* Protestant.

For Scripture opposes grace "not only to merit but to debt." Seeing that "all we are, or have, or can do, is of God and not of ourselves," it makes no sense to think of God as owing us anything whatever. Now "if he that worketh [should] claim any reward for his work"—even out of "promise made to the work"—he is nevertheless collecting on a debt. So

> if we claim to gather . . . comforts to ourselves from the promises made to good works wrought in us, and by us (though of grace) before we see our union with Christ and right to all the promises . . . in him; we then do receive them not of grace but of debt; and that in very truth must needs derogate from free grace. (98)

At the very least, the idiom is wrong. The Old Covenant returns Life for Works not in justice but only by divine stipulation. And—subtler still—the New Covenant does more than promise the elect some gracious assistance to perform Faith. God's ministrations to man can never escape the condition of grace, but their acceptation must somewhere stop sounding like works. And, in this regard, Perry Miller ought to have exempted Cotton from the ranks of those Covenant theorists who urged men to make God pay off on his promises.[28]

And so Cotton offers the elders his own "take" on the "main difference between the promises of the Law and the Gospel":

> In the Law, the promise is made to the condition or qualification of the creature, though given him of God; so that, give me the condition and I claim my right to the promise. In the Gospel the promise is made to Christ, so that give me Christ and I claim my right to the promise and to all the comforts and blessings thereof. (98–99)

Cynicism might suppose that "Christ," occupying the same position in the New clause as "condition" in the Old, is just another, yet more pious condition; but the "elderly" readers of this Rejoinder are not the men to reduce Christ to a grammatical marker. And Cotton feels sure he can make them sit still for the conclusion of his analysis:

> And therefore that which maketh the accomplishment of all the promises of Gospel to be of grace, is not because we have the condition from God and the promises from God, and the revealing of both from God (for so it is in a covenant of works) but because all the promises are given to Christ, and . . . fulfilled in Christ, and the revealing of both is by the revealing of Christ given of grace freely to the Soul. (99)

We can see, on the one hand, a condition graciously met in ourselves; or we can see, on the other—and as the very substance of faith—all conditions meet together in Christ. And surely a saint will prefer to talk about Christ, the "door that must be first opened to me . . . before I can see any assurance that the treasures of God's House belong to me" (99).

And if the elders' condition comes down, at last, to "thirst" after Christ, then they would do well to remember that no man has this condition "given to him, or revealed to him, but he hath had Christ first given and revealed to him freely who hath wrought these conditions in him" (99–100). Natural men may hanker mightily after they know not what; but only those already touched by Christ can know it is Christ indeed they have been needing. As Cotton will put the matter elsewhere, in the graphic language of Canticles, those who desire God's "kisses" are only such as "have felt the sweetness, yea, and the excellency of them above wine, before."[29] Evidently it takes God to want God. And, having known God, who would prefer to prose about terms and conditions?

If Cotton's eighth rejoinder dissociates his position from that of Bellarmine, his ninth invokes the authority of Puritans Perkins and Ames. It also reveals that both he and the elders are willing to pursue differences that seem unlikely ever to have become the subject of widespread dispute. It matters very intensely, to the kind of profession one made before this or that Puritan congregation, whether one spoke of being graciously led to meet some scriptural condition of sainthood or, more mysteriously, of seeing oneself wrapped up in Christ, sole heir to every promise. But, Adam having long ago soiled the nest, the difference between his original righteousness and our sanctification may seem gratuitous; nor can one imagine a popular outcry against making repentance "an act without a habit" (101). Yet we have already learned that there are more curious things in the heaven and earth of "Calvinism" than are dreamt of in our simple for-or-against philosophy. And, the elders having raised the issue, Cotton is only too willing to continue.

Cotton's editor suggests that the nice point concerns the question of "man's activity prior to grace,"[30] but the parties also disagree over the way we account for the virtue that is an effect of saving grace. Cotton takes the elders to hold that God's Spirit, given in response to a (grace-enabled) act of faith, becomes thereby the "procreant and conservant cause of our sanctification, by begetting and preserving the habit of sanctification in us," but to deny that the Spirit is himself the *primary* agent in "producing the acts of sanctification," with the result that "we ourselves produce the acts of sanctification by virtue of those habits received by us and preserved to us." This account does indeed identify us with Adam. But not, unhappily, with Paul, "who bringeth in Christ not only as a procreant and conservant cause of his spiritual life but as jointly concurring with him in every act of spiritual life as much as himself, yea more" (102). Barely repressed here—and more lively to our sense than who "jumpeth with Grevinchovino" and who may "join with Ames"—is the problem of human identity, which any strong theory of the "new birth" is bound to encounter sooner or later. No party to the present controversy has any use whatever for man's activity prior to grace. The difference concerns the nature of human agency in or after the grace required for man's salvation.

Having defined faith as our own (grace-assisted) response to Scripture's universal call, the elders wish also to insist that the sanctification which proceeds from the justification we have been given in return for faith continues to be a matter of our own (enabled) human activity. But Cotton—untroubled by the question of who is who—professes not only that the power of the Spirit must figure as a "formal ingredient in its healing of the Soul, which in Adam's [original] holiness it did not," but also that the Spirit is in an important sense the very "material" of our sanctification (102–3). Less scholastically, "the Holy Ghost hath not only an external efficacy in begetting and preserving our sanctification, but also an internal concourse and cooperation in [its] duties." It may seem compulsive to insist that the same "could not have been said of Adam . . . in the state of innocency"; but Cotton is sure of his emphasis: "Is not our sanctification the image of God renewed in us?" (103–4).[31]

The ninth rejoinder ends with a return to the question of Adam—and to the views of Perkins and Ames, whose power to authorize a radically spiritual notion of Christian identity may be more ambiguous than Cotton supposes.[32] But the work is already done. Independent of their authority, Cotton has won the right to his spiritist sense that, as faith may be thought of less "selfishly," as an insight rather than a choice, so Christian virtue may owe more to God's immanent presence than to the soul's "own" regenerated faculties. To be sure, that position threatens to unsettle the commonsense understanding of human identity, yielding our stubborn personhood to the miracle of God's immanence in regeneration. But then this is what conversionist theology is *for*. And if not in New England, then where?

———

But it is with his tenth rejoinder that Cotton settles in to challenge the entire ethos of sanctification. What has gone before is inevitable only in the sense that any system which seeks to link the mystery of unalterable divine favor to the equally mysterious question of quantum changes in authentic human discernment and efficacious moral capacity seems bound to discover an ambiguity here and there, whatever the idiom. And if, within any such idiom, anyone's reason seems lucid enough to bias our own (disinterested) preference, some small return of thanks is well in order: yes, Mr. Cotton, it does seem wrong for an aggressive religious protest to rest in a position only a *little* more spiritual than the sacralized moralism it sought to replace. But surely the Christian community in New England was predestined to decide exactly what premium men and women of faith were to place upon good works. And fortunate we are to find, just there, the discerning intelligence of John Cotton.[33]

Willing to concede a sort of mutual witness between justification and sanctification—the joyful practice of good works may well ensure that our reception of God's own spirit has been a fact of faith and not a flight of fancy and, conversely, that an experience of God's Spirit enables us to recognize our works as authentically spiritual and not hypocritical or merely anxious—Cotton has been dared to make this formula meaningful to earnest pastors of flocks who hate sin, love virtue, and yet "see no Christ" and who feel, accordingly, that using works to prove a faith already evident would be like getting a candle to see the sun rise. Now, to the question of whether "sanctification can be evident unless justification be first evident," he can only answer, with an honesty that may preclude conciliation, "I conceive not." For as

> the life of . . . faith is a necessary ingredient not only in every habit but in every act of sanctification, it is not possible that our sanctification or any duty of it should be evident to us to be wrought in God unless it first evidently appear to be wrought in faith; and then our justification will of necessity be evident to us before our sanctification can be truly evident. (104)

And with that observation, the battle for the conscience of New England is fairly joined.

Turning first to their metaphor, Cotton suggests they should have said "a candle to a candle"; for, as his irenic temper is still insisting, "there is not so great difference between sanctification and faith, as betwixt a candle and the sun." Unless of course the sun were taken to mean "the object of faith, Christ himself, and him revealed by the witness of the Spirit itself." This *ultimate* confirmation, better than finding one's name in Scripture—and satirized as such by Edwards[34]— is, to repeat, *not* to become the norm of church admission; but its very mention is enough to set the nerves on edge. And to enliven, perhaps, Cotton's own sense of free enfiguration: surely "it is no dishonor to sanctification to light his candle at justifying faith, which receiveth his light immediately from Him who is the light of the Wor[l]d" (105). Faith first, an experience in itself: a new, "spiritual" understanding of the necessity of an utterly gracious economy of salvation, able to identify itself as such; and able to nod its light to the nodding light of all works done in faith thereafter.

And if the elders stick on Bible passages "that hold forth evidence by sanctification . . . unto babes in Christ and such as believe and know not that they do believe," well perhaps we had all better sweeten our mouths with a morsel of Calvin. On Scripture's suggestion that "we know that we know him if we keep his commandments," the Genevan mentor comments:

> "We must not hence gather that faith doth rely upon works; for though every believer have a witness of his faith from his works, yet it followeth not that it is founded there. . . . [For] surely we do not know that we are Sons of God by any other means than because he sealeth to our hearts by his Spirit our free adoption." (105–6)

Cotton's intention is less to wrap his doctrine in the mantle of authority than to provoke the realization that the "sanctification" assurances of Scripture were not given as a way "to gather the first assurance" but are addressed in fact "to such only as are formerly assured of their good estates by the seal of the Spirit" (106). The point is that works have to testify to the validity of some *other* experience—of faith—that was both prior to those works and different in kind. They can help to *re*assure the Christian, in the days that follow *after* the surprising conversion, that their experience was as true as it was surprising. That the blessed motion was God's Spirit in very fact, and not the pickles and pie à la mode they served me; Granada I saw, not Asbury Park. *W* may help to prove that *F* was and remains identically *F,* but it cannot be used as the *only* evidence that *F* is truly there. The works of sanctification, that is to say, may confirm the truth of but may not at all substitute for an experience of the divine.

Nor are we to feel that, given such an encounter, the confirmation of works can be only an annoying supplement; for those sealed by the Spirit find such "holy fruits" to be "of notable use to declare" that their experience of faith "is not feigned nor themselves hypocrites" (106). The conclusion of their spiritual biography, that is to say, ought to have at least two parts: after the life of sin in the grain—and with or without the piercing preparation of contrition, compunction, and humiliation—the saint will experience a divine sealing, not necessarily of his very own election, but of the blessed freedom of God's ways in grace. But the emphasis continues to fall on Cotton's *positive* doctrine, of the necessity of faith in itself and as such. The Lord Jesus knows best "what milk to feed his babes," and he does not "send them to gather . . . assurance of their estates first from their . . . good works, but first from the knowledge of himself and of God as their father." And if any should ask "by what means" such a thing is known, the answer can only be, "by the unction which they have received by the holy one" (106–7). Not the Spirit's extreme unction, we know by now for sure, but better than a poke in the conscience with a sharp stick.

At this point the modern reader may feel that the contending positions have got close enough for government work: surely Cotton has made a place for sanctification and is not likely again to overemphasize its need to be strictly scrutinized; and surely the elders will not now encourage a man to know his faith by works alone. Yet Cotton is not the man to stop before he has made answer to all that has been asked. And even as we pause to reflect that *proving faith* by works is only somewhat like *earning life* that same way, Cotton seems eager to refine the whole discussion by moving the emphasis from the logic of actual Scripture to the tone of possible System. Authorities aside, what needs repetition, perhaps, is that there are, in the figure and the flow of Protestant thought, places where talk of works just sounds wrong. Cannot a latter-day Calvinism learn to be as literary, so to speak, as it is conscientious and precise?

Not that Cotton makes his transition explicit. But having said why our sanctification cannot be evident before our justification, he is clearly impatient with the question of whether that sanctification can be the "ground of our primitive comfort." No, obviously, and for the reason already given: "the same grounds upon which our first assurance is built, upon the same is our primitive comfort built" (107). And insofar as the elders' eleventh reply has inserted "any new matter," Cotton tends to address it in psychological terms. The elders suspect that Cotton's faith will be "suspected to be but a dead faith unless the presence of sanctification will be seen with it"; but Cotton has his own sense of case and cure: "In sad hours, if faith be suspected sanctification will be suspected much more. For seeing the Just live by faith, the life of faith putteth life into sanctification: If faith seem dead and suspected, sanctification cannot appear lively and evident" (109). Different therapists, different cures, our analytic sophistication may well conclude. But Cotton holds hard to his own: faithful works require faith to be known as such.

Nor will he have his position reduced: deriving "after comforts" from the true sight of sanctification does not at all "prejudice . . . free grace," but deriving "primitive comfort" there most certainly does, for "our first comforts spring from such blessings as go before all our works, as from effectual calling, adoption, justification":

> [A]nd as they are wrought together without works, so they are revealed
> without works. [F]or it is the glory of grace to conceal all mention of works
> there: and the free and gracious revelation of them without works be-
> getteth those works which flow from them, and which afterwards bear
> witness to them. (111)

And with that revelation we are at the sensitive heart of Cotton's studied system:
no talk of works *at first;* or at any moment which throws us back upon the sense
of the first. Cotton might as well have said: it is the genius of our system—don't
you see?—not ever to put works in a place of emphasis, particularly one that allows everything else to stand or fall.

Indeed, when he repeats, somewhat later, his crucial phrase about "the glory
of grace" (127), it will be in a context which again begs the elders not to adopt a
position so close to the Reformed Catholicism of Bellarmine. But surely they can
see the (ideal) point without the (political) threat: proving faith by works sounds
worksy. And so it may fairly be added that "when God acknowledgeth a good
work and speaketh comfort to it," he nevertheless directs a man to look for the
blessing and the comfort "not in the things themselves but in Christ" (112). A nice
point, perhaps, but what is the excuse of New England except to enact an epitome
of Reformed intelligence?

Subsiding for the moment, Cotton's twelfth rejoinder returns to the implication that many souls may *need* to prove their grace by their sanctification when
their "justification lyeth prostrate." First the quiet repetition: while I "cannot believe that my person is accepted in justification, I cannot believe that my works
are accepted." And then a reality check: we are to remember the difference between the "man that never saw his justification by any light of God's spirit" and
the one who has "sometimes seen it by the witness of the spirit . . . though now it
be hidden" (112): the sight of sanctification may help the latter but can in no way
assist the former; and even here the surer comfort is "not so much . . . to show
them the working of their sanctification within them, as to discover the face of
God." Suppose that "by chaffing the soul in a swoon you might revive the same
heat and life that was in him," still

> he will never be convinced to see life in his sanctification, till he see life in
> his justifying faith, which is that that putteth life and truth into his sanc-
> tification: he will ever fear that without faith his best works of sanctifica-
> tion are but *splendida pecccata,* goodly glistering beautiful sins. (113)

Or if we cannot in fact predict, beyond the energetic pursuit of virtue, this zero
degree of Protestant sophistication in our well-instructed population, then where

indeed have we so splendidly come? Is the end of our godly letters but to furnish a figure for Poe's "Ligeia"?

The argument is not that "justification should be first seen because it first is" but that "we cannot see our sanctification accepted" until we see it "quickened" (114). Nor does this sight require that *ultimate* revealing of the Spirit's "own work" but only in "applying Christ's works of ease and refreshing and child-like liberty to the soul" (115–16). Primitive comfort, that is to say, is nothing like knowledge to the power of conscious divine co-presence but "only"—if one dare risk offending the elders—the joyous insight that Christ has made salvation free. And how could one realize just this in the performance of a work?

———

The longest section of the "Rejoinder," number thirteen, seeks to answer the objections made to the "Propositions" into which Cotton had first thought to settle the question of who may be "going on in a covenant of works" (52). The process takes time and involves repetition, yet Cotton gathers confidence as he goes, and by the end of this essay he is once again singing his highest note—not just teaching a technical lesson to fellow professionals, but prophesying in a voice that can no longer repress its astonishment that so much latter-day Calvinism has come to rest in an emphasis that allows an emphasis on works even to arise.

Not without reason, perhaps, the elders suspect that Cotton's preaching of assurance by spiritual witness is being taken—by the enthusiastic, or the unwary, or the carnal—as a dismissal of the need for Christian virtue in some new Protestant order. And Cotton is doing what he can to reassure them. But he has his own fear, namely, that the faith of "too many professors" is not grounded "upon the righteousness of Christ nor upon the free promise of grace wherein that righteousness is applied to us, but only upon their own works." Which is certainly the case, as he continues to argue—with an energy that overrides the distraction of numbered answers to numbered objections—so long as men can produce "*only* the evidence of sanctification" (116; my emphasis). Once again Calvin is explicit: works are but a *posterior probatio accedere instar signi,* an afterproof, added ("accidentally," one is tempted to translate) as a sign.[35] The Publican (Luke 18) saw only "his corruption, and yet went home justified" (117). The text does not say he *saw* that justification, in the self-deprecation that Scripture counts to him as faith; but if and when he came to see such a thing, it had to have been in "something before" his sanctification (118). For when sanctification does indeed add to assurance, it is only by "the sight of God's free love revealed in it by his Spirit" (119).

And if the question concerns a consistency among the "Reverend Brethren," then hear one of their own "pithy expressions": "if a man holds forth rich treasure and cannot give account how he came by it, it is a shrewd sign either the treasure is counterfeit, or else he stole it" (120). Cotton names no names, but he feels free to appropriate and to complicate Shepard's own vigorously Protestant emphasis: the man who can offer *only* works in support of his sainthood evidently has no idea "how he came by his sanctification" (119). Yet Cotton has not meant, any more than Shepard himself, to "beat men off from the use of holy duties" but only to prevent their abuse "even in honest minds" which may, in their love affair with virtue, forget Calvin's teaching that "the right of all the promises" depends not at all "upon the performance of duties . . . but . . . wholly upon our union with Christ" (121); or which may turn not to Christ but to duties for their "comforts and enlargements," as Abraham once "looked for no other blessed seed than in the face of Ishmael" (122). To disallow a man's "betaking" himself to duties is not to discourage their "frequent and diligent use" but only to forbid a seeking the promise or a resting therein. Surely it is right and just for Protestants to remember that Christ himself is the "way" (123).

Readily accepting Calvin's *"posterior probatio"*—when the "witness of the Spirit in the promise of free grace hath gone before it"—Cotton continues to "beseech" the elders to think of it as a "divine testimony . . . only as it shall please the Spirit of God to bear witness in it" (125); our works are "but works" until we "discern . . . the light of the Spirit breathing" (126) in them. And if Cotton is lowering the threshold of what counts as a "going aside" to the Hagar of an outmoded covenant, his reasons are well considered; for in the arena of righteousness, God can look to the *perfect* righteousness of Christ only; and in declaring "his righteousness to be ours out of his Grace, then he will not declare it to us in the holiness of our works, nor in the promises made thereto" (127). Amongst all this familiar high-mindedness, the emphasis has to fall on the declaration *to us,* who are to take the mood of our salvation from the spirit in which God gives it; and so Cotton appeals again to his deepest conviction:

> It is the glory of Grace to dash all works out of countenance when the Lord sitteth upon a throne of Grace. . . . When the Lord declareth himself pacified to the soul . . . , he doth not bring our sanctification but our sins to remembrance, that we may be ashamed and confounded and never open our mouths any more. (127)

By God—the insight has to appear—I am saved in spite of my sin. Know this first, and the after-proof of works can take care of itself.

Nor will it do to imagine sanctification as the way we come to see, at last, that Christ is the "end and bottom on whom the peace of our justification is settled and grounded." Not first, but secondary; and not the last thing either. We come to God, always, with "halters about our neck," never with "golden chains of righteousness." Christ alone is "the door to open both the light of God's countenance and all the gracious work of sanctification to us"; nor can we find Christ "the end and bottom of our peace, unless we find him first, as well as last; the first ground of our peace as well as the chief top and end of it" (129). Certainly all will agree that men should seek not only to see the face and hear the voice of Christ but also to feel his gracious work; yet to trust to "the feeling of our sanctification" is at best a "building of hay and stubble upon a golden foundation." And surely Calvin—"counted a Master Builder in his time"—knew no such "way of building" (130). Then, as the talk returns to the example of Hagar, the pace and the power of Cotton's rejoinder rise up again, from the necessity of point counter point, to one of those climaxes which tempts the bemused observer—seeming always to have known that Paul had undone so many—to reflect instead that Cotton may indeed have discovered the way a sufficiently intellectual Protestantism "ought" to go. Or at least how an adequately self-conscious Calvinism had better learn to sound: confident in its promotion of piety to the place both common sense and reason always accord to virtue; and glorying in the discovery that works must take a lower place in line.

First off, not Cotton but "the Apostle saith, Hagar was a type of the Law or covenant of works." Nor is it anything but "tautology" for the elders to concede that "to go aside to a covenant of works to seek to see the promised seed is a going aside to a covenant of works." What needs fuller discovery, surely, is that seeking "assurance of our justification . . . by our works of sanctification" is making "such a use of works as is peculiar to the covenant of works." Obviously, all Protestants teach justification "neither out of works nor out of grace to works"; cannot we also agree that the *assurance* of justification must fulfill the same luminous condition? Surely the Apostle offers Abraham "and his justification and his faith and the grounds of it as a pattern to us all"; and "certain it is that Christ was seen of Abraham in a free promise of grace without works" (132). The "way of the covenant of Grace," it appears, first and last, is to offer assurance and comfort "without *mention* of works" (132–33; my emphasis). With all due respect—but with patience wearing thin enough to obscure the question of who is questioning whom—what game are we supposed to be playing here?

We do not know exactly who started the nasty business of accusing certain ministers of teaching a covenant of works, but here at least, with the Calvinist laundry still indoors, Cotton has decided not to hold back.[36] If we all "disrelish so much the name of works," then must we not learn to "disrelish the thing it-self"?—to forgo, that is to say, "all mention of . . . works of sanctification and of promises made to such works as the grounds and means and ways of obtaining our first assurance of justification." The fine points of theology may be fine in-deed, and all are no doubt agreed to do no harm, but

> seeing we all profess (according to the intentions of our hearts) to hold forth Protestant doctrine, let us hold it forth in the language of Calvin and others our best Protestants, who speak of purity of life and growth in grace and all the works of sanctification as the effects and consequents of our assurance. (133)

Such, Cotton recalls, is exactly what Bellarmine "chargeth . . . upon Protestants," and what Pareus has acknowledged to be "true of our first assurance." If we would indeed "speak as Protestants," we ought to stop talking about "good works as causes" of that assurance.

Our system has, no doubt, certain practical and competitive disadvantages: it can neither flatter nor silently co-opt the common sense of the ordinary well-meaning person who, when accosted upon the matter, can usually be got to con-cede that one must follow the good because it is better than the bad. And possibly some pastors have imagined an easier time with the Souls of Puritan Folk if they made as much of works as sound doctrine might permit. But our "way" is simply otherwise—historically, Cotton observes, and esthetically, one almost hears him suggest. The very difference of our system is to be silent about works in all the crucial places. Doing as they must, cautious and skeptical men will argue, down the corridors of a faithless future, both sides of the question of "Calvin and Cove-nant."[37] Cannot we, for our part, learn at least to sound like ourselves?

You elders may wish, upon challenge, elaborately to "deny good works to be the grounds and causes of our assurance of faith," yet you maintain that "a man may gather his first assurance of his justified estate from his works of sanctifica-tion." And from this "it will unavoidably follow that our works are the grounds and causes of our first assurance." Must I read you the lesson in logic?

> Such things from which our first assurance doth arise, and before which it was not, they are the causes of our assurance. But you make good works such things from which our assurance ariseth, and before which it was not (at least in a good many Christians) and therefore you make causes of our assurance. (133)

Or is the needful teaching in the department of rhetoric? Or in the emergent and allied field of theopolitics? Seeing your position is "disallowed by the chief Protestant writers," do you imagine that a mere "change of words" will enable you to "hold it forth for Protestant doctrine, that we may gather our first assurance of justification from our sanctification"?

> Call you our good works what you please, whether sanctification or gifts of grace or saving graces (or any such like) yet seeing our good works are indeed the same thing, the point is rather worse than better, to clothe unwholesome and popish doctrine with Protestant and wholesome words. (134)

With no apology, this time, the gathering consensus of Massachusetts can be made to look a lot less purified than one had imagined. And perhaps there is yet some point in learning to call things by their right names.[38]

"Popish" is just a word, of course, and Shepard had learned to hate the Man of Sin with a fervor hard to feign. "Protestantism" too is just a word, and orthodoxy is exactly what the synods will decide. Unless somebody should become convinced that the protest could discover its fundamental difference from the infamous thing it meant to crush and to defend that difference as more than one more saying under the sun. "Puritan" is one word for the degrees of that conviction and, within the context of New England, Cotton is the man who, for one long moment, held out for a *strictly* Protestant understanding of the way salvation had to be discovered: not from the acts which did or did not fit the standard of saintly behavior, for this did in the end make the knowledge—and also the tone—of salvation depend on works; but on some other sort of knowledge, like the springing up in the soul of the conviction that divine rescue without regard to human works is not only revealed but is also simply true, as a structure and indeed a limit possibility of human experience. The rarity of this insight might make the Church of the Future somewhat less encompassing than the one which sprawled from Rome, regaled itself at Westminster, and slouched now toward Cambridge; but "Catholic" too was just a word, and what sense in any event could one make of a universal remnant? Protestants remove the intermediaries, it says in all our notes. They can afford to, Cotton would have us add, because they know the Spirit of God.

———

Of course, Cotton cannot end just there: the thirteenth rejoinder has two more propositions to run, and there were sixteen questions in all. Further, his concern for the future of New England will hardly let him call a name and walk away. But in the fifteen pages that remain, he returns, with some sense of aftermath and almost of literary structure, to the less prophetic business of sharpening the professional sense of Protestant propositions. As if he knew that God alone works reformation all at once.

The rejoinder to the reply to Cotton's fifth proposition wishes to emphasize that our "renewed knowledge" (134) of the insignificance of our works is not the same as the Spirit's positive witness to God's "free love" (135); and to appropriate the sunlight/starlight imagery of a certain "learned Country-man."[39] "True, when the sun is set, star light may yet appear; and so may the graces of God's Spirit in us, when the sunshine" of God's countenance be hid;

> but yet, as he that should only see stars in the sky and had never seen or known the sun rising could neither conclude there was a sun in the other hemisphere, nor that it will arise in this: But if he do conclude there is a sun in the other hemisphere, it is because he has seen it arising in our hemisphere heretofore. (138)

Plato to the rescue, one more time. And to the discovery that the stars are but other suns, the answer would be, "Ah, yes, for God's Spirit is ever one with itself."

Cotton's defense of his sixth proposition begins with a denial that he holds that, in the covenant of grace, "no man seeth any thing to evidence his good estate, or seeth what he doth see but by the immediate witness of the Spirit itself" (138). Troubled by the notion of a *secondary* witness, of works, that seems weaker than the primary one, of the Spirit's own assurance, the elders are still having their candle-and-sun problem. But Cotton remains convinced that justification and sanctification can each give "good evidence to the other" and accuses the elders of thinking that "he that seeth any thing evidently and clearly by daylight, he seeth nothing by star light or candle light." Wishing to imply that his system is both more temperate and more subtle than their emphasis on works as a cure for agitation, he can do no better than restate his definitive conviction about the Christian's primitive comfort:

> neither the word of God nor any work of grace wrought by the soul . . . can give clear evidence unto faith, either of our justification or sanctification unless the Spirit of God do give him a clear sight of his justification in a free promise of grace in Christ, and a clear sight of his sanctification in any promise whether absolute or conditional. (139)

To the elders' worry that Cotton's "Spirit" will drive every other consideration out of the market, Cotton proposes "only" that Protestants need God's potent presence at every point.

The point can seem "purist," but more is at issue than the insertion of the adjective "spiritual" here and there. What Cotton insists upon—as the proper emphasis of Protestantism as such—is that human assurance rests not upon moral regeneration but upon a lively sense of what Edwards will call the glory of God in the work of redemption. It is tempting to say that Cotton's position is more "subjective" than that of the elders, but we need to take seriously his constant reminder that works themselves are ambiguous and must be looked at therefore with discernment. And in a curious way it is the elders who, in their fatal fascination with doubtful cases, too close for conscience to call, have made the problem of assurance more "psychological."[40] The Spirit, Cotton seems everywhere to imply, is an insight, not a complex mental state.

Lacking Edwards' fascination with the affect of the "divine and supernatural light,"[41] Cotton never goes on to "portray" the Witness of the Spirit, even in its ordinary task of testifying to the work of Father and Son. His interest is epistemological, as we might say, and it expresses itself as a critique of comparative systems: what must Protestants hold if they are to be anything more than headstrong apostates? And in the prosecution of these interests he is no less loyal to Scripture than are the elders. So considered, the problem is somewhat circular: the Spirit must be thought to have some worldly expression which men may judge; but the expression of works must be more spiritual than worldly, making the judgment a little more arcane than it might first appear. From the point of our accomplished disinterest, the point might appear undecidable. But Cotton's choice reveals somewhat more than personal bias: Catholic Christianity having made its own rather messy attempt to save the world through a way of pious works and their corporate corruption, does it not remain the part of Reformation to start with the ordinary working of the Spirit and live with the risk of its possible inflation?

Yet as the elders require "proofs," Cotton will add what he can—leaving it to Emerson to protest the relation of "'arguments' . . . to any expression of a thought."[42] Surely we have it from God that it is "the office of the Spirit . . . to clear up all things pertaining to spiritual sight" (139). Then too, as our regeneration is admitted to be an altogether spiritual affair, its reality can be discerned "only by . . . comparing spiritual things with spiritual things" (140); and here, where the argument threatens to become adjectival merely, we do well to remember that the elders are in no position to identify the pun; the breath of Antinomianism invites moral caution, not Deconstruction. Nor can one leave out of account "the nature of faith," which "cannot rest upon any object but upon the Lord and his free grace . . . and this revealed to us in some divine testimony." Scripture is full to overflowing with God's own truths, "yet the application of them . . . is not of divine force"

> unless the Spirit breathe in them and apply them to me. And the works of sanctification in me, though they be the works of God . . . in me, yet created things they be, and divine faith they cannot work to assure me of the Lord's acceptance of such sanctification, unless the Spirit of God before witness to them that they are wrought in him and accepted by him of his free grace. (141)

To *me*—the authentic religious subject, modern vulgarity may think to add— Scripture is true, not upon the bare reading, but only if some hermeneutic grace assist. With works, the same: they are "but works," unless the Spirit lend both its power and its light. And if the Spirit at all, then surely the Spirit first. And who, touched by the Spirit, would talk so much of works?

Again, one is not to hold out for the Spirit to bear witness "to his own proper work" but only "such a concourse of the Spirit as he doth more ordinarily put forth in every of those testimonies . . . whereof John speaketh" (141). The Father creates and decrees, the Son offers himself as price for the elect, but the Spirit alone teaches these truths with power. One who understands this fact may continue to say that believers shall be saved (rather than that the saved shall believe), but they will know, all the while, that "till the Lord say to my soul my sins are pardoned, I cannot believe, or see myself to be justified; nor can I see myself sanctified . . . till I see Christ made . . . my wisdom, righteousness, sanctification, and redemption" (142). Surely the coming to see just that will make a cogent enough conversion narrative.[43] And "[i]f this kind of arguing seems uncouth and strange to us," then hear again, in these "perilous times" the language of "our soundest divines":

> The Lord must prevent us in every work of grace or else we shall not follow him. If we cannot love him but he must first love us, neither can we see ourselves loving him, till we see him first loving us. And yet seeing the Lord preventing us with his grace first, as we have first argued from his grace to us, to conclude our good estates towards him, so afterwards from the effects we may argue to the cause, and from our faith and sanctification argue to the Lord's justification of us, and to his salvation reserved for us in the heavens. (142)

"Prevent" in the sense of "anticipate" sounds not yet uncouth in the seventeenth century; and if Emerson's "Grace" cannot forget the protective outworks of his own "preventing God," surely the elders can recall both Calvin and their own first love.[44]

Three more rejoinders: conscientiously for Cotton, briefly for the present. The fourteenth rejoinder reaffirms the claim that "a Christian is more active after regeneration than before"—provided one understands that before regeneration "we are not active at all" (143) and that our regenerate good works never do stop requiring God's *immediate* assistance. Once more the (Pauline) question of identity: "not we but Christ [is] said to live in us" (144). Hearing such enthusiastic speech, civil men will wonder what outrage next; the faithful will repair to Augustine for the piety of self-denial. And again to Calvin: "'The Spirit of God who acts upon you is the helper of those who act'" (145). Always so, if the act be one a man would wish to own. And who would not prefer a dependent self to none at all?

The fifteenth rejoinder rescues the elders' "practical reasoning" by passing its logic through the magic glass of the Spirit:

He that repenteth and believeth the Gospel shall be saved[;]
But I repent and believe the Gospel[;]
Therefore I shall be saved (and consequently am justified)[.]

"The conclusion is safe if the minor proposition be true." And the minor proposition is true only "if the Gospel [has] been first published . . . and applied to that soul, not only by the outward ministry of the Word but by the Spirit of God himself" (148). Practical men need practical means, one hastens to grant; and not all have had the course in logic. But Protestantism has mysteries of its own. And "I believe" is always one of those. "Our own spirit" may bear witness until our cows come home, but it remains "unsafe" until, miracle of miracles, it finds a second in "the testimony of the Spirit of God" (149).

And to conclude this dialectical inquiry into the "spiritual" mystery at the heart of Protestant epistemology, Cotton modestly affirms that a saint will more properly "press the Lord for spiritual mercies by arguments drawn from his own . . . infirmities rather than from the graces of Christ in himself" (150). Wishing to valorize *both* these ways of reasoning with God, the elders claim it would be "easy to show" from Scripture that graces and infirmities may together decorate the piety of "many a Christian prayer." Cotton thinks he can afford to wait: "When I see your Induction, I hope God will keep me from shutting mine eyes against the light." For the time being, however, he has not often "observed the saints in Scripture to urge the Lord in their prayers by arguments from their graces." Unless one thinks of their "dealings . . . toward men." For there they do often plead "their righteous and gracious dealings . . . to provoke the Lord to take their part against unjust and undeserved requitals which they have found from man" (151). Which practice Cotton would here decline. But the sentence reads just as well as a final point of Protestant instruction: in the battle of flesh for pride of place with flesh, a person might say just anything; but as to those who take themselves to be "in Christ," let them remember that "He that glorieth, let him glory in the Lord." A rule of piety it takes a nerve to violate, no doubt. And a rule of discourse as well, so long as spiritual protest shall think to weigh its words.

Of course, the mere scholar cannot read the rule to those whose faith alone survives. But—Pastor or Pontiff—there must be fifty ways to leave and, except for questions of sex and offspring, none all that interesting. And to the question, What next? Cotton thinks there had better be a cogent answer. Would it be enough to see, in a moment, that election alone offers a convincing account of religious difference and then leave our works as prominent as ever? Even if this *could* reveal our status? Could we—in the midst of recovering the language of the Spirit[45]—ever be comfortable praying "Be merciful to me, O Lord, a regenerated worker"?

We can deny neither the historical facts nor the scholarly consensus: the elders will go on to win the war; anxious preparation and determined sanctification will become the dominant (if not quite the only) Orthodoxy in Massachusetts; and both preparation and sanctification will count as assurance.[46] So be it: men will save themselves however they can; and Protestantism is what the ministers will teach. But even at this distance, amidst the din of other discourse, it seems well to remember that great books get written for all sorts of reasons. Not that Cotton meant at all to help invent the canon of American letters. But only to suggest that the secret of religious comfort may be more primitive even than the logic of the Covenant. And to make the simple case that saints know God.

PART THREE

REVISION

CHAPTER EIGHT

WIVES AND LOVERS

Reaction and the Gender of Puritanism

I. SHEPARD'S VIRGINS

Where such things are thought to matter at all, John Norton usually gets credit for trying to heal the split between the Spirit-first theology of John Cotton and the less elite conditional-promise, comfort-of-sanctification emphasis of the majority of New England ministers. In James W. Jones' familiar-sounding simplification, the whole controversy had been about "the delicate balance between God's sovereign initiative and man's own role in the drama of conversion." Omnipresent and indefatigable, apparently, such formulations may serve so long as we recall that the problem is one more of discernment than of fact and is not properly limited to the realm of the preparatory. On this account, it becomes the task of Norton to explain the nature of faith as a "consequent condition," a duty the convert must (and is graciously enabled to) fulfill, in such a way that "God's election" (and not any human action) figured as "the only cause of justification."[1] A younger and more vigorous Cotton might have asked even this handpicked successor in what *spirit* one discerned the authenticity of the performance of this consequent condition, but perhaps age and isolation made him grateful for such allegiance as seemed available. And for their part, modern readers may notice that, as further "Calvinist" distinctions reveal themselves, the "limits of human ability" are not expanding that much.[2]

But the question of reconciliation or possible compromise would not be the only reason for wishing to add *The Orthodox Evangelist* (London, 1654) to the necessary canon of godly letters in New England. For here, in a book of about three hundred fifty pages, which know themselves to be somewhat more than a gathering of regular sermons—and with a scholastic determination barely suggested in the six propositions of Shepard's *Sincere Convert*—we get, with prefatory apologies from both Cotton and Norton himself, a "pithy" and "compacting"[3] representation of the multiform theological system supposed to underlie the entire project of preaching and hearing the Word in New England. Ames' *Marrow* done anew, in retrospect, with a full sense of assembled Protestant history and emergent New England occasion, for the spiritual nourishment of anyone grown up to the need for the "strong meat" of theology as they know it in the schools.[4] And those who would observe that any such (catechetical) ambition is far from what modern discernment understands by the "literary" should ask themselves whether the *Summa* of Aquinas—assuming they have read around in it—is not part of the "literature" of the Middle Ages. (A pun, perhaps, but what is not, where two or more are gathered together.)

But if Spenser really is, as they say, a better moral teacher than Aquinas, then it may be the better part of valor to name Shepard's more dramatic sequence of sermons on the "ten virgins" as the work which—along with the later portions of Winthrop's "Journal"—reveals the most inspired response to the Antinomian Crisis. For even as the men who invented that complex event must be understood to have first focused upon and been most deeply upset by the wayward emphases of John Cotton, they never were without the sense that Cotton had a notorious female disciple; that her response to Cotton might be significantly gendered; and that Cotton's teachings might themselves be a suitable spur to the awakening of "woman's wit." Where Hooker openly sponsored "holy violence" and Shepard closed with Christ as a "Husband" only after resisting the temptation to "run [his] head against walls," Cotton calmly urged the steady task of spiritual discernment. True, a man might learn to "run the commandments"; but this was quite different from defining all of life as warfare and, when you came down to it, wading and then swimming in grace remained the better figure. Then too Cotton seemed far readier than Shepard to entertain the "kiss upon kiss" of the Bridegroom whose "bare" manhood would make women of us all. It would require a couple more New England centuries—and a reading of Milton and the sound of feminization in a new key—to wring from Hawthorne the warning that "women's . . . morality is not exactly the material for masculine virtue";[5] but puritanic men might suspect as much, even in the first New England century.

Given the emergent concern of the Antinomian Controversy—to learn to say just the right thing about the place of sanctification in the unfolding experience of Protestant sainthood—it comes as no surprise that Shepard would turn at once to the task of instructing the members of his own congregation in the role of moral vigilance for all the time that might lie between the formation of "virgin churches" and the long-delayed (second) coming of the Heavenly Bridegroom; and the conclusion of *The Sound Believer* already indicates an interest in the biblical parable of the ten virgins as a powerful resource.[6] Subtler to suppose, perhaps, but predictable as well from the gendered subtext of that controversy is the fact that Shepard will try to appropriate (and thereby control) some of the "womanish" logic, perhaps even some of the sexiness, of Cotton's sweetly passive position. Going right on from the somewhat hurried, "sanctificationist"[7] ending of *The Sound Believer, The Parable of the Ten Virgins* strenuously reiterates the proposition that, over time, saints sustain the knowledge of themselves as such by the self-renewing vigor of their virtue and by their use of "means." Responding as well to the allure of a gendered holiness—of the sort feminist readers have detected in Jonathan Edwards[8]—it also seeks to redefine the entire love and marriage plot of Christ and the soul.

This it does in one bold stroke. Converted, long since, to Christ as his very own "Husband," and possessed, now, of his own amply covenanted congregation—a "virgin church," if there ever was one, constituted by the professions he recorded in his own hand[9]—Shepard now makes haste to stipulate and makes conscience to repeat that God's grand plot of the apocalyptic marriage is far from over. Espousal to Christ there may well have been, for all those admitted without hypocrisy to the most pure churches of New England, but "the last consummation of this happy marriage"[10] is not yet. Postponed indefinitely, yet awaited with inspired immediacy, the prospect of that momentous event must arouse a fervor of sanctified moral effort which only the dread of irony can keep Shepard from calling preparation once more. For so it most assuredly is, though set in a new key, with ghostlier demarcations, keener works. But even as the prose account teeters on the verge of this embarrassing metonym—Hooker forever, without the courage of his one-term system—a strong poetic turn comes magically to the rescue. True enough, some ring or other well adorns New England's saintly hand, but with love's last expectation thus delayed, what virgin soul would let herself turn sloven?

———

Though the latter pages of Shepard's "Autobiography" take some pleasure in the (English) publication of his *Sincere Convert* (1640) and *Sound Believer* (1645), there is no reason to suppose that *The Parable of the Ten Virgins* (1660) was conceived as anything other than a sequence of sermons—or "lectures"—carefully designed to meet the needs of New England, his own congregation and other gathered churches, whose members might also be feeling a little let down when the tremulous excitement of a transoceanic migration began to subside and, with it, the enthusiasm of the "revival" that marked the ministerial and saintly arrivals of the years 1633–35. Especially if that enthusiasm were still running high in one particular church.[11] Nor can we safely assume that Shepard knew in advance that he was embarking on a course of lectures that would take almost four years to complete; or run to over six hundred pages in any properly readable type; or that, through the editorial efforts of Jonathan Mitchell, his successor at Cambridge, his *Ten Virgins* would establish itself as *the* work which taught the generations of New England, beset by evidences of ordinariness, how to keep their personal history holy,[12] from a reduced but still urgent "now" until the denouement of God's elongated plot; as long as sacred time might require.

Yet irresistibly, almost, an imitative fallacy asserts itself: the length of Shepard's address to the question of how a God-converted and self-confessed saint might expect to live out the days left until the end of the world—or at least until his own more timely death—is less a function of the problem's intellectual demand than of the time it might take to intimate the sense of time it might take for the end-times in fact to end. Thoreauvian deliberation may shorten two years into one, and the optative mood reduce all experience to an eternal now; but elsewhere life is very long. And transcendence occurs only when some other, more linear plot has lost the power of its paradox: live in constant expectation of the end; world without end, amen. But if suspense is the sustaining trope of Shepard's *Ten Virgins,* its love theme appears early enough. Shepard's pastoral art competes with life for length of days. Criticism may abbreviate.

Seven more or less methodical chapters prepare us—if anything can—for the love song of Thomas Shepard Sr. The parable itself (Matthew xxv.1–33) must be recited, contextualized, and pointed in the direction of proper interpretation: at issue in the short story of those ten attendant women, five of whom do not bother to prepare to meet the advancing bridegroom and who are thus shut out of the marriage feast, is the solemn question of the end of the world, its state at that time (including the morale of the churches), and the rule we must follow to avoid the closing in our faces of joy's holy door. Marked "Nevermore." The watchword, so to speak, is "watchfulness." And that continuously: "continuance and perseverance in it from a prudent foresight of the coming of Christ" (14).[13] Simple enough, we may think: even Boy Scouts and Marines are "always" something or other. But consider the question from the point of view of the particular church and note, in this context, that the women in waiting "are all virgins; virgin professors"; and, as they all in fact take their lamps, "They were all awake and watchful for some time" (15). Denied at the outset, therefore, to an audience of visible saints, is the problem of the "openly profane, corrupt, and scandalous" others; to the contrary, the foolish are to be found within the very ranks of those already "awakened for some season out of carnal security; lively Christians, not preserving their chastity and purity merely in a way of works, but waiting for Christ in a covenant of grace" (16). Here we all are, gathered with pains from the corruptions of the world and into that "kingdom" we call the "particular church," professing our desire to meet the Bridegroom, and some of the enemy appear to be us.

Happy we are, of course, to be visibly so called, but heedful we must be of "pull[ing] down this kingdom." Ignorance of certain sins may do just that; so may "a spirit of self" (21); so may the failure to bring forth "the fruits of the kingdom" (22). And, as we turn from the (churchly) place of the parable to the (end) time of its reference, let it be understood, here in "the latter part of those last days" (24), that when the "churches of Christ . . . shall grow virgin churches—all visible saints—when all members seem to be espoused to Christ, yet there will be found desperate folly in some, and in time great security will fall upon all" (25–26). Not "polluted within or without with the evils of the world," yet so far only "espoused" to Christ, Matthew's decrypted virgins are such churches or members of churches "as are divorced from all other lovers, and matched only to Jesus Christ." Divorced, in general, from that "idolatry [that] is called whoredom in scripture" (27); and divorced, more particularly, from "lusts after . . . any creature" (28) and—as "God's greatest plot [is] . . . to advance his free grace"—"divorced from the law" as a source of Christian comfort (29–30). Torn away from these natural loves, "The soul now comes to be espoused to the Lord Jesus":

> The soul, beholding the glory of the Lord Jesus, makes choice of him, as in all marriage bonds there is a choice made; and, if love be great, there is little standing on terms—let me have him though I beg with him; so the soul sees such a suitableness in the Lord Jesus, as that it stands not on terms—let me have him, though in prison with him, though in the garden of agonies with him. (30)

"Terms" may yet appear, in some other context; nor will "law" be forever out of fashion; but here, at the outset, Shepard is determined to sound his highest Protestant note.

And also, it appears, his loveliest. Choice there must be, for this unreconstructed prophet of Calvinist activism, but a choice that quibbles not about its divine enabling but rather rushes headlong into union. And to prove that the soul behaves just "like one espoused to her husband"—and perhaps to challenge

Cotton on his own ground—Shepard cites Canticles, however briefly: "'I am my beloved's.'" "Servants," he then reminds us, "give work for their wages, and masters give wages for their work, but husbands and wives give themselves" (31). And only the anxious critic will notice that Shepard's enthusiasm may have run just a little ahead of itself; for biblical virgins only promise and are promised the ultimate self-giving.

Shepard's own caution takes a more conventional form—reminding us, in a first "Use," of the "great error" of those "who think that they may love and embrace the world and the Lord Jesus too" (32) and specifying, in the second Use, that those who "never shall have everlasting communion with the Lord" are identically "those that never were espoused to him," who may know themselves as those "never yet divorced from all others." Continuing caution, aimed at the discovery of Bible Whores in Virgin Churches, explores the "signs" of any continuing "love with any lust" and, more important, any unannulled marriage "to the law" (33). For here he cannot but stay and make a pause: "When I speak of not being married to the law instead of Christ, I do not hereby exempt your selves from obedience to the law after you are in Christ"; nor do "I speak against all evidencing your estates from conformity to the law" (36). Only rank Antinomians would openly do the one and only oversubtle casuists like Cotton "obscurely" hold forth the other. But it is the romance of orthodoxy to know that "obedience to the law done by the power of Christ" is an "evangelical" and not a "legal" work. At issue, clearly, is not moral relaxation but the Lord's own saving plot—to make men seek salvation "out of themselves in another" (37). Let them fear, therefore, who cheer not in the presence of the Lord; or who mourn more "for want of grace . . . to remove sin" than "for want of Jesus Christ" (38); or who rejoice "more in a little they do than in all the Lord hath done" (39); or who perform their duty "to ease [their] conscience" (39); or who wear the law as "fig leaves" to cover "some lust" (40); or who fear to question their estate (41). All visible saints, that is to say, are but putative saints; those that are true will never fear, if only in silence, to pass their entrance test again.

Circumspect as well are the last of the chapters our emphasis has cast as preliminary. For all that has been said so far has also the (third) Use to persuade us "unto the love of Christ, and to be espoused to him." Have the outsiders, earnestly yet not quite faithfully in attendance, chosen not at all? Or have certain church members chosen amiss? Then choose again:

Is there no communion to be had with the Lord Jesus, unless virgins—unless espoused to him? O, therefore, here is a match for you; choose him, get your affections, if entangled, to come off if ensnared to any other thing, and set your hearts, bestow your love upon him. (41)

Readers of the "Autobiography" will recognize at once the anxious need to choose the Lord, again and again, as other loves appear and sadly pass beyond. But the need, we also observe, is general enough: some there be who "never yet loved the Lord Jesus, unless it be from the teeth outward"; others, doubtful souls, and known to pastors well enough, "have been striving . . . yet can not, to their own feeling," come all the way to love. Still others, lovers by their lights, find affections dried "and love is parched away" (42). Even here the test will tell: a visible saint is a proven saint until proven otherwise. Prove yourself again. Choose.

"Motives" abound. First of all, "the glory of the person": "Prince" of all the earth, appointed "Judge of quick and dead," "author of all the good" redemption knows; "everlasting wonderment of saints in heaven"; "delights and bosom love of God himself" (42–44). Consider too that such a one "makes love to thee": waive all doubts of heaven's "secret purpose"; the prophet speaks, as called upon to speak, the word of love to you, here, now. The love so made is "real love," "fervent, vehement, earnest love," "constant and continual" love, "pure love" (45–46)—love that will "set thee . . . in honor," "enrich thee," "counsel thee," "dwell with thee as a man must dwell with his wife," "rejoice in thee . . . as a bridegroom does over the bride," "comfort thee," "bear exceedingly with thee," and never on any account "part with thee" (47–48). Do you object that "If the Lord be so desirous of me, why doth he not overcome me?" Then hear again the activist theology of the *Sound Believer*: the Lord draws a soul by "cords of love"; and he requires thee to "get him" and then to "wait by faith on him to overcome thy heart" (49–50).

Beginning with the fourth Use of this doctrine of the love that is the soul of sanctification, chapter 7 is both quick and careful to remind us "to bring forth no spiritual act but from Christ, and for Christ"; for "if a woman bring forth children to any other but her own husband, that woman hath lost her chastity" (50). The point assumed—in deference to Cotton, as we may think—is that even the justified person does not perform the works of sanctification without *some* (debatable) form of spiritual assistance; and so, in point of lively practice, the saint will recognize himself as such in the sober recognition that Christ alone is glorified in man's performance.[14] And this in spite of the paradox that must be faced: on the one hand, "all men living nakedly, considered in themselves, have lost all power to any thing that is," in the final analysis, truly "good"; on the other hand, however, even the most "vile" of men are sometimes given a "power . . . to do many spiritual duties" (51). Note then the never-absent problem: as it is "most pleasing to man and agreeable to his nature to act only from himself" and because it is "so hard a thing to live upon another" (53), saint and natural man alike will be taking their virtue to be their very own, not realizing, in either case, that "all these works, though good in themselves, yet are most vile before the Lord" (54). Evidently the point will bear iteration: "the soul is to act wholly and only from the Lord Jesus Christ; and whatever fruits of love it shows to Christ, to bring them forth from Christ" (56). For only so, it appears, can one remain as strict a Calvinist after the fact of regeneration as before.

To be sure, there may be times when even the New England saint, not feeling Christ as his only motive, will have to perform his ordinary duties the best he humanly can; but what Sound Believer would think to take much self-satisfaction in that precise fact? Still, as the days of wonder dwindle down to the months and years of pious routine, it may be well to "consider of the *means* to act from Christ Jesus" (my emphasis). And where better to learn this consideration than from the pen of the man who has taken just this long, in Englands old and new, to discover, as the axis of his own turning, that "herein lies the skill and life of a Christian"? Shepard may wish the world to end—and Thy Kingdom come—quite as much as the adversary who would go on to inscribe that precise possibility.[15] But here, in the church that serves the town rewarded for its refusal to take up the ways of immediatism with the gift of Harvard College, Shepard has discovered the true malaise of the latter-day yet not quite end-time congregation: "Christ is full, and he is not for himself, but for those that want, and I come to Him when I want it, and yet I find no help; and hence many are brought to think either it is in vain to come to Christ, or else I have no faith in Christ" (59). Down in Connecticut, Brother Hooker may continue to preach preparation until, on some bright tomorrow, the soul will discover the authentic yesterday of his salvation. But Shepard's task is to theorize the entire space between Christ accepted and Christ realized. Glorification may be ecstasis, but Sanctification is a matter of means.

So we are to "Labor for a comprehending knowledge what is the love of Christ to thee," so that it shall be with us "as it is with women": "when the fullness of the husband's love is seen, it knits the heart invincibly to him, and makes her do any thing for him" (61). But while we reflect, with the astonished minister of *The Scarlet Letter,* on the "wondrous strength and generosity of a woman's heart,"[16] Shepard shows that New England's true interest is less to anticipate Hawthorne than to prevent Cotton; for in specification of a second means we are instructed not to content ourselves "with feeling a want of supply" but to "labor to feel a need of supply from the Lord Jesus" (63). Answered here, but not with overwhelming cogency, is Cotton's emphatic and reiterated teaching that I certainly may *not* "satisfy myself" with "such good desires, and hungerings and thirstings, and mournings after Christ as are in me."[17] But that spiritual satisfaction comes not indirectly and from some keenly perceived absence but uniquely from a Christ who is really present, there in the soul on purpose to satisfy all legitimate desires.

One could argue, at just this point, that Shepard's (slow) preparationism is simply a pausing to deal with the would-be saint one moment earlier than in Cotton's famous model of hunger and thirst *satisfied;* but that is merely to repeat the point that where Cotton calmly honors the accomplished Calvinist fact, Shepard is still struggling to find a language for proper Calvinist process. What Cotton opposes to the want or lack of assured spiritual satisfaction is God's wonderful filling up of the gnawingly empty human space: come to me, you that hunger and thirst, and *be satisfied;* and notice that satisfaction and assurance are identical. Shepard's rhetoric, taking the part of desperately hopeful but still insatiate Christian, flourishes in the space it opens between want and need: "many a Christian feels a want of grace from Christ" but feels no such "need of supply, so as he can not be without it." No wonder then that he "never finds supply, and wonders at it why it is so." Reprising the epistemology which in *The Sound Believer* made important distinctions among conviction, compunction, and humiliation, Shepard dares to imagine, here in New England, the virgin members who can say quite well what they obviously lack but do not feel, above all else, the need for that lack to be supplied from some magical source beyond the self. If only they did, then surely Christ would . . . For Shepard goes on to imagine Christ's own response: "I love you dearly, and I am content to give you any thing you need; but you do not need my grace, my Spirit, my presence; i.e., you feel not a need of it" (63). And he concludes this strategic section on "Means" with the discovery that, beyond the confession of evident lack, the keen affect of need—for supply from beyond the self—is "the great door at which Christ enters into the soul" (64–65). No end in itself, Shepard agrees with Cotton, it is the terminal stage of the soul's efficacious preparation: without which not; and *with* which the covenanted link with Christ's presence is most strongly forged.

Then, as if the last section of this tense and poised seventh chapter were less to summarize strict doctrine than to introduce typic imagery, Shepard warns his audience of visible saints to maintain the famous chastity of their virgin church in the face of all available temptations. No effectively converted person will experience that "spiritual defilement" which is the "forsaking of the husband, a total secret forsaking of Christ," but even true saints in virgin churches may slip into "neglect of private communion with him"—which is "whorishness in a wife." And who in New England has not experienced the "temptation to neglect private prayer and meditation, partly by want of room, partly by multitudes of businesses, and work, and cares hereabout, that being weary in the day, sleepy at night, busy in the morning" (65–66)? Of which homely subject Shepard promises more hereafter, but even now this unsettling question: "O beloved, have you such a husband as Christ in heaven, that loves thy looks, thy company, thy sighs, thy speeches, and will you neglect him thus?" "What!" he asks, sounding not a little like Edward Taylor trying to smell the perfume of Canticles, "no love?" For God's sake, O Virgins of New England, "Where are your hearts?" (66).

And besides this neglect, there is also love's competition, for virgins unfulfilled will be "bringing other lovers into the same bed"—worldly loves to vie with the one love beyond all others, especially here in New England where "most men have lost and sunk in their estates." Made "hungry and greedy" by want, a man sees "what he may gain by his labor of many acres, by his goats and cattle, in so many years," and so "casts himself into the world." Not daring to forsake Christ utterly, this halfhearted worldling must have his "corn, commodities, cattle . . . in the [same] bed with Christ" (66–67). Continuing in this same vein, familiar since Bradford, Shepard names also the "decaying in love to those whom Christ loves," namely, "his saints," as yet another form of "secret defilement." And he ends the long prelude to his latter-day theme of wives and lovers with the sharp reminder that those found "not greatly caring for posterity, that they may know and serve this God," is the spiritual equivalent of "letting a new generation of harlots into Christ's bosom" (67).

Were this all, there would be plenty of reason to wonder why Shepard is at pains to extend the love-and-marriage implication of his "virgin" material in every possible direction. But his main discovery is yet to be made, and we cannot read its sexual revisionism without the sense that Shepard is trying to one-up someone: to wrest the discourse of sexuality away from the proponents of an immediate, all-consuming, all-disrupting knowledge of God and wed it indissolubly to the cause of ordinary, prudential human behavior. For if even the veriest saints in this latter-day world are not to expect the consummation of their well-contracted marriage to Christ until his Second and more literal Coming, then— as all the chaste virgins of New England might plainly see—Cotton and his entire party of first hungering but then satiated holy lovers have surely been guilty of premature something-or-other.

———

Coming at last to the point which circumspection and suppleness of system have delayed, Shepard begins his raid on the storehouse of mysticism's favored language not with fleshly figure but with hermeneutic apology, deferred from the outset to the critical moment of a treatise only beginning to be, in the words of its most reverent editor, "somewhat lengthy."[18] Only at this moment of truth, that is to say, does Shepard bother to remind us that "much dispute is made," by popish interpreters and others, about the exact symbolic meaning of the well-worn lamps and oil and vessels; and to take the conscientious revisionist's modest credit for discovering "somewhat else more plainly and principally intended," of which other divines give only the barest hint, namely, "that by the lighted lamps and the taking of them is meant nothing else but the readiness of the churches to meet and to have fellowship with the Lord Jesus" (68).

Just so, he suggests, would the Lord "teach his people watchfulness" and "put them to a narrow search of themselves." For consider that he borrows a "similitude" from the

> custom of those times wherein their marriages were celebrated in the night; and hence the virgins (the only children of the bride chamber . . .) being to walk out in the night, took their lamps; and when they had kindled their lamps (usually the last thing that is done), now they are ready to go out. (68–69)

As if the Lord of love and of language had said to all that had ears to hear: all else in the world being performed and in readiness, light up the lamps of your virtuous love, ye virgin churches, and all ye that are duly congregated therein, and go forth to await the coming back to earth of your Lord and Savior, which shall be the consummation of a marriage with the very Husband of your virgin Soul. From such an understanding one readily raises the doctrine "That all those that are espoused unto Christ ought to be in a constant and continual readiness to meet Christ, and to have immediate communion with Christ" (69).

Do but consider the lit-up and glowing terms in which that communion ought fitly to occur. If to Thomas Hooker had fallen the commonsense task of insisting that Christ's initial converting appearance could hardly be expected to occur in a soul unprepared—as if a sovereign were to enter a house of squalor, or if a precious liquid were to be poured into a vessel not yet empty of its own vile contents—it remained to Thomas Shepard to insist that even the most consciously self-confessed saints had to bend all virtuous attempts to prepare for Christ's final and more literal coming. And to remind just such persons that, though both they and the earth might grow old in the waiting, there really was no other event left to expect; and no way to prepare for it except to burn with the gemlike flame of holy duty. But if Shepard's logic reflects the decorum of Hooker, the import of his language suggests more than the tropic inventions of that homely sage. Reaching past Cotton, who urged his charges not to be afraid to speak of earthly revelations, and who evoked those (elsewhere) as a few light kisses,[19] Shepard dares to grasp for the entire meaning of the typology of human sexuality. Why not, his revisionist instinct might have thought, for had he not set himself the task of explicating the connection between the soul's redeeming experience and its final earthly end?

And why not, again, if the entire argument could be made to sound like nothing but the frank observation of the most natural of men?

> A woman may be espoused to another, and yet she may be sometimes not ready to meet him; her foul apparel is on. So here, therefore, it is not enough to be espoused unto Christ but, being espoused, now you ought to be in a continual readiness to clasp the Lord in your arms, and to lay your heads in his bosom. (69)

In point of popular fact, the modern reader may have learned the same lesson already, in a more modern form, from a rather more secular source:

> Hey, little girl, better wear somethin' pretty,
> Somethin' you'd wear to go to the city;

Not the city of God, to be sure, and *surely* the jingle of modern romance owes little enough to the ardent preaching of Thomas Shepard; but what our two poetic observers share in common is the belief that the female soul must avoid a familiar error:

> Don't think because there's a ring on your finger
> You needn't try anymore.

No romantic, Thomas Shepard shows none of Burt Bacharach's concern that "Day after day, there are girls at the office," yet the very same (puritanic) knowledge that "Men will always be men" has already led him to lament the possibility that the alliterating loves of "corn, commodities, [and] cattle" might come to co-occupy the marriage bed with Christ. And both prophets press home the same urgent theme: the husband approaching, it's "time to get ready for love."

Yet what is nothing more than romantic counterfeminism in a trivial modern ballad is a strong theological stroke for Thomas Shepard. The visible saint of New England's virgin church, espoused to Christ as surely as anyone on earth can ever be, is just that, named and claimed by promises made and (with God's help) accepted, but not yet gathered up into arms of love. Perhaps we are to understand Shepard's "espousal" as what modern practice calls "engagement." The substitution will work so long as we remind ourselves that the act of becoming "affianced" was once taken with a much more nearly unbreakable seriousness than in our own world of falling in and out of love and climbing in and out of bed; the ring on the finger signifies a promise unbearable to break, but the night of bliss is still a wish and not a fact. Or maybe Shepard means that New England's virgin soul is married all simply: vows have been made and witnessed, and these are, on the side of the heavenly bridegroom at least, the very type and model of all lesser fidelity. Still, the point is the same. Something essential is still to occur: that very consummation without which no marriage, real or figurative—assuming that we, in the wake of Saint Paul and Jonathan Edwards, essay to decide which is which—can be said to be complete and indissoluble. Has the visible saint of New England thought it much to have answered *yes* to the urgent proposal of Christ through his ministry? Or to have the authenticity of his conversion witnessed by a chorus of those in whom Christ has created a mind of the same spirit? Stay with Shepard this day and learn what more is to be expected and also, more modestly, how to prepare.

Certainly a soul is *un*prepared for the long-delayed yet always imminent return of the heavenly bridegroom when given up to "strong fears and jealousies, and damping doubts of the love of Christ to him" (70). Or, more to the purpose of the prevailing figure, when it lacks "affections suitable to the majesty, and according to the worth and love of the Lord Jesus":

> Suppose a woman knows her husband's love; yet if she have lost her love to him, or if she love him, it is only as she loves another man, not according to the worth of her husband's person, or the greatness of his love. Is she fit now to appear before him, when no heart to receive him? (71)

Again, New England, "where is your heart?" Have you not in fact "lost your love, your first love, or second love?" And if you have love indeed, "is it not divided to other things, as wife, child, friends, hopes of provision for them, and too much care hereupon for that?" (71–72). Or, with less poignantly personal undertones, the soul is unprepared when, though with "some inward love to Christ," it yet "neglects and has no heart to do the work of Christ." Or when having done its work, it "grows puffed up with it" (72–73), for sanctification is never to be seen as satisfaction in our own moral accomplishments; and so a Christian cannot be said to be "ready for the Lord" until he is as ready as Cotton's own conscience might wish "to give all to free grace, and to adore that" (74).

Shepard calls his next emphatic point a "Reason," but it is also a chance to display once more the confidence he feels in his ability to envision the end-time expectation according to his analogy of espousal and consummation: a woman *not* set apart to be the consort of a prince may "go how she will, and do what she will"; but "she that is chosen to be next unto him" is never to plead that "she has so much business to do, and so many friends to speak with, that she can not make herself ready" (75). For a Use we are to observe the

> great unkindness of many a soul immediately after his espousing to Jesus
> Christ, who, having once given himself to Christ, and received comfort
> thereby, presently grows more careless than before he was matched unto
> the Lord Jesus, who should now stand in a holy watchfulness and readi-
> ness to receive Christ. (76)

"Wives," that is to say, "should always be lovers too." To which Shepard can think to add only that holy lovers will know themselves as watchers—watchers for the end they profess so ardently to desire and watchers after the standards of their be-havior in the long meanwhile.

Next, Shepard devotes a long chapter to a series of "Exhortations" to "all those especially that the Lord has espoused to himself" (77). Each exhortation is pressed by its own set of timely (but ultimately answerable) "Objections"; and each of these evokes a series of "Means" by which the once-eager yet now dis-tracted New England soul may learn to live out the suspense of waiting. And though the message is variously expressed, responding plausibly enough to a range of questions or complaints, the pressure of a single, overriding message is impossible to miss: after the moment of being matched to Christ, but before the moment of union, the only way for the soul of the saint to sustain the knowledge of itself as such is to go on, rejoicingly, in the saintly life; to express (if not to prove) its justification—whether known at first or not[20]—by the fervor of its de-termined sanctification.

The first exhortation is "to quicken up all those doubting, drooping, yet sin-cere hearts that much question the love of Christ to them, now to use all diligence to make [sure] their calling and election." Of course, it has to have been, on prem-ise of covenant, altogether "sure on Christ's part"; but Shepard admonishes the soul to "make it sure on your part too, else how can you be in a readiness to meet the Lord Jesus?" (77). Thus does sober pastoral observation confirm inspired poetic suspicion: someone is going to have to deal with the doubts certain to arise in the length of days "After the Surprising Conversions"—when those who have been "traders with the Lord long" and those who "have gray hairs on [their] heads" and are "near [their] graves" confess that in the end they "still doubt" (78). *Is* it true faith that has motivated all along the motions of their saintly life or only the mood of some curious moment long ago? And why, in Calvin's name, will some shepherd worry them to make their calling sure? Must they not wait "till the Spirit comes and speaks it?" Carefully, now, "It is true the Spirit only can do it; but yet the same Spirit that seals the elect, the same Spirit commands the elect not to sit idle and dream of the Spirit, but to use all diligence to make it sure." And again, "though there is an immediate witness of the Spirit of the love of Christ, yet it doth most usually and firstly witness by means" (78–79). Cotton's Calvin to the contrary notwithstanding.

And while on that subject, permit this pastor to "*give* you means, looking only to the Spirit of Christ to set them on"—and reminding your instructed scruples that

> Evangelical precepts have a power; for the gospel ministration of the Spirit consists not only of stories and promises, but commands, and the elect feel them. Hence carnal men under the law, yet pretending gospel, will profess the law is preached when [commanded] to any evangelical duty, because they feel not the power of the gospel, being not yet under it. (79)

Doing as commanded, therefore, he commands "a sad inquiry of . . . whether the Lord hath loved thee for his everlasting name's sake or no"; for if he has loved thee so, then

> as no good in thee moved him to love thee, so no sin . . . can quench that love; and if he hath manifested his love to be grounded on this, though but once, that same night when thou changest is not changed, but is still as dear to him, and ever before him to move him to love thee still. (79)

The perilous significance of this moment is heightened rather than obscured by the altogether uncustomary failure of syntax. Here, from his own imagination, is as far as we may go in Cotton's direction: recall, if you must, your (nighttime?) moment of High Protestant promise; well, trust it, and then get on with the main business of Christian love and obedience. Beware, in this regard, of building assurance from a "mingled covenant of works and grace" (81), imagining that "If I can believe in Christ, and perform universal obedience to all the commands of God, I shall be safe"; build, instead, "from your subjection to the second covenant." But remember, all the while, that though a Christian is "free from the law . . . as a covenant," he is "not free from it as a rule" (82) to which, from now until the end, he must always count himself strictly responsible.

Other "Means" abound: do not fear the worst if the Lord "hides his face, and departs sometimes from you; husbands remain so [even] when they depart, and leave the house for many a day"; and often a "Christian's purest and dearest love [often] appears in Christ's absence from him" (83). Remember always to "look to the tender-heartedness of the Lord Jesus," thereby thwarting that Satan who "presents him only in wrath" (84); learn to resist the fear that one's "faith" is simply a self-deception; and if none of this works, against "fears on fears, as wave on wave," look to see if there is not "some sin you . . . would give way to, if you had assurance of God's love." Or simply replay the central scene in the entire drama: "Bring thy heart to a strait, either to reject or receive him to be thine; he is offered to be King and Savior, and lord and husband" (86); choose again, as once before, in *The Sound Believer,* and let the act of choosing be the proof.

Yet even if the assurance of this reassurance were perfectly to endure, this confident subjectivity "is not all that which makes you ready for Christ"; one's love must be "set and fixed on him" (86). A little love, in time of affliction, falls well short of readiness: "your lamp is not yet in your hand" (87). Yet surely a proper ardor may be aroused by the lively awareness that Christ has "loved thee more than himself," loved thee "when he might have passed by thee" (88) and "although thou wrongest him," loved thee "in thy low estate"(89) and continues to love thee "constantly every moment" (90), with an "immeasurable love" from a place of "glory" (90–91), grieving "when any evil touches thee" (92), staying "not . . . long from thee" when he does depart; and—to bring the ample list to pointed conclusion—"He has from before all the worlds loved thee, when no reason for it" (93). The slow learner may ask the "Question": "How shall I come," in any answering sense, "thus to love the Lord?" But the patient minister will provide the careful and familiar answer: "The Lord only can plant, can water this grace; yet because the Lord does it by means, I will give you some now."

    I. Labor to find out the true sweetness, and to taste the bitterness of the deceitful sweetness of all creatures . . . (93)

    II. Taste the all-sufficiency of the love of Christ. A woman that is not content with her husband's love, she will not love him as is fit . . . (94)

    III. See the Lord Jesus as he is, and in truth this were enough to make any profane heart love him . . . (95)

Suitably instructed in the means, therefore, be exhorted to "recover your love." And just in case the sticklers are listening, "the Lord help you so to do" (95).

Moving away from his moment of poetic resistance—not to Cotton's specific formulations so much as to the observed tenor and suspected effect of his distinct disemphasis on sanctification—Shepard exhorts his visibly espoused audience "to do the work of Christ, to be daily at it, and [the] finishing of it" (95). Life goes on, it appears, well past the point of (re)assurance. And—whether it prove further (re)assuring or not—it is *commanded* to do one's duty. Strive, therefore, with a will on premise changed "after conversion," against the infirmity that is the permanent condition of our nature and against "the remnant of malignity" (101) as well.[21] Work tirelessly, but work in a suitably Protestant spirit:

> After you have done your work be ever humble, and be ready to give the Lord the honor of his grace, that ever he gave any thing to you, that ever he did any thing by you; for the last end of all the elect, it is to admire and honor the riches of God's grace. (102)

For this reason only "the fall was permitted [for] never should grace have been seen, if sin and misery had not come in" (102). And hence it is, Shepard insists, with a list designed to fill up the space of orthodoxy, that "the Lord saves by faith, and justifies by faith, and seals by faith, . . . and sanctifies by faith, and glorifies by faith." Surely work that does but express the life of faith can in no way discredit the Calvinist principle that salvation "is of faith that it might be of grace" (103).

––––––––

There are, of course, more than five hundred pages remaining in Shepard's last great work of systematic preaching, and now as well as then a person of theological taste might wish to savor their religious sense. But as the attention span of even the ideal insomnia appears to have shortened up over the years, modern readers will perhaps satisfy themselves with a few generalizations in place of a patient analytic summary—justified, perhaps, by the fact that we are now past the moment of surprising redefinition and into a region of predictable implication. As the weeks of the *Ten Virgins* pass into years, Shepard rehearses once again, though with a new urgency, his definitive sense that though faith is indeed an encounter with the Spirit, it is by no means a passive experience and that saintly assurance depends on the maintaining of an *active,* indeed an energetic Calvinism every step of the way. That work (re)done, he feels free to follow the lines and the logic of his parable until the End.

Chapter 10 returns us, briefly, to the love-and-marriage basis of Shepard's "take" on the Virgins. The "bridegroom" mentioned is indeed "the Lord Jesus Christ" (111), and "the object to which faith chiefly looks, and closeth with, is the person" of this same Lord. Eager here to agree with Cotton,[22] Shepard labors to make his point emphatic:

> It is the bridegroom himself that the virgins chiefly have to do withal; they are espoused to him as in a marriage; there is a giving of themselves one unto another; they make themselves ready for him, they go out to meet him. It is him they love, it is him they want, it is him they look for, it is him they close withal. (113)

A later state of religious taste might find this dwelling on the *person* of Christ a "noxious exaggeration,"[23]—not to say a source of gender confusion—but Shepard's old-time interest is to deny that saints choose Christ for the benefits. And in this cause his trust in the epistemology of the bourgeois marriage seems boundless: "Whorish lovers look not after him, but his; his peace to comfort them when in horror and fear, his mercy to save them from eternal flames; but virgins look to *him*" (113; my emphasis). So it is that Christ often keeps his own without the "spiritual blessings" they so desire—"that they might close with and be contented with the person of the Son" (115).

The possibility of such faithful closing depends, of course, on some real knowledge: "Did you ever see any espoused together that did not first see and know each other?" (120). And obviously this must be much more than knowledge "by report" or "from his works" (121) or from "the bare letter only of the word." Anxiously competing with Cotton—and happily anticipating Edwards—Shepard reminds us of the futility of giving "a blind man a description of the sun, or a tasteless man of honey" (122).[24] But though the "knowledge the saints have of Christ, it is not by bare word only, but also by the Spirit," this spiritual knowledge is merely initiatory: it must be followed by faithful works and, because even the saint's earthly knowledge of Christ is "as the knowledge of a thing in a glass" (123), it must never be confused with the consummate knowledge that comes in with end-time glory. Faith is, so to speak, an intimation of the final splendor, of which it is the duty of the saint constantly to anticipate, when "the Lord shall break out of heaven in such glory as shall amaze all the world" (124). Until then, one encompassing and undeniable exhortation to spiritual activity: "To close with the person of the Lord Jesus" (135), whose glory the Spirit reveals, in part, even now.

Will someone object, again, that "this is not a right course" because "we can not do it"? Then hear again the familiar answer: "the gospel has commands and entreaties wherewith Christ's Spirit goes to the elect"; the elect, that is to say, are precisely those who, sensing their own hopeless state of loss and having a glimpse of the glory of salvation in Christ, do, in some urgent now, actively respond to the Gospel call. And beyond that crucial moment, from now until the end, the "saints that have faith and power are quickened by the voice of the Son of God" (135). Only remember this: those who would "close with the person of the Lord Jesus" must truly feel the need—not just of comfort "but of his holy presence" (137). To become espoused, that is to say, is to accept, on the basis of a unique need, the proposal of Christ for his own bare beauty. And to wait for consummation, devoutly to be wished, as long as it may take for the divine lover to show himself again in person.[25]

Chapter 11 enforces the conviction that "true believers do with hope expect the second coming of Christ," that they indeed "go forth by hope and desire of him and his coming," implying that those "truly espoused to Christ, and made in any measure ready for Christ[,] . . . are no more of this world, but look out of it, and verily expect the second coming" (143). What they desire, among many other things, is that "their husband, at the marriage day, should take away [the] rags" of their own "vile bodies" and "make them like unto his glorious body" (149) and, in a figure Anne Bradstreet could appreciate and perhaps borrow, that they might exchange a "dunghill world" for their true "home" (151).[26] No wonder, then, in chapter 12, that true saints eagerly long for the "consummation of their marriage" (159). True, one may sin by a too simple despising of "this world" (161), but surely the greater temptation, even "in God's dearest saints," comes in the form of "their hungry lustings and dropsy desires after the sweet of the things of this world" (163). Hence "the great sin . . . of New England: Men come over hither for ordinances, and when they have them, neglect them" (169), preferring instead the rich opportunities of a new "this world." Cherish ordinances, therefore, as the instituted way to have earthly "fellowship" (171) with Christ and as an efficacious way to heighten the desire for that "perfect and immediate" (176) contact which is awaited.

Failures in this regard may point to the unhappy fact that "there are hypocrites in the best and purest churches" for, of the ten expectant virgins, "five were foolish." Not wishing "to wrack and torment parables," one is forced nevertheless to observe that though "a great part of them were sincere [yet] a great part of them were false" (13, 183). So it only makes sober sense to offer a chapter (14) "Containing a Discovery of Gospel Hypocrites" (191), giving this most evangelized audience the timely opportunity to search and try "whether you, or some of you, may not be evangelical hypocrites" (199). A rich list of "Signs" is produced, ending with the familiar "Antinomian" tendency "to cry for grace and Christ, and afterward grow licentious," living and lying "in the breach of the law" and taking specious "warrant . . . from the gospel" (203). Chapter 15 is as full as any disciple of Cotton could wish in "showing that there is a vast difference betwixt a sincere Christian and the closest hypocrite" (206),[27] confusing to many at first sight but easy enough to discern after the fact of a true conversion (207), and appearing well in the observation that "God's great plot" involves the sanctifying of his church, "by little and little here, until it 'appear without spot or wrinkle' at the last day" (208). Comfortably confuting Papists and Arminians alike, but declining to dispute the nicer questions of whether a work is required along with the word and the spirit in a man's "first com[ing] to know his estate" (216), and "whether the Spirit in the first or second place clears God's love," Shepard offers at last one practical certainty: "be sure you find out," as a definitive difference, "some work in you, that no hypocrite" can do (219).[28] Otherwise, all fine talk of the Spirit is surely a delusion.

Similarly, Shepard's scholasticism is forced to concede that, because conversion is in some important sense a kind of knowledge, there is an "Hypocrisy of the Heart" that "Proceeds from a Want of Saving Illumination in the Understanding" (16, 229). But he clearly understands that the cogency of his extended reading of the virgins parable—and indeed the efficacy of his entire ministry—rests on a correlative proposition in the practical or moral order, namely, that by and large and on the whole and in the end "Hypocrites Discover Themselves in an Ineffectual Use of the Means of Grace" (17, 238). And this is to say that, although the elongation of this vivid and resourceful sermon sequence involves Shepard in a fairly energetic attempt to meet and answer Cotton's "Rejoinder" in terms of the epistemology that underlies its reading of Scripture, its main thrust, determined by the sort of spiritual experience that made Shepard an inspired reader of his chosen text, is to offer professed New England saints a way to think of themselves in the long aftermath of their conversion (or perhaps their migration) experience. "Sanctification"—the last thing before glory itself—is the only way.

No doubt it is the mark of a basically irenic nature that this principal term of recent controversy is hardly ever mentioned. But we see the shape of the concept everywhere. And thus it is that hypocrites discover themselves not in the lack of a lamp, or of sufficient oil therein to cause the bright burning of some temporary faith;

but oil they take not in their vessels, the only means to preserve their lamps from going out, that so they may meet the Lord, and not be shut out from the Lord, as at least these careless virgins were. Search the church for the present, search the records of past ages; many have desired and looked for the Lord, and yet have lost the Lord, their end. Why so? They never had hearts effectually to use and improve the means to that end, either outward or inward. (239)

The point is not only that a life of prayer and service is the only way to *verify* the authenticity of faith's terrible moment, whether of active choice or of a more passive insight; it is also, and perhaps primarily, that, when the celebration dies down, saints have to have something to do—if not to evidence then at least to express their sainthood. No doubt this sense of *working* toward the end is what Pastor Shepard missed in Cotton's Teacherly precision. Where Cotton wants the saintly life to begin in nothing but a (tender enough) experience of God's own Spirit, Shepard wishes it go on and to thrive upon a mounting desire for the final consummation of the mystical marriage between the Christ-espoused soul and its only proper lover.

The end of Cotton's teaching—against sanctification as first evidence—is the inspired knowledge of God's revealed design for salvation; its locus is that luminous, unpsychologized place he called the soul. In direct enough response to this, the end of Shepard's preaching—on behalf of an inspired use of the means— is the lighted and ever-growing desire for the soul's final consummation; its locus, now that the means have been puritanized, is the church. No wonder if these two prophets could never quite reconcile. And if it would become Cotton's more or less official scholarly task to work out the biblical arithmetic by which the dread last day of the world might be faithfully predicted,[29] it continued to be Shepard's zealously self-imposed duty—for some twenty-three more chapters and beyond that—to continue to prepare the distinctly female soul of saintly men and women for the climactic meeting with the husband whom they have by faith and by covenant espoused. Sanctification will be defended, implicitly, in the doctrine that God's Spirit resides in the saint as a principle of life and action, somewhat in the manner of "oil in the vessel" (19, 268); and again, explicitly and as such, as part of a new six-part morphology of the converted life, from first preparation to final glory (21, 302–51). But then the nineteen chapters of the second part of *The Parable of the Ten Virgins* return the emphasis to the existential problem of all those New England Virgins in Waiting: grace uneasily presumed, gratification in an event deferred.

Also, unfailingly, to the problem of making his parable teach that a sanctified use of the means come to seem the inevitable way to prepare for God's end-time caress. Beware of "carnal security" in "virgin churches" (370), creeping in "by degrees" (384), and constituting "the last sin of good and bad" (391)—predictable, given Christ's long "absence" (403), but nonetheless a sign of "the vileness of the hearts of men" (405). And, though Jeremiahs you have always with you, do not the ministers' Gospel warnings amount to "Christ's awakening cry before his coming" (409)? The coming is a "certainty" (416); so is a certain attendant "awakening" of the "sleeping Christians" (430), together with a hasty "trimming" of lamps and lives into the style of "holiness," which is of course the Christian's down payment on "glory" (437). Foolish virgins will ask for the loan or sale of oil, willing in this inevitable but repressed moment to pay any price, but there will be none then to be had. Would it not make sense, therefore, to avail oneself of "the plentiful dispensing of grace in the gospel ministry" (494) *now*? Nor should one affect to be scandalized when ministers preach that the Gospel makes faith a condition of salvation; or that "sanctification is an evidence of justification" (503). Specially enabled, faith remains a choice. And it admits of proof in practice.

Eventually—as a very long work shows signs of its own winding down—the Lord will come, "as a Bridegroom to his own": a man shall indeed experience "a personal meeting between his spouse and himself, as it is in a marriage." As in the typic event, "before the marriage is consummated," the bridegroom first "sends letters and tokens, but then he comes himself" (514). Observe this token. And prepare. Will you say the Lord must do this? Yes, but "he doth it by means"; and though only he can make you willing, it is the part of his ministers to announce that if there is "earnest suit on the one side," there must indeed be "consent on the other" (521). Look not for your name in Scripture, but answer the call if you find you can. And do so at once, for "Christ will not tarry when once his time is come" (526), for "None shall enjoy Christ hereafter, but those that are prepared here" (549). Prepared for espousal, if that is indeed the moment of some hesitant hearer. Or prepared for consummation, as the professed, but still doubting, Christian can feed his flickering flame only with the oil of the means: "Labor to be in readiness, awaken out of your sleep, and get your garments on, your loins girt, your vessels full, your lamps burning, that you may indeed be ready" (561). For know it: the door, wide open today, will one day be shut, leaving earnest entreaty of "the other virgins" to be answered with a sovereign "I know you not" (575, 588).

Wide open indeed?—the skeptic is bound to ask—though the gate is said to be *so* strait and though so many more are called than are chosen? Again the Calvinist crux: make explanation, one more time, or be still and let the chips of election fall where they may. To repeat, then, salvation "is offered universally to all wherever it comes, and therefore personally to every man"—to the elect "with the power of it effectually[,] . . . yet offered it is also unto those that never shall have God" (596). Those who are to have it are, identically, those who have the will to receive it, and cavils with the logic or the justice of this position can be allowed to embarrass neither the minister's commanded duty nor the saint's enabled will. Where the herald of the kingdom is instructed to issue the call as forcefully as possible, and the elect of God are commanded to leave off analysis and feel the force of that call, the parsing of sentences would seem a very bad sign. Edwards may demonstrate,[30] but the saint is given to know: you can if you will. Therefore I say, to the authentic religious "subject" that puritanic Calvinism exists to create, receive Christ "with thy whole heart" (599), and question not "God's secret decree of election" (600). You may say to our ministry, in honesty as well as in Calvinism, "I can not but resist." Well enough, yet "give us leave to exhort you to believe" (618); who knows but that God may help? But "what if . . . not?" Then remember the square one of our sovereign theology: "Thou art unworthy, thou art his clay, he may and will do what he will" (619).

But enough questioning. The task of all hopeful or professed members of our virgin churches—which do well to make their "diligent and narrow search and trial," thus to anticipate Christ's own "very strict search and examination of wise and foolish" (626)—is not to quibble but to "watch" (633). Watch "against security, and dead-heartedness[,] . . . slightness and shallowness," and watch for "the blessed appearing and glorious coming of Christ" (633). Espousal accomplished, consummation deferred, "You have nothing else to look for" (634). Knowing this, that the espoused lover has promised to return, and that with his return he brings the soul's completion, who will hesitate to pray "Come, Lord, come quickly" (635). Or—in the larger structure of the complex invitation— whose desire for final holiness will scruple to prepare with all possible works of sanctity?

II. WOMAN AS HUSBAND

The "antifeminism" of Winthrop's various accounts of the heresies and social irregularities of Anne Hutchinson should, at this date, surprise no one.[31] Not quite so overt as that of Edward Johnson, who spares no sensibility in informing his reader that, in the unhappy events of 1636 and following, "the weaker sex prevailed so far, that they set up a priest of their own profession and sex" and that in "abominably wresting the scriptures to their own destruction, this master-piece of woman's wit" was suitably abetted by "the sorcery of a second, who had much converse with the Devil by her own confession,"[32] Winthrop nevertheless begins his own more temperate account with the remark that this dangerous "erronist" was "a woman of a ready wit and bold spirit" (193). And though the *Journal* actually works hard to focus on the problems caused by Cotton, Wheelwright, and others—and emphasizes, above all else, the danger to public peace and good order—there are clear reminders along the way that Winthrop is by no means blind to the question of gender.[33]

Under his urgent sponsorship, New England's first Advisory Synod would declare that, though several women may meet

> to pray and edify one another, yet such a set assembly (as was then in practice at Boston) where sixty or more did meet every week, and one woman (in a prophetical way, by resolving questions of doctrine, and expounding scripture) took upon her the whole exercise, was agreed to be disorderly, and without rule. (234)

Evidently women might meet to discuss but not to hear any one of their number profess and expound. Certainly his own court did not wish "to discourse with those of your sex."[34] Nor is a certain implication of female stubbornness absent when, on the occasion of Hutchinson's church censure and excommunication, "she impudently persist[s] in her affirmation" (250) that doctrines credibly and repeatedly ascribed to her open teaching were none of her own. When Winthrop makes his devastating connection between Hutchinson and Mary Dyer, "notoriously infected with Mrs. Hutchinson's errors, and very censorious and troublesome (she being of a very proud spirit, and much addicted to revelations)," all semblance of neutrality disappears: no wonder if all sorts of "rank familist[s]" (253) should give birth to monsters. And, famously, this same sort of gender bias shames (if it does not quite vitiate) the elaboration Winthrop provides in his *Short Story of the Rise, Reign, and Ruin of the Antinomians, Familists, and Libertines.* So much so that the irregular sexual history of Hester Prynne can be said to begin just here.[35]

Equally worth recalling, however, is the generous evocation of female affect that animates Winthrop's "Model of Christian Charity"—redeeming it, one might almost suppose, from the otherwise oppressive hierarchy of its conservative politics. Saints love one another, on Winthrop's studied account, with a sort of redeemed self-love. Themselves renewed in the image of Christ, they recognize in other saints the very same Christ-self. The religious delimitation is cautious, of course, as befits the rescue of self-love of any sort, resting on a page-long treatise of the nature of Christ's mystical body; and the theological derivation is careful and explicit, requiring an account of the difference between Adam's original and our own recovered righteousness. But then, at the moment of rhetorical climax, the example is unconstrained, full to the point of overflow. The love between "the members of Christ"—each discerning, "by the work of the spirit, his own image and resemblance in another"—is like

> Adam when Eve was brought to him. She must have it one with herself. This is flesh of my flesh (saith she) and bone of my bone. She conceives a great delight in it, therefore she desires nearness and familiarity with it. She hath a great propensity to do it good and receives such content in it; as fearing the miscarriage of her beloved, she bestows it in the inmost closet of her heart. She will not endure that it shall want any good which she can give it. If by occasion she be withdrawn from the company of it, she is still looking toward the place where she left her beloved. If she hear it groan, she is with it presently. If she find it sad and disconsolate, she sighs and mourns with it. She has no such joy as to see her beloved merry and thriving. If she see it wronged, she cannot bear it without passion. She sets no bounds to her affections, nor hath any thought of reward. She finds recompense enough in the exercise of her love towards it.[36]

Deep problems lurk, of course, and some of them may be the kind that persuade historians to leave such metaphorical stuff out of their anthologies.[37] Nevertheless, the enthusiasm of this effusion is unmistakable—as if Winthrop himself had written, from conjugal memory, but on behalf of the theology of the feminized soul, Hawthorne's tribute to the "strength and generosity of a woman's heart."[38]

But where Dimmesdale has a real woman overtly in mind, Winthrop's passion is supposed to be allegorical. And just here we seem to encounter a small but fascinating confusion. Attentive students immediately notice the lack of gender consistency at the outset: consider Adam when Eve was presented; "she must have it." With only limited success does the canny instructor suggest that the antecedent of "she" may be the soul, identified in some texts as the excited speaker in the next line; the Puritan soul, they are always to remember—as in Thomas Shepard's conversion, for example—is always female in relation to Christ. No difference, their scrupulous gender training insists: Eve in particular or the soul in general, Winthrop has shifted to a female point of view. What he wants to say, apparently, is that Puritan saints are to love one another the way an awakened woman loves a man. The students may be right. In any event the passion of this moment throws an instructive light on those occasions, which had been accumulating earlier in the "Journal," when Winthrop absolutely insists that warring political factionalists have simply got to kiss and make up before any further discussion can proceed. And it is worth noting that this ideal vision of mutual affection—along with its recognizably "feminine" model of social problem solving—persists well into the latter days of Winthrop's experience of saintly disagreement.

Yet not until the very end. For along about the middle of Winthrop's second decade as representative magistrate and inside historian, even the least sympathetic reader can sense that the strain of a plausible but not well-informed opposition has begun to wear out his patience. Whatever our politics, it comes as a needful literary catharsis when Winthrop is finally driven to tell his freemen—who came into his polity in such a remarkable manner—exactly where to get off. They may be surprised to learn that the less lovely side of Winthrop's politics involves the sort of "contractual absolutism" that makes the Puritan state look more like Leviathan than Love-in. And they might not be flattered to hear their resistance to the necessity of contractual obedience compared to the restive spirit of a wayward woman. But the reader who recalls the political lesson of Anne Hutchinson will not be entirely unprepared for this critical turn. Had he said that there was something overflowingly female about the quality of saintly love? Well, perhaps he needed to add that a saint's obedience is exactly that of the lawfully wedded wife.

On our way to a discussion of that paragon of freedom by way of subjection, it may be well to review Winthrop's encounter with the woman whose behavior most noticeably crossed his own theory and most fully aroused his political anxiety. Perhaps the nineteenth-century editor was wise to insert a portion of Winthrop's *Short Story* of Hutchinson and related matters at precisely the point where Winthrop indicates, in November 1637, that a full account of the proceedings against the Antinomian party was "sent into England to be published there," so that "our godly friends might not be discouraged from coming to us" (242). Different audiences, he would seem to suggest, but the same unfolding text. And if the *Short Story,* then probably the records of the trials as well, since the two together constitute a subtext to Winthrop's journal-becoming-a-history. The loss will be to our sense that, delayed until 1644, the publication of the *Short Story* occurred on the very eve of Winthrop's appearance as courtroom defendant; and we may need to remind ourselves of this curious reminder. The gain, on the other hand, will be a realization of the extent to which Winthrop's developing sense of

the way government needed to function among the regenerate is itself the principal "text" of first-generation New England.

———

Winthrop cannot be held responsible for all the gynophobia discovered or created
by the need to examine, to judge, and to sentence a surprisingly resilient Anne
Hutchinson on two separate occasions—once before Winthrop's own general
court, where he was himself clearly in charge, and again before the elders of the
church of Boston where, among the laymen, he certainly enjoyed the position of
primus inter pares. But he certainly can be expected to have remarked the gendered lesson that he and his masculine counterparts caused to emerge; and to
have added that to whatever connubial memories may have inspired his estimate
of the way some ideal "she" may lovingly defer to and actively pursue the welfare
of her heart's best beloved. Women may be nature's model of redundant saintly
love, but they can also misbehave.

   The trial led by Winthrop—"The Examination of Mrs. Anne Hutchinson
at the Court at Newtown"—does not end well. "All but three" of the magistrates
agree that the offending woman is "unfit for our society" and deserves to be
"banished out of our liberties" (E, 347).[39] Puzzled by this outcome, Hutchinson
"desire[s] to know wherefore I am banished," and Winthrop, out of patience after
a long and not entirely successful battle with this "woman of a ready wit and bold
spirit," merely resounds the note of his own magistracy: "the court knows whereof
and is satisfied" (E, 348). We may wish to notice that Winthrop refers to the state
from which Mrs. Hutchinson is banished as "our liberties," and that this figure
may well anticipate the terms of the "Little Speech" of 1645: evidently her offense involves the misuse of something Christ has made peculiar to his saints. But
more than this Winthrop will not venture. Having worked hard to arrange a
consensus, Winthrop's abrupt conclusion merely registers his sense that the defendant has placed herself beyond the pale.[40]

   Without defending this peremptory expression of judicial discretion, one can
discover something of what Winthrop thought the court knew. Matters of doctrine, from whimsical habits of expression to settled and dangerous heresy—
though clearly of great interest to Winthrop—could be left for the church to
resolve. But when those same matters pitted saint against saint, church against
church, turning a fledgling utopia into the sort of sectarian battleground in which
any man (or woman) might start up an invidious discussion about which of their
established prophets had got mired in a covenant of works, then clearly it was

time for the state to intervene. A liberal democracy can wait for the drama of debate to play itself out; but a commonwealth of congregationalists is forced to act. The provoking occasion is the fact that, inspired by a duly elected Teacher or not, Hutchinson has made herself a danger to the end for which God discovered New England. Magistrates, competing for primacy among themselves, have been learning how to kiss and make up. But when the disturbance comes not from magisterial dissent but from public dissension—and even from private persons who challenge the prevailing public wisdom—the representatives of that public wisdom find themselves forced to take positions on questions they had hoped would never arise.

If irreconcilable differences over fundamental matters constituted the reason to hold an examination, the defendant's inability to deny or excuse her part in sponsoring or exacerbating those differences caused the judgment to go immitigably against her. Did she aid and abet the "seditious" behavior of her brother-in-law Wheelwright?—the tropes of whose fast-day sermon (as Winthrop duly noted)[41] carried the sense that physical warfare might be both necessary and welcome. A case could be made, one supposes, but the issue drops away. Could she, then, beyond the existence of a local "custom," produce a "rule" to cover the religious meetings regularly held at her house, right across the street from the watchful eyes of Winthrop, whether a woman ever edified a man or not? Could her lively biblical knowledge produce more or stronger rules than could his more stolid wit? Or could it even be decided which side actually bore the burden to produce the rule? It got embarrassing. But the charge that would not go away, the one to which two of the accusing six ministers eventually agreed to take their oath, was that at one time or another, whether in the full hearing of her considerable audience or for the ears only of certain dutifully inquiring witnesses, she had indeed "disparaged all our ministers in the land that they have preached a covenant of works, and only Mr. Cotton a covenant of grace" (E, 318).

Where Thomas Shepard remembered her to have said that he and his cohort "were not able ministers of the new testament" and that he himself was "not sealed" (E, 323–24), her witnesses contended that she said only that the New England ministry "did not preach a covenant of grace so clearly as Mr. Cotton did" (E, 333). But even that might have been enough: the seed of invidiousness had indeed been sown. Autonomy of the "particular church" was a root presumption of an entire tradition of "Non-Separating Congregationalism,"[42] but loving consensus was the higher law of Winthrop's Holy City. So that, even if Hutchinson had not gone on to ascribe her skill in the distinguishing of spirits to the tuition of an "immediate revelation" (E, 337), her fate might already have been decided. Winthrop was no doubt overcome with judicial relief at her reference to a private "miracle." And even if she had meant only a "special providence"—a possibility Cotton found himself unable to "bear witness against"—Winthrop knew he could speak for the majority in declaring that the "marvelous providence" of the matter lay in God's having caused the defendant "to lay open her self and the ground of all these disturbances to be by revelations" (E, 341). For in these latter days any individual claim to transcendent spiritual authority can appear only as a dangerous aberration. In Winthrop's view, "It overthrows all" (E, 343). But so too, we readily infer, does any publicized resistance to the church-state consensus that was beginning to look like a "constitution."

We can say, if we wish, that the case was so much the worse because the recognized leader of the increasingly noisy dissent was a woman. But no such charge could be brought against Wheelwright, who fared little better at the hands of the unfolding Puritan system of justice. Not even the fact that, as a woman, she did not hold the union card of a Cambridge education ever clearly surfaces as a disqualifying condition.[43] Indeed, Winthrop's court is almost as careful as is his journal to root out the public facts and to refrain as far as possible from the available *argumentum ad feminam*. Something about our sense of the situation keeps us nervously expecting that, anachronistically or not, the whole "woman question" is about to break out in full career. But for the moment it is the part of caution merely to record our suspicion of their suspicion: how like a woman to mistake personal charisma for divine inspiration, or to offer it in the place of suitable training.

On the other hand, the semblance of gender neutrality drops away in the church trial of Mrs. Hutchinson. Perhaps gender lies closer to theology than to politics. Or perhaps, because church discipline seems more like a matter that is all in the family, everyone was more willing to let out their deepest anxieties. Whatever the reason, an undertone of antifeminism is audible from very near the beginning of the proceedings. And before these religious men have done their judicial worst, they have not only revealed their deepest fear of woman's intellect but also concluded that an entire set of assertions about a higher form of divine grace and a rarer form of religious freedom can be conveniently described and written off as woman's wit.

The trial begins with a strong reminder of the problem of the personal, of which the gendered may be the extreme case: judicious church members will this day "be content to deny all relations of father, mother, sister, brother" (T, 350),[44] so to arrive at a verdict biased only by the love of God's own truth. The reader may wonder that Shepard—representing a church other than that of Boston—is the first to charge Mrs. Hutchinson; but she herself objects that Shepard and others who had come to her "in private," professing "in the sight of God that they did

not come to entrap or ensnare [her]" (T, 352), had in fact done exactly that. Usually appearing as a mild-mannered man, Shepard shows here a very short fuse:
never meaning to "entrap," his visits left her, always, with "some testimony . . .
against her opinions," which he "did not publish" until, "seeing . . . her willingness . . . to sow her seed in us that are but highway side and strangers," he finds it
necessary to declare "her a very dangerous woman" (T, 353). In fact, as the truth
must now be known, he finds her the bearer of "the vilest errors" ever brought
into the church (T, 354). The sowing of the seed may seem, for the moment, like
a touch of gender confusion, but clearly Shepard thinks there has been some failure to control the female tongue. He could have said "dangerous person."

The vile error is, of course, her "mortalism"—the belief that God can raise
up on the last day whomever his sovereignty may please but that the soul of man
is of itself no more immortal than the beasts of the field. The issue may seem unrelated to those of her civil trial—maligning the condition-mongering ministers
and their evidences—but in fact the doctrine of "resurrectionism," as opposed to
that of "immortalism," is a fairly traditional way of affirming that the Creator in
fact has all the power, all the true being, and of trimming thereby the prideful
creature down to size.[45] Surely this had been the Cotton-inspired tendency of her
various doctrines all along: conversion is when the Spirit witnesses Christ to the
soul, and the works of grace are more truly those of God's Spirit than our own.
And so here: "The Spirit is immortal indeed but prove that the soul is" (T, 355).
From this theology of the highest tone, however, Shepard has been ready to infer
the worst. Pastor Wilson is quick to agree: "if we deny the resurrection of the
body then let us turn Epicures. Let us eat and drink and do any thing, tomorrow
we shall die" (T, 357). And, with a dose of Cambridge learning, Davenport also
agrees: the question "was disputed . . . before Adrian," who rightly concluded
that those speaking "for the mortality of the soul speak most for licentiousness"
(T, 358).

When a second version of the mortalist question leads Davenport to propose that "the Spirit is not a third substance but the bent and inclination of the
soul" (T, 360), it becomes clear that twenty-first-century readers are not the only
ones who have got in a little over their heads. But rather than wait for a clarification, Bulkeley desires to know whether the woman on trial holds "that foul,
gross, filthy and abominable opinion held by the Familists, of the community of
women." Before Mrs. Hutchinson can quite answer, a modern editor hastens to
assure us that the sixteenth-century "Familists" were *incorrectly* "supposed to believe in 'free love.'" But neither that belated information nor her own "I hold it
not" is sufficient to prevent her examiners from pursuing their own sense of the
ugly implications of her abstruse belief. If she denies the resurrection of the body,

then she *must* believe that Christ is already resurrected in his saints; and if this, then, as there will be, after the resurrection, "no more marrying or giving in marriage," she must also hold that "marriage is past"; so that "if there be any union between man and woman it is not by marriage but in a way of community" (T, 362). It does not seem that these alert moral censors are trying to entrap her. It appears, rather, that she has wandered—conscientiously, but with the naïveté often ascribed to Cotton—into an area of doctrinal overdetermination that can only be called "Munster-panic."[46] Somewhere, someone must be just about ready to turn Protestantism into a "moral holiday."

But not in the Model City of John Winthrop, who enters the discussion to assure a protesting Hutchinson that "the Familists" do indeed "practice the thing" she says she abhors and that they point to her very text "to justify their abominable wickedness." Ergo, your doctrine is "a dangerous error"—so pernicious that Eliot imagines it may be "dangerous to dispute [it] so long in this congregation" (T, 362–63). To Davenport, her position implies "the overthrow of all religion" (T, 364), and Shepard warns all who may share Hutchinson's mortalist opinions that she who "hath often boasted of the guidance of God's Spirit" is in fact following "a spirit of delusion and error." How indeed can her church not censure and then "watch more narrowly over her for time to come," for she is "likely with her fluent tongue . . . to seduce . . . many, especially simple women of her own sex" (T, 365). One hopes that "women of her own sex" is a scribal tautology, but in any event the lapses of gender may be only implicitly sexual: thus far the convicted Familist—a libertine therefore—has seduced only female belief.

Mr. Savage protests that his mother-in-law is not in fact charged "for any heinous fact but only for opinion"; but Cotton, past master of figures that transform and then consume their own literal meaning, and determined to prove it a poor argument that will not work both ways, reminds the group that there are "errors as dangerous and of worse consequence than matters of practice can be" (T, 366). And so the Teacher proceeds, thanking others "for bringing to light what our selves have not been so ready to see in any of our members" (T, 369), blaming Hutchinson's children for holding too hard to a natural attachment, accusing next the "sisters" of the congregation of trusting too much in the word of a person from whom they appear to have received "much good" but who is after all "but a woman" (T, 370), and then admonishing the principal offender herself.

Beginning with a little history: rumored to have made some problematic declarations on shipboard, she nevertheless gave her Teacher "such satisfaction that after some little stay to your admission you were received in amongst us"; after which—for the truth of history demands it—you have been "an instrument of doing some good amongst us." "A sharp apprehension, a ready utterance and ability to express yourself in the cause of God," has made you able not only "to instruct your children and servants and to be helpful to your husband," but to prevent many from "building their good estate upon their own duties and performances." Damn right. And Cotton's own cause, we hardly need be reminded. But now, unhappily, all of this is undone, for the "evil of your opinions," here discovered, "doth outweigh all the good of your doings" (T, 371). For consider that "if the resurrection be past," then you cannot evade the "filthy sin of the community of women and all promiscuous . . . coming together of men and women without distinction or relation of marriage" (T, 371–72). Then, at the risk of blurring his point about errors "of worse consequence than matters of practice can be," the following "logical" but otherwise gratuitous prediction:

> And though I have not heard, neither do I think, you have been unfaithful to your husband in his marriage covenant, yet that will follow upon it, for it is the very argument that the Saducees bring to our Savior Christ against the resurrection: and that which the Anabaptists and Familists bring to prove the lawfulness of the common use of all women. (T, 372)

One sure way to start a lively rumor, it appears, is to deny what nobody has yet imagined.[47]

Conscientiously, it is hard to tell whether Cotton's prediction concerns Hutchinson's own future behavior or that of her followers, whose lapses from strict marital purity Winthrop's journal will follow so assiduously. With no thought of Hester Prynne, perhaps he means to say only that, strictly speaking, things imply things, whether John or Jonathan sees a crack in the wall or not. Yet he too has decided to follow the low road of ugly inference: tenets equal to the same thing are equal to each other. Interrupted by a protest from the object of admonition, he recalls that he has often "feared the height of [her] spirit," and finds it therefore "just with God thus to abase [her]," showing that what may look like the highest form of glorifying God turns out to be but a familiar way to "set an open door to all epicurism and libertinism": "What need we care what we speak, or do, here if our souls perish and die like beasts" (T, 372). Then, lest no stone go unthrown, Shepard concludes a first day of hearings by observing that the object of all this fury did "interrupt when she ought to have attended, with fear and trembling" (T, 373). As if to make her manner of bearing censure as heinous as the matter of her teaching. A suspicion which a second day's hearing will do much to confirm.

Or else the second occasion might come to look anticlimactic; for the list of charges contains much that is familiar from the civil examination, for example, that there are "no created graces in believers after union," that sanctification is "no evidence of a good estate," and that "we have no grace in our selves but all is in Christ," and so there is "no inherent righteousness in us" (T, 374–75). Appearing both contrite and better instructed, Hutchinson is willing to recognize many of her errors, but she is also able to object, when appropriate, "I never held any such thing" (T, 376). When Wilson wants to know why, at the last examination, she denied holding any of her really dangerous opinions before her imprisonment, she replies that she was led to speak rashly in the face of accusation, but not then and not ever was it in her heart "to slight any man but only that man should be kept in his own place and not set in the room of God." Having heard his own distinctive note, Cotton translates her answer as a confession of defiance out of the "pride of her spirit"; and as to her "slighting the ministers," he declares her "heartily sorry for it." But Shepard, who ought himself to recognize the high note of Protestantism, can hear only a shifting of the blame and so declares himself "wholly unsatisfied" (T, 377).

Eliot agrees that she is holding back, and Cotton, at some peril to his own emphasis, feels forced to ask if there was not a time when she held there were "no distinct graces inherent in us." Hutchinson pleads a misunderstanding of the word, but Shepard is sure "she did not only deny the word inherent, but denied the very thing itself" (T, 378)—denying, that is, that converting grace makes any difference in the moral capacity of the elect individual. Besides that, the discerning deputy is sure "her repentance is not in her countenance" (T, 379). Peters asserts that she has been widely heard to magnify the female prophet of the Isle of Ely, known to be "a dangerous woman." Then, as the chorus of condemnation increases, the often-slighted Wilson gets his own full say: surely the cause of her present distress is the clear fact of her "slighting of God's faithful ministers and contemning and crying down them as nobodies." Though she may protest "the setting up of men in the room of God," and though she may well esteem one or two established preachers, "our teacher and the like," evidently her controlling motive has been to set herself "in the room of God," that she might be "extolled and admired and followed after . . . and undertake to expound Scriptures, and to interpret other men's sayings and sermons after your mind." Therefore, precisely, God hath "left you to your self" (T, 380–81). And with that speech the subtext of personal resentment comes once more plainly to the surface: Wilson, in his home church—and Shepard, fairly representing the cause of religion abroad—have been publicly disrespected and, one gets the strong sense, effectively upstaged. And by a woman.

Sensing an opportune rush to judgment, Shepard is quick to declare no further need of witnesses. But Eliot, pedantically to our modern sense, tries to return the discussion to the area of formal doctrine, the question of whether real human virtue must follow as the "gifts" of redemption. Hutchinson protests that she never held her views on this matter different from "our Teacher," and Dudley himself recalls a time in the long and arduous history of Hutchinson examinations, when "she held nothing but what Mr. Cotton held" (T, 381). Thus we are back to those abstruse matters to which the Puritan Mind is inevitably drawn but which, with or without Perry Miller, it can never solve: salvation, all agree, begins as a forensic transaction in which the righteousness of Christ is "imputed" to certain elect humans, from whom nothing like righteousness can possibly be expected; but this imputation is accompanied by a sort of divine in-dwelling—which either makes it possible for the elect individual to begin a life of true virtue or is so transformative that regenerate acts are more properly ascribed to divinity itself. Social morality, on the one hand, God glorified, on the other. So fatal is the attraction to this fault line that not even Wilson, in full cry of personal vindication, can resist the chance to occupy his old ground once more: Hutchinson has affirmed it "dogmatically" that we have "no graces in us but only the righteousness of Christ imputed to us, and if there be any acting in us it is Christ only that acts." Nor can Richard Mather forbear to remind to Hutchinson that she once said "I live, but not I, but Jesus Christ lives in me" (T, 382). As if it were a crime to quote Paul.

Then a reversion and a climax—in which Mr. Peters not only names the tune they have been lowly humming but also boldly announces the entire set of metaphorical equivalences which Winthrop's "Little Speech" will both presume and deploy. Become better "grounded in your catechism," Mrs. Hutchinson; and consider

> that you have stepped out of your place; you have rather been a husband than a wife and a preacher than a hearer; and a magistrate than a subject. And so you have thought to carry all things in church and commonwealth as you would and have not been humbled for this. (T, 382–83)

For the moment the surprise is merely that a single set of parallel categories, founded in and never breaking free of some metaphysics of gender, can so perfectly summarize Hutchinson's transgressions of person, state, soul, and church. Nor will we be surprised to see that metaphysic endure. The shock will come when Winthrop finds he can make virtually the same place-of-a-woman speech to his freemen. Who are in fact all men.

But even as we turn away, from a door closing like fate, the men in charge go on to press the advantage they have assumed and then enacted—to the limit which both defines their world and advertises it as one we can scarcely imagine: can a woman so deluded and so active in the delusion of others be considered any longer a "visible saint"? That is to say: is the issue not further admonition but excommunication? Which will amount, in this case at least, to reversing the awesome decision which once recognized, in loving regard for the love by which the saints recognize their own, a coequal member of Christ's own body.

The story told in David Hall's brave anthology never outlives its surprise: the outburst of "antifeminism" is expected at every moment, but the final, catastrophic delivery "up to Satan" is largely unexpected. Yet it too seems a matter of discovery and not of malice aforethought. Winthrop thinks that, because so many "sisters of the congregation have builded on [the] experience" of Mrs. Hutchinson, it might be a good idea to have her declare the grounds of her own "good estate"—"if not by ingrafting into Christ Jesus," then what, for in her view "a man may be ingrafted into Christ Jesus and yet fall away." And Shepard, in what may be his least attractive moment,[48] not only seizes the moment, but declares the stakes already raised:

> You have not only to deal with a woman this day that holds diverse erroneous opinions but with one that never had any true grace in her heart and that by her own tenet. Yea this day she hath showed herself to be a notorious imposter; it is a trick of as notorious subtlety as ever was held in the church, to say there is no grace in the saints. (T, 383)

There could of course be churches made up entirely of persons marvelously convinced that God's grace—and hence the capacity of true virtue—is never truly "inherent" in their humanoid selves. One such might even be *this* church, if Cotton had been able to convince everyone of his own subtle system. But Winthrop, Shepard, and most of the Boston elders make a pretty strong combination. And so Shepard's own "trick"—of taking Hutchinson's minority opinion at its face value rather than its pious intent—quickly turns the collective attention to the question of "whether ever [Mrs. Hutchinson] was in a good estate." Not often, we have learned to notice, but now and then, praise God, a Gospel hypocrite really does discover herself.

Wilson takes time to "adore" the providence that has allowed Hutchinson to expose herself but hurries on to notice the more than suspicious fact that "there was much love and union and sweet agreement amongst us before she came, yet since, all union and love hath been broken and there hath been censurings and judgings and condemnings one of another." The reason can only be "the misgovernment of this woman's tongue" (T, 384). And so—as he rushes toward his own vindication—the church must judge "how safe it is to suffer so erroneous and so schismatical and so unsound a member amongst us." Consider

> whether we may longer suffer her to go on still in seducing to seduce and in deceiving to deceive and in lying to lie and in contemning authority and magistracy still to contemn. Therefore we should sin against God if we should not put away from us this so evil a woman, guilty of such foul evils. (T, 385)

Oliver declares himself surprised that the church could "have come thus far so soon." But while the modern reader is registering some such thought in himself—troublesome, yes; proud, perhaps; impolitic, most certainly; confused, now and then; but "evil"?—Eliot seconds the motion: Hutchinson has "carried on all her errors by lies, as that she held nothing but what Mr. Cotton did," and others so pretending have already been "cast out of our church." How else correct the earlier error of admission?

Now Cotton, whose range or change of motives we may never understand, hastens to step aside. Points of doctrine are his proper business, but this "point of practice . . . belongs to the pastor's office" (T, 385). Yet he takes time to observe that Hutchinson's "pride of heart is not healed" but is causing her, in fact, to lie about her views on inherent righteousness; and for this "lie," on the strength of which they once "received her in amongst [them]," they ought now to "remove her from [them]." Davenport recalls that "God will not bear with mixtures"—of lies with the truth or of self-exposed hypocrites in his church. A loyal brother-in-law, Richard Scott, thinks it "better to give her a little time to consider," since she is not yet "convinced of her lie," but Cotton doubts the usefulness of this in a "point of fact or practice" (T, 386). And Shepard, sensing the desire of many "to stay her excommunication," challenges them to notice the gravity of what they have all witnessed: is it really tolerable "for one not to drop a lie, but to make a lie, and to maintain a lie: and to do it in a day of humiliation, and in the sight of God, and such a congregation as this" (T, 386–87)? Would they carry the judgment in charity on forever?

Some fuss ensues, about how many admonitions make an excommunication, and some "stranger" wants to know whether the excommunication "be for doctrine or for her lie." Wilson, the ox of whose "conditionalist" doctrine has been gored as badly as any other, insists it be for both, but Cotton passes over this implicit challenge and agrees only that the proceeding occur "forthwith without delay." After all, "as soon as ever Annanias had told a lie, the church cast them out" (T, 387). Yet the long-embarrassed officer in charge of "practice" insists upon vindication as well as revenge:

> Forasmuch as you . . . have . . . troubled the church with your errors and have drawn away many a poor soul and have upheld your revelations; *and* forasmuch as you have made a lie, etc. Therefore in the name of our Lord Jesus Christ and in the name of the church I do not only pronounce you worthy to be cast out, but I do cast you out. (T, 388)

There are, as we have observed, more than fifty ways to leave your pastor. Still— speaking on behalf of those who know excommunication as that one thing with or without which everything else remains the same—the language is meant to be tough.

But even as we hear a dull man deliver a witty woman "up to Satan"—that she might "learn no more to blaspheme, to seduce, and to lie"—and even as we hear her commanded "as a leper to withdraw [her] self out of the congregation," we remember certain ironies in which outcasts have ample refuge: *et hereticos pertinent ad ecclesiam,* as we used to say at school. Even heretics have to do with the church, possibly even with the congregation. So too, one gathers, do women, as they get to be preachers and not just hearers of the word. Yet in the end this court *too* was "satisfied": she lied about her original position on "inherent graces"; and also perhaps about having disrespected Thomas Shepard. And judges at this distance may hesitate to decide whether her repentance was "true." She seems quite sincere asserting that only in her imprisonment did she learn that her spiritist doctrine of conversion-as-resurrection made her a Familist de facto. And what wonder if even a saint became confused about how a matchless divine gift may yet become "inherent."

But even with the causes gone, the reason would still remain: a woman, only gradually coming to estimate her sphere of influence, had overestimated the power of her words to undo the force of religion's commitment to its principal overdeterminations.[49] Clearly Cotton had tested the limits of the power of the doctrine of the Spirit to upset the ordinary logic of salvation, even in a community that prided itself on protest. But he allowed himself to be taught that Winthrop's Model of Charity meant holy consensus: he let his notion of the Spirit's "witness to its *own* work" become the special and not the normative standard of authentic spiritual experience. But Hutchinson, whether or not she went beyond either the letter or the spirit of his teaching, remained unwilling to let the subtler sense of salvation recede into New England's wondrous background of theological white noise. And, partly at least, because she was not a Cambridge-validated male, she could be held to a much higher standard of proof for her doctrine or her practice, if either of these seemed to cause a stir; and of renunciation as well, if she could not be taught quickly enough to say her piece in words which all might use. Mrs. Hutchinson was by all accounts a quick study. Just not quick enough. Had her message remained entirely orthodox—Cotton too accepts the evidence of sanctification, carefully considered—she might well have got away with acting like "a husband." Yet had her message been entirely orthodox, what had been the point? For surely her protest was not given in the name of protest itself.

That is to say: it is not quite correct to think of Hutchinson as a "feminist." One might argue, with the aid of theorists whose names are French, that there is something "female" about her doctrinal emphasis;[50] but the more important point is that she passionately believed in things that neither favor nor oppose the agenda of NOW. Assisting at the scene of Puritan childbirth, she may or may not have performed third-term abortions; but this seventeenth-century woman would probably have been embarrassed by the tone in which her modern admirers have learned to say "our bodies, ourselves"; for one of the things that troubled her most deeply is how Christ could possibly be united "to these fleshly bodies" (T, 364). So it will be well for history to honor the complexity of her thought along with the strength of her protest.

On the other hand, however, it seems fair enough to characterize most of her judges as "antifeminist"—the negative position having a much longer life than its corresponding positive. Hutchinson's judges try hard to keep the argument up at the level of doctrine, where the state of the soul matters more than the shape of the bodily parts. They even go a certain distance in letting any soul have its prophetic say.[51] But they fail. They live comfortably enough, for the most part, with their (symbolic) sense that all souls are in some sense female—passive, that is, submissive, and, yes, even subservient when considered as a Bride of Christ. But having put themselves, relative to Christ, in the position of the woman, they cannot bear to see a woman put herself, relative to themselves or to any of their social structures, in the position of a man.[52] Nor is it unfair to conclude that, after the theological *i*'s have been dotted, Mrs. Hutchinson was convicted of acting like a husband. The surprise will come, however, when a large group of representative men are convicted of the same misbehavior. One might almost say deviance.

———

Not all that short, nor as much a narrative as students may wish, Winthrop's *Short Story of the Rise, Reign, and Ruin of the Antinomians, Familists and Libertines* is "essentially a collection of documents" with a commentary "so cursory" that, back in England, Thomas Welde "determined to add a preface 'laying down the order and sense of this story.'"[53] Evidently, in this touchiest of all first-generation matters, Winthrop remains willing to allow the record some large room to speak for itself. In any event Welde's "Preface" takes more than eighteen pages to tell the story, from the moment remarked in Shepard's "Autobiography," when God sent upon a barely established community a "storm" of "unsound and loose opinions" (*SS*, 201),[54] to that more terrible one in which certain Indians did slay Mrs. Hutchinson "and all her family." Thus freed from a "sore affliction," New England's prefacer can only "bow [his] knees to the God of truth and peace" (*SS*, 218). As a reader like Roger Williams was certain he would.[55]

Along the way we learn the phrase "a fair and easy way to heaven"[56]—to characterize a theology that would teach a man to "see nothing in himself" (*SS*, 203–4), either before or after the moment of grace. And we learn to realize how easy it is to "steal into [the] bosoms of the innocent" and to seduce them with "soul-ravishing expressions" like "free grace" and "naked Christ" (*SS*, 204–5), to begin the process with the "women," considered as "the more flexible, tender, and ready to yield" (*SS*, 205–6), to undermine "the good opinion of their ministers" (*SS*, 206), to "father their opinions upon" (*SS*, 207) famous persons, and finally to have a woman set up a lecture which, under cover of repeating the important points of a sermon, was actually bent on making faction and so to overthrow the gospel of conditional promises.

So much for the rise. As for the reign, consider that at public lectures, the "opinionists" let fly a volley of objections like so many "pistols discharged at the face of the preacher" (*SS*, 209); or notice their "turning their backs upon the faithful pastor" of the Boston church, "going forth from the assembly when he began to pray or preach"; or recall the preaching, on a day set aside for fast and for healing, of a sermon dividing "the whole country into two ranks, some . . . under a covenant of grace and . . . others under a covenant of works" (*SS*, 210). And as for the ruin, of which we have seen the result, let it be said to have begun with God's stirring up "all the ministers' spirits in the country to preach against" the "easy" way, to gather force in the "time and strength" spent "in conference with" the erronists, and to have entered its victorious phase with "an assembly of all the ministers" (*SS*, 212). Consensus discovered, deviance identified.

Winthrop's own work begins with a catalogue of the eighty-two "erroneous opinions" precipitated out by the "assembly" mentioned above. As no persons are explicitly identified with any of these errors, the *argumentum ad feminam* has no chance to appear. Distinguishing the Puritan Mind here, instead, is the daunting completeness of its list of ways of missing the truth—especially on what might be called the "high side," where enthusiasts have pressed the freedom of Protestant salvation beyond the possibility of orderly social enactment. Most familiarly, those in Christ "are not under the law," so that "Christ's life is not a pattern according to which men ought to act" and, more symbolically, that "the new creature . . . is not meant of grace, but of Christ." Most insultingly, "the whole letter of the scripture holds for a covenant of works" (*SS*, 220–21); "there is no inherent righteousness in the saints"; and "to be justified by faith is to be justified by works" (*SS*, 223–24)—and clearly so, if faith is construed as a performable condition like any other. Most relevant to the sensitive question of church admission, "there is a testimony of the Spirit . . . merely immediate, without any respect unto . . . the word"; "there is no assurance . . . unless it be without fear and doubting" (*SS*, 230); and that, as all "conditional promises are legal" (*SS*, 232), it clearly is a "dangerous thing to close with Christ in a promise" (*SS*, 235). Yet there plainly is a point to this obsession, so far beyond the familiar crux of sanctification as evidence of justification: all *possible* errors must be carefully confuted, lest the cynic suspect New England had only a pragmatic guarantee for its logic of moral anxiety and theological condition; or that Winthrop was *not* one of those "few" who "could see where the difference was."[57] The difference might be reduced to a "scantling," but it was fundamental. Even in his list Winthrop inscribes himself as one not put off by the sound of some finer Christian liberty.

The "proceedings . . . against Mr. Wheelwright and other . . . seditious persons" begin by noticing that, though Cotton has made his peace with the moral majority, Wheelwright and Hutchinson have continued in their old ways. To emphasize the "civil" (*SS*, 248) nature of the proceedings, the charge is that those who had signed the *Remonstrance* against the censuring of Wheelwright, for a fast-day sermon that heightened the tensions, are alike guilty of "sedition" (*SS*, 249); as also are those who now defend the signers. Wheelwright himself is instructed that the court "had not censured his doctrine" but only the "application," by which he implied that "the magistrates, and the ministers, and most of the people of God in these churches" were laboring "under a covenant of works" and thus were "enemies to Christ" (*SS*, 252–53). Winthrop's account of Hutchinson's civil trial (*SS*, 262) interrupts the case against Wheelwright, but when it is taken up again, Winthrop reiterates that "this case [is] not a matter of conscience, but of a civil nature" (*SS*, 283).[58] And, to the argument that Wheelwright has been urging his followers to a "spiritual fighting and killing, &c. with the sword of the spirit only," Winthrop replies that his "instances of illustration, or rather enforcement, were of another nature, as of Moses killing the Egyptian in defense of his brother [and] Sampson losing his life with the Philistines." A wittier man might have said "My tropes are tropes, but yours are not"; what he settles for is the observation that Wheelwright's "experience might have told him, how dangerous it is to heat people's affections against their opposites" (*SS*, 293)—by telling them, among other things, "that truth and external peace cannot possibly stand together" (*SS*, 295).

The "story" of the civil trial of "Mistress Hutchinson" is considerably shorter than the court record itself, but it suggests that the gender theory which emerged full-formed only in the church trial has found its way into Winthrop's explanation of the earlier occasion as well.[59] Except perhaps for Wheelwright, Winthrop begins by asserting, all these erronists "were but young branches, sprung out of an old root." "Dux foemina facti," he solemnly intones: "a woman had been the breeder and nourisher of all these distempers"—wife of an "honest and peaceable man," but herself "a woman of a haughty and fierce carriage, of a nimble wit and active spirit, and a very voluble tongue, more bold than a man" (*SS*, 262–63). Such, since her first mention in the *Journal*, is what her "ready wit and bold spirit" has grown up to be. Confident, now that he can have everything his own way, Winthrop churlishly adds that this voluble woman, more bold than a man and once his equal in dispute, is in fact "inferior to many women . . . in understanding and judgment" (*SS*, 263).

So informed, the narrative may now proceed without interruption. At the ceremony of entrance into the Boston church, the woman "dissembled . . . her opinions." Then, from her sensitive position as midwife, she "easily insinuated herself into the affections" of many unsuspecting women, whom she instructed in the need to get beyond a trust in "common gifts and graces" and to seek instead the "witness of the Spirit." "All this was well," Winthrop allows, as much of the public ministry "went along in the same way"; but then, having "prepared the way by such wholesome truths, she begins to set forth her own stuff"—the uselessness of sanctification as evidence and the need, consequently, of an "immediate revelation" in the Spirit; and then, as briefly noted in the *Journal* for 1636, she began to teach "the in-dwelling of the person of the Holy Ghost," along with a concomitant denial of "any . . . inherent qualifications" in the believer (*SS*, 263–64). An "Assembly" was able to quash many of these unsound inferences, but the premise of an "immediate witness of the Spirit" took hold and spread to a majority in the church of Boston; for they, along with "many profane persons," who found it "a very easy and acceptable way to heaven, to see nothing, to have nothing, but wait for Christ to do all." Close to home, perhaps, for a man pious enough to name a favorite son "Waitstill," but that is not what he had meant at all, and we can well imagine the across-the-street anxiety with which this professional Watcher watches when the self-appointed Reformer, determined that her main emphasis "should be spread," began to hold "open house for all comers" (*SS*, 264).

The pretense may have been but "to repeat sermons," but when that was done, Winthrop seems certain, Hutchinson would "comment upon the doctrines, and interpret all passages at her pleasure, and expound the dark places of Scripture," thus expressing her belief that the letter of Scripture holds forth only "a covenant of works" and enabling her own tenets, which tended to "quench all endeavor in the creature" (*SS*, 264). From this it was a short way to laying "near all the elders and most of the faithful Christians in this country" under a covenant of works, meaning thereby to "disclose and advance her master-piece of immediate revelations, under the fair pretense of . . . free grace." Woman's wit, indeed. Convincing to "some eminent persons," however, her opinions "began to hold up their heads, in the church assemblies, and in the court of justice," to the public embarrassment of Wilson, a good and faithful pastor but unable to skill in the discourse of grace without effort, and to the encouragement of Wheelwright, emboldened to declare war on many "enemies to Christ." Yet the "hand of authority, guided by the finger of divine providence," was able to break the snare and deliver this city from "this woman who was the root of all these troubles" (*SS*, 265).

Formally charged, now, with the creation of "public disturbances"—by her "erroneous opinions," by "encouraging such as have sowed seditions amongst us," by "casting reproach on the faithful ministers," and by "maintaining . . . public meetings"—she must know that the concern is not for "conscience" but for "practice," in violation of the fifth commandment—"to honor . . . all in authority" (*SS*, 266). The issue of her having "justified" Wheelwright's sermon leads to that of obeying God above all human authority, and Winthrop, remembering perhaps his own impatience, quickly moves to the question of the "warrant" for her "public meetings." Rule counters rule, and Winthrop again quotes Paul's categorical "I permit not a woman to teach" (*SS*, 266–67). Instances are multiplied, with Winthrop denying that her texts justify an edification quite so public as her own, and yet he faithfully preserves her own exasperation: "Must I show you my name" in Scripture? The court can conclude only that she walked by what she called "the rule of the new creature, but what rule that was, she would not, or she could not tell." Neither would she willingly "lay down her meetings" (*SS*, 269).

As the court moves on to "the reproach she had cast upon the . . . ministers," Winthrop reminds his readers of the conference all had had with Cotton, at which Hutchinson told them of the "wide difference" between his ministry and theirs, namely, that "they could not hold forth a covenant of free grace, because they had not the seal of the Spirit" (*SS,* 269–70). Nightfall interrupts, as does a next-morning dispute about whether the ministerial witnesses against Hutchinson need to be sworn to their testimony, and likewise a fruitless reference to certain exculpatory but missing notes. A pointed appeal is made to Cotton, who declares himself "grieved" at any invidious comparison his avowed disciple may have made "between him and his brethren," yet assures those same brethren that he had taken "her meaning to be only of a gradual difference," likening the majority of ministers to Christ's disciples "before the Holy Ghost was come down upon them" (*SS,* 271). QED, Winthrop implies: *some seal* was indeed said to be lacking. Then, while a weary court agrees to swear in the hostile witnesses, Hutchinson moves to the fatal account of her spiritual history, giving Winthrop less the evidence he needed for a censure and more the confidence that her facts could indeed be submitted to a candid world—that her account of immediate revelation and her prediction of miraculous rescue could amount to nothing less than the special providence of his own.

Once again, the tale of trouble and of searching: the gradual discovery that "the ministers of England were . . . Antichrists," the resistance to this terrible knowledge, the gradual turning of her own heart away from the "covenant of works," the reception of the gift of distinguishing among the teachers—"which was the voice of Moses, which of John Baptist, and which of Christ." When the only safe guides are silenced, it is revealed that she too must go to New England where, it is also revealed, she "should be persecuted and suffer much trouble" (*SS,* 272), but that, as she learns from place after place in Scripture, she is to rely for deliverance on the same hand "that delivered Daniel." Nor, by Winthrop's narrative account, will her delusion stop short of predicting of her persecutors that "God will ruin you and your posterity, and this whole state" (*SS,* 273): nothing about "blood to drink," to be sure, yet a prophecy dire enough that the faithful remembrancers of New England will long remain eager to show on which side the providence really does lie.[60]

For the moment, a flurry of questions tests the literalness of Hutchinson's belief in personal revelation and miracle. From a distance, the evidence seems a little mixed. On the one hand, yes, she knows her voice to be that of God in the very same way Abraham knew "it was the voice of God, when he commanded him to sacrifice his son" (*SS,* 273). As to the reality of her miracle—as distinct from an event "above common providence"—she answers with an assurance fit to astonish the anxiety of latter-day epistemology: "you know it when it comes." On the other hand, in answer to one of Cotton's careful distinctions, she answers that she expects to be delivered not "from the sentence of the court" but "from the calamity of it"—which sounds as though her miracle of deliverance might be essentially "spiritual." Unwilling to stay for further distinction, however, the court is satisfied that she has "freely discovered her self," and all those "except those of her own party" regard her surprising claim to miracle as in fact a "special providence" in their own behalf. Quite evidently, they (almost) all conclude, this woman walks "by such a rule as cannot stand with the peace of any state; for such bottomless revelations . . . if they be allowed in one thing, must be admitted a rule in all things"; and, "being above reason and scripture, they are not subject to control." Nor can any state with the soul of a church permit private citizens to declare which ministers are and are not "sealed by the Spirit" (*SS*, 274). Seeing the "sink" of self-flattery from which the "ill vapor" of Antinomianism has arisen, what wonder that "so many of her seduced party [do] loathe now the smell of those flowers which they were wont to find sweetness in" (*SS*, 275).

Just imagine: "she can fetch a revelation that shall reach the magistrates and the whole court, and the succeeding generations, and she hath scripture for it also, Daniel must be a type of Mistress Hutchinson." And lest the literariness of the moment lapse too soon, Winthrop answers Hutchinson's daring discovery of her scene in Scripture with a rare display of humor: "she vented her impatience with so fierce speech and countenance, as one would hardly have guessed her to have been an Antitype of Daniel, but rather of the lions after they were let loose." Then, as if to stifle the smile, an invocation once more of "the tragedy of Munster" (*SS*, 275); and of worse, for "Satan seemed to have commission now to use his utmost cunning to undermine the kingdom of Christ here," daring to "enterprise any such innovation under the clear light of the Gospel." Indeed, the like had scarcely been known in former ages, that "so many wise, sober, and well grounded Christians, should so suddenly be seduced by the means of a woman." And so the court—elsewhere merely "satisfied"—in this account "saw now an inevitable necessity to rid her away," unless they wished to be "guilty, not only of [their] own ruin but also of the Gospel" (*SS*, 275–76). Great issues, it appears, and not the sort of story an ideal planner might easily forget.

Not the whole story, to be sure. John Underhill, a signer of the petition favoring Wheelwright, has his own day in court. And not the court reporter but the moral historian turns aside to include the details of the "monstrous and misshapen" birth of "the wife of one William Dyer" (*SS*, 280), and to marvel that the discovery of this judgment upon a "father and mother [who] were of the highest form of our refined Familists" occurred the "very day Mistress Hutchinson was cast out of the church for her monstrous errors" (*SS*, 281). The proceedings against Wheelwright get their own "brief apology" (*SS*, 282), emphasizing once again their civil nature, but making it plain that the majority of "ministers in this country do walk in and teach such a way of salvation . . . as he describeth" (*SS*, 289), and reminding the world that the metaphorical nature of his appeal to violence might not appear to all concerned. How, given his insistence that "truth and external peace cannot possibly stand together," could the court believe his way of "holding forth Christ should bring the desired peace"? (*SS*, 295).

In the end, however, Winthrop's *Story* comes to its fit ending only when "the elders of Boston" come round to "deal with Mistress Hutchinson in a church way" (*SS*, 301). Where the records of the church trial are slightly longer than those of her civil judgment, the narrative of that procedure is noticeably shorter— as if Winthrop had finally become confident enough to tell the tale without so elaborately pointing the moral. Twenty-nine theological errors are identified, from the mortality of "the souls of all men" to the inappropriateness of asking any true saint "to work out [his] salvation with fear" (*SS*, 301–3). Along the way, the familiar emphases, once frightful but now utterly defeated: the absence of "created graces in the saints" (*SS*, 301), and hence the impossibility of any such thing as "inherent righteousness" (*SS*, 302); and of course the tried and untrue teaching that "sanctification can be no evidence at all of our good estate" (*SS*, 303). All of which, in this account, Hutchinson is said to "acknowledge she had spoken," but under circumstances in which entrapment had disguised itself as honest inquiry. She is also said to have flown "into passion against her pastor for his speech against her at the court after the sentence was passed" (*SS*, 303); but her charges are said to be confuted by Wilson himself and, with similar brevity, the assembled judges simply reject her claim that her errors came in with her imprisonment. Without the language of Hutchinson's bright and often provocative protests, it all seems very one-sided. And a little dull.

One expression of her mortalist heresy is swiftly cured by a stranger's distinction between "the soul and the life" (*SS*, 304),[61] but in other heresies she is more persistent: when one of the elders tries to show her, by biblical logic, that her position entails the "community of women," she tells him he "spoke like the Pharisees." Finding her "obstinate," the elders recommend an "admonition"; Cotton complies, warning also her sons not to let natural affection outweigh their "covenant." Later, he asks "the sisters of the church" to repent their involvement in her opinions and "to withhold all countenance and respects from her, lest they should harden her in her sin" (*SS*, 305). And so she is dismissed and appointed to appear again in a week.

In the interim Cotton and Davenport bring her to acknowledge most of her errors. At her second appearance, accordingly, she begins by admitting that she has "greatly erred, and that God left her to her self"—so that "the assembly conceived hope of her repentance." Yet she cannot satisfy them about the crucial question of "inherent righteousness" (*SS*, 306); nor will they allow her to make it a matter of semantics. They are distressed to hear her claim that, though she might have phrased her belief incautiously, she never differed in substance from the dominant belief, in real virtue in real saints. Indeed, the elders deem this denial a lie. And, Winthrop further alleges, there are "diverse women" who, except for their "modesty," might "have born witness against her" on this very point. Hearsay unheard—and with Cotton yielding to Wilson on the point of practice—she is excommunicated, not for doctrinal extravagance, but as one who would "make and maintain a lie." As she departs, a person standing at the door prays the Lord to "sanctify this unto you"; and she replies, in words that surely seal Winthrop's sense of an obstinate refusal to repent, "The Lord judgeth not as man judgeth, better to be cast out of the church than to deny Christ" (*SS*, 307).

But if this account of Hutchinson's fate at the hands of the Boston church is noticeably less dramatic than the "Report of the Trial," still Winthrop is unwilling to end his short *Story* without a studied account of its lesson—the discovery, namely, of "an instrument of Satan" so superbly "fitted . . . to his service for . . . poisoning the churches here planted, as no story records the like of a woman, since that mentioned in the Revelation" (*SS*, 307–8). No typology is invoked, but clearly Winthrop is willing to raise the history-of-salvation stakes as high as Hutchinson herself. He proceeds to observe the special marks of "her entrance, . . . her progress [and] her downfall." As the Devil is known to talk a pretty good game of Scripture: first, she "seemed" to lay her "foundation" in "Christ and free grace"; and, in maintaining this very high ground, she pretended to the rule of *sola scriptura* as discerned by "only the Holy Ghost." Her converse was largely with "Christians in church covenant," about "the things of the kingdom of God" and in a "way of righteousness and kindness" (*SS*, 308). Small wonder at her success, but then perhaps that is exactly what may be required to lead astray even the elect. Insinuating herself "into the hearts of . . . many of the wise and godly," she allowed herself to be looked at "as a prophetess, raised up of God for some great work now at hand," so that a great pride began to appear in her "framing a new way" of evidencing salvation, in her "despising" all other ways as a "covenant of works," in her taking upon herself "infallibly to know the election of others" (*SS*, 308), and in her "impatience of opposition." Yet with great "cunning" she "pretended she was of Mr. Cotton's judgment in all things," covered her errors "by doubtful expressions," concealed the true end of her "weekly meetings," unsettled all the comfort of "sanctification," and recommended to others her own way of assurance by "immediate revelation" (*SS*, 309).

Nor are the signs and significances of her downfall any less worthy of clear and formal recognition. On the one hand, she was brought to confess "the vanity of her revelations"; on the other, God gave her up to certain "delusions" and to a certain "impudence in venting and maintaining them" (*SS*, 309). But we read Winthrop's distinctive note in the confirming evidence in which he himself has been most personally involved:

> this American Jesabel kept her strength and reputation, even among the people of God, till the hand of Civil Justice laid hold on her, and then she began evidently to decline, and the faithful to be freed from her forgeries. (*SS*, 310)

Elsewhere, in this separated world of congregational independence, the hand of Civil Justice does best if it is mostly hidden. But not here. A due form of religion has positively required a due form of civil oversight; thus the magistrates, ever wary of religious theories that take men—and women—beyond the scope of ordinary political practice, have had to discern and effectively to oppose a fatal danger the pious themselves could not seem to recognize as such.

Like the freemen later, so the saints are warned against the abuse of words that appear to carry with them their own guarantee. Evidently we are to shun such values as are "insusceptible of embodiment in lasting institutions."[62] Let the issue be the occult entities of faith and spirit, the venue is still the human world: even God's holy lovers need to remember the difference between the rulers and those who are ruled; indeed, the distinguishing mark of lovely New England was its gracious capacity to *love* the rule by which they agreed to walk. So that if the memorable lesson of Hutchinson's church trial is that she has "rather been a husband than a wife, and a preacher than a hearer; and a magistrate than a subject," the hard-worked conclusion of Winthrop's *Short Story* is the parallel discovery that the woman's disregard for the place of law in religion and utter contempt for both its theorists and its executives went along just "as if God did work contrary to his own word, and loosed from heaven [what] his church had bound on earth" (*SS*, 310). As if God could first reveal and then abrogate his own law. Or allow, on earth, the specially instructed to live outside the "way of subjection."

III. WINTHROP'S WIFE

If it had taken a little time for Winthrop's out-setting "Journal" to discover its duty to watch for lapses from and recoveries of sweet accord, it takes only a moment more for his emergent "History" to identify the multiform but continuous threat to his utopian ideal of social peace through holy love: citizens and saints

alike, often the very same persons, do not seem to cherish the wholesome re-
strictions to which covenant and covenant's God entitle them. Clearly the social
stress of 1636 and 1637 mark an important crisis in the history of New England;
and one could organize much of the post-1638 portion of the "Journal" around
Winthrop's steady interest in the after-history of those who had involved themselves most vocally in the challenge offered to the morale of preparation and sanctification—including, of course, the providential punishments of Anne Hutchinson herself. What this would lack, of course, as a summary of Winthrop's developing thematics, is some word about the continuation of his now-familiar battle with the freemen over their charter rights. But perhaps the secular issue of
rights was not entirely unrelated to the question of the style and the language of
grace. Democracy is not the same thing as Antinomianism, of course, but Winthrop's account of how events in New England threatened to "shame the faces of
many of God's worthy servants"[63] is not the best place to learn this fact. To be
sure, Winthrop's exasperation with the pressure of the freemen for an ever greater
share of political power never issues in a full-dress exposé.[64] And Winthrop hesitates to reduce the clergymen's list of doctrinal extravagances to a single controlling error. But it is hard to miss his sense that a fundamental misunderstanding
of Christian liberty is threatening to undo state and church alike.

The political case is easy enough to grasp. Indeed, it is spelled out in the
more literal portions of Winthrop's justly famous "Little Speech on Liberty"
(1645): men who have agreed to the terms of their own governance—particularly
when that is by the grace of their own elected representatives—are not entitled to
quarrel with or arbitrarily to reinvent those very terms. Free to enter, by their
oath, a given social contract, and free to recall an official for serious breach of fundamental good faith, they are expected to submit, on a daily basis, to the political
determinations of their justly empowered rulers.[65] Most especially, one easily
imagines, in a holy state, where political wrangling is morally disedifying as well
as philosophically incoherent. If men do not understand this, they will need to be
taught—little by little, at first, in public remarks very justly recorded in any faithful account of the ebb and flow of political virtue in a model city, even if the
teacher and the recorder turn out to be the same subtle but enlisted observer; and
full bore, sooner of later, if the subtler tuition should fail to make its point. Even
if the experience compressed into the 1645 "Little Speech" should find a need to
revise, somewhat, the figure of love and duty so warmly sketched in the proleptic
"Model" of 1630. Even if, that is to say, the whelming enthusiasm of the holy lover
shall reappear as the circumspect obedience of the wedded wife.

The comparison with the *Ten Virgins* should thus be clear: where Shepard
sought to preempt, for the conservative cause of worldly virtue and churchly holi-

ness, the language which another style of Christianity has always associated with the mystical possibility, here on earth, of a direct, indeed a quasi-sexual relation with the transcendent God, the master stroke of Winthrop's later "Journal," in the aftermath of that Saturnalia of Faith we call the Antinomian Controversy, is simply to revise, in the direction of decent and lawful behavior, the gendered, indeed quasi-sexual language in which he himself proposed a surpassingly lovely morale for New England's holy "City." Cautious criticism rarely emphasizes, and sober history seldom even publishes, the part of Winthrop's famous "Model of Christian Charity" which suggests that the exemplary character of New England will consist in something more inviting than a replication of all the familiar hierarchies. So that when Winthrop writes his reactionary "Little Speech on Liberty," the effect can seem less revisionary than in fact it is.

True, the Winthrop of 1630 had assured his original New Englanders that some of them were still going to be somewhat richer than others. Nor were they to expect anything like democracy, in either political rule or social role. Yet if this were all, no observer with the scruples of a Hawthorne would have dared refer to the prospect of first-generation New England as a "Utopia of human virtue and happiness."[66] That note comes in with the expansive emphasis on holy love, which only a settled cynicism can refuse to see as the soul of Winthrop's famous "Model." Balancing Winthrop's well-publicized emphasis on hierarchy as a prime feature of the divine plan for this world is a rather lengthy and elaborate sense of what must follow, in any world that would dare call itself "Christian," from the fact of hierarchical differences: noblesse really does oblige, in the matter of lending and giving; and in that of forgiving, the standard has got to be higher than either justice or mercy might imagine. And on the subject of the nature and social exercise of the love that shall underlie and guarantee this social and economic departure from even the most "unstrained" standard of British experience, Winthrop can hardly come to the end of his theological articulation. Or his enthusiasm— according to which the members of his ideal community will be knit together by the irresistible attraction the Christ-possessing soul feels for the image of Christ in every other soul so possessed; an attraction of souls, to be sure, but one significantly like the overwhelming one felt by Adam and Eve, upon her first presentation unto him, in the Garden, well before any hint of serpentine temptation.

That this mythic Eve should dwindle to a wife over ages of historical time and anxious sacramental theory is probably not surprising. But that Winthrop should change his controlling figure—from the boundlessly loving and beloved woman to the more familiar figure of the obedient and submissive wife—may call for some attention. Especially if, in the time between, Winthrop had opportunity to learn that his holy lovers could also be political sticklers; and also to observe, in the rise and fall of a certain female prophet, that "woman's intellect should never give the tone to that of man."[67]

––––––––

But if the matter of the Woman is the subtext of the revisions Winthrop was to make in his gendered theory of New England, the provoking occasion is both less abstruse and more obviously political. Indeed, there is a sense in which the run-up to the 1645 impeachment of John Winthrop and its well-earned rebuke are entirely predictable. For some time the freeman of Massachusetts—enjoying that title by the grace of an initiatory decision to open the franchise to all church members—seem happy enough to have grasped what they regarded as their charter-given privilege to elect their own governor rather than have the elected assistants choose one of their own number. Nor were they especially grieved by the compromise of electing deputies who should, together with the assistants, make all necessary laws on their own behalf. But there remained, unhappily, the question of "the veto": namely, the ongoing claim of the assistants to constitute, in relation to the deputies, a sort of upper house, whose distinguishing power it would be to have the last word in matters legislative and judicial. That "constitutional" matter will get decided, in favor of the assistants, in 1644, in the aftermath of the contested pig of Goody Sherman. But there are other contests of liberty and authority along the way, plenty of occasions for positions to be occupied, tones to be taken.

In 1639, for example, the court elected Winthrop governor for the third straight time—even though some freemen feared that Winthrop, though "beloved," might be on the verge of becoming governor for life. Cooler heads came to realize, however, that "neither the governor nor any other attempted the thing" (292). Other "jealousies" arose, however, when Winthrop thought to propose his brother-in-law to fill a vacancy among the assistants: "though he were known to be a very able man . . . , yet the people would not choose him." Nor could all the people be got to agree that, with the number of deputies "much increased by the addition of new plantations," it was only fit "to reduce all towns [from three] to two deputies." Some feared a conspiracy which would, "in time," bring "all power into the hands of the magistrates." So at the next session "allegations were made" that the reduction "was an infringement of their liberty"; and only "after much debate" could the majority of these representatives be convinced that "their liberty consisted not in the number, but in the thing" (293).

Still, the next day a petition from Roxbury sought "to have the third deputy restored," so that objections had to be answered in writing; particularly as "the hands of some of the elders . . . were to this petition." Doubtless these "learned and godly men" had been drawn in "without due consideration," for—as Winthrop begins to anticipate the wording of his "Little Speech"—

> when the people have chosen men to be their rulers, and to make their laws, and bound themselves by oath to submit thereto, now to combine together . . . in a public petition to have any order repealed, which is not repugnant to the law of God, savors of resisting an ordinance of God; for the people, having deputed others, have no power to make or alter laws, but are to be subject. (293–94)

Or else, if this strict republicanism seem a little harsh to those in whom Winthrop might expect to recognize the image of Christ, let them at least "prefer some reasons . . . to the court," rather than "peremptorily to petition to have [an order] repealed," since this amounts to a "plain reproof of those whom God hath set over them, . . . against the tenor of the fifth commandment" (294). Still, as the model is of parents and children rather than of husband and wife, Winthrop is yet holding back from the formulation of his contractual absolutism.

One reason may be that there are, at this one court, so *many* occasions "of increasing the people's jealousy of their magistrates." Again, the question of lifetime tenure for the governor—raised by one of the elders as a matter for debate but seized upon by a suspicious populace "as if there had been some plot." Then, as one thing led to another, they wished to have it established that "no person chosen a [standing] counselor for life should have any authority as a magistrate, except he were chosen in the annual elections to one of the said places of magistracy established by the patent" (294). Winthrop takes time, he tells us, "to consider of it, before he would put it to vote." And then, after recording that "this order was after passed by vote," he takes pains to explain that, in yielding to this desire of the deputies, "they did more study to remove these jealousies out of the people's heads, than to preserve any power or dignity to themselves" (295). Peace, not at any price, perhaps, but well worth the sacrifice of Endicott's presumptive magistracy.[68] Or anyone's vanity.

Yet the patience of this beloved yet vaguely mistrusted leader is beginning to wear a little thin. Even the democrat may smile at the lapse of tone:

> And here may be observed, how strictly the people would seem to stick to their patent, where they think it makes for their advantage, but are content to decline it, where it will not warrant such liberties as they have taken up without warrant from thence. (295–96)

He mentions, for his own morose delectation, only the people's "strife for three deputies," where the "patent allows them none at all" (296). But he might also have reminded the ironic sense of some reader that the entire utopian affair had begun with his agreement that freeman might come to mean migrating church member rather than stay-at-home stockholder.

Yet not all the political battles of Winthrop's journal-turned-history are rationalized losses. The resist-and-delay foreign policy of this Non-Separating Congregationalism, hanging fire since the threats of 1634, and involving as much the course of English politics as the triumph of saintly reason, is written into the record as a singular success as of July 4, 1639:

> We were much afraid this year of a stop in England, by reason of the complaints which had been sent against us, and the great displeasure which the archbishops and others . . . had conceived and uttered against us, both for those complaints, and also for our not sending home our patent. But the Lord wrought for us beyond all expectations.

For the petition sent in response to the "order . . . for our patent . . . was well accepted" (298); and, thus justified, the influx of persons and provisions continued to be great. To be sure, local merchants such as "Mr. Robert Keane" find it hard not to take advantage of the market that results, but Cotton is quick to elaborate the "rules for trading" (308). More seriously, perhaps, the citizens of Winthrop's holy city continued to feel themselves "unsafe" without a "body" of positive law. Yet the magistrates—jealous perhaps of their "discretion," but also mindful that "our church discipline" would certainly "transgress the limits of our charter" (314)—manage to refer the matter to a process of proposal and review that will take several years to complete.

Meanwhile, and as if to recall the rituals of consensus that mark the earlier years of his "Journal," Winthrop records that he and several others, a minority in the Hutchinson matter, who might well have responded to their disaffection by "withdrawing themselves," were rewarded to see the Lord cause "the hearts of all the people to love and esteem them more than ever before" and to experience again that wave of political grace in which "all breaches were made up" (315). A more explicit crisis is narrowly averted when, after proposing (again) that there may be such a thing as too much preaching, Winthrop's court was only observing that people might well expect to get home from services "by daylight" and that "nothing was attempted herein against the church's liberties" (318). Furthermore, at the elections of 1640, the old fear of a lifetime governorship appears one more time; but the election of Dudley is attended with such professions of "sincere affections and respect towards" Winthrop that no offense can possibly be taken; and when "the old governor" expresses his wish to attend to private affairs, mentioning the cost of his public service, he speedily receives a number of "voluntary contributions," including the gift of "three thousand acres of land" (326).

The early months of 1641 find Winthrop approving the Dudley government's refusal to recommend itself to the newly restored Parliament—for "if we should put ourselves under [its] protection . . . , we must then be subject to all such laws as they . . . might impose" (346); and later noting that Parliament's intention to begin "a general reformation" has had the result of stopping the migration of saints to New England, thus making "foreign commodities . . . scarce, and our own of no price" (353). But 1641 also provides its local distractions: before John Cotton and Nathaniel Ward have quite finished their competing proposals for a body of positive laws, all registered moral teachers are called upon to decide how the "penetratio" of two prepubescent females compares with the mere "frictatio usque ad effusionem seminis" (372), on the one hand, and the less speakable sin of buggery, on the other. Nor does Bellingham, elected governor in May 1641—and refusing, thereupon, to step down and explain why he performed the rites of his own marriage, to a young woman otherwise "espoused"—seem quite the man to manage this delicate inquiry (367–74). Embarrassed but not unduly discouraged, the faithful historian can only conclude, with Genesis and Bradford, that "as people increased, so sin abounded" (374).

Not that departures were to be encouraged. Having opposed Hooker's move to Hartford, Winthrop is now happy to see that he cannot now be lured back to England, even temporarily, "to . . . advise about the settling of church government": why indeed should *anyone* wish to "go 3,000 miles to agree with three men"? (403). If not for reformation, still less might persons walk away in the name of worldly advantage: given "the sudden fall of land and cattle" resulting from the cessation of Puritan immigration, many of Winthrop's citizens fell into "an unsettled frame of spirit" and "began to hasten away" (414). God was not favoring their prospects, however, and Winthrop takes the occasion to question the idea of "liberty" that may underlie this new mobility. "Much disputation there was"—as at Plymouth—about "removing for outward advantages," but Winthrop's fear is that "many crept out at a broken wall." And he continues what seems a "little speech": "For such as come together into a wilderness," and "bind themselves to support each other, . . . how they can break from this without free consent is hard to find." Are we not also "straitly tied to all care of each other's good and of the whole"?[69] Then "ask thy conscience" if thou wouldst have plucked up thy stakes and brought thy family 3,000 miles if thou hadst expected that all, or most, would have forsaken thee there. Ask again, what liberty thou hast towards others, which thou likest not to allow others towards thyself; for if one may go, another may, and so the greater part, and so church and commonwealth may be left destitute in the wilderness.

Better, surely, "to suffer affliction with thy brethren than to enlarge thy ease and pleasure" (416). And were it not for the speech on liberty and authority, this carefully composed passage might well bear the theme of Winthrop's journal-turned-history.

Less solemn, the case of the pig that completed the constitution issues in a signal triumph for Winthrop's sense of what a saintly populace owes to its aristocracy of political talent. But only after some ugly moments. Surfacing again in 1642, this "great business upon a very small occasion" (395) went from a hearing "before the elders" all the way up to the General Court, which gave it "the best part of seven days" (396); and with no outcome, given the split between the magistrates, who favored the finder of the pig, and the deputies, who favored the loser. According to Winthrop, prejudice against the finder—the same Keane found guilty of profiteering—blinded some of the popular representatives; but in any case the lack of resolution caused many to speak irreverently of the magistrates, especially as "the report went that their negative voice had hindered the course of justice and that these magistrates must be put out, that the power of the negative voice might be taken away" (397–98). So Winthrop finds it appropriate to publish the true state of this case; and to reaffirm that, whatever the dissension, all involved "were the same in affection." Opposed by some of the plaintiff's party, the plan was "laid by"; but nothing prevents Winthrop from publishing "a declaration of the necessity of upholding" the negative voice (398). Leaving us a perfect model: loving consensus before all else; sovereign authority when that shall fail.

Quiet for a while, but then, in the midst of framing the confederation with Connecticut, the old "sow business" reappears one more time. Pressed "by some on the plaintiff's side," the matter eventually comes before a meeting "both of magistrates and elders . . . and some of the deputies" (451–52), where the elders discover such a "crossing of testimonies" as led them to desire "that the court might never be more troubled with it." To this weary conclusion the only objector is Bellingham, "who still . . . would have the magistrates lay down their negative voice." Bellingham's "singularity in opinion" is duly noted, but because "a principal end of the meeting was to reconcile differences" (452), the discussions must

go on anyway. And so there begins anew—though constitutional historians seldom feature this fact—the drama of Puritan disputants trying to declare a state
of holy love.

In the midst of the unhappy "sow business," Mr. Saltonstall had written a
treatise "against the council," and so stood "divided from the rest"; but now, as
the juices of the Puritan heart begin to flow, he is "brought to see his failings in
that treatise, which he did ingenuously acknowledge and bewail, and so he was
reconciled with the rest." Bellingham remains a holdout, in spite of the fact that
Winthrop offers himself ready for a "perfect reconciliation" (452). On the other
hand, however, Dudley "at last . . . did acknowledge" the fault of his recent speech
to Mr. Rogers, "and they were reconciled." Even the deputies "seemed now to be
satisfied, and the elders agreed to deal with the deputies of their several towns,"
so that the "cause might never trouble the court more" (453). Which ought to end
the whole sorry affair—unless the solicitor for the plaintiff, "an unsatisfied spirit,"
should prefer "a petition at the court of elections [May 1643] for a new hearing."
How could sane men not be "much grieved to see such a spirit in godly men,"
when neither magistrates, nor elders, "nor the loss of time and charge, nor the settling of peace in court and country could prevail with them to let such a cause
fall." As nothing could be discovered of a criminal nature, and as the suit could
scarcely amount to "forty shillings," one could only infer the existence of extrane-
ous factors: "the democratical spirit which acts our deputies" and "the desire of
the name of victory," which the magistrates, "for peace sake" (453), were willing
to let utterly scuttle and slide.

With the populace the remaining unhappiness seems to swirl around the
"20 pounds which the defendant had recovered against the plaintiff in an action
of slander for saying he had stolen the sow"—which cause they could not, in
Winthrop's view, keep separate from either the original issue or from their settled
bias against "a rich man" in court against "a poor woman"; so the court satisfies
itself with a plan to persuade the defendant to return to the plaintiff the "3 pounds"
he had taken "upon that judgment" (454). Then, in the name of *utter* reconciliation, the elders persuade their pliable governor to apologize for some things he
had earlier written upon this trivial but tortured case. Setting down his speech
verbatim, "to prevent misinterpretation, as if he had retracted what he had wrote
in the point of the case," Winthrop restates his view of the legal matter, a "point
of judgment . . . not at [his] own disposing," but profusely apologizes for the manner of his expression. Though provoked by the "adverse party," and though invited by others "to vindicate ourselves from that aspersion that was cast upon us,"
he had nevertheless been "too prodigal of [his] brethren's reputation" and "might

have obtained the cause . . . without casting such blemishes upon others." More particularly, he repents that in implying that others might be "void both of religion and reason" he did "arrogate too much to [himself] and ascribe too little to others" (454–55). And as if to repeal every hint of the merely personal, he confesses that his profession of honesty "before all the world" seems now, with a light refracted from the corporate conscience of the assembled elders, "a fruit of the pride of his own spirit" (455–56).

Pardon these faults and "pass them by," he lets yet another little speech conclude. And for his own part, he hopes he shall "be more wise and watchful hereafter" (456). From which the reader can conclude only that, along with his still self-stifled sense that in these latter days the ideals of his "Model" are not everywhere being honored, Winthrop wishes to express his own unrepentant loyalty to the utopian notion that, in a Christian commonwealth at least, lawyers should always be lovers too. Yet all this deference can hardly persuade us that there is not a puritanic hard line somewhere; or that, given sufficient occasion or provocation, Winthrop is not the man to speak it. Indeed, if the "Journal" were a novel, the accomplished reader would be on the verge of demanding some loss of political composure to relieve the text of its mounting repression. But who has ever anticipated that, when it finally comes, the authoritarian outburst will serve to remind the freemen of their status as submissive "wives"?

Provoked but not really caused by the "sow business," the question of the negative vote continues to haunt Winthrop's sense of how the saintly lover ought to run a country. His own treatise, arguing from both "the patent" and an "order of the general court in 1634," that the magistrates' negative voice was so fundamental that, without it, "our government . . . would be a mere democracy" (456), convinces no one not already convinced and draws forth an "Answer" which emboldens the deputies to press for a final determination of the issue. The magistrates urge caution upon an issue vital to "the very frame of our government" (457); Cotton writes "a small treatise," establishing the "unavoidable change into a democracy if the negative vote were taken away"; and this persuades Winthrop that "the deputies and the people also, having their heat moderated by time . . . let the cause fall" (457–58). "Too optimistic," comments Winthrop's editor, as "strong opposition to magisterial authority continued until 1645."[70]

Yet with Winthrop's own dismissal, the issue ceases to be an obsession, and the "Journal" seems momentarily freed up to consider at some length a variety of other matters: the marginal but enticing question of whether La Tour or D'Aulnay shall prevail in the contest for Acadia; the relation of various sachems and tribes to the Puritan confederation; the trial, sentencing, and eventual release of the rampant heretic, Samuel Gorton, who "reviled magistracy, . . . alleging that a man might as well be a slave to his belly as to his own species" (483); and one final encounter with Thomas Morton who, being too "old and crazy" to be whipped, is permitted to wander out of the court's jurisdiction, to die "poor and despised" (539). Along the way, the historic decision to divide the magistrates and deputies into two houses, a "compromise solution" to a protracted and invidious argument,[71] gets only six lines, ending "this order determined the great contention about the negative voice" (503)—as if Winthrop preferred not to comment on a settlement reached by division rather than by loving consensus.

More energetic is his opposition to the deputies' suggestion that a "commission" of some of themselves and some of the magistrates should "order all affairs of the commonwealth in the vacancy of the general court" (511)—refusing to concede for even a moment the deputies' contention that "the governor and assistants had no power out of court but what was given them by the general court" (512). More spirited still is his representation of the (August 1644) protest of Governor Endicott, bewailing "the great differences and jarrings which were upon all occasions among the magistrates, and between them and the deputies; that the ground of this was jealousies and misreports" (530–31). Endicott's "magisterial" interests are the same as Winthrop's, of course, and all the pending constitutional issues appear in the speech. The two appear to share, furthermore, the opinion that the clergy ought to be siding more univocally with the magistrates. But what appears to capture Winthrop's attention is Endicott's hatred of discord and his suggestion that the elders should serve as "mediators of a thorough reconciliation" (531). For how can law save civil men from the failure of love?

Yet if that is the way they *will* tend, then the outcome will have to be theorized. Or publicly promulgated, at least, in a land where the penalty of the Fall is understood as well as the privileges of Redemption. And so volume 3—as if to insist on a continuity of interest unaffected by differing editorial procedures—turns at once to the matter of calling in the elders "to reconcile the differences between the magistrates & deputies." A meeting is arranged, to determine once and for all whether magistrates are indeed, "by patent & election of the people, the standing council of this commonwealth in the vacancy of the general court" (554). The deputy turnout is insulting light, but Winthrop is gratified to report that the answer of the elders was "affirmative on the magistrates behalf, in the very words of the question" (555). This cleanly result is followed by a virtual orgy of questions and answers. In the end, however, almost all agree: "The magistratical power is given to the governor &c: by the patent: to the people is given by the same patent to design the persons to those places of government." Those "few leading men . . . still fixed upon their own opinions" only reveal how "hard a matter it is to draw men (even wise & godly) from the love of the fruit of their own inventions" (561). And were it not for a personal insult, this might well be Winthrop's bottom line: apparently it is easier to invent a government than it is to obey one already in place; and evidently Christ is not *all* that saints see in the souls of their fellows.

Then, as if this lesson in realism were too diminished a thing, the problem of the disputed election of the captain of the trainband in the town of Hingham, explained in ten pages of detail annoying enough to convey Winthrop's own sense of tedious disproportion. Never a strict constructionist, and confident, now, that magistrates can indeed operate as such "in the vacancy of the general court," Winthrop, in consultation with two other magistrates, intervenes in this local squabble and commits one faction "for contempt"; whereupon, in the words of Perry Miller, "the lower house of the General Court impeaches him for having exceeded his commission."[72] In fact, the wheels of an increasingly factitious Puritan justice grind just a little slower than this, the process requiring first that Winthrop be identified as the single target of the procedural protest. Eventually, however, that identification is made, and Winthrop presents himself as seated conspicuously apart from the rest of the magistrates, to indicate that he has stepped down from his familiar (if untenured) magisterial position—placing himself, where other criminals had stood, in "the most important power struggle in Massachusetts since the Antinomian Controversy in 1637."[73] Well does he suppose that something may be expected from him, even if cleared of all charges. The surprise is that he should take the occasion to revise, in a strikingly figurative way, the fundamental theory of his Utopia, not so much abandoning its original premise of regenerate love as sinewing that "holy pretense"[74] with a strict account of the loving obedience it had all along supposed.

———

Winthrop was indeed cleared, but not perhaps inevitably, and certainly not all at once. First of all, the General Court has to agree to hear the complaint of those from Hingham who felt they had been dealt with unfairly and in an arbitrary manner; and though the deputies speedily agree to the hearing, the magistrates marvel that the deputies would "grant such a petition without desiring conference first with them selves" (578). Eventually they too agree, in part because the accused himself, aware of the extent both he and the other magistrates "did suffer in the cause, through the slanderous reports" of the deputies, was himself anxious "that the cause might receive a public hearing" (579). With all due process, therefore, Winthrop begins by waving the several arguments he might make in favor of summary dismissal and proceeds instead to justify, to his own satisfaction, "all the particulars laid to his charge" (580). The first judgment falls out along party lines: "two of the magistrates & many of the deputies were of [the] opinion that the magistrates exercised too much power," jeopardizing thereby "the people's liberty": but the remainder of the deputies and "all the rest of the magistrates were of a different judgment," feeling instead that "authority was overmuch slighted" and fearing that the outcome of the tendency herein discovered could be nothing short of "mere democracy" (581).

Predictably, perhaps, the results of so fundamental a difference between the two "houses" of the evolving Massachusetts government were distinctly disedify-ing, especially to the consensualist sensibility of the magistrate on trial, as "each side [strove] unseasonably to enforce the evidence" in ways that "should have been reserved to a more private debate." Only after "the best part of 2 days was spent in this public agitation" did the two sides choose a "committee . . . of magistrates & deputies" which did, "with great difficulty," write up a statement of the case "as it appeared upon the whole pleading & evidence" (581). As stated just so, the magistrates and deputies agree to consider the matter "apart." Not even thus sepa-rated, however, can the deputies reach a consensus, sending "up to the magis-trates to have their thoughts about it." The magistrates—with deputy Governor Winthrop withdrawing himself—are quick to declare the entire petition "false & scandalous" and to suggest "that the deputy governor ought to be acquit." The deputies concede that some things may have been out of order, but they deny, in the words of Winthrop's editor, "that the charges against JW were causeless and unjust" (582). And so the proceedings wind on.

The deputies propose and the magistrates agree "to refer the cause to arbi-traters according to an order of court, when the magistrates & deputies cannot agree." The magistrates quickly name six elders from the neighboring towns and require the deputies to name their own, but these lower-house representatives, knowing well how the elders tend "to uphold the honor & power of the magis-trates," find themselves "now at the wall" and so desire to send six of their very own number. And these staunch protodemocrats, worn out perhaps by the law's delay, agree to fine all the petitioners and to declare "the deputy governor to be legally & publicly acquit of all that was laid to his charge" (583–84). Then, as fur-ther stipulated, a solemn public scene is arranged:

> after the lecture the magistrates & deputies took their places in the meet-ing house, & the people being come together, & the deputy governor plac-ing himself within the bar . . . , the governor read the sentence of the court,

> without speaking any more; for the deputies had . . . obtained a promise of
> silence from the magistrates. Then was the deputy governor desired by the
> court to go up & take his place again upon the bench. (584)

It would be impossible for any modern enactment of Law and Order to arrange
for itself a drama more charged with social meaning than this one-scene performance: when all has been said and done—and, as always, much more has been
said than done—the voice of the present leader of this remarkable experiment
announces the only terms on which an ever-complexifying corporate body could
proceed and be one body still; and the original guardian of this holy corporation
resumes his rightful place.

But then, just as "the court [is] about to arise"—and as we too are ready to
agree, with magistrate and deputy alike, that after days of personal stress and
public strife, the rest must indeed be some political faith nourished in silence—
the exonerated man desires "leave for a little speech" (584), which every apt observer since Cotton Mather has felt the need to quote and to apply, often with an
appropriate sense of drama, but seldom with anything like a full sense of context.[75] For once again, for good and for ill, and after fifteen years of more or less
impatient but self-stifled observation of the way even self-consciously godly individuals insist on ends that cannot consist with the good of the social body, the
voice of the theorist is heard in the land. A little too personally, at first, as the man
"publicly charged" and "publicly & legally acquitted" is of course pleased by his
"justification before men" (584, 586). But then, with a sense that duty rather than
vanity demands something further, Winthrop gives voice not only to the political
theory about which the unaccused magistrates had all agreed to remain silent,
but to the parts of the gendered theology which his "Model of Christian Charity"
had left unsaid—as if, in that inspired moment, anyone could doubt that holy
love subsumed and did not at all abrogate the need of submission and obedience.

First, as to the great question of the "authority of the magistrates," whether
from patent or from English precedent or yet from the sense of right which must
prevail in any system aware of the need to found itself upon the art of the possible,
it has a double source: from the men "who have called us to this office," to be sure,
but from God as well, as government is in itself an "ordinance" that has "the
image of God eminently stamped upon it." From this latter consideration it follows that contempt of the ordinance itself can expect nothing less than "divine
vengeance"; and from the former the timely reminder that, as men choose governors from among themselves, they will come with "infirmities" (586) quite like
their own—which ought to make the consent of the governed, if not generous,
then at least a little tolerant. Prudence, in any event, will "account him a good ser-

vant who breaks not his covenant," which obliges him to "govern you & judge your causes by the rules of God's laws & our own, according to our best skill" (586–87). Ordinary workmen are hired and recompensed according to their expertise, but as only God is a truly skillful ruler, men cannot be all the time protesting and petitioning where matters of political technique or of personal tact are at issue. Let them worry instead about issues of "faithfulness," of cases in which it is "clear to the common apprehension" that "the error is not in the skill, but in the evil of the will" (587). Or else, as in the present case, politics will come to consume the waking hours of every observant individual.

Sound advice, perhaps, for any society which does not endorse any special schooling for "The Prince"—where wrestlers and actors are elected to govern liberal states, and older actors, before they forget entirely who they are, get to be the president. The stickler might protest that the petitioners had begun by charging in fact some fundamental abuse of the contractual relation, and that Winthrop's sense of the good-faith demands of his covenant are a little more forgiving than the freemen's more scrupulous sense of responsibility to a constitution. But in the end, their deputies seem to have agreed to Winthrop's settled religious conviction rather than insist upon their own emergent political understanding. Besides, it is the second of Winthrop's two "great questions" that arouses the most resistance, as Winthrop's "liberty" has seemed to limit the citizens of Massachusetts to the performance of "those things that qualified magistrates like Winthrop and learned clergymen like Cotton and Hooker defined as the good, just and honest."[76]

Yet the literary critic, bound to find as much in Winthrop's metaphors as in his exact political slogans, cannot let it go with this rueful discovery of the real. As in the "Model" the lively image of the Woman matters as much as the rules for giving and for lending, so here the figure of the Wife who freely chooses a husband whom to obey tells us things Winthrop seems able to express in no other way. It points, for one thing, to the unmistakably affective center of Winthrop's otherwise crisp version of "contractual absolutism." And it reminds those readers who have a harder time discovering the binding emphasis of an event-oriented journal than following the sense of continuity built into some more consciously emplotted literary form that Winthrop's emerging *History of New England* is not without a beginning, a middle, and an end.

Not surprisingly, Winthrop reminds us that not even the most liberal theory can get along without the caution that the ideal of liberty is everywhere imperiled by the experience of license. In the state of nature man may, just like the "beasts & other creatures," have "liberty to do what he list," without "the least restraint," but in a contractual society, self-expression, even in the name of moral experimentation, has got to end somewhere; and as Winthrop's classical quotation is meant to suggest, conservative Christians are not alone in holding that "we all degenerate in the absence of control."[77] Nor are we particularly alarmed to hear Winthrop speak of a second, "civil or federal," sort of liberty. Natural man may have to give up his natural liberty in order to enjoy the benefits of a system of human regulation, but as the New England Utopia is neither *Leviathan* nor *Bellipotent,* it cannot truly be said that he is now become a slave to a system of mutual safety.[78] Free as ever in his capacity of choosing—the alehouse or the meetinghouse, as Hooker put the option—New England man has, by his participation in a multiplicity of overlapping covenants, formally promised to pursue the "good, just & honest" (587) exactly so far as this may be in him enabled. Of course, one might always slip and fall—like Dimmesdale, perhaps—but one had also promised to accept reproof and even punishment when the damaged and not fully repaired human nature has led his personal choices away from the unfolding consensus of what God's will ideally requires. Or, if one should experience a radical change of mind about the true nature of "the good, just & honest," one might always leave. As Hester herself was all along free to do. For where is it written that honest dissent will always acquire the power to work a "moral revolution"?[79]

Of course, there is some paradox in using the same word to refer to both an uninhibited self-expression and a hearty enjoyment of all "due metes and bounds."[80] But Winthrop is scarcely alone in regarding the gracious overcoming of self-indulgence as a sort of liberation. And, within the Christian orbit, only the enthusiast will tell us, in a moment of Antinomian hyperbole, to love God and do whatever we want. All we learn from this line of analysis is that Winthrop's ideal world attached less value to moral experimentation than have some others. And it is, finally, in a figure that Winthrop feels competent to explain himself with greatest cogency. To him—if not to Thomas Hobbes—it seems just like the question of love and marriage.

The liberty New England freemen are to "stand for, with the hazard . . . of [their] lives, if need be" is the kind of liberty that can only be "maintained & exercised in a way of subjection to authority." It is, this theologically disposed politician dares to suggest, "of the same kind of liberty wherewith Christ hath made us free." The way to understand *that* kind, he confidently continues, is simply to consider that

> the woman's own choice makes such a man her husband, yet being so chosen he is her lord, & she is to be subject to him, yet in a way of liberty, not of bondage; & a true wife accounts her subjection her honor & freedom, &

would not think her condition safe & free, but in her subjection to her husband's authority. (588)

It may take us a while to get over the historical shock of recognizing the old-fashioned theory of marriage laid out quite so plainly: Wither thou goest, I will wither; and they shall travel on to where the two shall be as one and an angrily negotiated fraction. But eventually the point does sink in: saints keep their covenants—with Christ, with a particular church, and (in this case) with a social arrangement agreed on all sides to have the soul of a church—in exactly the same spirit as the wedded wife keeps her vows. Free to marry or not, and free, on the terms of middle-class modernity, to marry this or that other suitor of her affection, she promises, as the very condition of the advantages offered by marriage, to *obey* as well as love and honor her husband. Willingly.

By which, of course, one could only mean lovingly. What the wife promises, on this account, is to redefine her freedom as the privilege to embrace the self-fulfilling terms of a solemn promise without the least hint of threat or coercion, on the one side, or of grudge or grievance, on the other. For obviously—to leap to the other extreme of Winthrop's comparison at once, without pausing to consider the probably unanswerable question of tenor and vehicle—that is exactly the way the regenerated soul, always female in this relation, must come to love the Bridegroom Christ. Not in the spirit of that unregenerate liberty which demands the right of continuing to do whatever reckless nature suggests, and most certainly not in the Antinomian desire to be free of the very notion of terms and conditions; but in the hard-won knowledge that God's will is our only safe way.

The issue here, to be sure, is neither the social nor the mystical marriage. But, as the lawyers love to say, the defendant's own remarks have opened the door. And what they clearly suggest is that Winthrop has taken the occasion of a local dispute to raise and to answer what he takes to be the fundamental question of civility itself, as that necessary condition of enduring humanity must be assimilated to, and never set against, the ideal of true religion. Declining to say—what quite easily he might have said—that the so-called freemen had a share in the governance of Massachusetts only because he had allowed their charter to be so (mis)interpreted; that he and a few other corporate share-holding officers might well have ruled as an oligarchy.[81] Having conceded thus early, however, that government of the saints indeed depends in some measure on the consent of the governed, he avoids entirely the argument from largesse and ingratitude. But he declines as well the opportunity to rehearse his case for the need for the oligarchic magistrates to have veto power over the democratic deputies. What he argues, instead, is the need for authority in general, and in terms which demand to

be called theological. In states just as well as in the churches they exist to protect, saints are those who agree to love the law, who understand their liberty by
analogy with that of "the church under the authority of Christ her king & husband" (588). What, after all, *could* the members of a church freely seek but the
will of their spiritual head?

Saints—which the freemen have needed to be, in order to be granted that
status in the first place—are those to whom the "yoke" of holy authority is as
"easy and sweet . . . as a bride's ornaments." Once again, as in the "Model," the
reference is being allowed to slide. And with it the gender of the audience. Regard the *female* aspect of this churchlike, saintly soul: "if through forwardness or
wantonness" she shake off, at any time, this easiest and sweetest yoke,

> she is at no rest in her spirit until she take it up again; & whether her Lord
> smiles upon her & embraceth her in his arms, or whether he frowns, or re-
> bukes, or smites her, she apprehends the sweetness of his love in all, & is
> refreshed, supported & instructed by every such dispensation of his au-
> thority. (588)

"Oh, brave new world that has such creatures in it." And oh, again, the "wondrous strength and generosity of a woman's heart." And whether we read this
miracle of fire and ice as needful supplement to John's loving correspondence
with Margaret Winthrop or as an ideal figment raised up out of Galatians, Ephesians, Revelation, and Matthew,[82] the fact remains that this is a remarkable speech
to be given to a bunch of local politicians aspiring to become constitutional theorists. Called into question, quite pointedly, on an issue of law, Winthrop has responded with a little sermon on love. As if the two were just the same.

Of course, the reader is anything but unprepared. Already adept at expressing love all around to his fellow magistrates, Winthrop has here but to kiss and
make up with the deputies as well. Nor can we forget the long-term preparation
of the "Model" itself: the only difference is that where saints were there evoked as
those required to love the other saints, in Christ, exactly as themselves, they are
here defined as those who love the law. Again in Christ—the supreme, indeed
the only reason, for asking more than nature can support. Then too, the logic of
this chapter still insists, the case of the Woman Hutchinson was resolved only
when there prevailed a Winthrop-led but community-endorsed decision that no
one here could ever set the love of Christ against the law. The law, say the lawyers,
lovingly, is what we saintly lawyers learn to love. Go in peace, therefore, to love
and serve the law.

Or are there, perhaps, dissenters from this holy consensus, preached at the outset, raised up to public drama by an early crisis, and then inscribed in all the works and days that followed? On the one side, those who stand for the "liberty wherewith Christ hath made us free." On the other side, "you know who they are that complain of this yoke & say, let us break their bands &c: we will not have this man to rule over us." That is to say, the "Speech" has its threat—not of historic scandal this time but of personal exposure:

> Even so brethren, it will be between you & your magistrates: if you stand for your natural corrupt liberties, & will do what is good in your own eyes, you will not endure the least weight of authority, but will murmur, & oppose, & be always striving to shake off that yoke. But if you will be satisfied to enjoy such civil & lawful liberties, such as Christ allows you, then will you quietly & cheerfully submit unto that authority which is set over you, in all the administrations of it, for your own good. (588)

At last identified: you know who you are; and we know where you live.

Our first thought, no doubt, is that the final note of Winthrop's message is more severe than even the bluntness of Perry Miller could quite express. It's not just that the so-called freemen are free but to follow the will of the suitably placed, but that in this particular mystification of the police forced, the authority of an eclectic, by some accounts motley, collection of men with the power to surveil and punish has been dressed up in the garments of Christ. Which collective figment has and exercises, ex officio, the power to turn freemen into women. On careful consideration, however, Winthrop's threat is more subtle, and less simply sexist, than it first appears. For as we parse the logic of his *if* and *then,* we detect the deep and perhaps characteristic temptation of that subjectivity which a majority of "qualified magistrates" and "learned ministers" had worked so tirelessly to establish: by your affect, if not quite by your actions, you will know you. As sainthood is suitably inferred from loving obedience, so—as the emphasis of Winthrop's clauses rearranges itself—so something quite the opposite would seem to reveal itself in resentful opposition. No one is perfect of course, but murmur too much, even in the jargon of strict construction, and someone may begin to suspect that, church members as you freemen undeniably are, the freedom you seek is merely a space for your natural corruption still. Go home now. But internalize that thought, colleagues and critics, before the next plenary session.

Off they all go, "to attend their other affairs." But Winthrop, as aware of "posterity" as he is of drama, holds on to his second, literary audience a little longer—for a review and a "memorial of . . . the workings of Satan," in the form of the

distempers [into which] a wise & godly people may fall in times of temptation: & when such have entertained some false & plausible principles, what
deformed superstructures they will raise thereupon, & with what unrea-
sonable obstinacy they will maintain them. (589)

Incredibly, as his tone seems to say, "some of the deputies had seriously conceived
that the magistrates affected an arbitrary government," which sought to have "an
unlimited power, to do what they pleased without control"; and that, in the dispute about the negative voice and elsewhere, they interpreted "all the magistrates
actions & speeches" (589) in this paranoic light. And so there followed a series of
radical proposals, all offered in the name of the charter, but all designed to limit
the power of the magistrates; and even a certain "treatise about arbitrary government," not widely known to be Winthrop's own, could do little to quiet the fears.
"Then fell out the Hingham case," wherein the deputies thought "either that the
magistrates had abused their authority, or else that their authority was [in fact]
too great to consist with the people's liberty" (591). Unfortunately, however, their
movement for redress was as flawed as their assumptions were diseased—as
twelve numbered observations all tend to suggest.

What Winthrop threatens to obscure, in his anticlimactic pursuit of *perfect*
vindication, is that the Devil was less in the details of procedure than in the
premise of suspicion. Magistrates too are saints, if anybody is. They too are obedient to the will of God. Submissive even. If they seem jealous of their "authority,"
this can as easily be in the name of the spiritual order as in their own pride of
place. How could his fellow saints have distrusted him so? Perhaps "posterity"
will do better. Remember him best, perhaps, not as a politician somewhat vain in
the exercise of power but in the milder construction of himself as a sensitive soul
in the type of Miriam: "If her father had spit in her face, . . . should she not have
been ashamed?" (586). Or else, if that is merely sentimental—or if we prove no
true posterity—it may be as well to remember him as the man who, in some high
sense which we can hardly now recover—and despite his unswerving opposition
to the life force of New England's most famous first-generation female—tried so
hard to express the values of sainthood in the figure of a woman.

———

Winthrop's "History" goes on, of course, looking again rather like a "Journal."
But this is not the place to confuse a modern reader's weariness with a Puritan
writer's failing powers; and a variety of important issues can be identified in the
years between Winthrop's "Little Speech," of July 3, 1645, and his final entries,

dated November 1648 and January 1649—the religious fallout of the Hingham matter, the arrival of a flood of books (and of a spirit of toleration) out of England, the first stirring and the final determinations of what would come to be called the Cambridge Synod, the missionary successes of John Eliot, the continuing dispute of doctrine and discipline with Samuel Gorton, and the constitutional crisis occasioned by the Remonstrance of 1646.[83] But one gets the impression that Winthrop, though far from losing interest in the unfolding history of New England, is aware that he has had his philosophical say. And for the purposes of theme and form, the tale is now pretty well complete: from the initiatory and perhaps naive ideal of saintly love on the model of the woman who will not bear any ill to befall the proper objects of her awakened affection, to the disturbing discovery of the life force of a real woman whose religious experience went so far beyond the reach of regulation as to threaten human authority itself, to the chastened reminder that even saints are under the law, distinguishing themselves not by scorning its demands but by embracing the identity it confers.

Only faith makes a saint, as all Protestants began by realizing. And, as the plot of New England elaborated itself, only saints came to vote in the general elections. But what exactly *was* this faith? One had to know. And to convince others as well. Shepard might fear that Winthrop's public expression of personal faith might sound a little thin; and readers of Winthrop have wondered whether he means to include himself among the "few" who could actually see any "difference" in the positions being debated;[84] but it seems impossible to deny this arch "magistrate" his intense fascination with the spirit of the premise that would so disturb the morale of his state. At the outset, that is to say, New England history is above all religious.

It seems proper, therefore, to understand the demand for the chartered "liberties" so vaunted by Winthrop's freemen as some faint fore- and aftershadowing of a protest on behalf of a covenant utterly free from the condition of works in any figure or relation. Not in the mind of the freemen themselves, perhaps, many of whom stood with the magistrates in their suppression of this radical theory of salvation. But quite credibly in the view of Winthrop—who probably thought his original "Model" had made both salvation and citizenship as "lovely" as possible, whose original interpretation of the charter had conferred significant civil liberties on a class of persons totally unused to self-governance, and whose moral suspicions were aroused by resistance to the duty of sworn obedience in whatever form. But however that may be, it certainly appears that, though his "Little Speech" is directed to citizens as such, its prime figure applies as well to, indeed is derived from, the mysterious region of sainthood itself; and that its self-conscious revision of the gendered, indeed the sexual bearing of the "Model"—

from the rosy world of prelapsarian love to the thorny bed of middle-class marriage—owes more than a little to Winthrop's experience with the Antinomians: to their general insistence on the Spirit's exemption from the law, no doubt; and not less to the curious consideration that the prime person so to insist was in fact a singular female personage.

Had Winthrop begun the history of non-Separatist salvation in New England with the observation that the affect of the saint was like the love of an awakened woman? Had he then had to listen to the ideas and the tone of just such a woman? It took him a while, but perhaps he had needed to say "wife" all along. Thomas Shepard, himself a noted lover of first one wife and then another, found his own way to learn the lesson of gender: New England churches and New England souls were virgins still, waiting long for the Bridegroom in faith and with moral energy undismayed; they had to keep garments very clean. Winthrop's female figure, splendid but singular, turns wedded wife in time, but only to affirm that a soul may love the law with as little resentment as woman comes to wait upon the will of the man she chooses. A pretty world and no doubt. Perhaps, at the end of the movie, these two could go off together.

CHAPTER NINE

MARCHING ORDERS

Johnson's Summary Syntax

I. THE MEANING OF NEW ENGLAND

The "plain style" has proven harder to describe than, on behalf of Puritan protest, merely to invoke. Latin quotations largely disappear, but biblical allusions, mostly overt but often artfully buried or subtly interwoven, more than fill their place—as if to prove that the function of second-level literacy can be fulfilled in more than just one way. And it would be hard to show that reformed pastors like Cotton and Shepard are not past masters of the rhetorical teachings of their age; or that each does not have his own way with the trope as well as the type. Still, variations have proved easier to identify and even enjoy than ordinary manifestations of the supposed norm: Hooker gets some credit for his way with the vernacular and his talent for everyday comparison, and Edward Taylor is easily recognized as the writer who worked these homely graces to the point of laughter.[1] And, while waiting for Cotton Mather's largely infelicitous innovations, now and then somebody will think of the witty style—or is it just the "Inkhorn terms"?—of Nathaniel Ward; even though no less acute an observer than Hawthorne once went out of his way peremptorily to reject his "empty wit of words."[2]

Overcome by the sentimental force of his story "The Gentle Boy," Hawthorne may for once have gone too far: *The Simple Cobler of Aggawam in America* (1647) may be said to express a version of Puritanism's "miserable distortions of the moral nature," but it has its moments of fun. Indeed, Hawthorne's invention of "Aubepine" may find its inspiration in the earlier Nathaniel's translation of himself as "Theodore de la Guard."[3] And no doubt one could begin a sampling of the conventional career of literature in New England with Ward's determined refusal to allow his saintly hatred of toleration to overshadow his secular philology.

Perry Miller's original anthology captured much of Ward's original energy, including his characteristic refusal of linguistic inhibition. Beginning with the anti-Antinomian premise that "The finer religion grows, the finer [Satan] spins his cobwebs," bestirring himself "to prevaricate evangelical truths," Ward's variable persona traces the spirit of innovation to a human source as well: anyone "that hath well-faced fancy in his crown, and doth not vent it now, fears the pride of his own heart will dub him duns forever." Still those who have heard New England "reputed a colluvies of wild opinionists" had better know it: Aggawam's "Cobler" is on the case, ready to discredit every "article of constipulation" that seeks to provide "free stable-room and litter for all kind of consciences, be they never so dirty or jadish." Recognizing that the Devil wants nothing but "liberty to enfranchise all other religions, and to embondage the true," the Cobbler will flatly oppose the wish for "lax tolerations upon state-pretences and planting necessities" (226–28).[4] What else makes sense in a world where Reformed Truth has sailed away to find its Due Form? Have not Familists and Antinomians ever had "free liberty to keep away," and do we not now allow our Anabaptists and other Enthusiasts leave "to be gone as fast as they can, the sooner the better"? (227).

Wishing to avoid the appearance of extremism, the Cobbler concedes that there must be "tolerations in things tolerable, exquisitely drawn out by the lines of the Scripture, and pencil of the Spirit"; these indeed are "the sacred favors of truth, the due latitudes of love, the fair compartments of Christian fraternity." Yet "irregular dispensations, dealt forth by the facilities of men, are the frontiers of error, the redoubts of schism, the perilous irritaments of carnal enmity." Nor are the logic of balance and the rhetoric of parallelism not the Cobbler's only resources, as his pure heart rejects not only religious mixing but social miscegenation in general:

> My heart hath natural detested four things: The standing of the Apocrypha in the Bible; foreigners dwelling in my country, to crowd out native subjects into the corners of the earth; alchemized coins; tolerations of divers religions, or of one religion in segregant shapes. (228)

No one has recorded the response of Native Americans to the second of these natural detestations, but perhaps even they were a bit Puritan at heart; for even the staunchest defenders of multiversity have had to overcome an initial preference for a little less otherness. Perhaps Ward may stand as an unembarrassed embodiment of our unreformed preference for the same.

On the score of our toleration of all sorts of religious possibilities, we are no doubt proof against Ward's prediction that our conscience will prove us "either an atheist, or an heretic, or an hypocrite, or at best a captive to some lust"; but it seems hard to deny that our perfect acceptance lies close to an equally perfect indifference, and that, on any premise other than perfect skepticism, it once made sense to think of religion as "*ignis probationis,* which doth *congregare homogenea & segregare heterogenia*" (228). And even if we deny that indifferentism argues neither atheism nor a willingness to "deal indifferently with God," we may afford a wry smile in response to Ward's perfect image of a world offering us the religion of our choice:

> I lived in a city, where a Papist preached in one church, a Lutheran in another, a Calvinist in a third; a Lutheran one part of the day, a Calvinist the other, in the same pulpit; the religions of that place was but motly and meager, their affections leopard-like. (229)

The present observer once taught in a college where the chapel had a button that caused several sorts of altars to revolve, from one Sabbath to another or through successive hours of a single Sunday. We smiled: it was, no doubt, the best we could do. But we often lamented that the same college was forbidden to have a department of theology or divinity—if only in memory of the time when religion was thought to matter.

Students who greet the Cobbler's witty rejections of the multicultural conscience with the predictable "That's not funny" are probably not part of the intended audience. His appeal must be to those who can remember the time when purity of heart was to will *one* thing. Nor, in a world where men are required to take courses in women's literature, can Ward expect a revival on the basis of his fun with the fair. To speak at all of women's fashions, this inspired social repairman must "borrow a little of their loose-tongued liberty, and mis-spend a word or two upon their long-waisted, but short-skirted patience." Professing to "honor the woman that can honor her self with her attire"—and persuaded that "a good text always deserves a fair margent"—this equable critic can even restrain himself when he sees a "trim, far trimmer than she that wears it." But this studied social patience has its limits:

> when I hear a nugiperous gentledame inquire what dress the Queen is in this week; what the nudiustrian fashion of the Court; I mean the very

newest; with egg to be in it in all haste, what ever it be; I look at her as the very gizzard of a trifle, the product of a quarter of a cipher, the epitome of nothing, fitter to be kicked, if she were a kickable substance, than either honored or humored. (232)

Domestic satire is one thing; kicking quite another. Let alone annihilation. And—even for those who love the word "nugiperous"—there's no excuse for domestic violence.

It may be of some interest to note that when the Cobbler wonders whether those women who "disfigure themselves with . . . exotic garbs" can have "any true grace," his point is esthetic and not theological; we may think we hear a pun, but it cannot survive the claim that women's fashion "not only dismantles their native lovely luster, but transclouts them into gant bar-geese" (233). Tasteless or not, this comic note may serve to remind us that Ward—who in another persona helped to frame a set of laws rather more secular than those imagined by John Cotton—wears the biblical conscience about as lightly as any writer from his generation.[5] Just so, in a sort of addendum on the tendency of Puritan *men* to wear long hair, the Cobbler honors Scripture precedent but relies at last on his own sense of masculine propriety:

> If those . . . termed Rattle-heads and Impuritans would take up a resolution to begin in moderation of hair, to the just reproach of those . . . called Puritans and Round-heads, I would honor their manliness, as much as the others' godliness, so long as I knew what man or honor meant. (30–31)[6]

Those were the days: men, who "use not to wear such manes" (31), were very men; and women dressed to please these men and not the queen of France.

We may wonder how to take the remark with which Ward ends the explicitly satirical portion of his book—that we are wrong if we imagine he has "spoken rather merrily than seriously" (29)[7]—but we need to notice that the remaining portion of the *Cobler* is devoted to a serious attempt to speak "a word over the sea" (31) on how, without sacrificing the interest of truth, the warring parties in England might reach a "seasonable and reasonable cessation of arms" (32). Surely, he argues in the first of four titled sections, "Reformation" has proceeded to the point where Parliament can manage to "commoderate" (33) the argument between Independent and Presbyterian; and soon, for while "public assemblies of divines cannot agree on a right way, private coventicles of illiterate men will soon find a wrong" (37). Reformed Truth being set in its rightful place, Parliament and Crown ought to work toward a "composition" of their differences, each modestly realizing that "moral Laws, royal prerogatives, popular liberties, are not of man's making or giving, but God's" (48). "Mutual cessation of arms" will then depend on nothing more than a "mutual and general forgiveness" (61).

In the end, however, if this simplified advice cannot be taken, the Cobbler must "speak briefly and indifferently still to both sides" a word about the further prosecution of hostilities. The "Royalists" need to try themselves in light of the knowledge that "foolish cowardly man . . . dreads and hates nothing in heaven or earth so much as truth" (64), and to be warned that they "will find it a far easier field to wage war against all the armies that ever were or will be on earth, and all the angels of heaven, than to take up arms against any truth of God" (65). And so, to the other side, to those "brave Englishmen" who press the cause of "truth and righteousness": "Go on undauntedly: as you are called and chosen, so be faithful" (65). And be assured that "we your brethren, though we necessarily abide beyond Jordan, and remain on the American sea-coasts"—declining even to send learned representatives to the assembly charged with the long-delayed reformation of our mother church—"will send up armies of prayers to the throne of grace." And, visionaries that we are, even under our mask of satire, "We will likewise help you believe that God will be seen on the mount" (67).

Confident that "it is all one with him to save by many or by few" (67), the Cobbler seems to be preparing his former countrymen for the possibility that, in the end, the remnant in New England may be enough. And for this reason of Puritan "foreign policy," if no other, it might have been well for Miller to have provided more of Ward's holy politics than his "quodrobulary" sayings (235) about emperors, kings, asses, and devils.[8] Ward has only a limited sense of how complicated the religious situation in England had become, even as the loyally professing emigrants were having the logic of Non-Separating Congregationalism pretty much their own way. But he really is concerned—enough to "compose half a dozen distichs" (42) concerning wars of religion—to register his sense that states do well to notify their people, by "some safe woven manifesto," what "flagitous crimes [are] prohibited by the light of nature" (49); to instruct (a still unbeheaded) King Charles to make conscience of matters such as "the sophistication of religion and policy in your time, the luxury of your Court and Country, . . . your forgetful breaches upon the Parliament, your compliance with popish dogs" (55); and to remind the unhappy monarch that the "will of a king is [so] very numinous" that "it were well for a king if he had no will at all" (59).

And yet, one might reasonably argue, Ward's devotion to reasonable behavior is never quite equal to his love of words:

Civil liberties ... are the *prima pura principia, propria quarto modo,* the *sine quibus* of humane states. ... People's prostrations of these things ... are profane prostitutions; ignorant ideotismes, under-natural noddaries. (46)

The Latin is there for intellectual authority, but the insistent usage of flagrant derivatives signifies—cobblerspeak be damned—a love of polysyllabic expression for its own sake; and "noddaries" means principally to advertise the polymorphous possibilities of early modern English. Probably it would involve no fatal risk of reputation if one were to ask students to read a little of Ward in the interest of the verbal might-have-been—wackier than Thomas Morton but clearer as well. Or, if that is to trivialize his incorrect politics, to read him in supplement to Jonson's characterization of Zeal-of-the-Land Busy or Butler's *Hudibras.* Satire of the Puritans, however telling, in no way precludes the possibility of their own satiric productions. Either way, our impression of the temperament of seventeenth-century Massachusetts, always in danger of reducing itself to cliché, can surely stand the reminder that a Puritan can also be a Cobbler.

Still, it is one (relaxed) argument of this chapter that Edward Johnson's *Wonder-Working Providence of Sion's Saviour* (1653)[9] is the work that ought to occupy the place we reserve for the bizarre exception that defines the conventional rule of Puritan style. For one thing, Johnson's book, though the product of a layman, is more continuous with the interests of history and piety expressed in the books generated by the problems inherent in New England's original theory and practice.[10] Poised near the moment of generational transition, Johnson's bravura performance maintains the old generic loyalties, as the whim-whams of Nathaniel Ward do not. Furthermore, where Ward's literary energy is given over to the task of discrediting innovation and instructing foreigners, Johnson's attention is focused on the glories of and dangers to "the good old way." And finally, where Ward's outrages of style seem altogether studied, expressing a desire for a linguistic performance that has outlasted the fashion of plainness, Johnson's sins against an emergent modern syntax impress us as the spontaneous marks of decorum whose overflowing zeal for the past, present, and future of New England can scarcely afford to pause for a period. Ward's satire neatly identifies emergent abuses. Johnson's enthusiasm simply runs on. Delightfully.

Johnson's history has, of course, a case to make. Largely it is conservative, agreeing with the preparationist/sanctificationist emphasis of Hooker and Shepard, and with the actions taken by Winthrop's government to foster and extend the sway of that emergent standard. Yet there are some surprises, as when Johnson sounds more like Cotton in expecting apocalyptic fulfillment than like Shepard in preparing the New England soul for survival over the long haul. And in a world discovering that there really were at least two "Orthodoxies in Massachusetts," the choice of episode and distribution of emphasis of an inspired layman are certainly worth our notice. In the end, however, Johnson's Wonderbook lives in the tone of his excited but underconstructed sentences. Which we ought to learn to read.[11]

———

Beginning with "A relation of the first planting in New England, in the year, 1628," *The Wonder-Working Providence of Sion's Saviour* loses no time in advertising the fact that its movement will more often be swift than subtle. Book I, chapter 1, announces the presentation of a subject familiar enough: "The sad Condition of England, when this People removed." But nothing in the richly various history of Puritan literature so far can possibly prepare us for the breathless pace and compressed intensity:

> When England began to decline in Religion, like lukewarm Laodicea, and instead of purging out popery, a farther compliance was sought not only in vain idolatrous ceremonies, but also in profaning the Sabbath, and by proclamation throughout their parish churches, exasperating lewd and profane persons to celebrate a Sabbath like the Heathen to Venus, Bacchus, Ceres; in so much that the multitude of irreligious lascivious and popish affected persons spread the whole land like grasshoppers, in this very time Christ the glorious king of his churches, raises an army out of our English nation, for freeing his people from their long servitude . . . ; and because every corner of England was filled with the fury of malignant adversaries, Christ creates a New England to muster up the first of his forces in; (23)[12]

And five or six more jam-packed lines besides. Johnson's (1910) editor inserts his first footnote after "Venus, Bacchus and Ceres," which is also the place of the passage's first all but useless semicolon; but as to the student-friendly plan of clarifying emphasis by regularizing punctuation, forget it. The various clauses of assumption and assertion do not add up to sentences: perfectly intelligible to the reader ready to relish the author's enthusiasm, they explicate but they do not parse. Indeed their refusal of subordination is endemic: these considerations all go together, all of first-rate importance.

Venus, Bacchus, and Ceres the more experienced reader will remember from their striking but inopportune appearance at Bradford's redaction of Morton's

Merry Mount; and imagination (or an instructed reading of Hawthorne's "May-pole") will easily work them back into the fabric of English religious life, where only a little wit was required to detect the pagan intention behind James I's "Declaration concerning Sports," which "encouraged the practice of playing games on Sundays."[13] But where, again, is Laodicea? How subtly does Jesus' express desire to "vomit" the lukewarm out of his mouth control Johnson's idea that someone was supposed to "purge" popery?—whatever precise practices that evidently unfriendly term may be thought to include, and however they may have spawned a positively Egyptian crop of grasshoppers. Of course, most of this has, by 1650, been said many times before, in one place or another; and Johnson gives us, from the outset, the impression of a man who, having swallowed whole too many Puritan sermons, cannot contain his wish to chew on them in public. But even the prepared reader is constrained to confess that the Puritan myth almost never comes on us quite this fast. The Puritan reader will know all this, we patiently reassure ourselves. Yet it seems as if Johnson's gift is excited expression of personal passion and not anxious concern for reader response.

Historical suspicion may linger to notice that, though *New* England is emphatically a providential creation rather than an opportune discovery, it figures primarily as a place for Christ "to muster up the first of his forces in": time alone will tell, that is to say, if the locus of the Puritan "Errand" will become an end in itself.[14] But when the energy of the prose is running so high, only the pedantic will pause. Others will need to be reminded that though "every corner of England was filled with the fury of malignant adversaries," and that though the "low condition, little number, and remoteness of the place made these adversaries triumph," still "in this height of their pride the Lord Jesus brought sudden and unexpected destruction upon them." Only with that assurance does Johnson make his first full stop: "Thus you have a touch of the time when this work began" (23). Whether Thomas Morton knew it or not. An exciting time, as we cannot now doubt. A full present if there ever was one.

The remaining paragraphs of chapter 1 are formally more dramatic than this opening, but even their military manner can hardly be more intense. Following Christ's intention "to manifest his kingly office . . . more fully than ever yet the sons of men saw," even to the end-time uniting "Jew and Gentile churches in one faith," and beginning his work with "our English Nation," he stirs up his servants to act as "Heralds of [the] King":

"Oh yes! oh yes! oh yes! All you the people of Christ that are here oppressed, imprisoned and scurrilously derided, gather yourselves together, your wives and little ones, and answer to your several names as you shall be shipped for his service, in the ... united colonies of New England, where you are to attend the service of the King of Kings." (24)

We wryly notice, perhaps, that the 1628 imagination of Christ extends to both the peopling and then the holy joining, in 1643, of the separate colonies of Massachusetts and Connecticut; or we may savor our understanding that to "attend the service" means to wait for the announced instructions rather than to hurry off to church. But less precious ears may wonder at once if they have heard the main intent:

> "Can it possibl[y] be the mind of Christ (who formerly enabled so many soldiers of his to keep their station unto the death here) that now so many soldiers disciplined by Christ himself ... should turn their backs to the disheartening of their fellow-soldiers, and loss of further opportunity in gaining a greater number of subjects to Christ's kingdom?" (24)

The point is understood but not well taken, for the proclamation merely resumes its own military confidence and pace: "What, creature, wilt not thou know that Christ the King crusheth with a rod of iron the pomp and pride of man, and must he like man cast and contrive to take his enemies at advantage?" (24).

Certainly not. The little "retreat" to New England may leave the adversaries of the Kingdom of Christ "glorying in the pride of their power" but—remembering how great Caesar could "so suddenly fetch over fresh forces from Europe to Asia, Pompy to foil"—consider "How much more shall Christ who createth all power call over the 900 league ocean at his pleasure such instruments as he thinks meet to make use of in this place" (24–25). Evidently this is no ordinary war. Indeed, the departing remnant must know, more certainly than John Robinson could preach it to the retreating *Mayflower,* or John Cotton or John Winthrop to the more self-important *Arabella,* that this *New* England "is the place where the Lord will create a new heaven and a new earth in, new churches, and a new common-wealth together; Wherefore"—as chapter runs on into chapter, with only a comma to stay the rush, we need to hear the details of "The Commission of the People of Christ shipped for New England, and first their gathering into Churches" (25).

As history, all this proclamation is supposed to involve repetition, but Johnson writes as though it is being said and heard for the first time, at the migrating moment itself.[15] The literary effect is one of original excitement, but the historiographic implication is a little more curious. Already—even before presenting us with the clear and precise terms of a fictional "Commission," which many a soul-searching Puritan would have been exceedingly grateful to hear preached in literal fact—Johnson is assuring us that all sorts of deep and obscure matters, meanings that took time to unfold, were clear from the outset. Obviously Johnson is inscribing the bold outlines of a History that will be known and repeated by a number of future remembrancers; but he may be misrepresenting both the clarity and the confidence of the original migrants. Certainly Winthrop cannot produce this tone in his 1629 rehearsal of his "Reasons"; even the glowing rhetoric of his "Model," bright with the hope of covenantal assurance, is shadowed with the thought of failure. Nor is Johnson's excited invention of the New English call to arms anything like what Shepard remembered as a "poise of spirit." Either Johnson is projecting backward, for the sake of his drama. Or else—more likely—he is realizing that what the original migrants could only take the risk to hope had come in sober experience to seem exactly so. To Bradford, Winthrop, and Shepard, New England meant *either* Holy History *or* a dumb mistake. To Johnson, the last, best, indeed the only hope, had come quite true.

No wonder, then, if the pace of this original repetition cannot control itself. Given the observable flourishing of the seeds of things once hidden in Divine Wisdom, how could one fail to share the excitement of their first historic planting? Puritans of 1650 may not be the final fulfillment of their own typic prediction, but surely they had the right to celebrate their destiny as if it were all one. And so they must hear—again, as it were—the call they all but knew they were answering, even before Winthrop defined their Covenant.

One effect of this missionary prolepsis is that we must wait until chapter 12 to learn the personal feelings of these enlisted saints. And even then, though Johnson does not spare us the scene of the "last farewell" of those embracing a "voluntary banishment" in the "western world" (50), his main interest is to assure us that the public motive can overcome the personal misery. Running on from a sentence about gathering together in Southampton—and purchasing a ship typologically named the *Eagle*—the voice of enthusiasm raises all the questions a skeptic could think to press: turn your backs on your "yearly revenue"? Abandon "your tables filled with great variety of food, your coffers filled with coin, your houses beautifully built and filled with all rich furniture"? Cannot you practice the "chief duties of a Christian" as well here "as any place in the world"? Only then, well assured that none of these "siren songs" can sway "the immovable resolutions that Christ continued in these men," does Johnson invite us to "pass on and attend with tears" (51) the farewell speech of his own epic representative.

A pious pilgrim, as full of tears as sentiment itself could require, will assure his friend that "as near as my own soul doth thy love lodge in my breast, with thought of the heart-burning ravishments that thy heavenly speeches have wrought." Himself recovering from a bout of weeping, the friend laments that he shall never "see thy face in the flesh again." Deeply moved, the pilgrim nevertheless calls a puritanic halt to this heart-rending drama of conflicted loves:

> What do you do weeping and breaking my heart? I am now pressed for the service of our Lord Christ, to re-build the most glorious edifice of Mount Sion in a wilderness, and as John Baptist, I must begin by crying prepare ye the way of the Lord . . . for behold he is coming again. (52)

Further tears ensue, to be sure, as the departing pilgrim and his bosom friend discover that their feelings are widely shared; just so would Johnson seem to give the "natural affections" their due. Yet the chapter ends with a lament that "the best choice our orthodox ministers can make is to take up a perpetual banishment from their native soil." As they depart, at the express command of Christ, through the door he has "opened upon our earnest request," their faithful historian proposes that "for England's sake they are going out of England to pray without ceasing for England" (53). Critics may suspect this patriotism,[16] but its effect is to move the emphasis off the pitiably personal.

And even in this blunted form, this sentimental indulgence has had to wait for five chapters of pure ideology and four more of tendentious prehistory. Chapter 2 spells out, as if in elaboration of Winthrop's "Model," the terms of the "Commission" these Christian soldiers have been given.[17] They are to "search out," first of all, "the mind of God both in planting and continuing church and civil government," being careful that "they be distinct, yet agreeing and helping the one to the other." Further:

> Let the matter and form of your churches be such as were in the primitive times . . . , neither national nor provincial, but gathered together in covenant of such a number as might ordinarily meet together in one place, and built of such living stones as outwardly appear saints by calling. (25–26)

Jameson notes that this précis of congregational polity is a little beyond what "the Puritans who planned the great Migration to New England had . . . in mind from the beginning,"[18] but Johnson charges ahead to require that ordained elders must be kept free of "anxious cares for their daily bread" and be learned enough to keep a congregation from being "wildered with strange revelations of every fantastic brain" (26).

Accordingly, "here are to be shipped among you many both Godly judicious and learned, who"—in chapter 3—will not "for lucre" admit sheep just because their "fair fleeces allure much," or, for the sake of filling the pews, knowingly admit any "wolves in sheep's clothing," or hinder "the increase of churches," or stop their ears against "the counsel of an orthodox synod" (26–27). Winthrop may well have hoped for but one church at the utopian beginning, which would not of course require anything like a synod.[19] But as the "increase of churches" is, as we shall see, both a narrative principle and a necessary theme in this history, Johnson is anxious to elevate his private passion to the level of theory. And—as only a comma splices this chapter to the next—he cannot resist the temptation to register as originary the principles his experience has taught him concerning "How the people in Christ's churches are to behave themselves": judiciously, first of all, in refusing to call "weak ones to office" and, as a further dimension of pro-lepsis begins to reveal itself, in rejecting the appeal of "silly women laden with di-verse lusts" (28); charitably, as well, in admitting new members and in "casting out such members as walk disorderly" (28–29); and humbly, in this same matter, "remembering yourselves were once aliens" (29). But charity is not the same as indifference, and the New England saint, called for "pulling down the kingdom of Antichrist," must not "set up for tolerating times." Far from contenting himself that he is "set at liberty," he must take up "arms, and march manfully on till all opposers of Christ's kingly power be abolished" (30). Apocalyptic expectations are thus planted at the outset, but also a predictive reflection of the toleration anxiety of the 1640s.

But as inspired prolepsis is Johnson's founding trope, militarism the maga-zine of his preferred rhetoric, the run-on sentence his characteristic form of per-sonal expression, so the power to (over)specify is also an essential part of his saintly syntax. Thus chapter 5—ostensibly a prediction of the sort of "civil gov-ernment the people of New England are to set up," and serving notice that the civil ruler is to enforce more than "the second table" (30)—thrives instead as a list of sectaries to be avoided: Gortonists, Papists, Familists, Seekers, Antinomians, Anabaptists, Prelacy (31). The chapter then trails off into the duty of the magis-trate to protect the church, picking up only when its "Lastly" (32) carries us over to a chapter on the maintenance of "war-like discipline": anticipating the final battle with Antichrist, the saints are to store themselves "with all sorts of weapons for war," to "furbish up [their] swords, rapiers, and all other piercing weapons." Not quite enough for the task, perhaps; but rather than retreat from his martial rhetoric, Johnson promises that Christ will yet provide the "great artillery" (33).

Then, as if to insist on the literalness of his apocalyptic militarism, this fur-ther instruction: "in the mean time spare not to lay out your coin for powder, bul-lets, match, arms of all sorts, and all kind of instruments for war." It may all seem incredible "now," in 1628 or 1629, but in time "you shall see in that wilderness, wither you are going, troops of stout horsemen marshaled, and therefore fail not to ship lusty mares along with you" (33). And, lest your "faith fail at sight of the great armies of Gog and Magog," you must appoint only "diligent" officers in your "New England regiments," and "keep your weapons in continual readiness" (34); for only after these great military convulsions shall come "the time of breaking spears into mattocks, and swords into scythes" (35). This complex vision—rather than coveting titles or grabbing land—is the only commissioned motive. Elsewhere, perhaps, world-weary followers of Thomas Shepard are yet rehearsing, to forestall the lengthening shadow of disillusion, the long-haul instructions of their latter-day prophet of inspired waiting. Here, however, in tones that bespeak other loyalties, Johnson's undaunted enthusiasm practices the curious effect of preaching immediate expectation to a set of pilgrims who hardly know where they are going.

Then, after reading de facto development as a priori instruction—and further to defer the moment of remembered departure—Johnson turns his attention from implied meanings and motives to actual circumstances. Under the observation that the Lord helped "his people to a large liberty in spiritual things, under the hopes of gain in earthly things" (36), chapter 7 notices that the 1629 charter to the Massachusetts Company might be looked upon as a joining of the "Worthies of Christ . . . with merchants and others, who had an eye at a profitable plantation"; and he promises that, "one way or another," the Lord will recompense all those in "any way helpful to his people in his work" (38). Changing the focus, chapter 8 notices all the "wonderful preparation" wrought for the Lord's people "in this western world": a comet observed in learned Europe, the first appearance of a ship to affright the natives of "this naked nation" (39), a favorable beginning of "a rich trade for beaver-skins" (40), the "great mortality" among the natives, by which God "not only made room for his people to plant, but also tamed the hard and cruel hearts of these barbarous Indians," so that a mere "handful of his people landing . . . in Plymoth Plantation found little resistance" (41–42).

Not in possession of the Bradford manuscript, but feeling himself "prevented" by the account of Edward Winslow, Johnson nevertheless recognizes Plymouth as a sort of holding place for the "brethren and fellow soldiers who arrived eight years after them" (42). And, fusing "into one the stories of Samoset and Squanto,"[20] he admires the timely appearance of an Indian prepared in England to offer the newcomers, in their own language, "Much welcome Englishmen." All this makes an impression of "present providence" so powerful that it "might not soon be washed off with the encumbered cares of a desert wilderness." Bradford himself would reach a far less happy conclusion.[21] But as Johnson is bent upon telling the story of success in a hostile world made safe for the planting of churches, his emphasis must fall on the fact that, after becoming "acquainted and reconciled with most of the neighboring Indians," the Pilgrim group

> planted a Church of Christ there, and set up civil government, calling the ... place Plymouth: under this jurisdiction there are ten churches at this very day, this being the first place any English resorted unto for the advancement of the kingly government of Christ in this western world. (43)

In thus honoring Plymouth, exactly as Bradford, in 1630, had hoped, Johnson is telling a story Bradford *might* have told—if only the multiplication of churches had not required the splitting of the original rock.[22]

There are, of course, many other churches to be counted off when, presently, the saints go marching in to this western world in their numbers. For the present, salvation's own historian must recognize the wisdom of the merchants who designated "Mr. John Indicat" to govern an advance party sent to the Massachusetts in 1629: "of courage bold and undaunted, yet sociable, and of a cheerful spirit, loving and austere, applying himself to either as occasion served." Other memorials capture less complexity, and fiction always wins the minds and hearts; but even Hawthorne will agree that Endicott was "a fit instrument to begin this wilderness-work" (44).[23] During which there must have seemed "little likelihood there was building the temple for God's worship": one recognizable Puritan "betook him to the seas again," and the other, also well remembered in Hawthorne, took up farming, "retaining no symbol of his former profession but a canonical coat" (46). Yet in the very next chapter, a quorum of saints—"by calling appearing so in the judgment of charity"—fasted, prayed, and then "joined together in a holy covenant with the Lord, ... promising by the Lord's assistance to walk together ... , and to cleave to the Lord with a full purpose of heart" (47). Not quite Bradford's formula, but close enough to satisfy the needs of recognition and of myth.

With continuing attention to the Scripture model of "particular churches," these sparse but highly motivated beginners "elected and ordained one Mr. Higginson to be Teacher of this first Church of Christ, set up in those parts," and then called "the Reverend Mr. Skelton" to the office of "Exhorting Elder." Jameson glosses this latter office as "Pastor," but Johnson's poems call both Higginson and Skelton the "first Pastor of the Church of Christ at Salem." And after praising both for the willingness to leave their native soil, Johnson rushes to announce that "this Church of Christ, being thus begun," has done nothing but "increase and fructify." Indeed, "every ear [must] listen, and every heart admire" the fact that in the time from 1629 to 1650, when "the great Jehova" was working such "fearful desolations" in England and among the natives—where the latter are reduced from "a populous Nation of 3000 able men" to a sorry remnant of "less than 300"—Christ has raised up "forty-three churches in joint communion with one another, professing one God, one Christ, and one Gospel, and in those churches about 7500 souls in one profession" (48–49). The miracle of supplantation seems the more remarkable as the new civilization has had to be "cut out of the woods and bushes" by men who passed through "a dreadful and terrible ocean" (49).

So we must "know," as the burden of chapter 11, that this is "but the beginnings of Christ's glorious reformation and restoration of his churches to a more glorious splendor than ever." And in Johnson's figure, the beacon is more fire than light:

> [Christ] hath therefore caused [the] dazzling brightness of his presence to be contracted in the burning-glass of these his people's zeal, from whence it begins to be left upon many parts of the world with such hot reflection of that burning light, which hath fired many places already, the which shall never be quenched till it hath burnt up Babylon root and branch. (49)

So we behold these "troops" of Christ, marking them well "man by man as they march, terrible as an army with banners." And others too must "crowd in . . . to see this glorious sight." And everyone eager for "his coming" must "hear what his herald proclaims" (49–50):

> Babylon is fallen, is fallen, both her doctrine and lordly rabble of Popes, Cardinals, Lordly-Bishops, Friars, Monks, Nuns, Seminary-Priests, Jesuits, Ermites, Pilgrims, Deans, Prebends, Arch-Deacons, Commissaries, Officials, Proctors, Sumners, Singing-men, Choristers, Organists, Bellows-blowers, Vergers, Porters, Sextons, Beads-men, and Bell-ringers and all others who never had name in the Word of God. (50)

One had not known Puritanism had undone so many. Not even from Bradford, whose class hatred is more than sufficient to mark reformation as a radical shift of culture. Where he announced the idea, Johnson wrote the list—in a supra-syntactic unit that goes on to reidentify erroneous movements and persons—Arians, Gortonists, Papists, Antinomians, Arminians, Familists, Conformatants or Formalists, Seekers (50).

Only now—after fifty pages of ideologically informed effort and providential success—does Johnson portray the sad affect of the "voluntary banishment."

Fearing everywhere that the necessary and sustaining loves of the flesh will turn to that idolatry in which the Puritan defines himself as loving the creature more than the creator, Johnson offers us the tearful separation of friends and the sad disruption of families only after the rare devices of his rhetoric has done all it can to assure us that the triumph of holy history can more than repay the keenest loss of personal love. To be sure, his zeal rushes to promise the very most we may expect, and in a term short enough for memory to compare and measure. To offer anything less, he appears to feel, would be to disguise gratuitous dreariness as spiritual joy. And the pleasure of resignation is no part of his plot.

———

Johnson seems to have designed the first (longest) book of his exemplary work to run as far as the challenge and defeat of the Antinomians. Indeed, that crucial episode draws forth some of his finest run-on rhetoric. But between the tears of the "last farewell" to friends (50) and the "heart-easing moan" of his "serious meditations" on the "sorrowful condition of the people of Christ" (133) when encountering these dread erronists lies just less than a third of Johnson's entire volume. Nor is Johnson's imagination slow to discover sufficient matter of enthusiasm for the time between.

Chapter 13 totals up the "charges expended by this poor people," and all "to enjoy Christ in the purity of his ordinances" (54)—namely, "one hundred ninety-two thousand pounds," quite apart from the "pittance" laid out by the Adventurers, the mere availability of which must be read as a "memorable providence" (55). Memorable too is the "wonderful preservation" of this generously self-sacrificing host as they crossed what Johnson believes to be "the largest ocean in the world" (56), where seasickness, the death of cattle, and outbreaks of disease serve only to strengthen their reliance upon the Lord. And though Johnson tends to pass over the trials of the ocean passage, he cannot omit to take "a short survey of all the voyages by sea, in the transportation of these armies of the great Jehova" up to the year 1643, when England herself "began to endeavor after Reformation" and when indeed "some of the chief worthies of Christ returned back." Of ships, 298—or 198, as the next chapter corrects the figure—and of "men, women and children passing over this wide ocean" about 21,200. Whose example inspires chapter 15 to exhort "all people, nations, and languages, to advance the Kingdom of Christ" (58). With feeling:

And now all you whose affections are taken up with wonderful matters (attend) and you that think Christ hath forgotten his poor despised people (behold) and all you that hopefully long for Christ's appearing to confound Antichrist (consider) and rejoice all ye his churches the world throughout, for the Lamb is preparing his Bride, and oh! ye the ancient Beloved of Christ, whom he of old led by the hand from Egypt to Canaan, through the great and terrible wilderness, look here, behold him whom you have pierced, preparing to pierce your hearts with his *Wonder-Working Providence*. (58–59)

The penetration of the history of New England by the poetry of Israel is not complete, perhaps, but deep enough to redeem what is yet a "little handful."

Especially in view of the glory that lies ahead. "Weak worms," for now, they are only "the porch of the glorious building in hand." If so much wonderful providence now, what works to expect "when the whole nation of England" shall set upon Reformation? And well beyond even that, for "assured confidence there is also for all nations." The winter being past, and the rain being "changed and gone," let all the English brethren "come out of [their] holes": "fear not because their number is but small, gather into churches and let Christ be your King." And more:

Ye Dutch, come out of your hodge-podge, the great mingle-mangle of religion among you [that] hath caused the churches of Christ to increase so little. . . . Oh, ye French! fear not . . . the croaking frogs in your land, Christ is reaching out the hand to you . . . ye Germans that have had such a bloody bickering, . . . cast off your loose and careless kind of Reformation [and] gather into churches . . . oh Italy! The seat and center of the Beast, Christ will now pick out a people from amongst you for himself. . . . Oh! Ye Spaniards and Portugals, Christ will show your nations the abominations of the beastly Whore. (59)

And "finally"—when all the world will be like America in the *end*—a call to "all ye nations." The "Seed of Israel" especially must "grow together as one tree." As the "bloody battle of Gog and Magog" approaches, judge in conscience "whether these poor New England people be not the forerunners of Christ's army" (60), and whether he has not sent them "to proclaim to all nations the near approach of the most wonderful works" the sons of man have ever seen. "Will you not believe," he demands, "that a nation can be borne in a day?" (60–61). Believe it, and you shall see far greater things as well. And soon.

In the meantime, however, we are to "look on the following discourse": of providential deliverances at sea in chapter 16, where only one of those 198 ships "ever miscarried" (61); of the first establishment of a civil government and the happy admission of about 110 church members to the status of freemen (66). Then, as the very substance of his midworld discourse in these latter days, the regular foundation, in 1631, of the second, third, fourth, fifth, sixth, and seventh Churches of Christ, duly gathered, chapter by chapter, at Charlestown, Dorchester, Boston, Roxbury, Lynn, and Watertown. Modern footnotes reassure the reader that his own memory of the ordering may be more faithful than Johnson's,[24] but the local geography and clerical personnel are accurate enough. The sequence is repetitious, to be sure, as all the churches begin "with a small number in a desolate . . . wilderness"; and, as the wilderness itself turns slowly but surely into a garden, the mercy of Christ turns them all into so many "fruitful fields" (68). But the prose remains alive, as each chapter/church has its distinguishing details—and its own celebratory poem. Dorchester, for example, is "frontier town" where some "ancient traders" who "came for other ends" tried to resist the work, but the "hand of Christ" (69) overcame. And Roxbury shows that God can not only bring "fruitful fields and gardens" out of "dismal swamps and tearing bushes" (72) but also raise up, in John Eliot, a prophet who can "heathen people teach / In their own language, God and Christ to see" (72).

We may find these facts "discursive," but what did we expect the discourse of salvation to be like? This, evidently, is the way the world begins to end: not (yet) with a bang, but with a series of gatherings of particular churches, formulaic in intention and uniform in expression, but each marked with congregational particularity. All supported by the government of Winthrop and Dudley, all bearing "the penuries of a wilderness" with a "great cheerfulness" (75), all holding the line against the appearance of a "greedy desire for land" (77). And all guaranteed by the Lord's gracious protection—"from the barbarous cruelties of the Heathen" (78), from the constant press of hunger, from the "weekly snows" (84) of an unseasonably cold winter, and from "extreme parching heat of the sun" (86) in the season that followed. For the timely rescue from which, "this poor people" declared in October 1633 a day of solemn thanksgiving and were much edified on that day not only by the Reverend John Wilson's reasonings on providence but also by the humility with which he welcomed "the Reverend Mr. John Cotton" (88).

The almost casual reminder of this recent arrival reminds us that Johnson has been faced with the problem of maintaining his soteriological enthusiasm across a stretch of months in which not much is happening. But now, after Cotton gets his welcoming poem, bigger things begin to move. Chapter 28 gives us the "Eighth Church of Christ," gathered at Cambridge, in 1633, around the "golden tongue and pen" of Thomas Hooker, whose "rhetoric shall people's affections whet" (90–91) and goes on to note that in 1634, while Dudley was being chosen for the first time as governor, a certain "well smooth'd Stone" (93) was added as teacher to the Cambridge congregation. Chapter 29, honored by its inclusion in Miller's anthology, violates Johnson's intention to speak of departures from England only in a "general relation" in order to savor the remarkable preservations of John Norton and especially "that soul ravishing minister Mr. Thomas Shepard" (94). His establishment at Cambridge, in the space left by Hooker and Stone, must wait its turn, as now the Lord gathers a "Ninth Church," at Ipswich, under the leadership of "that soldier of Christ Master Nathaniel Ward" (97).

The church at Newberry is also said to be "gathered," though its principal officers differ somewhat "from all the former, and after mentioned Churches in the preeminence of their presbytery"; indeed, Johnson's ecumenism points to their working presence as an example that might have prevented many "hot contentions . . . about Presbyterian and Independent government in churches" (98). The removal of the congregation of Hooker and Stone to a place "well stored with meadow" (105) is duly noted, but the new churches, at Hartford and New Haven, do not count in Johnson's ongoing tally; and their notation comes only after Johnson has thought to wonder—amidst an influx of migrants—whether "purity, peace and plenty [can] run all in one channel" (102). Nevertheless, Shepard's replacement congregation at Cambridge is counted as the eleventh gathered in Massachusetts (107). Concord, the "Twelfth" (110), requires two chapters, as this "first in-land town" calls forth "a short epitome," in sentences that stretch over whole pages, "of the manner how [this people] placed down their dwellings in this desert wilderness, the Lord being pleased to hide" from their eyes the "difficulties they are to encounter" (111). And Johnson's "Thirteenth Church," gathered at Hingham in 1636, holds for him the lesson about the New England constitution: the "un-brotherly contention" that will break out there in 1645, calling forth Winthrop's "Little Speech" and refusing to be healed by soothing words of neighbor churches, provides ample proof that particular churches "ought . . . never to take up such an Independent way as to reject the advise and counsel of each other"; for although the Lord has given "full power to every particular church," he has "so dispensed his gifts, that when one want, the other shall abound" (116).

In noticing the election in 1636 of Sir Henry Vane along with the gathering of a church "at Sandwich in Plymouth patent" (118), chapter 28 reminds us that the colony has been filling up with all sorts of refugees from the wars in England. Lacking any longer a sense of who may be loyal to what, we may not be surprised to hear "Of the first appearing in the field of the enemies of Christ's people in point of reformation." Trusting to his original figure, Johnson himself seems prepared to take the shock in full narrative stride: "Christ having safely landed many a valiant soldier of his on these western shores, draws hither also the common enemies to Reformation." And grasping for a type, he recalls that as the Lord "sometime drew Sisera, the Captain of Jabin's army, to the River Kishon for their destruction; only herein was a wide difference, that Sisera was delivered into the hands of a woman, and here Sisera was a woman" (121). Evidently we are approaching a moment planned from the outset. The weapons may have to be "spiritual," but the word is still war.

Thus far Johnson's "masculism" has expressed itself in largely unselfconscious ways—by the implication of his military figure and by his steady emphasis on soldierly *men*. Of all the "godly women that came through the perilous seas to war their warfare," we have heard of only a certain Mrs. Sarah Simmes, a "virtuous woman, endued by Christ with graces fit for a wilderness condition." Now, having presented us with her "nurturing up her [ten] young children in the fear of the Lord" as a "certain sign of the Lord's intent to people this vast wilderness" (100–101), Johnson prepares to offer his counterportrait, of a woman of quite "another kind of spirit" (127). Not quite as a gender cliché, however, and only after very careful preparation.

—————

After a certain flourishing of trumpets and rattling of drums, Johnson advises us that, could anyone bring the "disorderly work" of the enemies into "some order," it would "make much for the good of God's people the world throughout": it would in fact discover "the last (I hope) but most subtle practices of Satan to hinder the restoration of the purity of Christ's ordinances in his churches in all places" (121). With Johnson's rhetoric in mind, Cotton Mather will, in his own time, imagine 1693 as the fatal year in the history of the Devil's earthly reign,[25] but Johnson will have that moment in 1636: knowing that "at the fall of Antichrist he must be chained up for a thousand years," Satan now "strives with all the wicked craft his long experienced maliciousness could possibly invent," to uphold his earthly sway. And, seeing no other way to mislead those "resolved soldiers of Christ in New England" who seek "not only the final ruin of Antichrist . . . but also the advance of Christ's kingdom," he responds by stirring up "instruments to cry down Antichrist" even more than most (122). On this account the Devil not only quotes Scripture, but offers to provide a finer version than the orthodoxy.

Itself a work of considerable subtlety. Having liberty now "to deliver their master's mind," the "Ambassadors of Christ . . . preach unto all the doctrine of free grace, beseeching them to be reconciled unto God in Christ"—reminding them that "faith is a gift of God, and none can come unto Christ but such as the Father draws," but insisting in the end on "the fruits of faith which worketh by love, and that love will be obedient to the commands of Christ, who saith, if you love me keep my commandments" (123). Calvinism, once again, without the feckless plea of inability. And yet "this good old way would not serve the turn with certain sectaries." Naming no names, now or later, Johnson merely invokes the strategy of these "cunning sophisters":

> seeing the bent of the people's hearts . . . was to magnify the rich grace of God in Christ, they began to tell the people . . . that the . . . ministers among them preached a covenant of works, either coarse or fine, and with a what do you say to this, they began to spread their errors and heresies.

Johnson is ready to provide two chapters on the "dividing principles of the erronists"—but only after premising that, "the easier to deceive," the Devil's dupes have laid their foundation "as near the truth as possible" (124).

No wonder, Johnson observes, if errors are "like those feigned heads of Hydra, as fast as one is cut off two stand up in the room"; still, the principal point at issue was "the uniting of a soul to Christ by faith" (124–25). In this the sectaries have attempted to invoke the teaching of Cotton, but he—by the time of Johnson's writing—has spoken for himself in his answer to Mr. Bailey. Admitting "some little difference between him and the elders," which the sectaries could "enlarge at their pleasure," Johnson nevertheless imagines his own scenario of misrepresentation:

> I'll tell you Friend, Neighbor, Brother, if you will forebear to speak of it till you hear farther, this is the judgment of M. Cotton, when he, it may be, had never heard of it, or at least wise, when they brought their bastardly brat to him, they put another vizard on the face of it. (125)

With the reference to some illegitimate doctrine as a "bastardly brat," the experienced reader senses that Johnson, with knowledge of the (gendered) history of the Antinomians, is laying a foundation for his own (sexist) contribution.[26]

Undaunted by the terrors of theology, however, Johnson accuses the sectaries of "dividing those things the Lord hath united in his work of conversion," and that in "four particulars." First, "in dividing between the word and the word"—meaning, it appears, setting the Law against the Gospel. Calling them "legal preachers" who insist on "any preparation work," they express themselves in form of an either/or which Johnson runs his sentence on to refute:

> Here's nothing, says one of them, but preaching out of the Law and the Prophets, truly says another of them I have not heard a pure Gospel sermon from any of them, but sure they were both troubled with the lethargy, or read not the Gospel themselves, for they may find the apostles, yes, and Christ himself, preached good Gospel sure, out of the Law and the Prophets. (125)

If this first error might also be called separating the word from the work, so too could be their second, of "separating Christ and his graces," which "they say makes much for the magnifying of free-grace" (126). As elsewhere, the familiar issue is whether the saints, possessing Christ, also possess any virtue that is strictly speaking *their own*. Which the orthodox insist is necessary to maintain a premium on virtue *at all*.

One sectary is made to say that though the orthodox speak of "inherent grace, and of a man being made a new creature," he is sure "the best of them go on in their legal duties and performances still." Another is quick to raise the ante: "Tush, man,"

> I was discoursing with one of their scholastical preacher's disciples, . . . yet when he came to pray, he beg'd for forgiveness for his sins, I asked him why he used that vain repetition, since he did believe he was justified by Christ already, and he made me an answer not worth repeating, but when I told him God could see no sin in his people, . . . he told me I spake little less than blasphemy, so ignorant are these men, and their learned guides also; who persuade them the more they have of the in-dwelling of the Spirit of Christ, the better they shall be enabled to these legal duties. (126)

Hypothetical or remembered, this dramatic exchange is remarkable for the sophistication it accords those who scoff at the association of salvation with virtue and of virtue with the works of the law. Evidently this concession is necessary if we are to understand "how these . . . heretical persons batter off the fruit from the goodly branches of Christ's vine and make bare the flourishing trees planted in the house of the Lord" (126).

Posing as "scholars of the upper form," those who would deny that sanctification is the true and necessary fruit of justification are nothing but "orchard robbers," who should remember that it is an offence

> far beyond petty larceny, to rob Christ's garden, let your pretences be what they will: can it possibly be for the magnifying of Christ's grace that the

branches growing upon his root should remain fruitless? no assuredly, herein God is glorified that his people bring forth much fruit. (126)

Johnson is willing to concede that "hypocrites [may] have a seeming show of saints' graces"; but because "felons and traitors coin counterfeit gold," is that a reason "true gold should not pass for current?" (126–27). Already the energy of the prose is running pretty high: evidently moderation in defense of virtue is no virtue.

The "two latter dividing principles" of these erronists require a separate chapter (41); and as Johnson proceeds to discuss the separation between "the Word of God, and the Spirit of God," we find him moving closer to the heart of his own antienthusiastic enthusiasm. Here, we are told, "these sectaries had many pretty knacks to delude withal, and especially to please the female sex, they told of rare revelations of things to come." Though devised "to weaken the Word of the Lord in the mouth of his ministers," thus to put "ignorant and unlettered men and women in a posture of preaching to a multitude," the new views possessed a certain democratic as well as gendered appeal:

> Come along with me, says one of them, I'll bring you to a Woman that preaches better gospel than any of your black-coats that have been at the Ninneversity, a Woman of another kind of spirit, who hath had many revelations of things to come, and for my part, saith he, I had rather hear such a one that speaks from the mere motion of the spirit, without any study at all, then all of your learned scholars. (127)

Just here, where we sense that the treatment is becoming a little less analytic, Johnson inserts his famous caveat: "Gentle Reader, think not these things feigned because I name not the parties." And while we are wondering whether this omission makes his mounting literary opposition less "personal," he tells us the tale of a man "in one of the farthest towns . . . where they have no ministers," who scolded a fellow frontiersman for missing *his own* sermon. Thus would he illustrate "how these sectaries love preeminence," scoffing all the while at the "scholar-like way of preaching" (127–28).

Even the nameless "Woman," the "grand mistress of all the rest, who denied the resurrection from the dead," is set down as a prophet "against learning" who, nevertheless, "to show her skill that way," would affect to discover the "fallacy" in some orthodox "syllogism." As would also, later, a certain Gortonist—"as shallow a pated scholar" (128) as Johnson himself—pretending to solve problems requiring a knowledge of languages of which Johnson knows only enough to know he knows not enough. What makes him even more angry, however, is what goes along with this studied ignorance as its proper accompaniment, namely, "the strange revelations told both of men and women, as true some of them said as the Scriptures." Indeed, Johnson observes, "had this sect gone on awhile, they would have made a new bible." But instead of theorizing the abstruse relation between the Word and the Spirit, he ends his third point with other dramatic instances of private inspiration:

> and their chief mistress, when she was shipped for N. England, what will you say, quoth she, and it hath been revealed to me that we shall be in there six weeks, and one of the female Gortonists said, she was a prophetess, and it was revealed unto her, that she must prophesy unto the people in the same words the prophet Ezekiel did. (129)

Nor, at the risk of blurring his emphasis on the gender of inspiration, can he omit the case of the "lusty big man" who explained before his pastor and the entire congregation that "the spirit of revelation came to him while he was drinking a pipe of tobacco" (129).

But if the tendency to transcend the text has its humorous side, the fourth attempt of the sectaries, to "divide between Christ and his ordinances," most certainly does not. Moving away from what we can recognize as a distinctly Hutchinsonian emphasis—and promising us more details for the "years (43) and (44)" later—Johnson records a certain protest against baptism: having "cast off the cross in baptism," one heretic is reported to have said, "you should do well to cast off baptism itself." And also against the Lord's Supper, where to make "the juice of a silly grape to represent the . . . blood of Christ . . . [is] as bad as necromancy." Perhaps Johnson has Roger Williams in mind when he asks us to note that those persons who were "first bewildered in the denial of infants being baptized, could neither find [a] right faith to be baptized unto, nor yet any person rightly constituted to baptize" (129); and so they remained "Seekers." Yet not without attempting to "shoulder out the officers Christ hath ordained, and set up in his churches" (129–30). And this emphasis on the necessity of learned authority all but swamps the second of Johnson's chapters on the sectaries' "dividing principles."

The cry "against a learned presbytery" shows itself as a masterpiece of the Devil's cunning precisely because it follows hard upon

> the lording Prelacy, Popes, Cardinals, Bishops, Deans, etc., [who] were ordinarily brought up at the university to learning, and have most tyran-

nically abused it, usurping over the people of Christ, and exercised most inhumane and barbarous cruelty upon them.

The very difficulty of throwing off such influences, both in the "wilderness-work" of New England and in "that bloody war so long continued in our native country," gives a "very fair bottom" for those who would have "the sluice of authority of the officers of Christ's church plucked up, that so their errors might flow in like a flood" (130). Indeed, the point is crucial enough to warrant a direct address: "My friend, cast off as much of thy own power as thou canst, and beware of lording it over God's heritage, but I pray thee let Christ alone with his." No more than Winthrop, it appears, is Johnson willing to let an aroused, "Puritan" resistance to authority run on to its dangerous limit. Christian liberty ends not in holy anarchy but in established authority. The power to elect church officers rests with the particular church, and this (inalienable right) "no man may take from them, nor yet they themselves cast off " (131).

Caught up in this layman's zealous attempt to defend the claims of his religious rulers, the reader may be surprised by Johnson's abrupt return to the more famous matter of 1636—namely, that from the "four dividing Tenets" there followed some "fourscore gross errors" which proved "very infectious to some of the churches of Christ in their members." Yet it is with this abrupt transition that Johnson leads us to consider, in chapter 42, the "sad effects of the pitiful and erroneous doctrines broached by the sectaries" (131). And indeed his emphasis falls upon the *effects* rather than the doctrines themselves. As he had veered off from an arid defense of the sacraments to a somewhat juicier justification of religious authority in general, so here this Puritan Man of Feeling is interested in matters a bit less specialized than the overdetermined propositions which scholastic acumen could tease out of spirited utterance.

Once the "infectious persons" had drawn "a great party on their side," including "some considerable persons," they began to "dare question the sound and wholesome truths delivered in public by the ministers of Christ" (131–32). Church meetings grow "full of disputes in points of difference, and . . . love-feasts are not free from spots." In the "courts of civil justice some men utter their speeches in matter of religion very ambiguously," and on all sides there is "a great talk of new light" which, as in "the city of Munster," proved but an "old darkness." "Dolorous" indeed was the condition of these infant churches, and a great part of "this new transported people stood still many of them gazing one upon another, like sheep let loose to feed on fresh pasture, being stopped and startled in their course by a kennel of devouring wolves." The light might yet prevail, but for a time "the weaker sort wavered"; even established Christians "hardly durst discover the truth."

> The fogs of error increasing, the bright beams of the glorious gospel of our Lord Christ in the mouth of his ministers could not be discerned through the thick mist by many, and that sweet refreshing warmth that was formerly felt through the spirit's influence was now turned . . . to a hot inflammation of their own conceited revelations. (132)

Bad enough, as we may think, when the worst are full of passionate intensity. But all this is only preparing us for Johnson's own worst—when . . .

Without the distracting interruption of a period, he records that the "frenzy or madness" of the enthusiasts caused "the congregation of the people of God to be forsaken" and—worst-case scenario come real—

> the weaker sex prevailed so far, that they set up a priest of their own profession and sex, who was much thronged after, abominably wresting the scriptures to their own destruction; this master-piece of women's wit drew many disciples after her, and to that end boldly insinuated her self into the favor of none of the meanest, being also backed with the sorcery of a second, who had much converse with the Devil by her own confession, and did, to the admiration of those that heard her, utter many speeches in the Latin tongue, as it were in a trance. (132)

An editor's learned footnote identifies the "second" as "Jane Hawkins, the midwife," and refers the dutiful reader to the appropriate passages in Winthrop's *Journal,* but a lesser degree of compulsion will satisfy itself with the thought that the tone of the name-naming Winthrop is everywhere more restrained than that of Johnson.[27] Scientific modesty requires the latter historian to confess ignorance of the precise workings of the "drinks" given by this second "to other women to cause them to conceive"; enough to know that "sure there were monsters born not long after" (133).

And to cry out, as to an audience of lively participants, "Oh ye New England men and women, who hath bewitched you that you should not obey the truth?" Women, presumably, but in the end of course Satan. Only observe again how "to make sure work with this semblance of preaching the doctrine of free-grace by his instruments, [he] makes show of out-bidding all the orthodox and godly ministers in the country, pretending their preaching to be but a covenant of works." This to silence the faithful ministers "without a bishop" and to create the impression that "these erroneous persons with their new light were the only men and women that were pure gospel preachers." In the sad result,

> the poor people of Christ . . . having expended their estates to voyage far through the perilous seas, that their eyes might behold their teachers . . . began to deem themselves in a more dolorous condition then when they were in the commissaries' court and prelates' prisons. (133)

"The hideous waves . . . were nothing so terrible . . . as was this flood of errors. . . . The wants of this wilderness, and pinching penury in miss of bread put them to no such pain . . . as did the miss of the administration of Christ in his Word" (133). Evidently, if we are to trust this outbreak of figure, it was the controversy of 1636 and 1637, not the ocean crossing or the starving time, that gave the Great Test to this first Great Generation.

However that may be, what Johnson offers us as the first emotional climax of a book notable everywhere for its nervously heightened affect is the "sorrowful complaint of a poor soul in miss of its expectation at landing" (133). We might imagine the moment of chapter 43 as the one immediately after that of the arrival of Thomas Shepard—who debarked just in time to be dismayed by and then to strike out against the first awakening of an "Antinomian" protest. Less highly placed, Johnson's dramatic sufferer can only cry out. A version of himself, perhaps, as he returned to New England after a voyage to fetch over his family to the Place of Grace, he is both shocked and morally bewildered to find he cannot confess his salvation in the language of the new light. When he had first arrived, and when he left on his domestic countererrand, preparation, the conditional covenant, and the high-stress pursuit of sanctification as evidence were all but established as the authentic language of salvation. Now, in the heat of a protest against anything at all resembling a human work, the old language is in danger of losing its currency, leaving this far-marching migrant bereft of assurance and guilty of false tone.[28]

Thus, when the arriving marcher finds "the good old way of Christ rejected" by the theological novelists, and that he himself cannot "skill in that new light, which was the common theme of every man's discourse," the only response seems to be the language of complaint: whose country have I come to now? And how will my story of urgency and manful strife strike the ears of a congregation that honors rapture and openly disrespects "the true sight of sin"? Or, if we should take the complainant to be Johnson himself, already received into an established congregation, what of his family? Can they learn the new language? Even if so, what will they think of his adherence to the "old way"? And so this strenuous and not noticeably "subjective" victim of theological change can only take his case to the woods—to a "narrow Indian path, . . . where none but senseless trees and echoing rocks make answer to his heart-easing moan."

> Oh quoth he where am I become, is this the place where those reverend preachers are fled, that Christ was pleased to make use of to rouse up his rich graces in many a drooping soul; here I have met with some that tell me, I must take a naked Christ. Oh, woe is me if Christ be naked to me, wherewith shall I be clothed. (134)

Johnson might be brought to admit that there was nothing in his naked hand, not even the works of preparation, to offer Christ in exchange for the grace of salvation, but he does not at all like to think that, beyond His own lovely self, Christ has nothing to offer him, as the content or the consequence of salvation. If Christ's merit, or some measure of his capacity for perfect virtue, does not come as a gift to the saint, then what's the point? The naked and the dead are all one.

And what *of* the Gospel need for godly sorrow, as the very substance of the preparation God conducts in the soul of him whom he would save, or as the heightened sense that enabled virtue is subject to repeated lapses? What could be clearer than the need to make straight God's ways in advance of his coming and then to prove the love by keeping the commands? Well may I wonder, therefore, when "they tell me of casting of[f] all godly sorrow for sin as un-beseeming a soul that is united to Christ by faith, and"—with only a comma for a pause—

> there was a nimble tongued Woman among them, who said she could bring me acquainted with one of her sex that would show me a way, if I could attain it, even revelations, full of such ravishing joy that I should never have cause to be sorry for sin, so long as I live, and as for her part she had attained it already; a company of legal professors, quoth she, lie pouring on the law which Christ hath abolished, and when you break it then you break your joy, and now no way will serve your turn but a deep sorrow. (134)

Evidently the way of joy, as opposed to that of conviction and humiliation, is the way of The Woman, and the rugged Edward Johnson does not expect to be edified by the results.

Where some quasi-magical certainty of the divine favor becomes the norm of churchly experience, one can expect "little increase in the graces of Christ, through the hearing of his word preached, and other of his blessed ordinances."

And how like the "cunning Devil" to use the "pretence of a free and ample gospel" to shut the soul out from the true mysticism—of such a union with the Spirit as creates and continues God's uplifting "graces in the soul" (134). Clearly preferring the strenuous morale of the "good old way," Johnson's inspired protester breaks out again, in a speech which may reveal the fundamental reason why the "fair and easy" alternative did not in the end carry the minds and hearts of enough of the original saints in Massachusetts:

> my dear Christ, it was thy work that moved me hither to come, hoping to find thy powerful presence in the preaching of the Word, . . . and also by the glass of the Law to have my sinful corrupt nature discovered daily more and more, and my utter inability of any thing that is good, magnifying hereby the free grace of Christ; who of his good will and pleasure worketh in us to will, and to do, working all our works in us, and for us. (134–35)

Surely we did not march all this way for an easing or indeed an erasure of conscience. Rather for a heightening and deepening. Thomas Shepard may write the thought in more correct "English," but neither he nor Hooker nor Bulkeley can name the tune of New England's Preparationist-Sanctificationist-Calvinist orthodoxy in fewer notes.

Or say its sense with more conviction: we came here—did we not?—to cultivate the true sight of sin and, brought low by this sad self-knowledge, to accept a Gospel call if offered, and to prove the authenticity of our response by the intensity of our pursuit of godliness, denying all the while that true virtue is a thing any of us can do of ourselves. Is this not Calvinist enough? Evidently not, for "here they tell me of a naked Christ." Yet we would ask them: "What is the whole life of a Christian upon this earth? But through the power of Christ to die to sin, and live to holiness and righteousness, and for that end to be diligent in the means" (135). The "good old way" is, evidently, the strenuous way, the active way, indeed the manly way. The moral equivalent of war. And we should not be too surprised to find ourselves suspecting that, in the seventeenth century at least, many men (and probably some women too, religious but male-identified) found this way in fact "easier" than the one they explicitly satirized as such. For, as Milton and Emerson will compete to express the fact, the love of virtue lies deep in the nature of reflective human beings. And, though it is plainly ended now, there seems to have been, in the history of consciousness, a long-enduring episteme in which the source of the world's ill was seen to lie in an unruly and recalcitrant "self" whose nature was most likely to appear under the aspect of "sin."[29] An unhappy fact, to be sure, and likely to raise all sorts of difficult questions about cause and effect; but better provided with homely language than was the relief one might feel if God should come with a surety that blotted out all conditions of giving and getting.

Speaking for the strenuous majority, Johnson's bewildered pilgrim moves from painful complaint to happy discovery. Following his woodsy course to the next town, he is summoned by the sound of a drum, whose significance he does not at first recognize, to the place where "one Mr. Shepard" may be heard to lecture. Ah, yes, remembers this veritable newcomer, the very man the New Lights have identified as preaching "a finer covenant of works" than the rest of the "legal preachers" (135). Yet he must hear for himself. Then, being smitten, he provides a "review" of the preaching such as more learned disciples might clarify but never outdo. Staying "while the glass was turned up twice, the man"—whether speaker or hearer—"was metamorphosed,"

> and was fain to hang down the head often, lest his watery eyes should blab abroad the secret conjunction of his affections, his heart crying loud to the Lord's echoing answer, to his blessed spirit, that cause the speech of a poor weak pale complexioned man, to take such impression in his soul at present, by applying the word so aptly, as if he had been his privy counselor, clearing Christ's work of grace in the soul from all those false doctrines which the erroneous party had affrighted him withal. (135–36)

So that, as we once again sort out who is who, the reassured pilgrim now "resolves . . . to live and die with the ministers of New England" (136). Who did not, so far as we know, pay for the publication of Johnson's book. But who could not but love its spirit.

What Johnson's first climax suggests is that laypersons in New England could be just as vigorous in support of the way of anxiety—and of morality—as the majority of ministers and magistrates. If this were not the case, the history of New England would look entirely different. Indeed, we can scarcely imagine how even a consensus maker like John Winthrop could have composed a situation in which ordinary men and women opposed their leaders' uniform demand for regular behavior with their own wayward desire to experience revelation and express love, even the love of God, without let or hindrance. The way of revealed certainty is in fact "easy" only to those who have the gift of lovely speech, rarer and more poetic, we are to understand, than the gift to migrate and to raise up one's metaphors along that courageous path.

But the reckless excitement of Johnson's prose also suggests that hating sin and loving virtue—marching along, as it were, to the martial music of the Law— can be productive of its own enthusiasm. If, on the one hand, the dangers of the Antinomian position lose none of their emotional thrill in Johnson's parodic but never pedestrian evocations, his prose also shows itself perfectly equal to the task not only of registering his anger at the temporary seductions of mere subjectivity but also of expressing the rare pleasure a self-conscious soul may take in the idea of its own discipline. Did we come all this way for a moral holiday? Or was it not to beat our brains with meditation on the nature and the power of sin and, with the help of God, to bend our wills, as we would bend our backs, to the pursuit of what is good, just, and honest? End times are coming, to be sure, but battles come before the milk and honey. And so we continue the march, in step with the over-whelming majority of the pious "ministers of New England, whom"—as any pilgrim might see—"the Lord had . . . made zealous to stand for the truth . . . and not to give ground one inch" (136). Theme enough to raise the spirit.

––––––

Anticlimactically, perhaps, but in studious good faith, Johnson ends his first book with two further chapters, one on the fair and rational discipline of the "Congregational Churches" (136) and the other on the mild and nurturing "civil government in N. England" (139). The point of both is to assure the "Christian Reader," back in England as it clearly appears, that both church and state in New England have shown themselves particularly well suited to deal with those "erroneous spirits" who have "dogged the sincere servants of Christ, when ever they have set upon a thorough reformation." Prelates may boast that only their own "lordly power" (136) has been able to control error, but they have kept God's own truth in check as well; and the facts will reveal that, in providence, the New England Way has more than proven its worth.

First of all, no one who saw the "loving counsel" which the congregational churches exhibited in dealing with the recent threat would ever again "stand for classical injunctions" (137–38). Indeed, Johnson assures us, "the days are at hand when both Jew and Gentile churches shall exercise this old model of church government"; then universally (as in New England now) "shall the exhortation on one church to another prevail more to reformation than all the thundering bulls [and] excommunicating lordly censures . . . in the world." Nor should pious Independents conclude that the New England Way has been "too strict in dealing with persons for their sinful opinions" (138). They must know, as they cannot from the mouths of the offenders themselves, what the entire experience of New England, down to the moment of writing in 1651, has taught, namely, that in the context of churches already well reformed, "errors and heresies are not broached and held out by tender consciences," but such self-styled adepts as would "teach the most ablest Christian among us another gospel." Further, our erronists "will not suffer us quietly to enjoy the ordinances of Christ, for which we hither came," but will be "buzzing our people in the ear with a thing they call liberty." And once they say that word, they can no longer abide the authority of either "synod, or gathering together of able, and orthodox Christians, nor yet of communion of churches." And as for the authority of civil government, "they deem religion to be a thing beyond their sphere" (139).

The last chapter of Book 1 begins with an assurance that, in "the vernal of the year 1637," the election of Winthrop and Dudley was an example of "the Lord graciously providing for the peace of his people" (139). A further preamble works hard to refute the charge that "New England government doth persecute the people and churches of Christ": aiming but "to enjoy the liberties of the Gospel of Christ," no wonder if the men of Massachusetts continue to elect to government "such men as mostly endeavor to keep the truths of Christ pure and unspotted." To this end they have labored to keep away or to expel all religious enemies, so "that here might be none left to hurt or destroy" the precious consensus, and civil officers have been known to "put the churches in mind of their duty" in this regard. But never do they "exercise civil power to bring all under their obedience to a uniformity in every point of religion," but only strive "to keep them in unity of the spirit and the bond of peace" (140). Johnson's editor calls attention to the "artless speciousness of this defense."[30] But even liberals need to notice a truth we did not know a priori—that neither Reformation nor yet America could hold a liberated populace to the terms their covenants could imagine in advance.

Johnson proceeds to define the "supreme power of this little commonwealth" as a "mixt company, part aristocracy, and part democracy of magistrates, that are yearly chosen by the major vote of the whole body of the free-men throughout the country; and deputies chosen by the several towns" (140–41). Then, instead of clarifying the ambiguities of this description, or recounting the painful process that lay beneath its evolution, this faithful precursor of Cotton Mather proceeds to record the name of many of the deputies providence has provided to the towns, as "stones to build up the walls of Jerusalem" (141). Finally, to end a "Book" that has already wandered past its moment of keenest personal encounter, Johnson repeats what he takes to be the moral of that drama: elsewhere men may decide that "all sorts of sectaries . . . should be tolerated by civil government" (144), but the men of New England have learned otherwise: "from Scripture" they have been taught to choose as governors only "men truly fearing God"; nor have they found a way to believe that any such person could learn to tolerate "all sorts of sectaries"—doing evil, in his own mind, that "good may come of it." Others might find wisdom in dividing utterly the interest of civil government from that of the churches, "yet the people of Christ, who are the natural mothers of this government, resolve never to see their living child so divided." Conscientious Englishmen, therefore, must find a way to "bear with them in this point" (145).

Or, should any meditate force, prepare to see their American cousins daring to move on to "the backside of this desert." Or else to stand and fight—

> resolved to keep the government our God hath given us, and for witness he hath done so, let this History manifest: for we chose not the place for the land, but for the government, that our Lord Christ might reign over us, both in churches and in commonwealth. (145–46)

New England may seem, by the Lord's good pleasure, a garden now, but the "land in it self is very sterile" and—John Smith and the esthetics of empire not-withstanding—the truth of Christ "is the chief cause why many have hitherto come" (146).[31]

Then, as if this consideration of lives and fortunes and sacred honor were not enough to raise argumentative prose to a climax of its own, the reader is to consider also the gathering sense that "the downfall of Antichrist is at hand." With "the kingdom of the earth" about to become "the kingdom of our Lord Christ in a more peculiar manner," what wonder if our magistrates, already "ruling for Christ, dare not admit of any bastardly brood to be nursed up upon their tender knees." The "increase of trade" (146) may seem a marvelous inducement to some, but the meaning of New England lies in its apocalyptic link to the New Heavens and the New Earth. And Johnson ends the first book of his holy history with a promise that, against all odds and all old world advice to compromise, it means to maintain that end-time identity.

II. THE END OF THE WORLD

If the *Wonder-Working Providence* were nothing but a position paper, it might well conclude its effort with the climax and concluding rationale of Book 1. But as its argument rests on a reading of actual events as well as a promulgation of ideal meanings, it goes right on, bravely enough, with two more "Books" of militaristic explanation and social defense. Together, they require of Johnson about as many pages as his bold initial foray: Book 2 carries us, in twenty-six chapters, from the Pequot War to a series of military preparations in the mid-1640s, and Book 3 takes us from there, in twelve chapters only, to Johnson's own moment of expectant writing and waiting when, as we have already sensed, the defeat of Gortonists in the mid-1640s serves to reinforce the warlike lessons of 1636–37. And, as New England men march ever further into the end times, Johnson will miss no opportunity to sound the drums of the final battle.

Like other sponsors of New England's Covenant, Johnson treats the Antinomian Controversy and the Pequot War as parallel events in the logic of special providence: in order to manifest his mercies, "The great Jehova . . . causeth the dark clouds of calamities to gather about" his people. Looking to the right, they behold the "damnable doctrines, as so many engines set by Satan to entrap their poor souls"; to the left, "the terrible wilderness affright[s] them"—out of which comes news of "cruel murders committed by a barbarous and bloody people called Pequods." All of this is to presage "some terrible tempest to follow" (147), but the present danger is serious enough: "swollen with pride," and "trusting in their great troops," the Indians renew a "quarrel . . . as ancient as Adam's time, propagated from that old enmity between the Seed of the Woman and the Seed of the Serpent"; this "grand signor of [the] war in hand" would gladly have given his minions a "large commission, had not his own power been limited" (148) by the God who lays out the plan of salvation history. "Continually at home" in "woods [that] are as welcome to them as their wigwams," this formidable enemy is nevertheless frustrated at the outset by the timely warning by "one of the English" (149) who discovered their design.

Yet the providence is not perfect, and its unpredictable twists lead Johnson into some odd reflections on both gender and race. Several of the "weaker sex" spend valuable time disputing the news of the Pequot approach and, as if to seal the truth of the evil tidings "with their dearest blood," three of their number are abducted by the attackers. One of them resists with scratching and biting, causing her captor to "beat out her brains with his hatchet" (149). The other two prove unable to make gunpowder and are returned as

> nothing so precious a pearl in their eyes as before; for seeing they exceeded not their own squaws in art, their own thoughts informed them they would fall abundantly short in industry, and as for beauty they esteem black beyond any color.

Wherefore their squaws use that sinful art of painting their faces in the hollow of their eyes and nose with a shining black, out of which the tip of their nose appears very deformed. (149–50)

Sensing but not quite reconciling its odd mixture of issue and effect, chapter 1 of Book 2 closes with a sentence that scorns the sort of "beauty esteemed by them," notices the Pequots' increasing pride and defiance, and records the fact that it was in fact Dutch traders who "procured the maids' liberty again" (150).

Retreating from current event to everlasting design, chapter 2 records only the "courageous resolutions" of the Lord's people—beginning with their "petition" to the "supreme judge of all the world . . . who they knew right well stood not as an idle spectator beholding his people's ruth and their enemies' rage," but as an actor working "to bring to naught the desires of the wicked." Aware that the God of history is also the true cause of every natural effect, "guiding every shaft that flies, leading each bullet to his place of settling," this people of God can express their dependence only by "casting themselves down at his feet in the sense of their own unworthiness," desiring him "to do his own work in them" (150). Before the answer can be declared, however, all men must "lay down [the] interest they suppose they may have in procuring it . . . that the glory of our Lord Christ may appear in its splendor." Then strict Calvinism passes over into apocalyptic zeal:

for the day of his high power is come, yea his appointed time to have mercy on Sion is at hand, all you whose eyes of pity so see her in the dust stream down with pear-like drops of compassion, a little mixture of the inconceivable joy for the glorious work of Christ, Now, now, [ay] now in hand for the exalting of his glorious kingdom, in preparing his churches for himself, and with his own blessed hands wiping away the tears that trickle down her cheeks, drying her dankish eyes, and hushing her sorrowful sobs in his sweet bosom. (151)

"This rightly believed," Johnson assures us, "will make the narrow affections of body too little to contain the present apprehensions of his soul." "Wanting a vacuum to contain the strength of this new wine, wonder not if it vent itself with swift thrilling tears" (151). As if the writer would confess: the sentence is too little for the love.

So much so that the first "thematic" chapter of Book 2 has to end with a self-conscious apology for the emotional depth of the writer's commitment, entreating the "Charitable Reader" to forgive his folly "in meddling so meanly with such weighty matters"; blinded by emotion, "he lost sight of his great inability to the work, when he first set pen to paper." Yet the matter of his enthusiasm unabashedly remains: "As the Lord surrounded his chosen Israel with dangers deep to make his miraculous deliverance famous throughout and to the end of the world, so here behold . . . a small handful of his people . . . in a forlorn wilderness": stripped "naked of all human helps" and plunged "in a gulf of miseries," they are now to "swim for their lives through the ocean of his mercies, and land themselves safe in the arms of his compassion" (151). So justified and rededicated, Book 2 may now proceed apace.

Chapter 3 assures the cautious reader that the Lord saved his people "from the floods of errors that were bursting in among them" not by some miracle but by "the use of his means," in this case the calling of themselves "to gather together as one man in a synodical way" (152) and, in preparation for this decisive event, the searching out not of "men and women's persons, but their errors" (153). Filling in part of the meantime, chapter 4 briefly notes the "liberal supply" provided by the Lord to his "New England people" (153). A much longer chapter then discusses the "deliverance" of this people from a third threat, not quite parallel to that of the sectaries and the wilderness, namely, the "malignant adversaries, who forced them to this wilderness" in the first place. The specific problem, here in 1637, is that the infamous Thomas Morton may further prejudice the "lording Bishops" (154) against the wilderness people; but though the Lord delivers "this wretched fellow into his people's hands again," Johnson is unwilling to rest his case. After reminding the reader that the antiprelatical motive of this migration was the very "means" (155) God was using in the work of Reformation, and that its perfection waits only "the prayers of his people" (156), Johnson turns directly to the enemy, whose power remains a lively memory:

> Oh you proud bishops, that would have all the world stoop to your lordly power, the heathen Romans your predecessors, after they had banished John . . . , suffered him quietly to enjoy the revelation of Jesus Christ there; here is a people that have betaken themselves to a newfound world, distanced from you by the widest ocean the world affords, and yet you grudge them the purity of Christ's ordinances there. (156–57)

For Bradford, Moses and Paul had a worse time of it in prosecuting the salvation project. Johnson adds John to the venerable list of partial predecessors.

The remainder of chapter 5 is dedicated to the "wonder" that must accompany "the sudden and unexpected downfall of these domineering lords" (157), despite their defense at arms. Encouraging the faithful to go on with their countercampaign of prayer and fasting, Johnson interprets a recent earthquake, which spread from west to east, as an appropriate sign of God's intention to "shake the kingdoms of Europe's earth" (160). And he observes that such signs of the times, delivered in direct answer to prayer, have "caused some of this little handful with resolute courage and boldness to return again to their native land"—forgivingly, for "it matters not indeed who be the instruments," so long as "the eye of faith" (160–61) can see the hand of the Lord at work.

With chapters 6 and 7, Johnson returns to the "parallel" dangers of the 1630s—"barbarous Indians" (161) and the "cursed errors" that "dog the reforming churches" (170). In the case of the Indians, providence appears first in the decision of the Narragansetts not to league with the Pequots against the English who, "though strangers to the woods, swamps, and advantageous places of the wilderness," are nevertheless "advantaged by their weapons of war" (163). Even more clearly, providence fills the English soldiers "with a spirit of courage and magnanimity to resist not only men, but devils; for surely [Satan] was more than ordinarily with this Indian army" (165). Again, however, there is a natural means, as the stirring speech of John Wilson pits against the "swelling pride" of the adversary nothing less than "the lives, liberties, and new purchased freedoms, privileges, and immunities of the endeared servants of our Lord Christ Jesus" (166). After such inspiration, the battle goes on savagely but well, the Indians withdrawing from "a great slaughter" into a dismal swamp. Even then, however, providence must deprive the enemy of the knowledge of "how much weakened our soldiers were at present [or] they might have bourne them down with their multitude" (168). Nor is it dumb luck that "some of them spied an Indian with a kettle at his back going more inwardly into the swamp," enabling the English to make a "passage of their soldiers" and bringing the war to a period. When a straggler is taken captive and carried about, like a "Pope . . . on men's shoulders" (169), it requires all the skill of "the nimble Captain Davenport" to effect his rescue. But in truth it is "the Lord in his mercy" that has so utterly destroyed "these bloody barbarous Indians." And struck "trembling terror into all the [others] round about, even to this very day" (170).

Back in the settlements, "the first synod holden in New England" attends to the other clear and present danger. Fortified with a number of newly arrived ministers, "the synod sat at Cambridge" and, listing errors rather than persons, demonstrated that "the weapons these soldiers of Christ warred with" was nothing other than "the sword of the Spirit." Declining once again to list the eighty errors (eighty-two, actually, but who indeed is counting?), Johnson prefers, whimsically and something in the manner of Nathaniel Ward, to imagine "four sorts of persons [whose] passage out and home again to England" he would gladly have paid, that they might testify of both truth and method "to their own colleges at their return." First, "prelates," who might "have made their own eyes judges," whether in the "suppressing of error" or in the "advancing of unity in the true worship of God," their "commanding power backed with the subordinate sword of princes" was any match for "the Word of God cleared up by the faithful labor and indefatigable pains of sincere servants of the Lord Christ" (171). Second, more briefly, "the godly and reverend Presbyterian Party" who might have seen in this paradigmatic expression of the New England Way a sufficient reproof of their repeated attempts to slander the "Congregational or Independent Churches." Third, all "those who with their new stratagems have brought in so much old error." Truly, Johnson confesses, there had been such a party "here," but they dared not "bring their New Light to the Old Word, for fear it would prove Old Darkness." And who would not have been edified to see the ministers of Christ?— "so experienced in the scripture that some of them could tell you . . . chapter and verse," (172) where your extravagant interpretation was plainly put to rout.

Indeed, Johnson's excitement continues, the New England cadre has "been clearing up the truths of Christ clouded by . . . errors and heresies, as has not been done for centuries." Then, sensing that his praise of the religious intelligence of New England may sound partial, he ventures to ask the "reverend and highly honored" preachers who have remained in England to consider why "their fellow brethren have done so worthily" in the western world: "It is well known to all our English nation, that the most able-preaching ministers of Christ were most pursued by the lording clergy." Then too, besides "their continued practice in studying and preaching the ways of truth," there is the fact they have had to meet "so many crafty . . . errors, whose first foundation was laid cheek by jowl with the most glorious, heavenly, and blessed truths" (172). This last consideration throws the emphasis off of Johnson's wish to instruct English exponents of the New Light, but it reinforces his sense that the high theological tone of the Antinomian challenge was a particularly devilish effect; and that its exposure by New England's "valiant champions of the truth" (173) could not be other than a work of rare and providential intelligence.

But Johnson's enthusiasm for apposite learning appears in a simpler way as well. "The fourth and last sort of persons" whose presence he could have desired at the first of New England's exemplary synods, and more than "all the other three," are "those whose disease lay as chiefly in despising all physicians" on the ground that "some for filthy lucre sake have nursed diseases rather than cured them." Distressingly, "many pamphlets have come from our countrymen of late" seeking "scurrilously to deride all kind of scholarship, presbytery, and synods." Yet New World "experience hath taught" otherwise: abuse never discredits the right use, and anyone who had "been at this synod" would have noted, along with "the humility of the most learned of these servants of Christ," the salutary effect of "the framing of arguments in a scholar-like way" (173). A compromise between Presbyterian authority and Congregational independence and a cornerstone of the New England Way as it responded to problems not entirely foreseen, the Advisory Synod can easily be made to seem but another curious folkway in the social history of religion.[32] To Johnson, however—and probably to Winthrop, whose authority had agitated such a thing into being—it was a recognizable feature of end-time practice.[33] Indeed, this phase of history could end not when the "tradition of our forefathers," nor yet "man's reason" prevailed, but only when "the revealed will of God" was properly opened by "instruments" (174) prepared for the purpose. Even as Johnson's history has witnessed.

Means, once again, and not miracles: God's Instruments will be but "earthen vessels, men subject to like infirmities with ourselves." Yet "these did the Lord Christ cause to be trained up in learning and tutored at the universities, and that very young, some of them, as the Reverend Mr. John Cotton, at 13 years of age. The mighty power of God sanctified and ordained them for this work" (174). Johnson's wonder at the youthful beginning of Cotton's intellectual career may amuse anyone familiar with the sociology of education in the sixteenth and seventeenth centuries;[34] as will his happy surprise, earlier, that so many ministers knew the Scriptures by heart. And probably Johnson would have been dismayed to learn just how close Mr. Cotton had come to falling outside the blessed circle of those called by God to solve the dark problem of this world in the plain reading of a handy book. Yet Cotton was in fact saved for consensus and could therefore be counted a worthy member of the "little handful" called to be "a model of [the] glorious work . . . of dispersing [the] smoke which of a long time hath filled the Temple," hindering the influx of "converts which shall flow in at the fall of Antichristian errors" (174). And why not? All it had taken was the transoceanic migration of a self-selected remnant, the majority of whom were wise enough to know they could not themselves devise the things their betters had studied early and long to know.

Johnson ends his chapter assuring us that, though the civil government of Massachusetts had taken the lead in "looking after such as were like to disturb the peace," there had been no violation of the necessary separation of powers: the persons banished were those who had "remained obstinate," to the disturbance of society in general, so that

> the synod, civil government, and the churches of Christ, kept their proper place, each moving in their own sphere, and acting by their own light, or

rather by the revelation of Jesus Christ, witnessed by his Word and Spirit, yet not refusing the help of each other. (175)

Thus an episode that might have ended in calamity, destroying the dream of government by the Word and for the end of Holy Love, resolved itself instead into a demonstration that, complex as it was becoming, the New England Way was meant to be.

————

Freed, now, of its besetting fears, New England begins to expand without anxiety. Chapter 8 records "the planting of the fourth colony of New England's godly government called New Haven" (176), centered in the church of Theophilus Eaton and John Davenport; and the next three chapters inscribe the names of the fourteenth, fifteenth, and sixteenth Massachusetts churches, at Dedham, under the "heavenly-minded Mr. John Allen" (179); at Weymouth, which has some trouble keeping a settled minister; and at Rowley, whither, in 1638, "the zealous affected and judicious servant . . . Mr. Ezekiel Rogers" had led a "holy and humble" group of about "three-score families." And just in case this sort of worldly fact should turn out to matter in a world preparing for its martial end, Johnson includes the peaceful detail that these were "the first people that set upon making of cloth in this western world" (183).

This same year a "great earthquake" shakes the houses of New England but, far from rattling Johnson's morale, it lends a certain cautious confidence to his account of the "sad end" of the (ever unnamed) Anne Hutchinson. Exiled with her party to "Rhode Island, where having elbow room enough," they soon "hampered themselves foully with their own line" (185). And there this "mistress of them all," still "deeming the Apostle Paul to be too strict in not teaching a woman to preach in the public congregation . . . ordinarily prated every Sabbath day, till others, who thirsted after honor in the same way with herself, drew away her auditors." Withdrawing again, she and her family "came to a very sad end" at the hands of the "Indians in those parts." Though conceding that the Lord is "secret in all the dispensation of his providences," Johnson is nevertheless sure that "much can be learned" (186) from this signal instance of the slighting of the ordinary way: trusting in private revelations of her own safe rescue, she found herself instead "cruelly murdered." Then too, had not the Lord already pointed at the sin of her sect by the "fearful monster that another of these women brought forth"? (187).

In any event, the same year brought forth the plan of Harvard College as well, so that the march of God's much-threatened but well-protected saints goes on in full career: "the seventeenth Church of Christ at the Town of Hampton" (188) and, as an offshoot, an "eighteenth church at . . . Salisbury" (189). The established "Church of Christ at Watertown" is further provided with the labors of "the reverend, judicious, and godly-affected Mr. John Knowles" (190). The Lord also sends, in the same year, a "very sharp winter," and Johnson finds "the sad hand of the Lord" in the fate of two persons who suffered death by freezing; but the same providence accounts for the "great supply of godly ministers" (191–92) introduced in chapter 16. And for the planting of the "nineteenth church" (195) at Sudbury, or of the "twentieth" (197) at Braintree, or, skipping ahead a chapter, of those at "Gloucester" and "Dover" (205). Having found a way to count proliferation as success, Johnson is more than satisfied to count off the march of the New England congregations. And, as all that stands "between" numbers 20 and 21 is a further account of the founding of Harvard College, there seems just no interruption at all. For it is no small part of Johnson's brief for the exemplary success of Reformation in New England that each of its particular churches is served by a learned minister. Exactly the sort Harvard was founded locally to provide.

Indeed, Johnson argues, of all the "passages of this history" in which the "Wonder-working Providence of Sion's Savior" has aptly appeared, it shines

> more especially in this work, the fountains of learning being in a great measure stopped in our native country at this time, so that the sweet waters of Shilo's streams must ordinarily pass into the churches through the stinking channel of prelatical pride. (199)

So notorious has been this corruption of the sources of "godly learning"[35] that the Devil has used it as a "means to persuade people from the use of learning altogether, that so in the next generation they might be destitute." At issue is not polite accomplishment but "such helps as the Lord hath been pleased hitherto to make use of, as chief means for the conversion of his people and building them up in the holy faith" (199). As providence does not in these latter days mean miracle without means, so grace itself must dip down to touch the ordinary ways of civilized man. Nor can the saving knowledge of God and his ways rely upon the Spirit alone.

Reminding us in his Harvard poem to "Expect not miracles, lest means thereby you over-run" (203), Johnson stresses as well the practical difficulties in the creation, by a "poor pilgrim people," of a university in the midst of a "desolate wilderness" (199), especially in an age when many people . . . are out of conceit with learning." While refusing to allow that New Englanders count "ignorance the mother of devotion," he nevertheless admits that they are by and large a "people wholly devoted to the plow"; and they, more than willing to allow that "learning should plead for it self," find it proper to leave the planning to "those who had tasted the sweet wine of wisdom's drawing" (200). As such men well understand the power of "spiritual learning . . . to sanctify the other, and make the whole lump holy" (200–201), they wisely choose to locate their seminary of learning in Cambridge which, "under the orthodox and soul-flourishing ministry of Mr. Thomas Shepard," had been kept free of the Antinomian infection. Established with the "conveniences of a fair hall, comfortable studies, and a good library" (201), the college was not slow to bring forth and nurse up "very hopeful plants, to the supplying [of] some churches here" (201–2)—just in case the world lasts longer than Johnson has reason to hope. And, giving the hint once again to Cotton Mather, he recites the names, as of 1651, of some of the distinguished graduates.[36]

The truth of history constrains Johnson to mention "the sudden and unexpected fall of cattle," the very moment when the interruption of Puritan migration suddenly shrunk the market for all such commodities. Yet the bulk of his twenty-first chapter is devoted to the "wonderful alteration" that, by 1642, had in fact occurred in his "nation . . . born in a day" (209). Though not quite ready to switch without notice from the ordinary world's expected end to the beauty of its fertile continuance,[37] he certainly allows its present prosperity to complicate his prediction of martial climax:

> This remote, rocky, barren, bushy, wild-woody wilderness, a receptacle for lions, wolves, bears, foxes, rockoones, bags, beavers, otters, and all kind of wild creatures, a place that never afforded the natives better than the flesh of a few wild creatures and parched Indian corn inched out with chestnuts and bitter acorns, now through the mercy of Christ become a second England for fertileness in so short a space, that it is indeed the wonder of the world. (210)

As if Bradford's fulfillment fulfilled itself in produce as well as in churches. Not a miracle exactly, but a wondrous transformation of diet, raiment, and dwellings: from wilderness to garden in one generation.[38] Which the comfortable ought to "declare . . . to their children's children" (210). Either here or in some newer Heaven and Earth.

A long chapter 22 takes the occasion of the establishment of the "three and twentieth" Church of Christ in the Massachusetts government—at Woburn—to clear from Presbyterian slander the true "manner of planting towns and churches in New England" (212). Indeed, those learned in Scripture are invited to "lay the actions of N.E. to the rule" (212–13). Indicating first that a New England town, its "bounds fixed by the General Court," ordinarily comes into existence by means of a grant given to "seven men of good and honest report" who promise to "erect house for habitation thereon," Johnson further specifies that these men have, in turn, the "power to . . . grant out lands unto any persons willing to take up their dwellings within the said precinct," including an "ample portion both of meadow and upland" (213). Since this Woburn is to be Johnson's own town, he is generous in his familiar description of its seat and setting, including the situation of its meetinghouse, "in a small plain, where four streets meet" (214). Then to the disputed case of church foundation.

Though it is as "unnatural for a right New England man to live without an able ministry as for a smith to work his iron without a fire," one is never to imagine such men as "rashly running together themselves into a church, before they had hopes of attaining"—and supporting—"an officer to preach the word and administer the seals unto them" (214). They choose, rather, to "continue in fellowship with some other church for their Christian watch" (214–15). Then, on the morning of August 24, 1642—after "the Reverend Mr. Symmes had continued in preaching and prayer" for four or five hours, "the persons that were to join in covenant" made open profession "before the congregation and messengers of divers neighbor churches." Among them were Cotton, Wilson, Shepard, and Mather, plus Mr. Increase Nowell to represent the magistrates, not only to prevent "disturbance" by sectaries but also to assure the people of God that "under them they may live a quiet and peaceful life, in all godliness and honesty" (215). And so

> the persons stood forth and first confessed what the Lord had done for their poor souls, by the work of his Spirit in the preaching of the Word, and providences, one by one; and that all might know their faith in Christ was bottomed upon him, as he is revealed in his Word, and that from their own knowledge, they also declare the same, according to that measure of understanding the Lord had given them; the Elders . . . present questions with them, for the better understanding of them in any points they doubt of, which being done, and all satisfied, they in the name of the churches to which they do belong hold out the right hand of fellowship unto them, they declaring their covenant, in words expressed in writing to this purpose. (215–16)

Puritans, in both Old England and New, have written more correct English, but few have captured in one expanded sentence more of the competing motives of the Congregational Moment. As if purity of heart could will a unity beyond syntax.

The Woburn Covenant is somewhat longer than other versions with which we are familiar, but Johnson is careful to assure us that "Every church hath not the same for words, for they are not for a form of words" (216).[39] Then, after touching on the ordaining of "Mr. Thomas Carter," Johnson is careful to detail the admission of further members, each by his own confession, first to the pastor and then to the "charitable approving" of the entire congregation, of "the manner of his conversion . . . and the work of the Spirit in the inward parts of his soul." Beyond expressing his own enthusiasm for the project, Johnson is eager to stress that this admission by faithful confession need not be a stumbling block to Presbyterians: of the bashful, "less is required" and, in Johnson's own congregation at least, "women speak not publicly at all" (217); indeed, the only issue is to ensure that those who take the Lord's Supper "do not eat and drink their own condemnation." And any who suppose the New England Way less evangelical than some broader path need to consider that, between 1642 and 1650, the number of professors in the Woburn congregation had grown from seven to seventy-four; and that all these had confessed conversion by "the preaching of the Word in N.E." and had experienced the covenant as efficacious "not only for the building up of souls in Christ, but also for converting of sinners" (218). For what could stir the soul of the would-be Christian like the desire to gain admission to a group sworn to uphold one another in "mutual love" (216)?

Satisfied with this definition of the institution of religion in New England, Johnson moves on, in chapter 23, to the confederation of the four English colonies in New England. Massachusetts will have to bear a disproportionate expense in any "chargeable war with the naked natives," yet Johnson indicates that his chosen commonwealth is more than willing—"so long as [the other] governments maintain the same purity in religion" (219). Then, after ascribing a battle between the Narragansetts and Mohegans to the fomenting activities of a company of "vagabond English" (220), Johnson turns to Samuel Gorton, the "ringleader" (223) of those vagabonds. Refusing to answer charges involving Indians and the land, Gorton instead "vomits up a whole paper full of beastly stuff":

> one while scoffing and deriding the ignorance of all besides himself, that think Abraham, Isaac, etc., could be saved by Christ Jesus, who was after born of the Virgin Mary, another while mocking at the sacraments of Baptism and the Lord's Supper, in an opprobrious manner, deriding at the

elements Christ was pleased to institute them in, and calling them necro-
mancers that administered them at all. (223–24)

In official response, the governors of Massachusetts "resolved to send forty persons well-appointed with weapons of war for apprehending of him" (224).

As the government of Massachusetts made the Gorton affair the occasion of
"extending its jurisdiction unwarrantable over the Shawomet region," Johnson's
editor sees this "harrying" as "one of the most discreditable episodes of early Massachusetts history" (222), but Johnson himself continues to witness the overriding
interest of religion. Indeed, the banishing of the Gortonists seems rather lenient
to a man who came to New England to enjoy "Christ Jesus and his blessed ordinances" and who writes on behalf of those who "had rather lose their lives than
suffer them to be thus blasphemed." To be sure, "some have favored them, and
endeavored to bring under blame such as have been zealous against their abominable doctrines," but is this unhappy fact itself not a sign of the times?—

> that in these days, when all look for the fall of Antichrist, such detestable
> doctrines should be upheld, and such persons suffered, that exceed the
> Beast himself for blasphemy, and this to be done by those that would be
> counted reformers, and such as seal the utter subversion of Antichrist.
> (225)

Small wonder, then, that the year of 1644 began with "another earthquake."

Otherwise, however, the "march" goes on—in the planting of the "twenty-
fourth Church of Christ at the town of Reading" (225) and the "twenty-fifth" at
Wenham, this latter figuring as a "little sister" to Salem, which "nourish[ed] her
up in her own bosom, till she came of age" (226); and, less domestically, in putting the entire "country" of New England "in a posture of war, to be ready on all
occasions" (227). The title of the chapter with which Johnson concludes his Book
2 points to "the forts of Boston, and Charles[town]" and to the "castle erected
anew by the six nearest towns" (227); and Johnson makes it clear that the guns of
New England are "to make many shot[s] at such ships as shall offer to enter the
harbor without their good leave" (232). Yet the bulk of chapter 26 is devoted to a
recording of the names of the military officers of all the various counties and
towns. And in other ways too Johnson makes it clear that, in the war for which
his countrymen are preparing, the men matter more than the materiel.

The chapter begins with the stout claim that the "soldiers of Christ Jesus . . .
[are] resolved to stand it out" against any who should try to rob them of the religious "privileges" the Lord has "purchased for them at a very high rate." And

though it concedes that "the chiefest work of these select bands" has all along been "to mind their spiritual welfare," it also asks us to remember that the "temple was surrounded with walls and bulwarks," and that God's people "did prepare to resist their enemies with weapons of war, even while they continued building" (227). Thus Johnson's attempt to balance the military and the spiritual draws its conviction from the same sort of (re)vision that makes it so hard to tell New England from Jerusalem.[40] In the end, however, after naming all the (latter-day) names of those chosen to lead the saintly troops that are to be "exercised and drilled eight days in a year" (228), Johnson seems to reverse his emphasis. The military remains in place, boldly and as such: "Thus are these people with great diligence provided for these days of war, hoping the day is at hand wherein the Lord will give Antichrist the double of all her doings" (232); *but*—with the emphasis falling now on matters which military preparedness could only protect and dimly figure—

> that which gives greatest hope concerning this particular is this, that these times afford more soldiers depending on the Lord Christ through faith for deliverance and true valor than any age since Antichrist began to fall, without which all these preparations were but so many traps and snares. (233)

Which is to say: saints are to resist invasion, but only in the name of Christ; and martial rhetoric is but vain glory unless it find redemption as typology.

Trusting, therefore, that the March of the Churches promises victory quite as much as the drilling of the trainbands, Johnson is content to end his second book on a note of defiance that is expansively typological:

> let all people know that desire the downfall of New England, they are not to war against a people only exercised in feats of war, but men who are experienced in the deliverances of the Lord from the mouth of the lion, and the paw of the bear. (223)

Regeneration through Violence, one sort of analysis might conclude.[41] And indeed Johnson's pairing of the native bear with the familiar biblical figure of the lion may mean to say that he has been to the frontier. But having been to the older of his two testaments as well, he knows where to look for assurance: "When the same God that directed the stone to the forehead of the Philistine guides every bullet shot at you, it matters not for the whole rabble of Antichrist on your side, the God of Armies is for us a refuge high" (233). In truth Johnson wants The War: his God has been, from the outset, a God of Armies. But he also indicates

that they also fight who only resist the appeal of false doctrine and fill the churches
with faith.

———

The final book of Johnson's *Providence* is by far the shortest of the three—covering in just twelve chapters "the passages of God's Providence . . . from the year
1645 till toward the latter end of 1651" (234). From the example of Bradford we
might expect that, as Johnson comes nearer to his own narrative present and begins to avail himself of the year-by-year method, he might also fall prey to certain
doubts and fears, as piety wanes and as the focus of strategic revision becomes
shorter and shorter. Remarkably, however, something like the reverse is true:
problems continue to arise but, having decided at the beginning of his latter-day
composition that the meaning of New England has been clear from the outset,
and that his story can have only one—apocalyptic—ending, Johnson presses ever
more fervently toward that climax. Even if, in order to be of any earthly use, his
book must see the light of publication before the actual dawning of that last day.

Familiarly, but with an urgency we have been instructed to respect, chapters
1 and 2 report the formation of churches 26 and 27, at Haverhill and Springfield
respectively. Apropos of the first of these, "lying higher up than Salisbury, upon
a fair and large river of Merrimack," Johnson observes with content that the "constant penetration farther into this wilderness hath caused the wild and uncouth
woods to be filled with frequent ways, and the large rivers to be over-laid with
bridges" (234). The truth of history requires him to notice as well "an over-
weaning desire in most men after meadow land," but he assures us that though
"the people are laborious after gaining the goods of this life," still they are "not
unmindful of the chief end of their coming here, namely, to be made partakers of
the blessed ordinances" (235). And it never occurs to him to connect the "constant
penetrating" (234) with the need to prepare for renewed war with the "native inhabitants" (235), emphasizing instead that the avoidance of such war was owing
to the "acts of the Lord Christ in awing these . . . heathens" (236). Just so, the
penetration of Mr. Pyncheon to Springfield "upon the river of Canetico" (236–37)
provokes no anxiety of supplantation,[42] but only the report that this wilderness
people "deemed it now high time to implore the Lord for his especial aid" (238).

Yet as if to express this besetting Puritan unconscious, Johnson—or perhaps
the morale of the people—insists that *this* form of spiritual inventory be as searching as possible. Daring not to presume on "former deliverances," a people pray
instead that the memory of these may "refresh their frozen affections and move a
melting heart in their barren breasts, that began to dry up with a lazy lethargy."

More specifically, at the invitation of the "godly government the Lord . . . had peaceably placed among them," each church held its own day of public repentance. The "Jeremiad" occasion, clearly enough. Yet Johnson cannot quite manage to keep his emphasis on his people's "sinful provocations." What moves his prose to its customary extravagance is the scene of faithful remembrance: as Jacob over Jordan,

> so they came over this boisterous billow-boiling ocean, a few poor scattered stones newly raked out of the heaps of rubbish, and thou Lord Christ hast now so far exalted them as to lay them sure in thy Sion, a-building, to be the wonder of the world; orderly are they placed in five and forty several churches, and that in a wilderness, where civility scarce ever took place, much less any religion, and now to the Lord earnestly they cry to be delivered from the cruel hands that would destroy both . . . the bird and her young together. (238)

As in the sermon at the end of *The Scarlet Letter,* not man's failings but the unfolding of God's plot becomes the theme of Johnson's day of humiliation.

Johnson's dramatic outburst ends with the reminder that it is the people themselves who did "thus . . . plead with the Lord." And no doubt it will be possible to discover the sermon sources from which Johnson has edited his own supra-sentences.[43] But the literary energy of this latter-day vision of timely accomplishment and end-time expectation that will not be surrendered is all his own: "so now shall these and the like sister-churches spread the whole earth, the Lord Christ reigning as King and Lord for ever over them." And though the modern reader cannot account for the hectic shifts in point of view, or identify all the tag-ends of ecstatic Scripture, still it is easy enough to recognize the voice—of the man who has taken in too many sermons:

> Then why do the heathen rage, and the people imagine a vain thing, seeing the time of the Lord's arising to have mercy on Sion is come, yea his appointed time is at hand; and he who walks in the midst of his golden candlesticks, whose eyes are as a flaming fire, will not suffer his churches to be trodden under feet of that Antichristian lordly prelacy any longer, nor yet defiled with any transformed saint-seeming angels of light with their painted doctrines. (239)

Of course the heathen will rage, when more than at the end of his sway? But neither he nor any more refined shapes of the Devil can be expected to prevail. For the divine denouement is as familiar as the earthly *agon.*

As to the "success" of these fast-day prayers, historical estimates vary.[44] But Johnson shifts his emphasis to the need for the churches to continue the process and—to avoid the drama of ritualistic confession in the face of the mounting interest in worldly business as usual—he calls attention to the beauty of the prayerful scene itself:

> these New England churches are near one hundred miles distant one from another, and yet communicate, counsel, care, love, joy, grieve with and for one another, dismiss some and commend others . . . to the Christian care and watchfulness, from one to another, and why may not this be practiced the world throughout, even from Jerusalem . . . to Illyricum? (239)

And, by implication, he raises a question certain modern warriors might well consider: when all the world has joined together to extirpate the agents of Evil, is not the drama of history as good as over already?

If chapter 3 sees the Devil in the form of a petition rather than that of a firework, the issue must have seemed serious indeed. In fact, the New England Way itself: against the provision that only church members vote in general elections and that only those openly professing conversion be admitted as church members, the petition of Robert Childe and others has demanded, in the words of Johnson's editor, that "all members of the Church of England and . . . Scotland be admitted to the communion of the New England churches," and that all those formerly "debarred from suffrage and from civil office" for reasons of nonmembership be enfranchised.[45] Johnson scoffs at the idea that the petitioners actually "cared for a Presbyterian Church," for such they might well have found in England, and holds instead that they were merely trying to embarrass the local establishment. While the government delays in meting out a penalty "for their seditious . . . words and practices" (240)—clearly justified in the eyes of all but "such as are all for liberty, and nothing for government"—the petitioners charge other "gross matters." When the plot is publicly exposed, Johnson can only conclude that "it was the Lord's gracious goodness to quell their malice against his people" (241). Nor have "the proud bishops," or "any other hitherto prospered who have maligned these poor churches of Christ." Still, with the case of Gorton still pending in England, the colonies find it prudent to send over "the honored M. Winslow to manifest and declare the naked truth of things." And though Gorton is permitted to return to New England, and though Winslow remains in England to take a hand in important matters there, Johnson rests his case upon the blasphemy: "the devil showed his horns in that book he printed, wherein he takes upon him a monstrous interpretation" (241) of the Lord's Supper.[46]

Johnson's next two chapters take up the question of codification—dangerous, still, as the special features of the New England Way challenge most Protestant practice and violate some English law; but necessary, as the reports of what
one scholar has called "Puritan Radicalism in New England" are gaining it the
reputation as a "colluvies of sectaries."[47] In "the second synod holden at Cambridge," the churches of Christ meet "to hold forth the doctrine and discipline of
Jesus Christ, according to the rule of the New Testament"; they conduct a "disputation" that is "plain and easy to be understood of the meanest capacity, clearing up points that were most dubious" and (eventually)[48] publish their results.
Evidently the New England churches are "not ashamed to make confession of
their faith to all the world" (242). As before, there are opposers: first, those so
used to "the broad beaten path of liberty that they fear to be confined in the
straight and narrow path of truth"; second, those whose will is "wedded to some
singular rare conceited opinion"; third, and more honest, those "scared" with the
"big words" of those who tell them of the "popish and prelatical synods, what a
deal of trash and canon laws they have brought in." Either the opposition to the
"advisory synod" has died down or Johnson has himself become more comfortable with this compromise measure. Yet his opposition to all extraconsensual theology remains undiminished—as "two parelii, or images of the sun," are referred
to those whose New Light expectations announce "another sun, yet indeed had
no light in them, but vanished away no man knew how" (243).

Chapter 5 salutes the completion of the process, begun in 1635, of compiling
and publishing a set of laws for Johnson's "little commonwealth." Building on
"The Body of Liberties" adopted in 1641, a series of committees finally has their
work approved by the General Court in 1646 and 1647 and committed to the
press in 1648, so that "the General Laws and Liberties concerning the inhabitants
of Massachusetts"

> are now to be seen of all men, to the end that none may plead ignorance,
> and that all who intend to transport themselves hither may know that this
> is no place of licentious liberty, nor will this people suffer any to trample
> down this vineyard of the Lord. (244)

Though specified and promulgated only "now," Johnson nevertheless sponsors
what had been the implicit policy of this religious establishment from the very
beginning: a covenanted state, as understood and implemented by godly ministers and magistrates, from which all those who think otherwise have always been
entirely free to stay away.

Belated, perhaps, but cogent enough, for the time and place—unless it be the natural right of every man to live in Boston:

> for it is no wrong to any man, that a people who have spent their estates . . . and ventured their lives for to keep faith and a pure conscience, to use all means that the Word of God allows for maintenance and continuance of the same, especially they have taken up a desolate wilderness to be their habitation, and not deluded any by keeping their profession in hugger-mug, but print and proclaim to all the way and course they intend, God willing, to walk in. (244–45)

The questionable plea of "nonseparation" notwithstanding, no one has ever accused Winthrop's original "Model" of "huggermug." Liberalism is not yet, and a deep separation of godly possibility from the "City of Man" is the province of the prophet of Rhode Island, now back in the England of Gorton and Winslow. Here and now, therefore, would it not "savor too much of hypocrisy"

> that any people should pray unto the Lord for the speedy accomplishment of his Word in the overthrow of Antichrist, and in the mean time become a patron to sinful opinions and damnable errors that oppose the truths of Christ, admit it be but in the bare permission? (245)

At issue, finally, is not only the legitimacy of New England but also the meaning of the Reformation itself: is it not the duty of the present age finally to get religion right?

Turning back to the way of the world within the plot of God, Johnson devotes chapter 6 to the providence that fitted "this people with all kinds of manufactures" (245). Praying for the end, he cannot yet turn away from the way the Lord has *continued* to turn "one of the most hideous, boundless, and unknown wildernesses in the world in an instant, . . . to a well ordered commonwealth." Of course, the wealth and good order are "all to serve his churches" (248), of which "the three last" (249) are duly specified in chapter 7. The third of these—"The Old North Church, afterward famous as the church of Increase, Cotton, and Samuel Mather[49]—results from a necessary division of the church of Boston, the mention of which leads Johnson to record the death of the "honored Governor, John Winthrop Esquire, whose indefatigable pains in this wilderness-work is not to be forgotten" (251–52). Nor are the works and days of many other "personages," duly praised in chapter 8: Hooker of Hartford, Philips of Watertown, and above all "the holy heavenly, sweet-affecting, and soul-ravishing Minister M. Tho. Shepard, Pastor of the Church of Christ at Cambridge, whose departure was heavily taken by all the people of Christ round about him." And only now does Johnson turn from the "heaps upon heaps of the riches of Christ's tender compassionate mercies" to stern possibility of his "approaching rod" (252).

An "army of caterpillars" has destroyed the "husbandman's hope," rebuking his "over eager pursuit of the fruits of the earth." So too was the Lord "pleased to command the wind and seas to give us a jog on the elbow, by sinking the very chief of our shipping in the deep" (253), the more remarkable as "the Lord was pleased to forbid any such things to befall his people in their passage hither." Surely all the people of New England are to read "as in great capital letters, their sudden forgetfulness of the Lord's former mercy"; but especially warned are such "men of trade" who are

> so taken up with the income of a large profit, that they would willingly have had the community tolerate diverse kinds of sinful opinions to entice men to come and sit down with us, that their purses might be filled with coin, the civil government with contention, and the churches . . . with errors." (254)

So it may be easy enough to understand why the Lord has been "pleased . . . to let in the King of Terror among his new-planted churches."

Untimely deaths of children, from "an unwonted disease," show the Lord "now smiting many families" (254–55), and, in a definitive anamnesis, they remind "these pilgrim people" of their forgetfulness of the "worthies that had died not long before" and more especially of "the little regard [they] had to provide means to train the children." But Johnson cannot maintain the Jeremiad strain for very long; for these signs actually *work* to stir up the Lord's people to prepare for "the overthrow of Antichrist,"

> which in all likelihood is very suddenly to be performed; as also in stirring up all the young ones that remain to consider for what end the Lord had spared their lives, when he cut off others by death, namely, to prosecute the work that he hath given them to do. (255)

Johnson may be extending the lest-you-forget message of Shepard's autobiography to an entire generation of children lucky enough to be left alive but, unlike the Jeremiahs of the second generation, he *records* and does not merely pray in high anxiety for the reformation devoutly to be wished. This may be, as one readily supposes, pure wish fulfillment, but the need of Johnson's rhetoric to carry through from wakeup call to actual awakening seems a distinctive feature of his peculiar zeal.

Fatal disease continues from 1650 to 1651. Johnson notes that "so small a sickness might not be taken notice of in other places," but a people in covenant will—"many of them"—perceive that if they tread in "the same steps of riot and excess" as other men, "in the plenty he hath given them," then "with the men of this world he will lay the same sicknesses and disease upon them" (255–56). Of course the prophetic speaker must always "perceive plainly" the logic of the covenant problem and solution; and now and then some otherwise strident Jeremiah will stipulate, to stop the mouth of invidious comparison, that New England still has many "praying Saints."[50] But the problem of "Declension in a Bible Commonwealth" is largely a matter of spiritual blindness: the inspired speaker cannot quite believe that his audience does not see where their wayward behavior is leading them. Here, however, a significant portion of the audience is said in fact to see and understand. And with this reversal of proportion comes a reversal of emphasis: backsliding there unquestionably is, but God's methods are actually working.[51]

Understanding the punishment of their worldliness as the predictable, indeed the necessary response of a God who is serious about his earthly engagements, Johnson's percipient "many" can "further perceive" that God "hath some further great work to do." Further still, Johnson shares with his historical subjects the knowledge that God is "beginning again to awaken, rouse up, and quicken them with the rod of his power." And as a sign of this shared sense they "begin to reason with themselves":

> when the Lord was pleased to expose them, their wives, and little ones to the troubles of a tempestuous sea in so long a voyage, and the wants of a barren wilderness . . . , he brought forth by his mighty power and stretched-out arm the glorious fabric of his New-England Churches; and therefore now again they look for some farther extraordinary work of his, if he shall once again refine them in this furnace. (256)

By the decade of the 1660s, in the wake of the Restoration and the Half-Way Covenant, the Jeremiahs of New England will have decided that New England's troubles signify unquestionably her backsliding. Still looking for some more dramatic conclusion to New England's astonishingly successful experiment in church-making, Johnson is certain they mean that God is still making his people strong for war. So certain is he of his New England certainty that he can only wish for the Lord Christ to "confirm our brethren in England in like faith by our example"; and to suggest that his own book—which ought to be volumes longer to do its proper job—is nevertheless sufficient to prove the "almost miraculous" character of the present place and age, "as if the Lord did intend to make his power known more abundantly than ever the sons of men" (256) have seen.

Then, stepping back from his confident ascription of proper spiritual discernment to a moral majority of New England—and from the chauvinism it has so evidently bred—Johnson suggests that New and Old English alike may profit from the self-accusing sentiments of the (annotated) verses which are identically his ninth chapter. In the first four (six-line) stanzas, he grieves that "Grief comes but slack" for the "ill requital" of the Lord's "infinite and undeserved mercies" (257–58). Four more repeat the acknowledgment of "The rod of God toward us in maritime affairs" (258): "No wonder then thy works with eastern wind / On seas are broke" (258). Recognition of "the Lord's hand against our land affairs" requires a full eight stanzas, citing both the "countless crew of caterpillars" and certain "fearful fires"—blaming both his own soul's weak faith and also the habits of "our meaner sort that metamorphos'd are, / With women's hair, in gold and garments gay" (259); and promising "The world's embrace, our longing lust for gain, / No longer shall us into corners draw" (260). Seven final stanzas reprise the death lament for Winthrop, Hooker, Shepard, and others, pondering the significance of this separation of "men and means," and suggesting, if only in a prose paraphrase,[52] *either* that the Lord means to raise up another people to himself to do his work *or*—the preferred alternative, clearly—that he means to "raise us up by his rod to a more eager pursuit of his work, even the planting of his churches the world throughout" (261).

So much for the "wailing muse" (257). Now, perhaps, Johnson's credentials as advance man for the Jeremiad are complete: early (and astonishing) success in the name of Providence, repeated and multiform warnings against the erosion of end-time faith by the good-time experience of this world, and the possibility that the covenant with New England might be just about over.[53] Yet perfection of form is not the same as exhilaration of spirit, and Johnson—whose real poetry is always in his prose—hastens in chapter 10 to assure us that not all are slack in their "endeavors . . . to enlarge his kingdom the world throughout" (261). Peters and Wells, famously, but many others as well, have "steered their course for England, so soon as they heard of the chaining up of those biting beasts who went under the name of spiritual Lords." And as for "the Indian people," who were at the first coming of the English "very barbarous and uncivilized, going for the most part naked" (262) and who, as to "religious observation, . . . were the most destitute of any people yet heard of," working out their salvation with "Squantam [as] a bad Devil, and Abbanocho [as] their good Devil" (263), one has only to mention the works of the "godly Mr. John Wilson, who visited their sick," Mr. Eliot, who studied to instruct them "in their own Wigwams," and "the Reverend Mr. Mayhew," who gathered an Indian church "at a small island called Martins Vineyard"—about all of whom much is "already published" (264).

Consider too the missions of New England to both Virginia and the Bermudas. True, their efforts in Virginia were repulsed, but let "all you Cavaliers and malignant party the world throughout" consider: "Oh poor Virginia, dost thou send away the ministers of Christ with threatening speeches? No sooner is this done, but the bloody Indians are let loose upon them" (265). And though the "gathered" church at Bermuda was "banished . . . to one of the southern Islands," it is well known how God's people contributed to "supply their necessity"—so that the aid of New England was recognized as the hand of God. Small evidence, perhaps, when nothing less than a "gathering" of churches worldwide will serve, yet Johnson's need to accentuate the positive forces from it his own sense of an ending:

> so that as this book began with the wonderworking providence of Sion's Savior, in providing so wonderful graciously for his churches the world throughout; so it here endeth with the same. (267)

Of course, it is "to be desired that the churches of Christ in Europe would gather" their own list of "wonderful providences" including, especially, "those in our native country." For there as well as here—and in spite of the counterclaims of the "antichristian party"—the story of the reform efforts of so many persons could hardly fail to reveal itself as "the very finger of God" (268).

And would it not strengthen the end-time faith of those "appointed of the Lord for the overthrow of Antichrist"? Not the faith of Johnson himself, a true believer if there ever was one. But those in England, perhaps. Or even in New England, should any of the holy exiles be confused, given the religious upheaval in England, about where the Final Battle is likely to break out. Here, if the signs of the times promote revival in fact; and if there—or elsewhere—only as "another people" can learn from New England. Consider again the "finger of God" in the safe establishment of all those "gathered churches." And know that "the time of his having mercy upon Sion is come" (268).

———

Unaware, perhaps, of his own best gift—for a prose whose excitement defies the laws of its own creation—Johnson ends his book with another long poem as, into twenty-one of his customary six-line stanzas, Johnson compresses his own version of "God's Plot." Decorous in diction, utterly obedient to the laws of iambic meter and inverse poetic syntax, perfectly sober in its expression of an (elsewhere unruly) apocalyptic desire, his concluding poem leads us calmly from a recognition of Christ's great work, "poor captives to redeem" (272), to a reminder that these captives can soon expect the liberating Christ to "crown [their] heads with lasting glee" (275). Along the way we learn it has been Christ's plan not only to save souls but also to purchase churches, of which he is now "come down possession for to take." And though his "wrath is kindled," none who "walk in [his] way" need fear "his anger" (272); nor the "fury of men or devils" either, since "Christ among you takes his daily walk." Yet all such are to avoid pride at this "exaltation," for it is "Not thou but Christ triumphs his foes upon" (273).

The people of the original Israel are given their own special instructions: expect that a returning God will "your heart not member circumcise"; but know as well that, once converted, your task will be to convert the entire Moslem world, freeing all "poor Christians" (273) there held prisoner. As to the "Nations," they are to observe that "Christ comes you near" and to "seek his face" while yet "the battle's but begun." Then, as the poem beseeches Christ to place such newly gathered Nations in his "strong Armies newly gather'd, / Thy churches," we begin to suspect that Johnson can revel in the energy of his military metaphor whether he lives to see any actual battle or not. Or, rather, that the effort to cast down "all antichristian power" is of its very nature a warlike act. As salvation itself was nothing less than freeing of the soul from a sort of military captivity, so the final "battle," to settle the entire world into the ranks of gathered churches, will soon be won whether or not anyone blows up the Vatican. And even if Satan himself never appear at the head of his Legions.

And if we find ourselves a little let down—Oh, you mean it was all a metaphor?—we only betray thereby our failure to appreciate the typic power of Johnson's latter-day vision. Which could hardly be more excited if a literal Christ had, along about 1629, turned up in England in the form of a recruiting sergeant. If salvation is, in one available orthodoxy at least, the proper outcome of a life-and-death struggle of the Spirit, then surely the meaning of the triumphant march of the churches is a prime part of the war to end all wars. Which even now the spiritual eye can see:

> Oh blessed days of Son of Man now seen,
> You that have long'd so sore them to behold,

March forth in's might, and stoutly stand between
   The mightiest sword, and Christ's dear flock enfold.
     Undaunted close and clash with them: for why?
      'Gainst Christ they are, and he with thee stands by. (274)

So that if there is indeed any "confusion" about the conclusion of Johnson's book,[54] it is chiefly that his "poetic" is so much more proper than everything else.

Including the prose pages of the final chapter—on "the time of the fall of Antichrist and the increase of the gentile churches, even to the provoking of the twelve tribes to submit to the kingdom of Christ." Has it been the "longing expectation of many, to see . . . [Christ] casting down that man of sin who hath held the whole world . . . under his lordly power"? Then let all such "take notice the Lord hath an assured set time for the accomplishment of this work," even if the detection of the precise moment has so far eluded the searches of a number of "reverend ministers." And though no less a luminary than John Cotton "hath declared that some sudden blow [is] to be given to this blood-thirsty monster," yet it remains true that "the Lord Christ hath inseparably joined the time, means, and manner of this work together" (268); so that "all men that expect the day must attend the means" (269). How absurd, therefore, to affect concern for the certain denouement without taking part in the necessary plot.

Yet one does fairly come, at last, "to the time of Antichrist's fall" and, not to put too fine a point upon it, "that time is come, and all may see the dawning of the day." Now, as the issue is as much one of means as of discernment, all those "that long so much for it, come forth and fight [for] who can expect a victory without a battle?" And for that matter, who can fail to notice a battle of principles already under way?

> the lordly Prelates . . . are fled into holes and corners; Familists, Seekers, Antinomians and Anabaptists, they are so ill armed that they think it best sleeping in a whole skin, fearing that if the day of battle once go on, they shall among Antichrist's armies: and therefore cry out like cowards, If you let me alone, I will let you alone; but assuredly the Lord Christ hath said, he that is not with us is against us.

The first principle of the present war, therefore, is that "there is no room in his army for tolerationists," who appear to insist on worldly peace at any spiritual price.

Some will say, "We will never believe the day is come till our eyes behold Babylon begirt with soldiers" (269). But let such literalists think again:

hath not the Lord said, come out of her, my people? etc.; surely there is a little space left for this, and now is the time, seeing the Lord hath set up his standard of resort; now, come forth of her and be not partakers of her sins: now is the time, when the Lord hath assembled his Saints together; now the Lord will come and not tarry. (269–70)

Think with precision about the typological prediction: as there needed to be both Moses and Aaron before the Lord would "deliver his people and destroy Pharaoh lest they should be wildered indeed in the wilderness,"

so now it was needful that the churches of Christ should first obtain their purity, and the civil government its power to defend them, before Antichrist come to his final ruin; and because you shall be sure the day is come indeed, behold the Lord Christ marshalling of his invincible army to the battle. (270)

To those who imagine all this "only to be mystical, and not literal at all," Johnson concedes that "assuredly the spiritual fight is chiefly to be attended"; but he also insists that "the other" cannot be neglected, "especially at this time." For we are to understand "the ministers of Christ who have cast off all lording power" as "field-officers, whose office is . . . to encourage the fighting soldiers." Blow for blow, Johnson thinks, defiance of the prelates has hardly been "mystical." And, given the English example, is Christ not already making use of "kings, rulers, or generals of earth's armies"? (270).

Finally, however, a word to those established doubters who "will not believe the day is come till they see them engage battle with Antichrist":

Verily, if the Lord be pleased to open your eyes, you may see the beginning of the fight, and what success the armies of the Lord Christ have hitherto had; the forlorn hopes of Antichrist's army were the proud prelates of England; the forlorn of Christ's army were these N.E. people, who are the subject of this history, which encountering each other for some space of time, ours being overpowered with multitude, were forced to retreat to a place of greater safety, where they waited a fresh opportunity to engage with the main battle of Antichrist, so soon as the Lord shall be pleased to give a word of command. (271)

The problem is partly in recognizing that England's "proud prelates" are, though no longer agents of Rome, avatars of Antichrist in fact. And also in being able to see the truth of saying that the struggle so far has been a war indeed. To be sure, reforming work remains to be done in England and beyond, and some of it by armies altogether literal. But those who can see the justice of saying that already the Lord Christ has "pleased to command the right wing of his army to advance against the left wing of Antichrist" can also recognize that "Babylon is fallen" (271).

And now a series of admonitions. To Christ's army an encouragement: where there is "such a certainty of victory," who will hesitate to be a "soldier on Christ's side"?—particularly when "every true-hearted soldier that falls by the sword in this fight shall not lie dead long, but stand upon his feet again and be made partaker of the triumph of this victory." To the enemy a warning: "Christ will never give over the raising of fresh forces" until the army of Antichrist is "overthrown root and branch." To the "ancient people of Israel" an assurance: not only that the Lord Christ "is certainly come . . . to put life in your dry bones," but

> here is a people not only praying but fighting for you, that the great block may be removed out of the way, . . . that they with you may enjoy that glorious resurrection-day, the glorious nuptials of the Lamb: when not only the Bridegroom shall appear to his churches of both Jews and Gentiles, (which are his spouse) in a more bright array than ever heretofore, but also his Bride shall be clothed by him in the richest garments that ever the sons of men put on, even the glorious graces of Christ Jesus, in such a glorious splendor to the eyes of man, that they shall see and glorify the Father of both Bridegroom and Bride. (272)[55]

Again the reckless run-on—of an enthusiasm that cannot stay to mend the fences of its own syntax, and of Bible poetry brought in to assert that an early life of high religious adventure, far from settling to the dread regime of the ordinary, has its climax still ahead. In a miraculous future, beginning in the providential now.

Less poetic "verses" are to follow, formally to end a narrative marked by its triumphant disregard of very many settled forms. The more conventional poetry is there, it seems, to aid those prosy souls who may stumble at the idea of the Lamb who is a Bridegroom to Churches. In the end, however, these may be as far beyond help as those who cannot grasp the essentially military nature of their own experience. Perhaps—as the enduring world of New England was elsewhere discovering from the experience of its children—you had to be there, when Christ recruited soldiers for service overseas. Unwilling to let his own Greatest Generation pass on quietly, however, Johnson argues to the last that, from the first, New Englanders marched into history by believing that militant church reform was warfare indeed. And that the Archenemy was about to fall. What a waste, otherwise, of all those wonderful providences.

CHAPTER TEN

GOVERNMENT IN EXILE

Williams and the Decay of Dialogue

In one sense, nothing could have been more timely than the appearance, in 1644, of Roger Williams' *Bloody Tenet of Persecution:* conceived as an answer to Winthrop's *Short Story,* it was put together in the England of Milton's *Areopagitica* and brought to New England by the same hands that carried a charter for the "tolerationist" colony at Rhode Island; and it arrived on the eve of the definitive controversy between the Holy State of Massachusetts and the supporters of the Remonstrance of 1646, who looked to England for aid and comfort on the question of permissible dissent. Surely this was a moment when the unfolding modern world might try out, in an available Protestant code, the "Jeffersonian" proposition that not only consensus but Truth itself is discovered only at the end of free and open discussion. Even Winthrop was learning, however unhappily, to hear the voices of citizens who understood their freedom differently.

In another sense, however, the *Bloody Tenet* was hopelessly belated, as the arguments that bore most heavily on the quasi-theocratic understanding of "The Theory of the State and of Society" in the communities of Massachusetts and Connecticut had been won and lost long since. Essentially there had been two key issues: how, in a holy commonwealth, will the protective state relate to the purified church? And, granting the crucial—"medieval"—premise of a protective state,[1] how will the churches assure themselves of a membership, from out of a world of sinners, of persons worthy to go about under the name of Saints? The answer to the second, more "spiritual" of these questions had been effectively settled by 1636, when an inaugural synod agreed that church membership in New

England should be tied to the public rehearsal of the candidate's gracious experience. And the entire matter of the Antinomians can be understood as the literary
solution to the entailed question of how anxious and conditional or how subjectively assured the normative account of Faith ought to sound. The first question
had been decided even earlier when, at the spring 1631 meeting of Winthrop's
General Court, it was decided that freemen, who possessed the right to vote in
charter affairs, might henceforth be taken to mean church members; and, though
there must have been some discussion of this radical divergence from English
practice and charter intent, the available records are remarkably silent. Even Williams, arriving just a little too late to dissent from this original unseparation,
seized upon other issues. And this fact makes the cases of Williams and Hutchinson more different than they have often been made to seem.[2]

Not to blame Williams, but had he not run off to Narragansett Bay, in winter 1635, with the assistance or silent assent of Winthrop, the cases might have
come to look similar indeed. That is to say, if the infant colony of Massachusetts
had had to conduct, at just that tense and dangerous moment, the same sort of
knock-down, drag-out examination and trial of Williams as it found itself forced
to endure in the case of Hutchinson, then the first cornerstone of New England's
Puritan Constitution—call it "Member Franchise"—might well have had as full
an airing as its second, discovering that "Regenerate Membership" does not at all
imply perfect assurance. To be sure, some letters get exchanged, between Williams for the prosecution and John Cotton for the defense of the New England
understanding of "conscience"; nor does Winthrop omit to record his response to
Williams' original critique.[3] But he is forced to prepare no documentary account
of the judgment against Williams; and by the time Williams responds to the
Short Story that did get written, the decision to understand Massachusetts as a
state with the constituency of a church was a fact so well accomplished and prosperous that, quite like Nathaniel Ward, the official Puritan Mind could understand Williams' increasingly frustrated critique as no more than the recommen-
dation of a compromise they had no need to make.

It is simply contrary to fact, of course, to suppose that the political history
of New England would have been quite different if the exclusions underlying
what not all agreed to call "persecution" had got a full intellectual thrashing in
the years 1634–35. The *literary* history would certainly look a little different—
as neither Winthrop nor any other inquisitor could have relied upon their control of tone to carry the day against this subtle man who held the same degree
they all respected. And this may help us to understand why Winthrop may
have been willing to allow Williams to slip away: to avoid a divisive—indeed a

scandalous—confrontation.[4] Down the road apiece, William Bradford was sore-ly puzzled by the positions Williams was taking, but he could scarcely assign this conscientious man to the Devil's party.[5] Perhaps Winthrop faced a similar problem: having failed to compose the sort of brotherly consensus that marks the only acceptable outcome of saintly controversy, what remained but saintly stalemate, the public disclosure that fundamentals themselves remained open to debate? Perhaps Williams, who knew that the truth was meaningless unless the man really believed it, was himself not quite prepared for this epistemic new de-parture, though we will forgive him if he merely thought it prudent to construct his alternative world in practice before giving it the full defense of theory.

In any event, the belated *Bloody Tenet* can mark a terminus. Johnson's Won-derbook is a later entry into the canon, as are both the formal climax and the ac-tual ending of Winthrop's "Journal"; but the Williams controversy goes on until 1652, when his *Bloody Tenet Yet More Bloody* supplies the needful response to Cotton's *Bloody Tenet Washed* (1647). One way or another, Williams deserves to have the place, if not of finality, at least of settled resistance. *The Bloody Tenet Yet More Bloody* "makes confused reading,"[6] but its earlier incarnation is definitive enough: the first version of the last word, a good enough place to discover whether the New England prophet we most honor has found a way to write as good a book about religious inquiry and political peace as those whose more spotted fame was earned in the pursuit of a truth they supposed would redeem and annul the entire realm of social difference.

———

Students of American Studies may wish to consider the significance of Roger Williams for the "American Tradition" if only for the fact that his antiestablish-ment writings provided the source of Perry Miller's most obvious historical mis-take and offered, thereby, the occasion of the most enduringly useful correction of Sacvan Bercovitch. Williams' debate with Cotton does, for a moment at least, turn on the interpretation of the specific New Testament parable of the wheat and the tares and also, more generally, on the issue of biblical typology. The ques-tion, however, involves different *styles* of typological interpretation and not, as Miller kept insisting, on the presence of typology in Williams and its absence in Cotton. Indeed, the typological imagination of John Cotton is as rich—one might almost say flagrant—as any in New England, and Miller's error seems as funda-mental as it is inexplicable.[7]

That said, it remains to notice that Miller was exactly right in identifying Williams, whose Puritan radicalism could hardly have been less like the Enlightenment liberalism of Thomas Jefferson, as the man who steadily resisted the notion that the Puritan exiles in New England were entitled to think of themselves as living out a special, predicted, and perhaps perfected repetition of Jewish history, and who would deny at the outset the otherwise irresistible implication that there was, in the grand scheme of Providence, something "exceptional" about the American opportunity. On one account, historical ironists like Hawthorne and Melville will come to figure as signal disciples of Williams' profound Augustinianism; on another, Williams stands virtually alone in denying that Americans can show their name in Scripture.[8] In either case the argument of this aboriginal "un-American" deserves the closest attention, even if this means close-reading a "dialogue" made up to bear the author's sense of political disagreement rather than to satisfy the reader's desire for pointed exchange. Williams having sworn his own opposition on the altar of God, we may not feel the need to "polish." But—failing to read his thought as written out *in extenso*—are we sure we really understand?

A character named "Truth" begins the more dramatic portion of the *Bloody Tenet* by inquiring of her would-be partner "Peace," "In what dark corner of the world . . . are we two met?" (55). But the book as a whole offers us no such dramatized beginning. The first of three prefatory gestures sets forth, unintroduced, twelve separate propositions touching the argument of the book—from the pious observation that all the blood spilt in the "religious" wars of the present and the past is neither "required nor accepted by . . . the Prince of Peace" to the political claim that "true civility and Christianity may both flourish in a state or kingdom, notwithstanding the permission of divers and contrary consciences" (3–4). A second preface offers to instruct "both Houses of . . . Parliament" in the separation of their duties: "as Christians" their task may be to save souls, but "as Magistrates" their concern is limited to "the bodies and goods of others." Men "eminent for ability and piety, Mr. Cotton and the New English ministers" (5) may oppose this distinction, but men famous for "unparalleled wisdom, courage, justice, mercy, in the vindication of your civil laws" will want to recall what "oppressing, plundering, ravishing, murdering, not only of the bodies but the souls of men," (6) worldly rulers have carried out in the name of religion. Parliaments have changed allegiance "according to their consciences" (7) and persecuted accordingly. But those Fathers being dead, let it never be told "at Rome nor Oxford" that the present Parliament "hath committed a greater rape, than if they had forced or ravished the bodies of all the women in the world" (9).[9]

The final preface warns "every Courteous Reader" that the present protester against "the bloody doctrine of persecution" and all who agree to champion his cause may themselves "prepare to be persecuted" (11). Still it pleads for agreement on four "particulars." First, those who cannot bear to see schismatics and heretics go unpunished must know that "there is a sorer punishment in the Gospel for despising of Christ than Moses." Next, the "purest" religious observances "practiced without . . . true persuasion" are simply "sinful" (12). Then too, "without search and trial no man attains this faith and right persuasion"; in vain, therefore, will Bibles have been opened to the search of "the simplest men and women" if they are to be "forced (as if they lived in Spain or Rome . . .) to believe as the Church believes." And finally, whatever the cost, "we must hold fast" (13) to the faith which search and trial have won. Truths *we* hold to be self-evident—so that we do not often pause to estimate the multiform text they introduce but do not quite generate or epitomize.

Obviously, a proper hermeneutics is inseparable from Williams' lengthy unfolding of his politics of separation, and few have wished his Old Testament readings longer. The teachings of John Cotton too are of the essence: as Cotton's theology sharpened and defended itself in response to the "Sixteen Questions" put to him by the New England elders, so Williams uses his conflict with Cotton to explain why he dissents so fundamentally from the sanctocracy of Massachusetts. But there are differences. The pressures of time and place, for one. Slow to detect a danger, perhaps, Cotton comes to realize that he is fighting for his position and reputation, if not for his life; turning peril to inspiration, his "Rejoinder" gathers the plausible but imprecise doctrines of the elders into a tense and testing exchange with his own. Williams' differences with Cotton, though profound in their implication, have something of the sense of old news. The two have been disagreeing in New England, episodically, for almost a decade, and Williams takes the opportunity of an available printing press in England to go back over the whole history of their debate. From the tone of their exchanges, Perry Miller has inferred that "Cotton hated Williams," yet one may observe something excessive in Williams' need to refute Cotton at every point: obsession normalizing itself as rational exchange.[10]

Having already printed and answered "a haughty letter" written by Cotton in summer 1636,[11] Williams finds further materials to preface and to delay the dialogue between Truth and Peace. Certain "Scriptures and Reasons written long since by a witness of Jesus Christ"—beginning with Christ's command to let "the tares and wheat" grow up together "until the harvest" (29), invoking the "meekness" (30) that characterizes the spiritual kingdom of Christ, and referring to a host of authorities both secular and sacred (31–39)—have somewhere required "The Answer of Mr. John Cotton of Boston." And it is this thirteen-page letter, seeking to complicate the concept of "persecution for cause of conscience" (41), that generates the first long section of dialogue. Not psychologically, perhaps, like the "haughty" letter, but formally, as a passive-aggressive Peace will permit a scrupulous Truth to leave no stone unreturned.

Infamous from anthology appearances, Cotton's reply wishes to permit religious differences, in both doctrine and practice, in all matters less than "fundamental" (41), unless they are held "with such arrogance and impetuousness, as tendeth . . . to the disturbance of civil peace" (42). Anne Hutchinson would fail, of course, on both these grounds. And—begging the entire question, in the eyes of modern epistemology—Cotton hastens to assure us that it is certainly "not lawful to persecute any for conscience sake rightly informed." Nor could one persecute "an erroneous and blind conscience" either, even in "fundamental and weighty points . . . till after admonition once or twice." Had not Winthrop required Hooker thus to sit down and reason with Williams?[12] Would not they all discuss beforehand the "sanctification" issue to the point of stultification, even of their own immense capacity? For, given the remarkable experience of consensus formation in New England, was it not reasonable to suppose that the person holding out against the unfolding of end-time and special-place Truth must be acting "not out of conscience, but against his conscience"? Accordingly, such a person is "not persecuted for cause of conscience, but for sinning against his own conscience" (42). And, as the point has been disputed in the domain of figure, let it be understood that, though tares are not wheat, neither are they "briars and thorns." Tares signify "hypocrites, like unto the Godly, but indeed carnal" (43); and as their case is almost always too close to call, Christ has declared it the part of wisdom to learn to live with their presence in even the purest of reformed churches.

Cotton's "Answer" goes on to consider all the arguments and authorities in the "Scriptures and Reasons," and Williams will force Peace to persuade Truth to follow him everywhere. But already we see the problem. With a keen (Augustinian) sense that there no longer *are* any special places, even in the end times; or with an especially acute conviction that authentic Christianity can nowhere flourish under the patronage of civil government, however pious its intention; or simply because his dangerous rejection of the mixed multitudes of the Church of England had excluded him from a place on the inside of the consensual process evolving in the New World, Williams can only reject the notion that conscience can ever be anything but individual; and, lacking a well-developed language of religious subjectivity, repeat his insight in the available idiom of the "spiritual." Including the sort of typology which sees Christ and, by implication, the life of the redeemed soul as the poetic and only fulfillment of the "land," the "people," and the "worships" of a literal Israel that has lapsed. And the power of the insight is almost great enough to redeem the labors of its language.

———

"Peace"—clearly female, but sounding a lot like the straight man—is quick to second the observation of "Truth" that "this present evil world" appears to have banished them both from the earth: " 'Tis lamentably true," she reflects, that "the foundations of the world have long been out of course" (55). To Truth's discovery that Peace must have "left the earth and fled to heaven," her response can only be "O where's the promise of the God of Heaven, that Righteousness and Peace shall kiss each other?" (56). The reader thinks of Moses kissing Aaron, perhaps, over there in Boston, or wonders if Righteousness demands to be a character in her own right, but Truth knows better what we need to hear: "Patience (sweet Peace) these heavens and earth are growing old, and shall be changed like a garment." Then shall the "Eternal Creator ... gloriously create New Heavens and New Earth, wherein dwells righteousness." Only then shall "our kisses have their end-less date of pure and sweetest joys." Till then, the "fury of the Dragon's wrath" (56).[13] And a little friendly dialogue. Only a few may yet be "valiant for the truth," fears Truth, who seems to be a man, but Peace could "spend eternal dates ... in listening to the precious oracles of [his] mouth" (57). Fit audience, unless a little too easy to convince.

Unable to suspect herself that way, Peace pours out her "sad complaints": the most sober proponents of toleration are everywhere said to be "contentious, tur-bulent, seditious" enemies of Peace, whereas those whose bloody persecutions truly disturb the peace cover their crimes with the cry of "holy war"; nor do they "dare to plead ... Christ for their author," appealing instead to "Moses and the prophets" (58). Truth responds with a little disquisition on "strife"—quite un-necessary "in most cases" in a world where "it is the express command of God that peace be kept." From that default setting only two departures are permitted: taking up "earthly weapons to defend the innocent and rescue the oppressed," and learning to "fight the fight of faith with ... spiritual artillery" (59). Truth's own complaint lends voice to "the cry of the whole earth, made drunk with the blood of its inhabitants, slaughtering each other in their blind zeal ... for reli-gion" (60). Then, when it begins to seem that Williams' most compatible per-sonifications have met together merely to love love and hate hate, Truth notices that Peace is holding a copy of some "arguments against persecution for cause of conscience" and also a certain "answer to such arguments." Truth ventures to hope that both sides proceed "from godly intentions," yet he is already aware of "a marvelous different style and manner": where the arguments against persecution, written by a prisoner deprived of ink, were known to have been written (literally) in milk, "the answer for it (as I may say) in blood" (61).[14]

After the two tease this conceit for a moment, Truth begins to attack the series of definitions by which Cotton had hoped to blunt the force of the charge of persecution for cause of conscience. First of all, his distinction between doctrine and practice is "not full and complete," as a man may be persecuted for *not* yielding "obedience to such doctrines and worships as are by men invented" (63). Less formally, the distinction between matters "fundamental" and others that are "less principal" runs the risk of condemning outright all those "ten thousands" of righteous persons who lived between the falling away of the church from its "first primitive Christian state" (64) and its recent, reformed recovery, including those left in the "parish churches in England" (66), from whom "the New-English particular churches" (67) do not officially separate. Indeed, this same consideration might well disqualify Cotton's own most conscientious ministry in Old England. Surely it is safer to hold that "there may be inward . . . fellowship with God" when *all* the forms are wrong. Perhaps the fundamentals are not "so clear." Or perhaps "Cotton measures" to others what he "would not have had measured to himself" (70–71).

That consideration, however, besides being ad hominem, is also a little ahead of the argument, which Williams is content to let Cotton dictate. So we come next to the (touchy) question of the "manner" of the persons holding heterodox views, even if in points "less principal." Technically, of course, the question raiser is Peace, who still holds Cotton's offending "Answer" in her ever-gentle hands; and we can well imagine her concern for the difference between those who hold forth their views "in a meek and peaceable way" and those who offer them with such "arrogance . . . as of itself tendeth to the disturbance of civil peace" (71). Yet Truth, who appears to know that an abiding concern for the bodies of men does not make one automatically a respecter of persons, must tell it like it is. First of all—in an early recognition of the legitimate autonomy of the purely secular— civil peace can mean nothing but that "pax civitas" which has been known to exist in "so many glorious and flourishing cities" (72) where religious views appear hopelessly mixed. A church is, to a city, like a "College of Physicians" or indeed a trading company, like those that first spied out the commercial possibilities in what John Smith named New England. The members of any such group may dissent, divide, break into schisms and factions, sue and implead each other at the law, yea wholly break up and dissolve into pieces and nothing, and yet the peace of the city not be in the least measure impaired or disturbed; because the essence or being of the city, and so the well-being and peace thereof, is essentially distinct from those particular societies. (73)

Religion matters, of course, uniquely so within its own (interior) domain; but Life must and can go on, even where Theory fails to solve the case—as if the fate of Los Angeles depended on the morale of the English Department at UCLA.

As to the question of arrogance, the truth of history requires Truth sadly to observe that Cotton has decided "to take up the common reproachful accusation of the accuser of God's children" (75). In point of fact, God's people have often "proclaimed, taught, [and] disputed" about their new religion, and in this they have been "zealous for their Lord" (75). Further, they have been "resolved to the death in refusing to submit to false worships," and they have "openly and constantly" taught that no civil official can have "any power over the souls . . . of their subjects" (76). The sum of all their glad-news preaching, however, was merely that "God anointed Jesus to be the sole king" of all his people "in spiritual and soul causes" (77). And, where this authority has been grossly usurped, "no wonder if sore eyes be troubled at the appearance of the light." Nor, on the score of tone, can we forget that "persons of soft and gentle nature" can teach "falsehood with more seeming meekness . . . than [did] the Lord Jesus . . . hold forth the true and everlasting Gospel" (79).

None of these preliminaries is without a certain contextual interest. But the drama of this sentence-by-sentence reply to Cotton's "Answer" has not been running very high;[15] and when Williams comes, finally, to Cotton's essential contention—that punishing a blind and erroneous conscience is, after suitable instruction, not properly persecution at all—many readers may wish Williams had seen fit to vary his measured pace. Not that he could drop the patience-enforcing device of a truthful yet peaceful dialogue, but could he not have come to the heart of the matter more swiftly? The point, we wish to hear him say, is that the truth of all matters of the Spirit, including those delivered in so many books written by so many hands over so many years, and all so many years ago—the Truth, my dear Mr. Cotton, is, as I have been implying, not nearly "so clear" as you appear to imagine. What the soul requires, quite obviously, is not discipline but inquiry. And the lucky success of an opinionated majority in New England proves nothing to the contrary. Perhaps the lack of any such killing outburst ought to give us pause. Perhaps that fundamental point, as utterly lost on Cotton as on certain popes one could name—that to characterize any conscience as right or wrong is to beg the very question to which "conscience" is the only honest answer—was itself not quite so clear to Williams as it has become to us. And we do not feel the strength of his point until we see that he means that those who, by God's own Spirit, know their own position to be true are obliged, as a function of their own righteousness, to extend all possible civility to those whose position they know, by that same Spirit, to be false. Charity, it would appear, defers epistemology.

Still, wherever Williams may be thought to stand in the history of Christian skepticism, he now and then comes close enough to the modern tonality. After lamenting that both rightly informed and blind consciences have indeed been persecuted, Williams makes his first rhetorical stand on Cotton's teaching that "it is not lawful to persecute any for conscience sake rightly informed": why bother with a truth so utterly self-evident, Williams wants to know, for no one, from Pharaoh to the "Devil himself" has ever professed to "persecute . . . Christ" without some pretense (82). Christ they call a "seducer of the people"; "Christians are schismatical, factious, heretical" (83). Nobody ever persecutes the truth as such; persecution is meaningful, by definition, only to the perception of error. Thus far, in the negative at least, Williams understands and is able to register appropriate surprise at the lack of substance in Cotton's distinction.

But then, as Williams addresses Cotton's theory of punishing heretics "after admonition" on the ground that, since "the Word of God is so clear in fundamental and weighty points," the properly instructed person stands "condemned of himself" and may be "'persecuted for sinning against his own conscience,'" intellectual outrage turns again to moral lament and exegetical competition. As Cotton's "Answer" invokes the authority of Titus 3.11, the character of Truth can only observe that Satan, who often "takes up the weapons of Scripture," has raised a "palpably gross . . . mist and fog" (84) about this one in particular. When Peace calls upon her instructor to "scatter these mists," Truth feels obliged to perform and, after clearing up the matter of the biblical definition of "heretic" (87–88) and of the internal nature of "self-condemnation" (88–89), he arrives at the practical questions of "admonition" and "rejection." Neither, he holds, involves the magistrate in any way, so that the "rejecting" spoken of in Titus can only mean "excommunicating" (91).

Still the anti-Cotton animus of the *Bloody Tenet* is such that it cannot even take yes for an answer: Cotton is correct to sponsor toleration "in points of lesser moment," but his reason, that "God may be pleased to reveal his truth to him" (92), has a much wider application; indeed, any soul "sensible of mercy received to itself in former blindness . . . cannot but be patient and gentle" toward Jews, Turks, and Pagans, to all of whom "God may peradventure at last give repentance" (92–93). Then too the stickler will observe that in the texts quoted in support of his own stingy version of toleration Cotton regularly makes "the churches of Christ at Phillipi and Rome all one with the cities of Phillipi and Rome," as if to imply that "what these churches must not tolerate, that these cities . . . must not tolerate" (93–94); from which it will follow that "these cities . . . were bound not to tolerate themselves." How much more logical—and more sweet—to recall that "as the lily is amongst the thorns" (94), so stands the Church to the World. And, as Peace remarks, those who would restrict toleration to "persons but holding lesser errors" appear to have forgot that the merciful are blessed precisely because "they shall obtain mercy." Of which they certainly "have need" (95), as Truth cannot but agree.

With some sense of finality, then, Peace receives Truth's assurance that disturbers of civil peace really do deserve appropriate civil punishment and, with Truth's renewed warning that it has been all too easy for misguided persons to "cry out for prison and swords against such who cross their judgment . . . of religion" (96), she observes that the two "are now come to the second part" of Cotton's "Answer," which examines "such grounds as are brought against . . . persecution" (97). The "first sort," of course, are scriptural, and though these occupy more than seventy-five pages of the remaining hundred or so explicitly devoted to the text of Cotton's "Answer," the reader may trust Miller's sense that Williams' debt to Scripture is well represented by his attempt to defeat Cotton's reading of Matthew 13.30, 38—about letting certain "tares" grow up in a field of wheat "until the Harvest" (97). But though the tropic life of "the wheat and the tares" takes us as near the heart of Puritan practice as anything before the dispute of Taylor and Stoddard over "the wedding feast,"[16] it represents only one moment of Williams' attempt to destroy Cotton's moral authority. Once again it appears that Cotton's many errors make up the difference between Williams' crucial insight and the length of his book.

Cotton wants "tares"—as distinct from "briars and thorns"—to be either close and careful "hypocrites," very like the saints to the view of all but God, or else "doctrines or practices" (97) that, though corrupt, greatly resemble the truth. And all such cases, too close to call, as we might say, Cotton is perfectly willing to allow to continue until the end, when the Just Judge himself shall make the proper discrimination. Williams, appealing to the authority of Calvin and Beza, and not willing to "imagine any deceitful purpose in the Answerer's thoughts" (98), can only suffer the pain this position threatens to inflict on the briars and thorns. And then try to show that these tares signify "persons in respect of their religion and way of worship, open and visible professors, as bad as briars and thorns; not only suspected foxes, but as bad as . . . greedy wolves." And though their mouths must be stopped, "yet no carnal force" is to be used against them

(99–100). First of all, as the Lord himself interpreted "the good seed to be persons" (100), so too must consistency interpret the tares. And as to the possibility of hypocrites, the Greek word for these "tares" suggests, metaphorically, people as are "known to be manifestly . . . opposite to the true worshipers of God" (101); and even the common reader can see that the parable turns on the idea of dissimilitude that is immediately recognized, as "every husbandman can tell which is wheat and which is tares and cockle, &c" (103).

Even more crucially, perhaps, "these tares cannot signify hypocrites in the church" because the Lord's "own interpretation" identifies "the field in which both wheat and tares are sown . . . [as] the world, out of which God . . . calleth his church." To be sure, the church is called aside from a world which "lies in wickedness," but the warfare that arises from this opposition is waged by spiritual means alone. And though a bumper crop of false religions spring up in this wicked world, right alongside the true, "the meek Lamb of God commands a permission of them . . . until the time of the end of the world" (104). Some lively opponent might protest that in this reading Williams' "persons" have silently become whole churches, but a favoring Peace remarks only that "some excellent worthies . . . have labored to turn this field of the world into the garden of the church"—leaving Truth to scorn the absurdity of "calling the world the church." And to relate the present matter to the "former parable" in which "Jesus compared the Kingdom of Heaven to the sowing of seed": in that place the "four sorts of ground" signify four sorts of "hearts of men, which . . . cannot be supposed to be of the church," where there is only "one, to wit, the honest and good ground" (105). Or so it would have to be in any church to which this purest of the Puritans would sign his name.

Accordingly, the tares are "such sinners as are . . . contrary to the children of the kingdom visibly so declared" (107). Peace proposes that "drunkards, thieves, unclean persons, &c." are also "opposite to God's children" (108), but to these, Truth reminds his innocent friend, the civil state must duly attend. Sinners of another sort, however—"idolaters, false-worshipers, antichristians"—are precisely those "who without discouragement to true Christians must be . . . permitted . . . to grow and fill up the measure of their sins" until at "the great harvest" the "heavenly reapers" (angels) shall make clear "the difference" (109). Those who "imagine that the time . . . is long," and that in the meantime these spiritual criminals "may do a world of mischief," need to keep several things in mind: the civil state is armed just in case these tares "attempt ought against [its] peace and welfare"; the "church or spiritual state" maintains its own armory of spiritual weapons; and the promise of the "Lord Himself" is proof that "his chosen cannot perish nor be finally deceived" (111). Finally, from the parable itself, toleration is necessary so that, by human mistake, no "good wheat be plucked up . . . out of this field of the world" and also, with a little less unction, so that *this world,* miserable and not to be redeemed by any remnant, may grow "ripe in sin" (111–12). And this final "vindictive" emphasis may serve—along with his indefatigable interest in torturing the one true text—to remind us that the theology of this noble exile may be as different from our own as from that of the orthodox fathers in New England.[17]

Still the vision appeals. Unable to be persuaded that the successful prosecution of a sanctocracy, willed into being in the space some king had imagined as the overseas project of a home-based trading company, had so altered the movement of the universe that a new Israel had come into being—"in a day," as the hyperbole of Edward Johnson would celebrate the case—Williams remained true to that form of Christianity which held that God alone held the keys to his end-time Kingdom and that, until he himself opened the gates, his saints would have to suffer the civil discontents of the City of Man along with everyone else.[18] Or that those believers who did happen upon a position of power, by setting out for the territories a step or two ahead of the rest, might well prove the authenticity of their calling by founding a city secure enough in its holiness to extend the blessing of civility to every sinner God had made, knowing that they too were caught up in what the poetry of America would call "the checkerwork of Providence,"[19] wherein any sinner might one day find grace, and even if not, knowing that God was not kidding when he said "Sovereign." With God alone responsible for last-analysis justice, surely his people could afford a little elbow room for conscience. The state was there to arrest all its really threatening experiments, and who knows what else its free exercise might discover? In times and places all the same, from the moment of Redemption to the End, bitter enough, by all accounts, to satisfy the demands of a Justice writ large as you please.

———

Forgiven by Peace for having been so large in "vindicating" a text of such "great consequence," Truth nevertheless promises to be "briefer in the Scriptures following" (113). Still, he pauses to give a brief "recapitulation" (118) of his reading of the parable of the wheat and the tares before turning to the second text which Cotton has said does *not* tell against the civil discipline of religious irregularity. The going now is pretty heavy: Cotton had felt the need to answer each of the original prisoner's scriptures against persecution, and Williams can imagine no alternative to refuting each of Cotton's answers. Still, there are moments even in this most "professional" section of the *Bloody Tenet* when Williams looks up from the terms to which an existing controversy has committed him and expresses one of his own fundamental insights with memorable clarity and force.

For example, Cotton has rejected the relevance of Jesus' instructing his disciples, in Matthew 15.14, to let his Pharisee tormentors alone—giving as his reason "that the blind lead the blind, and both shall fall into the ditch," and observing that the words were "spoken to his private disciples and not to public officers in church or state" (119). The hairsplitter in Williams wants to argue that "if it had been an ordinance of God, that all civil magistrates were bound to judge in causes spiritual," then it would follow that "the disciples and Lord himself" were bound to perform this same duty as "faithful subjects" (120). Yet while the reader is puzzling over this division of civic responsibility, Williams comes closer to his own deepest beliefs:

> had it been the holy purpose of God to have established the doctrine and kingdom of his Son this way . . . , he would have furnished commonweals, kingdoms, cities, &c., . . . with such temporal powers and magistrates as should have been . . . fit and competent: for he could have had legions of angels. (121)

In a real-life dialogue Cotton might well have answered that, in the gradual unfolding of the divine plan, a competent magistracy, lapsed since the nation of Israel, had just now come back into being, in the model city of New England, from which the future might everywhere take example. But there the two get stuck: Cotton believes, from his own experience, in the biblical identity of New England; Williams, from some profound historical a priori, does not.

Williams could only repeat his "typological" conviction that the practices of Israel are "not to be matched or paralleled by any . . . but the spiritual state" (116); or plead again his (exile's) conviction that the kingdom really is not of this world. Or remind the vindictive that, though for the present the punishment of spiritual criminals is "deferred," yet the punishment inflicted on them will "amount to an higher pitch than any corporal punishment in the world" (122)— in ways a separate chapter will specify. There is, of course, "that blindness which forever to all eye-salve is incurable" (123), but also that "bottomless pit of everlasting separation" (124). No mention is made of hellfire, as the order of the spiritual strives to maintain itself as such. But Williams is willing to match the magistrate's death sentence with his own "vengeance of a dreadful judgment both present and eternal" (125).

The matching, however, is mostly interpretive, and so we have to go on, in a book whose subtext is not the different stories a soul might tell in the name of conversion or even the events an historian might select in the name of providence, but the things a Theocrat had said to answer a Prisoner. The Prisoner has observed that, in Luke 9.54, 55, the Lord reproved his disciples for wishing "fire [to] come down from heaven, and devour those Samaritans that would not receive him" by reminding them that "the Son of Man is not come to destroy men's lives, but to save them," and also, elsewhere, that "the servant of the Lord must . . . be gentle toward all men" (129–30). Cotton has replied that both these Scriptures are "directions to ministers of the Gospel how to deal not with obstinate offenders in the church who sin against conscience, but with men without as the Samaritans were" (130). As such, Cotton contends, they say nothing about how "the minister of the Gospel [is] to proceed in a church way against church members, when they become scandalous offenders . . . [and] much less do they speak at all to the civil magistrates" (130–31). Williams, taking the "disciples" here to be neither ministers nor magistrates but simply followers of Christ, is bound to reply that where, as in New England, the "civil magistrate be a Christian," a disciple or follower of the meek Lamb of God, he is "bound to be far from destroying the bodies of men" and is by these texts "forbidden to . . . inflict any corporal judgment" (132) on those who reject Christ without breaking the civil peace.

Then, as rhetoric appears to be an altogether spiritual weapon, Williams sees no reason to repress a generalizing outburst:

> It is indeed the . . . blind zeal of the second Beast . . . Rev. 13.13, to persuade the civil powers . . . to persecute the Saints, that is, to bring fiery judgments upon men in a judicial way, and to pronounce that such judgments of imprisonment, banishment, death proceed from God's righteous vengeance. (132–33)

In this context Peace seems to know that differing styles of typology are only part of the problem—that there is also, as one might say, the general tone and tenor of the New Testament as the "blessed" have always received it: "Doubtless such fiery spirits are not of God" (133). Indeed, Truth himself may have meant to implicate Cotton in the Lord's observation that his own disciples often "know not of what Spirit [they] are" (130). And Miller does well to remind us that Williams has written in the margin, in just this place, that "patience and meekness [are] required in them that open Christ's mysteries."[20]

Wisely anthologized as well is Williams' observation that religious power in the hands of a magistrate exempt from the canons of meekness is a great way to make "a whole nation of hypocrites," but that to "recover a soul from Satan" requires nothing less than "the sword of the Spirit." For a case in point, Truth asks his audience "to seek no further than our native soil": "within a few scores of years, how many wonderful changes in religion" have occurred, and all "according to the change of the governors thereof";

> Henry the 7 finds and leaves the kingdom absolutely Popish. Henry 8 casts it into a mold half Popish half Protestant. Edward 6 brings forth an edition all Protestant. Queen Mary within a few years defaceth Edward's work, and renders the kingdom . . . all Popish. Mary's short life and religion ends together: and Elizabeth reviveth her brother Edward's model. (136–37)

But with the advent of New England . . . , we hear the excluded voice interrupting to declare. No exception, comes back our own disillusioned reply: just more real estate, granted by the king in the name of trade and hardly to be redeemed by the fantastic overdetermination called Non-Separating Congregationalism. No such ironist, Peace alone can answer in our stead: Old England or New, one more fulfillment of the type of "Nebuchadnezzar's bowing the whole world in one most solemn uniformity of worship to his golden image" (137).

Peace and Truth cannot but approve the first part of Cotton's reading of Micah's famous prediction that "they shall break their swords into plough-shares" (139): this prediction shows first that "the Nations" shall be won to the Gospel "not by fire and the sword . . . but by the power of the Word," and also that Christians shall not be to one another as "lions or leopards." But what are they to make of the further conclusion that such texts in no way prevent Christians from driving "ravenous wolves from the sheepfold" (140)? Peace must beg a "clearer opening of this mystery" (141), and Truth, predictably, can only limit the driving away of wolves to "the elders or ministers of the Church" (142). For, clearly, a magistrate in this capacity would be claiming the ability "to discern . . . who are spiritual sheep" (143). Surely the whole bloody business of having wolfish "brains knocked out" to protect the sheep is long since discredited. As to handing the task over to any civil magistrate, "Is not this . . . to make [Christ's] kingdom of this world?" (145). And is not the attempt "to bound out new earthly holy lands of Canaan" but to "set up Spanish Inquisitions in all parts of the world?" (145–46).

And more to the same purpose. "The weapons of our warfare are not carnal" (146) persuades Cotton only that church officers are forbidden to use physical force, but this interpretation leads to a protest against *anyone's* using "civil weapons . . . in matters of the spiritual state" (147), reminding us that using physical force "to batter down idolatry, false worship, heresy, schism, [and] blindness" is not only improper but "vain" (148), and—predicting Hawthorne's Endicott—asking us whether Jesus did ever "join to his breastplate of righteousness the breastplate of iron and steel?" (149). More of this war talk lies ahead, as Williams will find it necessary to distinguish "four sorts of swords mentioned in the New Testament" (160), but that will come in the midst of a commentary on Romans 13. Because both the "Answerer" and many other "excellent servers of God have insisted upon" using it in defense of their "persecution for conscience" (150), Peace begs Truth for his "pains to enlighten and clear this scripture" (151). And Truth, with the aid of Calvin, puts himself at pains to show that Paul's command that Christians "be subject to the governing authorities" implies nothing about the power of magistrates in matters spiritual.

There is indeed a "sword of civil justice" so that, as Paul calmly observes, "authority does not bear [it] in vain." But its legitimate exercise is in "material" issues such as "the defense of persons, estates, families, liberties of a city" (160).

> It cannot according to its utmost reach . . . (now under Christ, when all nations are merely civil . . .) I say, it cannot extend to spiritual and soul causes, spiritual and soul punishment, which belongs to that spiritual sword with two edges, the soul-piercing . . . Word. (160–61)

Again the essence of Williams' position: since the coming of redemption in Christ, the political practices of Israel may well figure things which happen in the soul of a saint, but they are no model for civic repetition. Now until the end of time, the kingdom of God is within. In a world pretty much in shambles, the state exists to provide police protection. Christians, for their part, try to love even their intellectual enemies. And where the soul of man is concerned, civil rulers must learn—not to make a bad situation worse—to stand aside and let the Word do its work. A powerful conception, as Miller has indicated, of salvation and survival in a world unable to save itself. But also, as he implies, one Williams could enhance mostly by repetition.

Some interest may attach to Williams' pragmatic answer to Cotton's suggestion that "we must not do evil that good may come thereof" (164) and that "it is evil to tolerate seditious evil doers" (165). "It is one thing," he first replies, "to command, to conceal, to counsel, to approve evil and another thing to permit and suffer evil . . . without approbation of it." But it also occurs to him that the end of this "sufferance" is nothing less than "God's own glory" (165) and that, in the conduct of the universe, a long-suffering God seems to be our very model. Further to complicate Cotton's logic, he goes on to write in the margin that though "evil is always evil, yet permission of it may in case be good."[21] But while Williams is helping us to consider that the universe may be a more complex affair than we may have thought, Peace reminds us all that a perfectly God-like toleration on the part of human rulers would turn the civil world back into a "wilderness" (167). This leads Truth back to his well-worn distinction that the sword of the civil magistrate is of course competent to cut down the crime rate. And we know a section is ending when he appeals once again to the lesson of the weeds and the wheat—the latter being permitted, as always, "for a common good of the whole" (169).

A criticism less cautious than that of either Miller or Bercovitch might suggest that Matthew's tares had become, for Williams, less the typic key to a learned style of reading the Old Testament than something in the nature of a founding trope. A trope of messiness, as it were: in a world not invented, as Emerson might say, by a God with the napkin of a divinity student at his neck, things grow up and mature together. Good is better than bad, by long chalks; and true churches, if there are yet to be any such, will have to observe a standard of purity that even other Puritans would find fantastic. Then too, as his own world matured, no doubt this most admirable of all the exiles from Winthrop's model city would live long enough to let the peace-talking but trouble-seeking Quakers get his goat.[22] Yet something there is, the *Bloody Tenet* seems to say, that does not love a wall: though "Christ's lilies" are indeed called aside from "the daughters and wilderness of the world" (175), yet the church so constituted "must necessarily be mingled and have converse with" that very world. And if—while trying to hold the plantation of Rhode Island together long enough to become a colony—the ideal state of which he saw himself as the ideal governor were to have a motto, it might well be "Let them alone."

Williams' commentary on Cotton's "Answer" to the protests of the Prisoner ends with some forty-five pages on the "Reasons from the profession of famous princes against persecution for conscience" (175). Miller's remarkable little anthology generously includes a few pages of this less godly material, which Williams justifies with the observation that "precious pearls" are often found in "muddy shells" (180).[23] Yet his bolder claim—that when "state policy and state necessity" have the end of preventing "rivers of civil blood" they will be found "to agree most punctually with the rules of the best politician that ever the world saw, the King of Kings" (178)—is actually a concession that many of the arguments here are versions of things we have heard before, without benefit of the king of Bohemia. And the reader is likely to agree with Cotton's contention that a "prince's profession and practice is no rule of conscience" (177).

Of greatest interest in this section, perhaps, are the clarifications Williams makes concerning his theory of history. Agreeing with Cotton's observation that

"Christianity fell asleep in Constantine's bosom," Williams argues that the persecution of "erroneous persons" such as Arius injured the cause of Christ more than the earlier persecution of Christians themselves, for now "by degrees the gardens of the churches of saints were turned into the wilderness of whole nations." Doubtless various emperors and bishops intended to exalt Christ, but "not attending to the command . . . to permit the tares to grow in the field of the world, they made the garden of the church, and the field of the world to be all one." The result was not only the zealous mistake of persecuting "good wheat" but, worse almost, the creation of that anomalous, indeed oxymoronic thing called "Christendom" (184). As if souls were to be saved a world at a time. Then too, in point of private experience, Christianity began to fail "not when Christians lodged in cold prisons, but down beds of ease" (187).

As to the state of England—and touching the lurking question of truth versus certitude—Williams argues that "if Queen Elizabeth . . . did well to persecute according to her conscience," then James I did no less well in persecuting Puritans "according to his" (187). The New England question is implied of course and, after a dispute of the thoughts of Hilary (193), Tertullian (196), Jerome (198), Brentius (200), Luther (202), "the Papists themselves" (204), Augustine (206), and Optatus (209), the subtext is finally permitted to surface, even if at first only in outline. According to Cotton's largest concession, "none but such as truly fear God should enjoy liberty of conscience" (213). From this it will follow of course that "the inhabitants of the world must either come into the estate of men fearing God, or else dissemble a religion in hypocrisy, or else be driven out of the world" (213–14). In actual debate, Cotton might wish to argue that New England's way of testing for grace was but an earthly approximation, admitting that true discernment was indeed "only the gift of God" (214). Then too he might wish to argue not only that gifted dissemblers had their proper "use," keeping up the moral tone.[24] Or he might suggest that to be denied citizenship in a specially theorized and well-advertised experiment in the practice of godliness as a uniform standard was hardly the same as exclusion from "the world": England remained an option, on the one hand, and beyond it the whole range of the Old World; on the other hand, the entire region of the frontier. Surely men might try to find *some* space where dissent might not seek opposition and then complain.

In one's own book, however, one has one's own way. And so this archprophet of dissent gets to formulate the question: "Since there is so much controversy in the world, where the name of Christ is taken up, . . . I ask who shall judge[,] . . . who be they that fear God" (214). If the church alone, then Williams remains free to float around New England as he chooses, holding on to a post at one or another church more inclined to separatism. But if Winthrop and his General Court are allowed into the picture, then clearly he will have to leave. Winthrop might distinguish between fear of God and fear of arguments that tempt invasion by the forces of Archbishop Laud,[25] but Williams gets to repeat his arguments against the civil magistrates judging in spiritual cases. And if his own case seems too ancient or too tangled, then consider a recent answer from "the ministers of the churches of New England," admitting to their honored Presbyterian brethren that if "other godly people . . . coming over to them should differ in church constitution, they then could not . . . advise the magistrates to suffer them to enjoy a civil being within their jurisdiction" (215–16). "Hear, O Heavens, and give ear, O Earth" (216), an astonished Truth cries out. And in the England of 1644, what further need of witnesses?

Peace is quick to point out that the same New England "Answer" expresses the assurance that sweet accord would surely be reached by all concerned were they all exactly in the same situation, but Truth can only recall "what lamentable differences" have separated these same men when ministers of the Church of England, "some conforming, some leaving their livings, friends, country, life, rather than conform"; and then, with the substance of Winthrop's *Short Story* in mind, points out "how great [are] the present differences even amongst them that fear God, concerning faith, justification, and the evidence of it." And so he offers his (counter-)Americanist conclusion: "Let none now think that the passage to New England by sea, or the nature of the country can do what only the Key of David can do, to wit, open and shut the consciences of men" (217).

Truth goes on from here, briefly, to the case we well recognize as that of Williams himself—admonished, once or twice, without the desired effect and so "esteemed obstinate" and banished, though his "godliness was acknowledged." Evidently Winthrop was not privy, in 1635, to the entire scope of Cotton's doctrine. Nor, on the other hand, does Winthrop get a chance to say that church doctrines all but calculated to arouse the enmity of England are not without consequences to the peace of the city. But not to press the personal point, Truth passes on to another case. A "godly" and otherwise "most desirable person" who, wishing "to dwell in a certain town in New England," has met with this abrupt response from "the chief of the place": "This man differs from us, and we desire not to be troubled." Let the "poor man" be never so "godly, useful, and peaceable," still he cannot be "admitted to civil being and habitation on the common earth in that wilderness amongst them" (218). Winthrop would wish to deny, of course, that the king's charter had left New England in the condition of "common earth"; and no doubt he also believed that a series of overlapping covenants had materially altered its status as "wilderness." These issues, however, form no part of the discussion, and Williams' simpler point remains: while Cotton was developing his doctrine of whom and what to tolerate, the Winthrop establishment felt free to do pretty much as it pleased.

After these pointed instances, we are clearly ready for a conclusion of sorts. Peace notes that Cotton concludes his "Answer" by registering a "confident persuasion" that he has cleared up the disputed issue of "persecution for cause of conscience" (218). Truth responds, "with fear and trembling," that he has not only "contradicted the spirit and mind and practice of the Prince of Peace" but further involved himself in the heinous crime of "soul rape." Peace agrees, assuring Truth that his own "lips drop as the honey-comb" (219). Then, as the two consider "how long" before the world shall realize that "Christ is not delighted with the blood of men," Truth promises that acceptance of his own doctrine would deck every house with "olive branches." Encouraged, Peace thinks of craving the "patient ear and holy tongue" of Truth once more. "Error's impatient and soon tired," she observes, "but thou are light, and like the Father of Lights, unwearied in thy shinings" (220). Students of controversy may judge otherwise, as Cotton can keep the pot boiling as long as anyone. And as to the reader's patience, students of literary form are entitled to their own judgment. In any event, it is only mildly comical when, after the intervention of a new title page, Truth asks Peace, "What hast thou there?" (221).

What she has, begging for rehearsal and refutation, is *A Model of Church and Civil Power,* composed by several ministers in the Bay Colony—*not* including Cotton—and sent to the church at Salem in 1636 to quiet their uneasiness about the power of the General Court to summon a synod. Williams' own title makes Cotton one of its authors and labels this *Model* "a further confirmation of the bloody doctrine of persecution for cause of conscience."[26] In Peace's own editorial reply, "Here is a combination of thine own children against thy very life and mine," a model of church and state such as "wakens Moses from his unknown grave and denies Jesus yet to have seen the earth." A familiar charge but then an ongoing issue. Evidently no word *ascribed* to John Cotton can go by Roger Williams unanswered. The reader may quail, but "sweet Peace" can only be urged to "read and propound."

———

For the student of New England institutions, Williams' close examination of this second occasional text has the advantage of referring not to a general discussion of the state's interest in the matter of heresy but to a defense of the relation of church and state in the developing "constitution" of Massachusetts. Then too, as the construction of Miller's anthology indicates, Williams further develops his special sense of the (invisible) church as the only antitype of the nation of Israel, and with this comes a further attack on typological pretensions of Winthrop's holy state, which Williams seems to sense were present from the beginning. But the simulation of dialogue is unchanged, and so is the structure and pace. With the reader wishing for a sustained vision of the life of the church as the pure spouse of Christ, destined to converse with yet hold herself off from a world that is altogether lost yet fully entitled to maintain a life of its own, Williams prefers to go on refuting "Cotton," addressing himself, one by one, to each of the sixteen heads that organize the ministers' *Model*. And he continues to have a supra-dialogic authority named Truth preach to a choir called Peace.

The *Model* begins with the prefatory stipulation that as "God hath given a distinct power to church and commonweal," the obvious problem is to determine "how the civil state and the church may dispense their several governments without infringement" (222). But as it has also posited, as a matter of New England fact, that "every member of the commonweal" is also "a member of the church," problems arise at the outset. Rather than protest this identity of separate citizenship, however, Williams pursues at some length the question of where, when push comes to shove, the sovereignty is really going to rest. Offering a case that begins much like his own at Salem, he imagines a magistrate charging a particular church with having "made an unfit and unworthy choice" and proceeding to make it "void." The church complains of this violation of "her privileges," cries out against such persecution and, "not prevailing with admonition," proceeds to excommunicate this (Christian) magistrate. Unconvinced, the magistrate proceeds against his churchly enemies as "obstinate abusers of Christ's holy ordinances . . . in civil court" and "according to the pattern of Israel cuts them off by the sword" (230). What help for "any poor church"? "Shall [she] here fly to the Pope's Sanctuary?" (231).

Absent from this scenario, obviously, is any account of just how prudentially, even ritualistically careful of one another the churches and the commonwealth of Massachusetts learned they had to be. Listening to an elaborately reasoned mix of ideal possibility and established practice—and not wishing to exile its corporate self—Salem came to be satisfied with the consensus, even if Williams himself was not. Nor can Williams allow that, as in his own case, the conflict may indeed have had implications for the peace of the city. The reader, however, may well imagine that the same Winthrop who appears to have warned Williams to make his escape may easily have felt that one man's evident godliness counted less, as a reason of state, than the continuing goodwill of the British. As in the case of Wheelwright, whose rhetoric appeared to threaten an uprising, the General Court could claim that its actions were entirely civil.

Next to be seized upon, in the "third head" of the *Model,* is the phrase "all godliness and honesty" in reference to both the state's duty to increase "external and temporal peace" and the church's parallel obligation to increase "internal and spiritual peace" (232). Here again, very near the outset, Williams identifies the Massachusetts tendency to make "the garden and the wilderness . . . all one": if the last end of both church and state is in fact "godliness" (233), are they then not somehow the same? Questionable also is what in this context someone might mean by "internal": does it mean "within the soul, which only the eye of God can see," or does it refer to "matters of God's worship"? Then too there is the question of "godliness and honesty"—but before Truth can decide whether this pairing is a distinction or a repetition, Peace has to express her agitated response to the inquiry so far, namely, that the theorists of New England seem "never to have seen a true difference between the church and the world":

> these worthy authors seem to make a kind of separation from the world and profess that the church must consist of . . . regenerate persons, and so make some peculiar enclosed ordinances, as the Supper of the Lord, . . . yet by compelling all within their jurisdiction to an outward conformity of church worship . . . and maintenance of the ministry thereof, they evidently declare that they still lodge and dwell in the confused mixtures . . . of the flock of Christ and herds of the world together. (234)

At this point Cotton might well detect Williams' narrowing sense of a church even *more* carefully gathered than those of New England.[27] Or he might think to ask what really lies at the base of Williams' unshakable conviction that "this world" is never in time to be redeemed. Williams, however, returns to the question of "godliness and honesty," which he finds *not* to signify "the first and second table" (235).

Clearly Christ does not command magistrates to enforce the First Table. First of all, witness "those Caesars," who were "professed worshipers . . . of the Roman gods or devils" (237). Nor is "great pretense of Israel" at all relevant as a counterexample since, as we have heard before, Jesus himself has established "a more spiritual way of worship all the world over" (239). Constantine, Theodotius, and Henry VIII to the contrary, the utterly inward church of Christ can risk no such "Defender of the Faith" (241); as their states are but a "commonweal of families," so their authority can never exceed that of the husband, who might wish his wife to believe as he does but must be as "far from forcing her from her conscience unto his" as from forcing her "to tarry with him" (242). For, as has been clear from the third preface, "without . . . an upright heart . . . , neither magistrates nor subjects can please God" (245). And, on the other hand, a magistrate may clearly be "good," in the same sense as a lawyer or a physician, without being in the least "godly"; so Cotton and his cohort are simply wrong to "deny that there can be . . . a good magistrate, except he see all godliness preserved" (246). Indeed, the same "civil honesty which makes a good citizen must . . . make also a good magistrate" (247).

Historians of government might be interested in the curious twist Williams gives to the familiar doctrine that "the sovereign, original, and foundation of civil power lies in the people" (249). From this it will follow, Williams suggests, that if governments are to have any power over the church it must come from the people. This argues that man himself must have a "power to govern the church, to see her do her duty, to correct her, to redress, reform, establish." And this is "to pull God and Christ and Spirit out of heaven and subject them unto natural, sinful, inconstant men, and so consequently Satan himself, by whom all peoples naturally are guided" (250). Another reminder that Williams is not the perfect democrat. Powerfully dedicated to defending the peace and security of a world he takes to be of the Devil, his principal ambition remains, as Miller long ago agued, the protection of the church.[28] Or—what amounts to the same thing—the protection of the right of conscience to find not its own but rather God's well-advertised yet precious rare sense of godliness. Peaceably, on his own part, and without any misguidance from the men who run the league of neighborhood self-protection.

The (fourth-head) proposition, that "outward civil peace cannot stand where religion is corrupted" (251), Williams takes to be false de facto. He concedes that civil governments may pass laws restraining the activity of certain religions notorious for uncivil behavior, but he proudly announces that "the very Indians abhor" (252) to disturb Papists, Jews, or Turks at their peaceful worship. Under their "fifth head" the men of Massachusetts contend that, though a civil magistrate may "apply such civil laws as . . . either are expressed in the word of God . . . or are to be deduced therefrom," he may not violate individual conscience by legislating about "indifferent things" (254–55). Taking for granted, now, that Israel is no "typic" model, Williams seizes instead on the second half of the Massachusetts teaching:

> If the civil magistrate have no power to restrain or constrain their subjects in things in their own nature indifferent, as in . . . wearing this or that garment . . . , it will be much more unlawful and heinous in the magistrate to compel the subjects unto that which . . . is simply unlawful. (257)

That is to say, if the magistrate cannot "constrain me to . . . a garment" in divine worship, how can he "command me to the worship it self?" (258).

The difference, once again, is that where the men of Massachusetts have written from the point of view of those who still felt confident, not in themselves exactly, but in the arranged clarity of Scripture's teaching in all essentials, Williams remembers the position of the sincere person who cannot find in himself the power to read with the majority, however painfully achieved their consensus. Outsider that from the outset he became, his epistemological Truth cannot fail to impress the corresponding Peace with the sense that New England practice must imply a number of guilty embarrassments: either they believe such a "doctrine of freewill" as makes it possible for subjects "to believe upon the magistrate's command"; or they suppose that, upon the command of a magistrate, God is "to be forced or commanded to give faith" to a subject so commanded; or they must live with the "guilt of the hypocrisy" of a people commanded "to act . . . in matters of religion . . . against the doubts and checks of their consciences" (258). To indicate that this last is the likely case, Peace concludes that "with less sin ten thousand fold may a natural father force his daughter, or the father of a commonweal force all the maidens in the country to the marriage beds of . . . men whom they cannot love" (259). Evidently no party to the multiform Puritan protest went without some version of the love trope.

Past this moment of tropic competition, Williams' Truth can hear in the practice of requiring a magistrate to "establish and ratify such laws . . . as Christ hath appointed in his Word" (261) only a pathetic echo of the Israelites' "Make us a king that may rule over us after the manner of the nations" (262)—inspiring Peace to reflect on how hard it is "for flesh to forsake the arm thereof!" (264). Where Massachusetts glories in the public pronouncement of the fact that its magistrates worship the same sovereign authority as its ministers, Williams, unimpressed by this rare historical accident, takes greater comfort in an enhanced sense of the autonomy of the authentically spiritual: "Christ's truth, and the two-edged sword of his Word, never stood in need of a temporal sword" (267).

Question 6 passes in only a couple of pages: church members are of course subject to civil punishment if they violate any just civil law; but if Cotton's colleagues continue to hold that the state must punish, by death, "heresy, blasphemy, &c.," they should consider that somewhere all Jews, "whose very religion blasphemeth Christ," will have to be "immediately executed" (270). Peace may feel the "poisoned daggers stabbing at [her] tender heart," but Truth must pass on to the seventh head, concerning the "order" in which the magistrate may "execute punishment on a church or church-member that offendeth his laws" (271). Once again Williams rejects the proposition that repeated church instruction turns the heretic into one who sins against his own conscience; naive and sophistical, it begs the very question of conscience understood as the subject's own self-binding conclusion. Do the men of Massachusetts not recall that "God's people themselves" have often stood by a "deluded" conscience? Do they not recognize the mood in which convinced (but mistaken) consciences "walk on confidently . . . even to the suffering of death"? (272). Surely excommunication is the punishment both appropriate and sufficient, for it delivers the heretic up to "Satan his jailer, and he keeps him in safe ward until it pleaseth God to release him" (274). Does any Protestant imagine the church instruction to work *ex opere operato* (275), apart from personal assent? Or is the habit of Inquisition just too deep?

Heads eight and nine concern the power of the magistrate to "gather" churches and to provide them with officers. Surely "none at all" would be the answer of any congregational true believer prior to the unique situation of New England. "Reformation without tarrying" for any human magistrate is the purest form of Puritan immediatism. Or, in the gradualist scenario, the conscientious gathering of saints, in a space Parliament shall have declared safe for just such mutual empowerment. But then no one had yet imagined what practices might unfold in an entirely new setting—in a land declared to be in covenant and watched over by a magistrate as pious and principled as John Winthrop. A settled disbeliever in any earthly City of God, Williams could imagine New England only as a smaller, less complicated version of the Old, growing up gradually to its own advanced state of plurality and competition. For their part, the men of Massachusetts may well have been astonished at the worldly success of their separated version of Non-Separating Congregationalism. And though they too surely knew that Israel was a state of history and of providence never seen before or since, they were at the same time unable to discredit their own success. New England too seemed to be a nonesuch. And they were not the men to vote for confusion when a holy unity seemed so near their grasp.

So they fear not to publish their policy of expecting their ruler "to encourage . . . such persons as voluntarily join themselves in holy covenant, both by his presence . . . and promise of protection"; to "forbid all idolatrous and corrupt assemblies"; and to "compel all men within his grant to hear the word," though not at all to "compel all men to become members of churches" (278–79). Judging always from without, Williams can only make his dissent more and more pronounced. First of all, magistrates should indeed "protect the persons of the church from violence, disturbance, &c.," but where they decide to suppress worship other than their own the result is almost always that the Lord Jesus is driven "out of the world." Nor will the supposed example of David's resolution "to cut off all the wicked and evil doers" (280) prove otherwise for, as Williams cannot repeat often

enough, there is now "no holy land or city of the Lord . . . but the church" (281)—
from which *of course* heretics may be excluded. To deny this essential metonymic
shift, from Old Testament to New, is to imply that, everywhere, "not only such as
assay to join themselves . . . in a corrupt church estate, but such as know no church
estate . . . must be hanged or stoned as it was in Israel" (282). And if, happily,
New England does not follow its logic to this extent, still their self-contradiction
involves the refusal to separate from the Church of England, that "Mother
Whore" with whom they communicate back in Old England but to whose "profane ordinances" (283) they allow no free exercise in the New.[29]

As to the "natural" reason for compelling nonmembers to hear the word,
Williams replies that "nature leadeth men to hear that only which nature con-
ceiveth to be good for it" (287), and here only conscience can decide. Further, in
point of fact, the clear bent of "congregational" preaching in New England is directed not to the conversion of unbelievers but to the "edification, exhortation,
and consolation" (289) of those already within the particular church. And though,
from deep inside the congregational theory of voluntary entry by conscious covenant, it makes perfect sense to proclaim that "persons are not to be compelled to
be *members* of churches, nor the church compelled to receive any," yet Williams'
outsider logic is bound to ask whether the religion people are forced to entertain
"all their days" does not become in fact "this people's religion" (289). Either that
or admit that they are compelled "to be of no religion at all, all their days" (290).
To this powerful critique the best New England answer might be, eventually, the
theory of halfway membership—anxious preparation for the one true religion
being preferable to complacent attendance upon the false.

Williams spends more time on the ninth head of the *Model* than later interest may require. New England magistrates have, of course, no more power to
provide officers for the congregations than any Puritan dissenter from the ways
of the English church might wish; but Williams would make the task of recom-
mending the formation of new churches the exclusive concern of an apostolic
ministry, for which he can detect no place in the congregational theory that "two
or three godly persons may join themselves together" (293) and so become a
church. And he certainly cannot pass over the question of "maintenance" (297):
church members of course are bound to support their faithful pastor, but how
is it reasonable to force the payment of tithes from those forced to hear a preaching they neither seek nor approve? Further, opposing the enforced support of
"schools" (305), Williams recalls how readily "the seminaries or seed-plots of all
piety" have "changed their taste and color to the prince's eye and palate" (306).
And as to the supposed dependence of the church on such schools, Williams
finds that in Scripture the only "schools of prophets" are the churches them-

selves, in which "it may please the Lord again to clothe his people with a spirit of zeal" (307).

Only a characteristic refusal to take agreement at face value causes the tenth head to be discussed at all; for no one privy to the discussion would grant the magistrate any power at all "in matters of doctrine": "'That which is unjustly ascribed to the pope is as unjustly ascribed to magistrates'" (308). But Williams cannot pass by the opportunity to taunt the protest of today with the conformity of the past. Grant that King Edward caused certain "homilies [to be] thrust into the room of the Word of God" (310); and that he persecuted those who, after pious "admonitions," resisted still. Was he not merely seeking Reformation, "being constantly persuaded by his clergy" of a duty "received from Christ"? And if so, what in the New England position makes the magistrate now "exempt" (311) from a similar introduction of new doctrine under the head of reformed worship? The very lesson of history, they might think to reply. But where they discern enlightenment in the history of Reformation—the progressive recovery of some pristine Christian purity—Williams can discern only further dispute and continued bloodshed. New England, it appears, was seeking an aboriginal and perfect form.[30] Williams wished to recover, more simply, a certain Spirit—of difference from all that had gone before.

———

With a consideration of the eleventh head—which occupies more than a third of his entire reply to the *Model*—Williams comes to the heart of his argument, explaining in detail that Christians fulfill the multiform typology of "Israel" not in the civil organization of their towns and countries but only in that mysterious "city" which is the (largely invisible) church or else, even more internally, in the mysterious depths of their Christ-inhabited souls. Yet even here, where the early modern revival of Augustine might call forth an effort of history or of vision that breaks free of the political propositions that have drawn transcendent faith into local controversy, the logic of the *Model* continues to set the pace, as if to imply that when error appears abroad and advertises itself in the guise of grand design, the only ground safely occupied by truth is personal resistance and public critique. Word for Word.

Working somewhere between the antique precedent of a peculiar religious history invested with remarkable valeur and a present practice evolving in a situation no prophet of comparative folkways could possibly have predicted, the New England *Model* proposes that magistrates "ought," in Williams' summary, "to reform the worship of God when it is corrupted," "to establish a pure worship of

God," and "to defend it by the sword" (314–15)—restraining idolatry and cutting off offenders. Proofs from the New Testament and from "the practice of kings of other nations" Williams dismisses as unworthy of reply. "The practice of the kings of Israel and Judah" has also been rejected before, of course, but so much weight "lies upon this precedent of the Old Testament" that Williams is willing once again "to declare how weak and brittle this supposed pillar of marble is to . . . sustain such a mighty burden." All he needs to prove is that

> the state of Israel as a national state made up of spiritual and civil power . . . was merely figurative and typing out the Christian churches consisting of both Jews and Gentiles, enjoying the true power of the Lord Jesus, establishing, reforming, correcting, defending in all cases concerning his kingdom and government. (316)

Not the clearest piece of controversial prose ever written, perhaps, but fortunately we have already seen a large part of Williams' position: Israel being absolutely unique in the unfolding history of Salvation, its practice of offering secular support for institutions of the Spirit is just no rule for anybody else.

At first it might appear that Williams has to show only that the Israelite example has no binding force on later practice, that no degree of reformation is *required* to imitate the luminous paradigm. But this would leave New England free to follow the Jewish example not necessarily, so as to realize itself as an antitype, but only plausibly or prudentially, as something that once had God's approval might well be tried again—especially when conditions seemed favorable. But as Williams is opposed to the cozy kissing of Moses and Aaron under any pretense, he needs to argue in fact that, given the *spiritual* nature of New Testament revelation, the precedent of Israel must never be followed anywhere. Religion having moved inside the soul, the nearest approach to discipline of that soul must come from an institution whose ends and means are avowedly spiritual. Where the Jewish state existed to protect and to discipline the public religion of Israel, the church exists to deal with the soul, by the sword of the Spirit alone. The odd man here, the state, is not by any means out; but it is reduced to the function of protecting the bodies and estates of all civil men. Glimpsing this nice problem, the reader only hopes Williams' prophecy can get there from New England's propositions.

Peace can hardly wait to hear the view of Truth concerning "that . . . most unimitable state of Israel" (316). Thus her own view that even the "precedents of Cyrus, Darius, and Artaxerxes are strong against New England's tenet and practice" delays only for a moment the more necessary argument. First, as to "the very land ... of Canaan itself," it was specifically "chosen by the Lord out of all the countries of the world to be the seat of his ... people"; now, however, as the Lord himself testified to "the woman of Samaria" (John 4) "there is no respect of ... places or countries" (317); in the old dispensation "the tribes were bound to go up to Jerusalem to worship," but now in every nation "he that feareth God and worketh righteousness is accepted with him, Acts 10.35" (317–18). Then too, the former inhabitants of Canaan "were all devoted to destruction by the Lord's own mouth," but since then "it hath not pleased the Lord to devote any people to present destruction"; so that when, "in a spiritual antitype" God's people slay their enemies, it is only by the "two-edged sword of God's Spirit" (318). Once, it appears, there was indeed a Holy *Land,* where the idols of gold and silver were "odious and abominable and dangerous." Now, however, gold and silver are lawfully used and, except as they signify any of the things that may "draw us from God in Christ," they and all things else "are made ... pure (in all lands) to the pure" (319).

Once God might speak of "his own land" in the literal. Now, in light of the universalist goal of the new order of preaching, such language is proper only "unto the spiritual Canaan, the church of God." A "partition wall" having been "broken down," there is now no "difference between Asia and Africa, between Europe and America, between England and Turkey, London and Constantinople." The "Jerusalem from above" having become "not material ... but Spiritual," it is only the Antichrist who christens "all those countries where the Whore sitteth" with the title of "Christian land" (320). Add a few arguments concerning the spiritualization of Sabbath and of Jubilee, and Truth can fairly conclude that "Israel's parallel and antitype" is now no literal country but only that "mystical nation the church of God, peculiar and called out to him out of every nation and country" (322); and for his peaceful easy listener to agree that "Canaan Land was not a pattern for all lands: it was a none-such, unparalleled and unmatchable" (323).

If the land was unique, so too were the people: "all the seed ... of one man Abraham." Now in fact "few nations of the world but are a mixed seed," and in reformed theory only "the new-born are but one" (323). Besides that, "this people was selected and separated to the Lord, his covenant and his worship, from all the people and nations of the world"; but where in the Gospel has God "separated whole nations and kingdoms as a peculiar people? ... Yea where [is] the least footing in all the Scripture for a national church after Christ's coming?" (324). Further, the seed of Abraham "was wonderfully ... brought from Egypt's bondage through the Red Sea and the wilderness." Peace observes that the English are "apt to make themselves the parallels, as wonderfully come forth of popery" (325); but Truth is not impressed, and no one is there to make the case.

Less restrictive in some respects, the *New* English might suggest that their own exemplary migration amounted to just such a divinely authorized separation—which Scripture could hardly narrate so long before the fact, but which all those not closed to the idea of God's making an end-time place for his people in the world itself might piously discern. Indeed, Williams' dogmatic refusal to allow "Christianity" a *literal* life might make his spiritualism look a bit insensitive to the poetry of early modern history. For writers like Bradford, Shepard, Winthrop, Cotton, and Johnson had not wished primarily to return to anything like the formality of the Old Covenant; but only to believe that God might yet find a way to prepare at least a portion of this world to receive his very saints. For why, on Williams' theory, had there needed to be a world-shaping Reformation at all? Surely God had always known ways to save any number of individual souls, spiritually and as such. Which is to say: no party to the controversy is reading Scripture without the bias of one or another theory of history. To be sure, Augustine had learned to protect Christianity from the charge that its cogency depended on the sum of social evil it managed to prevent. But Cotton was not the only believer unwilling to surrender the desire to see, if not cedars sprouting in Sinai, then at least a garden in the wilderness.

Unchallenged by any assertion of this countervision—that God's plan is in the end to save *this world* as well as a few scattered elect—Williams "spiritualist" typology is free to unfold itself apace. In the new dispensation, only the "circumcised in heart" are the antitype of Israel, "the holy nation wonderfully redeemed from the Egypt of this world." Once upon a time, a whole people were, "in typical and ceremonial respect, . . . holy and clean"; but "where is now that nation or country . . . thus clean and holy unto God"? At present, "all the nations of the earth [are] alike clean unto God, or rather alike unclean," until God shall "call some out to the knowledge and grace of his Son" (327). The proof is clear in Acts 10 where the Lord informs Peter "of the abolishing of the difference between Jew and Gentile in any . . . clean or unclean respect." In this way the "people of Israel in that national state" become the type of "all the children of God in all ages," and thus it is that "Christians now are figuratively in this respect called Jews." And these are called from "all nations, tongues, and languages" (328). And with this dispersed aggregation of Spiritual Jews, individually called out of the world and into a church as universal as it is invisible, there exists no covenant permitting the slaughter of those who "according to the rules of the Gospel are not born again" (329). Then, an elect nation fought its enemies with all the ordinary weapons of war. Now, the "faithful witnesses" of Christ use only "spiritual . . . weapons" (330). Everywhere the elect realize more and more the truly internal nature of the kingdom, but neither the discovery of America nor the selective peopling of New England moves This World any closer to its rescue by and for the saints.[31]

But if the outward imitation of the onetime Israel is a "profanation" (329) leading to the "slaughters both of men and women," still all those "who willingly submit unto the Lord Jesus as their only king and head may fitly parallel . . . that Israel in the type" (330) without danger of hypocrisy. Which is to say: Israel is a type not only of the church but also, and more important, perhaps, of the regenerate soul. Of this poetic equivalence we could use a little instruction. First of all, some things occurred of old for which it might be hard to find the spiritual equivalent: not everyone translated the going aside into Hagar in exactly the same way.[32] Then too, because Williams had been, famously, finding it harder and harder to locate the church in *any* visible manifestation, we might require of him a special emphasis on the most spiritual branch of his typological doctrine.[33] But the *Bloody Tenet* is a political and not a spiritual book: its author returns to implications of his doctrine for the institution of civil magistracy; and only the most determined readers will be able to fetch a corollary from the memory of a repetition.

The notion that the church and the commonwealth are like "Hippocrates twins"—"born together" and destined to "grow up together, laugh together, weep together, sicken and die together"—Williams regards as "a witty, yet a most dangerous fiction"; for (once again) there have been and continue to be "many flourishing states . . . which hear not of Jesus Christ" (333). Only the determined student of antique folkways will much relish Williams' distinction between the "kings of Israel and Judah" (336) and "all other kings and rulers of the earth" (338). Williams asks us to recall the case of Solomon who, acting as "King of the Church" and thus "a figure of Christ" (340), remitted the civil punishment of Abiathar but removed him from the priesthood: would the General Court of New England feel free to exercise the same power? Peace loves this sort of *reductio* and begs her champion to "glance upon Josiah" in relation to the "worship of God" (342), but the interest of the ordinary reader picks up only when Truth decides to reprise "England's imitation of Josiah's practice" (344):

Henry 7 leaves England under the slavish bondage of the Pope's yoke. Henry 8 reforms all England to a new fashion, half Papist, half Protestant. King Edward 6 turns about the wheel of the state, and works the whole land to absolute Protestantism. Queen Mary . . . brings forth an old edition of England's Reformation all Popish. Elizabeth . . . plucks up all her sister Mary's plants and sounds a trumpet all Protestant. (344–45)

Metaphor aside, Williams seems to have earned the right to his repetition: "What sober man stands not amazed at these Revolutions?" Indeed, what reader of *actual* history could expect from the heirs of all this confusion "another impression and better edition of a National Canaan"? (345).

Yet no reader of biblical prophecy ever denied that redemption history was going to go through some ugly stages and, from Columbus to America's Romantic Historians, the Puritan migrants were far from alone in imagining that the addition of America made absolutely no difference to the proper understanding of God's plot.[34] Cotton and his cohort may have to explain why the course of reformation has shown no "steady unretracing progress"; but they might ask Williams why, in these latter days, a revival of spirituality should have no chance to redeem the times. Perhaps—in the formula of Edmund Morgan—it was his subjectivity and not their public testing that would take the Church too far from the World.[35] Forswearing the redemption of this world, however, Williams thought "a twofold exaltation of the Lord" was enough—"one in the . . . souls of men" and one "in his church and congregation," this latter being the extent of his "kingdom here below." Thus the "Kings of Israel" predicts not any future rulers with both civil and religious power but only "the spiritual King of Israel, Jesus Christ" (347).

At issue, of course, is not the Lord's worldly power to make laws and "ordinances to his saints and subjects" but the claim of some men to have a "deputed" (348) share of that power. Such is the pretense not only of "the arch-vicar or Satan, the pretended Vicar of Christ on earth" but also of the civil magistracy, supported here and there by "the prelacy" (349), "the presbytery" (350), and even such Independents as "pretend to receive their ministry from the choice of 2 or 3 private persons in church-covenant," yet would "fain persuade the mother Old England to imitate her daughter New England's practice" (350–51). Beyond these parties which look to some worldly power to enforce their present consensus lie those who separate from one or another of these groups, dividing themselves into "several professions" (351), seeking earnestly to "come nearer to the ways of . . . God" and who ought be permitted "to enjoy the common air" (352).

More than convinced of the crucial difference, Peace can only wonder when this distinction between the search of the soul and the ways of the world will come clear to the general mind. Truth urges patience, and uses its presumption to iterate for another twenty-five pages or so. First of all, as the land, people, and worship of the Old Testament are "types and figures of a spiritual land, spiritual people," so the "saviors, redeemers, deliverers, judges" must also have "their spiritual antitypes" or the "essential nature of types . . . [is] overthrown" (353). Spiritual antitypes *only,* he seems to mean. Yet if we accept this restriction, then Miller was right all along: Williams alone was the true typologist; Cotton and all the rest were merely knee-jerk imitators of an outmoded regime.[36] Perhaps we ought to think of another way to state the difference—namely, that the new religious dispensation was so entirely "spiritual" or interior that no worldly arrangement could approximate it except in gross external parody. Which a cautious piety might hesitate to express but which a strict logic might very well imply.

And so the differences run again to a lengthy list: the New Testament makes no thought to "compel whole nations to true repentance" (353); for the "sword of steel" can scarcely "reach to cut the darkness of the mind" (354); accordingly, that revelation offers "not one tittle" to support the idea that the older magistrates predict new ones of the same order, resting instead in an understanding that the duties of the civil magistrate are entirely civil, denying any "addition of power from [his] being a Christian," and "expressly mentioning" as the magistrate's sole concern "the duties of the second table." Further, if magistrates *did* have "the power to establish, correct, reform" (355) the church, they could only have it from the people; and this would be to define reformation as what the people will vote. Conversely, we *do* expressly find in the New Testament "a spiritual power . . . in the hands of his saints, ministers, and churches, to be the true antitype of those former figures" (357). Peace may not feel her "kind encouragement" is being presumed upon, but other readers may doubt that even she realizes when we have reached a fourth and then a fifth class of differences: who in after-time would claim the special status of Moses, "the law-maker or law-publisher or prophet, as Moses calls himself" (357), or what latter-day ruler would dare assume that "eternal life" was the "reward of the observation" (360) of any law on his books? Peace wants to hear the typical character of the various wars of Israel: assailed without, betrayed within (361), they yet achieve victories "contrary to those of the world, for when they are slain and slaughtered, yet then they conquer" (363).

Impressed by differences such as only a proper typology can mediate, Peace raises the possibility the reader herself has imagined: if not type, then at least precedent? And on this score Williams is willing to admit that, apart from all typology, modern states are free to imitate whatever was "simply moral, civil, and natural in Israel's state," but he is quick to add that "since civil constitutions are men's ordinances," no one can "question the lawfulness of other forms of government" (364). Against New England's contention that the laxity of princes has been the cause of untold "corruption in the worship and temple of God," Williams replies that the state of affairs which might be called "the Pope's Christendom" can never be deduced from the inactivity of princes; indeed, he counters, it argues "idleness and faithlessness in such as profess to be messengers of Christ Jesus, to cast the heaviest weight of their care upon the . . . rulers of the earth" (365). Then too he asks—with no special eye to the rare gifts of John Winthrop—who can suppose that civil rulers, well burdened already with concerns of public safety, will also be "furnished with . . . spiritual and heavenly abilities?" (366). Finally, Christ himself has taught how "unsuitable is the commixing . . . of the civil with the spiritual charge": "If ever any in this world was able to manage both the spiritual and the civil, . . . it was the Lord Jesus. . . . Yea he was the true heir to the crown of Israel . . . ; yet being sought by the people to be made king, he refused and would not give precedent" (367). And as to the actual record of princes, even New England has confessed that it was "under Constantine [that] Christians fell asleep on the beds of carnal ease." True, one might blame not the "assuming" but the "ill-managing" (368) of spiritual power, yet the actual existence of such ill management surely makes a weak precedent.

As to the prediction that kings shall be "nursing fathers," Peace is satisfied that "many excellent pen-men" fight about "those prophecies" (371). In the meantime—which New England refuses to recognize as such—the civil magistrate may lawfully give "countenance" (372) to that religion his conscience recognizes as true; and of course he must protect the persons and estates of all "true professors." Yet he owes this same protection to the professors of a religion he deems to be false; he cannot give it "approbation," but he certainly owes it "permission" (373). Peace then permits Truth to end his discussion of the "eleventh head" by turning their prince-in-the-ship metaphor into another advertisement of the internal nature of Christianity. Not actually disagreeing that a prince may reprove a pilot if he "manifestly err in his action" and also may "in due time and place punish him" (376), Williams is more interested in emphasizing that, within the ship-church, the "officers . . . appointed by the Lord Jesus are . . . above the prince himself" (378), and indeed that "every Christian . . . ought to be of higher esteem . . . than all the princes in the world" (378–79). A "democratic" doctrine, but entirely spiritual.[37]

———

The final five heads of the *Model* require less than ten pages each, much of which is taken up by quotations from this ad hoc constitution itself. The twelfth head concerns "the magistrate's power in the censure of the church" (380). Williams would of course deny any such power and, in the New Englanders' attempt to circumscribe it, he finds only paradox and self-contradiction. But his principal complaint is that New England practice lays "a deep charge of weakness . . . upon the church"; for what in truth need be added to "the cutting off from Christ"? (385). As to the "power magistrates have in public assemblies of churches" (389), Williams finds the *Model* presents something like a "double picture" (392). On the one side, in the churches' "power to assemble . . . for the performance of all God's ordinances, without or against the consent of the magistrate" (389), Williams finds "a most fair and beautiful countenance of the pure and holy Word" (392–93). On the other, "a most sour and uncomely deformed look of a mere human invention" (393): the defense of "extraordinary" assemblies cannot rest on the example of Josiah since Israel has been shown to be "a none-such"; and as to those that are "yearly and monthly" (401)—of which "we find not any such in the first churches" (402)—they had better not mean that magistrates may "give [this] liberty only unto themselves" or that they may force "the elders" (401–2) to participate.

Williams knows, of course, that when the several congregations of New England could not agree on the outlines of the authentic narrative of faith, Winthrop's timely suggestions to the clergy had been hard to refuse. And he seems untroubled by the concern that the proliferation of individual, potentially antithetical congregations can never add up to anything more than a "sect-type" religion. For a man whose chief interest is the purity of the individual faith, centralization is never an ally. In this preference for authenticity above all semblance of order Williams may indeed be a little like the Jefferson with whom he has often been associated.[38]

Equally evident, in his brief response to the *Model*'s fourteenth head, is his more than Puritan refusal to take the approximate for the exact. Judging Massachusetts' arguments that a particular church may censure a member who happens to be a magistrate as "immoveable" as "Mount Zion," Truth yet finds that "a query or two will not be unseasonable": by "the church" (407), do they mean with or without "the elders and governors"? And if the latter, "why name they not the governors at all, since that in all administrations of the church their duty lies not upon the body of the church, but . . . properly upon the elders"? (407–8). Surely they *do* mean to include the elders. But what looks like a discovery that no one here intends congregationalism most pure may also be read as another expression of Williams' desire to prove that no real-world government need fall into the compromises that mark the New England Way. Indeed, this is a large part of what one might mean by thinking of Williams' reactive critique as nothing less than the constitution of a government in exile.[39] Cotton and the others had the ample opportunity to do right; but they have let the surprising fact of a strong

Christian magistrate—in possession of an empowering paper from an earthly sovereign—blind them to the political implications of the New Testament's revolutionary definition of "the Kingdom of God." Expelled as a result of their blindness, Williams nevertheless possessed the true ground plan. Which he has elected to write as a critique of theirs.

That critique begins to run down with a commentary on their fifteenth head—applauding the "tenderness" which would move a church to be slow in the excommunication of any magistrate but serving a sharp rebuke to the special instructions given in a case where "the commonweal consists of church members" (411). And it ends with a peroration attached to the second of two chapters devoted to the sixteenth head, touching the very foundation of the Massachusetts "theocracy"—that "all magistrates ought to be chosen out of church-members"; and that the "free men" who do the electing be themselves "only church-members" (412).[40] Given the foundational importance of these two principles, one might expect a more extended treatment. Yet the basis of their rejection has already been well elaborated. And though the tenor of thought in Williams' *Bloody Tenet* is altogether brave and free, no man ever wished it longer.

Ever the grammatical logician, Williams insists on quibbling with the nature of the Massachusetts "ought": this choosing magistrates who are church members, do they mean to recommend it as a good idea or to require it absolutely? If the latter, how will this apply to states "where no church of Christ is resident"? (414). Or where "there may not be found in a true church of Christ"—which can after all be quite small—"persons fit to be either kings or governors"? (414–15). And should magistrates be "deposed when they cease to be of the church"? Bloody precedent for this, especially among the "Papists." In fact, Williams knows but too well what they mean: when you have the luck of forming a self-selected community of saints, of course they must elect one of their own. Yet he requires principles that will apply in general. And even in the actual Massachusetts case, where the civil may be as churchly as anyone could desire, he insists that the churchly requirement is nothing less than a way "to turn the world upside down." Where Cotton had come to agree with Winthrop that the "Model of Christian Charity" implies something very like the present "Model of Church and Civil Power," Williams brands that model a perverse refusal to let the world be itself. Where the men of Massachusetts see a unique opportunity for the greatest possible harmony, Williams discovers only a plan "to turn the garden . . . of the church into the field . . . of the world" and thus "to reduce the world to the first chaos and confusion" (415).

Here Peace congratulates Truth with having "conquered" and predicts that he will indeed "triumph in season" (415). And, as if in summary, Truth takes credit for having "fully . . . declared the vast differences between that holy nation of typical Israel and all other lands and countries" (415–16). There remains a "second branch" to this sixteenth and final head, namely, that "all freemen . . . be only church members," but as this is declared to rest on the "sandy and dangerous ground of Israel's pattern," Williams is willing to let it pass without further comment, offering instead only a prayer that the "Father of Lights" might discover the Israelite fallacy "to all that fear his name":

> then would they not sin to save a kingdom, not run into the lamentable breach of civil peace and order in the world, nor be guilty of forcing thousands to hypocrisy, in a state worship, nor of profaning the holy name of God and Christ by putting their names and ordinances upon unclean and unholy persons; nor of shedding the blood of such heretics . . . whom Christ would have enjoy longer patience and permission until the harvest. (416–17)

Amen to all that, saith the modern conscience—in faith, perhaps, but also in weariness.

Lacking altogether the sense of ending, Peace requests of Truth his "faithful help" in "2 or 3 Scriptures . . . we have not spoken of" (417). Yet the reader knows when he has heard Williams sing his highest note and so is more than willing to move on to the final two pages (of chapter 138), which offer themselves plainly enough as a formal conclusion.[41] Peace, despite her tin ear, is allowed to announce the ending—and also to concede a fact the reader did not know she knew: "We have now . . . clambered up to the top of our tedious discourse." Truth considers it "mercy unexpressible" that the two have been permitted "so long a breathing time" (423), thus shifting the emphasis from literary *longueur* to political respite. And no doubt Peace herself had meant chiefly to lament the length of time that multiform error requires of steadfast duty. Still, we are glad to know that our sense of time is not simply one more mark of our own fallenness: Williams' *Bloody Tenet* is a long book; longer in psychological time, perhaps, than Hooker's indefatigable *Application*. Reassured, we readily allow Truth and Peace to trade a few maxims of sorrow and of hope and are even pleased by the last-page appearance of our speechless "Sister Patience, whose desired company is as needful as delightful" (424). If Williams' truth took so many bloody centuries fairly to appear, no doubt its official publication may be granted the right to take its own time. And ours.

Of the strengths of the *Bloody Tenet* it may *still* not be possible to say enough. First of all, it discovers and promulgates, at the very outset of the Age of Epistemology, precisely that fallible yet inalienable authority of conscience which alone makes the practice of religion meaningful. "Private" the operation of that conscience must necessarily be, yet socializing in its recognition that no human being may be deprived of its constitutive function. Next, if it soberly forswears the earthly triumph of true religion, it bravely recommends a regard for the integrity of "this world" as the place where honest searching for some truth that may point beyond it must necessarily occur.[42] It reminds those who most sincerely testify to the discovery of transcendent truth that it is still a "private" faculty that has made this awesome discovery; forbidding them, thereby, to foreshorten the process of search by any other conscience; making the world safe, in the process, for that state of doubt which—as Emerson would remind us[43]—always mediates our passage from an earlier to some more mature belief. And, by refusing to pass over in silence the complex and self-revisionary history of Christian thought itself, it may actually advertise the conscientious possibility of a more or less settled skepticism. As if the last act of Puritan belief were to license its Melvillean opposite.

Nor should it be forgotten that many of the faults of Williams' definitive book are as much a function of genre as of sensibility or literary strategy. It has been hard to praise the stilted use of an explicit dialogue form; indeed, we might even conclude that there is more genuine give-and-take in those sermons of Shepard and Hooker where an imaginary auditor is never slow to voice some touchy "Calvinist" objection. Yet a studied comparison of the *Bloody Tenet* with Cotton's *Keys of the Kingdom,* or Hooker's *Survey of the Sum of Church Discipline,* or Norton's *Responsio* (to the *Consideratio* of William Apollonius), or Shepard's *Defense* of the *Answer* John Davenport had returned to John Ball's *Questions* about the churches in New England—might produce a different sense of its relative effect.[44] No one has ever suggested that any of these treatises should be read for their originality of figure or resplendency of wit. And no doubt critique's exaggerated concern to identify and discredit error will cloy no sooner than dogma's determination to pass off curious folk invention as the end time's fated form.

But then that faint praise would seem to be part of the point—namely, that the first-generation American Puritans do their best work not in the polemics necessary to attack or defend the churchly arrangements but in the more visionary genres of history, understood as the account of a more-than-individual attempt to discover and empower some version of godliness in this world; of autobiography, which could be nothing but the record of the way God's recovery of a private soul put him or her in the way of participating in the larger plot of world redemption; and of sermons and cycles of sermons, in which a living exemplum of gratuitous salvation tries his human best to serve as God's occasion for further acts of grace. These efforts—it has been the working assumption of all the previous chapters—produce in first-generation New England the highest sort of imaginative stress and bring forth from that condition a product we can appreciate as literary even if we identify its ideas as the expression of a mentality that no longer controls the laws of our own thought. Not wishing to return, we might yet find ourselves, in Hawthorne's cautious formula, "happy to have had such ancestors."[45]

Not every writer invents an episteme. Some only give vivid expression to the most inspiring possibilities of the one they inhabit. Such is the enduring accomplishment of writers like Bradford, Winthrop, Shepard, Cotton, Hooker, and Johnson. If we value Williams for seeing through to what was illusory at the core of their excited belief, we need not at the same time suppose that the experiment which stirred their imaginations did not deserve in the name of Reformation to be tried, or that his precocious insight has made their literary productions unreadable or irrelevant. It might be too simply ironic to thank them for projecting so strongly the vision that awakened Williams from his dogmatic slumbers. Perhaps it will be enough to realize that critique can seldom afford to be quite so venturesome as visionary projection. And to understand the sort of appreciation that is appropriate to each.

EPILOGUE

CHAPTER ELEVEN

"GOD'S ALTAR"

The Fall to Poetry

Of course there is some irony in the subtitle. Not everyone in the world loves poetry, to be sure, and many experienced teachers of "literature" will testify that a certain resistance to the way of verse is beginning to get a wide enough expression in modern students of "English." But professionals are supposed to hold the line against this literary failure to thrive, and enthusiasts are still entitled to affirm, with Emerson, that the day I discover a new poet "shall be better than my birthday."[1] Nor will the students who cannot see the fun of Edward Taylor be among the first to ask if they may go *back* and read more of Hooker on sin or Shepard on faith. Still, there may be a place to hear the devil's advocate, even in the discourse of godly letters.

The point, in its simplest formulation, might be something like this: bewildered beginners in the subject of American Studies usually welcome the knowledge that the seventeenth-century American Puritans wrote poetry, and many even choose to write about it, as somehow more proper to their allied interest in "English"; yet they are forced to confess that the writerly urge of the first generation appears more energetically in history, autobiography, and sermon sequence. For example: most of these novices feel suitably instructed to learn that Bradford, who gave up on his book about Plymouth, lived on to write a couple of verse laments on the lapse of New England from its original religious "glory" to an ordinary interest in "wealth and the world," and that he saw the "great and wealthy town of Boston" as leading the way down. And if in fact they read the small poems provided in a first-week handout, a few at least will notice that Bradford's self-authored epitaph, anticipating the "happy change" from earth to heaven,

539

bears comparison to Bradstreet's better-known farewell to her life, "As Weary Pilgrim";[2] but they never doubt that *Plymouth* is Bradford's essential and necessary work, and indeed that his representative "poem" is the two-page prose meditation on his "poor people's present condition" upon arriving at Plymouth. The aboriginal Puritan poem, that is to say, is the power of vision to inspire historical record, to which versification can appear only as supplement.

And even more so, perhaps, in other early cases. John Cotton remembered the life and death of his daughter Sarah tenderly enough to record her last words, spoken to him alone but addressed in all probability to a higher authority: "Pray, my Dear Father, let me now go Home." Yet given the events and issues of Cotton's own life, the offspring we best remember is that "Seaborne" son he would not baptize until properly admitted to a particular reformed church. And though it fills out the portrait of this man in love with the word to notice that he complimented the prose of his "Reverend Dear Brother M. Samuel Stone" with a few well-turned verse conceits on the type of the "stone," still the *raison* of the poem is not this contemporary's life or death but his cold-prose view of *A Congregational Church [as] a Catholic Visible Church*.[3] Somewhat more challenging at first glance are the verses interspersed throughout Johnson's *Wonder-Working Providence*. What they seem to signify is that Johnson knows his theme is indeed "poetic"— worthy, that is, of an expression most considered and dignified. Yet the poetry is already there in the excitement of sentences that cannot come on fast enough; and indeed the too correct summaries of Johnson's verse can only retard the double-time march of his prose toward the end of earthly days. One way or another, the spontaneous overflow of Puritan emotion is into prose.

More nearly essential are the little poems that end the various chapters of Roger Williams' *Key into the Languages of America* (1642). Perhaps these condensed efforts can stand for Williams' interest in the expressive as such— redeeming, if possible, the misplaced literariness of the *Bloody Tenet*'s deadly dialogue. Certainly these poems arrest the attention of the modern reader, expressing as they do, in summary form, the essential insights of the cultural openness that marks Williams' Berlitz-style introduction to the speech and folkways of Algonkian culture. Further, these pithy products often refine to a point exactly the sort of insult the dominant majority of Puritans seem to have been courting. Yet after we have noted the poetic application of the doctrine that pagan gifts alone have made Native Americans noticeably more "humane and courteous" than their nominally Christian supplanters, and savored the spiritual democracy of the teaching that birth-proud English are made "of one blood" with their "brother Indian," very much remains to be said about the Puritans' enthusiastic affirmations and about Williams' skeptical denial. We may lament the fact that, after

Williams, we have to wait for Mary Rowlandson to observe the interest of various native practices—foodways, sleepways, workways, sexways—but the fact remains: Williams well understands that each of his little poetic exercises is generated by his prosier work of cultural linguistics.[4] Thus epitome itself appears in the mode of the supplement. And poetry, as anything like a for-itself, comes along rather late in the life of this vigorous and highly literate culture.

———

Perhaps it is an accident, yet it seems somehow revealing that very few of Anne Bradstreet's "Puritan" poems were produced early in her career. Indeed, so many of the poems we customarily emphasize were written after the publication of her *Tenth Muse Lately Sprung Up in New England* (1650) that students often place her in the Wigglesworth generation, needing to be reminded that she, along with her father and husband, came over on Winthrop's original *Arabella*. Of course, we feature its "Prologue": invoking classical example to clear a space for female writing, this American and feminist original has powerfully attracted modern attention; but the closed-minded attitudes it firmly resists seem to spread wider than the Puritan patriarchy to which her father and husband both significantly belong and from whose ranks her book drew so many prefatory poetic compliments. It might be too much to suggest that her work is being praised for standing apart, somehow, from the political and religious issues that had driven the Puritans to drive the presses in the 1630s and 1640s but, from the title on, it is certainly her unlooked-for poetry and not her presupposed Puritanism that is being praised. Though not at all devoted to the kitchen subjects avowed by this prologue, the principal poems of the *Tenth Muse* propose nothing that might arouse the suspicion of censors of doctrine like Thomas Shepard. The "Good Anne," as others have noticed.

Nearer to the center of puritanic interest—and written in 1642, when Hooker and others were declining to "travel 3000 miles in order to agree with 3 men"—"A Dialogue Between Old England and New" has no trouble giving the last word on the end-time aims of holy history to her own land of chosen refuge; but it does as much as the new-migrating Winthrop himself to deny that nothing like separation from the "dear Mother" (179) had ever been the intention.[5] At the New England's invitation, the Old Mother pours out grief for public sorrow and repentance for political sin, including such "idolatry" and "superstitious adoration" as made the "Gospel trodden down"; but her Daughter, whose "flying for the truth was made a jest" (182), both admits the fact of her own "guilty hands" (183) and blesses the "nobles," "commons," "counties," and "preachers" (185–86) who stand at the present moment for radical reform. All that remains is to make an Earth's Holocaust of the "miters, surplices, . . . copes, rochets, crosiers, and such empty trash" as *all* true Englishmen associate with "Rome's whore" (186). Call this Puritanism 101; but notice that it must share pride of emphasis with an account of English history that goes back to "Hengist and Canutus" (180), as if historical learning were as much a part of the project as religious discrimination.

Certainly it is worldly learning, such as a fostering father might have both proffered and insisted upon, that seems the distinguishing mark of the 3,500+ lines of "The Four Monarchies": one can easily imagine Old and New England striving to compete or cooperate for the part of that famous "Fifth Monarchy" under the millennial rule of the benign King Jesus, but in fact the prodigious (heroic) couplet fragment ends with the expulsions of the Tarquins from the kingship of Rome—and with "An Apology" (177) that a concluding effort, much encouraged but long delayed, came at last to nothing when the laborious yet perhaps beloved papers "fell a prey to th' raging fire" (178). Nor does the impression of worldly learning change with the four "Quaternions": attempts to allegorize their late Renaissance identities have been unable to relieve the impression that Elements, Humors, and Ages debate themselves chiefly for the sake of keeping the exiled mind sane or the marginalized poetic faculty alive. There is, to be sure, some suggestion that, as the opposition of nature's elements and humors subsides to cumulative cooperation among the four ages of human life, and then to the necessary circularity of the four seasons, Bradstreet is searching for a theme, testing the capacity of her own voice to express the Greek ideal of moderation, harmony, and the golden mean and, beyond that, to valorize Ecclesiastes' notion of the vanity of all things, whether in or out of all due proportion.

Accordingly, "Air" ends the four-part harangue of the Elements with the peacemaking pun that she at least "dare not go beyond [her] element" (32). And phlegm, her "humorous" counterpart, ends the versified self-advertisement of "The Four Humors in Man's Constitution" with an explicit plea for harmonious resolution:

> Let's now be friends; it's time our spite were spent;
> Lest we too late this rashness do repent,
> Such premises will force a sad conclusion,
> Unless we agree, all falls into confusion. (50)

Winthrop himself could not have said it better; and Bradstreet, hearing no objection, proceeds to declare that eight things, taken two at a time, are equal to "A golden ring, the post UNITY." Which teaches the natural world a wholesome lesson:

Not jars nor scoffs, let none hereafter see,
But all admire our perfect amity;
Nor be discerned, here's water, earth, air, and fire,
But here's a compact body, whole entire. (50)

Phlegm may be merely phlegmatic, but her moral pleases all the others so well
that she is judged "for kindness to excel": Miss Congeniality of 1650.

What follows next, with far less competitive strife, is the revelation that
"Childhood," "Youth," "Middle," and "Old Age" all have their pleasures as well
as their problems and that all are necessary to a full and complete life. Still, as Old
Age is wise enough to discern, it is, all of it, "vanity" and "vexation of mind" (63).
So we are not too surprised when the four seasons posture and preen themselves
hardly at all: each season is presented "in season" (65) and, before the four-times-
four performance ends, with apology for lack of invention, we sense only that the
year's "cycle," hardly pausing until that fall we call the Fall, has run its natural
"round," leaving us and it "where first it did begin" (72). Wiser, perhaps, but only
with the wisdom of natural insignificance. And what this hypothesis would suggest is that Bradstreet's mature and properly puritanic poetry begins with "The
Vanity of All Worldly Things": concluding the *Tenth Muse,* and proceeding from
the moralized physics of the Quaternions in about the same way the "Old England and New" poem completes the history of the Monarchies, this short-course
meditation on the Augustinian completion of Ecclesiastes, that the *"summum
bonum"* which alone will "stay" (220) the human mind lies beyond any element,
humor, age, or season, however made or mixed by the classical efforts of human
reason.

But whatever the case of intention or development, it is simply a matter of
fact that most of Mrs. Bradstreet's recognizably "Puritan" poems come to us from
a period of her life well after the 1650 publication of the *Tenth Muse*—from a revision and enlargement she seemed to be planning and from a manuscript not
printed until 1867. The same is true, of course, for the many of her "family"
poems, inserted by her executors into a posthumous edition of her work in 1678;
and though some critics have wished to take these intensely personal poems as
Bradstreet's essential poetic product, this gesture may have the ironic effect of
enforcing the conclusion that she aimed not at the "bays" but only at a "thyme or
parsley wreath" (17). The place of the "poetess," that is to say, is in the kitchen
or the private room of birth or death. But another view is also possible: her
unabashed poems of human love and grief stand as a challenge to her own,
frequently expressed and well internalized view that the one real sin is the "idolatry" of loving any creature more than God. She makes the general case in her

"Meditation" on the fact that, as some children are "hardly weaned" from the mother's milk, so many Christians "are so childishly sottish" as to be "still hugging and sucking" at the empty breasts of worldly satisfaction that only God's timely and deliberate "affliction" (279) can grow them up. And she applies it to herself in her autobiographical letter to "My Dear Children." There, intent upon convincing them of the tough-love doctrine of "affliction"—and willing enough to lay upon them, Shepard-like, a heavy enough burden of familial guilt—she humanizes her message with the confession that she too has "been with God like an untoward child" (242). But only well along in her poetic life does she take up the default-setting Puritan point and hold it against herself. As if poetry had seemed at first a stranger to the province of salvation.

And even then she refrains from pressing the doctrine of unruly love very far into the bosom of her family. Flesh and Spirit are said to be "sisters," but both are parts of Bradstreet's own (Pauline) personality; and if Spirit is predestined to win this debate about who is and who is not getting enough of whatever it is our (Augustinian) "hearts are made for," the victory will not come before the earthly desiderata of "honor," "riches," and "pleasure"—added to the "beauty" and "wisdom" already advertised in the "Vanity" poem (219)—are permitted to challenge the shadow life of "meditation," "contemplation," and "speculation" (215). We may have to take it on faith that the "royal robes" she expects to wear in heaven, where the streets are "transparent gold," are essentially different from their earthly counterparts, but in no case does Bradstreet anticipate a withering away of all desire.

Desire of some sort is certainly the condition of her poem "Upon the Burning of Our House"—not sexual desire, perhaps, although the poem remembers the place where she and her earthly bridegroom "long did lie"—but certainly the possessive feeling that attached not only to the house as the treasured scene of familiar love but also to all those "pleasant things" (292) brought along from a richer life in England, to stabilize with a sense of the "mine" that personal identity without which a woman may lapse into a household symbol or a function. More poignantly personal than the abstract "riches" already spoken into vanity, and fully realized only in the loss, such desire is surely a given of nature, to be repressed only at great psychic danger and not to be sublimated without extreme effort. Which Bradstreet puts forth in a degree that may shock even the reader biased to believe she is merely going through the pious motions.

The "house on high" may seem to go without saying—the sort of familiar quid pro quo which persuades Spirit to trade "meat" for "manna" and to exchange any supposable earthly city for one with "stately walls . . . of precious jasper stone" and streets which feeble human sense can only call "transparent gold."

Yet there is unexpected substance in both poetic places: gold or not, the heavenly city knows nothing of "sickness and infirmity" (217); and absent "withering age," its "beauty shall be bright and clear" (218). So impressive is this turn to the physiological that one begins to suspect Bradstreet believes the thing which makes earthly life a vanity is not that it lacks the perfect object of heart's desire but merely that it grows old and dies. However that may be, the attraction of the heavenly house is not its metonymic substitutability for the one on earth and not even the fact that it has been both "framed" and "furnished" by God the "mighty Architect." Deeper down, the attraction is that it "stands permanent," even though the one on earth "be fled." And deeper still, from an imagination not easily diverted from the facts of human life, is the thought that "It's purchased and paid for too" (293)—by the bloody sacrifice, we readily understand, of that God-come-to-earth, whose "person" suffered time, pain, and death so that these might by his elect be overcome.

Yet the most shocking conceit drawn forth by the burning of her house, a lamentable event in the life of any committed homemaker, is altogether earthly in nature. Passing by the ashes of her earthly treasure in the length of days thereafter, and aware that she scarcely can keep her concupiscent eyes from straying aside to view and to regret that ruin, she becomes keenly aware that, as our deepest wishes are our truest prayers, her own must be arising to the throne of God, like the summer steam from a pile of animal dung nearby, with a none-too-pleasant aroma.

> Didst fix thy hope on mold'ring dust?
> The arm of flesh didst make thy trust?
> Raise up thy thought above the sky
> That dunghill mists away may fly. (293)

What else can she mean? Necessary grieving to Dr. Freud, her lingering desire can be nothing but an oblique but recognizably blaming of God to her Puritan conscience. And as such, a stink to his nostrils. And who will deny her the knowledge that our attempts to hold on to our own stuff are, well, a little shitty?

Of *course* she still loves her house. How not? And what but this subtle fact of sinful inevitability can be the structural meaning of a poem that twice tries to end before it fairly can? Part 1: I awoke to shouts of "Fire" and cried aloud to God—as would many a man or woman who politely reserves his name for just such emergent occasions; I watched the devastation as long as I could and then—composing my thought—"I blest His name that gave and took." That's what we all believe: what can I tell you? But ending here would leave the subtext all exposed: "The Lord giveth, the Lord taketh away;/With friends like that . . . " And so we continue the self-consolation: what he took was his own, after all; so we content ourselves to find "sufficient for us left." And still—Part 2—these desiring eyes, which appear to have a life of their own. And the small but irrepressible voice of happy memory, whose name is now "no more" (292). "Adieu," therefore, recalling only what the Preacher taught: "all's vanity." Except, as things vain before the silence of God may not be so in the words of a poem, I did delight in "guest" at "table" with a "pleasant tale," in candle "shine" and "bridegroom's voice." And so it all begins again: this time God and Christ are required to provoke her recoil from the odor of the selfish until, humbled at last, a prayer for affection well weaned: "The world no longer let me love" (293). Desire without end, Amen.

Even as the "Vanity" poem explicitly had declared: "While man is man, he shall have ease or pain" (210). Not only ineradicable, but wide as the world itself, as Nature itself allures the poet's hard to regulate "Contemplations"—giving us yet another poem which virtue tries to shut down before affect has had its full say. Autumn's glory, the "aspiring oak," and most of all "the glistering sun" (205) not only imply but in fact express divinity in a way the human poet can only hope to emulate. But never match—as even the "grasshopper" and the "cricket," both separately and together, "resound their Maker's praise" (207) while the musing human woman can only worry the thought of how much more glorious than nature the God of nature surely is. Why should this be? Why this paradoxical defect in the efforts of *conscious* praise? Ah, the Sin of Adam and the bloody history of his fallen progeny: "Cain and Abel" (208) the epitome; and after them, an entropic history, surely, as modern men appear to live lives both shorter and less vital than their testamentary counterparts. And just so—with or without the example of Andrew Marvel—"unawares comes on perpetual night" (209). The Puritan Nightmare: Sin without Grace.

To end here, however, would be to allow oneself to be overcome by an insight that answers a more ultimate question than the one being asked. Not, is human life at worst a bloodbath and at best a vanity? But, what are we to make of our odd "poetic" preference of Nature's way above our own? And so, recovering from its premature universal, the verse begins to meditate again: "the heavens as in their prime"; "the earth (though old) still clad in green"; and everything else in the natural system altogether "insensible of time": "If winter come and greenness then do fade," can Shelley's "spring" be far behind? A cyclical illusion, perhaps, but preferable in thought to the counterplot in which "man grows old, lies down, remains where once he's laid." "More noble," supposedly, than all creatures beside, yet "by nature and by custom cursed" (209), it makes one almost wish to have been born a natural creature simply, or not to have been born at all; unless one remembers, beyond all cyclic renewal, the saving thought of "immortality" (210). Thank you and welcome to that endless Christian day.

Except that "Under the cooling shadow of a stately elm," one's thoughts of nature's perfect world take up again their well-established course—like eyes that cannot be made *not* to look—and swell to a Romantic flood, almost, as streams now compete with trees to be the scene and sign of natural pleasure. So much so, that if only "the sun would ever shine, there would I dwell." Just as we suspected: time and change alone make nature vain. Not vain, surely, is the lesson of the streams that cannot be prevented from arriving at their "beloved place" in the ocean. And not alone, but with all their tributaries, so that the poetic observer can only wish for a similar power to lead her own "rivulets" to rest in heaven. Nor is it all a matter of "emblem": envy the fish themselves, taught their way by nature, unconscious of their great "felicity,"

> Look how the wantons frisk to taste the air,
> Then to the colder bottom straight they dive . . . (211)

It may require two centuries—and a more elaborated plan of natural observation—but this is the very mood that will inspire Thoreau: "Surely joy is the condition of nature."[6] And it is only a small stretch to suppose that it was the "protoromantic" Bradstreet who taught nature poet Bryant the prime theological distinction of his epochal "Inscription":

> The primal curse
> Fell, it is true, upon the unsinning earth,
> But not in vengeance. . . .

"Misery" being "yoked to guilt" alone, the woods are still "the abodes of gladness" in which

> the thick roof
> Of green and stirring branches is alive
> And musical with birds, that sing and sport
> In wantonness of Spirit.[7]

Sooner or later, it appears, America too will have a literary history all its own.

Meanwhile, as we wonder whether the latter-day Romantic or the finally-just-about-Puritan is more likely to speak more innocently of wantonness, Bradstreet moves from fish to bird—to nightingale, in fact, whose "melodious strain" causes the would-be prophet of Vanity to become so "rapt . . . with wonder and delight" as to risk the emphasis of a six-beat on an altogether wayward fantasy: "[I] wished me wings with her a while to take my flight." The flight of poetic desire may predict Keats, but the next moment's reflection both honors and challenges the New Testament, at just the place Thoreau himself would take it up: "Consider the birds"; or any natural creature that "neither toils nor hoards up in thy barn"; considers not what to wear or to eat and, in philosophical fact and heavy hexameter, "Reminds not what is past, nor what's to come dost fear." And the thought continues through another stanza—not that Providence takes care of *even* the birds of the air, but that their songs innocently "prevent" each "dawning morn," all summer long, until they all fly south, "Where winter's never felt by that sweet airy legion" (212). And just so, a poem bent on realizing the Puritans' own default doctrine of the vanity of every creaturely thing goes as far as it can—further than it ought, perhaps—in the discovery that the way of nonhuman Nature appears a good deal *less* vain than that of man himself.

And now of course the poem *must* turn, one final time, to the final implication of that paradoxical fact: less attractive in many ways than the Nature that surrounds and supports him, Man's only preeminence is the claim of his spirit to an immortality that is at last not cyclical. Which it behooves him to consider, more soberly than that "mariner" who sings and "steers his bark with ease" until "suddenly a storm spoils all his sport" (213). Time does not *worry* Nature, it readily appears, yet it is in the end a "fatal wrack of mortal things," outlasting all things else, and speaking the last word over the dust of everyone except "he whose name is graved in the white stone" (214). "Graved" is, of course, a masterful pun—redeeming, perhaps, some earlier, less happy adventures in poetic diction and all but justifying an ending that is far from a surprise. Not well modulated by any careful "turn" from Nature's innocent splendor to man's ignorance and weakness, it seems necessary only in a world where poetry's variable affect had better not stray too far from the changeless truth of prose. The wonder that it strayed so long. Long enough to require unweaned affection to seek the discipline of meditation. And why *not* in verse?—the place where doctrine and difference might learn, each one, to say without fear the other's name.

———

Clearly it was to verse that Bradstreet turned, again and again, to express the breadth and height of her earthly loves and the depth of her worldly losses. Now

and then the love of her "Dear and Loving Husband" seems to escape measure-
ment by the essential standard of the Heavenly Bridegroom. And never, it must
be confessed, is the love contest quite as piercing-earnest as in the case of Thomas
and Joanna Hooker Shepard—or later, in Taylor's "Wedlock and the Death of
Children." But often enough to be recognized as the rule, her sad response is cautious, ruled by a "proper" sense that no human person, however near and dear,
may be allowed to oust the Lord himself from the throne of Absolute Love.

Thus in the poems on the grandchildren, the death in 1665 of one "dear
babe," allowed to become her "heart's too much content," reminds this grieving
parent's mother that earthly days are only "lent" and that it is not quite proper to
"bewail [the] fate" of one well "settled in an everlasting state." Trees and plants do
not ordinarily die until "thoroughly ripe," but when any "buds new blown" are
found "to have so short a date," we recognize "His hand alone that guides nature
and fate" (235). In 1669 a second death in the same family causes her to observe,
even more self-consciously, not only that the heavens once again "have changed to
sorrow my delight," but that by now she should have learned her lesson:

How oft with disappointment have I met
When I on fading things my hopes have set.
Experience might 'fore this have made me wise,
To value things according to their price. (236)

The price of a "Dear Grandchild [Named] Anne Bradstreet" may have been
high enough in its own right, but it was not infinite; and, though it seems cold to
say so, by the standard of that "stable joy" and "perfect bliss" we crave, a human
namesake is a "withering flower," a "bubble," or a "shadow." So powerful is the
need to remind herself of the vanity of her earthly loves that she momentarily
forgets the significance of death to the one dead; and, catching herself, once
again, past the verge of the usual mistake, she remembers only the orthodox lesson to herself: "More fool then I to look on that was lent / As if mine own, when
thus impermanent." Only belatedly does she remember to cheer her "throbbing
heart" with the assurance of placing the child "with [the] Savior . . . in endless
bliss" (236).

Then, as if the death of this three-year-old namesake had been a kind of crisis, the death of her one-month-old sister, five months later, gets a shorter, less
personalized farewell—not only a dangerous repining of yet another loss but also
a necessary summary of a lesson well taught but never quite accepted: "No sooner
came, but gone," so that now we weep for "Three flowers, two scarcely blown, the
last i' th' bud." The flower formula suggests Taylor's later response to the hard

fact of repeated childhood deaths, as does the conceit according to which all have been "Cropt by the Almighty's hand." Less convincing, however, is the explicit self-reminder: "yet is He good." In fact, the human response seems a little less than overflowing love:

> With dreadful awe before Him let's be mute,
> Such was His will, but why, let's not dispute,
> With humble hearts and mouths put in the dust,
> Let's say He's merciful as well as just.

As recompense to the living lies in some mysterious future, however, the best a committed poetic faith can do is commend this "pretty babe" to "rest with sisters twain" and there "in endless joys remain" (237). But the modern reader, with an ear trained to hear ironic remainder as the undersong of necessary resolution, the "Let's say" appears to give the game away:

> Let's say that our little show is over, and so the story ends.
> Why not call it a day, the sensible way, and still be friends?

For Bradstreet, however, the friendship in question is with God, and who can she turn to if he turn away? And so the sound again of patient orthodoxy: "Go pretty babe, go rest with sisters twain; / Among the blest in endless joy remain" (237). Never having "lost as much but twice," what other note to sound?

Of course she is not perfectly reconciled. Shall we say, on her behalf, that a God who had wished on purpose to establish enduring enmity between himself and his human seed could not possibly have done better than to arrange for infant death to follow hard upon the process of awkward-hopeful childbearing and painful-joyous childbirth? Puritan piety, when it finally arrives, is but the earnest effort to say something *else*. And what if they had been her own babes?

To those "eight birds hatched in one nest," all alive in 1659 when she remembered having "nursed them up with pain and care" (232), her only word is to offer a good-bye that meditates her own death. Yet the question of human relation lies just beneath the surface of the poem "To the Memory of [the] Dear Daughter-in-Law" who, at age twenty-eight, added her own name to the list of losses, leaving the poetic observer in shock: "And live I still to see relations gone, / And yet survive to sound this wailing tone." Branches lopped, tree itself fallen, the "bruised heart" of the near and necessary observer "lies sobbing at the root." If this to the mother-in-law, what to the "dear son"? "I lost a daughter dear, but thou a wife, / Who loved thee more (it seemed) than her own life" (238). What else to make of a love that continued to bear life unto death? And how will the "fainting bleed-ing heart" of the son compare this love with that of "Him alone that caused all this smart"? Better for him, perhaps, to hear but not to have to say "He knows it is the best" (239). And better for the piety of the poet bent upon the same to be excused from writing epitaphs for those dear enough to challenge in fact the love of God.

Simon Bradstreet—the beloved husband and busy official whose distin-guishing mark is that he lived long enough to pose, in 1689, for a spectral portrait of Hawthorne's "Gray Champion"—may seem hardly worth the love expressed; but then poetry may be supposed to have a life of its own. In any event, when Bradstreet's marital love is moved to "count the ways," including a way that "riv-ers cannot quench," she is nonetheless careful not to overlook the otherworldly dimension: "Then while we live, in love let's so persevere / That when we live no more, we may live ever" (225). Worldly love is in effect insatiable, but it may never become inordinate. Yet other efforts to express a love nothing on earth can satisfy or repay are a little less guarded, leaving the clear impression that familiar death aroused Bradstreet's Puritanism more effectively than an ongoing, if now and then interrupted, heterosexual relationship. The "loving hind" knows only that she "wants her deer"; the "pensive dove" cannot but "bemoan . . . her love and lov-ing mate"; with less scruple still "the loving mullet . . . launches on that shore, there to die / Where she her captive husband doth espy." And there appears to be only one cure for this unnatural lack: "Return my dear, my joy, my only love" (229). Elsewhere, to be sure, there are appropriate Christian petitions for bless-ings "Upon My Dear and Loving Husband His Going into England" (265); for comfort "In My Solitary Hours in My Dear Husband in His Absence" (267); and "In Thankful Remembrance for My Dear Husband's Safe Arrival" (270). Here, however, the only significant fact is the absence of a one and "only" love. And upon "Another" such occasion of enforced separation, the prayer is not to God for a safe return but to "Phoebus" to haste away, as "silent night's the fittest time to moan" (227). Apparently the temporary absence of the partner in wedlock does not arouse the same religious scruples as the death of children.

In fact, the paradigmatic "Letter to Her Husband Absent upon Public Em-ployment" deploys a symbol system so inherently secular as to defy typological redemption.[8] First, by a conceit of local geography, head and heart, separated by "but a neck," should not lie so far apart. Next come, without apology or embar-rassment, the pagan signs of the planets:

I, like the Earth this season, mourn in black,
My Sun is gone so far in's zodiac,

Whom whilst I 'joyed, not storms, nor frost I felt,
His warmth such frigid colds did cause to melt.
My chilled limbs now numbed lie forlorn;
Return, return, sweet Sol, from Capricorn. (226)

Then, as if to keep us from missing the sexual implications of this seasonal heat and cold, the reflection that, in the sun's absence, the chilly devotee can only "view those fruits which through thy heat I bore." The figure system precludes any reference to her own heats, but no inhibition prevents the expression of her wish that when the Sun

     . . . northward to me shall return,
I wish my Sun will never set, but burn
Within the Cancer of my glowing breast,
The welcome house of him my dearest guest. (226)

Immortal earthly love is incompatible with "nature's sad decree," of course, but again we get the sense that, did the possibility exist, Anne Bradstreet would not declare it altogether vain. Nor does the biblical self-identification—"Flesh of [her husband's] flesh" and "bone of [his] bone"—manage to keep Simon Bradstreet from postponing all thought of the last-day bridegroom supposed to be the only fitting answer to all the heart's desire.

Theological innocence is also the distinguishing mark of a moving meditation "Before the Birth of One of Her Children." "All things within this fading world hath end," one can always premise, and not much wisdom is required to know one can always die in childbirth. Nor are any ties strong enough to withstand "death's parting blow." And yet, full in the face of this evident vanity, natural love bids the expectant, fearful mother to address some "farewell lines" to the beloved husband and father. So that "when that knot's untied that made us one, / I may seem thine, who in effect am none." Flesh of thy flesh no more: what else to say? God grant you the long life denied to me. Bury my faults, but let "any worth or virtue . . . live freshly in thy memory." And then, more poignantly, "when thou feel'st no grief, as I no harms, / Yet love thy dead, who long lay in thy arms." Keep me alive in loving memory, as literally as possible—as if life renewed in the Bosom of Abraham were not quite comfort enough. Or else, if I am indeed to be replaced in that loving posture, protect "my little babes . . . from step-dame's injury"; and, as a minimum recognition of the inextinguishable wish to endure, "kiss this paper for thy love's dear sake, / Who with salt tears this last farewell did take" (224). Evidently not all Puritans are beyond love's need for natural reassurance.

Students, in search of moments they are pleased to identify as "the human," may set down this unabashed forget-me-not as one such—as if the master plot of American literary history were to find the moment when someone unhappily placed in history manages to stop being a Puritan. Yet a subtler observation could also be made: what we have here, in Bradstreet's just-in-case request, is a version of what Thomas Shepard does *not* record as his wife's actual last words. Which, we assume, his humanity wanted her very much to say. Either way, the point is pretty much the same: Bradstreet's most poetic moments are not necessarily Puritanism's highest moral note. Even though, in the end, the poetic career composes itself into the figure of orthodoxy. For when she consciously arranges to bid formal farewell to her life "As Weary Pilgrim," the only lover she can remember is the same Bridegroom a bereaved but well-weaned Shepard watches his own beloved wife go off to meet.

Vanished from this last accounting is any record of the loves that have bid fair to give the lie to the power of "vanity" as a universal claim. Present, instead, and fully willing to insist upon itself, is the memory of earthly suffering. The first listing, of the conditions remembered by some "weary pilgrim, now at rest"— "dangers . . . and travails," "burning sun," "stormy rains," "briars and thorns," "hungry wolves," "erring paths," "wild fruits . . . instead of bread," "thirst" to parch the tongue, and "rugged stones" to gall the feet—may seem at first conventions, yet the reader is expected to realize that the literal of Bradstreet's own life has not been far off from the poetic paradigm: *any* sensitive person's journey from earth to heaven is supposed to make sense under the aspect of pilgrimage, but here the speaker's migration from the settled estates of the Old England to the frontier condition of the New has made her conventional figure come very close to the literal. Thus we feel a kind of double force in the poem's turn to the familiar allegory: the "sins" and "sorrows" with which the "Pilgrim I" has been vexed are an extension of as well as a counterpart to the conditions of travel on foot through unfamiliar and unfriendly terrain.

In fact, having made the necessary but obvious connection to the life of the spirit, the poem immediately turns back, as it were, to the details of physical suffering—which we easily recognize not only as real but in fact the accumulated reason why this worldly-enough person is *so* eager at last to be rid of it all:

By age and pains brought to decay,
    And my clay house mold'ring away[,]

Oh, how I long to be at rest
And soar on high among the blest. (294)

Encountering there the dearly departed Sara Cotton, no doubt; perhaps even the homesick Emily Dickinson. Yet the communion of triumphant saints appears only a small part of Bradstreet's otherworldly longing. The driving concern is one of release from the house of pain:

This body shall in silence sleep,
  Mine eyes no more shall ever weep,
No fainting fits shall me assail,
  Nor grinding pains my body frail,
With cares and fears ne'er cumb'red be
  Nor losses know, nor sorrows see. (294)

What might appear elsewhere as a sort of programmatic *contemptus mundi* amounts here almost to a death wish. Yet Bradstreet evidently feels that her life of deprivation, loss, and physical pain has earned the right. And no doubt it were bad form if we, who have scouted so closely her temptation to love the world too much, now turned to accuse her of exactly the opposite failing.

An available piety asserts the proposition that death is, after all, a bed that Christ himself "did perfume"; and, more reassuring still, that

. . . when a few years shall be gone,
  This mortal shall be clothed upon.
A corrupt carcass down it lays,
  A glorious body it shall rise. (295)

And thus, with all due respect, we confirm our sense that Bradstreet's "vanity" attaches not to created—that is, imperfect—being as such: evidently the body does not *have to* suffer, sicken, and die; in its resurrected and "glorified" form it will do no such thing. In that form, of course, it will "of [its] Maker have the sight," along with "such lasting joys . . . / As ear ne'er heard nor tongue e'er told." Certainly not her own tongue, however poetic. And when, in a conclusion echoing the love language of Canticles, she anticipates the day on which she can say "come, dear Bridegroom, come away" (295), a perfect orthodoxy is marred not by any lingering love of husband and children, but only in our all-but-repressed suspicion that what Bradstreet most requires of heaven is a body that does not ache or bleed.

Which undergraduate naturalism is entitled to applaud, and other post-Puritan observers are in a weak position to criticize. Except perhaps to observe that it would be easy enough to reverse the emphasis of the customary student evaluation: the ineradicable humanism of Bradstreet's imagination represents less a happy separation of her deepest wishes from the dogmatic prescriptions of the historic creed that threatened to imprison her and more a failure to press her poetic expression to the level at which the deepest tensions of that creed could be credibly expressed. This was a poet, and no doubt, as the diction now and then insists, but not at the pitch it is possible to imagine. Educated (evidently) as a classicist, Bradstreet began with some big poems that versify the lore of a world which did not much engage the soul of the Puritan movement; and when she moved to disclose the vanity of that world (and, now and then, of the worldly motions of her own wayward soul), she wrote along the baseline of Puritan moral culture. Experiences of Nature's vanity she regularly inscribed—credibly, because set in tension its powerful temptation. But of the ambiguities of conversion or the self-delusion that haunts the life of sanctification we hear just nothing at all. Nor would the story told in her letter "To My Dear Children" have answered all the questions a scrupulous congregation might think to ask. Shepard might sympathize with her leanings toward the vanities, but where was an account of her Christian experience as such? And were he permitted to read her unpublished poems, he might well find himself wondering if she did not in fact honor that sunlike husband rather too much?

Yet the point is not to diminish but to distinguish. The body of American literature in the seventeenth century would be painfully diminished if Bradstreet had not lived or made bold to write; certainly its *general* interest would undergo a very drastic reduction. Still it is worth remembering how little is said about Bradstreet in the writings of Perry Miller—and how little the excitement of that incomparable form of literary criticism suffers from this fact. The prose of the first American Puritans is by itself an enormous literary fact: self-conscious in the understanding of its duty to the will of God, it remains committed to the project of disturbing, guiding, and reassuring a plain populace with the subtle and dramatic publication of an accumulated Christian psychology and with all the wit a godly task could well permit. Literary historians, accustomed to wonder why this culture produced so little poetry, used to explain that a colonial, indeed a frontier enterprise has other things to worry about. Yet what other colony, in the history of the world, can show an overflow of powerful expression to compare with the godly letters of first-generation New England? One might even risk the suggestion that if those same historians had had the wit to appreciate the astonishing prose product of the Puritans, they might have worried less about the paucity of their poems. Or tempted others, in response, to overstate somewhat the culture's openness to and achievement in the specialized department of poetry.

Eventually, perhaps, in the matchless inventions of Edward Taylor, it may be possible to observe that the highest form of intellectual inquiry and self-analysis is being represented in the lines of the poems; but the fact remains that Taylor writes with as much insight and wit in prose as in verse; and the connoisseur is tempted to suspect that the "meter-making argument" of his typological medita-tions has often been worked out elsewhere, independent of rhyme and meter. Taylor's rare mind does subtle work in almost all the writings he has left us, but it has been suspected that in his poems he often "preaches to the choir."[9] And, in the meantime, few have been tempted to overpraise the dogmatic verse of the Reverend Michael Wigglesworth, self-appointed laureate of the second genera-tion. Absent John Milton, it evidently took the life of poetry a little time to catch up with the way of New England.

———

Doggerel by some accounts, "The Day of Doom" is purely a joy to those who re-ally do relish the discovery of a new poet: nothing like this in Cotton, Shepard, or Hooker, my children; Calvinism 101, for a new generation, who appear to have been fatally attracted to this dramatic expression of their deepest fears and who needed to see if they could pass as well as their zealous parents the still-emerging but virtually definitive test of a willingness to be damned for the glory of God. Or whether, deep down, they would find themselves siding with one or another of the objections brought forth to oppose the last-day outcome of what Sovereignty has from the beginning decreed. For "The Day of Doom" does less to justify than simply to promulgate or advertise the ways of God—and then to discover with extreme prejudice an element of bad faith in the anxious expression of each of these self-justifying questions.

Accordingly, it has been a serious misprision to characterize Wigglesworth's most memorable effort as "flaming and sulfurous." It believes in a pretty literal hell, of course, and presses that reality upon those protouniversalists who protest that a good God could not possibly "delight in such a sight / as sinners misery" (89).[10] But only near the end of this long and very "talky" poem do we catch the pungent scent of burning flesh; and only briefly there. What stretches the poem out—from a melodramatic beginning in which the "carnal reason" (55) of thoughtless sinners is astonished by the untimely arrival of that last day to the final assignment of Saints and Others to their predestinated places—is a stage-managed discussion of enough of the sore points of Calvinism to convince even the least sympathetic reader that Wigglesworth is fully aware that his creed is a long string of hard sayings. And even at the end, another (quite familiar) question challenges the emphasis of the "wail, and cry, and howl" (109). All but conclusive, in fact, is Wigglesworth's own version of the defining test of weaned affections.

The scene, of course, is the breakup of families—not at the hour of a lamented departure by death but at the last-day separation into the rank of sheep or goat. In one moment nature and grace combine to make every true lover extremely solicitous of the fate of all the best beloved, whether husband or wife or child. Then, on a sudden, all is changed utterly: preference for any outcome other than that manifested in divine decree can appear only as unredeemed desire. As no such thing can appear in the Saints, it will remain for a certain Belle of Amherst to issue Nature's protest: I cannot rise with you, "Because Your Face / Would put out Jesus'"; here, instead, an excruciating but now outmoded test of affective discipline that is too strong for its own language:

> He that was erst a husband pierc't
> with sense of wife's distress
> Whose tender heart did bear a part
> of all her grievances,
> Shall mourn no more as heretofore
> because of her ill plight
> Although he see her now to be
> a damn'd forsaken wight. (106–7)

Even Shepard stops just short of this profession, as he watches his "dear, precious, meek, and loving wife" die into the arms of the bridegroom he knows they both have lived to love the best.[11]

And if Wigglesworth has the honor of provoking Emily Dickinson more sorely, he also enjoys the distinction of laying bare a number of telling arguments against Calvinist orthodoxy to which either the subtlety of his mind or the flexibility of his verse was not able to answer. The effect is very curious: the objections are mostly quite real, and often enough they are expressed with an admirable vigor; and the responses do the best they can, so that we never suspect the author is playing an ironic game of silent self-sabotage. Yet, as the answers often fall short of entire conviction, we get the distinct impression that the point is less rational illumination than faithful acceptance: the reader will recognize himself as a saint (or not) in his ability to accept a pointed version of some well-reputed group belief, *even though* the powers of the general reason—or perhaps only the local rhetoric—are inadequate to put to rest all the arguments against. Indeed, the poem seems to imply that a distinguishing mark of "carnal reason" is its inability to grasp and apply home the very doctrines in which an infallible Scripture most affronts the expectations of ordinary moral wisdom. No doubt the sense of distance between necessary difficulty and available solution is increased in the mind of the modern reader, not mindful of the prose places where more elaborate versions of the same arguments are presented; who cannot appreciate, that is, the power of the "fourteener" to make simple as well as memorable. But as the natural man's "Arminian" expectations have not changed very much from that day unto this, the difference is only relative. The ways of the Calvinist God have *never* been that easy to justify. And no doubt Wigglesworth deserves credit for making the difficulties of his system as explicit as he does.

Then too, as we have already remarked, the real point is to reveal how many degrees of bad faith can disguise themselves as rational objection. The classic case, perhaps, is that of the "civil honest men," those paragons of civic and domestic virtue who are, as Edmund Morgan long ago remarked, "on [the] way to Hell."[12] Their self-characterization, in Wigglesworth's ready vernacular, is just about perfect:

> Our way was fair, our dealing square,
> we were no wasteful spenders,
> No lewd toss-pots, no drunken sots,
> no scandalous offenders.

Still less have they been Whoremongers, Murderers, Idolaters, or Adulterers. No scandal to the commonwealth—or even to the purest church. But consider their tone:

> We hated vice, and set great price,
> by virtuous conversation:
> And by the same we got a name,
> and no small commendation. (79)

From which we readily infer that publicity has been their mode and social approval their motive; so that the reward they sought has already been awarded: good deeds have their place in the orthodox Puritan scheme, but never with so shallow a meaning. So that we scarcely require the voice of Christ to remind us that "piety" is required "no less than honesty"; or, if we are indeed willing to play the game of works, then "justice demands" not just a fair show of natural virtue but nothing less than "perfect obedience" (80).

Centrally placed in the poem's ongoing conversation, the "civil, honest men" serve as a sort of paradigm of spiritual impercipience: plausible but imperfect doctrine is everywhere exposed as just the sort of thing the not-*quite*-religious person is likely to think; or at least self-righteously to say, when a moment of self-justification offers itself. And many other protesters undo themselves in much the same way. Bible hypocrites point with pride to their "painful teaching, and pow'rful preaching," but the pride suggests that their fair works have been in fact quite "dead" (73). Recognizable church members recall their regular participation in the Lord's Supper—only to learn that, without the proper motives, this seal of grace is sacrilege. Subtler communicants avow an acceptance of God's "gracious promises" but give the lie to this *sola fides* by stressing too much the way they "prayed and wep't [and] fast days kept" (76). And Christ—unaware that he is creating a text for Edward Taylor[13]—readily observes that they ". . . did presume that to assume / which was not yours to take /And challenged the Children's Bread / yet would not sin forsake" (77) /Again it appears that one thing Puritan rhetoric can always accomplish is to detect the damning note of self-interest in any human claim to have fulfilled the well-publicized conditions of salvation. In the face of mystery, evidently the convert has to learn the lesson of silence.

Yet it must be confessed that Wigglesworth himself had not quite learned it. For Christ himself, unequipped with the acumen of Jonathan Edwards, cannot quite explain why moral inability, an effect of the Fall, is not a fair objection to something or other: "Ne can they grieve, nor yet believe, / that never were elected" (93). Tensely, we realize, an earlier moment is repeating itself: there, unchallenged as yet by any consideration other than his own concern for godly coherence, Christ explains that as election is simply a divine prerogative, no cranky questions need be asked. And, indeed, "all silence keep" while Christ recalls the Father's choosing "before the world's foundation" (65), his own suffering to redeem exactly those so chosen, the irrelevance of the actual sin of those redeemed, and, finally, the freedom of Sovereignty from the duty of self-justification:

My grace to one is wrong to none / none can election claim,
Amongst all those their souls that lose, / none can rejection blame.
He that may choose, or else refuse, / all men to save or spill,
May this man choose, and that refuse, / redeeming whom he will. (66)

Here, one feels, is the poem's safest Calvinist ground: who are we to demand of the universe an account of its peculiar justice? God knows and is satisfied. And the strength of this position is only emphasized by later attempts to explain.

The various replies to the questioners quoted above all have the effect of deferring the definitive answer from one version of the problem to another: "I damn you not because / You are . . . not elected" but because "you have broke my laws"; and those "God will save, such he will have / the means of life to use" (93); and God's decree does not compel anyone "against their will to good or ill" (94); and "Not for his Can . . . But for his Will" is any man "adjudged to hell" (95). Generations later, the prose of Edwards will work long and hard to demonstrate that the causes of willing, hidden from experience, are irrelevant to the moral quality of our actions. Wigglesworth can only assert as much, in verses meant to be more memorable than profound, in the form of a hard saying: reprobates are damned for the sins they did in fact intend; saints are saved in spite of those same sins. And if the point is indeed to offer the second generation, understood as having things a little too easy, an opportunity to measure their capacity for self-abnegation, then clearly it is a mistake to elaborate too fully. God is God. What did you think was meant by "sovereign"?

Nowhere is the problem of saying too much more drastically evident than in the infamous case of the hell-bound infants: some born dead, others dying before any available psychology could judge them capable of any "actual sin," they put their case with reason as well as pathos: If damned for sin in our own will, fair enough;

> But Adam's guilt our souls hath split, / his fault is charged on us;
> And that alone hath overthrown, / and utterly undone us.
> Not we, but he, ate of that tree / whose fruit was interdicted;

yet we share his punishment. Explain this: "How could we sin that had not been?" Or, if that is indeed inexplicable, by God *or* Edwards, then

> . . . how is his sin our,
> Without consent, which to prevent / we never had a pow'r?

And if you appeal to our corrupted nature, we'll simply ask, "O great Creator," why was that nature made so "depraved and forlorn," so "defiled . . . whilst we were yet unborn?" You'll say Adam, we suppose, but

> Behold we see Adam set free, / and saved from his trespass,
> Whose sinful Fall hath split us all . . . (99)

How is that supposed to work?

Well, let's see, so far there are two principal theories of original sin: Adam was both your "public head," designed to stand or fall on your behalf in some paradigmatic test of obedience, and also your "common root" (100) which, if self-corrupted, could only corrupt its branches.[14] You've heard the news: he fell. Had he stood, you'd hardly be quarreling now with the justice of your fair inheritance. Further—as the Infinite Mind seems to know all, not only all futurables but also all past contraries to fact—

> Had you been made in Adam's stead / you would like things have wrought,
> And so into the self-same woe, / yourselves and yours have brought.

Then, while we are waiting for infant wisdom to wonder if that more-than-statistical fact does not argue a depravity of nature prior to its alleged corruption by Adam, of which God alone could be the author, God suddenly moves back to his higher, safer ground: quite simply, I am *free* to save "the chief offender" and not his offspring or "Else my Grace would cease to be Grace." Salvation being "due to none," whom do I injure in choosing just some? "Am I alone of what's my own, / no master and no lord?" (101). Sinners—by nature if not by human act—may expect sin's well-known wages.

And yet a weakening God finds himself forced to concede that the infants may have a point: surely the sin of natural inheritance is "much less" than the sin of willful act. No Softy, he is not about to concede heaven to anyone unredeemed by grace; and limbo, like purgatory, is but a Papist fantasy. What to do? Oh dear, thinks the reader, better avoid this point altogether: let the sentimental disputants in the Wood-n-Ware Controversy face the argument from childhood innocence, in some kinder, gentler epoch.[15] But no: the nineteenth century did not invent the problem of sympathy; even Calvinists have a Mother. So here goes: original sin is sin indeed,

> . . . therefore in bliss / you may not hope to dwell;
> But unto you I shall allow / the easiest room in Hell. (102)

It is hard to imagine anyone satisfied with this answer—to a question so succinctly posed. So much so, that were there any other evidence, it would almost seem that there is something subversive about Wigglesworth's Calvinism.

Yet if Wigglesworth is helping to give the game away—like the tender-minded men explicitly charged with this offense in Joseph Haroutunian's account of "Piety Versus Moralism"[16]—surely the effect is unintended. Consciously, one supposes, this most public poet is sufficiently sure of his audience to offer them even *this* opportunity to prove that their moral fiber is still pretty tough. One more chance, that is to say, to affirm that they love God's will more than their own babies. Which the rediscovered novel of Susan Warner will still be trying to establish, against the flood tide of domestic affection in fiction.[17] Evidently one diametric antagonist of Calvinism is Sentimentality.

Surviving its own predictions, "The Day of Doom" became Wigglesworth's "best-seller," but "God's Controversy with New England" appears even better calculated to address the problem of second-generation Puritanism as such. And on a good day it can be bracing to demonstrate that, though also a fairly heavy-duty threat, it is in no sense just another version of "The Day of Doom"—any more than is "God's Determinations Touching His Elect." Some things are "Jeremiads," some things are not, even in America. Seventeenth-century men and women could hardly spare any of the various expressions of their passionately placed (then oddly sliding) convictions. And neither can we, unless we have decided to abandon all question of literacy and culture and begin our account of the world sometime yesterday afternoon.

And so we can surely spare the time to notice that Wigglesworth's nearly paradigmatic Jeremiad begins with a personalized "request" for the "Good Christian Reader" (42) not to feel accused if not actually guilty of the faults found to be flourishing in New England, not to think the author means to spare himself, and above all not to forget that the prophet speaks not from his own sense of what is acceptable behavior in a covenanted people but with the voice of God, imitated from his own works heard in the past on occasions similar enough to be considered typologic. That prefaced, Wigglesworth rehearses an extremely favorable view of the founding and first flourishing of his own dear New England: armies of saints were led into a wilderness from whence, at their approach, "darkness sad / Soon vanished away"; depending on the character of their response, natives were destroyed, sent fleeing, or "brought to civility" (44); and here, while Europe overflowed with blood, a covenanted people enjoyed such peace as permitted "Poor travelers" to sleep in desert places "as free from danger as at home." Home rule made possible the selection of rulers for their "wisdom and true piety" (45); temporal blessing "did abound" right along with the spiritual; and such was the delight taken by King of Kings in the placement of his throne and tabernacle that, as the "morning stars" of the Congregational Way shone brightly into the "noon-day" of the holy experiment, "many thought the light would last, / And be perpetual" (46).

Yet Hooker and Cotton did *not* live to see the second coming and, worse fate, a "strange and sudden change" came over the entire aspect of New England; so that an aging remnant of the original leaders covered themselves with "sack-cloth"—leading the prophet of the present to offer this metaphor of his own darkening vision:

> . . . I beheld and saw
> Our welkin overcast,
> And dismal clouds for sunshine late
> O'erspread from east to west.
> The air became tempestuous;
> The wilderness 'gan quake. (46)

What wonder, then, if he should hear "from above with awful voice" the response of the Almighty?

What the thunder said would make more sense to Perry Miller than to other interpreters of modernism. For want God asks, in a meter a little more sober than the fourteener employed so far, is the no-real-answer question with which a generation which merely inherited the effects of those great deeds of Christ in an earlier America seemed doomed to torture itself: "Are these the men?" Are these still the ones that "Forsook their ancient seats and native soil / To follow me into a desert land" (46)—and that out of love to "purest ordinances"? "Are these the men that prized liberty / To walk with God according to their light"? That I led safe across an ocean, planted on a "western shore," swept clean by "my fatal broom"? "Are these the men whose gates with peace I crown'd," whose natural life I "blest with bounteous store" and in whose heavens I placed those "glist'ring sun-like stars"? Whose "souls I fed . . . with finest spiritual food" and "With whom I made a Covenant of peace"? "Are these the same? *or* are some others come in place" (48)? Perfect dichotomy though this last question creates, the answer is simply, painfully *yes:* yes the same and yes different. A new generation, in all demographic fact, and yet—God willing—the very same people, constituted as such and preserved, as we still have reason to hope, by God's own covenant which—God knows—we renew on every suitable occasion. Confess we do, both our obligations and our shortcomings; confess we would our faith as well, if only that precious gift were given. And in the meantime, what? Is it not fitting for us to pursue our worldly callings with all due diligence?[18]

Different, of course, as the grace of God has turned wilderness into garden, yet not deaf to the chorus of calls to maintain a wilderness mind—a "mind of winter," shall we say?—in the midst of this very garden, remembering that comfort and satiety wait not in any New English Canaan but across the Jordan that separates Life and Death. And the same, surely, in church polity: panting indeed for pure ordinances, have we not solemnly entreated baptism for our own seed? And do we not wait, most of us, in that condition of aroused preparation which will one day lead, or so we pray, to the gift of faith and to the communion of saints embosomed therein?

Well, then, if so much the same, "how is it that I find / Instead of holiness carnality," "indifferency," and "dead-heartedness"? Whence comes in "pride, and luxury / debate, deceit, contention, and strife"? How explain "security," "sloth" (48) and, most fearful of all, "dissembling shows of holiness"? Let no fate willfully misunderstand: New England's the right place for grace, and some indeed "maintain a real root" thereof, requiring only "due correction." Others, though not enough, "still retain / Their ancient vigor and sincerity" and to such "praying saints I always have respect." On the other hand, you evident backsliders, "think not / That I shall still your evil manners bear," especially those that are "The seed of such as name my dreadful name" (49). The children of Christians being "an holy seed," heaven and earth must stand amazed to hear the report—"I children nourisht, nurtur'd, and upheld: / But they against a tender Father have rebelled." More for them could scarce have been done, but where I looked for "meekness" and "humility" I find instead

> An iron neck, a proud presumptuous hand;
> A self-conceited, stiff, stout, stubborn race,
> That fears no threats, submits to no command:
> Self-will'd, perverse, such as can bear no yoke;
> A generation ripe for vengeance stroke. (50)

Like the Israelites—except that they misused a "darker light and lesser means." Warned before, "by my ministers / To gird your selves with sack cloth and repent," what remains but to threaten to "strike at once an all-consuming stroke" (51). For the failure of New England might just *be* the end of the world.

"He ceased," as they say in their epics, and nothing remained to the faithful reporter but to watch the consequences: wave after wave of uncustomary sickness failing to call the people back, "fruitful seasons" are turned to barrenness by "parching drought" or "rain's excess" (52); so that "all things a famine do presage." See what thou hast got, O New England, "by riot and excess" (53). And prepare for worse.

> Or God, or thou, must quickly change;
> Or else thou art undone:

Wrath cannot cease, if sin remain,
Where judgment is begun. (54)

And—except for the final upturn, which opens up the space between Perry
Miller and Sacvan Bercovitch—there it all is: bright original glory, sad evidences
of a sorry falling-away, urgent calls to repent, clear evidences of God's displeasure
at the general failure to heed those calls, and a final threat of the end of the covenant and perhaps of the world, unless the backsliding is reversed. Soon. There is
not much reason to suppose that other latter-day Puritan prophets, with names
like Mitchell, Stoughton, Danforth, Shepard Jr., had recourse to the pattern of
Wigglesworth in constructing their own inventories of a failing identity; the
books of Jeremiah and Isaiah would have served their prose as easily as a poetic
estimate. But the fact that Wigglesworth's effort was then and is now the best remembered of the New England Jeremiads strongly suggests that poetry could became as popular as preaching; and, with the example of Milton still some years
off, that poetry was not at all incompatible with theodicy.

As to the final upturn, it seems significant that Wigglesworth—in the meter
of God's own dramatic speech—returns to the personal note of his "Author's request unto the Reader." The prophet is bound to carry out God's business of
judgment and threat, of course, and God alone knows how it's all going to end;
but meantime, and as for himself, the mood is one of hope, based in part at least
on patriotic love:

Ah dear New England! dearest land to me;
Which unto God hath hitherto been dear,
And mayst be still more dear than formerly,
If to his voice thou wilt incline thy ear. (54)

Wigglesworth may have contributed, that is to say, to the crazy-making sense
that his culture had to repent and scourge itself for the very things it felt otherwise obliged to do; and he certainly helps to create the feeling that, as the time to
repent is now, so the moment of glory is just a day away; but his intention, much
more simply, is to rally love of place in the service of a renewed dedication to the
vision that had brought it into being. "Consider well" the meaning of "the rod"
to the experience of a people in covenant: it means there still is time. And remember that "Thou still hast in thee many praying saints, / Of great account, and precious to the Lord." Not a claim to be presumed upon, to be sure, but not an
insignificant fact in the reading of the signs of the times.

The last word, then, is one of hope and love, not only to saints but also to
those who would be such:

Cheer on, sweet souls, my heart is with you all,
And shall be with you, maugre Satan's might:
And wheresoe're this body be a thrall,
Still in New England shall be my delight. (54)

The turn here may be less than the positive swerve—from end-time desire to local satisfaction—that marks the context of Samuel Sewall's prose poem to Plum island. But surely it is significant to see so solemn a verse duty end in pleasure. And, whatever else there may be to say about the motive and effect of Wigglesworth's efforts in and out of the common meter, we ought to observe that Puritan poetry has set itself the task of catching up with the work of its prose.

————

Reach begins to approach grasp, it might be argued, only in the rare performances of Edward Taylor—a literary figure sufficiently complex and accomplished to resist conclusive treatment in the coda to an epilogue. Yet perhaps the reader will accept with grace a few conclusions added to work done elsewhere, with the neck of appreciation pretty well extended.[19] The point again: in coming to love Shepard and Cotton more, we need not love Taylor less.

The eight occasional poems that appear in the Taylor manuscript as "Occurrants" have tended to loom somewhat too large in most anthology representations of Taylor's work—as if to emphasize the fact of the poem-as-such; and this at the very moment when developing Puritan sensibility was experimenting with the possibility of treating its own brand of theodicy in verse well beyond the model of Wigglesworth and of realizing that religious meditation, a lifelong project surely, was quintessentially a poetic task. Yet, where undergraduates rule, no harm, no foul. And some of these poems are indeed "representative." Certainly no one else currently taught in Departments of English could have written Taylor's lines "Upon a Sweeping Flood": explication may have a little trouble explaining the logic by which rain, pouring down in stanza one to quench the flames of that "carnal love" for which we could shed not one tear turns into the heavenly "excrements" of stanza two; or how our sins have turned from flames to laxative and emetic "pills," administered by our pride, as if we thought the "heavens sick." But no one misses the shock of this sudden insult—to a decorum that, even in the Jeremiad, may have become more polite than efficacious. And there can be no doubt how those excrements ought to affect the way we carry, henceforth, "our lofty heads" (471).[20]

Representative too, in the same minimalist sense, is Taylor's self-explicating tale "A Spider Catching a Fly" (464). The outcome of the drama enacted between these figures of a powerful Satan and a hapless natural man is perfectly predictable, of course, but the presence of a wasp, not prepared for in the title, complicates this miniature beast fable considerably: the spider's standing off from the more dangerous prey assures us that somewhere or other Satan has met his match—and leaves us wondering what to think if this little allegory does indeed imply Christ: Father Hopkins' windhover has stretched our imagination, perhaps, but Christ as a wasp seems a bit bizarre. Altogether more decorous, we think, is the more naturalistic appearance of that wasp, when "Chilled with Cold" (465). Appearing to be dead of the early morning chill, the little body stretches out, graphically, almost imagistically, to gather in the sun's increasing warmth until capable of movement, even flight, once more. Rather like Bradstreet envying the songs of natural praise instinctively sung by the cricket and the grasshopper, Taylor wishes that his human reason were as well attuned to heavenly influence as the wasp to its natural source of life. And of course Taylor's special decorum of the "homespun" effectively governs the diction, and even the conceit of his two poems on the life of grace as a sort of "Huswifery."[21] The better known of the two even manages to spin itself into a perfect Calvinist prayer: use my faculties as a spinning wheel on which to knit the garment with which my spiritual nakedness needs to be covered; only so can I be "clothed in holy robes" (467) for a glory that begins in the wedding feast of the Lord's Supper. Not even a perfect Puritanism, it appears, is so specialized as to defy poetry.

Though it trades somewhat oddly on a metaphor of a metaphor, "The Ebb and Flow" is nevertheless competent not only to convey a credible sense of the hot-and-cold fluctuations that must have characterized many a Puritan's search for satisfactory assurance but also to intimate, more personally, the paradox by which Taylor's piety seemed to reduce itself from a wildly out-flaming tinder box to the flameless fire of a little "censer" at the very time he became a priest to God's altar, charged with the duty of offering the "sweet incense" of public prayer up to God. And some reader, aware of the difficulty of inferring the presence of fire beneath the layer of ash that surrounds so ambiguously the spark once lit, is supposed to see the humor in calling the breath of God's own Spirit a "bellows"; for even a very dim and ash-covered faith will glow red-hot when that Big Wind is brought to bear. "Then"—*of course*—"thy fire doth glow" (470). The test, perhaps, would be to trust the presence of faith in other, calmer times.

And do we need to add that "Upon Wedlock and the Death of Children" is, along with Shepard's farewell to his second wife, a sort of high-water mark in the

Puritan expression of its peculiar sort of nonhumanism? Children are born and appear to flourish, like flowers in a garden, each in the joyful sight of the other, and both too young to suspect that some "hellish breath" might come along to "singe their plumes." What actually happens—though it may be a matter of interpretation—is that "a glorious hand from glory came" to crop one of these delightful flower-children, resulting in a sorrow that "almost tore [up] the root" of the father's own faith: a "dolesome, darksome hour" indeed. But down the path of resentment lies the way of madness, and so the same vision which detected a "glorious hand" rather than a "hellish breath" reminds itself, whether the garden is the instituted Church or merely the Christian family, the little slips planted there were God's more truly than his own. And so the first reassurance:

> Christ would in glory have a flower, choice, prime,
>   And having choice, chose this my branch forth brought.
>   Lord, take't. I thank thee, thou takest aught of mine,
>   It is my pledge in glory, part of me
>   Is now in it, Lord, glorifi'd with thee. (469)

Clearly he knows just what to say, at least as well as Bradstreet; and if the "sweet" that "perfumed [his] thought" seems a little too sweet, we need to remember what it answers and compensates: a grief that all but tore him up.

And then—as if God himself had begun to learn that Puritan management of grief involved a poem that had to stop and then start itself again—a second visitation of that same heavenly hand. At which the reader wants to rage: keep your flower-picking hands out of my garden of children! And Taylor himself adjusts the verse to match the grief. In the first instance: we had two children, "But oh!" one died. Here, however, a movable "Oh!" slides to a different moment of emphasis entirely: praying about our life of sex and sainthood, we were gifted with two more children; again one died,

> But oh! the tortures, vomit, screechings, groans,
>   And six weeks fever would pierce hearts like stones. (469)

What Thomas Shepard no doubt repressed, in recalling the death of his first son named Thomas, Taylor has caused in one graphic couplet fiercely to appear. A token, no doubt, from which the worst may be inferred: "Grief o'er doth flow," more than just a little; what wonder if "nature fault would find"? What submission will require, evidently, in a line made to parallel the list of terrible symptoms, is to discover in the divine will "my spell, charm, joy, and gem" (469). Only then, it appears, can the faithful father safely repeat his chosen form of comfort:

> That as I said, take, Lord, they're thine.
>   I piecemeal pass to glory bright in them.
>   I joy, may I sweet flowers for glory breed,
>   Whether thou gets them green, or lets them seed. (470)

A moment like that of Bradstreet's "dreadful awe" gives way not to some pious wish to "say he's merciful" but to express poetic joy in remembering that the Garden of the world is God's.

Beyond this famous "complaint," the same battle of natural affect and Puritan wisdom is evident in Taylor's various essays at the formal elegy. The five-part poem "The Death of . . . Mr. Samuel Hooker" overstays the length of the poet's personal grief, but the same remark has been made in Milton's "Lycidas"; and, as a self-conscious successor to poetic amateurs like Bradford and Cotton, Taylor makes it clear that when "grief" truly is "a duty," its proper poetic vent must involve more than "non-sense sobs" (476). As a practiced poet, therefore, Taylor offers first "To New England," then, more specifically, "To Connecticut," to "Farmington," and "To the Family Relict," including both the "mourning widow" (483) and the "stems of his root, his very flesh and bone" (484), the comfort appropriate to loss of this "pastor very choice," this "loving husband," this "tender father" (479). What the effort may lack in the way of personal poignancy, it more than makes up for in the civilized sense that poetry is what somebody has to do when, in the face of death, there is nothing else to be done. Bosom friend or not, an important personage has passed away; and, with more conviction than he could have commanded in any of the elegies he wrote at Harvard,[22] his effort expresses the premise that "It surely would / Be sacrilege [his] worth back to withhold" (477).

Too formal by half is the diagrammatic love poem that springs up from the "Dove Letter" written to Elizabeth Fitch: curious for its representation of a heart that looks alarmingly like a cunt,[23] it may serve as a reminder, for those who need it, that Emblems, in innocency and then in decadence, were things they used to write back in England. But that was then. And well may the same plain-dealing Elizabeth Fitch have been wondered whether, according to the logic of the tribute beginning "Were but my muse an huswife good," her suitor loves her more or less for her not making the same demands on him as does, say, a poem of John Donne. Our conclusion here, at a minimum, is that we have seen this sort of thing done better elsewhere and that we are still fairly far off from discovering, in a poetry worthy of the name, the sort of intense and sustained intellectual work the Puritan Mind was born to do. Can it be that Puritan ministers *also* feel the need to plead for sex? Well, then, be it so. Buy flowers and candy, Ed; lose the verse. Or, if writing only floats her boat, cease at least to "affect the metaphysics."[24] It's way old.

On the other hand, only the slightest hint of necessary performance tinges Taylor's three-part outcry at the death of that same beloved Elizabeth. And none at all in the very personal "Part 1." Aware that he is at the fault line of Puritanism's domestic theology, Taylor is anxious to proceed with caution. Indeed with permission:

> My gracious Lord, I license of thee crave,
> Not to repine but to drop on the grave,
> Of my dear wife a tear, or two; (471)

God having summoned her soul away, the bereft husband asks only the right "in salt tears . . . to embalm her clay." And to raise the question Bradstreet could only hold off at arm's length: does death in fact "the true love knot untie"? He hardly *feels* it so. In fact,

> I do but find it harder tied thereby
> My heart is in't & will be squeezed therefore
> To pieces if thou draw the ends much more.
> Oh strange untying! It tieth the harder: What?
> Can any thing untie a true love knot? (472)

Nothing *so far,* a buried logic seems to suggest: we buried "five babes" together, and these arrows shot into the bowels scarcely went unnoticed; but what makes this loss "strike and stab . . . in the very heart" is that it has removed the "bosom friend" he held as a "comfort." What consolation now?—unless the poem find some other way to turn.

As of course it must: "Yet my Lord I kiss thy hand," it faithfully confesses. And though the language is all his own, the reader recalls the Shepard plot: "I her resign'd, thou tookst her into thine / Out of my bosom" (472). And if "yet she dwells in mine," call that natural remainder not the settled idolatry of an affection unweaned but the inevitable entailment of the cunning and "curious knot God made in paradise" (468). A conundrum, perhaps: can God tie a knot so tight that even he cannot undo it? Or perhaps simply a temptation: can a type forget its own first loveliness? Consoled, no doubt, by an honest belief that "her precious soul now swims in bliss," the poet finds nevertheless his "harp is turned to mourning" (472). Of which there may well be too much, of course; but also, by some other standard, too little:

> Grief swelling girds the heart strings where it's purst,
> Unless it vent the vessel sure will burst.

"A little ease," as Melville knows enough to ask of no one but his song. But perhaps even the most jealous God ever imagined may be entreated for a moment's respite:

> My gracious Lord, grant that my bitter grief
> Breathe through this little vent hole for relief. (110)[25]

The alternative, he manages to imply, would not be edifying. And at this moment of truce, so to speak, we measure again the breaking point of its all-but-unbearable regimen. Less intense, Parts 2 and 3 of this composite "Funeral Poem" retreat from the frontier of Puritan grief-work in order to perform other essential functions. To complete, first of all, a literary task begun long ago:

> What[!] shall my preface to our true love knot
> Frisk in acrostic rhymes? And may I not
> Now at our parting, with poetic knocks
> Break a salt tear to pieces as it drops? (111)

Indeed: if derivative absurdity then, why not a little sober reflection now? But also, taking the duty of poetry in a more general sense, to make sure that true worth, equal in its own less visible way to that of Samuel Hooker, does not go unrecognized. How otherwise "shall thy babes, & theirs, thy virtuous shine / Know, or pursue unless I them define"? And thus, in the hope that "some angel may my poem sing / To thee in glory," Taylor sets out to dress "in hyperboles" (111) a suitable recognition of her extraordinary qualities as faithful wife, prudent housekeeper, tender mother, courteous neighbor, and exemplary church member—no "gaudy Christian" but a "real Israelite indeed" (113).

Taylor also writes of his own death, of course, but with a prolepsis that seems less inspired than merely determined and dutiful. A fifty-line reflection "Upon [his] recovery out of a threatening Sickness in December, 1720", convincingly expresses a pilgrim-like wish to be "free of the world brim full of sin & woe" (218).

Somewhat more famously, "A Fig for thee Oh Death" is successful enough in staring down the "King of Terrors" with the "ghastly eyes" (261), confident that destruction of the mortal body is the worst thing that last menace can threaten. But the two separate versions suggest neither heightened poetic effect nor deepening insight but merely the need to keep thinking sanely about a subject that presses upon age and failing vigor. The various versions of the various "Valedictory Poems" suggest a person somewhat too intent on putting his spiritual (and poetic) house in order—as if the insult of Death could be prepared for in the same way as the blessing of the Lord's Supper. And no injustice will be done if the reader forms his impression of the final stages of Taylor's poetic career from the last contributions to the long sequence on Canticles which ends his Second Series of *Preparatory Meditations*; for as he had realized, very early on, it was not the common fact of death but the rare gift of the Lord's Supper that made him a poet and sustained his effort over a life more than long enough for boredom or distraction to set in. And that inspired him, in both the "Meditations" and that rare epitome of Puritanism he called *God's Determinations Touching His Elect,* to dare in verse a set of language effects equal, finally, to the great prose works of the first New England generation.

————

Milton is an American poet only if somebody's reputation for academic eccentricity depends on it.[26] And surely Shakespeare's "brave new world" has fewer original literary creatures in it than our Americanist philosophy might wish. Taylor is what we have—to express the fading wish for a poetry that might be an *acknowledged* legislator of the world; or else, at the very least, that it might defend itself against the minimalist definitions of Edgar Poe. One wonders, for example, what impression Taylor's regular preparations for each communion Sunday, had they been published, might have made on Solomon Stoddard; for, certainly, to open the Supper were to stop the mouth of this prolific model of meditation, whose special gift it was to associate assurance of salvation with an ever more joyous appreciation of Scripture's rich typology of feasting and celebration. Stoddard seemed certain that the way of Taylor and the Mathers was sure to turn sacrament Sundays into "days of torment"; but Taylor's soul seems pretty sure of its "wedding garment" logic.[27] And indeed his meditative performance is almost sufficient to persuade one of the wisdom of counting Canticles into the canon.

And what might a generation of anxious "professors" have made of the "double standard" offered up in *God's Determinations*?—a poem which, in the beginning, makes appropriate fun of Milton's attempt to have God and Christ reason themselves, like schoolmen, out of the tangled logic of foreknowledge, freedom, and fall; and which, at the very end, reminds a not quite coherent John Bunyan that we neither walk to salvation nor go there solemn and alone, but ride in a coach, with other saints, all singing. One way, obviously, to be sure of God's acceptance is God's immediate promise, well represented in the trope of whispered words: "Peace, Peace, my Honey." But perhaps there is another way, for those "duller scholars of the Mysterious Bard" not caught up in the rapture of John Cotton, to be sure *enough*: "To learn the transport by the pain." The *via negativa,* that is to say, as it survived from the earnest proposal of Thomas Shepard to the wry rejection of Emily Dickinson.[28]

Of course, there are moments when Taylor's high argument lapses from inspired poetic translation to needful explanation merely—as when Satan's aside reminds too much of the audience that, in barking the sheep back into the fold, he is of course only playing the part a wiser and more powerful God has assigned him. But there are also moments when the snake really does have all the lines—as when he notices the common fact of "temporary faith":

> Soon ripe, soon rot. Young Saint, Old Devil. Lo
> Why to an empty whistle did you go?
> What[?] come uncalled? And run unsent for? Stay,
> It's children's bread: hands off: out, dogs, away. (407)

Or with reference to the interior discoveries to be made by an honest conscience:

> Nay, nay, what thoughts unclean? lascivious?
> Blasphemous? murderous? And malicious?
> Tyrannic? wrathful? Atheistic rise
> Of evils, new and old, of e'ry size?
> These bed and board here, make thy heart a sty
> Of all abominable brothelry. (410)

And if, in this poem as elsewhere, the decorum governing doctrine and diction borders on what the students want to call the "goofy," our response can only be to ask ourselves where else, in or out of Puritanism, we might look for the sort of divine comedy which everywhere knows that—stuck as we are with tropes, even if they happen also to be types—the task of theology is one we must strive to meet, even if our very best efforts are doomed to parody.[29] The problem is not Calvinism but language: we *must* yet we really *cannot* talk about God. What wonder if it took some time for Godly Letters themselves to reach the conclusion that, with proper mimesis out of the question, one might as well go with the astonished affect? Thus creation might as well compare itself to bowling and original sin come to seem not unlike a fall in the mud.

The point, once again, is not to slight an interest in the Puritan Origins of American Poetry, but merely to insist that poetry is not the aboriginal product of Puritan culture; that it reaches its full expressive capacity rather late; and that, early or late, it does only a small portion of the work a vital and energetic society requires its verbal expression to perform. Let the Puritan soul be as keenly attuned to the beauty of the world as anyone might require—and poetry as important a cause as anyone pleases—there remain other tasks for high-level literacy to perform in the name of complex culture.[30] Nor did the Puritans rest silent, waiting for their representative man to appear. Indeed, they all but knocked one another down in the effort proclaim God's piercing word as their own top note.

And so to say it all at once: the original generation of New England represents as vital and energetic an experiment as we are likely to find anywhere within the modern world of repeated new departures. No sober reader of Bradford can doubt that his "Pilgrims" really meant to continue their communal experiment in exemplary Christian living, and that they were themselves quite surprised when expanded economic opportunity, itself made possible by the flourishing of further Puritan migrations, turned the peopling of the Kingdom into the settlement of America. Only the drowsy will fail to notice that Shepard found that life forced certain choices upon him—first for Christ, next for New England, and finally for a theology of sanctification—in ways he could never have predicted; and that his various explanations of the ways in which certain choices are first impossible and then wondrously enabled amount to a body of religious reflections that leave us feeling foolish if we object too much to the egotistical premise of his own election. Or that Hooker's enormous, "preparatory" preface to Shepard's luminous moment of enabled volition constitutes a "variety" of religious experience it were folly to disregard: for what if the true sight of sin is the most that the democracy of divine grace can predictably and on a large scale accomplish in this life? Or doubt that if there is *indeed* something more of salvation truly to be known, that Cotton's studied (epistemological) denial that sanctification may figure as the (poor doubting) Christian's "primitive" comfort represents a necessary prolegomenon to any future Protestant theology. Or that these questions lie at the heart of the history of the Puritan project in America which, whatever our after-the-fact reservations, seemed demanded of them in the name of God. Not to that minority of one we know as Roger Williams, to be sure, but to enough of a population of enthusiastic emigrants that neither John Winthrop, present at the creation, nor Edward Johnson, anxious to recoup it all again before the moment should pass, can imagine that their story makes sufficient sense to any eye or ear but that of God, whose life they knew to be longer than any art of theirs.

With a new generation, a new set of writerly motives; and also, no doubt, a radically new sense of audience: the theory of New England life having already been made luminously clear, little remained but to offer judgment on its sustained embodiment or puzzling failure to thrive. Bradstreet endures, as if to bear private witness to the continuity of the question of worldliness. Taking the matter public, Wigglesworth writes the nostalgic wish "to live ancient lives"[31] very well—just not better than Jonathan Mitchell, Thomas Shepard Jr., or Samuel Danforth. And we might well learn to think of Taylor as studying to do something *other* than the Jeremiad. Which he learns to do, uniquely. But we can pay him no higher compliment than to claim that, against considerable odds of time and place, he wrote his way up to the level of the Founders—for whom the writing of an appropriate religious literature seemed less to augment than to constitute the godly life, and whose rare life product a serious modern reader might yet learn to value. Not a godliness for its own sake; and nothing like an art *as such*. And yet, all unpredictably, a Godly Letters like none other.

NOTES

AL	American Literature
ALH	American Literary History
ATR	American Theological Review
AQ	American Quarterly
AzQ	Arizona Quarterly
CH	Church History
EAL	Early American Literature
EIHC	Essex Institute Historical Collections
EL	Essays in Literature
FS	Feminist Studies
HTR	Harvard Theological Review
JA	Jahrbuch für Americastudien
JEH	Journal of Ecclesiastical History
MP	Modern Philology
NCL	Nineteenth-Century Literature
NDEJ	Notre Dame English Journal
NEQ	New England Quarterly
NHR	Nathaniel Hawthorne Review
PMLA	Publications of the Modern Language Association
SAH	Studies in American Humor
SN	Studia Neophilologica
WMQ	William and Mary Quarterly

PREFACE

1. Palpable in American Colonial Studies before the recent shift of interest to a more secular political paradigm, the influence of Miller may be conveniently reviewed in David D. Hall, "Understanding the Puritans," in *The State of American History,* ed. Herbert J. Bass (Chicago: University of Chicago Press, 1970), pp. 330–49; and Michael McGiffert, "American Puritan Studies in the 1960's," *WMQ* 27 (1970): 36–67. Rereviewing the problem in 1987, Hall remarks that, though much has changed, "Perry Miller's structure of interpretation remains a focus of discussion" (p. 194): see "On Common Ground: The Coherence of American Puritan Studies," *WMQ* 44 (1987): 193–229. The only comparable

paradigm-creating force in American literary study would be that exercised by the period-creating power of F. O. Matthiessen's *American Renaissance* (New York: Oxford University Press, 1941); see my "American-Renaissance Renaissance," *NEQ* 64 (1991): 445–93.

2. For Douglass' abandonment of the paradigm of American declension from purity, see William L. Andrews, *To Tell a Free Story* (Champaign-Urbana: University of Illinois Press, 1986), pp. 123–38, 214–39; and cp. David Van Leer, "Reading Slavery," in *Frederick Douglass: New Literary and Historical Essays,* ed. Eric J. Sundquist (Cambridge: Cambridge University Press, 1990), pp. 118–40.

3. For the place of Bradford's *Plymouth* in a plausible narrative of the search for community in American literature, a search consciously continued in Hawthorne's *Blithedale Romance* (1852), see A. N. Kaul, *The American Vision* (New Haven: Yale University Press, 1963), pp. 9–18. For the signal (and predictive) failure of that vision, see Robert Daly, "William Bradford's Vision of History," *AL* 44 (1973): 557–69.

4. If ever the verbal product of one generation daunted the creativity of the next (and the next), such was certainly the inhibitory power of the overflowing achievement of original New England. And this literary effect may be the most important form of what is everywhere called "declension": unable to write their way up to the originary standard, sons and grandsons could only play variations at the words of the Founders.

5. Reviewing the Richard S. Dunn edition of *The Journal of John Winthrop* (Cambridge, Mass.: Harvard University Press, 1996), Sargent Bush suggests that "there is no other document like Winthrop's Journal for its combination of factual data about the colony and personal revelation of a central figure's character"; see "A Text for All Seasons," *EAL* 33 (1998): 97.

6. For the "Reasons" Winthrop gave himself for deciding to head the Puritan expedition to New England, see *Winthrop Papers,* vol. 2 (rpt. New York: Russell and Russell, 1968), pp. 138–45. And for the group's claim of nonseparation, see, in the same volume, "The Humble Request," pp. 231–33.

7. In the revised edition of *God's Plot* (Amherst: University of Massachusetts Press, 1994), Michael McGiffert has included the various "Confessions of Lay Men and Women" (pp. 149–225) given in Shepard's Cambridge church and written out in his own hand. Those confessions form the basis of Patricia Caldwell's *The Puritan Conversion Narrative* (Cambridge: Cambridge University Press, 1983).

8. My sense of the development of the recent origin and development of the ideology of the esthetic is based on the complementary work of M. H. Abrams and Terry Eagleton—opposing, at least implicitly, the "traditionalist" account of Murray Krieger. See Abrams, "Art-as-Such" and "From Addison to Kant," in *Doing Things with Texts* (New York: Norton, 1989), pp. 135–87; Eagleton, *The Ideology of the Aesthetic* (London: Basil Blackwell, 1990), esp. pp. 1–101; and (in contrast) Krieger, *The Theory of Criticism* (Baltimore: Johns Hopkins University Press, 1976), esp. pp. 98–148.

9. The doctrinal passages in *The Pilgrim's Progress*—e.g., the conversation of Christian first with Hope and then with Ignorance—make Bunyan's strict Calvinism apparent. The drama of his narrative, on the other hand, requires an all-but-Arminian sense that Christian's "free" choices are the only factors in the story of his salvation; nowhere does Bunyan explain that the choices will of course be grace assisted.

10. See Sargent Bush Jr., *The Writings of Thomas Hooker* (Madison: University of Wisconsin Press, 1980), pp. 152–85.

11. In no less a critic than Northrop Frye, one notices with chagrin an echo of the weary complaint, virtually universal in early modern philosophy, that, compared to the sciences, the humanistic disciplines have never really advanced; see *Anatomy of Criticism* (Princeton: Princeton University Press, 1957), pp. 3–29.

12. For the criterion of unity as a condition of esthetic experience, see Krieger, *Theory of Criticism,* pp. 98–148.

13. Building on the suggestions of Sargent Bush (see note 10 above), my reading wishes to notice that a Puritan treatise, like any work of considerable length, discovers the need for both rhetorical invention and philosophical self-editing in order to make an insight sustain itself to the length of a book. A phenomenon we might call "Doctrine and Difference."

14. Famously contending that "there is no document of civilization that is not also a document of barbarism," Walter Benjamin protests the literary historian's exclusive emphasis on "cultural treasures"; see "Theses on the Philosophy of History," in *Illuminations,* ed. Hannah Arendt (New York: Schocken Books, 1968), p. 258. Yet it would seem lazy and impercipient not to identify the existence and certify the power of works of verbal genius as such.

15. A book on second-generation Puritanism might discover "declension" to be as much a literary as a social fact. My treatment of Taylor's brilliant rise to the challenge of the first generation presumes work done elsewhere; see "Christ's Reply, Saint's Assurance," in *Doctrine and Difference* (New York: Routledge, 1997), pp. 27–60.

16. E. D. Hirsch has attempted to revive, from Renaissance usage, the term "bonnes lettres" to account for works of significant intellectual impact that have become canonical quite apart from the (modern) premise of esthetic pleasure; see *The Aims of Interpretation* (Chicago: University of Chicago Press, 1975), pp. 124–25. The concept is put to good effect in Richard E. Brantley, *Anglo-American Antiphony* (Gainesville: University of Florida Press, 1994). The Emerson reference is to "Experience"; see *Essays and Lectures* (New York: Library of America, 1983), p. 484.

CHAPTER 1.   A COSTLY CANAAN

1. The treatments in question are, in historical order, Charles Francis Adams, ed., introduction to *New English Canaan* (rpt. New York: Burt Franklin, 1967), pp. 1–105; William Carlos Williams, *In the American Grain* (rpt. New York: New Directions, 1956), pp. 75–80; Richard Slotkin, *Regeneration through Violence* (Middletown, Conn.: Wesleyan University Press, 1973), pp. 58–70; and Donald F. Connors, *Thomas Morton* (New York: Twayne, 1969), pp. 36–122.

2. Though the two subjects sometimes overlap, the official bibliography of the Modern Language Association currently lists fifteen items on Morton published since 1963, compared to thirty-eight on Bradford. The most recent edition of the *Norton Anthology of American Literature* affords three times as much space to Bradford as to Morton; and in the more revisionist *Heath,* the proportion is still two to one.

3. For a suggestive account of Morton's discourse as "a loser's case," see Daniel B. Shea, "'Our Professed Old Adversary,'" *EAL* 23 (1988): 52–69.

4. For the self-reflexive allegory in the "May-pole," see Michael J. Colacurcio, *Province of Piety* (Cambridge, Mass.: Harvard University Press, 1984), pp. 251–82.

5. Citations of Morton's text refer to *New English Canaan* (New York: Da Capo, 1969), a facsimile reprint of the Jacob Stam (Amsterdam) edition of 1637. The reader may find it more convenient to consult Jack Dempsey's more recent edition, *New English Canaan* (New York: Digital Scanning, 2001). For the context of American landscape gendered female, see Annette Kolodny, *The Lay of the Land* (Chapel Hill: University of North Carolina Press, 1975), esp. pp. 3–25.

6. See William C. Spengemann, *The Adventurous Muse* (New Haven: Yale University Press, 1977), pp. 14–65.

7. For the identification of trees as the "real Sirens" of Columbus' response to the New World, see Tzvetan Todorov, *The Conquest of America* (rpt. New York: Harper, 1989), pp. 24–27.

8. For the beginnings of an esthetics of the list, see Wayne Franklin, *Discoverers, Explorers, Settlers* (Chicago: University of Chicago Press, 1979), esp. pp. 1–19.

9. See John Seelye, *Prophetic Waters* (New York: Oxford University Press, 1977), pp. 166–80; and cf. Slotkin, *Regeneration,* pp. 58–70.

10. Quoted from Todorov, *Conquest,* pp. 24–25.

11. Quoted from Todorov, *Conquest,* p. 25.

12. Howard Mumford Jones famously pointed out the power of the literary convention of the pastoral to (de)form eyewitness accounts of the New World; see *O Strange New World* (New York: Viking, 1952), pp. 1–34.

13. Citations of Smith's text are taken from volume 2 of Philip L. Barbour, ed., *The Complete Works of Captain John Smith* (Chapel Hill: University of North Carolina Press, 1986); page numbers are those of the original (1624) edition of Smith's *Generall History of Virginia, the Somer Isles, and New England*. For Smith's identity as "Evangelist of Fish"—as well as his invention of "the true colonist and the true colony"—see Evelyn Page, *American Genesis* (Boston: Gambit, 1973), pp. 124–38; and cf. Everett H. Emerson, *Captain John Smith* (New York: Twayne, 1971), pp. 103–9.

14. For the idea of wonder as the common note of New World reporting, see Stephen Greenblatt, *Marvelous Possessions* (Chicago: University of Chicago Press, 1991), esp. pp. 52–85.

15. Citations of Wood's text are from Alden T. Vaughan's edition of *New England's Prospect* (Amherst: University of Massachusetts Press, 1977).

16. In the view of his editor, Wood's occasional passages of verse are "not entirely successful as poetry"; see Vaughan, ed., *New England's Prospect,* p. 9.

17. For Williams' poems on "Indian" ways, along with his significant appreciation of Native American culture, see his *Key into the Language of America,* ed. John Teunissen and Evelyn Hinz (Detroit: Wayne State University Press, 1973), pp. 99, 104–5, 108–9, and passim.

18. See Colacurcio, *Province,* pp. 272–75; and cp. J. Gary Williams, "History in Hawthorne 'May-pole of Merry Mount,'" *EIHC* 108 (1972): 173–89.

19. Apologizing for many important "omissions" from the journal that enabled his *Week on the Concord and Merrimac Rivers* (Princeton: Princeton University Press, 1980), Thoreau excuses the oversight on the ground that "to write is not what interests us" (p. 332).

20. The identity of Morton himself remains rather vague—compared, for example, with that of Bradford, even though his *Plymouth* is, famously, a very unsubjective book. Clearly Morton fails the "Thoreau" test: "I, on my side, require of every writer, first or last, a simple and sincere account of his own life." Foucault, be still.

21. For the prepublication history of the Bradford manuscript, which did not appear until 1857, see Samuel Eliot Morison, ed., *Of Plymouth Plantation* (rpt. New York: Modern Library, 1967), pp. xxvii–xl. When Morton's *Canaan* was published (in Amsterdam, 1637), Bradford's work was still very much in process.

22. Tracing the error—of "French" for "Indians"—to an 1836 reprint of the *Canaan,* Dempsey accuses Charles Francis Adams of knowingly reprinting the error and then accusing Morton of "confused and misleading statements" (Dempsey, ed., *Canaan,* p. 106).

23. Unlike undergraduate sarcasm or professional cynicism, literary satire requires a generally accepted standard of behavior; see M. H. Abrams, *A Glossary of Literary Terms* (New York: Harcourt Brace, 1985), pp. 187–90.

24. For Bradford's treatment of the Weston story, see Morison, ed., *Plymouth,* pp. 134–38.

25. See Morison, ed., *Plymouth,* pp. 204–5.

26. See Lawrence, *Studies in Classic American Literature* (rpt. Garden City, N.Y.: Doubleday, 1951), p. 14.

27. For Bradford's treatment of Lyford and Oldham, see Morison, ed., *Plymouth,* pp. 146–69.

28. For useful efforts to dispel the murk of "Rise, Oedipus," see Robert D. Arner, "Mythology and the Maypole of Merry Mount," *EAL* 6 (1971): 156–64; and Edith Murphy, "Solving the Riddle of Thomas Morton's 'Rise, Oedipus,'" *WMQ* 53 (1996): 755–68.

29. For Endicott's "hysterical" response to the maypole at Merry Mount, see Colacurcio, *Province,* pp. 265–69.

30. See Connors, *Morton,* p. 102; also Dempsey, ed., *Canaan,* p. 152. As to Master Bubble, Connors repeats Morison's speculation that he may refer to Mr. Rogers, whom Bradford found "crazed in his brain" (p. 150).

31. The official Puritan account of the final disposition of Morton's second banishment is provided by John Winthrop; see Richard Dunn, ed., *The Journal of John Winthrop* (Cambridge, Mass.: Harvard University Press, 1996), pp. 535–39.

32. For speculations on the classical context and possible abstruse meanings of Morton's final *"Cynthius aurem vellet"* ("Apollo will pluck your ears"), see Shea, "Adversary," pp. 65–66; and cf. Dempsey, ed., *Canaan,* p. 199.

33. For Franklin, Bradford's *Plymouth* is the epitome of "Settlement Narrative"; see *Discoverers,* pp. 165–78.

34. For Smith's complicated and shifting relation to the Virginia project, see George F. Willison, *Behold Virginia* (New York: Harcourt Brace, 1951), pp. 44–104.

35. For Bradford's account of what his editor titles a "New Deal," see Morison, ed., *Plymouth,* pp. 184–88.

36. In the judgment of Willison, the various members of the council in Virginia were interested "only in themselves and their petty ambitions" and thus "spent their entire time bickering, quarreling, and scheming against one another" (*Behold Virginia,* p. 36).

37. Other prime examples of the power of Pilgrim self-representation are the sermon delivered to the departing members of the Leyden congregation by the Reverend John Rob-

inson and the discouraged letter of Robert Cushman to Edward Southworth; see Morison, ed., *Plymouth,* pp. 368–71, 54–57.

38. The tone of Bradford's arrival scene has been misread as really and simply— rather than strategically—pessimistic; see, e.g., Ursula Brumm, "Did the Pilgrims Fall upon Their Knees . . . ?" *EAL* 12 (1977): 25–35.

39. John Seelye's *Prophetic Waters* may be regarded as the exemplary attempt to begin American literary history well before the arrival of the Pilgrims: Columbus, Cartier, and Smith get their originary due, but once Seelye gets to New England, the Puritans take over.

40. See Daly, "Bradford's Vision," pp. 565–69.

41. For the "primitivist"—or at least the recuperative—desire of the New England Puritans, see Theodore Dwight Bozeman, *To Live Ancient Lives* (Chapel Hill: University of North Carolina Press, 1988), esp. pp. 3–50.

42. In Connors' memorable formulation, it is not at all surprising that Morton's *Canaan* has had "little or no influence on nineteenth- and twentieth-century writing": this "lesser Lyly" was capable of the "witty phrase and the slashing epithet," but the "language and form of his book, like many of its ideas, belong to the past" (*Morton*, p. 130).

43. For a reading of Cabeza de Vaca's "Narrative" that makes it highly comparable to the Puritan interest, see Kun Jong Lee, "Pauline Typology in Cabeza de Vaca's *Naufragios,*" *EAL* 34 (1999): 241–62. For a more cosmopolitan approach, see E. Thompson Shields and Dana D. Nelson, "Colonial Spanish Writings," in *Teaching the Literatures of Early America,* ed. Carla Mulford (New York: Modern Language Association, 1999), pp. 97–111.

CHAPTER 2.   ADVANCING THE GOSPEL, DIVIDING THE CHURCH

1. Quotations of Bradford are taken from the Modern Library version of the Samuel Eliot Morison edition: *Of Plymouth Plantation, 1620–1647* (New York: Modern Library, 1967).

2. For the "theology" of travel, see William C. Spengemann, *The Adventurous Muse* (New Haven: Yale University Press, 1977), esp. pp. 6–67.

3. By his own account, Bradford first began his "scribbled writings" concerning Plymouth "about the year 1630"; the rest, he says, was "pieced up at times of leisure afterward"; see Appendix I of *Plymouth,* p. 351. Morison believes that Bradford finished only "through Chapter X" in 1630 (*Plymouth,* p. xxvii); but even if this is correct, the "vision" of 1630 informs all the annals up to that year; see Emory Elliott, "New England Puritan Literature," in *Cambridge History of American Literature,* ed. Sacvan Bercovitch (Cambridge: Cambridge University Press, 1994), pp. 84–89. For Bradford's "modesty," see Moses Coit Tyler, *History of American Literature* (rpt. Ithaca: Cornell University Press, 1949), pp. 100–109; Kenneth Murdock, *Literature and Theology in Colonial New England* (rpt. New York: Harper and Row, 1963), pp. 78–84; and, more recently, Alan B. Howard, "Art and History in Bradford's *Plymouth,*" *WMQ* 28 (1971): esp. 256–58.

4. This chapter builds on the foundational work of Robert Daly in "William Bradford's Vision of History," *AL* 44 (1973): 557–69; and on the brief analysis of William J. Scheick in *Design in Puritan American Literature* (Lexington: University of Kentucky Press, 1992), pp. 6–15.

5. For the discrepancy between Bradford's representation of the moment of arrival and that given in *Mourt's Relation,* see Ursula Brumm, "Did the Pilgrims Fall upon Their Knees . . . ?" *EAL* 12 (1977): 25–35. And for emphasis on the triumph of the arrival scene, see David Laurence, "William Bradford's American Sublime," *PMLA* 102 (1987): 55–65.

6. Quite likely the "Magnalia" of Cotton Mather is a conscious translation of Bradford's "wonderful works."

7. Morison, ed., *Plymouth,* p. 54. For a more generic account of Bradford's use of letters, within an episteme of "true relation," see Philip H. Round, *By Nature and by Custom Cursed* (Hanover, N.H.: University Press of New England, 1999), pp. 53–64.

8. Morison's *Plymouth* prints the farewell letter of Pastor Robinson as Appendix IV, pp. 367–71. The Francis Murphy adaptation of the Morison edition prints it in the body of the text; see *Of Plymouth Plantation* (New York: Random House, 1981), pp. 55–58. For a defense of the proposition that the letters Bradford has assembled are an important part of his greatness as a historian, deserving to be printed in the body of his text, see David Levin, "William Bradford: The Value of Puritan Historiography," in *Major Writers of Early American Literature,* ed. Everett H. Emerson (Madison: University of Wisconsin Press, 1972), pp. 11–31.

9. Winthrop is quoted from Alden T. Vaughan, ed., *The Puritan Tradition in America* (New York: Harper and Row, 1972), p. 31. Attempting to turn aside this objection, Winthrop argues that "Though miracles now be ceased, yet men may expect more than ordinary blessing from God upon all lawful means, where the work is the Lord's and He is sought in it according to His will, for it is usual with Him to increase or weaken the strength of the means as He is pleased or is pleased with the instruments and the action, else we must conclude that God hath left the government of the world and committed all power to the creature" (*Puritan Tradition,* p. 32). Facing a less drastic objection, Bradford says of the Pilgrims' decision to migrate that "their condition was not ordinary, their ends were good and honorable, their calling awful and urgent; and therefore they might expect the blessing of God in their proceeding" (p. 27).

10. In noting that Cushman and his family were among those returning to England when the Pilgrims lost the use of one of their two ships, Bradford observes that their "heart and courage was gone from them"; but after this, Bradford also observes, "he continued to be a special instrument for their good" (p. 54).

11. A UCLA graduate student of Native American descent, Betty Donohue, has referred to this incident as the seventeenth-century equivalent of knocking over the local 7-11 on one's first visit to the neighborhood.

12. Smith mentions his "salvation" by Pocahontas only once, briefly and long after the supposed fact (of 1607), in chapter 2 of the Third Book of his *General History* (1624); see Philip L. Barbour, ed., *The Complete Works of Captain John Smith* (Chapel Hill: University of North Carolina Press, 1986), p. 151.

13. For a comparison between Bradford's sense of providence and that of three other Pilgrim documents, see Kenneth Alan Hovey, "The Theology of History in *Of Plymouth Plantation* and Its Predecessors," *EAL* 10 (1975): 47–66.

14. See "The Relation of Man to the Globe," in *The Early Lectures of Ralph Waldo Emerson,* ed. Stephen Whicher and Robert Spiller (Cambridge, Mass.: Harvard University Press, 1959), vol. 1, p. 49.

15. The classic study of what Samuel Danforth would evoke as "New England's Errand into the Wilderness" is, of course, the title essay of Perry Miller's *Errand into the Wilderness* (Cambridge, Mass.: Harvard University Press, 1956), pp. 1–15. But see also Andrew Delbanco, *The Puritan Ordeal* (Cambridge, Mass.: Harvard University Press, 1989), esp. pp. 81–117; Theodore Dwight Bozeman, *To Live Ancient Lives* (Chapel Hill: University of North Carolina Press, 1988), pp. 81–119; and, for a more secular account, David Cressy, *Coming Over* (Cambridge: Cambridge University Press, 1987).

16. Miller, *Errand,* pp. 3–4.

17. One might well read, in Melville's *Pierre,* the skepticism about the lucid integrity of the reflecting human subject in the light of Puritanism as well as that of Deconstruction.

18. As M. M. Knappen makes clear, even this Father of English Separatism "looked forward to the day when the magistrate should support and defend his system against all adversaries"; see *Tudor Puritanism* (Chicago: University of Chicago Press, 1939), p. 305. See also William Haller, *The Rise of Puritanism* (rpt. New York: Harper and Row, 1957), pp. 181–90.

19. For the range of Winthrop's motives, see his "Reasons for Forsaking England," in Vaughan, ed., *Puritan Tradition,* pp. 25–35; and cp. his widely reprinted "Model of Christian Charity." For commentary, see Edmund S. Morgan, *The Puritan Dilemma* (Boston: Little, Brown, 1958), pp. 18–53; and Darrett B. Rutman, *Winthrop's Boston* (Chapel Hill: University of North Carolina Press, 1965), pp. 3–22.

20. Daly's formulation bears repeating: "Whatever the Pilgrims' initial motives for their journey, it is clear that by the time he came to start his account, Bradford believed that they had been sent on an errand and that they were succeeding" ("Vision," p. 561). See also Jesper Rosenmeier, "'With my owne eyes': William Bradford's *Of Plymouth Plantation,*" in *The American Puritan Imagination,* ed. Sacvan Bercovitch (Cambridge: Cambridge University Press, 1974), pp. 77–106, esp. pp. 78–98; and Peter Gay, *A Loss of Mastery* (Berkeley: University of California Press, 1966), pp. 26–52.

21. Both of Miller's widely used anthologies—*The Puritans* (1938; rpt. New York: Harper and Row, 1963) and *The American Puritans* (1956; rpt. New York: Columbia University Press, 1982)—begin the Bradford selection with the outbreak of Reformation in Bradford's own "North parts." Collections that follow Miller's lead include the earlier editions of both the Bradley-Beatty-Long and the Baym-Franklin-Gottesman versions of the *Norton Anthology of American Literature.* For the importance of Bradford's beginning, see Howard, "Art and History," esp. pp. 242–48.

22. For a modern account of what resources of intellectual explanation are lost by outlawing the Devil, see Andrew Delbanco, *The Death of Satan* (New York: Farrar, Straus and Giroux, 1995).

23. For the special religious destiny of England, see William Haller, *Foxe's Book of Martyrs and the Elect Nation* (London: Jonathan Cape, 1963).

24. See Daly, "Vision," pp. 557–60.

25. The classic statement of the debt of the English and American Puritans to Saint Augustine is Perry Miller's chapter "The Augustinian Strain of Piety," in *The New England Mind: The Seventeenth Century* (Cambridge, Mass.: Harvard University Press, 1939), pp. 3–34. More important for this study, however, is the work which seeks to disimbricate

the Christian vision of Augustine's *City of God* from that of the earlier *Ecclesiastical History* of Eusebius of Caesarea and the later *Ecclesiastical History* of Socrates Scholasticus, who extended the work of Eusebius from 309 to 445: see Robert Hanning, *The Vision of History in Early Britain* (New York: Columbia University Press, 1966), pp. 20–37; and Sacvan Bercovitch, "Typology in Puritan New England," *AQ* 19 (1967): 166–91. For Foxe's influence on Bradford, see Norman Grabo, "William Bradford: *Of Plymouth Plantation*," in *Landmarks of American Writing*, ed. Hennig Cohen (New York: Basic Books, 1969), pp. 3–19.

26. For the significance of the calendar of English holidays, see Leah S. Marcus, *The Politics of Mirth* (Chicago: University of Chicago Press, 1986); and David Cressy, *Bonfires and Bells* (Berkeley: University of California Press, 1989).

27. A parenthetical remark in the annal for 1620 points to a date fourteen years after 1630, and this has led some scholars to conclude that Bradford wrote nothing on the *Plymouth* between 1630 and 1644; see Murphy, ed., *Plymouth*, p. xv. But the parenthesis suggests an afterthought, inserted at the time of making a fair copy from some form of notes; and, given Bradford's words about having "pieced [things] up at times of leisure" after 1630, we need not assume that all the annals were written consecutively. The fullest consideration of the importance of the 1630/1644 composition is Rosenmeier, "'Owne eyes,'" pp. 77–106; see also Levin, "Bradford," pp. 25–30; and Walter P. Wenska, "Bradford's Two Histories: Pattern and Paradigm in *Of Plymouth Plantation*," *EAL* 8 (1978): 151–64.

28. For an epitome of the myth of the Mayflower Compact, see George Bancroft, *A History of the United States of America*, vol. 1 (Boston: Little, Brown, 1976), pp. 242–44. For an oppositional reading, see Mark Sargent, "The Conservative Covenant," *NEQ* 61 (1988): 231–51. For a more balanced account of the problem of "Puritanism and Democracy," see Perry Miller, "The Puritan State and Puritan Society," reprinted in *Errand*, pp. 141–52. And for a general survey, see Ralph Barton Perry, *Puritanism and Democracy* (rpt. New York: Harper and Row, 1974).

29. In the novel *Hobomok* (1824), Lydia Maria Child presents the title character as "conjured" by the romantic magic of her rebellious heroine, but his own religion seems a pristine form of Deism.

30. For the foundational account of the Pilgrim's First Thanksgiving, the reader must turn to *Mourt's Relation* (1622); see the edition of Dwight B. Heath (New York: Corinth Books, 1963), pp. 81–84.

31. See *The Blithedale Romance* in *Nathaniel Hawthorne: Novels* (New York: Library of America, 1983), p. 846.

32. Doubtless there was some truth to Lyford's charge that the church (if not the government) of Plymouth did in some manner "distaste" persons "who were not of the Separation" (p. 153); and surely a different sort of religious establishment would have rested less easily in a "want of both the Sacraments" (p. 142). For Bradford's handling of the exposure of Lyford, see Round, *Nature and Custom*, pp. 60–62.

33. In the breakup of the Company of Adventurers, the men of Plymouth had been accused of "dissembling with His Majesty . . . and with the Adventurers" about the exact nature of their religious theory and practice (*Plymouth*, pp. 170–72).

34. Morison, ed., *Plymouth*, p. 181.

35. Morison's title (p. 184) suggests the "creeping socialism" of the Roosevelt administration, whereas something like an opposite political movement is actually taking place.

36. For a fuller account of the ambiguities involved in the story of Merry Mount, see my *Province of Piety* (Cambridge, Mass.: Harvard University Press, 1984), pp. 251–77.

37. For the politics of the Maypole, see J. Gary Williams, "History in Hawthorne's 'May-pole,'" *EIHC* 108 (1972): 173–89; and Colacurcio, *Province,* pp. 272–75.

38. See Colacurcio, *Province,* pp. 258–72.

39. The formula—of D. H. Lawrence, in his 1923 *Studies in Classic American Literature* (rpt. New York: Doubleday, 1951), p. 14—may well have been suggested by Melville's characterization of Benjamin Franklin (in *Israel Potter*) as "Jack of all trades . . . and mastered by none." The point here is that Bradford imagines Morton as inviting Wollaston's indentured servants to become "free from service" and "live together as equals" (p. 205).

40. For the slender basis of the official charges against Morton, see John P. McWilliams, "Fictions of Merry Mount," *AQ* 29 (1977): 1–30; and Michael Zuckerman, "Pilgrims in the Wilderness," *NEQ* 50 (1977): 255–77.

41. The credibility of the "-L-10 in a morning" charge is challenged by Minor W. Major, in "William Bradford versus Thomas Morton," *EAL* 5 (1970): 1–13.

42. Morison, ed., *Plymouth,* p. 213.

43. See Bradford, *Plymouth,* pp. 213–14.

44. Morison, ed., *Plymouth,* p. 184.

45. Quoted from Morison, ed., *Plymouth,* p. 233.

46. On the leaders of the Great Migration to Massachusetts Bay as de facto Separatists, see Morgan, *Dilemma,* pp. 51–53.

47. Upon arriving in England from Scotland, King James I declared that he found in his new kingdom, among other things, "but one religion, and that which by myself is professed, publicly allowed and by the law maintained"; quoted from Perry, *Puritanism and Democracy,* p. 69.

48. Though he covers other matters of interest, Johnson disposes his narrative around the formation of twenty-seven separate congregational churches: see J. Franklin Jameson, ed., *The Wonder-Working Providence of Sion's Savior* (New York: Scribner's, 1910).

49. See Morison, ed., *Plymouth,* p. 224.

50. For the development of a theory of "Non-Separating Congregationalism," see Perry Miller, *Orthodoxy in Massachusetts* (Cambridge, Mass.: Harvard University Press, 1933), esp. pp. 73–101.

51. Miller's *Orthodoxy* may be thought of as written back against the implication that the intellectuals of Massachusetts had to copy the practice of Plymouth, and may have learned a thing or two from the visit of Thomas Fuller. For the argument in favor of this position, see Williston Walker, *History of the Congregational Churches in the United States* (rpt. New York: Burt Franklin, 1985), p. 85; and Larzer Ziff, *The Career of John Cotton* (Princeton: Princeton University Press, 1962), pp. 74–80.

52. It is just possible that the unhappy dispersal of the Plymouth church (in 1644) goaded Bradford to try to finish his account. That would explain the tone of the annals for the 1630s and 1640s, but it would throw an odd light on the 1620s; for the unlikely successes of that decade would have to be celebrated in full knowledge of the later failure.

53. For Cotton's end-time predictions, see his full-length *Exposition on the Thirteenth Chapter of the Revelation* (rpt. New York: AMS Press, 1982). For the cautious mood of the

1650s, see Perry Miller, *The New England Mind: From Colony to Province* (Cambridge, Mass.: Harvard University Press, 1953), pp. 3–15. And for the view that a sense of failure began with the founding of a number of towns and churches, see Rutman, *Winthrop's Boston,* esp. pp. 3–40.

54. See Cotton Mather, *Magnalia Christi Americana* (rpt. New York: Russell and Russell, 1967), p. 27.

55. What Bradford himself testifies to is his surprise at the swift and radical course of Reformation in England: "Full little did I think that the downfall of the Bishops . . . had been so near, when I first began these scribbled writings"; see Morison, ed., *Plymouth,* Appendix I, p. 351. Perhaps this was also part of the impetus for writing in the 1640s— including the frustrated desire to have Plymouth ratified by England as well as by Massachusetts.

56. The felicitous phrase is that of Michael Walzer; see *The Revolution of the Saints* (rpt. New York: Athenaeum, 1968), p. 309.

57. According to the calculations of George D. Langdon, "By 1640 there were ten thousand [non-native] people living in the New England, where before 1630 the settled inhabitants had numbered less than 500"; see *Pilgrim Colony* (New Haven: Yale University Press, 1966), p. 44.

58. See Richard D. Brown, *Modernization: The Transformation of American Life, 1600–1865* (New York: Hill and Wang, 1976), esp. pp. 3–48.

59. Morison, ed., *Plymouth,* p. 253.

60. For Winthrop's fuller response to the disturbing ideas of Roger Williams, see the Richard S. Dunn edition of his *Journal* (Cambridge, Mass.: Harvard University Press, 1996), pp. 50, 82, 102–3, 107–9, 137, 144, 149–51, 153, 158, 163–64.

61. Morison, ed., *Plymouth,* p. 264.

62. The confidence of Winthrop's "Reasons" derives in part from his assumption that land "which lies common and hath never been replenished or subdued is free to any that will possess and improve it"; quoted from Vaughan, ed., *Puritan Tradition,* p. 28. For the history of this most political ecology, see Cecelia Tichi, *New World, New Earth* (New Haven: Yale University Press, 1979), esp. pp. 1–36.

63. For Winthrop's initial resistance to the removals to Connecticut, see Dunn, ed., *Journal,* pp. 125–28.

64. For the "genocidal" implication of the Pequot War, see Ann Kibbey, *The Representation of Material Shapes in Puritanism* (Cambridge: Cambridge University Press, 1986), pp. 1–4, 92–120. For other accounts of this brutal war, see Alden T. Vaughan, *New England Frontier* (Boston: Little, Brown, 1965), pp. 122–54; and Gary B. Nash, *Red, White and Black* (New York: Prentice Hall, 1974), pp. 74–86.

65. For Michael Wigglesworth's rather restrained evocation of hell, see stanzas 208–13 of *The Day of Doom,* in Harrison T. Meserole, ed., *Seventeenth-Century American Poetry* (Garden City, N.Y.: Doubleday, 1968), pp. 109–10. More curiously, perhaps, Bradford's graphic description of blood quenching flames predicts the redemptive suffering of Christ in Edward Taylor's "Meditation I.1"; see Donald E. Stanford, ed., *The Poems of Edward Taylor* (New Haven: Yale University Press, 1960), p. 5.

66. The classic study of the inability of "civilized" Europeans to respect the culture of the Native Americans is Roy Harvey Pearce, *Savagism and Civilization* (rpt. Baltimore: Johns Hopkins University Press, 1967), esp. pp. 19–35.

67. See Hawthorne's "May-pole," in *Tales and Sketches* (New York: Library of America, 1982), p. 365; Melville's vision of savages dancing in the fire is from the famous chapter 96 of *Moby-Dick*, "The Try-Works."

68. The ceremonial posting of Babo's severed head in Melville's "Benito Cereno" may thus refer back further than the instance of Massasoit at the close of "King Philip's War."

69. Besides arguing, from the first, that the English needed to purchase their lands from the native population, Williams repeatedly served as a mediator between Massachusetts and the Indian tribes with which he was familiar; and his *Key into the Languages of America* (1643) is truly remarkable for its sympathetic insight into native culture; but perhaps not even he saw that the problem of supplantation was not a question of fairness but simply of numbers.

70. Chapter 1 of *The Scarlet Letter* refers to the need for a prison in "whatever Utopia of human virtue and happiness" the Puritan founders may have projected, but the inevitability seems unrelated to economic systems; see *Hawthorne: Novels*, p. 158.

71. For Daly, the foundation of the Puritan belief that godly men "may expect more than ordinary blessing" on their work derives from the Old Testament Book of Deuteronomy; see "Vision," pp. 557–58.

72. The point is important enough to complicate any general account of what we call "metahistory"—as the mode of any "emplotment" radically depends on the mood of the "moment towards which"; see Hayden White, *Metahistory* (Baltimore: Johns Hopkins University Press, 1973), pp. 1–42.

73. Bradford's very brief treatment of the hard questions raised by Roger Williams (p. 257) and Charles Chauncy (pp. 31–14), and virtual omission of the Samuel Gorton controversy, clearly proceed from his initial sense that abstruse theological speculation is the Devil's work.

74. For the connection to *The Scarlet Letter*, see "The Woman's Own Choice," in Michael J. Colacurcio, *Doctrine and Difference* (New York: Routledge, 1977), esp. pp. 205–17. For Winthrop's account of the matter of the rape and the awkward example of Bellingham, see Dunn, ed., *Journal*, pp. 361, 367, 370–76.

75. Morison's edition assigns many of the letters Bradford mentions to a long series of "Appendices"; for the other letters to Bellingham from the elders at Plymouth, see his Appendix X, pp. 404–13.

76. For the place of the Granger episode in the production of nonheterosexual behavior in the early modern period, see Jonathan Goldberg, *Sodometries* (Palo Alto, Calif.: Stanford University Press, 1992).

77. According to Emerson, there is in heroism "somewhat not holy"; see "Heroism," in *The Early Lectures of Ralph Waldo Emerson*, ed. Stephen Whicher et al. (Cambridge, Mass.: Harvard University Press, 1964), vol. 2, p. 331. For the difference between Bradford's "Life" of Robinson (1626) and that of Brewster (1643), see Rosenmeier, "'Owne eyes,'" pp. 93–94. And for the example Bradford handed on to his successors, principally Cotton Mather, see Cecelia Tichi, "Spiritual Biography and the 'Lords Remembrancers,'" in Bercovitch, ed., *Puritan Imagination*, pp. 56–73.

78. Where Bradford ascribes the role of heroic leadership to Brewster, Cotton Mather will famously declare that Bradford himself was the "Moses" of the Plymouth movement; see *Magnalia*, I, 113.

79. In Morison's words, the exemplary death of Miantonomo "has lain heaving on the New England conscience ever since" (*Plymouth,* p. 332). And see Vaughan, *Frontier,* pp. 155–66.

80. In the summary formulation of Robert Daly, Bradford "simply ended his account, left it whole but incomplete, and, in consenting to lose his book, gained it" ("Vision," p. 569).

81. See John Griffith, "*Of Plymouth Plantation* as a Mercantile Epic," *AzQ* 28 (1972): 231–42. For other responses to the economic emphasis in Bradford's *Plymouth,* see David Read, "Silent Partners," *EAL* 33 (1998): 291–314; and, most recently, Michelle Burnham, "Merchants, Money, and the Economics of 'Plain Style' in William Bradford's *Of Plymouth Plantation,*" *AL* 72 (2000): 695–720.

82. For the more sober history of migration out of Plymouth, see George F. Willison's chapter "Diaspora" in *Saints and Strangers* (New York: Reynal and Hitchcock, 1945), pp. 312–43; and Langdon, *Pilgrim Colony,* pp. 38–57. For Bradford's constant, worried attention to the "children," see Rosenmeier, "'Owne eyes,'" pp. 102–4.

83. For the function of the Jeremiad in the middle and late seventeenth century, see Perry Miller, "Declension in a Bible Commonwealth," reprinted in *Nature's Nation* (Cambridge, Mass.: Harvard University Press, 1967), pp. 14–49; Miller, *Colony to Province,* pp. 19–146; Sacvan Bercovitch, *The American Jeremiad* (Madison: University of Wisconsin Press, 1978), esp. pp. 3–92; and Sacvan Bercovitch, "The Ends of Puritan Rhetoric," in *The Rites of Assent* (New York: Routledge, 1993), pp. 68–89. For the special function of Cotton Mather, see "Cotton Mather and the Vision of America," in *Rites of Assent,* pp. 90–146.

84. Morison, ed., *Plymouth,* p. 33.

85. The major text on "preparation for salvation" as a lifelong process is of course Thomas Hooker's *Application of Redemption* (London, 1656).

86. Besides his hesitancy to identify any ideas as specifically his own and his constant reference to himself in the third person, criticism has noted his omission of all mention of the death of his wife, Dorothy, sometime after the first arrival at Cape Cod; see Murphy, ed., *Plymouth,* p. xiii.

87. The early observation of A. N. Kaul remains apt: "The important thing to Bradford was the religious Community"; see *The American Vision* (New Haven: Yale University Press, 1963), p. 13. And that may measure Bradford's distance from the Dreamwork of Poe: "I have been happy—tho' but in a dream I have been happy—and I love the theme."

88. In Daly's formulation, "Bradford's tone, once confident and even exuberant, has become elegaic" ("Vision," p. 568); see also Gay, *Loss,* p. 52. For a rejection of the "elegy" in favor of "irony," see Murphy, ed., *Plymouth,* pp. xv–xix. And for the argument that an embattled Bradford vigorously renews his inquiries into the meaning of history in his late "Dialogues," see Mark L. Sargent, "William Bradford's 'Dialogue' with History," *NEQ* 65 (1992): 389–421.

CHAPTER 3. "A STRANGE POISE OF SPIRIT"

1. Where Perry Miller had emphasized the crazy-making potential of a rhetoric which precluded success and failure alike, Sacvan Bercovitch has suggested that the American Jeremiad proceeds from the moment in which recovery from declension is always just

about to be; see Miller, "Declension in a Bible Commonwealth," reprinted in *Nature's Nation* (Cambridge, Mass.: Harvard University Press, 1967), pp. 14–49; Miller, *The New England Mind: From Colony to Province* (Cambridge, Mass.: Harvard University Press, 1953), esp. pp. 27–52, 173–90; and cf. Bercovitch, *The American Jeremiad* (Madison: University of Wisconsin Press, 1978), esp. pp. 132–75; Bercovitch, *Puritan Origins of the American Self* (New Haven: Yale University Press, 1975), esp. pp. 136–86; and Bercovitch, *The Rites of Assent* (New York: Routledge, 1993), esp. pp. 68–89.

2. As Bradford's nephew, Nathaniel Morton might be expected to honor his uncle's account as nearly as possible; by the time of Mather's *Magnalia,* however, many another scenario might have suggested itself; see Morton, *New England's Memorial* (Gainesville, Fla.: Scholars' Facsimiles, 1937), pp. 1–82; and cf. Cotton Mather, *Magnalia Christi Americana* (rpt. New York: Russell and Russell, 1967), pp. 39–73.

3. See Perry Miller, *Orthodoxy in Massachusetts* (rpt. Boston: Beacon Press, 1959), esp. pp. 15–101.

4. See Edmund S. Morgan, *The Puritan Dilemma* (New York: Little, Brown, 1958), esp. pp. 18–53.

5. No doubt Winthrop's famous evocation of the neobiblical "City upon a Hill" is less a prediction than a challenge; and that his sense of the possibility of failure is real and graphic; see "A Model of Christian Charity," in *Winthrop Papers,* vol. 2 (rpt. New York: Russell and Russell, 1968), pp. 282–95. For Winthrop's experience of political life in England, see Morgan, *Dilemma,* pp. 17–33; George L. Mosse, *The Holy Pretence* (London: Basil Blackwell, 1957), esp. pp. 88–106; Darret B. Rutman, *Winthrop's Boston* (Chapel Hill: University of North Carolina Press, 1965), pp. 3–22; and James G. Moseley, *John Winthrop's World* (Madison: University of Wisconsin Press, 1992), esp. pp. 13–40.

6. On Miller's famous account of the ambiguity of motives in the Great Migration, the adventure in New England might have been undertaken in the name of England and might, therefore, be temporary; see his "Errand into the Wilderness," reprinted in *Errand into the Wilderness* (Cambridge, Mass.: Harvard University Press, 1956), pp. 1–15.

7. See *Winthrop Papers,* vol. 2, pp. 138–45.

8. The modern editor of Shepard's "Autobiography" has taken his title—"God's Plot"—from Shepard's repeated use of the phrase in the "Journal"; see Michael McGiffert, ed., *God's Plot* (Amherst: University of Massachusetts Press, 1972), pp. 119, 141. *The Sound Believer* also suggests that God's "great plot" in permitting the fall of man was that "thereby way might be made for the greater manifestation of God's grace in Christ"; see John A. Albro, ed., *The Works of Thomas Shepard* (Boston: Doctrinal Tract and Book Society, 1853), vol. 1, p. 145.

9. Thus the Narrator of *The Scarlet Letter* formulates his response to Dimmesdale's dubious sighting, in the chapter called "The Minister's Vigil," of his own scarlet *A* blazoned on the midnight sky.

10. The quote is from Emerson's essay "Experience"; for discussion of Emerson's own quasi-Puritan problem of love and religion, see Eric Selinger, "'Too Pathetic, Too Pitiable,'" *ESQ* (1994): 139–82.

11. All quotations from Shepard's "Autobiography" are taken from McGiffert, ed., *God's Plot.*

12. Daniel B. Shea supposes that Shepard's preliminary address may have been written as late as 1649, the last year of Shepard's life, when Thomas Jr. would have been about

thirteen years old; see *Spiritual Autobiography in Early America* (Princeton: Princeton University Press, 1968), p. 142. But it is just as likely to have been written at or near the same time as the rest of the "Autobiography" proper; which, though it stretches out to include events up to 1646, seems to have been conceived and organized from the standpoint of arrival, settlement, and first preservation in New England (i.e., 1637–39). And for the incompleteness of all such arguments, see Walter J. Ong, S.J., "The Writer's Audience Is Always a Fiction," *PMLA* 90 (1975): 9–21.

13. *The Sound Believer* and (more noticeably) *The Sincere Convert* often sound as if the energy of ministerial rhetoric were by itself sufficient to turn the sinner into the way of salvation; but they usually go on to apologize for giving that impression. For example: "It is true, God hath elected but few, and so the Son hath shed his blood, and died for but a few; yet this is no excuse for thee to lie down and say, What should I seek out of myself for succor?" See John Albro, ed., *The Works of Thomas Shepard* (rpt. Ligonier, Pa.: Soli Deo Gloria, 1991), vol. 1, p. 54.

14. The burden placed on Shepard's surviving son has been well recognized: "spared by a merciful Providence, standing in the place of his brother, and given life by a mother who offered up a holy curse in his name before she died of his 'frowardness,' [the surviving son] had been given much to contemplate in his father's autobiographical directive"; see Shea, *Spiritual Autobiography*, p. 144. Suggesting that the burden was one he learned to bear would be the fact that his Election Sermon of 1672 ("Eye-Salve") represents a perfect completion of the Jeremiad argument laid out in Samuel Danforth's more famous "Brief Recognition of New England's Errand into the Wilderness" (1670). For the Danforth sermon, see A. W. Plumstead, ed., *The Wall and the Garden* (Minneapolis: University of Minnesota Press, 1968), pp. 54–77. The "answering" sermon of Thomas Shepard Jr. is usefully excerpted in Alan Heimert and Andrew Delbanco, eds., *Puritans in America* (Cambridge, Mass.: Harvard University Press, 1985), pp. 247–60.

15. McGiffert, introduction to *God's Plot*, p. 5.

16. Beginning with Miller's own dramatic treatment, critics have sought to determine the extent to which New England's "declension" was real or merely "rhetorical"; recent works that argue for the latter position include Mark Peterson, *The Price of Redemption* (Palo Alto, Calif.: Stanford University Press, 1997), esp. pp. 4–7, 12–19; and Darren Staloff, *The Making of an American Thinking Class* (New York: Oxford University Press, 1998), esp. pp. 141–68.

17. Augustine famously rejects—as a sort of epitome of the old, unredeemed self— the young man's love affair with rhetoric and disputation whereby "I was led astray myself and led others astray in turn"; see *Confessions* (rpt. New York: Penguin, 1961), p. 71. For Shepard's close dependence on the Augustinian model, see Thomas Werge, *Thomas Shepard* (New York: Twayne, 1987), pp. 16–22.

18. For the notable place of Cambridge in the Puritan movement, see William Haller, *The Rise of Puritanism* (rpt. New York: Harper & Row, 1957), esp. pp. 3–127; and cf. Patrick Collinson, *The Elizabethan Puritan Movement* (rpt. Oxford: Clarendon, 1990), pp. 122–30. For an account which gives Oxford its own (lesser) place in the Puritan story, see Mark Curtis, *Oxford and Cambridge in Transition* (Oxford: Clarendon, 1959), esp. pp. 165–226.

19. Albro, "Life," in *Works*, vol. 1, pp. xiii–xiv.

20. McGiffert, introduction to *God's Plot*, pp. 3–4.

21. See Perry Miller and Thomas H. Johnson, eds., *The Puritans* (rpt. New York: Harper & Row, 1963), vol. 2, pp. 471–72; and cf. Perry Miller, ed., *The American Puritans* (Garden City, N.Y.: Anchor, 1956), pp. 226–27. Criticism has noticed that Shepard's is the only autobiography represented in the Miller anthologies—or noticed in Kenneth Murdock's *Literature and Theology in Colonial New England* (rpt. New York: Harper & Row, 1949); see Shea, *Spiritual Autobiography*, p. 139; and cf. Mary Cappello, "The Authority of Self-Definition in Thomas Shepard's *Autobiography* and *Journal*," *EAL* 24 (1989): 49. Equally important, perhaps, is Miller's reduction of Shepard's long and painful conversion to its melodramatic beginning.

22. For the tradition of interrelated conversions at Cambridge, see Haller, *Rise*, pp. 49–82.

23. For the origin, functioning, and eventual suppression of the privately endowed lectureship, see Albro, "Life," pp. lxix–lxxx; and cf. Paul Seaver, *The Puritan Lectureships* (Palo Alto, Calif.: Stanford University Press, 1970).

24. For the importance of the example of Augustine to the entire tradition of Puritan autobiography, see Owen C. Watkins, *The Puritan Experience* (New York: Schocken Books, 1972), esp. pp. 37–88. And for Shepard's position at the head of an important American tradition, see Emory Elliott, "New England Puritan Literature," in *The Cambridge History of American Literature,* ed. Sacvan Bercovitch (Cambridge: Cambridge University Press, 1994), vol. 1, pp. 206–12.

25. See Albro, "Life," pp. lxiii–lxvii.

26. For an account of Laudian measures against suspected nonconformists, see Tom Webster, *Godly Clergy in Early Stuart England* (Cambridge: Cambridge University Press, 1997), esp. pp. 180–214; for the view that Laudian tactics may actually have *created* Puritans, see Albro, "Life," pp. lxxvi–lxxx.

27. For the function of "meditation" in both Reformation and Counter-Reformation theory and practice, see Louis L. Martz, *The Poetry of Meditation* (New Haven: Yale University Press, 1954), esp. pp. 1–20, 118–24; and for a contemporaneous—Puritan—account, see Thomas Hooker, *The Application of Redemption . . . The Ninth and Tenth Books* (London, 1659), pp. 210–17.

28. There is something Milleresque in Albro's appeal to Shepard's preface to *The Defense of the Answer* at the moment when he wishes to evoke the difficulty of the Puritan decision to remove to New England; see "Life," pp. xc–xci.

29. Quoted from Miller and Johnson, eds., *Puritans,* vol. 1, p. 119.

30. Quoted from Miller and Johnson, eds., *Puritans,* vol. 1, p. 121.

31. For the argument that partial loves are inherently "selfish" and likely therefore to become a scene of discord, see Jonathan Edwards, *The Nature of True Virtue,* in *The Works of Jonathan Edwards,* ed. Paul Ramsay (New Haven: Yale University Press, 1989), vol. 8, esp. pp. 551–60, 600–618.

32. For John Cotton's instructive, indeed originary act of delaying the baptism of his son, Seaborne, until the sacrament could be administered in a properly constituted particular church, see Richard S. Dunn, ed., *The Journal of John Winthrop* (Cambridge, Mass.: Harvard University Press, 1996), pp. 95–96.

33. Students are often upset to discover that the nurturing Anne Bradstreet was not herself above the "guilt trip," particularly as her letter "To My Dear Children" is addressed

from beyond the grave, to be read "when I am no more with you"; see Jeannine Hensley, ed., *The Works of Anne Bradstreet* (Cambridge, Mass.: Harvard University Press, 1967), p. 240.

34. The logic of the Jeremiads makes it clear that, by the 1660s, New England's "Errand" was thought to have been carried out not in the name of the Church of England but of the offspring of the founders; but—quite like Shepard's prefatory dedication to his son— the inheritance was seen not as burden but as liberation; see Thomas Shepard Jr., "Eye-Salve," in Heimert and Delbanco, eds., *Puritans,* esp. pp. 254–58.

35. For the New England context of Shepard's appearance on the scene, see Winthrop, *Journal,* pp. 156–57, 168–70. And cf. Samuel Eliot Morison, *Builders of the Bay Colony* (Boston: Houghton Mifflin, 1930), pp. 111–19.

36. For a learned and original account of the attempt at an identity of public and private selfhood in Puritan New England, see Sacvan Bercovitch, *The Puritan Origins of the American Self* (New Haven: Yale University Press, 1975), esp. pp. 35–71.

37. In the second edition of *God's Plot* (1994), McGiffert includes a generous selection of the public professions made by persons seeking to enter Shepard's particular church at Newtown (later, Cambridge) and recorded in Shepard's own hand. Fifty-one such testimonies were first printed in 1981; see George Selement and Bruce C. Wooley, eds., *Thomas Shepard's Confessions, Colonial Society of Massachusetts Collections,* 58 (Boston, 1981). For a review of this important publication, see Norman Pettit, "Grace and Conversion at Cambridge," *NEQ* 55 (1982): 596–603; and for the bearing of these documents on the much vexed question of elite versus popular religion in New England, see George Selement, "The Meeting of Elite and Popular Minds at Cambridge"; David D. Hall, "Toward a History of Popular Religion in Early New England"; and Darrett B. Rutman, "New England as Idea and Society Revisited"—all in *WMQ* 41 (1984): 32–61. We have been aware since the publication of Edmund S. Morgan's *Visible Saints* (New York: New York University Press, 1963) that the requiring of such professions was a distinguishing feature of New England Congregationalism, but a sampling of the professions themselves has enabled a new understanding of the popular reception of the inventions of rare religious sophistication. For important studies using these materials, see Patricia Caldwell, *The Puritan Conversion Narrative* (Cambridge: Cambridge University Press, 1983); and Janice Knight, *Orthodoxies in Massachusetts* (Cambridge, Mass.: Harvard University Press, 1994), esp. pp. 130–97.

38. To refer to the party of Anne Hutchinson (which Shepard takes to include John Cotton) as "Familists" is to associate them with the perfectionism of Hendrik Niclaes and to imply that their "Family of Love" might be expected to sponsor some form of experimental free love; see William K. B. Stoever, *"A Faire and Easie Way to Heaven"* (Middletown, Conn.: Wesleyan University Press, 1978), p. 232; and cf. Philip F. Gura, *A Glimpse of Sion's Glory* (Middletown, Conn.: Wesleyan University Press, 1984), pp. 54–56. Winthrop also invokes the same damaging name—in his *Short Story of the Rise, Reign and Ruin of the Antinomians, Familists and Libertines* (London, 1644).

39. For arguments in favor of changing the traditional name, see Michael P. Winship, *Making Heretics* (Princeton: Princeton University Press, 2002), esp. pp. 1–11.

40. *The Sincere Convert* first appeared in 1641, *The Sound Believer* in 1645.

41. As Andrew Delbanco observes, "The antinomian position implies a denial of [Shepard's] whole theory of psychology"; see "Thomas Shepard's America," in *Harvard Studies in Biography,* ed. Daniel Aaron (Cambridge, Mass.: Harvard University Press,

1978), p. 171. Indeed, the most grievous experiences in Shepard's conversion experience pivot on the recollection of the tempting thought that the Familists' "glorious state of perfection might . . . be the truth" and that anything else was so much legalism (pp. 42–43). For the "enthusiastic" backdrop of "the Antinomian Controversy," see Emery Battis, *Saints and Sectaries* (Chapel Hill: University of North Carolina Press, 1962), pp. 18–45; and cf. Gura, *Sion's Glory,* pp. 49–92, 237–75.

42. For the "prehistory" of Edwards' conversion experience, see his "Personal Narrative," in *A Jonathan Edwards Reader,* ed. John E. Smith, Harry S. Stout, and Kenneth P. Minkema (New Haven: Yale University Press, 1995), pp. 281–83.

43. On the development of a well-articulated "morphology of conversion," see Morgan, *Visible Saints,* pp. 64–73; Caldwell, *Conversion Narrative,* esp. pp. 163–86; and Knight, *Orthodoxies,* esp. pp. 164–97. One notices with chagrin that so faithful a shepherd as David D. Hall has elected to omit the conversion experience from the selection of the "Autobiography" included in his (otherwise) masterful anthology of New England writings; see *Puritans in the New World* (Princeton: Princeton University Press, 2004), pp. 37–52.

44. The suggestive phrase is from the "Coon Song" of A. R. Ammons.

45. English and American Calvinists understood their position in opposition to the version of "Arminianism" condemned at the Synod of Dort (1619). In these terms, faith could be an act of the will (as well as a free gift), but it could not be one the unaided will of the natural man could make as such.

46. For Shepard's particular emphasis on "contrition," "compunction," and "humiliation," see *The Sound Believer,* in Albro, ed., *Works,* vol. 1, pp. 115–90. For Shepard as a proper "Preparationist," see Perry Miller, "'Preparation for Salvation' in Seventeenth-Century New England," in *Nature's Nation* (rpt. Cambridge, Mass.: Harvard University Press, 1967), pp. 50–77; and cf. Norman Pettit, *The Heart Prepared* (New Haven: Yale University Press, 1966), pp. 101–14.

47. For the setting and use of Samuel Hopkins' formula of the "willingness to be damned for the glory of God," see Bruce Kuklick, *Churchmen and Philosophers* (New Haven: Yale University Press, 1985), pp. 43–55.

48. An essential feature of biography in the "Augustinian" tradition is that, given the postconversion point of view, a new personality tells the story of an older, unredeemed self from the standpoint of regenerate insight; things that may have looked one way then, to the old self, appear in their true light only now; see Werge, *Shepard,* esp. pp. 17–19.

49. The foundational study of Puritan attitudes toward romantic and familial affection is Edmund S. Morgan, *The Puritan Family* (rpt. New York: Harper & Row, 1966), esp. pp. 29–86. Important modern studies include Philip Greven, *The Protestant Temperament* (Chicago: University of Chicago Press, 1977), esp. pp. 21–148; David Leverenz, *The Language of Puritan Feeling* (New Brunswick: Rutgers University Press, 1980), esp. pp. 70–161; Charles Lloyd Cohen, *God's Caress* (New York: Oxford University Press, 1986), esp. pp. 75–110; Ivy Schweitzer, *The Work of Self-Representation* (Chapel Hill: University of North Carolina Press, 1991), esp. pp. 1–39; see also my essay, "The Woman's Own Choice," in *Doctrine and Difference* (New York: Routledge, 1997), pp. 205–27.

50. Shepard would almost certainly have agreed with the pronouncement of the Continental Reformed theologian Francis Turretin that "The absolute decree of saving individual persons does not make it impossible for conditions for gaining [salvation] to be wisely required of man, because God decreed salvation absolutely and antecedently

without the intervention of any preceding cause, but not consequently without means; indeed means are necessary for obtaining it"; see *Institutio Theologiae Elenticae,* in *Reformed Dogmatics,* ed. J. W. Beardslee (New York: Oxford University Press, 1965), p. 417. And cf. William Ames, *The Marrow of Theology* (Boston: Pilgrim Press, 1968), esp. pp. 152–71.

51. In the aftermath of the Calvinist Synod of Dort, one became an "Arminian" if one were moved to concede that, in the last analysis, the problem of salvation lay as much in the ambiguity of human will as in the mystery of predestination. For Arminius, it was enough to hold that God had "decreed to save" those whom "He knew from all eternity" would believe and persevere; and he dared to demand of the Orthodox whether the gift of faith ceases to be a pure gift just "because the beggar extends his hands to receive it?" Quoted from R. T. Kendall, *Calvin and English Calvinism to 1649* (London: Oxford University Press, 1979), pp. 142–43. Cf. Carl Bangs, *Arminius* (Nashville: Abingdon, 1971), pp. 206–21; and Keith L. Sprunger, *The Learned Doctor William Ames* (Urbana: University of Illinois Press, 1971), esp. pp. 145–52.

52. "Condign" and "congruous" are the terms used by Thomas Aquinas to distinguish between the sort of strict merit that can obtain only between equals (and hence not ever between God and man) and a more analogous sort, in which the party of superior status freely chooses to invent and abide by a "fitting" set of conditions to be fulfilled; see *Summa Theologica,* "Treatise on Grace," Q. CXIV.

53. Only with Emerson, perhaps, will the promises of 1 Corinthians 3 be applied to man himself; in the meantime, see Edward Taylor's "Preparatory Meditations," I, 30–36, in Donald E. Stanford, ed., *Poems* (New Haven: Yale University Press, 1960), pp. 48–60.

54. The quotation is from Edward Johnson's *Wonder-Working Providence of Sion's Savior* (rpt. New York: Barnes and Noble, 1967), p. 134. In the analogy of John Cotton, "a woman in true conjugal affection [will] look at no more but at the very bare man"; see *Christ the Fountain of Life* (rpt. New York: Arno Press, 1972), p. 53.

55. See McGiffert, ed., *God's Plot,* pp. 71–84. Kenneth Murdock gives 1637 as the *terminus ad quem* of the "autobiography proper"; see *Literature and Theology,* pp. 111–12.

56. Such is the project of Mary Cappello ("Self-Definition"). And for an attempt to read the tendency of Shepard's life out of the sermons as well as the explicit self-writings, see Delbanco, "Shepard's America."

57. For Edward Taylor's striking version of a Shepard-like story of love and death, see "Upon Wedlock and the Death of Children," in Stanford, ed., *Poems,* pp. 468–70.

58. Cappello notes a certain "tension" in many of Shepard's attempts to total up his private losses and public losses and his gains; see "Self-Definition," p. 37.

59. For an instructive example of the (post)modern attempt to read "mourning" where the historicist would see the problem of "weaned affections," see Mitchell Breitwieser, *American Puritanism and the Defense of Mourning* (Madison: University of Wisconsin Press, 1990).

60. One thinks of the example of Anne Bradstreet: "To My Dear and Loving Husband" perfectly conforms its marital passion to the expectations of sainthood and immortality, whereas the poem "Before the Birth of One of Her Children" ends in the worry over her own "dear" remembrance; see Hensley, *Works,* pp. 225, 224.

61. In Edwards' memorable formulation, "Not only would affection to a private system, un-subordinated in regard to Being in general, have a tendency to opposition to the supreme object of virtuous affection, as its effect and consequence, but would become *itself*

an opposition to that object"; either "God," Edwards seems to mean, or something else in the place of God; see *The Nature of True Virtue,* in Paul Ramsey, ed., *Works of Jonathan Edwards: Ethical Writings,* (New Haven, 1989), p. 556.

CHAPTER 4. THE CHARTER AND THE "MODEL"

1. In the words of Darrett B. Rutman, "The Winthrop migration was a lay movement, not clerical"; see *Winthrop's Boston* (Chapel Hill: University of North Carolina Press, 1965), p. 19 and passim, pp. 3–22. This lay character began radically to change, presumably, with the arrival of Cotton, Hooker, and Stone in September 1633.

2. See Richard S. Dunn's introduction to his (and Laetitia Yeandle's) edition of *The Journal of John Winthrop, 1630–1649* (Cambridge, Mass.: Harvard University Press, 1996), p. xxiii. Dunn's introduction rewrites his earlier essay, "John Winthrop Writes His Journal," *WMQ* 41 (1984): 185–212. For the argument that the representation of Winthrop's work as a journal rather than as a history has retarded "literary" treatment, see Stephen Carl Arch, *Authorizing the Past* (DeKalb: University of Northern Illinois Press, 1994), pp. 20–23, 196.

3. For the editing of Winthrop's *Journal,* see Richard S. Dunn and Laetitia Yeandle, "Editorial Method," in *Journal,* pp. xli–li. For the whole history of Winthrop's editing, see pp. xi–xvi; and cf. Lee Schweninger, *John Winthrop* (New York: Twayne, 1990), pp. 67–70.

4. In addition to the matchless work of Richard Dunn—and to the attentions of historians of seventeenth-century New England—one can notice the following attempts to "read" Winthrop's *Journal* in a more or less connected, thematic way: Schweninger, *Winthrop,* pp. 67–98; James G. Moseley, *John Winthrop's World* (Madison: University of Wisconsin Press, 1992), pp. 41–118; Arch, *Authorizing,* pp. 20–50; Alan Howard, "The Web in the Loom" (Ph.D. diss., Stanford University, 1968); and Rachelle Elaine Friedman, "Writing the Wonders" (Ph.D. diss., UCLA, 1991).

5. The first two quotations are from Winthrop's "Particular Considerations" in reference to the migration to New England; see *Winthrop Papers* (Worcester: Massachusetts Historical Society, 1931), vol. 2, pp. 126, 125; the third and fourth are from the famous "Model of Christian Charity," quoted from *Winthrop Papers,* vol. 2, p. 294.

6. In the case of a journal, the "author function" is perfectly clear: it is the name we invoke the moment we discover the vagaries of discourse have been redeemed by an act of personality. For the analogous case in the philosophy of selfhood, see Immanuel Kant, *The Critique of Pure Reason,* trans. Norman Kemp Smith (New York: St. Martin's, 1965), pp. 129–75.

7. Wherever possible, this essay cites from Laetitia Yeandle's abridged edition of the Dunn-Yeandle *Journal,* indicated by the letter "Y" before the appropriate page numbers (in the text). Citations of the unabridged edition are indicated by page numbers only.

8. Moseley speculates that "By not including his ["Model"] in the text of the journal or even referring to its delivery, Winthrop did not confuse telling about his design with showing how the events to which it gave rise unfolded"; see *Winthrop's World,* p. 42. For a strenuous but inconclusive attempt to fix the moment of the sermon's composition and delivery, see Hugh J. Dawson, "John Winthrop's Rite of Passage," *EAL* 26 (1991): 219–31. For

culturally emphatic readings of the "Model," see Loren Baritz, *City on a Hill* (New York: Wiley, 1964), pp. 13–17; Harry S. Stout, "Word and Order in Colonial New England," in *The Bible in America,* ed. Nathan O. Hatch and Mark A. Noll (New York: Oxford University Press, 1982), pp. 19–38; Rutman, *Boston,* pp. 3–14; Theodore Dwight Bozeman, *To Live Ancient Lives* (Chapel Hill: University of North Carolina Press, 1988), pp. 90–93; Edmund S. Morgan, "Winthrop's 'Modell of Christian Charity' in a Wider Context," *HLQ* 50 (1987): 145–51; Andrew Delbanco, *Puritan Ordeal* (Cambridge, Mass.: Harvard University Press, 1989), pp. 72–74; Schweninger, *Winthrop,* pp. 42–46; Scott Michaelsen, "John Winthrop's 'Modell' Covenant and the Company Way," *EAL* 27 (1992): 85–100; and Arch, *Authorizing,* pp. 8–20.

9. See "Model," in *Winthrop Papers,* vol. 2, pp. 282, 290, 293.

10. Beginning with an account of the voyage from England to the "land which we deemed to be Cape Cod," the journal—of William Bradford and John Winslow—titled *Mourt's Relation* (London, 1622; rpt. New York: Corinth Books, 1963) proceeds in a matter-of-fact way to detail the outward events of the settlement of Plymouth in 1620 and 1621. For its interest as a "contact text," see Philip H. Round, *By Nature and by Custom Cursed* (Hanover, N.H.: University Press of New England, 1999), pp. 216–22.

11. Dunn points to these "tantalizing" sentences as the beginnings of the problem of where exactly to plant and, if in various places, who would be expected to live where (Y, 29).

12. Dunn notes the emotion in Winthrop's letter to his wife: "My son Henry, my son Henry, ah poor child" (Y, 30).

13. Y, p. 30.

14. For the first assignment of judicial powers to the assistants, see Nathaniel B. Shurtleff, ed., *Records of the Governor and Company of Massachusetts Bay* (Boston: William White, 1853), vol. 1, p. 74. Dunn (p. 38) cites the same material in *Records of the Court of Assistants of the Colony of the Massachusetts Bay, 1630–1692,* ed. John Noble and John F. Cronin (Boston, 1901–28), vol. 2, pp. 1–3.

15. For the logic by which the free, unmerited salvation of individuals came to be applied, conditionally, to the entire New England community, see Stout, "Word and Order," esp. pp. 23–31. And for the argument that Winthrop's "Model" was "merely transposing into covenant theology the actual history, legal status and terms of the charter issued to the Puritans in 1629," see Michaelsen, "Company Way," esp. pp. 88–90.

16. By Dudley's account, all the assistants had agreed "to build houses . . . a mile east from Waterton"; see Dunn, unabridged *Journal,* p. 42.

17. Dunn, unabridged *Journal,* p. 44.

18. See Perry Miller and Thomas H. Johnson, eds., *The Puritans* (rpt. New York: Harper and Row, 1963), p. 137; and cp. Perry Miller, ed., *The American Puritans* (Garden City, N.Y.: Doubleday, 1956), p. 41. Less typical than the humor of modern skepticism may prefer to assume, the observation of such minor miracles might actually have the effect of weakening, back in England, a writer's "cultural capital"; see Round, *Nature and Custom,* pp. 17–22.

19. Dunn, unabridged *Journal,* p. 48.

20. The records of court for April 1631 refer to a number of practical matters regarding defense and the use of arms, but they make no mention of either Williams' ideas or their own initial venture into controlling the organization of a particular church; see Shurtleff, ed., *Records,* vol. 1, p. 85.

21. See Dunn, unabridged *Journal*, p. 50.

22. The loyalty-professing text in question is an open letter from "the governor and Company late gone for *New* England" to "their Brethren in and of the Church of England"; see "The Humble Request," in *Winthrop Papers*, vol. 2, p. 232. For the possible obliquity of this document, see Edmund S. Morgan, *Puritan Dilemma* (Boston: Little, Brown, 1958), pp. 52–53.

23. In Morgan's summary judgment, "The history of Massachusetts during Winthrop's lifetime is very largely the history of his efforts to meet the various dangers presented by separatism"; see *Dilemma*, pp. 75–76. For the tract Winthrop wrote against Williams, see *Winthrop Papers*, vol. 3, pp. 10–14.

24. Shurtleff, ed., *Records*, vol. 1, p. 87.

25. The 1629 "Charter" which created the Massachusetts Bay Company is reprinted in Shurtleff, ed., *Records*, vol. 1, pp. 3–20; or, more conveniently, in Alden T. Vaughan, ed., *The Puritan Tradition in America* (New York: Harper and Row, 1972), pp. 54–58.

26. "Charter," in Vaughan, ed., *Puritan Tradition*, p. 57.

27. See "Model," in *Winthrop Papers*, vol. 2, p. 288. For discussion, see Morgan, *Dilemma*, pp. 88–96, 155–73.

28. See, e.g., the characterization in Vernon Louis Parrington, *Main Currents in American Thought* (New York: Harcourt, Brace, 1927), vol. 1, pp. 38–50. Even so faithful a reader as Edmund Morgan tends to regard Winthrop's emphasis on "the love that flows from regeneration in Christ" as subserving his "appeal for subjection to authority" ("Wider Context," p. 145).

29. For the romance of this real estate, see John Seelye, *Prophetic Waters* (New York: Oxford University Press, 1977), pp. 133–38.

30. For the observation that "reconciliation" might be considered the "method" of Winthrop's *Journal*, see Arch, *Authorizing*, pp. 23–27.

31. See Peter Oliver, *Origin and Progress of the American Rebellion* (MS dated 1781; San Marino, Calif.: The Huntington Library, 1961), esp. pp. 10–22.

32. See "Model," in *Winthrop Papers*, vol. 2, p. 283.

33. A staple of historical commentary on Winthrop's *Journal* has been the rehearsal of the process by which the freemen of Massachusetts "recovered" the powers conferred by the Charter—and how the chartered assistants and the invented deputies eventually became a sort of bicameral legislature; see Samuel Eliot Morison, *Builders of the Bay Colony* (Boston: Houghton Mifflin, 1930), pp. 65–96; and cf. Morgan, *Dilemma*, pp. 84–100.

34. See "Model," in *Winthrop Papers*, vol. 2, p. 294.

35. The abridged (Yeandle) edition of the *Journal* reprints the mouse episode (Y, 48) but omits the local politics.

36. For a close account of the where-to-live debate between Dudley and Winthrop, see Rutman, *Winthrop's Boston*, pp. 30–32.

37. Note: The abridged text of the *Journal* fails to note an ellipsis between "After dinner" and "the deputy then demanded" (Y, 49).

38. See "Model," in *Winthrop Papers*, vol. 2, p. 292. On Rutman's account, the "Model" had implied a single community, but Winthrop saw early on that this plan would have to be abandoned; see *Winthrop's Boston*, pp. 23–40. Dunn says only that Winthrop was "possibly . . . planning to build a single community for all the incoming colonists" (p. 36).

39. In the interest of peace, the ministers "ordered that the Governor should procure them a minister at Newtown, & contribute some what towards his maintenance for a time" (pp. 79–80).

40. For the importance of the Dudley relationship to Winthrop's concern for harmony among the magistrates, see Schweninger, *Winthrop,* pp. 72–74; and cf. Moseley, *Winthrop's World,* pp. 53–56.

41. As Dunn summarizes the early movements of Williams' New World career: "Having been blocked from the Salem pulpit [in April 1631], Williams came to Plymouth where he stayed about two years; he then quarreled with the Pilgrims and returned to Salem in 1633" (Y, 51).

42. Dudley protests that the document in question refers to the "reverend Bishops," that it indicates acceptance of "all the Articles of the Christian Faith . . . of the Churches of England," and that it "gave the king the title of Sacred majesty" (p. 94). Evidently a little of the Williams spirit lived in the deputy.

43. Suitably advertised here is Cotton's lasting love affair with the allegory of Canticles—which culminated, years later, in his *Brief Exposition . . . upon the Whole Book of Canticles* (London, 1655).

44. The standard account of the American origin of churches which tested for sainthood is Edmund S. Morgan, *Visible Saints* (New York: New York University Press, 1963), esp. pp. 64–112; see also Patricia Caldwell, *The Puritan Conversion Narrative* (Cambridge: Cambridge University Press, 1983), esp. pp. 45–80.

45. Moseley happily observes that Cotton went to work "complementing John Wilson's work as pastor and guardian of discipline" (*Winthrop's World,* p. 61), but surely the complement was more formal than real.

46. Dunn, unabridged *Journal,* p. 193.

47. For the suppressed issue of preparation in the Antinomian Controversy, see Perry Miller, *The New England Mind: From Colony to Province* (Cambridge, Mass.: Harvard University Press, 1953), pp. 53–67.

48. Dunn, unabridged *Journal,* p. 103.

49. See David D. Hall, *The Antinomian Controversy* (Middletown, Conn.: Wesleyan University Press, 1968), pp. 10–20.

50. For the view that the reference to King Charles as a "Christian Monarch" lies close to the center of Williams' initial clash with Winthrop and the authorities of Massachusetts Bay, see the editorial note of Glenn W. LaFantasie in *The Correspondence of Roger Williams,* vol. 1 (Providence: Brown University Press, 1988), pp. 12–23.

51. Winthrop deletes this passage and writes a second, more complex account of the Stone murder for the date of November 6, 1634 (pp. 133–34); and Dunn refers the reader to Alfred A. Cave, "Who Killed John Stone?" *WMQ* 49 (1992): 509–21.

52. For the final resolution of "the veto question," in the aftermath of the famous "stray sow" matter of 1642, see Dunn, unabridged *Journal,* pp. 394–98, 451–58, 503. But Winthrop's most irritated response to the continual pressure from the freemen and their deputies comes in 1639, after a lengthy dispute about the proper number of such deputies and the functioning of the magistrates as a standing council: "here it may be observed how strictly the people would seem to stick to their patent, where they think it makes for their advantage, but are content to decline it, where it will not warrant such liberties as they have taken up without warrant from thence" (pp. 295–96).

53. Moseley writes admiringly of Winthrop's "tendency to hold strong convictions and also to be open to change in the political arena," of his understanding that "an organization's strength depends on an appropriate distribution of power" (*Winthrop's World,* pp. 63–65).

54. See "Model," in *Winthrop Papers,* vol. 2, p. 292.

55. See Dunn, unabridged *Journal,* p. 126. And cf. Miller's steady assessment in "Thomas Hooker and the Democracy of Connecticut," in *Errand into the Wilderness* (Cambridge, Mass.: Harvard University Press, 1956), pp. 16–47.

56. For the (relative) complexity of Williams' "separatist" position, see my essay on Hawthorne's "Endicott and the Red Cross," in *Province of Piety* (Cambridge, Mass.: Harvard University Press, 1984), pp. 221–38.

57. According to the logic of Winthrop's "Reasons to Be Considered," "That [land] which lies common, and hath never been replenished or subdued is free to any that possess and improve it"; see *Winthrop Papers,* vol. 2, p. 140. Winthrop's "Reasons" are conveniently reprinted in Vaughan, ed., *Puritan Tradition,* pp. 25–35. For a history of the "ecology" embedded in Winthrop's geopolitical claim, see Cecelia Tichi, *New World, New Earth* (New Haven: Yale University Press, 1979), esp. pp. 1–36.

58. See "The Theory of State and of Society," in Miller, ed., *Puritans,* pp. 181–94.

59. For a sample of an uncautious praise of Williams, one might consult George Bancroft's estimate, in volume 1 of his *History of the United States* (Boston: Little, Brown, 1856), pp. 348–82; Parrington, *Main Currents,* vol. 1, pp. 62–75; and Samuel Hugh Brockunier, *The Irrepressible Democrat* (New York: Ronald, 1940), esp. pp. 3–128. For a more controlled estimate, which takes into account the extremism of some of his views, see Edmund S. Morgan, *Roger Williams* (New York: Harcourt Brace, 1967).

60. Quoted from Dunn, whose note (Y, 87) indicates that Williams' letters to Winthrop suggest that "he saw JW as a secret benefactor and continuing friend"; and see *Winthrop Papers,* vol. 3, pp. 314–18. The same letter appears in the *Correspondence of Williams,* vol. 1, pp. 65–72.

61. See "Model," in *Winthrop Papers,* vol. 2, p. 290.

62. See "Model," in *Winthrop Papers,* vol. 2, p. 290.

63. For a sober reflection on how we might behave ourselves in the face of conflicting "myths of concern," see Northrop Frye, "The Critical Path," in *The Critical Path* (Bloomington: Indiana University Press, 1971), usefully anthologized in Hazard Adams and Leroy Searle, eds., *Critical Theory since 1965* (Tallahassee: Florida State University Press, 1986), pp. 252–64.

64. The reader who wishes to make the experiment for himself will find the limited pleasures of both *The Bloody Tenet of Persecution* (1644) and *The Bloody Tenet Yet More Bloody* (1652) fairly represented (and amply introduced) in Perry Miller, ed., *Roger Williams* (New York: Bobbs-Merrill, 1953), pp. 108–56, 168–92. Intervening between these two volumes, of course, and provoking the second volume, is Cotton's less edifying *Bloody Tenet, Washed and Made White in the Blood of the Lamb* (London, 1647).

65. The reference by the "Model" to the "near bond of marriage between [Christ] and us" may seem conventional enough, but the easy reference to "Cohabitation and Consortship" (p. 293) may be noteworthy in this context; and, as we shall see, the enthusiasm of Winthrop's comparison of the saints' mutual love to the transport felt by "Adam when Eve was brought to him" (p. 290) can hardly fail to raise the stakes of communal affect.

66. In Hawthorne's exact words, the men who judge Hester Prynne—"good men, just and sage"—are singularly incapable of "sitting in judgment on an erring woman's heart."

67. See "Model," in *Winthrop Papers,* vol. 2, pp. 293–94.

68. For Winthrop's change of title in the manuscript, see Dunn's introduction, pp. xv–xvi.

69. As we shall see in a later chapter, an insistent motif of Winthrop's *Journal* after 1638 is the repeated moral (often sexual) lapses of various persons who had been in sympathy with the Antinomian campaign against sanctification. For the denomination of quondam Puritans as "hot protestants," see Michael P. Winship, *Making Heretics* (Princeton: Princeton University Press, 2002), esp. pp. 2–3.

70. See Thomas Shepard, "Autobiography," published as *God's Plot,* ed. Michael McGiffert (Amherst: University of Massachusetts Press, 1972), p. 65.

71. Shepard judged, in 1639, that "Mr. Cotton repents not, but is hid only" (*God's Plot,* p. 74); but modern commentators are convinced that, at the very least, Cotton was made to concede the practical danger of slighting sanctification.

CHAPTER 5. DOUBT'S VENTURE, FAITH'S CALL

1. See "Autobiography," in *God's Plot,* ed. Michael McGiffert (Amherst: University of Massachusetts Press, 1994), p. 67.

2. "Autobiography," p. 48.

3. "Autobiography," p. 75. "Arminianism," in this context, would signify the belief in the competence of the will of man to accept a salvation freely offered; see Carl Bangs, *Arminius* (Nashville: Abingdon, 1971), esp. pp. 206–21.

4. Ralph Waldo Emerson, "Experience," in *Essays and Lectures* (New York: Library of America, 1983), p. 482; and see my essay "Puritans in Spite," in *Doctrine and Difference* (New York: Routledge, 1997), pp. 231–34.

5. All citations of Shepard's *Sincere Convert* (and *Sound Believer*) are taken from volume 1 of the John Albro edition of *The Works of Thomas Shepard* (Boston, 1853), as reprinted by the Soli Deo Gloria Press (Ligonier, Pa., 1991).

6. Norman Pettit has put the Shepard case as a "dilemma of covenant theology": "God alone can bend the heart to grace; [yet] man must enter the covenant of his own free will." What this means in practice, Pettit correctly observes, is that "if the baptized covenanter can find 'the condition or qualification within himself,' he may conclude that the absolute promise is 'his own'"; see *The Heart Prepared* (New Haven: Yale University Press, 1966), pp. 105, 111.

7. "Autobiography," p. 67.

8. In the tradition of William Ames, Shepard clearly believes that "Theology is the doctrine or teaching [*doctrina*] of living to God"; see John Dykstra Eusden, ed., *The Marrow of Theology* (Boston: Pilgrim Press, 1968), p. 77; and cf. Keith L. Sprunger, *The Learned Doctor William Ames* (Urbana: University of Illinois Press, 1972), pp. 127–42; and Janice Knight, *Orthodoxies in Massachusetts* (Cambridge, Mass.: Harvard University Press, 1994), pp. 52–60.

9. Emerson, "Self-Reliance," in *Essays,* p. 269.

10. For the morale—and the pitfalls—of preparationist theology, see Perry Miller, "'Preparation for Salvation' in Seventeenth-Century Massachusetts," reprinted in *Nature's Nation* (Cambridge, Mass.: Harvard University Press, 1967), pp. 50–77; and *The New England Mind: From Colony to Province* (Cambridge, Mass.: Harvard University Press, 1953), pp. 57–67. In both these places Miller emphasizes the role of preparationist preaching in a process he calls "Expanding the Limits of Natural Ability." Based on a failure to observe how awkwardly careful the preachers were to point out that preparation is itself a work of the Spirit, some of the same tendency appears in Pettit, *Heart,* esp. pp. 1–21. For criticism of this tendency, see R. T. Kendall, *Calvin and English Calvinism* (London: Oxford University Press, 1979), pp. 4–5; also William K. B. Stoever, *"A Faire and Easie Way to Heaven"* (Middletown, Conn.: Wesleyan University Press, 1978), pp. 212–13.

11. In my most respectful view, Perry Miller overstates both the centrality and the subversive power of the covenant idiom in Puritan thought: certainly Shepard (and Hooker too) can go for many pages without reference to this divinely initiated relationship; and when he does mention it, the emphasis is on the certainty it affords, not on the freedom it appears to imply. In fact the first-generation American Puritans are often excruciatingly careful to point out—painfully, but in strict loyalty to the logic of "Calvinism"—that the decision to accept the terms of the covenant is one that requires a specially enabling divine grace. What this suggests is that the covenant idiom functions with less elegance in Calvinist than in other Christian systems. For Miller's excited misprision, see "The Marrow of Puritan Divinity," reprinted in *Errand into the Wilderness* (rpt. Cambridge, Mass.: Harvard University Press, 1956), pp. 48–98; and cp. *The New England Mind: The Seventeenth Century* (Cambridge, Mass.: Harvard University Press, 1939), pp. 365–97. Attempts to correct Miller's emphasis include Everett H. Emerson, "Calvin and Covenant Theology," *CH* 25 (1956): 136–44; Jens G. Moeller, "The Beginnings of Puritan Covenant Theology," *JEH* 14 (1963): 46–67; Pettit, *Heart,* esp. pp. 218–21; John Coolidge, *The Pauline Renaissance in England* (London: Oxford University Press, 1970), pp. 99–140; Michael McGiffert, "American Puritan Studies in the 1960's," *WMQ* 27 (1970): 36–67; also "The Problem of the Covenant in Puritan Thought," *New England Historical and Genealogical Register* 130 (1976): 107–29; David D. Hall, "Understanding the Puritans," in *Colonial America,* ed. Stanley N. Katz (Boston: Little, Brown, 1971); Kendall, *Calvin and English Calvinism;* Stoever, *"Faire and Easie Way,"* esp. pp. 81–87; and most thoroughly, John von Rohr, *The Covenant of Grace in Puritan Thought* (Atlanta: Scholars Press, 1986).

12. In Augustine and his close followers, "integrity" names the harmonious and hierarchically ordered condition of all Adam's disparate powers and faculties before the Fall; the resulting disintegration we experience as the (Pauline) warfare between spirit and flesh—so that we do not the good we would and do the evil we would not.

13. As Edwards perfectly recognized, the organizing insight occurs in Romans 5: "just as sin came into the world through one man," so "much more surely have the grace of God and the free gift in the grace of one man, Jesus Christ, abounded for many." For Edwards' Pauline argument, see *Original Sin* (New Haven: Yale University Press, 1970), pp. 306–49.

14. According to the logic of Anselm (*Cur Deus Homo,* 1098), man might offer God as infinite offense—the degree depending on the dignity of the party offended—but it would require a being himself of infinite worth to perform the deed of adequate atonement;

see Jaroslav Pelikan, *The Growth of Medieval Theology* (Chicago: University of Chicago Press, 1978), pp. 106–8.

15. For the idioms available to express the mechanics of the Fall, see H. Shelton Smith, *Changing Conceptions of Original Sin* (New York: Scribner's, 1955), esp. pp. 1–9.

16. Edwards will do better than most, but even his strongest argument is negative merely: in a world where personal identity is a perfect mystery, no one can be perfectly sure he is not, in some abstruse sense, really Adam; any more than he may or may not be identical with himself in some parallel universe; see my "Example of Edwards," in *Doctrine and Difference,* esp. pp. 83–108.

17. Thomas Hooker, as we shall see, comes even closer than Shepard to making the completion of a successful reparation into the reality of conversion; see below.

18. Miller, *Colony to Province,* pp. 53–67.

19. For Calvin on the spiritual "stupor" of the reprobate, see his "Commentary on the Epistle to the Romans," in *Calvin's Commentaries,* ed. D. W. Torrance (Grand Rapids, Mich.: Eerdmans, 1973), pp. 243–44.

20. As should be evident, the logic of covenant may have several different uses. One is to establish that God has to agree to treat with man in any terms at all—which a truly "sovereign" deity might well decline to do; and thereafter to assure man that his promises are firm. So far so good. Beyond this area of certainty lies a major ambiguity: to the Arminian (or to a schoolman like Aquinas) the covenant promises a certain reward to actions (even subtle ones like faith) of which created and fallen man is presumed to be capable; to a strict Calvinist, however, it can offer only a way to know—from his own actions, perhaps—whether God has indeed enabled a man to perform the stipulated condition. Von Rohr names this difference "causative" versus "declarative" (*Covenant,* p. 20). Loyal to Calvin, the Synod of Dort (1619) ruled against the more simply voluntary or causative version.

21. For Edwards' inventory of evidences of the Fall, see *Original Sin,* pp. 105–206. And for a defense of the "empirical" nature of this vision, see Perry Miller, *Jonathan Edwards* (rpt. New York: Sloane, 1959), pp. 265–82.

22. The lapse of vital Calvinism in America—somewhere between Edwards and Channing—has been described in terms of the substitution of energetic good works in the place of a sense of man's absolute dependence on God; see Joseph Haroutunian, *Piety versus Moralism* (rpt. New York: Harper and Row, 1970). For a more forgiving view of the same historical transition, see Conrad Wright, *The Beginnings of Unitarianism in America* (Boston: Star King Press, 1955).

23. For the controversy over "striving," see Haroutunian, *Piety,* pp. 48–57.

24. See Edwards, *Freedom of Will* (New Haven: Yale University Press, 1957), pp. 156–67.

25. For the problem of separating the popular from the elite mentality in early New England, see David D. Hall, *Worlds of Wonder, Days of Judgment* (New York: Knopf, 1989), esp. pp. 21–70.

26. In the "Autobiography" Shepard accepts *The Sincere Convert* (London, 1640) as part of his own literary accomplishment (p. 71), but elsewhere he complains that this "collection of notes delivered in a dark town" had been published "without [his] will or privity" and that he suffers chagrin at its "many typographical errors"; see Albro, "Life of Thomas Shepard," in *Works,* vol. 1, p. clxxxvi.

27. For Laud as "scourge," see "Autobiography," p. 51. Shepard's "other things" may recall the end of John's Gospel, where the "other things" that Jesus did were of such a number that "the world itself would not contain the books that would be written."

28. "Autobiography," p. 67.

29. "Autobiography," p. 71.

30. For the context and status of Shepard and Hooker as preparationists, see Pettit, *Heart,* pp. 86–114.

31. Ames is in many ways the fountainhead of New England doctrine, though not of style or emphasis; see Eusden, ed., *Marrow,* esp. pp. 77–174. Excluded from this study (but just barely), *The Gospel-Covenant* (1651) of Peter Bulkeley offers the best support for Miller's emphasis on a Calvin-subverting sense of contractual bargaining; as McGiffert has put the case, "Bulkeley maintains the substance of sound doctrine, [yet a] devilish *quid pro quo* teases the margins of his mind" ("Problem of the Covenant," p. 129).

32. Registering a certain medieval and early modern tendency to ascribe to Christ many functions earlier theorists assigned to the Spirit, the phrase—*Christificierung des Geistes*—expresses Geoffrey Nuttall's sense of the scene of Puritan reaction; see *The Holy Spirit in Puritan Faith and Experience* (London: Basil Blackwell, 1946), esp. pp. 1–19.

33. Traditionally, Christ atones, and the Spirit applies in practice the results of that atonement. Further problems may lurk in Shepard's repeated reference to "the Spirit of Christ."

34. Prior to a full encounter with his *Application of Redemption,* the reader may note Hooker's emphasis on discerning the true nature and powerful presence of sin in either of Perry Miller's anthologies—both of which offer a passage Miller titles "A True Sight of Sin"; see Perry Miller and Thomas H. Johnson, eds., *The Puritans* (rpt. New York: Harper and Row, 1963), pp. 292–301; or Perry Miller, ed., *The American Puritans* (Garden City, N.Y.: Anchor, 1956), pp. 152–64. The reliance of Edwards on the "sensationalist" example of Shepard may weaken the argument for Edwards' dependence on Locke; see Edwards, "Divine and Supernatural Light," in *A Jonathan Edwards Reader,* ed. John E. Smith, Harry S. Stout, and Kenneth P. Minkema (New Haven: Yale University Press, 1995), pp. 105–24; and cp. Miller, "The Rhetoric of Sensation," reprinted in *Errand into the Wilderness* (Cambridge, Mass.: Harvard University Press, 1956), pp. 167–83; also *Edwards,* pp. 32–34, 64–66. The connection between Shepard's *Convert* and Edwards' "Sinners in the Hands of an Angry God" has been pointed out by Thomas Werge, *Thomas Shepard* (New York: Twayne, 1987), pp. 56–57.

35. Quoted from Miller and Johnson, eds., *Puritans,* p. 292.

36. As R. T. Kendall has suggested—and as we will notice in the next chapter— a mark of the more radical preparationism of Thomas Hooker is its more frank willingness to see salvation already present in its preparatory stages; see *Calvin and Calvinism,* pp. 125–40.

37. The "Autobiography" indicates that Shepard and his father *both* saw some significance in the fact that he was born on "powder treason day" (p. 39).

38. In Hawthorne's prime study of intellectual dissociation ("The Christmas Banquet"), the protagonist appears trapped in what Kierkegaard would call "the aesthetic stage": see my "'Life within the Life,'" *NHR* 30 (2004): 1–31.

39. Placing herself between Miller's emphasis on a single ("covenant") orthodoxy—see "Marrow of Puritan Divinity"—and Philip Gura's insistence on the many varieties of radical dissent rampant in seventeenth-century Massachusetts—*A Glimpse of Sion's Glory* (Middletown, Conn.: Wesleyan University Press, 1984)—Janice Knight sketches out two competing strands of theological emphasis, one stressing conditional promises and sanctification, the other standing firm on the acceptance of Christ without condition (or *necessary* ethical consequence); see *Orthodoxies in Massachusetts* (Cambridge, Mass.: Harvard University Press, 1994), esp. pp. 1–33.

40. Ignored on the question of the Church and the World, the power of Augustine's teaching on God as the only satisfying goal of human life is everywhere evident in the tenor of Puritan spirituality; see Perry Miller, "The Augustinian Strain of Piety," in *Seventeenth Century,* pp. 3–34. See also Werge, *Thomas Shepard,* pp. 10–48.

41. One remarkable fact about the experience described in Edwards' conversion experience is that his deep sense of sin and self-abasement is not preparatory at all but comes only *after* his sense of the perfect inevitability—and the sweetness—of the sovereignty of God; see "Personal Narrative," in Smith, Stout, and Minkema, eds., *Reader,* pp. 283–95.

42. It seems highly likely that only Hooker's departure for Connecticut in 1635 kept his extreme emphasis on preparation from becoming a major source of public disagreement in the "free grace controversy" of 1636–38. For the view that it mattered nevertheless, see Michael P. Winship, *Making Heretics* (Princeton: Princeton University Press, 2002), pp. 69–71.

43. The closest study of day-to-day events in the free grace controversy is Winship, *Heretics,* but it has almost nothing to say about performance and placement of *The Sound Believer.*

44. Luther's emphasis on the idea that man, saved while a sinner, continues in his own person to be a sinner after conversion, is most emphatic in his "Commentary on Galatians": "homo christianus simul justus et peccator, sanctus, prophanus, inimicus et filius deus est": for a convenient English version, see John Dillenberger, ed., *Martin Luther: Selections* (Garden City, N.Y.: Anchor, 1961), pp. 99–165.

45. Proof of the complexity—perhaps even the fluidity—of the doctrinal situation in Massachusetts may be drawn from the fact that Cotton can also cite William Pemble (*Vindicatio Gratiae,* 1629) on the crucial question of the "passivity" of faith; see Winship, *Heretics,* pp. 255–56.

46. Marking a prime difference between the famous journey of Bunyan's classic and Melville's revisionist version of the pilgrim's progress (in *The Confidence Man*), this final justification makes it perfectly clear that Shepard knows the preaching cannot cause conversion but only map the stages along its (almost always) tortuous way.

47. David D. Hall has identified the emphasis on "labor" as the heart of Shepard's "evangelism"; see *The Faithful Shepherd* (Chapel Hill: University of North Carolina Press, 1972). But it has not been shown that Shepard's "labors" were more successful than Cotton's less activist efforts in the pulpit.

48. This overriding emphasis on God's sovereign and mysterious will in the matter of salvation was, for Perry Miller, the prime fact of Calvin's own teaching—which covenant theology, on his account, had acted to weaken. His "Calvin" has been called a "stage figure" (see von Rohr, *Covenant,* p. 19), but that figure is stronger than many men of straw; and in

any case Miller's more essential error was to understate the determination of the original American Puritans to be loyal to Calvin's own spirit; see "Marrow," esp. pp. 60–68.

49. That is to say—again—the Calvinist use of covenant can only be declarative. Miller's clearest recognition of this fact comes in his 1956 anthology, *American Puritans:* "This Covenant of Grace did not alter the fact that only those are saved on whom God sheds His grace, enabling them to believe in Christ; but it made clear why and how certain men are selected, and prescribed the conditions under which they might reach a fair assurance of their own standing" (p. 144).

50. Perhaps Emily Dickinson's poem about "look of Agony" (#241) means to invoke some "Convulsion" like the near-despair depicted in Shepard's "Autobiography" (p. 45).

51. In the well-substantiated view of R. T. Kendall, the Shepard-led majority of American Puritans depart most from Calvin in turning "assurance" into a psychological problem in the first place; see *Calvin and Calvinism,* pp. 151–83.

52. See John Cotton, *Christ the Fountain of Life* (rpt. New York: Arno, 1972), p. 27. This crucial passage appears just *after* those reprinted in Miller's anthology *The Puritans,* pp. 327–34.

53. See Edward Taylor, "Gods Determinations Touching His Elect," in *The Poems of Edward Taylor,* ed. Donald E. Stanford (New Haven: Yale University Press, 1960), p. 414.

54. For the evidence that many in Shepard's congregation felt a certain letdown after the excitement of their migration for Christ and ordinances, see Patricia Caldwell, *The Puritan Conversion Narrative* (Cambridge: Cambridge University Press, 1983), pp. 119–34.

CHAPTER 6.   REGENERATION THROUGH VIOLENCE

1. On the account of John Winthrop, the primary issue was—as at Plymouth earlier—meadowland for grazing; see Richard S. Dunn, ed., *The Journal of John Winthrop* (Cambridge, Mass.: Harvard University Press, 2001), p. 126. Perry Miller long ago suggested the issue of "personal rivalry": see "Thomas Hooker and the Democracy of Connecticut," reprinted in *Errand into the Wilderness* (Cambridge, Mass.: Harvard University Press, 1956), p. 17.

2. For Hooker's service as co-moderator of the "formal inquiry into the spread of Antinomian opinions," see Sargent Bush, *The Writings of Thomas Hooker* (Madison: University of Wisconsin Press, 1980), pp. 77–78; and Frank Shuffelton, *Thomas Hooker* (Princeton: Princeton University Press, 1977), pp. 245–47. For the inference of the (displaced) importance of preparation in the controversy, see Perry Miller, "'Preparation for Salvation' in Seventeenth-Century New England," reprinted in *Nature's Nation* (Cambridge, Mass.: Harvard University Press, 1967), esp. pp. 60–66; and cp. Norman Pettit, *The Heart Prepared* (New Haven: Yale University Press, 1966), pp. 125–57. For a refusal of this emphasis, see William K. B. Stoever, *"A Faire and Easie Way to Heaven"* (Middletown, Conn.: Wesleyan University Press, 1978), pp. 192–99; and for a subtle compromise, see Michael P. Winship, *Making Heretics* (Princeton: Princeton University Press, 2002), pp. 69–70, 268–69.

3. Scorning the notion of any "democratic" intention, Miller yet emphasized that Hooker had originally favored a lower standard for church admission, so that "even if more

hypocrites were accepted, still fewer of the regenerate would be held out" ("Democracy," pp. 31–32). Shuffelton concludes that Hooker was willing to accept all who could give "satisfactory evidence, 'in the judgment in charity,' that they might belong to the external covenant" (*Hooker,* p. 169). Bush quotes Hooker's pained confession that denying baptism to the children of non–church members was against his own "secret desire and inclination" and suggests that "it was somewhat easier to gain membership in his congregation than in some others where 'rational charity' was not so actively invoked" (*Hooker,* pp. 121, 125). Citing Cotton Mather's report that Hooker left the test of faith "unto the elders of the church," Andrew Delbanco infers that Hooker evidently treated "conversion relations . . . as a matter of less than ultimate concern"; see *The Puritan Ordeal* (Cambridge, Mass.: Harvard University Press, 1989), p. 179. And yet, Patricia Caldwell has duly noted that, in *The Saint's Dignity and Duty,* at least, Hooker's sense of the incommunicability of deep and authentic religious experience is offset by his belief that when "I can best discover it to another, then do I know that which I never before understood"; see *The Puritan Conversion Narrative* (Cambridge: Cambridge University Press, 1983), pp. 90–92. This powerful if inchoate epistemology—of speaking and being heard, with charity yet with discernment—may take us further into the *raison* of Congregationalism than much that has been written about the abstruse imbrication of the covenants; see my "Certain Circumstances," in *New Essays on Hawthorne's Major Tales,* ed. Millicent Bell (Cambridge: Cambridge University Press, 1993), esp. pp. 51–59.

4. According to the now-standard account of the two principal soteriologies at issue in early New England, Hooker stands with Shepard and the majority of ministers in holding to the line of English Puritans like William Ames, which emphasized the necessity of preparation, the function (within the covenant) of conditional promises to works of faith, and both the moral and the evidentiary value of sanctification; Cotton's loyalty is to the more immediatist, more "spiritual" tradition of Richard Sibbes and John Preston; see Janice Knight, *Orthodoxies in Massachusetts* (Cambridge, Mass.: Harvard University Press, 1994), esp. pp. 34–71. And yet, as Shepard and Cotton did agree to live together in *some* sort of agreement about the promises made to works of grace, it might make sense to think of Hooker, down there in Connecticut, still preaching preparation while Shepard was trying to make the churches of Massachusetts safe for the logic of sanctification, as the odd man out.

5. As Cotton Mather noted, Hooker went over his salvation scheme three separate times but did not live to complete, in *The Application of Redemption,* its final, considered, and textually authoritative version; see *Magnalia Christi Americana* (rpt. New York: Russell and Russell, 1853), vol. 1, pp. 347–48. Shuffelton concludes that Hooker wished his *Application* to "supersede his other earlier books covering the same material" (*Hooker,* p. 253). Arguing for a development in Hooker's tone and vision, Delbanco nevertheless concedes that many "parallel passages" reveal only "small differences" (*Ordeal,* p. 175). This evident continuity of project well justifies Bush's large-scale attempt to describe the shape of Hooker's total system; see *Hooker,* esp. pp. 146–230, 251–75.

6. All citations of the first eight books of Hooker's *Application of Redemption* refer to the Arno Press (New York, 1972) reprint of the London edition of 1657.

7. Bush confidently asserts that, given the model of *The Soul's Preparation* (1632) and *The Soul's Humiliation* (1637), only death at age sixty-one kept Hooker from writing "a companion volume to *The Application of Redemption, the Ninth and Tenth Books*" (*Hooker,* pp. 186–87); but it could have taken a while, and it might not have made the task of provid-

ing an account of "vocation"—the noetic counterpart of "implanting" or "ingrafting"—any more comfortable. In any event, Bush treats the soul's "Humiliation" (pp. 186–203) and "Vocation" (pp. 204–30) from earlier (English) works bearing those titles. And then, in one chapter, called "Going Beyond Faith," the more mysterious topics "Union, Justification, Adoption, Sanctification" (pp. 251–75).

8. Ramus' notorious "method" might well have the unintended effect of causing the Not-A term of an A/Not-A dichotomy to be left uncomfortably behind: if, for example, one went on to break down Preparation for Salvation into a further series of proliferating dichotomies, it might seem inelegant, spatially or visually, to come "back" to its actual accomplishment. For commentary on the aim and historical significance of the method, see Perry Miller, *The New England Mind: The Seventeenth Century* (Cambridge, Mass.: Harvard University Press, 1939), pp. 116–53; and cp. Walter J. Ong, S.J., *Ramus, Method, and the Decay of Dialogue* (Cambridge, Mass.: Harvard University Press, 1958), esp. pp. 171–213.

9. Most strikingly absent from the last elaboration of Hooker's system is not the "Christ's Prayer for Believers, on John 17," promised as a "last" of eleven "books" in the 1657 edition of his *Application* (p. D3), but some account of what happens to the psyche just after this record-length Preparation.

10. Bush, *Hooker,* p. 77; see also George Leon Walker, *Thomas Hooker* (New York: Dodd, Mead, 1891), pp. 111–13.

11. On internal evidence, Bush concludes that the seven sermons that comprise *The Saint's Dignity and Duty* (1651) "came out of the 1636–38 disputes." With a preface by T. S.—almost certainly Thomas Shepard—it emphasizes that younger colleague's view that faith is significantly "active," yet carefully reminds the audience that God *enables* the elect "to do whatever he commands them to do"; see *Hooker,* pp. 78–95.

12. The sermons of *The Saint's Dignity and Duty,* some of which may well have been given in Boston, appear to coincide with the critical events of 1636–38 and thus with the earlier sermons in Shepard's *Parable* of Sanctification; back in Connecticut, however, Hooker returned to—and stuck with, from 1638 to 1640—the beginning: Preparation.

13. The Arno Press facsimile edition of 1972 bears the date 1657 but appears to be the same as the original of 1656.

14. *Application,* "To the Reader," p. D2.

15. In Pettit's words, "the preparatory phase was by far the most important single activity in Hooker's conception of conversion. Rarely did he preach to his covenanted community without exhorting the unconverted to prepare for grace" (*Heart,* pp. 100–101).

16. For the epistemology of the Ramist dichotomy, see Ong, *Ramus,* pp. 83–167.

17. Shuffelton concludes that, in his *Application*—begun "before June 1638"—Hooker tended to rely on "the same scriptural texts" as in his earlier works and even to illustrate his doctrines with "the same favorite tropes"; and yet "he did tailor their expression for a postantinomian New England" (*Hooker,* p. 254).

18. Thus the orthodox account theory of the "atonement," from its perfection in the eleventh-century *Cur Deus Homo* of Anselm of Canterbury to the post-Reformation "governmental theory" proposed by Hugo Grotius; see Jaroslav Pelikan, *The Christian Tradition* (Chicago: University of Chicago Press, 1978), vol. 3, pp. 139–44; vol. 4 (1983), pp. 325, 360–61.

19. For Calvin's teaching that, though only some are elected to salvation, Christ nevertheless died for the sins of all, see R. T. Kendall, *Calvin and English Calvinism* (London: Oxford University Press, 1979), pp. 13–28.

20. Perry Miller's prime point, still worth considering, is that the scholastic (and somewhat rationalistic) Puritans do not present the arationality of Divine Decree with the same "Gallic clarity" as the Calvin of *The Institutes;* see "The Marrow of Puritan Divinity," reprinted in *Errand into the Wilderness* (Cambridge, Mass.: Harvard University Press, 1956), esp. pp. 50–53; and cp. *The New England Mind: The Seventeenth Century* (Cambridge, Mass.: Harvard University Press, 1939), esp. pp. 64–108.

21. Shuffelton, *Hooker,* pp. 253–58.

22. Everett Emerson long ago reminded us that, in his sermons at least, Calvin himself gave generous attention to the covenant idiom; see "Calvin and Covenant Theology," *CH* 25 (1956): 136–44. Yet a theoretical point may remain: self-conscious Calvinists require the Covenant to assure themselves of God's steady intentions in the arena of salvation, but they may use it to energize the human will only with care and qualification. For the classic qualification (offered by John Norton), see Knight, *Orthodoxies,* pp. 125–27.

23. Though Kendall is correct in claiming that, for Hooker at least, "preparation for faith is tantamount to assurance of election," he probably makes too much of the abilities of Hooker's natural man. Any well-instructed would-be saint can put himself in the way of the means, but grace alone makes the means effective and that in the elect alone; see *English Calvinism,* pp. 4–5, 125–38. Thus the observation of Everett Emerson remains cogent: the various phases of preparation are "just as much God's actions as the Effectual Calling itself"; see "Thomas Hooker," *ATR* 49 (1967): 190–203.

24. Not a "voluntarist" in the matter of man's salvation, Calvin is most certainly so on the classic question of the primacy of will in God's nature, holding, apropos of reprobation, that the "will of God is the highest rule of justice; so that what he wills must be considered just, for this very reason: because he wills it"; see Hugh T. Kerr, ed., *A Compend of the Institutes of the Christian Religion* (Philadelphia: Westminster, 1939), p. 132. Or, in another version: "The will of God is the highest rule of righteousness, so that everything which he wills must be held to be righteous by the mere fact of his willing it"; see *Institutes of the Christian Religion,* trans. Henry Beveridge (rpt. Grand Rapids, Mich.: Eerdmans, 1972), vol. 2, p. 227.

25. Rejected once and for all at the Synod of Dort is the idea that salvation is, in the last analysis, conditional upon man's own free choice; see Keith L. Sprunger, *The Learned Doctor Ames* (Urbana: University of Illinois Press, 1972), pp. 52–70.

26. As Perry Miller well understood, Calvin's predestination is, in God, a great mystery and, for man, "an inextricable labyrinth"; and so—with "Gallic clarity"—"it is not right that man should with impunity pry into things which the Lord has been pleased to conceal within himself"; see *Institutes,* vol. 2, p. 204. For Hooker's learning experience with the inspired depression of Mrs. Joanna Drake, see Shuffelton, *Hooker,* pp. 28–68.

27. No Puritan theorist would deny that, logically speaking, preparation and sanctification are quite different: at the very least, different orders of grace were involved. Yet in widespread New England practice they might have *felt* pretty much alike: moral anxiety before and moral anxiety after saving grace are both moral anxiety. And if, as in Hooker's theory, the moment of that grace was itself rather easy to miss, then how did one know which side one was on? Consider, in this context, Winship's suspicion of Hooker's "inability to intuitively experience grace" (*Heretics,* p. 70).

28. In the long history of philosophical improbability in the West, the Catholic priest named Nicholas Malebranche usually gets the credit for an "occasionalism" in which,

thanks to Descartes' radical separation of the substances, God has to create the appropriate "idea" every time a human being experiences a "sensation." But Puritan evangelical theory keeps God very nearly as busy: the minister furnishes the Word but, just in time, God alone makes it into a converting experience.

29. In Hooker's Latin, *Johannis Ministerium, nec plane Propheticum, nec plane Apostolicum, sed intermedium quondam Ministerium fuit*—not just prophet and apostle, but a certain intermediary; and see *Institutes,* vol. 1, p. 367.

30. The shock ought to be less jarring in the region of theology than Jacques Derrida has made it seem in that of philosophy—God being on premise a transcendent being and Scripture offering (therefore) a plentitude of tropes—yet privileged figures have a way of coming to seem literal in relation to the figures they generate. For the timely insult to philosophy, see "White Mythology: Metaphor in the Text of Philosophy," in *Margins of Philosophy,* trans. Alan Bass (Chicago: University of Chicago Press, 1982), pp. 207–71.

31. At moments like this, perhaps, one feels the force of the suggestion that we call the "Antinomian" affair of Cotton, Hutchinson, Wheelwright, and Vane the "Free Grace Controversy"; see Winship, *Heretics,* pp. 1-27.

32. See Kendall, *English Calvinism,* esp. pp. 6–7, 21–25, 67–75, 143–45.

33. The alert reader will notice that the numbering in the text in question skips from p. 174 to p. 195.

34. Against the obvious objection about preaching to the predestined, even an Immediatist like John Cotton maintains the "occasionalist" position of Perkins and Ames: the God who alone confers salvation also commands men to seek and ministers to offer salvation; so that, "While we are thus speaking to you, God many times confers such a spirit of grace into us, as gives us power to receive Christ"; see *Christ the Fountain of Life* (rpt. New York: Arno, 1971), p. 173. (A better text might clarify the pronoun references without removing the creative ambiguity of doctrine.)

35. For the pervasive influence of William Perkins' *Art of Prophecy,* see Lisa M. Gordis, *Opening Scripture* (Chicago: University of Chicago Press, 2003), pp. 1–36.

36. The preeminent work on Hooker's style—including his manner of negotiating the sensitive relation between biblical types and the tropes of ordinary rhetoric—is Gordis, *Opening Scripture,* pp. 73–96. In this sensitive reading, Hooker's sermons are always "In dialogue with the Word" (p. 84). Gordis thus concurs with Knight, that Hooker's ideal preacher is "to employ rather than to unfold biblical texts"—so that he himself "always places Scripture in the service of his own narrative of the soul's pilgrimage" (*Orthodoxies,* p. 174). For early recognition of this tendency, see Alfred Habegger, "Preparing the Soul for Christ," *AL* 41 (1969): 342–54.

37. Thus the Puritan version of an *Ars* more venerable than the *Arte* of Perkins: weep if you wish me to weep.

38. Even as a "Puritan," Edwards is often praised for a prescient understanding of "modern" theories of motivation; see, for early examples, Perry Miller, *Jonathan Edwards* (New York: Sloane, 1949), esp. pp. 234–63; and, less extravagantly, "Jonathan Edwards on the Sense of the Heart," *HTR* 41 (1948): 123–45. For notice of Hooker's psychological emphasis, distinguishing him from a preparationist predecessor such as William Perkins and dramatized as an "adventure," see Bush, *Hooker,* esp. pp. 129–85; and cp. Shuffelton, *Hooker,* pp. 28–120.

39. Knight observes that in his pastoral project, "Hooker seems to expect resistance—his preacher must have courage to chastise" (*Orthodoxies*, p. 172).

40. For Emerson as forerunner, see Michael J. Colacurcio, "Pleasing God," in *Doctrine and Difference* (New York: Routledge, 1997), pp. 129–76.

41. For John Winthrop's long-delayed, yet still abrupt dismissal of Anne Hutchinson, see David D. Hall, ed., *The Antinomian Controversy* (Middletown, Conn.: Wesleyan University Press, 1968), p. 348; and for Edward Taylor's imitation of Christ's tender reassurance to the "poor doubting Christian," see *Poems* (New Haven: Yale University Press, 1960), p. 414.

42. Thus the "preparationist" opening of John Donne's "Holy Sonnet XIV."

43. Well made in his sermons "The Covenant of Grace" (1636), the point is central enough to have been selected for anthology representation: see Phyllis Jones and Nicholas Jones, eds., *Salvation in New England* (Austin: University of Texas Press, 1977), pp. 43–58. And see Charles Lloyd Cohen, *God's Caress* (New York: Oxford University Press, 1986), pp. 83–85.

44. Miller comes closest to expressing this important point (and thus in redressing the imbalance of his "Marrow") not in the introduction to its republication in *Errand into the Wilderness* (Cambridge, Mass.: Harvard University Press, 1956), pp. 48–50, but in his brief headnote to a selection from Thomas Shepard's preface to *The Gospel-Covenant* (1651) of Peter Bulkeley: the "Covenant of Grace did not alter the fact those only are saved upon whom God sheds His grace," but pledged in every other way "not to run tyrannically athwart human conceptions of justice"; see *American Puritans*, p. 144. But—academic attention span being what it is—paradigms shift, and new questions arise before the old ones are quite answered. What ought always to have been clear is that Arminians are entitled to presume in human "nature" an ability sufficient to accept the astonishing Grace that is salvation; Calvinists need to keep reminding themselves of the separate grace required to accept that Grace. Closest to this point is Stoever, who treats the problem of "Covenant Theology and Antinomianism" as a "Dialectic of Nature and Grace"; see *"Faire and Easie Way,"* pp. 3–20 passim.

45. In his 1838 "Address" to the Harvard Divinity School, Emerson solemnly pronounces that "the doors of the temple stand open, night and day, before every man" on the sole "stern condition" that religious truth be received by "intuition" and never "at second hand"; see Joel Porte, ed., *Emerson: Essays and Lectures* (New York: Library of America, 1983), p. 79.

46. For the famous discussion of religion as "ultimate concern," see Paul Tillich, *The Dynamics of Faith* (rpt. New York: Perennial, 2001). The classic analysis of determinism as bad faith is the work of Jean-Paul Sartre; see *Being and Nothingness,* trans. Hazel Barnes (New York: Philosophical Library, 1956), esp. pp. 457–85.

47. Stoever treats Hooker only in passing, yet this most "scholastic" of the American Calvinists might lend himself best to the nature-and-grace analysis; see *"Faire and Easie Way,"* esp. pp. 106, 116.

48. For Taylor as a reader of Hooker, see John Gatta, "Edward Taylor and Thomas Hooker," *NDEJ* 12 (1979): 1–13. Never is Taylor more the advocate of "holy violence" than in "Meditation I, 3," where the soul, seeking sweetness but smelling only the stench of sin, needs a solid knock on the head; see *Poems,* pp. 7–8.

49. For Augustine's doctrine of God and evil, freedom and the disorder that results from sin, see Etienne Gilson, *The Christian Philosophy of Saint Augustine* (rpt. New York: Vintage, 1967), pp. 143–48.

50. For Edwards' exposure of the regress involved in "willing to will," see *Freedom,* esp. pp. 171–79.

51. Citing Bush and Knight, Winship remarks that in his "fascination with preparation" Hooker "dismissed even the Sibbesian conception of the witness of the Spirit" (*Heretics,* p. 70).

52. Cotton's (supportable) contention that, of all the New England elders, he is the most consistent expositor of Calvin should not be allowed to obscure the express loyalty of Hooker and the others.

53. Delbanco refers Hooker's "delight that God chooses vigorous bodies to contain the gift of grace" to a certain "instinct for the muscular" (*Ordeal,* p. 173).

54. The repetition of this phrase links Hawthorne's "Egotism" with its partner, "The Christmas Banquet"; for relevant commentary, see my "'Life within the Life,'" *NHR* 30 (2004): 1–31.

55. The logic of the negative volition is noticed nowhere so well as in Melville's "Bartleby the Scrivener"—where, in sight of Locke, Priestley, and Edwards, and with the silent endorsement of Schopenhauer, the title character prefers, in the name of freedom, to prefer himself out of particular existence; see Walton Patrick, "'Bartleby' and the Doctrine of Necessity," *AL* 1 (1969): 39–53; Daniel Stempel and Bruce M. Stillians, "'Bartleby the Scrivener,'" *NCL* 27 (1972): 268–82; and Allan Emery, "The Alternatives of Melville's 'Bartleby,'" *NCL* 31 (1976): 170–87. For a convenient set of comparisons for this early modern question, one might consider the element of negativity in the theories of Augustine and Aquinas on the one side and Jean-Paul Sartre on the other.

56. Emerson, *Journals* (Cambridge, Mass.: Harvard University Press, 1965), vol. 5, p. 471.

57. Understandably, Edmund S. Morgan questioned whether the enthusiasm of the American Puritans did not lead "the Church" (of professing Saints) too far from "the world" of ordinary sinners; see *Visible Saints* (rpt. Ithaca: Cornell University Press, 1965). But William James had long since raised the more fundamental issue—of the extent to which "twice-born" standards could ever be the norm; see *Varieties of Religious Experience* (rpt. New York: Modern Library), pp. 320–69, 475–509.

58. Cp. the puzzled but pragmatic conclusion of Soul (Ranks Two and Three) in *Gods Determinations:* If certain "blessed motions" are indeed "from Christ, Oh! Then thrice happy me. / If not, I'st not be worser than I be" (*Poems,* p. 432).

59. For the bibliographic problems connected with Hooker's sermons and published works, see Gordis, *Opening Scripture,* pp. 217–20; and cp. Winfried Herget, "Preaching and Publication," *HTR* 65 (1972): 231–39; also "The Transcription and Transmission of the Hooker Corpus," in *Thomas Hooker: Writings in England and Holland,* ed. George Williams et al. (Cambridge, Mass.: Harvard University Press, 1975), pp. 253–54; and Sargent Bush, "Establishing the Hooker Canon," in Williams et al., eds., *Writings in England and Holland,* pp. 390–425. No exception to the puritanic law of books written out of need—or serendipity, or providence—Hooker's career provides a wonderful proof that literature often moves in strange ways.

60. For the centrality of the "true sight" in an actual conversion experience, see Cohen, *Caress*, pp. 176–78.

61. In the famous formula of Augustine's *Confessions*, "Our hearts were made for Thee, O God, and will not rest until they rest in Thee." For the general case of Puritanism as a prime manifestation of "The Augustinian Strain of Piety," see Miller, *New England Mind*, pp. 3–34.

62. See Louis Martz, *The Poetry of Meditation* (New Haven: Yale University Press, 1960), esp. pp. 25–39.

63. Miller, ed., *Puritans*, vol. 1, pp. 306–9.

64. What we have, meanwhile, is Sacvan Bercovitch's brilliant chapter on the way a historical language of sin could constitute an inevitable sense of self; see *Puritan Origins*, pp. 1–34. Also, more recently, Andrew Delbanco's urgent book *The Death of Satan* (New York: Farrar, Straus and Giroux, 1995).

65. Cotton's baroque evocation of the heart pierced through and bled out—a high point of his style in *The Way of Life* (London, 1641)—has been anthologized in George Horner and Robert Bain, eds., *Colonial and Federalist American Writing* (New York: Odyssey, 1966), pp. 91–98.

66. See Miller, ed., *Puritans*, pp. 309–14.

67. See Ernest W. Baughman, "Public Confession and *The Scarlet Letter*," *NEQ* 40 (1967): 532–50.

68. Quoted from Jones, *Synthesis*, p. 32. The question also figures in the account of David D. Hall, *Faithful Shepherd* (Chapel Hill: University of North Carolina Press, 1972), pp. 162–75.

69. One place to begin, perhaps, would be with Heinrich Heppe, *Reformed Dogmatics*, trans. G. T. Thompson (London: Allen and Unwin, 1950), which makes clear that the Calvinist tradition was not slow to develop its own scholasticism.

70. This "Edwardsian" emphasis is explicitly maintained by all the preachers in this study (as by Bulkeley, Norton, and Davenport as well); and this is the fact creatively obscured by Miller's "Marrow."

71. For the three feel-bad phases of preparation in Shepard, see above and cp. Pettit, *Heart*, pp. 105–14.

72. For readings of *The Soul's Humiliation*, see Bush, *Hooker*, pp. 187–203; and Shuffelton, *Hooker*, pp. 78–97. At this point the reader can probably agree with Kendall that Hooker's relentless system of Preparation leaves "Christ's coming into His temple . . . but a step away" (*English Calvinism*, p. 135).

73. All citations of "The Soul's Ingrafting" refer to Everett H. Emerson, ed., *Redemption* (Gainesville: University Press of Florida, 1956).

74. See Bush, *Hooker*, pp. 204–30, 251–75. Strikingly, Bush treats "The Soul's Ingrafting" as a "transition," thus reinscribing Hooker's own tendency to move from one process to another, sliding past (if not eliding) what might be a vital center.

75. Though Miller associates Hooker with the logic by which the Covenant undermined Calvin—and awards him ambiguous pride of place in expanding the limits of natural ability—both of his anthologies present him, much more simply, as the man who kept insisting that the bad news of sin in all must come before the good news of salvation for some; see *Puritans*, vol. 1, pp. 290–314; and cp. *American Puritans*, pp. 152–71.

CHAPTER 7. PRIMITIVE COMFORT

1. The most balanced and useful study of Cotton's career remains that of Larzer Ziff, *The Career of John Cotton* (Princeton: Princeton University Press, 1962). This chapter attempts to redeem what Ziff considers a naive idealism about many of Cotton's positions.

2. See Everett H. Emerson, *John Cotton* (New York: Twayne, 1965), p. 43; Phyllis M. Jones and Nicholas R. Jones, eds., *Salvation in New England* (Austin: University of Texas Press, 1977), p. 119; and Ann Kibbey, *The Interpretation of Material Shapes in Puritanism* (Cambridge: Cambridge University Press, 1986).

3. John Cotton, *The Way of Life* (London, 1641), p. 105; further quotes are from this edition. And see Perry Miller and Thomas H. Johnson, eds., *The Puritans* (rpt. New York: Harper and Row, 1963), p. 318. For a subtle description and appreciation of Cotton's distinctive way with the words of Scripture, see Lisa M. Gordis, *Opening Scripture* (Chicago: University of Chicago Press, 2003), pp. 37–55.

4. Cotton, *The Way*, p. 126. And cp. George Horner and Robert Bain, eds., *Colonial and Federalist American Writing* (New York: Odyssey Press, 1966), pp. 91–98.

5. Jones and Jones, eds., *Salvation*, p. 121.

6. And see Perry Miller, ed., *The American Puritans* (Garden City, N.Y.: Anchor, 1956), pp. 171–82.

7. Quotations are from *Christ the Fountain of Life* (London, 1651). This work was published ten years after *The Way of Life*, but the chronology of Cotton's English preaching seems uncertain: Ziff assigns *The Fountain* to the years "between 1612 and 1632" (*Cotton*, p. 263); Emerson places both *The Way* and *The Fountain* in the period 1624–32 (*Cotton*, p. 163); Kibbey presses hard to assign *The Way* to the years 1630–32 but is silent about *The Fountain*. My own arrangement is thematic rather than chronological.

8. For Cotton's sense of the totalized authority of Scripture, see Edward H. Davidson, "John Cotton's Biblical Exegesis," *EAL* 17 (1982): 119–38. See also Teresa Toulouse, *The Art of Prophesying* (Athens: University of Georgia Press, 1987), esp. pp. 39–42; and Eugenia DeLamotte, "John Cotton and the Rhetoric of Grace," *EAL* 21 (1986): 49–74.

9. Cp. Miller and Johnson, eds., *Puritans*, pp. 332–34. Surprising too is the fact that the closest modern student of the Antinomian (or Free Grace) Controversy cannot find in Cotton's English sermons "the critical position that generated so much controversy in Massachusetts"; see Michael P. Winship, *Making Heretics* (Princeton: Princeton University Press, 2002), p. 30. Perhaps Winship is thinking of Cotton's distinctive doctrine of spiritual witness.

10. For a full reading of what is (probably) the most authoritative and relevant text of Cotton's New England preaching on the Covenant of Grace, see R. T. Kendall, *Calvin and English Calvinism to 1649* (London: Oxford University Press, 1979), pp. 167–83. Kendall agrees with Ziff and Emerson that *A Treatise of the Covenant of Grace* (1659)—reprinted in 1671 and enlarged from *The New Covenant* (1654) and *The Covenant of God's Free Grace* (1655)—is the closest we can get to Cotton's preaching in 1636. A revealing portion of the 1659 version is reprinted in Jones and Jones, eds., *Salvation*, pp. 43–58.

11. All citations of Cotton's 1636 preaching on the Covenant are to *A Treatise of the Covenant of Grace* (London, 1659).

12. Especially interesting—as Winship suggests—would be the irenic sermon Wilson preached in the Boston church just after receiving a "grave exhortation" from Cotton; see *Heretics*, p. 103.

13. See David D. Hall, ed., *The Antinomian Controversy, 1636–1638* (Middletown, Conn.: Wesleyan University Press, 1968), pp. 24–42. For Cotton's public presence, see Sargent Bush Jr., "Epistolary Counseling in the Puritan Movement: The Example of John Cotton," in *Puritanism: Transatlantic Perspectives*, ed. Francis J. Bremer (Worcester: Massachusetts Historical Society, 1993), esp. pp. 129–30.

14. Hall, ed., *Controversy*, p. 46. All citations from the various parts of the "Sixteen Questions Controversy" are to this important gathering of texts.

15. Cotton, *Treatise*, p. 44.

16. Winthrop quoted from Hall, ed., *Controversy*, p. 60.

17. On Ziff's account, it took an "amazed John Cotton" quite a long time to "realize what the elders of the other churches [were] so disturbed about" (*Cotton*, p. 134).

18. Emerson's private parody of the elders' problem takes place in his journal for October 1, 1832, on the eve of his break with his Unitarian congregation; see William H. Gilman et al., eds., *The Journals and Miscellaneous Notebooks of Ralph Waldo Emerson* (Cambridge, Mass.: Harvard University Press, 1964), vol. 4, p. 45. For commentary that looks back to the Antinomian Moment, see my "Pleasing God," in *Doctrine and Difference* (New York: Routledge, 1997), esp. pp. 133–54.

19. For Shepard's tendency to make anxiety count as assurance, see Michael McGiffert's introduction to the "Autobiography," edited as *God's Plot* (Amherst: University of Massachusetts Press, 1972), esp. pp. 19–26; and cp. Winship, *Heretics*, pp. 16–21. For Hooker's rejection of a way of "sweetness," see "The Soul's Ingrafting into Christ," in *Redemption*, ed. Everett H. Emerson (Gainesville: Scholars' Facsimiles, 1956), pp. 101–9.

20. Significantly, Cotton was the only first-generation minister to preach a whole cycle of sermons on the inviting text of the Song of Solomon: see *A Brief Exposition . . . on the Whole Book of Canticles* (London, 1655). For Cotton's place in a tradition running counter to this way of anxiety, see Janice Knight, *Orthodoxies in Massachusetts* (Cambridge, Mass.: Harvard University Press, 1994), esp. pp. 109–29.

21. Hall, ed., *Controversy*, p. 78.

22. For a full account of the gradual development and special emphases of Cotton's spiritist position, see Winship, *Heretics*, pp. 31–36.

23. Cotton, *The Way*, p. 105; and cp. Miller and Johnson, eds., *Puritans*, p. 318.

24. Hall (*Controversy*, p. 93) identifies David Pareus (1548–1622) as the author of *Roberti Bellarmini . . . De justificatione . . . Explicati et Castigati studio* (Heidelberg, 1615). Apart from Cotton's notice of this confrontation, the significance of this little-known reformer has been hard to estimate.

25. The clear teaching of Cotton's *Treatise* is that no one can "thirst after Christ . . . if Christ had not wrought" that thirst, and that Christ will never "leave the soul to quench his thirst with his thirst" (pp. 161–62).

26. A three-volume edition of *The Works of Thomas Shepard* (with the 180-page "Life" by John Albro) was published in Boston in 1847 by the Massachusetts Sabbath School Society and was reprinted in 1853 by the Boston Doctrinal Tract and Book Society. The 1853 edition was reprinted in 1967 by the AMS Press; a further reprint is currently available from Soli Deo Gloria Press, 1991. A curious twist in the history of Puritan reputations lies

in the fact that Edwards' principal treatise on the discerning of God's Spirit represses its debt to Cotton and—ending with an emphasis on "Christian practice"—parades its debt to Shepard; see John E. Smith, ed., *Religious Affections* (New Haven: Yale University Press, 1959), pp. 52–57 and footnotes passim.

27. For the substance of Bellarmine's neo-Catholic position, see his treatise "De Justificatione," in Roberti Bellarmini, *Opera Omnia* (Frankfurt: Minerva, 1965), vol. 7, pp. 743–60.

28. The impression given by Perry Miller's chapter "The Covenant of Grace" is that one might almost quote from *Puritans* indiscriminately; see *The New England Mind: The Seventeenth Century* (Cambridge, Mass.: Harvard University Press, 1939), pp. 365–97. The situation is not much remedied in his familiar "Marrow of Puritan Divinity," reprinted in *Errand into the Wilderness* (Cambridge, Mass.: Harvard University Press, 1956), pp. 48–98. It is against Miller's view of a more or less unific declension from Calvin's sovereign to the Puritans' self-limited and self-entailed God that arguments in favor of Puritan varieties appear most cogent.

29. Cotton, *Brief Exposition*, p. 5.

30. Hall, ed., *Controversy*, p. 103. And for the importance of the "Adam" question— as the key to a crucial difference in soteriology—see Jesper Rosenmeier, "New England's Perfection: The Image of Adam and the Image of Christ in the Antinomian Crisis," *WMQ* 27 (1970): 435–59.

31. Hall's emphasis on "man's activity before grace" (and his loose explanation of material and formal in the matter of Christian sanctification) seriously reduces the question at hand—from the nice one of exactly who may be thought the prime agent in the human performance of sanctified works to the well-worn one of whether man without grace ever initiates anything truly spiritual. An allied simplification is offered by William K. B. Stoever, who regards the Antinomian Controversy as a chapter in the history of Nature and Grace; see *"A Faire and Easie Way to Heaven"* (Middletown, Conn.: Wesleyan University Press, 1978), esp. pp. 3–57.

32. If Janice Knight is correct—that "Ames's discourse, like that of his famous teacher William Perkins, seems consistently caught in the undertow of legalism" (*Orthodoxies*, p. 93)—then Cotton might have to content himself with the authority of Pareus and Calvin.

33. Though it has been possible to conclude, in a summary account of their contents, that "The Elders' Reply" and "Cotton's Rejoinder" reveal the collapse of an earlier moderation without shedding "any new theological light" (Winship, *Heretics*, p. 99), it seems truer to say that the elders not only provoked a final and necessary clarification of crucial discursive differences but also drew forth from their embattled opponent a major explication of Protestant logic as such.

34. *Religious Affections*, pt. 3, Fourth Sign, esp. pp. 266–69.

35. Hall (*Controversy*, p. 117) suggests that the place in Calvin is the *Institutes*, III, xv; but, assuming that Cotton is merely paraphrasing, III, xiv, suggests itself as well: "confidence in works has no place unless you have previously fixed your whole confidence on the mercy of God": see *Institutes of the Christian Religion* (Grand Rapids, Mich.: Eerdmans, 1972), vol. 2, p. 86.

36. For the subtler significance of this charge—and for Cotton's own use of the old covenant—see Winship, *Heretics*, pp. 31–33.

37. Against Perry Miller's repeated insistence that the Puritans' covenant does not sound much like Calvin, see Everett H. Emerson, "Calvin and Covenant Theology," *CH* 25 (1956): 136–44; and, at greater length, John von Rohr, *The Covenant of Grace in Puritan Thought* (Atlanta: Scholars Press, 1986), esp. pp. 155–91.

38. In a world where everyone is trying hard to be loyal to the Synod of Dort, Cotton appears to lack any sense of "Calvinism" as an issue; his appeal is simply to our "best Protestants," and his interest is in a coherent position for Protestantism as such.

39. Not identified in Hall. Presumably William Ames, though the quote is not from his *Medullae Theologica* (Amsterdam, 1623); and possibly William Perkins, whose *Golden Chain* (Cambridge, 1612) ends with an apt consolation from Beza: "At night the sun setteth, but in the next morning it riseth again" (p. 116).

40. For the turn of the "Calvinist" mind toward the "Puritan" question of assurance in the individual case, see Kendall, *English Calvinism*, esp. pp. 29–41, 79–140; and cp. Winship, *Heretics*, pp. 12–27. For epitome or parody, consider Thomas Hooker's early experience with the spiritual distraction of Mrs. Joanna Drake; see Frank Shuffelton, *Thomas Hooker, 1586–1647* (Princeton: Princeton University Press, 1977), pp. 29–68; and compare Shepard's lively interest in the resolution of *Certain Select Cases* (London, 1648).

41. Predicting and preparing for his defenses of the Awakening such as *The Distinguishing Remarks of a Work of the Spirit* and *A Treatise Concerning Religious Affections*, Edwards' early sermon "A Divine and Supernatural Light" (1734) marks the beginning of his ongoing attempt to define faith as a particular sort of (esthetic) experience; see John E. Smith, Harry S. Short, and Kenneth P. Minkema, eds., *A Jonathan Edwards Reader* (New Haven: Yale University Press, 1995), pp. 105–24.

42. For Emerson's famous rejection of "arguments," see his letter to Henry Ware Jr. of October 8, 1838; in Ralph L. Rusk, ed., *The Letters of Ralph Waldo Emerson* (New York: Columbia University, 1939), vol. 2, pp. 166–67. For an evocation of the moment and its epistemology, see Colacurcio, "Pleasing God," in *Doctrine and Difference*, esp. pp. 129–61.

43. For an authoritative account of the more anxious sort of professions, based primarily on the recovery of those recorded by Thomas Shepard in his own church, see Patricia Caldwell, *The Puritan Conversion Narrative* (Cambridge: Cambridge University Press, 1983).

44. Clearly the opening of Emerson's early poem "Grace" translates Augustine's sense of that "prevenient grace" which anticipates and thus annuls a moment of overwhelming temptation: "How much, preventing God, how much I owe / To the defenses thou hast round me set."

45. In the cogent argument of Geoffrey F. Nuttall, Protestant theology, especially as epitomized in radical Puritanism and its Quaker offshoot, represents a major reversal of a long medieval tendency to underrepresent the function of the Holy Spirit in the account of human salvation; see *The Holy Spirit in Puritan Thought and Experience* (London: Basil Blackwell, 1946), esp. pp. 1–33. In these terms the position of the elders looks indeed like a backward turning. Or perhaps one might see this tendency—in the terms of Edmund Morgan—as a refusal to take the church even further from the world; see *Visible Saints* (rpt. Ithaca: Cornell University Press, 1965), esp. pp. 139–52.

46. Preparing the way for Knight's splitting the New England Mind into two contending *Orthodoxies* (esp. pp. 1–87) are Andrew Delbanco, *The Puritan Ordeal* (Cambridge, Mass.: Harvard University Press, 1987), esp. pp. 118–83; and McGiffert, introduction to *God's Plot*, esp. pp. 9–26.

CHAPTER 8. WIVES AND LOVERS

1. See James W. Jones, *The Shattered Synthesis* (New Haven: Yale University Press, 1973), pp. 23, 19.

2. Beginning with Miller's stress on the "rationalist" element in Puritan thought—and especially the "conditional" element in their rhetoric of covenant—criticism has spent inordinate energy trying to detect a sort of creeping Arminianism; see "The Marrow of Puritan Divinity," in *Errand into the Wilderness* (Cambridge, Mass.: Harvard University Press, 1956), pp. 48–98; "'Preparation for Salvation' in Seventeenth-Century New England," in *Nature's Nation* (Cambridge, Mass.: Harvard University Press, 1967), pp. 50–77; and *The New England Mind: From Colony to Province* (Cambridge, Mass.: Harvard University Press, 1953), pp. 53–67. See also Norman Pettit, *The Heart Prepared* (New Haven: Yale University Press, 1966), pp. 86–124. For appropriate resistance to this tendency, see R. T. Kendall, *Calvin and English Calvinism to 1649* (London: Oxford University Press, 1979), esp. pp. 1–9.

3. See the (unnumbered) second page of Cotton's prefatory remarks "To the Judicious Christian Reader," in John Norton, *The Orthodox Evangelist* (London, 1654)—reprinted as volume 11 of the Library of American Puritan Writings, series ed. Sacvan Bercovitch (New York: AMS Press, 1982).

4. See the (unnumbered) fifth page of Norton's "Epistle Dedicatory" to his *Orthodox Evangelist*.

5. See "Mrs. Hutchinson" in Hawthorne's *Tales and Sketches* (New York: Library of America, 1992), p. 18.

6. See Thomas Shepard, *The Sound Believer* (rpt. Boston: Doctrinal Book and Tract Society, 1854), vol. 1, p. 282.

7. I employ the term "sanctificationist"—on the model of "preparationist"—to describe the emphasis that begins with the ending of Shepard's *Sound Believer* (pp. 255–63 and esp. pp. 275–84) and dominates the extended argument of the *Ten Virgins*.

8. For the presence of the feminine in the rhetoric of Jonathan Edwards, see Sandra Gustafson, "Jonathan Edwards and the Reconstruction of 'Feminine' Speech," *ALH* 6 (1994): 185–212.

9. The formal "professions of faith" transcribed by Shepard for his Cambridge church are included in the second edition of Michael McGiffert's *God's Plot* (Amherst: University of Massachusetts Press, 1994), pp. 149–225. These professions form, in large part, the basis of Patricia Caldwell's *Puritan Conversion Narrative* (Cambridge: Cambridge University Press, 1983).

10. See Jonathan Mitchell's preface to Shepard's *Parable of the Ten Virgins* (Boston: Doctrinal Tract and Book Society, 1852), vol. 2, p. 10.

11. As David D. Hall interprets the situation, correctly in my judgment, the excitement aroused by so many new and important arrivals in New England produced a sort of "revival" or "period of exaggerated piety"; see his introduction to *The Antinomian Controversy* (Middletown, Conn.: Wesleyan University Press, 1968), p. 13; see also Lisa M. Gordis, *Opening Scripture* (Chicago: University of Chicago Press, 2003), pp. 147–48. Michael P. Winship is right to connect certain passages in Shepard's *Ten Virgins* with important moments in the "Free Grace Controversy"; see *Making Heretics* (Princeton: Princeton University Press, 2002), pp. 108 ff. But it seems clear that sanctification is the topic we are promised at the end of *The Sound Believer* and that the *Ten Virgins* speaks to the more encompassing concern of enthusiasm and disillusion.

12. Shepard's loyal successor at the anti-Antinomian church of Cambridge, Thomas Mitchell, saw to the publication, in 1659, of a series of "sermons preached by the author in a weekly lecture, begun in June, 1636, and ended in May 1640." And though he addresses his prefatory remarks "especially to the inhabitants of Cambridge," he clearly has an interest in extending the influence, in space and time, of Shepard's "true middle way of the gospel, between the Legalist, on the one hand, and the Antinomian or loose gospeler, on the other"; see *Ten Virgins,* pp. 8, 5, 9.

13. All citations of Shepard's *Parable of the Ten Virgins* refer to volume 2 of the 1852 edition (Boston: Doctrinal Tract and Book Society) and are identified by page numbers in the text. This edition has been reprinted in the twentieth century (Morgan, Pa.: Soli Deo Gloria Press, 1990).

14. Always the doctrinal purist, Cotton strenuously insists that "Though the graces of Christ in his members be in part like to the graces of Christ in himself, . . . yet they are not therefore in us as they are in him, active of themselves without further help"; see "Cotton's Rejoinder," in Hall, ed., *Controversy,* p. 144.

15. For Cotton's more immediate expectation (and prediction) of the end of the world, see *An Exposition upon the Thirteenth Chapter of the Revelation* (London, 1655). And see Larzer Ziff, "The Time of the Fifth Vial," in *John Cotton* (Princeton: Princeton University Press, 1962), pp. 170–202; and Everett H. Emerson, *John Cotton* (New York: Twayne, 1965), pp. 95–99.

16. See Nathaniel Hawthorne, *Novels* (New York: Library of America, 1983), p. 176.

17. See John Cotton, *Treatise of the Covenant of Grace* (London, 1655), quoted from Phyllis M. Jones and Nicholas R Jones, eds., *Salvation in New England* (Austin: University of Texas Press, 1977), p. 56.

18. See Mitchell, "Preface," p. 7.

19. John Cotton, *Covenant of Grace* (London, 1671), pp. 177–79; and cp. *A Brief Exposition . . . upon the Whole Book of Canticles* (London, 1655), pp. 4–5.

20. For the question of whether justification must always be known first (and as such), see the elders' exchange with Cotton over "Sixteen Questions of Serious and Necessary Consequence," in Hall, ed., *Controversy,* pp. 51–52, 68–69, and esp. 107–12.

21. Where Shepard ascribes the familiar Pauline sense of not being "able" to do the good we "would" to the state of man both before and after conversion, it is a distinguishing mark of Cotton's theory that such doomed desires are themselves a mark of converting grace.

22. Cotton writes: "All conditions before union with Christ are corrupt and unsavory, . . . and all conditions after union with Christ are effects and fruits of that union." And again, "We cannot find Christ the end and bottom of our peace, unless we find him first as well as last"; see "Rejoinder," in Hall, ed., *Controversy,* pp. 92, 129.

23. See Ralph Waldo Emerson's 1838 "Address" to the Harvard Divinity School, in *Essays and Lectures* (New York: Library of America, 1983), p. 81.

24. John E. Smith, editor of the Yale edition of Jonathan Edwards' *Religious Affections* (New Haven: Yale University Press, 1959) emphasizes its loyalty to the thought and rhetoric of Shepard; see pp. 52–57 passim. Indeed, by the time Edwards reaches his concluding "Twelfth Sign," the "exercise and fruit" of holy affections in "Christian practice," the debt to Shepard's *Parable of the Ten Virgins* is evident and insistent. Earlier signs, how-

ever, particularly the Fifth—"Spiritual conviction of the judgment, of the reality and certainty of divine things"—show a far greater loyalty to Cotton's emphasis on the Spirit as its own evidence.

25. Even if an individual believer should *not* last until the day of general judgment, that individual was certainly to expect, in addition to an individual judgment at the moment of personal death, a replay of that judgment on the last day; see William Ames, *The Marrow of Theology* (rpt. Boston: Pilgrim Press, 1968), pp. 214–16.

26. Bradstreet's famous poem "Upon the Burning of Our House" flourishes as a not-quite-successful attempt to label her uncontrolled longing for her lost worldly possessions a "dunghill mist"; yet any continuing problem of "weaned affections" is clearly resolved in the death-wishful "As Weary Pilgrim"; see Jeannine Hensley, ed., *The Works of Anne Bradstreet* (Cambridge, Mass.: Harvard University Press, 1967), pp. 292–95.

27. For Cotton's "barnyard" instructions on the discrimination of hypocrites, as goats and the "washed swine," see Perry Miller and Thomas H. Johnson, eds., *The Puritans* (New York: Harper and Row, 1938), vol. 2, pp. 314–18.

28. In Cotton's formulation, on the other hand, salvation is "revealed without works" just as much as it is "wrought without works." Indeed, in his view, "It is the glory of Grace to conceal all mention of works" just here. See "Rejoinder," in Hall, ed., *Controversy*, p. 111.

29. Preached "as weekly lectures . . . at the end of 1639 and the beginning of 1640"—just as Shepard was finishing his own "lectures" on the Ten Virgins—Cotton's careful calculations render 1570 and also 1655 as banner years in the war against "the Beast" of Roman Catholicism; see Emerson, *Cotton*, pp. 95–99.

30. Only with Jonathan Edwards' argument that we are responsible for an act if we did indeed will it—regardless of how we came to do so—does Puritan apologetics acquire a strong response to the intuitive criticism that necessity and morality are incompatible; see Paul Ramsey, ed., *Freedom of the Will* (New Haven: Yale University Press, 1957), esp. pp. 149–67.

31. Winthrop's editor concedes that "the scholarly literature on the Antinomian crisis is [too] extensive" for him to cite in full. Yet one could do worse than to begin the study with his own generous footnote (*Journal*, pp. 193–94). Feminist readings include Amy Schrager Lang, *Prophetic Woman* (Berkeley: University of California Press, 1987), pp. 1–51; Marilyn J. Westerkamp, "Anne Hutchinson, Sectarian Mysticism, and the Puritan Order," *CH* 59 (1990): 482–96; Lyle Koehler, "The Case of the American Jezebels," *WMQ* 31 (1974): 55–78; Ben Barker-Benfield, "Anne Hutchinson and the Puritan Attitude toward Women," *FS* 1 (1972): 65–96. See also my "Footsteps of Anne Hutchinson," in *Doctrine and Difference* (New York: Routledge, 1997), pp. 177–204.

32. See Franklin Jameson, ed., *Johnson's Wonder-Working Providence* (rpt. New York: Barnes and Noble, 1910), Bk. 1, p. 132.

33. For a learned attempt to displace Anne Hutchinson as the single center of the Antinomian or Free Grace Controversy of 1636–38, see Winship, *Heretics*, esp. pp. 44–169. For an equally serious attempt to throw the emphasis back on Hutchinson—and not simply as a victim of male prejudice—see Gordis, *Opening Scripture*, pp. 145–66. The most patient account of Hutchinson's beliefs—as coded in the "confession" given during her trial before the General Court—is Michael G. Ditmore, "A Prophetess in Her Own Country," *WMQ* 57 (2000): 349–92.

34. See "The Examination of Mrs. Anne Hutchinson," in *The Antinomian Controversy,* ed. David D. Hall (Middletown, Conn.: Wesleyan University Press, 1968), p. 314. As Winship remarks, this is the "only time during Hutchinson's court session" that Winthrop tried "to invoke patriarchal control" (*Heretics,* p. 170).

35. See "Footsteps," esp. pp. 182–96.

36. See "Christian Charity: A Model Hereof," in *Puritan Political Ideas,* ed. Edmund S. Morgan (New York: Bobbs-Merrill, 1965), pp. 87–88. Morgan's is one of the few modern anthologies to print the entire text, from *Winthrop Papers,* vol. 2 (Worcester: Massachusetts Historical Society, 1931), pp. 282–95.

37. For the convenience of students, the paperback (abridged) version of Winthrop's *Journal* includes *almost* all of Winthrop's "Model" but elects to omit the passage here in question; see Richard S. Dunn and Laetitia Yeandle, eds., *The Journal of John Winthrop* (Cambridge, Mass.: Harvard University Press, 1996), pp. 1–11.

38. A brief selection of Winthrop's love letters (to Margaret) is included in Miller and Johnson, eds., *Puritans,* vol. 2, pp. 465–71. For a fuller representation, see *Winthrop Papers,* vol. 2.

39. All citations of "The Examination of Mrs. Anne Hutchinson at the Court at Newtown"—abbreviated E—are taken from Hall, ed., *Controversy,* and are noted by page numbers in the text.

40. Commentators have long agreed that Hutchinson held her own against Winthrop very well—until she betrayed herself with the confession of an "immediate revelation," the implication of which is explored best by Ditmore, "Prophetess," pp. 371 ff. Yet if this was the move that ended the game, the chargeable issue remained the "traduction" of the New England elders; see Winship, *Heretics,* pp. 183–84; and cp. Gordis, *Opening Scripture,* pp. 173–78.

41. In the words of the *Short Story of the Rise, Reign, and Ruin of the Antinomians, Familists & Libertines,* Wheelwright's "instances of illustration, or rather enforcement . . . as of Moses killing the Egyptian" were not all that spiritual; see Hall, ed., *Controversy,* p. 293.

42. For the intellectual history of those proto-Congregationalists who, unlike Bradford, never admitted to being anything like Separatists, see Perry Miller, *Orthodoxy in Massachusetts* (Boston: Little, Brown, 1933).

43. On the question of lay participation in the dialogic process of interpreting, see Gordis, *Opening Scripture,* pp. 97–111; and, specific to the Hutchinson controversy, pp. 152–62. For the thriving institution of the "lay conventicle," see Stephen Foster, "New England and the Challenge of Heresy," *WMQ* 38 (1981): esp. 626–30.

44. Citations of "A Report of the Trial of Mrs. Anne Hutchinson before the Church in Boston"—abbreviated T—are taken from Hall, ed., *Controversy,* and are noted by page numbers in the text.

45. For the triumph of the doctrine that, given a soul, man is himself somehow immortal, see Jaroslov Pelikan, *The Christian Tradition,* vol. 1: *The Emergence of the Catholic Tradition* (Chicago: University of Chicago Press, 1971), pp. 47–52, 153–54, 164–65, 272–73, 282–84. And for the Reformation context, see J. F. Maclear, "Anne Hutchinson and the Mortalist Heresy," *NEQ* 54 (1981): 74–103.

46. In the words of G. R. Elton, the "extraordinary episode of Munster [was] happily unique in the history of Anabaptism but [was] unhappily doomed to rest upon its shoulders for ever after"; see *Reformation Europe* (New York: Harper and Row, 1963), p. 99. Also

evident at this point in the making of a heretic is a certain "tendency to tell the accused what they ought to believe as a result of their principles" (Foster, "Heresy," p. 635).

47. Explaining, at her church trial, the implications of Mrs. Hutchinson's Familism, Cotton both denies the fact and predicts the inevitability of some adultery; yet it seems a feminist exaggeration to claim that "Everywhere in the court examination, one finds the insinuation that Hutchinson is, like Jezebel, guilty of fornication"; see Lang, *Prophetic Woman,* p. 43.

48. While modern commentary (e.g., Knight, *Orthodoxies*) often evinces considerable sympathy with the position of Cotton, Winship's careful study is remarkable for its portrait of Shepard as a relentless and mean-spirited heresy hunter; see *Heretics,* pp. 203–9 and passim; he also cautions modern interpreters to refrain from party preference "unless they are prepared to play for the participants' stakes" (pp. 228–29). Agreeing that the Antinomian heretics were "made," but resisting the "temptation" to blame Shepard, Foster cites instead the "rising sectarian temperature of the Bay Colony in the later 1630's" ("Heresy," pp. 655–56).

49. Accepting the rough justice of Hutchinson's church trial, Winship finds it crucial that a surprisingly combative Hutchinson was "inadequately socialized as a theologian" (*Heretics,* p. 193).

50. Modern feminism appears to divide itself—American from European (especially French)—on the question of the essential reality of gender qualities. Jacques Lacan and Julia Kristeva, for example, might be somewhat more tolerant of Winthrop's sexual essentialism than would their American counterparts, one of whom has informed me that "gender is particularly important if you are a noun in an inflected language."

51. Against Mrs. Hutchinson's appeal to the practice of "prophecy" within and around the established New England churches, Winthrop answers that this was not a "rule" but "only a custom in Boston" (E, 315).

52. Ditmore observes that, in her gratuitous yet perhaps not quite spontaneous "confession" to the General Court, Hutchinson presented herself in the figure of a man—to male judges who had to see themselves as female in relation to Christ the Bridegroom; see "Prophetess," esp. pp. 359–75.

53. Hall, ed., *Controversy,* p. 200.

54. All citations of the *Short Story of the Rise, Reign and Ruin of the Antinomians, Familists & Libertines*—abbreviated *SS*—are taken from Hall, ed., *Controversy,* and are noted by page number in the text.

55. Truth and Peace will return to haunt Orthodox New England as the speakers in the dialogue that constitutes Roger Williams' *Bloody Tenet of Persecution* (London, 1644).

56. The ironic and condescending formula of Thomas Welde's preface to the *Short Story* (p. 203) lends itself as the title of the important study of the Antinomian Controversy by William K. B. Stoever, *"A Faire and Easie Way to Heaven"* (Middletown, Conn.: Wesleyan University Press, 1978).

57. See John Winthrop, *Journal,* ed. Richard S. Dunn (Cambridge, Mass.: Harvard University Press, 1996), p. 216.

58. Where Winship emphasizes the embarrassments produced by the court's insistence that it was not censuring Wheelwright's doctrine (*Heretics,* pp. 120–25), Gordis proposes that the magistrates were availing themselves of the distinction between a sermon's abstract "doctrine" and its practical "application" (*Opening Scripture,* pp. 157–66).

59. In Winship's view, Hutchinson's confession of her immediate voice gave Winthrop a way to recast the entire free grace controversy, with Hutchinson's own female peculiarities at the source and center (*Heretics,* pp. 184–85).

60. Edward Johnson, for example, is careful to distinguish the "providence" to which the orthodox understanding of New England had such constant reference from the "miracle" of rescue and of validation Anne Hutchinson seemed to expect; the difference appears to involve the use of ordinary, intelligible "means," as when the American natives express their own cruel and savage nature in destroying Hutchinson and her family; see *Providence,* pp. 186–87.

61. The "Report of the Trial" identifies the soul/life distinguisher as "Mr. Damphord," probably John Davenport; see Hall, ed., *Controversy,* pp. 358–62.

62. The political theorist in question is Melville's Captain Vere.

63. "Model," in Morgan, *Political Ideas,* p. 93.

64. The evidence of Winthrop's authorship of the *Short Story,* sometime in the critical year 1637, remains presumptive. But as it has been hard to think of another with the same degree of familiarity—and the same intense interest in defending "the hand of Civil Justice" (p. 310)—the ascription remains fairly safe.

65. For the text of this classic piece of Puritan political theory—more correctly known as Winthrop's 1645 "Speech to the General Court"—see Dunn, ed., *Journal,* pp. 584–89, noted by page numbers in the text.

66. Hawthorne, *Scarlet Letter,* p. 158.

67. Hawthorne, "Mrs. Hutchinson," p. 18.

68. As Dunn explains in a useful footnote, the issue centers here on the person of John Endicott: "chosen to the Standing Council in 1637, [he] had not been elected a magistrate in 1638, but continued to sit with the assistants in his capacity as standing councilor" (p. 295).

69. See William Bradford, *Of Plymouth Plantation* (rpt. New York: Modern Library, 1952), p. 35.

70. Dunn, ed., *Journal,* p. 458.

71. Dunn, ed., *Journal,* p. 503.

72. See Perry Miller, ed., *The American Puritans* (Garden City, N.Y.: Anchor, 1956), p. 89.

73. Dunn, ed., *Journal,* p. 578.

74. For a study of the tough and practical side of Winthrop's politics, see George L. Mosse, *The Holy Pretence* (New York: Howard Fertig, 1968), pp. 88–106.

75. For Mather's recognition of the importance of Winthrop's "Little Speech" as a sort of epitome of Puritan anti-Antinomianism, see *Magnalia Christi Americana* (rpt. New York: Russell and Russell, 1852), vol. 1, pp. 126–28.

76. Miller, ed., *American Puritans,* p. 90.

77. Dunn, ed., *Journal,* p. 587.

78. For the secular analogue of Winthrop's theory of "contractual absolutism"—one leaves the state of nature voluntarily but is afterward quite bound, without appeal back, by the contract then enacted—see Thomas Hobbes, *Leviathan* (rpt. New York: Penguin, 1985), esp. pp. 223–88. The classic American text with the deepest debt to Hobbes is Melville's *Billy Budd*—where Vere's militaristic and finally cynical reliance on the absolutist

implication of his "buttons" reduces (elevates?) him to a position that can be maintained only by the Calvinist God.

79. For the "national" implications of Hester Prynne's failure to provoke an overt struggle to realize, at once, "the whole relation between man and woman on a surer ground of mutual happiness" (*Scarlet Letter,* p. 344), see Sacvan Bercovitch, *The Office of the Scarlet Letter* (Baltimore: Johns Hopkins University Press, 1991), esp. pp. 73–112; and cp. Bercovitch, *The Rites of Assent* (New York: Routledge, 1993), pp. 194–245.

80. The self-consciously moralist formula is that of Emerson's "Experience" (in *Essays,* p. 483).

81. See Edmund S. Morgan, *Puritan Dilemma* (Boston: Little, Brown, 1958), pp. 84–100.

82. See Dunn, ed., *Journal,* p. 588nn.4, 5.

83. Beyond the final, enforced resolution of the matter of Samuel Gorton and the calling of a second synod—which devised and promulgated the Cambridge Platform—the principal issue of Winthrop's "Journal," post-1645, is the "Remonstrance and Humble Petition" of William Vassall, Robert Child, and others "that we might be wholly governed by the laws of England" (p. 624), which eventually raises the question "in what relation we stood to England" (pp. 647–48). For commentary on this crucial matter, see Robert Emmet Wall Jr., *Massachusetts Bay: The Crucial Decade, 1640–1650* (New Haven: Yale University Press, 1972), pp. 157–224.

84. See Morgan, *Puritan Dilemma,* p. 142.

CHAPTER 9.   MARCHING ORDERS

1. Critical study of Puritan stylistics may well begin with Perry Miller's chapters "Rhetoric" and "The Plain Style," in *The New England Mind: The Seventeenth Century* (Cambridge, Mass.: Harvard University Press, 1939), pp. 300–362. Important modifications include Babette May Levy, *Preaching in the First Half-Century of New England History* (rpt. New York: Russell and Russell, 1967), pp. 131–56; Wilbur Samuel Howell, *Logic and Rhetoric in England* (Princeton: Princeton University Press, 1956), pp. 116–37; Walter J. Ong, S.J., *Ramus, Method, and the Decay of Dialogue* (Cambridge, Mass.: Harvard University Press, 1958), pp. 283–88; Boyd M. Berry, *Process of Speech* (Baltimore: Johns Hopkins University Press, 1976), pp. 1–19; John G. Rechtien, "Logic in Puritan Sermons in the Late Sixteenth Century and Plain Style," *Style* 13 (1979): 237–58; Jesper Rosenmeier, "'Clearing the Medium': A Reevaluation of the Puritan Style in the Light of John Cotton's *A Practical Commentary upon the First Epistle General of John,*" *WMQ* 37 (1980): 577–91; Michael Srigley, "The Lascivious Metaphor: The Evolution of the Plain Style in the Seventeenth Century," *SN* 60 (1988): 179–92; and, returning the question again to its classical context, Debora K. Shuger, *Sacred Rhetoric* (Princeton: Princeton University Press, 1988), esp. pp. 3–54. For the defining importance of differing patterns of biblical citation, see Lisa M. Gordis, *Opening Scripture* (Chicago: University of Chicago Press, 2003), esp. pp. 1–100. And for the place of humor in the stern business of Puritan conversion, see John Gatta, *Gracious Laughter* (Columbia: University of Missouri Press, 1989), esp. pp. 1–62.

2. A deleted remark, quoted from the original version of "The Gentle Boy," as published in *The Token* (1832); for commentary, see Seymour L. Gross, "Hawthorne's Revision of 'The Gentle Boy,'" *AL* 26 (1954): 196–208; and cp. Michael J. Colacurcio, *Province of Piety* (Cambridge, Mass.: Harvard University Press, 1984), pp. 106–202.

3. For Hawthorne's self-translation into French, see his brief (but not always reprinted) headnote to "Rappaccini's Daughter," in *Tales and Sketches* (New York: Library of America, 1982), pp. 975–76.

4. Quoted from Perry Miller and Thomas H. Johnson, eds., *The Puritans,* vol. 1 (rpt. New York: Harper and Row, 1963). Further citations are indicated by page numbers in the text.

5. As John Winthrop reports, the matter of a "body of laws" to protect "the people" from the "discretion of the magistrates" was referred to "Mr. Cotton and Mr. Nathaniel Ward, ... each of [whom] framed a model"; see Richard S. Dunn, ed., *The Journal of John Winthrop, 1630–1649* (Cambridge, Mass.: Harvard University Press, 1996), p. 314. As Dunn's footnote observes, "Ward's draft was preferred to Cotton's" and had more influence on the "Body of Liberties, approved in December, 1641." See also George Lee Haskins, *Law and Authority in Early Massachusetts* (New York: Macmillan, 1960), esp. pp. 113–40.

6. Quoted from P. M. Zall, ed., *The Simple Cobler of Aggawam in America* (Lincoln: University of Nebraska Press, 1969). Further citations are indicated by page numbers in the text.

7. As Miller points out, the explicit question of speaking "rather merrily than seriously" is added in the *Cobler*'s third edition (Miller and Johnson, eds., *Puritans,* vol. 1, p. 235).

8. Ward's modern editor complained in 1969 that this "'first American Satire' or 'first humorous book written in America'" is known only from anthology selections (Zall, ed., *Cobler,* p. ix); and in 1992 William J. Scheick refers to the fact that it has "received very little attention from literary scholars" as an "evasion"; see *Design in Puritan American Literature* (Lexington: University of Kentucky Press, 1992), p. 69. For a further sample of modern responses, see Patricia L. Bradley, "The Unifying Pauline Sub-text of Nathaniel Ward's SCA," *EAL* 34 (1999): 32–47; William J. Scheick, "The Widower Narrator in Nathaniel Ward's SCA," *NEQ* 47 (1974): 87–96; James Egan, "Nathaniel Ward and the Marprelate Tradition," *EAL* 15 (1980): 59–71; Jean F. Beranger, "Voices of Humor in Nathaniel Ward," *SAH* 2 (1975): 96–104; Robert D. Arner, "SCA: Nathaniel Ward and the Rhetoric of Satire," *EAL* 5 (1971): 3–16; and Janette Bohi, "Nathaniel Ward, a Sage of Old Ipswich," *EIHC* 99 (1963): 3–32.

9. As Stephen Carl Arch recounts the publication history of Johnson's text, its 1653 edition bore the date 1654 "to anticipate the book's appearance in London bookstalls"; see *Authorizing the Past* (DeKalb: Northern Illinois University Press, 1994), p. 201.

10. In the conservative formulation of Emory Elliott, "Johnson's *History* stands out as the most complete and coherent report on the first twenty-five years of the colony before Cotton Mather's monumental *Magnalia*"; and this in a "lively and energetic style," marked by "brisk narration and colorful personality"; see "Personal Narrative and History," in *The Cambridge History of American Literature,* ed. Sacvan Bercovitch (Cambridge: Cambridge University Press, 1994), vol. 1, pp. 219–20.

11. The foundational studies of *Wonder-Working Providence* (abbreviated *WWP* below) are Ursula Brumm, "Edward Johnson's WWP and the Puritan Conception of History," *JA* 14 (1969): 140–51; and Sacvan Bercovitch, "The Historiography of Johnson's

WWP," *EIHC* 104 (1968): 138–61. Other important treatments include Stephen Carl Arch, "Edifying History," in *Authorizing,* pp. 51–87; Arch, "The Edifying History of Edward Johnson's WWP," *EAL* 28 (1993): 42–59; Jesper Rosenmeier, "'They Shall No Longer Grieve': The Song of Songs and Edward Johnson's WWP," *EAL* 26 (1991): 1–20; Ormond Seavey, "Edward Johnson and the American Puritan Sense of History," *Prospects* 14 (1989): 1–29; Dennis R. Perry, "Autobiographical Role-Playing in Edward Johnson's WWP," *EAL* 22 (1987): 291–305; Cecelia Tichi, "Edward Johnson and the Puritan Territorial Imperative," in *Discoveries and Considerations,* ed. Calvin Israel (Albany: State University of New York Press, 1976), pp. 152–88; Cecilia Tichi, "Edward Johnson's American New Earth," in *New World, New Earth* (New Haven: Yale University Press, 1979), pp. 37–66; Edward J. Gallagher, "The WWP as Spiritual Biography," *EAL* 10 (1975): 75–87; Edward J. Gallagher, "An Overview of Edward Johnson's WWP," *EAL* 5 (1971): 30–49.

12. All citations of the Johnson text refer to J. Franklin Jameson, ed., *Johnson's Wonder-Working Providence* (New York: Barnes and Noble, 1910).

13. Jameson, ed., *Providence,* p. 23.

14. For Perry Miller's famous ambiguating of the Puritan "Errand"—was the "great migration" an ancillary mission undertaken on behalf of others, or was it a powerful end in itself?—see "Errand into the Wilderness," in *Errand into the Wilderness* (Cambridge, Mass.: Harvard University Press, 1956), pp. 1–15. And for a well-considered—yet not entirely conclusive—attempt to trace the growth and development of the Puritan sense of mission, see Andrew Delbanco, *The Puritan Ordeal* (Cambridge, Mass.: Harvard University Press, 1989), esp. pp. 1–27, 215–52.

15. Brumm notices that in Johnson's style of history "the preterit is not the dominating sense" and that, instead, his repeated use of the present tense is "more than an intimation that something is happening now"; see "Puritan Conception," pp. 140–41.

16. For a more realistic view of the "loyalty" of the migrants of 1630, see Edmund S. Morgan, *Puritan Dilemma* (Boston: Little, Brown, 1958), pp. 34–53.

17. Arch recognizes the possibility that Johnson may well have been on the *Arabella* with Winthrop but presses only general similarities between *WWP* and Winthrop's "Model"; see *Authorizing,* pp. 56–65.

18. Jameson, ed., *Providence,* p. 26.

19. For the early defeat and revision of Winthrop's original hopes, see Darrett B. Rutman, *Winthrop's Boston* (Chapel Hill: University of North Carolina Press, 1965), pp. 3–40.

20. Jameson, ed., *Providence,* p. 43.

21. By the disillusioned account of Bradford's entry for 1644, including its conclusive marginal note, the providential meaning of his enterprise was washed off all too soon; see *Of Plymouth Plantation* (rpt. New York: Modern Library, 1967), pp. 333–34, 33.

22. For an account of Johnson's expansionism in terms of environmental reform, see Tichi, "Territorial Imperative"; also "New Earth," esp. pp. 37–54.

23. In "Endicott and the Red Cross," Hawthorne permits Endicott's challenge to Roger Williams to go unanswered: "My spirit is wiser than thine, for the business now in hand"; see *Tales,* p. 547.

24. For a more correct account of the order of founding of the churches, see Jameson's footnotes to the Johnson text, pp. 67–71.

25. According to Cotton Mather—who from hindsight learned only the obvious— the Devil's unleashing of a plague of witches upon New England represented "an attempt

so critical that if we get well through, we shall soon enjoy Halcyon Days with all the Vultures of Hell trodden under our feet"; see *The Wonders of the Invisible World* (rpt. Amherst: Amherst University Press, 1862), p. 14.

26. For purposes of the printed word at least, the association of Anne Hutchinson's doctrinal misconceptions with her gynecological history appears to begin with the suggestion, in Thomas Welde's preface to *A Short Story of the Rise, Reign, and Ruin of the Antinomians, Familists & Libertines,* that "as she vented misshapen opinions so she must bring forth deformed monsters"; in David D. Hall, ed., *The Antinomian Controversy, 1636–1638* (Middletown, Conn.: Wesleyan University Press, 1968), p. 214. For its historical and literary ramifications, see my "Footsteps of Anne Hutchinson," in *Doctrine and Difference* (New York: Routledge, 1997), pp. 177–204; and Amy Schrager Lang, *Prophetic Woman* (Berkeley: University of California Press, 1987), esp. pp. 1–71.

27. Jameson, ed., *Providence,* p. 132.

28. For Johnson's manipulation of his own experience in *WWP,* see Perry, "Autobiographical Role-Playing"; and for Johnson's history as an attempt to fuse "the individual and the communal," see Gallagher, "Spiritual Biography," p. 75.

29. For the argument that seventeenth-century Puritans were most likely to encounter the "self" under the aspect of "sin," see Sacvan Bercovitch, *Puritan Origins of the American Self* (New Haven: Yale University Press, 1975), pp. 1–34.

30. Jameson, ed., *Providence,* p. 140.

31. The entire pre-1630 portion of Bradford's *Plymouth* may be understood as an idealistic reply to the realist doubt of John Smith's *Description of New England* that "any other motive than wealth will ever erect there a commonwealth"; see John Lankford, ed., *Captain John Smith's America* (New York: Harper and Row, 1967), p. 141. For a subtle account of an "esthetic" motive, see John Seelye, *Prophetic Waters* (New York: Oxford University Press, 1977), esp. pp. 3–95.

32. For the emergence of the "Advisory Synod" as part of an "emerging orthodoxy" that moved away from any pure form of Congregational Democracy, see Dunn, *Boston,* pp. 98–134; for Winthrop's leadership in the process, see Morgan, *Dilemma,* pp. 142–47.

33. For Winthrop's own account of the events requiring the first "Advisory Synod" in New England, see Dunn, ed., *Journal,* pp. 194–235.

34. For the structure of the late medieval university (and its pedagogic implications), see Ong, *Ramus,* esp. pp. 149–67.

35. For the insistence of "orthodox" Puritans on the absolute necessity of a learned ministry, see Miller, *New England Mind,* esp. pp. 64–88; and John Morgan, *Godly Learning* (Cambridge: Cambridge University Press, 1986), esp. pp. 79–141, 172–200.

36. Of all the early histories of the Puritan venture in New England, Johnson's *Wonder-Working Providence* most nearly anticipates Cotton Mather's "biographical" emphasis on the importance of faithful persons; it also appears to have prepared Mather's emphasis on the importance of an "ecclesiastical history"; see *Magnalia Christi Americana* (rpt. New York: Russell and Russell, 1852), pp. 25–38.

37. Ever since the publication of Perry Miller's shorter anthology, *The American Puritans* (Garden City, N.Y.: Anchor Books, 1956), Samuel Sewall's sudden hymn to the beauty and fertile continuance of Plum Island, in the midst of a book about the world's apocalyptic ending, has stood as an important marker of the way Puritan otherworldliness was imperceptibly overtaken by "the earthly" (p. 213).

38. For the second generation's attempt to make it clear that a rugged morale must be maintained even when the generosity of God has turned the literal wilderness into a pleasant garden, see Samuel Danforth, "A Brief Recognition of New England's Errand into the Wilderness," in *The Wall and the Garden*, ed. A. W. Plumstead (Minneapolis: University of Minnesota Press, 1968), pp. 54–77; and Thomas Shepard Jr., "Eye-Salve, or a Watch-word from Our Lord Jesus Christ unto His Churches in New England"; suitably excerpted in Alan Heimert and Andrew Delbanco, eds., *The Puritans in America* (Cambridge, Mass.: Harvard University Press, 1985), pp. 247–60.

39. For Bradford's (abbreviated?) version of the Covenant which brought into existence the "particular church," see *Plymouth*, p. 9. In a spirit Johnson would clearly have approved, Bradford also reports on the covenant formation of New World churches at Salem (pp. 224–25) and Boston (pp. 235–36).

40. For the thoroughness of Johnson's deployment of what may be called a "linear typology," see Bercovitch, "Historiography," esp. pp. 141–47.

41. Richard Slotkin makes no mention of Johnson's *WWP* in his provocative *Regeneration through Violence* (Middletown, Conn.: Wesleyan University Press, 1973); but Tichi's analysis of the real wildness of the literal wilderness in Johnson certainly points in that direction: see "New Earth," pp. 43–47.

42. For the "brassy assurance" of Johnson's territorialism, see Seelye, *Prophetic Waters*, pp. 228–31.

43. One thinks first, perhaps, of the *fictional* farewell sermon of Hawthorne's Dimmesdale—which, as the Narrator of *The Scarlet Letter* suspiciously remarks, differs from its Old Testament prototypes by its "mission to foretell a high and glorious destiny for the newly gathered people of the Lord." In this context and others, one might wish to recover the lost Election Sermon given by Thomas Shepard in 1649, the last year of his life.

44. In Miller's famous formulation, the "Protestant Ethic" of the Puritans of New England doomed them to constant pursuit of the very ends their prophets identified as "declension"; see *Colony to Province*, pp. 27–67.

45. Jameson, ed., *Providence*, p. 240.

46. For an account of the nature of Gorton's challenge, see Robert Emmet Wall Jr., *Massachusetts Bay: The Crucial Decade, 1640–1650* (New Haven: Yale University Press, 1972), pp. 121–56; and Philip F. Gura, *A Glimpse of Sion's Glory* (Middletown, Conn.: Wesleyan University Press, 1984), pp. 276–303.

47. For a scholarly account of the radical image—and also the actual varieties—of religious theory and expression in first-generation New England, see Gura, *Glimpse*, esp. pp. 155–234.

48. Though Johnson treats the "second Synod holden at Cambridge" in his chapter for 1646, the meetings went on until 1648, and only in 1649 did the colony cause to be published the Cambridge *Platform of Church Discipline*.

49. Jameson, ed., *Providence*, p. 251.

50. A classic instance of the patriotic stipulation of a faithful remnant is *Gods Controversy with New England* by Michael Wigglesworth; see Harrison T. Messerole, ed., *Seventeenth-Century American Poetry* (Garden City, N.Y.: Anchor, 1968), p. 49.

51. Bercovitch has made the New England Jeremiad occasion seem much less desperate than had Perry Miller: on his revisionary account, the halcyon days of America are always just about to begin; but even he stops short of suggesting that a proper Jeremiad marks

the actual beginnings. See Miller, "Declension in a Bible Commonwealth," in *Nature's Nation* (Cambridge, Mass.: Harvard University Press, 1967), pp. 14–49; and *Colony to Province*, pp. 19–39. And cp. Sacvan Bercovitch, *The American Jeremiad* (Madison: University of Wisconsin Press, 1978), esp. pp. 31–92.

52. As Jameson explains, each grouping of stanzas is marked, here and there, with capital letters which correspond to a series of "footnotes," A through E. It is only in his final note that Johnson raises the possibility of "another people" (*Providence*, p. 261).

53. For the essential elements of the New England Jeremiad, see Miller, *Colony to Province*, pp. 29–35.

54. For the view of Johnson's ending as confused, see Delbanco, ed., *Ordeal*, pp. 189–93. For the friendlier view, from the same critic, that *WWP* is "perhaps the literary masterpiece of first-generation New England," see *Puritans in America*, pp. 112–13.

55. For the importance of the language of Canticles throughout *WWP*, see Rosenmeier, "Song of Songs."

CHAPTER 10. GOVERNMENT IN EXILE

1. On the continuity of assumptions about the cooperating function of church and state, see "The Theory of the State and of Society," in *The Puritans*, ed. Perry Miller and Thomas H. Johnson (rpt. New York: Harper and Row, 1963), vol. 1, pp. 181–94.

2. For early warning of the secularist tendency to read Jefferson back into Williams, see Perry Miller, *Roger Williams* (New York: Athenaeum, 1965), pp. 25–30. Miller might well have had in mind a book like Oscar S. Straus' *Roger Williams, the Pioneer of Religious Liberty* (New York: Century, 1894); or, nearer to his own moment, Samuel Hugh Brockunier's *The Irrepressible Democrat, Roger Williams* (New York: Ronald Press, 1940). For a more cautious estimate of Williams' relation to liberal political theory, see Edmund S. Morgan, *Roger Williams: The Church and the State* (New York: Harcourt, Brace, 1967); and Timothy D. Hall, *Separating Church and State: Roger Williams and Religious Liberty* (Urbana: University of Illinois Press, 1998).

3. For Winthrop's first response to Williams' teaching against the right and duty of the secular power to enforce the "First Table" of the Ten Commandments, see Richard S. Dunn, ed., *The Journal of John Winthrop, 1630–1649* (Cambridge, Mass.: Harvard University Press, 1996), p. 50.

4. For the likelihood that Winthrop helped Williams to escape deportation, see Dunn, ed., *Journal*, pp. 163–64.

5. For Bradford's evocation of Williams as godly but "unsettled in judgment," see the Samuel Eliot Morison edition of William Bradford, *Of Plymouth Plantation, 1620–1647* (rpt. New York: Modern Library, 1967), p. 257.

6. See Miller, *Williams*, p. 166. Not that the *Bloody Tenet* is itself an easy read; Miller praises its greatness while conceding that it is "one of the most gnarled and incoherent utterances . . . in the language" (*Williams*, p. 101); in a similar vein Henry Chupack calls it "disjointed and repetitious"; see *Roger Williams* (New York: Twayne, 1969), p. 84.

7. For the strange misrepresentation of the Cotton-Williams debate as turning on the fact that Williams was a typologist and Cotton not, see Miller, *Williams*, esp. pp. 33–38. For the conclusive correction—that the issue involved competing styles of typology—see

Sacvan Bercovitch, "Typology in Puritan New England," *AQ* 19 (1967): 166–91. The differences are explored further in Jesper Rosenmeier, "The Teacher and the Witness," *WMQ* 25 (1968): 408–31; and Richard Reinitz, "The Typological Argument for Religious Toleration," *EAL* 5 (1970): 74–110. For the importance to Williams of idioms *other* than that of typology, see Christopher D. Felker, "Roger Williams' Use of Legal Discourse," *NEQ* 63 (1990): 624–48; .and John J. Teunissen and Evelyn J. Hinz, "Roger Williams, Thomas More, and the Narragansett Utopia," *EAL* 11 (1976–77): 281–95. And for a current and innovative account of Williams' use of Scripture, see Lisa M. Gordis, *Opening Scripture* (Chicago: University of Chicago Press, 2003), pp. 113–44.

8. With a respect for the work of Sacvan Bercovitch bordering on awe, I remain convinced that Hawthorne and Melville are powerful exceptions to his universal law of the American Jeremiad. For Hawthorne as Williams-like exception, see my *Province of Piety* (Cambridge, Mass.: Harvard University Press, 1984), esp. pp. 130–53; 205–82, 389–482; and for a reading of Melville as an exception to that offered in Bercovitch's *The American Jeremiad* (Madison: University of Wisconsin, 1978), see John Samson, *White Lies* (Ithaca: Cornell University Press, 1989), esp. pp. 143–45, 159–202.

9. For the sexual figure of persecution, see Michael W. Kaufmann, *Institutional Individualism* (Middletown, Conn.: Wesleyan University Press, 1998), pp. 55–62.

10. Miller, *Williams,* p. 164. Apropos of the time lag between the outbreak of the Cotton-Williams argument and the publication of Williams' *Bloody Tenet,* Miller writes that "there is something both pathetic and sublime" in Williams' storing up the relevant documents and "hoarding his thoughts until God's providence gave him his opportunity" (*Williams,* p. 77).

11. For the text of the Cotton-Williams letters of 1636, see Samuel L. Caldwell, ed., *The Complete Writings of Roger Williams,* vol. 1 (rpt. New York: Russell and Russell, 1963), pp. 298–317. Miller reprints the exchange in *Williams* (pp. 86–100). For analysis, see Anne G. Myles, "Arguments in Milk, Arguments in Blood," *MP* 91 (1993): esp. pp. 135–44; see also Edwin S. Gaustad, *Liberty of Conscience* (Grand Rapids, Mich.: Eerdmans, 1991), pp. 38–44.

12. For Winthrop's report on the relations among Williams, the General Court, and the efforts of Thomas Hooker, see Dunn, ed., *Journal,* p. 158.

13. For the "end times" in Williams' thought, see W. Clark Gilpin, *The Millenarian Piety of Roger Williams* (Chicago: University of Chicago Press, 1979).

14. For this important "discursive" difference, see Myles, "Arguments in Milk," pp. 133–60.

15. Miller, *Williams,* p. 144.

16. In a short list of New England's founding tropes, Edward Taylor on the "Wedding Garment," though a little later, might be almost as important as Cotton and Williams on the "Wheat and the Tares" and Thomas Shepard on the "Ten Virgins." For the question of the differing Puritan patterns of selecting and opening the texts of Scripture, see Gordis, *Opening Scripture,* esp. pp. 13–36, 115–21.

17. Readers who claim Williams for "liberalism" might do well to understand his career of defending the necessity of open inquiry in the rise of modern "skepticism": some of his most moving passages concern the impercipience of those who imagine that, after the spilling of so much ink (as well as blood), conscientious and "spiritual" readers of the Bible are about to discover sweet consensus.

18. As Bercovitch and others have shown, it is to Augustine's *City of God* that later Christians repeatedly turn for the powerful conviction that God's kingdom must wait until after the end of this present—fallen and never-to-be-perfectly-redeemed—world of sin and confusion; see "Typology," esp. pp. 176–84; and cp. Robert W. Hanning, *The Vision of History in Early Britain* (New York: Columbia University Press, 1966), pp. 20–37; see also Karen E. Rowe, *Saint and Singer* (Cambridge: Cambridge University Press, 1986), pp. 1–23.

19. See Edward Taylor, "Gods Determinations," in *Poems,* ed. Donald E. Stanford (New Haven: Yale University Press, 1960), p. 450.

20. Miller, *Williams,* p. 129.

21. Miller, *Williams,* p. 133.

22. For Williams' dealings with the Quakers, see Miller, *Williams,* pp. 240–53; and cp. Morgan, *Williams,* pp. 56–61; and David S. Lovejoy, "Roger Williams and George Fox," *NEQ* 66 (1993): 199–225.

23. Miller, *Williams,* pp. 135–36.

24. In Cotton's memorable formulation, a certain sort of hypocrite—not the "washed swine" but the "goat"—will, for all his "capricious nature," prove to be "a clean creature and of much good use"; quoted from Miller and Johnson, eds., *Puritans,* p. 315. For comment on this view of the "usefulness of hypocrites," see Perry Miller, *The New England Mind: From Colony to Province* (Cambridge, Mass.: Harvard University Press, 1953), pp. 79–80.

25. For Winthrop's sense of the danger of Williams' "foreign policy," see Dunn, ed., *Journal,* pp. 107–9.

26. For the occasion and audience of this jointly authored *Model,* falsely ascribed to Cotton, see Miller, *Williams,* p. 75.

27. For Williams' place in the context of separatism, see Hugh Spurgin, *Roger Williams and Puritan Radicalism in the English Separatist Tradition* (Lewiston, Pa.: Edwin Mellen, 1989), esp. pp. 123–41.

28. Miller, *Williams,* pp. 27–32.

29. Edmund S. Morgan is surely right to suggest that "The founders were so dazzled by the godly purpose and unique opportunity of their mission . . . that they could not acknowledge their departure from England as in fact a separation"; and that their disavowal of separatism sounds "a little too eloquent"; see *The Puritan Dilemma* (Boston: Little, Brown, 1958), pp. 52–53. Yet Winthrop clearly understood that nonseparation was a nonnegotiable premise of New England's foreign policy; and a man like Thomas Shepard was keenly aware that, for all its remaining corruptions, the Church of England had indeed been the nursery of many New England saints.

30. For the Puritan association of the perfection of Christian form with its primitive format, see Theodore Dwight Bozeman, *To Live Ancient Lives* (Chapel Hill: University of North Carolina Press, 1988).

31. In the resistant reading of Jesper Rosenmeier, Cotton was not without a considered position of his own, one which held that, while waiting for the second coming, "spirit and flesh must not be separated" quite so radically as Williams appeared to think ("Teacher," p. 410).

32. For Cotton versus the elders on the "allegory" of Abraham and Hagar, see David D. Hall, ed., *The Antinomian Controversy, 1636–1638* (Middletown, Conn.: Wesleyan University Press, 1968), pp. 55–56, 73–74, 131–34.

33. Winthrop himself was quick to notice Williams' tendency toward the position of "Seeker": his *Journal* entry for March 1639 notes Williams' involvement in the practice of rebaptizing (p. 286); and the longer entry for June–July 1639 reports that, having first "denied communion with all others," he had come round to a willingness to "preach and to pray with all comers" (p. 300).

34. Not even Columbus, it may help to recall, could resist the thought that his discovery of the "Terrestial Paradise" ("Third Letter") had been reserved in Providence until the last days and even had his own part revealed to him "as in a swoon" ("Fourth Letter").

35. See Edmund S. Morgan, *Visible Saints* (rpt. Ithaca: Cornell University Press, 1965), pp. 1–32.

36. One might suggest that, inspired by Williams, Miller was a victim of the profundity of his own spiritual insight; for clearly Williams thought that, as such, typology always involved that change of phase called spiritualization and not merely historical elaboration. As Miller put the case, Williams was a "maverick among the intellectuals of New England because he interpreted the relation of the Old Testament to the New not as an unfolding through time of an enduring covenant between God and man ... but as a radical break" (*Williams*, p. 32).

37. Brockunier founds Williams' "irrepressible" democracy on the relatively egalitarian land policy of Providence in 1636, itself an effect of "frontier" conditions; see *Irrepressible Democrat*, pp. 106–8, 165–67. For the more cautious view of Williams' politics as generally conservative, see Spurgin, *Radicalism*, pp. 52–54.

38. Except that Williams would have said "conscience," he too might well be thought to have "sworn on the altar of God" Jefferson's own opposition to "every form of tyranny over the mind of man."

39. For the actual—often troubled—workings of the colony at Rhode Island, see Teunissen and Hinz, "Narragansett Utopia," pp. 281–95.

40. For Cotton's initial defense of a government that might be called a theocracy—though better still a sanctocracy—see his 1636 Letter to Lord Say and Seal, reprinted in Miller and Johnson, eds., *Puritans*, pp. 209–12.

41. Miller's anthology of Williams sets the last two pages of chapter 138 apart and labels them a "Conclusion"; see *Williams*, pp. 154–56.

42. Like Rosenmeier, Keith W. F. Stavely suggests that Williams' *contemptus mundi* was perhaps extreme, with the consequence that "the only social vision he ever succeeded in clearly projecting was the strictly negative one of a state that would not persecute 'for cause of conscience'" (p. 259); see "Roger Williams and the Enclosed Garden of New England," in *Puritanism: Transatlantic Perspectives,* ed. Francis J. Bremer (Worcester: Massachusetts Historical Society, 1993), pp. 257–74.

43. Emerson's "Montaigne" suggests that, though men are "natural believers," yet a certain skepticism is the "domain of equilibration" through which every honest mind will pass, on its way from a simpler to a more adequate belief; see *Representative Men* (Cambridge, Mass.: Harvard University Press, 1987), p. 97.

44. Available versions of the texts mentioned are as follows: John Cotton, *The Keys of the Kingdom,* in *John Cotton on the Churches of New England,* ed. Larzer Ziff (Cambridge, Mass.: Harvard University Press, 1968), pp. 69–164; Thomas Hooker, *The Survey of the Summe of Church Discipline* (rpt. New York: Arno Press, 1971); John Norton, *The Answer to the Whole Set of Questions of the Celebrated Mr. William Apollonius* (rpt. Cambridge, Mass.:

Harvard University Press, 1958); the "rare" book of the set, Shepard's *Defense of the Answer,* must be consulted in microform.

45. See "Main-street," in *Hawthorne: Selected Tales and Sketches* (New York: Library of America, 1996), p. 1037.

CHAPTER 11. "GOD'S ALTAR"

1. Emerson, "The Poet," in *Essays and Lectures* (New York: Library of America, 1983), p. 452.

2. Bradford's poetry is quoted from Harrison T. Meserole, ed., *Seventeenth-Century American Poetry* (Garden City, N.Y.: Anchor, 1968), pp. 387–90.

3. Cotton is quoted from Meserole, ed., *Seventeenth-Century American Poetry,* pp. 381–82.

4. For the proper venue of Williams' poetry, see his *Key into the Languages of America* (rpt. Detroit: Wayne State University Press, 1973), pp. 99, 133, passim.

5. All citations of Bradstreet's works refer to Jeannine Hensley, ed., *The Works of Anne Bradstreet* (Cambridge, Mass: Harvard University Press, 1967).

6. See "The Natural History of Massachusetts," in *The Transcendentalists,* ed. Perry Miller (Cambridge, Mass.: Harvard University Press, 1950), p. 326.

7. William Cullen Bryant, "Inscription for the Entrance to a Wood," in *American Poetry: The Nineteenth Century,* ed. John Hollander (New York: Library of America, 1993), vol. 1, p. 126.

8. In a subtle attempt to account for the conflict of love and of language in Brad-street's "Letter," William J. Scheick seconds the early (1974) conclusion of Ann Stanford—that "the ardor with which Bradstreet addresses her husband . . . threatens to overshadow a proper love of God"; see "Logonomic Conflict in Bradstreet's 'A Letter to Her Husband,'" *EL* 21 (1994): 166–85.

9. See Carol M. Bensick, "Preaching to the Choir," *EAL* 28 (1993): 133–47.

10. All citations of Wigglesworth refer to Meserole, ed., *Seventeenth-Century American Poetry.*

11. See Shepard's "Autobiography" in *God's Plot,* ed. Michael McGiffert (Amherst: University of Massachusetts Press, 1994), p. 72; and for analysis, see above.

12. See Edmund S. Morgan, *The Puritan Family* (New York: Harper and Row, 1944), p. 1.

13. For Taylor's investment in the problem of presumption and despair, see my "God's Determinations Touching Half-Way Membership," *AL* 39 (1967): 298–314.

14. For the (two) available idioms in which Wigglesworth might formulate the relation of all men to Adam, see H. Shelton Smith, *Changing Conceptions of Original Sin* (New York: Scribner's, 1955), esp. pp. 1–9.

15. For a notice (and brief sample) of the dispute over original sin and the moral status of infants, see H. Shelton Smith, ed., *American Christianity* (New York: Scribner's, 1960), vol. 1, pp. 502–7. For commentary, see Joseph Haroutunian, *Piety versus Moralism* (rpt. New York: Harper and Row, 1970), pp. 208–16.

16. For early evidences of the unwillingness of certain latter-day Calvinists to uphold the rigors of their inherited system, see Haroutunian, *Piety,* pp. 43–156.

17. Recovered for feminist reasons, *The Wide Wide World* (1850) of Susan Warner may better serve the literary historian as a record of puritanic survival—as a morale somewhat older than domestic sentimentalism prompts the mother of the young heroine to swear that she loves God more than her own daughter; and to force from her daughter correlative confession.

18. For Perry Miller's telling account of the painful nature of the Puritans' worldly success, see "The Protestant Ethic," in *The New England Mind: From Colony to Province* (Cambridge, Mass.: Harvard University Press, 1953), pp. 40–52.

19. In supplement to my 1967 essay on "God's Determinations," see "Christ's Reply, Saint's Assurance," in *Doctrine and Difference* (New York: Routledge, 1997), pp. 27–60.

20. All citations of Taylor "Occurants" and of "God's Determinations" refer to Donald Stanford, ed., *The Poems of Edward Taylor* (New Haven: Yale University Press, 1960).

21. The wag who first said "burlap Herbert" might better have said "homespun"—not just for the alliteration but for the prediction of American economic and literary policy as well: use native materials.

22. Taylor's Harvard elegies celebrate "Richard Mather," "Mr. Sims," "Fran[cis] Willoughby," "John Allen," and "Charles Chauncey"; see Thomas Davis and Virginia Davis, eds., *Edward Taylor's Minor Poetry* (New York: Twayne, 1981), pp. 19–24, 30–33.

23. See Davis and Davis, eds., *Minor Poetry,* pp. 40–41.

24. Thus, at the outset of a famous contest of literary definition, did John Dryden's *Discourse of Satire* (1693) seek to stigmatize the more elaborate love efforts of John Donne.

25. Further citations of Taylor's poetry refer to Davis and Davis, eds., *Minor Poetry.*

26. For *Paradise Lost* as "Milton's American Poem," see William C. Spengemann, *A New World of Words* (New Haven: Yale University Press, 1994), pp. 94–117.

27. Perry Miller's second Puritan anthology—*The American Puritans* (Garden City, N.Y.: Anchor, 1956)—represents Stoddard's opposition to the strict communion policy of Congregational New England with a pithy example of his revisionist view "Concerning Ancestors" (pp. 222–24). Equally telling are his remarks on the painful effect of that policy on anyone *at all* unsure of their election; see *The Doctrine of the Instituted Churches,* reprinted in *Increase Mather vs. Solomon Stoddard* (New York: Arno Press, 1972), p. 22.

28. For the "double standard" by which Taylor vivifies the way of moral anxiety as well as the way of spiritual certitude, see Colacurcio, "Christ's Reply" (note 19); and for the cogent (if belated) response of Emily Dickinson, see Colacurcio, "Puritans in Spite," in *Doctrine and Difference,* pp. 241–48.

29. For the inspired critical notion of "reverent parody," see John Gatta, *Gracious Laughter* (Columbia: University of Missouri Press, 1989), esp. pp. 1–32.

30. For the definitive defense of Puritan culture against the repeated charge of being inherently "unpoetic," see Robert Daly, *God's Altar* (Berkeley: University of California Press, 1978), esp. pp. 1–81. In a politely resistant review, Larzer Ziff suggests that the very power of this defense leaves us less able to explain why the first American Puritans honored poetry so little in the observance; see *AL* 51 (1979): 111–12. For a more recent review of the poetic product of the American Puritans, see Jeffrey Hammond, *Sinful Self, Saintly Self* (Athens: University of Georgia Press, 1993).

31. For the larger context of the Puritans' ecclesiastical and social primitivism, see Theodore Dwight Bozeman, *To Live Ancient Lives* (Chapel Hill: University of North Carolina Press, 1988), esp. pp. 3–80.

INDEX

Author's note: Bold type indicates especially important, extended discussion on an individual.

Johnson, Edward (*cont.*)
  on Shepard, 442, 455, 463, 465–66,
  478, 488, 490; special providences,
  449, 452–54, 470, 473, 476–77, 479,
  483, 487, 491, 495; synods, 448, 468,
  472–75, 486; syntax, 442–43, 448, 465,
  480, 495; wilderness/garden, 448–49,
  454–56, 463, 469–470, 472, 477–78,
  483–84, 487, 489, 494; Word/Spirit,
  459–60, 473–74, 479–80
Johnson, Isaac, 71, 155
John the Baptist, 224, 229, 261, 263, 266,
  267, 270, 274, 364, 411, 447, 472
Jonah, 24; as Jonas, 25
Jones, Howard Mumford, 8, 579n12
Jones, James W., 369
Jones, Nicholas and Phyllis, 331–32
Jonson, Ben, 12, 442
Jordan, 23, 461, 484, 563
Judas Iscariot, 208, 226, 299

Kant, Immanuel, xvii, 595n6
Keane, Robert, 420, 422
Keats, John, 548
Kendall, R.T., 263, 603n36, 605n51,
  608n23, 612n72, 613n10
Kennebec, Maine, 67, 74, 82, 84, 87, 175
Kibbey, Ann, 331, 613n7
Kierkegaard, Søren, 222, 603n38
Knight, Janice, 604n39, 609n36, 610n39,
  615n32; *Orthodoxies in Massachusetts,*
  223, 443, 616n46, 621n48
Knowles, John, 477

Laodicea, 292, 443–44
Las Casas, Bartolomé de, 7
La Tour, Charles, 424
Laud, Bishop William, xv, 24, 83, 107, 112,
  118–21, 214, 246, 279–80, 331, 515,
  591n26, 603n27
Lawrence, D. H., 17, 63, 585n39
Lazarus, 289
Leyden, Holland, 45–46, 59–60, 66, 88,
  70–71, 76, 78; congregation of, 41, 59,
  65, 69, 580n37
Libertinism, 399–400

Locke, John, xiv, 199, 295, 603n34, 611n55;
  *An Essay Concerning Human
  Understanding,* xiv; *Two Treatises of
  Government,* xiv
London, Engl., 15, 29, 41, 55, 61, 75, 84, 99,
  113, 118, 128, 168, 525
Loyola, Ignatius, 312
Lowell, Robert; "After the Surprising
  Conversions," 241, 383
Ludlow, Roger, 163
Luke, 280, 357, 510
Luther, Martin, 26, 138, 264, 439, 514,
  604n44
Lyford, John, 17, 40, 58–59, 65, 99, 580n27,
  584n32
Lynn, Mass., 454

Machiavelli; "The Prince," 429
Macedonia, 120
Marian Exiles, 50, 123
Markpurge, 50
Merrimack River, 483
Martins (Martha's) Vineyard, 491
Marvel, Andrew, 546
Mary, Queen, 50, 123, 521, 528
Masconomo, Sagamore of Agawam, 153
Mason, Capt. John, 167
Massachusetts, xiv, 22, 25, 45, 53, 56–57,
  62, 64, 66, 70, 72–3, 76, 81, 82, 98, 177,
  184, 189, 366, 443, 445, 481, 500, 521,
  531–32, 586n55, 587n69, 598n50.
  See also individual towns
Massachusetts Indians, 15, 57
Massasoit, 56, 587n68
Masters, John, 164
Mather, Cotton, xix, 98, 106, 302, 428, 437,
  456, 468, 478–79, 487, 572, 582n6,
  587nn77–78, 588n83, 589n2, 605n3,
  622n75, 624n10, 625n25, 626n36
Mather, Increase, 487
Mather, Richard, 189, 402, 633n22
Mather, Samuel, 487
Mayflower (ship), 96, 445
Mayflower Compact, 37, 53–54,
  584n28
Mayhew, Thomas, 491

MICHAEL J. COLACURCIO

is Distinguished Professor of English

at the University of California, Los Angeles.

He is the author of a number of books and articles

on classic American literature,

including *The Province of Piety: Moral History in Hawthorne's Early Tales*

and *Doctrine and Difference: Essays in the Literature of New England.*